SAGA OF THE SILKMEN

# A History of
# Macclesfield Town Football Club

GRAHAM PHYTHIAN

Carnegie Publishing Ltd

Published by Carnegie Publishing Ltd
Carnegie House, Chatsworth Road
Lancaster LA1 4SL
+44 (0) 1524-840111
*Publishing*: www.carnegiepub.co.uk
*Book production*: www.wooof.net

*British Library Cataloguing-in-Publication data*
A CIP record for this book is available from the British Library

ISBN 1-85936-087-4

Designed and typeset in Goudy by Carnegie Publishing
Printed and bound in the UK by Cromwell Press, Trowbridge

# Contents

# MACCLESFIELD TOWN
## F O O T B A L L   C L U B   L T D

Main Official Sponsor: **Bodycote** Metal Technology

Ground & Registered Office: Moss Rose Ground, London Road, Macclesfield, Cheshire SK 11 7SP.
Tel: 01625 264686   Fax: 01625 264692

A full history of Macclesfield Town football Club is long overdue.

A book such as this will be of great interest not only to football fans, but also to local historians and devout Maxonians. Mr. Phythian stresses the part that the football club has played in the development of the town of Macclesfield as a community.

The story is a fascinating one, which will appeal to those who like "rags to riches" tales. From the humble Victorian beginnings of the rifle volunteers of Chestergate trying their hand at the new Association game, to the glorious Cheshire League days of the thirties, fifties and sixties, to giant killing and the climbing of the non-league pyramid to the Football League status – it's all here.

One notable skill of the author is bringing to life all the crucial matches throughout the club's history – "as if you are there". This is helped by the collection of many fine photographs reproduced here.

The book is monument to a fine club. For me it will remain a lasting memento of my six and a half years spent at the Moss Rose.

Sammy McIlroy MBE

Manager Macclesfield Town
May 1993 to January 2000

Incorporated in England No 415853

**saga** *n.* **1** a long story of heroic achievement

# *Preface*

My first visit to the Moss Rose ground was not on the occasion of some crucial cup or promotion match, nor in the free-scoring Cheshire League days of old. (How I envy those who can recall the *wunderteams* of the 'sixties!) No; it was merely to organise (for that read delegate) the selling of programmes at the annual 1998 Macclesfield Cub Scouts Champions *v*. Rest of the League match. My brother, League Secretary, had offered me a successful bribe.

My defining memory of that May evening – the seed from which this book has sprung – is of a six foot-plus Nigerian in a bandana happily and unhurriedly signing autographs for a seemingly endless queue of awestruck kids, without an agent or sponsor in sight.

The gentleman was, of course – as I found out later – Efe Sodje, one of the figureheads of those delirious years when the Silkmen finally, and deservedly, climbed into the Football League and then rose to Division Two the following season.

The autograph signing seemed to exemplify something, which only recently have I been able to come close to analysing. Here, I felt, was something other than what was on offer at those bloated conglomerates masquerading as Premier League football teams. Here was evidence of links between club and community, closer than any I had ever encountered. I had watched the big clubs, standing or sitting anonymous among the thousands; also, if I may be forgiven a dip into the ridiculous, I had played (for want of a better word) for one or two local and University soccer teams. But this, for me, was something new. The writer in me sniffed a story.

Or as it turned out, a 125-year saga.

The further my research took me, the more excited I became about celebrating the history of a fine club, with fine traditions.

The club-community links have enjoyed an inspiring continuity for well over a century. The Silkmen style of keeping their head and playing quality football, when all around are losing theirs and dishing up hustle and muscle, can be traced from the 1870s even unto modern times. The strength of the away following, discernible down the years, is another aspect of which the club is justifiably proud.

I started to watch the Silkmen in 1999, originally out of a scribbler's dedication, but soon became hooked. These days I enjoy everything about my trips in from Manchester: the pint(s) in the local, where supporters from both camps amicably mingle; the genuine wit (as opposed to the scurrilous rant we have all heard elsewhere) of the Silk contingent on the terraces, again something of a tradition; and above all, the team's insistence on playing constructive, progressive football, with some purple patches – well worth waiting for – which could easily grace a higher division. I even tolerate Roary.

I appreciate that there may be those who will look askance at a non-Maxonian writing such a book as this. Admittedly, I cannot claim the degree of involvement of, say, David Lafferty, Neil Howarth, and Paul Atherton in their excellent *Against All Odds* (see bibliography). If this book is not already on your shelves, then it darn well ought to be. But as they say, an 'interested outsider' is often the best placed person to give a rounded view. In any case, I welcome comments and criticisms of any kind. My e-mail address is at the end of the book. Feel free.

G. P. P.

## Post-script

It was with a great deal of sadness that I learned, in March 2001, of the recent death of Dave Jones, Silkman goalkeeper 1953–61. He remains the only player of the professional era to have represented Macclesfield at both cricket and football.

I was privileged to meet him only once, when he loaned me photographs for this publication, and reminisced about his playing days. The chapters on the fifties owe a lot to those couple of hours spent in the *Old Millstone* on Waters Green the previous spring.

## Acknowledgements

I would like to thank the following for their invaluable help and support:

ex-Silkmen Nat McKinstry, the late Dave Jones, Keith Goalen, Brian Booth;
Richard Evans, of the *Macclesfield Express*;
the *Express* for permission to use many of its photographs;
Mike Rance for support and liaison;
John Rooney, official club photographer, for generous loan of his photographs;
John Harman, for statistics for the Conference years;
Tom Read, for loan of programmes, statistical help, and fine-tuning for 1984–98;
Geoff Knights, for suggestions and corrections;
Rob Hooley, for help with photographs;
Steve Hulse, for information on Cheshire Cup matches;
Gary Jackson for photos;
Colin Garlick for access to club archives and liaison;
and the staff of the local history/reference sections of the following libraries:
Macclesfield
Newcastle-Under-Lyme
Northwich
Chester
Wythenshawe
John Rylands, Manchester
Manchester Central
Stockport
Altrincham
Sale, Trafford
And Nick and Janine for encouragement, computer services, and doughnuts.

## Note

After 1919, the clubs with teams in the Football League usually fielded their reserve sides for non-league competitions. So, unless otherwise stated, in the Cheshire League and Cups (and where applicable, in the Staffordshire Cup), Macclesfield played against the reserves of the following:
Chester
Crewe Alexandra
Port Vale
Stockport County
Tranmere Rovers
Wrexham
To save space and to avoid unnecessary repetition this point is not made in the ensuing text.

# I

# A Call to Arms

'The "silk lads" who played for sport and the honour of their native town.'
John Earles, *Fifty Years of Football*

## Origins

The beginnings of Macclesfield Town Football Club can be traced, at least in part, to the endeavours of a group of young men known as the 8th Cheshire Rifle Volunteers. They would meet at the Drill Hall off Chestergate, where concerts and tea parties were also held, as fund-raising measures. Their Drill Field was off Boughey Lane (now Victoria Road). Prospective members had to be at least 5ft 5½ ins. (1m. 65) tall, and have a chest circumference of at least 34 ins. (86 cm.) – though this was later reduced to 32 ins. (81 cm.)!

1873 seems to have been a year of sporting activity for the Riflemen. Gymnastics and athletics clubs were formed, almost certainly in response to the clarion call of two letters that appeared in the *Macclesfield Courier* in the January of that year. One calling himself 'Hereward' urged the adoption of team games:

> ... in friendly contests courage and pluck is developed, and above all a spirit of discipline is instilled.

This would be 'a wholesome recreation for the people ... a refreshing influence on those who toil in our shops and crowded factories'. The next week another correspondent – 'Zingari' – added weight to the argument:

> There is no greater honour (says Homer) than that he should be accomplished in the use of his hands and feet ... Athletics ... strengthens the muscles ... braces the nerves and exercises every joint.

Whether or not the writers had football in mind, within a matter of weeks the Volunteers had risen to the challenge and mustered a team that took on the boys of the Free Grammar School (now King's School). The Grammar School, who had been playing a form of Association for some years, won fairly easily, by 3–0. The report on the game criticised the Volunteers for frequent handling offences and lack of cohesive play.

The date of this encounter was 29 March 1873.

So the footballing story of the Volunteers might have ended. They were unwilling to play the skilled Grammar School team again just yet, and it was difficult to find games against other sides. Those few and far between groups who had tried out the Association game often played to significantly differing sets of rules. The unification which would be partly brought about by the emergent FA Cup was still some years off.

However, there was another group of sportsmen in the town who were keen to learn the Association game as played by the Volunteers.

The 'Olympic Cricket Club', whose home was a field off Boughey Lane adjacent to the Drill Field, were looking for an activity to keep them occupied in the winter months. On 22 November 1873 an area on their terrain was roped off to enable the Riflemen to play the Cricket Club at football. After a hard-fought game of around two hours, neither side, of fourteen and fifteen players respectively, had scored. This time it was the cricketers who were lambasted for handling. The Volunteers' captain, who had done much to organise the game, was one Lt. Walter Thorp. The Olympic goalkeeper was Harry Froggatt: not a brilliant cricketer – out for a duck when batting against his first team earlier that year! – he was to become a mainstay of the early town football team.

The Rifle Volunteers played host to nearby Prestbury one week later. Here again, though, was evidence that universal concordance of the laws of the game was still some way off. A set of rules was agreed upon with the visitors before commencement of play, but it soon became apparent that this pre-match contract was to be shown a cavalier disregard by certain of the Prestbury team. Kicking at opponents and ignorance of the offside law were just two of the peccadilloes noted. The result of a fractious game was 1–1.

The Volunteers registered their first win in the New Year, 1–0 against Adlington Yeomanry. The game lasted from 3.15 pm until 5.30 on a January afternoon, by which time it was presumably too dark to see much. The scorer of the Macclesfield goal was Peter Bond.

In February the Riflemen played two games against a Macclesfield select: one at rugby ('hacking and tripping allowed') and the second at Association. The Volunteers won the rugby game fairly easily (Walter Thorp, who was soon

to represent Cheshire at the sport, captained), but once again the round-ball game finished a goalless draw. Most of the town side were members of the Olympic Cricket Club.

At the end of the Riflemen's first season, it would be as well to cast a glance over the state of Association Football across the nation at that time. It would have been barely recognisable as the game we know today, with its two umpires, absence of goal nets and pitch markings, tapes instead of crossbars, frequent scrimmages in front of goal, and as we have seen, its confusing jumble of codes. Numbers on a team could vary from eight to twenty, depending on how many were able to turn up! Ends were changed after each goal scored, and a kick-in from touch was the norm in some regions. The corner-kick did not exist, unless you were playing the Sheffield rules of the time. It is unclear which regulations were adhered to by the Macclesfield players; there is evidence to suggest that there was some variation even here, from year to year, or depending on what was agreed by the teams beforehand. Uniformity would not occur until 1877, when the London rules became the accepted national norm.

## Early games with Stoke

We have already seen the role played by Lt. Walter Thorp in bringing to fruition the first of these games. Later that year he brought off a remarkable *coup* by persuading the illustrious Stoke club to pay a visit to Boughey Lane.

Stoke Football Club had been born as long ago as 1863, originating as St Peter's School. North Staffordshire railway workers, possibly under the aegis of some Old Boys of Charterhouse School, had formed an autonomous club by 1868. There was, therefore, a considerable gap in experience and skill between the two teams. Moreover, the Macclesfield side had chosen its players from a few dozen members of a Rifle Corps, whereas Stoke, at least in theory, had the population of a major Potteries town to call upon. The game, not surprisingly, was one-sided, with the more estab-

lished club running out winners by 7–1. Far from losing heart, however, the beaten side resolved to learn from the experience:

> The point the Volunteers ... have to study more is how to pass the ball on and send it across the ground from one to another, playing in a line, rather than altogether in a body. *Courier* (14/11/74)

The return was set for the New Year: 16 January 1875, at the Victoria Ground, Stoke.

That the Volunteers were determined pupils was indicated by the notice in the *Courier* later that month, concerning the team for the forthcoming match with Langley: 'Names in the reading room, and plan of places on the field.' Clearly they were taking another vital step away from the rollicking free-for-all that had typified folk football, and were approaching the game with some measure of military precision and science.

The day arrived for the Riflemen's return match with Stoke. On the team that day there were several players who were to figure greatly in Macclesfield football in years to come: Lt J. W. T. (Walter) Thorp, his younger brother Sammy, James Davies, Peter Bond, J. Robinson, W. Heathcote, and from Langley, Sam Morton. Stoke fully expected to run up double figures against the new arrivals on the Association scene, and when they quickly attained a 3–0 lead, it appeared that this would be the case. However, the Macclesfield men rallied at that point, finally started to put theory into practice, and to the surprise of the home team and its supporters, began to dominate. Peter Bond scored, and the game ended with the Volunteers having the better of the exchanges, but unable to translate that supremacy into further goals.

Nevertheless, a tradition had taken root, and the Stoke-Macclesfield games were soon to be eagerly-anticipated events on the sporting calendar.

A fortnight later, the Riflemen played the Grammar School once more. With two years' experience and match practice beneath their belt, this time it was the Volunteers who handed out the lesson, winning 3–0. The Grammar School side included the brothers H. and F. W. Paul (who the following year was to be awarded a Scholarship at Wadham College, Oxford), Alfred Holcroft, and Arthur Thorp. This last player, the third of the Thorp brothers, would also appear for the Volunteers later in the season. This was before professionalism tied a player to any one club, and a footballer would quite often openly guest for another local team without any hint of defection or duplicity.

It was in March 1875 that the Riflemen and a 'Macclesfield 15' engaged in an enthralling Association tussle. In the event, 14 men played 11:
*Macclesfield*: H. Paul (capt.), F. W. Paul, S. Clive, W. Warren, Wood, Smith, Crowder, Holcroft, Stringer, McDonald, Bradburn, Watts, Davenport, A. Bancroft

8th CRV: J. Robinson (capt.), P. Bond, Downes, S. Downes, W. Heathcote, Grubb, Riddlesworth, A. Hunt, Sampson, S. Morton, R. A. Thorp

It is fairly certain that much of the cream of the town's footballing fraternity was on view that day. The hotly-contested game finished 2–2, after the 14 had taken a 2–0 lead through Stringer and Crowder. Bond and Arthur Thorp equalised for the Volunteers.

Peter Bond, incidentally, was the town's sporting superstar of his day. In the previous year's 8th CRV Athletic Festival, he had entered all four distance races – closed and open 880 yards, closed and open mile – won three, and come third in the other! He added cycling to his activities the following summer, finishing runner-up in the final.

Games against Stoke had become the touchstone for progress. For the next season's encounter, in November, Lt. Walter Thorp was determined that he would, for the first time, bring together the town's finest in one team to make the trip to the Potteries. A sizeable number of supporters accompanied the team, in trains that departed from the new Waters Green Station shortly after midday.

Stoke had won every game played so far that season, and once again expected to win this one fairly comfortably. The Silkmen, however, repulsed every home attack, and came close to winning in the last minute with a Peter Bond shot that barely cleared the Stoke cross-tape. The result of 0–0, in the circumstances, was looked upon as a victory for the visitors.

It is worth recording the team on that historic day: 27 November 1875. Perhaps this is the first ever 'Macclesfield Football Club' line-up, in the proper sense of the term. The Volunteers, the Cricket Club, the silk mills, Langley, and the Grammar School, had all contributed their share of players:
Lt J. W. H. Thorp, H. Paul, F. W. Paul, J. Davies, J. Robinson, W. Bradley, P. Bond, S. Morton, J. Morton, A. Holcroft, A. Hunt, W. Heathcote, R. Hill

Within the next year or so, as the Volunteers and the Cricket Club moved towards joining forces, Macclesfield as a whole saw a startling mushrooming of smaller teams. Football had started to absorb the leisure hours of the town. The Wakes week – the first week in October – signalled the end of the cricket season, and thereafter soccer began in earnest. Although supposedly banned, street football games continued for those who could not wait to take part in an organised match. It is recorded that Mr Hooley, the water bailiff, was taking tea one April afternoon in his house in Black Road when a ball was kicked through his window. Three of the perpetrators were caught and subsequently fined one shilling (5p) – it was either that or seven days' imprisonment!

Happily, most players could now get a proper game: Macclesfield Victoria, Wanderers, Reliance, Alexandra, Charles St, Chester Road Mill, St George's Rangers, and both Free and Modern Grammar Schools were able to field teams. Chester Road Mill had a small but uncompromisingly tough full-back by the name of Abram Bancroft, who, bearing the nickname 'Yab Pickles', would make his mark in the first great Macclesfield team around the turn of the decade.

## The joining of forces

It was on 21 October 1876 that the following announcement appeared in the *Courier*:
MACCLESFIELD FOOTBALL CLUB – For some years past the Volunteers have been the principal exponents of the Football game in Macclesfield, and have been successful in making it very popular in the town and district. This season, however, a meeting of all football players has been held, and the Volunteers and Cricket Club having been amalgamated, football will henceforth be carried on under the auspices of the 'Macclesfield Football Club'.

One week later the so-called 'inaugural game' was held. Once again the opponents were the powerful Stoke outfit. The match took place on the Free Grammar School playing fields, on Coare St One further step had been taken towards modern-day football, in that, although the teams were 12-a-side, both sides adopted a 2–2–6 formation, with the captain acting as a rudimentary *libero*. For the first time, Jim Morton from Langley – Sam's brother – kept goal, and Harry Froggatt partnered W. Bradley at full-back. Sammy Thorp was at half-back; he was rapidly developing into a forceful, elusive dribbler. Arthur Thorp captained. The result was a victory for Stoke by a single goal.

These early friendlies were truly convivial affairs, with a pub – originally the *Pack Horse* on Jordangate – used as a basis for changing rooms and the after-match meal. Macclesfield had a reputation for competitive but fair play, and the renown of the town's hospitality ensured that it was a popular venue! Northwich Victoria (0–0) were entertained the following month, and the long-awaited visit of the Manchester Association took place in the New Year.

London rules were played, probably for the first time by the home team. There were 11 players per side. The offside rule stated that three (not one) players had to be between the attacker receiving the ball and the defenders' goal-line. The corner kick, co-opted from the Sheffield canon, existed, as did the one-handed throw-in. In a matter of months these rules would be the official, national code, putting an end – at least in theory – to regional variations. In reality, local idiosyncrasies persisted, by mutual agreement and for non-competitive matches, for some years.

The match with Manchester, described by one reporter as 'one of the hottest and pleasantest games ever played at Macclesfield', saw the beginning of the end of the goal drought. The team were deploying the 2–2–6 system with a fair degree of expertise, and a creditable 2–2 draw was achieved, playing unfamiliar rules against strong opponents who had recently been one of the first provincial teams to compete in the FA Cup.

The new combined team continued their unbeaten run until March. The club was now charging admission – 1 penny (½p) – to all home games, although ladies were admitted free. Games were advertised in the *Courier*, and crowds of between 100 and 200, depending on the weather, made the journey out to Boughey Lane to watch.

The first annual dinner of Macclesfield Football Club was celebrated on 12 March 1877. Lt. Thorp congratulated those present on their foresight in deciding to join forces. The Secretaries – Arthur Thorp and Harry Froggatt – stressed the economic soundness of the move. A bazaar had been organised, in an attempt to raise the necessary £400 for ground improvements. (The cricket terrain possessed the minor eccentricities of a mound and six trees.)

Articles in the *Courier* reflected the sudden mania for the game. Strategical hints were published, including this illuminating description of contemporary attacking play:

... *Forwards* should work in couples. Bear in mind that any two ordinary players can take the ball past the most brilliant dribbler, if they act in concert.

After a potted history of both Rugby and Association, the writer concludes with an analysis of football's burgeoning local popularity, even among non-players:

The game ... in both its forms is now pre-eminently one of skill and science, of discipline and good manners, of patience and observation. Mere violence and brute force play but a very secondary part in it.

Towards the end of the decade the rapid development of Association football in the town was defined by two conflicting trends.

On the one hand there was the proliferation of sides, brought about by the desire for weekly games (and Wednesday afternoon had just been granted as an extra holiday, creating even more free time that many eagerly filled with football). The advantages of playing locally were obvious: minimal organization, and no travel costs to speak of.

On the other, amalgamation was in the air. After further mergers involving the best players from other town sides, there arose 'Macclesfield United', soon to be re-named 'Macclesfield Hornets', after their team colours of amber and black stripes. First captained by ex-Grammar School athlete Alfred Holcroft, they would record an impressive series of results.

MACCLESFIELD CRICKET & FOOT BALL CLUBS.

THE First Annual DINNER will take place at the Pack Horse Hotel, on Monday, March 12.

Dinner at Seven o'clock prompt.

Tickets, 2s 6d each, may be obtained from J. H. Wood, Jordangate.

J. H. WOOD, Hon. Sec., M.C.C.
A. R. THORP, } Hon. Secs., Macclesfield
H. FROGGATT, } Foot Ball Club.

FOOTBALL MATCH.

MACCLESFIELD v. ASHBOURNE.
(Association Rules.)

To be played MARCH 10th, SATURDAY,
Macclesfield Cricket Ground, Boughey Lane.
Admission, 1d each ; Ladies Free.
Kick off at 2 45.

Front page, 10 March 1877. (*Macclesfield Express*)

## Further afield

However, the move towards unification was hampered by the frequent parochial tussles. On occasions a Macclesfield select team travelling to an away game would find itself significantly weakened. The worst instance of this was the game with Talke Rangers – another strong Potteries outfit – in December 1876. Only eight Silkmen were able to make the journey, other regular players preferring to be involved in other games back home. Talke generously offered to supply substitutes to make up the number, but the visitors' pride was at stake, and they refused. The eight men played thirteen, and unsurprisingly Talke won by six goals to nil.

There are two happier footnotes to this debacle: a tradition of Macclesfield – Talke Rangers games was started, and when a full Macc. team took the field against the 'Blue Caps' the following year, the Cheshire team ran out clear winners by 3–0.

The next season (1877–78) saw Macclesfield enter their first trophy competition: the Staffordshire Association Challenge Cup. The Cheshire

equivalent would not begin for another two years. The Round One visitors were Mount Pleasant from Stoke. Despite conceding an early goal, Macc. fought back to 2–2, and clinched the tie with a Heathcote goal near the end.

In this, their first ever Cup run, they performed creditably, eventually reaching the semi-finals, where they lost narrowly to Talke Rangers.

A notable win that year was the 5–0 drubbing of Leek, in which the Volunteers' Heathcote notched a hat-trick. The report of the game noted 'A. Slack's dashing play'.

The following season Alfred Holcroft gained recognition for his sound defensive play as captain of the Hornets by being selected to represent Cheshire in their Association's inaugural game against Staffordshire at Crewe. Boosted by the presence of many members of the powerful Stoke side, the Staffs. XI were easy 6–1 winners. Within a few years, however, these inter-Association games would witness a remarkable *volte-face*, which would in some measure reflect Macclesfield's first great run of results.

Alfred Holcroft bore the nickname 'Pin John', after his ingenious innovation in the silk mill managed by his father. Noticing the wastage involved in the strips of silk dropped on the floor and subsequently disposed of, he advocated the pinning of these pieces on a board, to be used in later work. He was also a useful runner, having won the 440 yards on the same day as Peter Bond's near-monopoly of the distance events at the Volunteers' Athletics Festival.

Two drawn matches with Cobridge marked the end of the club's flirtation with the Staffs. Association Cup. Unwilling to make another trip to Burslem for the second replay, the Silkmen had to concede the tie, to the eventual beaten finalists. In future years, such problems would not hinder the team's progress, as in 1880 the Cheshire County Challenge Cup competition would begin.

On a bitterly cold day in January, whilst the town was warming to the acrobatics and pantomime of *Fosset's New Grand Hippodrome and*

Team colours have undergone many changes over the years:
1877–1882: amber and black stripes, black shorts
1882–1890: red shirts, white shorts
1890–1891: red, yellow and blue stripes, black shorts
1891–1897: blue shirts, white shorts
1897–1915: red shirts, white shorts
  *alternate: white shirts, red shorts*
1919–1928: black and white stripes, black shorts
1928–1947: white shirts, black shorts
  *alternate: blue shirts, white shorts*
1947–1969: royal blue shirts, white shorts
  *alternate: 1940s and '50s: red shirts, white shorts; 1960s: tangerine shirts, white shorts*
1969–1970: blue and white stripes, white shorts
1970–1973: royal blue shirts, white shorts
1973–1975: blue shirts with broad white stripe, white shorts
1975–1976: tangerine shirts, black shorts
1976–1999: royal blue shirts, white shorts
  *alternate: all white*
1999–2001: all blue
  *alternate: 1999–2000: gold shirts, blue shorts; 2000–2002: all scarlet*
2001–2002: all blue, with yellow trim

*Circus* on Chestergate, the football team travelled to Blackburn. Playing one of the premier teams of the time evidently held more kudos than the Staffs. County Cup. On a ground covered in thick snow, in a game shortened to sixty minutes because of the conditions, Macclesfield and Blackburn Rovers fought out a vigorous, attacking game. The final score (0–0) did not reflect this; moreover, the visitors had a goal disallowed for an unclear hand-ball offence. Once again the Silkmen came away with a moral victory against top-class opposition.

Perhaps the best result of that season, though, further evidence of what the town's finest could achieve when resources were pooled, was the 1–0 victory over Manchester Wanderers, a side that was to enter the FA Cup within a matter of months. The team that day, 30 November 1878, was a mixture of newcomers and old faithfuls:

J. T. Robinson (8th CRV – goal)
A. Bancroft (Chester Road Mill – full back)
W. Bradley (Langley – full back)
A. Goldthorpe (Hornets – half back)
P. Warren (Hornets – half back)
R. Ward (Chester Road Mill – forward)
J. Howarth (8th CRV – forward)
R. A. Thorp (8th CRV – forward)
R. S. Comberbach (8th CRV – forward)
J. Watts (Hornets – forward)
J. Hall (Hornets – forward)

Despite the muddy conditions, several hundred spectators made the trip out to Boughey Lane.

Team captain R. A. Thorp scored the all-important goal.

Jack 'Mush' Howarth, another of the great characters of that early side, was a big, hefty fellow, and a runner of some renown. John Earles recalls him as being 'always in the thick of the fight. He could play a rough game if needed, as his opponents quickly found to their cost'. His play was typified by a 'bulldog impetuosity'. On Abram Bancroft: 'He was a safe tackler, he never played a dirty game'.

By February, both Bancroft and Robinson had joined the Macc. contingent on the County team. Within a year Warren (playing in goal) and Watts ('some splendid passing and dodging' – *v.* Lancs. November 1879) had swelled the ranks. It was but the first trickle of the forthcoming steady stream of representative honours.

The club's record against 'out-of-town' opposition that season is worth recording:

| | | |
|---|---|---|
| Fenton (Stoke) | A | D 0–0 |
| Talke Rangers | H | W 4–0 |
| Goldenhill | H | D 1–1 |
| Burslem | H | W 4–0 |
| Leek | A | W 2–1 |
| Mow Cop | H | W 5–1 |
| Talke Rangers | A | D 0–0 |

So began a new decade, which was to see further dramatic changes in the Association game, and which would end with Macclesfield Football Club taking its place among the County's élite.

# 2

# Crossroads

'I have heard it whispered that Macclesfield are preparing a splendid reception, both on and off the field, for their old and respected opponents, Stoke, today. This is a very old fixture, and one regarded with high favour by the Macclesfield players. Will Bromley-Davenport play?'
*Staffordshire Sentinel* (23/2/84)

'Every effort is being made to put down professionalism.'
Football Association AGM (22/3/84)

### Cheshire County FA

One of the recurring themes of Cheshire soccer in the 1880s would be the struggle for supremacy between Northwich Victoria and Macclesfield.

The 'Saltites' had started life much as had the Macclesfield Football club. They were originally an offshoot of the 3rd Cheshire Rifle Volunteers (22nd Battalion), and the name of their ground – the Drill Field – bears witness to this fact to this day. In the early years of the Cheshire Association, they were the team to beat: perennial winners of the County Challenge Trophy, Welsh FA Cup Finalists, quarter-finalists in the English Cup in 1884, and they were even to spend a couple of (largely forgettable) years in the new Second Division of the Football League early in the next decade. Another claim to fame was that they were the first English club of a brilliant young Welsh winger by the name of Billy Meredith, before his transfer to Manchester City, and greater glories.

A rising Silkman star of those years was one Jimmy Bates, originally a member of the Chester Road Mill team. He had made his debut in the 4–0 victory over Talke Rangers in November 1879. Instead of the position in which he was to make his mark in the coming decade – centre-forward – he had assumed the new role of centre half-back. Playing with a third man in midfield, incidentally, was a revolutionary idea at the time;

Macclesfield were one of the first Association teams to switch from the 2–2–6 system, before 2–3–5 became all the rage in the 'eighties. It was seen as the perfect vehicle for the new concept of Association as a cohesive, passing game, and results were soon to bear this out.

But to return to James Rigby Bates: by January 1880 he had shifted to left wing, from where he gave some indication of his prodigious shooting and lay-off skills. He was soon to take up his rightful position as prolific scorer of goals in central attack. 'O rare Jim Bates!' as former school friend John Earles was to write nearly fifty years later; 'The idol of the crowd ... a better man the good old town of Macclesfield never produced'. It was not long before Bates was to don County colours alongside the other Silkmen.

After the formation of the Cheshire County Association in August 1878, the next logical step was to introduce a knock-out competition, in the style of the FA Cup: the County Challenge Cup was born in January 1880. Macclesfield were drawn against Bowdon, away, in the first round. As none of the sources consulted mentions the match after 24 January 1880 – the date it was due to be played – one must assume that for some reason the tie did not take place. In any event, no more matches in that competition were played by Macclesfield (or Bowdon) until the following year. Northwich

Victoria carried off the inaugural trophy – the first of six consecutive triumphs – in the final against Birkenhead.

The next season was slow in getting under way, but was quickly to gain in tempo. In November the newly-formed Macclesfield Football Association proposed a competition open just to local teams, and again based on the popular knock-out format. Because of the cost of trophies, it was decided to award the members of the winning team a silver medal each, the runners-up receiving a bronze medal each. Clubs were charged an entrance fee of ten shillings (50p).

Most of the cluster of town teams formed a few year previously had disappeared, swallowed no doubt by the growth of the robust few. Only eight entered the first round draw:

Macclesfield 1 *v.* Hurdsfield
Macclesfield 2 *v.* Baptists FC (Sutton Hall)
Bollington *v.* King Edward's FC (Upton)
St George's *v.* Rainow

By the end of the month both of the Macclesfield club's sides were through to the semi-final. Hurdsfield had been disposed of 7–0 (Bates and Howarth shared four of the goals) and the Baptists had withdrawn.

In December the town once more played host to the Manchester club. In another thrilling game the visitors took an early lead, which was cancelled on the stroke of half-time by a long shot from Ward. Dunkerley had supplied the pass to the wing, from a free kick. The score remained at 1–1.

Hopes were high, then, for the first match of the New Year, in the first round of the Cheshire Cup, even though the opponents were the holders, the redoubtable Northwich. The general feeling throughout the county was that any meeting between these two sides was tantamount to the final. Several hundred Macc. supporters, confident of victory, travelled by train or bicycle to Northwich. The local newspaper reported that the visitors had brought 'an unusually strong team':

Morton; Bancroft, Goodfellow; Comberbach (c), Goldthorpe, Dunkerley; Ward, Sadler, Seed, Watts, Bates

The crowd of nearly a thousand, anticipating a close struggle, were not to be disappointed. Macclesfield attacked virtually from the kick-off, and for a while penned their opponents. Musgrave in the Northwich goal, however, was more than equal to the task, and half-time arrived with no score. The Saltites had come close to scoring from a free kick a matter of yards in front of the visitors' goal, but mass defending by the Silkmen saved the day.

Soon after half-time it was a rapid and intricate piece of close passing that placed Earlam of the Vics. in front of the Macc. goal. It was a relatively easy chance, and Earlam did not shirk it. Once more the visitors attacked with a will: Ward, Seed and Bates worked their way into promising positions, but each time were foiled by Musgrave, who was in excellent form throughout. In the end, it was Northwich who scored again through Capper, after a long run during which, his adversaries claimed, he handled the ball. Protests were over-ruled, and the final score was 2–0 to the Vics.

## Silver medal competition

Back home, the next opposition were Bollington in the semi-final of the Silver Medal Competition. Giving expression to the frustrated ambition of the previous week, the Silkmen were clear 6–2 winners. Bates notched two, and the other scorers were Watts, Howarth, Morton and Ward.

St George's Rangers had beaten the Macc. reserves in the other semi-final, a rough, niggly affair by all accounts. This second team – 'The Juniors' – nonetheless was a useful side: they were to astound onlookers by beating the first team 2–0 in an end-of-season kick-about. They certainly played a vital nursery role in the development of the club.

The final with St George's was, as expected, another one-sided game (4–0). The Macclesfield team, in fact, had won all their Silver Medal matches so convincingly that the Association introduced the rule that, for the following year, the inaugural winners had to give opponents a goal start!

The Association reported a profit of £4 over the season, and it was suggested that a trophy could be supplied for the next year's competition, with gate profits going to the Infirmary fund.

The club rounded off its season with a 1–0 victory over Manchester Wanderers, a goalless draw with Goldenhill – 'the premier club of North Staffs'. – and a fighting, high-scoring match at Eagley (Bolton), one of the top Lancashire sides of the day. Although playing with ten men, as goalie Jim Morton was unable to travel through illness, the visitors were amazingly leading 3–1 at half-time. The longer the game went on, though, the more the home side was able to capitalise on the extra man, and eventually won 6–3. The Cheshire side received their due praise for a gutsy performance.

The next season (1881–82) was not to disappoint.

The draw for the Silver Medal Competition attracted a couple of familiar faces:

Macclesfield 1 *v.* Macclesfield 2
King Edward's *v.* Total Abstainers
Baptists FC *v.* Chester Road
Bollington *v.* Rainow
Hurdsfield *v.* Langley Rovers

The season was starting ever earlier: in the opening game on 1 October, Macc. cancelled their imposed one-goal deficit within minutes, and went on to score three more. True, their opponents were their own reserves, but it must be remembered that four of the first team's best players – Bancroft, Bates, Goldthorpe and Dunkerley – were playing for Cheshire on that day, at Stoke against the Staffordshire eleven. The result of that inter-county match was a 1–1 draw: the tide was beginning to turn.

One of Dunkerley's notable skills, which he had used to great effect in the match with Eagley, was the long one-armed throw-in. Each team aspired to have one such specialist, before the two-handed throw-in rule was introduced in September 1882.

Dunkerley, later to inherit the directorship of a silk mill, was to captain Cheshire before too long. County honours were soon to follow for Rev. W. Seed, the curate of St George's, who guested for the town side against 'foreign' opposition. New-comer Alfred Sadler would join him on the County team; Sadler was an exponent of the spirited wing run and spectacular shot on goal. John Earles notes that Sadler attained a first class Honours in Silk Manufacture at the Technical School, being awarded £5 and a silver medal. Sadler, as well as Bates, was to score for Cheshire against North Wales in February 1882. Other Silkmen of those years to gain County honours were Sammy Thorp and Arthur Goldthorpe.

## Cup semi 1882

Victories against Hurst (6–0) and Crewe Alexandra (2–0) were recorded before the end of November. A return match at Northwich resulted in a goalless draw. There was talk of entry for next year's 'little tin idol' as the original FA Cup was often termed. The previous season's defeat at Northwich had surely been a rare off-day?

A sense of proportion was restored in December, when the Silkmen travelled to Blackburn to play the famous Olympic club. At the time considered to be at least on a par with the great Rovers, they were to win the FA Cup itself in 1883, surprising the pundits with their 2–1 defeat of the otherwise all-conquering Old Etonians. On a mudbath of a pitch – for which the home side were to gain a nationwide reputation – Macclesfield held out for nearly an hour. Then the floodgates opened, and Olympic hit six in quick succession. Once again, though, the beaten side learned from the defeat: in the next match, against Leek, the report stated that they 'worked more vigorously together'. The result was a 4–0 win, in which Leek were 'completely overpowered'.

In the Cheshire Cup, Macc. reached the semi-final, where once again they met Northwich Victoria. In an earlier round, against Hartford St John's, it was Sadler who had opened the scoring after a 'beautiful run' down the right wing. The final score had been 4–2.

The circumstances of the semi-final ties would these days be looked upon as bordering on the farcical. In one match, the two strongest teams in the county were shaping up for their usual hammer-and-tongs battle. In the other, a club called Witton Novelty – a team name from a bygone age, if ever there was one – had a bye into the final!

The early days of the FA Cup had not been spared similar eccentricities. The lay-out of the rounds of such knock-out competitions often had a threadbare look about them, especially if the original number of competing teams was not a power of two. So sometimes, an initial entry of twelve would be whittled down to a semi-final comprising three.

Once again, then, the Silk-Salt battle was looked upon as the equivalent of the final. On 25 March 1882 the teams met on Northwich's home soil. William Bramham, secretary of Blackburn Olympic, was referee. Macclesfield brought the usual strong team, with Rutland drafted in from the reserves as centre-forward. Bates and Sadler were on opposite wings.

A large number of supporters had once again trekked across the Cheshire plain. Three special trains had been laid on, and once more the new-style bicycle was put to good use. Unconcerned by the 6–4 odds on quoted for Northwich, the Silk fans were loudly confident.

F. W. Hughes, the Northwich captain, had been selected to play for Wales that day, but he had heeded the call of his club instead, anticipating a strong challenge from Macclesfield. He was right, but not quite in the way he had imagined. Early on in the game, with the away team pressing, he clashed with Comberbach. The result of this was that Hughes was knocked flying, and had to be helped from the pitch, in a state of some distress. Any hopes the visitors may have had of playing the rest of the game against a depleted foe, however, were soon dashed: after 'a good rubbing and a nip of brandy' Hughes reappeared and took up his position once more.

In the event, it was not the return of Hughes that won the day. Despite constant attacking from the Silkmen, and many shots that skimmed cross-bar and post, it was Northwich who possessed the striker who had the purple patch on the day. One George Plant found the target on four occasions as the Vics. ran out 5–1 winners. Even the local reports agreed that the match was a lot closer than the score suggested. Rutland hit the solitary Macc. goal, from a precise cross by Goldthorpe.

Needless to say, Northwich were easy winners against Witton Novelty in the final.

## New horizons

Before the end of the season, Leek was the scene of some hostility between a band of local supporters and the Macclesfield players. Taking exception to both the result (2–1 to Macc.) and some robust challenges by Howarth, a portion of the home crowd pursued the visiting team, showering them with stones and clods of earth. All of the Macc. eleven made a quick getaway, apart from Goldthorpe, who suddenly found one of the home supporters in front of him, squaring up for a fight. The *Courier* reporter, showing something

less than a professional detachment, described the sequel thus:

> Goldthorpe ... no ways daunted by his isolated position, 'went' for his opponent, whom he speedily rendered *hors de combat* by some straight hits carefully distributed over his countenance. *Courier* (18/3/82)

We are still in the soccer version of the Wild West, and the confrontation is a reminder, if one is needed, that altercations between spectator and player are nothing new. The incident was to have unfortunate repercussions, however, when the teams met in the FA Cup a couple of years later.

Such rare shenanigans apart, it had been a mostly successful season. At least the finances were healthy enough for the club to take the plunge and enter the FA Cup the following autumn.

Macclesfield, as expected, won the Silver Medal Competition with ease for the second successive year, beating Baptists 3–1 in the final. £8 was taken on the gate, and the *Courier* saw this as 'a good lift for the Medal Association'. Nonetheless, this was to be the last time that the town's premier club would take part. The Silkmen were obviously out of their class, and had their eyes on more distant and lucrative horizons.

An acrimonious meeting between members of the Association's teams took place in August. Macclesfield FC, not unreasonably, could not give a cast-iron guarantee that they would play all local teams in the coming season. They were then accused of 'treating the Association with contempt', and a number of clubs moved for their exclusion from the Silver Medal Competition. Several letters, over which can be detected the tang of sour grapes, were written to the *Courier*, reiterating this demand. In the end, to avoid further unpleasantness, Macclesfield took it upon themselves to withdraw. F. W. Sheldon, the club Secretary, had the last word, pointing out that he Association was in such a healthy financial state mainly due to the presence of his club. He estimated that Macc. FC were responsible for two-thirds of all gate money accrued in the course of the Silver Medal Competition. He concluded:

Macclesfield are ever zealous to further the interests of football, as shown by their past

> The earliest mention of payment for playing football for the club is in the minute book for November 1886: two professionals from another town were to be engaged.
> The going rate for away matches was fixed at two shillings (10p) expenses, with a shilling bonus if the team won. However, the following month it was recorded that Jim Bates was to receive eight shillings (40p) per match.

indomitable perseverance during the first few years of their infancy. *Courier* Correspondence (23/9/82)

Season 1882–83 was to see further developments. A new team strip was introduced, red jerseys replacing the old amber and black stripes. They were first worn into battle at the end of October, against the Manchester Association. It seemed to be a most favourable omen, as the Silkmen trounced the opposition 7–0. Only the play of Turner, the Manchester full-back, prevented the score from reaching double figures.

It was to be a year of high scoring: In the Cheshire Cup, Rainow were beaten 6–0. Bates, despite a knee strain, hit three. In the quarter-final, Middlewich were disposed of 10–2.

The County side caught the habit. Against Staffordshire that autumn, with Jim Morton, John Dunkerley and Jimmy Bates participating, Cheshire were clear 7–2 winners. Bates scored only one, but was involved in much of the approach work for the other six.

The Lockwood Brothers arrived from Sheffield on 4 November 1882 to contest the first round of that year's FA Cup. The teams were:

*Macclesfield*: J. Morton; Bancroft, Dunkerley; Downie, S. Morton, Comberbach (c); Goldthorpe, Bates, Hall, Rutland, Sadler

*Lockwood Brothers*: W. Beard; Buttery (c), Rutherford; Cutts, Thorpe, Harris, West, J. Beard, Housley, Sellars, Wood

Although nominally a works team, the Lockwoods were apt to help themselves to players from other Sheffield sides, notably the powerful Wednesday. This was before professionalism obliged a player to remain with a specific club – one of the many advantages, incidentally, of legalising pay for play. Although the Lockwoods were vociferous in their condemnation of professionalism – witness their refusal to play the Lancashire clubs whose stance on 'players' expenses' was well known – they were not above borrowing a few ringers if it helped their cause. Almost certainly four of the above team: Buttery, West, Housley and Wood, appeared regularly for the Sheffield or the Wednesday clubs.

It was to be a baptism of fire, but once again confidence was high. A crowd of well over a thousand lined the pitch, now 108 yards long with new goalposts; although a newly-formed puddle 'twenty yards across' made the approach to one goal fraught with difficulty.

The Silkmen attacked their illustrious opponents from the kick-off. Only three minutes had elapsed when Sadler sent in a high cross from the right wing. He followed it in, and when the ball was cleared into his path once more, he struck one of his famous 'screw shots' into the goal.

Within ten minutes it was 2–0. Goldthorpe crossed from the opposite wing, and Sadler was on hand to score a goal similar in style of execution to the first. (Some reports credit this goal to Goldthorpe.) Then, perhaps due to lack of experience at playing at such an exalted level, the home side committed the cardinal error of not pressing home their advantage. The Lockwoods' half-back line was allowed to enter the fray. Some skilful inter-passing presented Sellars with an opportunity of reducing the arrears, which he duly took. A few minutes before half-time Downie, a new recruit from the Juniors, had a rush of blood to the head

> Contrary to popular opinion (and John Earles' memory) Macc. did not play and beat Blackburn Olympic during the Lancashire club's FA Cup-winning season of 1882–83. The teams met twice:
> 3 December 1881:
> Blackburn Olympic 6, Macc. 0
> 19 February 1887:
> Macc. 3, Blackburn Olympic 2

and miskicked a clearance. West was able to profit from the error, and equalised matters.

Still the home team were not finished. Sadler took the ball on a tricky run from the wing, and worked his way into a scoring position. The lead was thus regained, with what the match report termed 'the neatest goal of the day'. So Macclesfield led 3–2 at half-time.

Perhaps it was the Sheffielders' greater stamina that swung the pendulum in the second half; in any event, the Lockwoods scored twice more without reply. Thus the Silkmen's first ever FA Cup campaign was at an end, with a narrow, pluckily fought defeat.

There remained the Cheshire Cup. In the semi-final for the second successive year, Macc. met the rapidly improving Crewe Alexandra. Once again the Silkmen took the lead, from a Bates headed goal; once again things were allowed to slip, and Crewe were eventual 3–1 winners.

For the rest of 1883, the club appeared to be going through a transition stage. New faces arrived from the reserves, notably McDonald and Mellor the half-backs, and Jones in defence. In the FA Cup they fell again at the first hurdle, losing 0–2 to Davenham, one of the Northwich cluster of teams. That same month Jim Morton, quite out of character, left the field in protest when a disputed goal scored against him by the Norton team was allowed to stand. Dunkerley took his place, and the ten men won 3–2. On a happier note, Over Wanderers were thrashed 4–0 in the Cheshire Cup in December, in a match in which Jim Morton hardly had a save to make.

## Amateur and professional

Nationally, the Canute-like efforts to stem football professionalism continued. Earlier that year the FA had passed a resolution: 'any member of a club receiving remuneration of any sort above his actual expenses, shall be barred'. The ways around such a statute, though, were legion, and becoming increasingly blatant. Whether Macc. players risked expulsion in this way is impossible to prove one way or the other. There would certainly be no records left lying around which would help any modern day researcher! It seems fairly clear, though, that some money was changing hands in a playing context, and had been for some years. One telling piece of evidence emerges from a report of a 'hare and hounds' event in March 1878. The participating club is given as 'Macclesfield *Amateur* Cricket and Football Club' – the first time such a title had been used. This was also the year in which Macclesfield United first made an appearance, which suggests that players' expenses of some sort was the bone of contention which caused the secession of the 'United' from its parent organisation.

In any case, in January 1884 legalised professional football was only eighteen months away.

Yet ironically, it was a player in the mould of the great amateurs who, as briefly and as brilliantly as a shooting star, was to light up the town's soccer scene that spring. William Bromley-Davenport, of the celebrated Capesthorne Hall clan, had played for Eton and Oxford University. He was to be selected twice for England, and scored two goals against Wales in March 1884.

He was a central attacker of the old school, with his penchant for fast and penetrative dribbling, in that twilight of the amateur day.

Bromley-Davenport made his debut for the Silkmen against Chester St John's in January. It was another Cheshire Cup match. Already something of a local hero (he had scored for his regular club, London Swifts, in the FA Cup Third

Round some days previously) his presence no doubt swelled the gate to a – for then – massive 1,800.

His impact on that particular game was considerable, in that he scored three goals in his side's 4–0 win. However, one can sense a certain tension between Bromley-Davenport's breathtaking individual charges on goal – which elicited 'round after round of applause' from the spectators – and the habitual interplay of the other members of the team. One report stated that the players were 'in awe of' the newcomer's skills.

The match was as good an indication as any of the crossroads at which English football found itself mid-decade. On the one hand the dashing individual style of the glorious amateurs; on the other the cohesive team game associated with the emergent professionals. Whether Bromley-Davenport would have integrated into his side's game plan is one for the speculative historians to argue about. The next week he returned to London, to help the Swifts overcome Old Forresters in the next round of the FA Cup. He was to play for the Silkmen again on Easter Monday, in a friendly against Northwich Victoria. He was more subdued, partly through illness, partly through a willingness to play a more unselfish role. The Vics. won narrowly.

> The career of William Bromley-Davenport out-dazzled even his footballing days. Later to receive the DSO in the Boer War, elected Lord Lieutenant of Cheshire and knighted in 1924, he was also a minor poet and popular and able MP for Macclesfield for many years.

## Silkmen in the USA

The town was doing its bit in the spreading of the soccer gospel around the globe. One of the founder members of the club, Peter Wright,

who had been present at the inauguration of the Cheshire Association, wrote to the *Courier* from Patterson, New Jersey. He had formed a football club, composed almost exclusively of ex-pat Silk-men who were working in the town's mills. He records with barely-concealed delight a recent victory over a team of émigré Scotsmen.

Beating teams originating from north of the border was always cause for celebration. Inviting them down for a game was at least a financial *coup*, as showed by the Langley club when they played host to Dumbarton, the Scottish Champions. The match was played on the Victoria Road pitch, and was the first time a team from Scotland had played in Cheshire. Warren and Bates guested for Langley. The result, as expected, was a clear win for Dumbarton, by 5–0. The Silkmen would fare better against Caledonian opposition in future years.

In the meantime, preparations were already under way for the following season. Every Wednesday and Saturday throughout September was dedicated to training, and an open invitation to attend was offered to all the town's footballers. Peter Wright returned from the USA, and before long the club had found another attacker of no mean ability: the Rev. Cobbold, of the Grammar School. Team committee meetings were now held in the Drill Hall every Monday night.

The season began well: Chester College, the previous year's Cheshire Cup semi-finalists, were beaten 4–0. At Old Trafford, the Manchester Association succumbed by the same score. Hopes were again high for the first round of the FA Cup, against Hartford St John's in November. This Northwich-based side had been drawn at home, but had requested that the match be played at Macclesfield, as the Victoria Road ground could accommodate a larger crowd.

In a strong wind the Silkmen ran riot and scored nine goals without reply. Wright celebrated his return with a hat-trick, and Howarth, his usual rugged style curtailed by a sprained hip, showed the more sophisticated skills in his repertoire,

notably some invasive wing runs and accurate centres.

In the next round Macc. were drawn at home against Leek. They would be playing the Staffordshire club for the first time since the set-to two years previously.

Mindful of the possibility of lingering bad blood, the clubs' respective committees decided it might be a good idea to play a friendly, at Leek, one week before the FA Cup tie. As usual, it is easy to be wise after the event, but the decision, made of course with the best of intentions, turned out to be a short-sighted one. Antagonism was increased by some blatantly home-biased refereeing by a Mr Gwynne – 'and he proved to be a proper "G-wynne" for them' as the *Courier* report wryly stated.

The teams met again, then, for the Cup tie the following Saturday. Matters were evenly contested for the first thirty minutes, then Vickerstaff opened the scoring for Leek. Soon after this the first of many dubious Leek challenges resulted in Bates receiving a blow to the head and having to retire from the game. A second goal for the visitors soon followed, Morton dallying too long with a straightforward save. After half-time Macc. rallied, and Howarth centred for the Rev. Cobbold to reduce the arrears. For a while the ten men had the better of it, until Cobbold sustained a 'back-handed blow to the face'. He also had now to leave the field with a suspected broken nose. Against a demoralised nine men, Leek were now able to score three more goals without reply.

There remained, again, the Cheshire Cup.

One week later, as if to exorcise the previous game's demons, Macclesfield catapulted into the next round of the County Association competition by defeating Crewe Olympic 9–0.

Confidence thus restored, the Silkmen entered the New Year of 1885. It was to be a watershed year of some significance.

# 3

# *Cheshire Champions*

'Not even when Mafeking was relieved or when the Armistice was proclaimed on
11 November 1918 was there such a display of enthusiasm.'
John Earles, *Fifty Years of Football*

## *Some memorable FA Cup matches*

Northwich Victoria, as expected, won the Cheshire Cup that year, making it six in a row. Reasonably enough, they then asked the Association if, in keeping with tradition, the club could be allowed to hold the trophy in perpetuity. The celebrated Wanderers, it was pointed out, had been offered the FA Cup after their mere hat-trick of wins the previous decade.

The Association's ruling – by a handful of votes – was that Northwich could keep the trophy, but only on condition they fork out for a new one equal in value! The Vics. bit the bullet and asked for subscriptions to the cause from the other clubs in the county. The *Staffordshire Sentinel*, in waspish mood, wondered if the Crewe district would be as forthcoming with their donations as other areas. (The current Crewe–Northwich rivalry was approaching the obsessive.)

In any case, sufficient capital was gathered in, so that the Vics. could order a fresh trophy from the Birmingham silversmith Messrs. Faughton and Son. The original may still be seen in the Drill Field trophy cabinet.

The switch was symbolic: within a year, a new team would be Cheshire Champions. This was not to be Macclesfield – not just yet.

During the year, the Silkmen continued to experiment with team members. Newcomers George Gaskell, George Millington, and Jack Hindley were given a run. The reserves – christened 'Swifts' after the Stoke 'A' team – were supplying a steady influx of new faces. It was to prove a sound policy, with the occasional spectacular success.

The date was the last day of October, 1885.

Old – and so far dauntingly resilient – rivals Northwich had arrived on the Victoria Road ground to contest the First Round of the FA Cup. All the signs were in the away team's favour: they had just completed a 15-match unbeaten sequence during which one of the scalps had been West Bromwich Albion, Cup Finalists within the year. Moreover, when Goodfellow inexplicably did not turn up, leaving two comparatively inexperienced players – Millington and Downie – in the home half-back line, the visitors could perhaps be excused for already planning ahead to the next round.

What followed was pure *Boys' Own* stuff.

Banner, who had played the occasional reserve game, was spotted in the crowd, and hastily kitted out with borrowed boots and jersey, to take Goodfellow's place in midfield.

The game began, and Macclesfield hit their opponents like a whirlwind. Within three minutes Wright had opened the scoring. Six minutes later it was 2–0 from a cracking shot from Cartwright from the wing. The forwards, inspired, worked harder for one another than ever before, and the Northwich defence was run off its feet. The delighted *Courier* reporter asserted that the visitors had 'caught a Tartar'. Before half-time Bayley had made it 3–0. In the second half the Vics. rallied, and pulled one back after 65 minutes. The Silkmen

16

had the last word, though, with 'a lightning shot very high up' from Millington.

One of the major factors of the win was the industry of the half-back line. All three concerned were to receive their reward: Banner and Downie could now command a first team place, and George Millington would be team captain on another glorious day, four years hence.

Astonishingly, this would be the last victory of any note in the FA Cup competition proper – notwithstanding some worthy wins in qualifying rounds – for another eighty years. The next one though, as we shall see, would be well worth the wait.

The next round, a fortnight later, was an inexplicable reverse, against bogey team Davenham. Giving an unusually sluggish display, Macc. were routed 8–1. 'About four' of the eight were own goals, according to a brief, dismissive report in the *Courier*.

The Silkmen now went ten games without defeat, a run which took them to the semi-final of the Cheshire Cup once more. Notable results in this spell were: a 6–0 win over Park Grange (recently finalists in the Sheffield Cup, losing narrowly to the Lockwood Brothers); a creditable 3–3 draw in a friendly at Northwich; a similar score at Manchester against relative new boys Newton Heath (soon to be re-named Manchester United); and a record 15–0 demolition of Chester St Mary's in the quarter-final of the County Cup.

Generally, the legalisation of professionalism – finally brought out of the shadows by a series of FA rulings the previous August – seemed to be working in Macclesfield's favour. Players now had to register for the season with their club, and only those born within a twelve-mile radius of the ground, or who had lived within the area for at least two years, were eligible to play. It took a while and a couple of setbacks, but eventually the new stability of professionalism helped Macclesfield build what was to become, in County terms, a formidable team. There was a good deal of natural footballing talent in the town, and now that those involved were being paid – legally –

The Cheshire Senior Cup.
The competition was inaugurated in 1879. The original trophy is in the Drill Field boardroom, Northwich. This trophy, the current one, has been won by the Silkmen a record 21 times. (*Macclesfield Express*)

The record Silkmen winning score is 15–0. This they achieved twice, both times in the Cheshire Senior Cup:

6 February 1886: *v*. Chester St Mary's

12 November 1887: *v*. Barnton Rovers

Some big hauls from the twentieth century:

26 January 1901: Prestwich 3, Macc. 8

8 September 1906: Macc. 8, Berry's 0

14 September 1907: Newton Heath 1, Macc. 7

8 March 1913: Macc. 8, Bacup 0

5 October 1923: Macc. 8, Witton Albion 0

6 October 1928: Macc. 9, Manchester North End 1

17 October 1930: Sandbach 2, Macc. 7 (0–0 at half-time!)

4 December 1931: Macc. 8, Nantwich 4

22 April 1933: Macc. 7, Northwich Vics. 0

2 September 1933: Stockport Co. 1, Macc. 8

24 February 1934: Macc. 7, Altrincham 2

28 September 1934: Macc. 9, Prescot Cables 0

2 March 1935: Macc. 9, Winsford 1 (and see Chapter 11)

2 January 1937: Macc. 10, Hyde Utd. 1

3 October 1937: Macc. 8, Hurst 4

20 August 1949: Macc. 7, Buxton 1

21 September 1950: Macc. 7, Droylsden 2 (after a 5–5 draw!)

17 December 1960: Macc. 9, Wigan Rovers 3

15 May 1963: Macc. 8, Witton Albion 0 (see Chapter 16)

21 November 1964: Macc. 9, Oswestry Town 2

23 September 1965: Macc. 9, Witton Albion 0

16 September 1967: Macc. 7, Bacup Borough 0 (0–0 at half-time!)

1 September 1979: New Brighton 1, Macc. 7

17 September 1983: Tamworth 1, Macc. 6

21 September 1985: Macc. 7, Caernarfon 2

8 October 1985: Macc. 7, Colwyn Bay 1 (but *see* Chapter 23)

6 August 1994: Wednesfield 1, Macc. 10

28 January 1995: Macc. 7, Blakenhall 0

9 March 1996: Macc. 7, Halifax Town 0

20 January 1997: Macc. 9, Kidsgrove 0

for a job well done, the arrival at the top was only a matter of time.

The draw for the semi-final of the Cheshire Cup pitted Macc. against the strongest remaining team: the high rollers of Davenham (Welsh Cup finalists 1887). This was another club who had benefited from the new system: George Plant, the Northwich forward who had hit four against the Silkmen in another semi four years previously, was now in Davenham's colours. Macc. were trying out a new goalkeeper, Barnshaw; perhaps a game of such importance was not the best scenario in which to make a debut.

The game was played at the Drill Field, North-wich, in front of 2.000 spectators, three hundred of whom had caught the special train from Mac-clesfield.

The result was a victory for Davenham by 4–1. It seems that scars from the FA Cup encounter had not yet fully healed. Barnshaw was described as 'very nervous', and the rest of the team failed to play with its usual cohesion. Davenham went on to win the final over Crewe Alexandra, thus breaking the Vics.' stranglehold on the trophy.

Macc. were to meet Davenham again in a friendly on Victoria Road the following October. For the West Cheshire team it was the fifth match of the season; for the home side, it was but the first. The progress of the Silkmen was evident, in that after a close struggle Davenham scraped home 3–2.

On the surface, it was not to be a brilliant season, as Macclesfield fell at the first hurdle in both FA and Cheshire Cups. In the former, how-ever, defeat was eventually sustained in circumstances that came close to the surreal.

They had been drawn way against Goldenhill, who for a while were challenging Stoke for the role of premier Potteries team. Macc. had met them before on several occasions, and the usual outcome had been a close-fought game. On the day of the first round match, the visitors arrived late, to be told that the Midlands side had already kicked off, 'scored', and were claiming a victory! Whether this was intended as a ploy to rattle the opposition is unclear, but upon the immediate protest from the travelling team, Goldenhill at once agreed to play the match.

After a rough game, which was stopped five minutes before time following a violent tackle on Downie, the home side claimed a 4–2 win. Alfred Sadler, now the Macc. Secretary, sent a written protest to the FA asking for the match to be replayed. One of the issues was the size of the pitch, 'too small for a cup tie'. The FA upheld the protest, and ordered a replay on a neutral ground.

The venue did not have the happiest of connotations for the Silkmen: it was at Leek, a fortnight later, that the re-match took place. Banner opened the scoring, and in an open, exciting match – in marked contrast to the first one – both teams had chances before Goldenhill levelled matters just before half-time.

In the second half Macc., playing downhill, gained a succession of corners. With their constant pressure it seemed certain they would win, especially when Downie scored a second. Then, a couple of minutes before full time, and against the run of play, Goldenhill snatched another equaliser.

Darkness was descending, but it was decided to carry on for another half-hour. 'There was now no good play, the ball being very rarely seen', said the *Courier* report. In the symbolic gloom Goldenhill hit the winner.

In the Cheshire Cup Macc. performed their usual trick of being knocked out by the eventual winners. This year (1886–87) it was Crewe Alexandra.

## Effects of the popular game

Victoria Road continued to be a popular venue, reflecting the club's progressive view of the game. Mr Howarth, of local catering fame, had obtained the franchise for a coffee stall which he erected on match days. At half-time, until then simply the occasion for an immediate change of ends, the players would take the time for a cuppa. (The changing rooms were now in the *Spread Eagle* on Chestergate, fifteen minutes' walk away.) The pitch was of a good size, and not beset with a slope, so that the ground was often the choice for a neutral cup venue, and for County games. John Earles recalls with affection one aspect of the care and pride that was the hallmark of the club:

> Mr Riddlesworth, whose duty it was to look after the footballs, who carried them about like a good nurse carrying a baby, gave them their nightly bath of oil, blew them up with an air-pump, gave then their nightly massage, put them to bed, and in every possible way attended to their welfare. *Fifty Years of Football*

Nationally, Blackburn Rovers had just completed their hat-trick of FA Cup wins. The Manchester-born player Turner, who had guested briefly for the Silkmen as full-back partnering Bancroft, was a member of the winning Rovers team in '85 and '86.

Another one-time Macclesfield man was Levi Johnson, who had left for Wolverhampton in his twenties in 1876. Mr Johnson, later to become mayor of the Black Country town, was instrumental in the rise of the Wolves.

The late Victorian 'drift to the cities' had its knock-on effect in the football world, and was soon to prove a drain on the club's resources. (The population of the town had peaked at 37,514 in 1881, and would not reach this total again until well into the next century.) Fortunately, the town's reservoir of footballing talent would prove capacious enough to overcome the difficulties of the next couple of years.

1887 began with a visit from the celebrated Scottish club Vale of Leven, national Cup finalists three times in the past four years. 2,000 spectators lent their support, and saw Macc. win by 3–1. New face Dourdon, a guest from Lancashire, scored all three goals. He was to settle locally for a while, and make his mark as a prolific goalscorer, the perfect ally for Howarth on the wing.

The pitch, though, was in an awful state, ironically due to its constant use as a neutral venue. Its drainage was poor, and during the Vale of Leven game had a 'pond of water six inches deep by one of the uprights'. The ice on this had recently been broken, rendering play dangerous. It got worse. When Park Grange arrived the following week, ice-skaters were using the pitch as an outdoor rink! The footballers were compelled to transfer the game to an adjacent field, despite its knee-length grass and occasional hole. The Arctic wind discouraged many spectators, scores of whom withstood the biting cold for a few minutes, then decided to head for shelter. Despite the appalling conditions, and the 2–1 victory for Park Grange, the *Courier* reporter was steadfastly positive in his summing-up:

Play throughout was of the happiest nature, quite devoid of that horseplay which frequently mars these contests. Sheffield left for home in the evening taking victory with them, but leaving behind pleasant reminiscences of a very friendly meeting. *Courier* (22/1/87)

## Another near-miss

That spring the County Association inaugurated the Cheshire Junior Challenge Cup, open to reserve and amateur teams. The competition was to be based on four areas: Chester, Northwich, Crewe, and Macclesfield. Winners from each area would go forward to the County semi-finals. The Swifts entered, hopeful of victory. From the eastern edge of town, just before the foothills began their march up to Cat's Tor and Shutlingsloe, there came one Hallefield FC, an unsung side of amateurs. Within ten years they would take centre stage, but for the moment a defeat at the hands of St George's Rangers on Dane's Moss was their lot. In the grand final, on the last day of April, Macc. Swifts drew 2–2 with Crewe Alexandra Reserves, despite having been two goals to the good. They lost the replay.

The first team continued to play host to illustrious clubs. Visitors in February were Blackburn Olympic. Although their glory days were clearly in the past, as only two of the Cup-winning side of 1883 remained (half the team had crossed the town and joined the Rovers, where wages were higher), the old dog still had some teeth, as the close game showed. Macc. shaved a 3–2 win, with goals from Bates (2) and Howarth.

Other notable results that spring were victories over Manchester (4–1), Stafford Rangers (4–0), and a 2–2 draw with Northwich, in which Macclesfield had the better of the play.

The next season started auspiciously enough, with a 4–3 win away at Rossendale. The Lancashire club had been playing for several weeks, but once again it was the Silkmen's first match.

Immediately after Wakes week, Macc. were back in the lions' den with their first round FA Cup tie against Shrewsbury. Armitt, a recent replacement for Dourdon, scored for Macclesfield after just two minutes. Howarth hit the post soon after. Here again, however, the Silkmen flattered to deceive. By half-time Shrewsbury had equalised, and they went on to score twice more in the second half.

There was the usual backlash in the Cheshire

Cup: this year the victims were Barnton Rovers, dismissed by 15–0 in the first round the following month. At the end of an erratic season Macc. would reach the semi-final once more. Trailing 0–3 with six minutes left, they forced a series of corners. The constant pressure paid off with two goals in quick succession, one of them a fine long shot from Millington that sneaked in under the bar. Unfortunately the rally was not quite enough: the opposition broke away in the last minute and scored a fourth.

The opponents in that semi-final were Crewe Alexandra. They went on to demolish Chester 9–0 in the final. Chester had scraped home 1–0 against Northwich in *their* semi. So a simple calculation was enough to persuade the Macc. contingent that the coveted trophy was within reach.

But there were further breakers ahead.

Despite the 'name' teams that had visited Victoria Road, and the sizeable crowds, the club was in financial difficulties. It was announced at the AGM in August 1888 that Macclesfield FC would, at least for the time being, revert to being run on amateur lines. This was the signal for several players to move on: notably Jimmy Bates, who was the first of many Silkmen to register with the Stockport club.

## The fightback

Macc. boldly published a fixture card for the whole of the coming season, with every Saturday taken up from mid-September to the end of April. The mood of Leagues was in the air: the Football League would be launched within weeks, with the innumerable offshoots (Alliances, Combinations, etc., etc.,) to follow in its wake.

In September the club played host to Davenham. The team bore little resemblance to that of two seasons before:

Kent; Corbishley, J. Hall (c); Gaskell, Upton, Birchenall; Dean, Hindley, Hall, Jepson, Burgess

These were indeed the 'silk lads who played for sport and the honour of their native town'. If Davenham thought that the apparently cobbled-together team of amateurs would prove easy meat, they were soon to discover they had a fight on their hands.

Davenham opened the scoring early in the game, but Jepson equalised. The visitors regained the lead, and so the score remained at half-time. Dean, and then Jepson again, notched further goals. With one minute left, the Silkmen were amazingly leading 3–2. Then a last-gasp attack from Davenham restored credibility to the proceedings. 'If the whole team can be kept together,' stated the *Courier*, 'we shall hear of their doings with satisfaction.'

*If the whole team can be kept together ...* the underlying implication, as ever, was that good players could be lured away by more lucrative offers. Nevertheless six of the above team – plus Millington and Howarth – would be representing the club in their first ever Cheshire Cup Final the following year. Loyalty would be seen to attract other, more tangible, rewards.

The rest of the 1888–89 season was a chequered affair.

Macc. lost at Chester in the first qualifying round of the FA Cup. The score was 2–2 after ninety minutes, and because the visitors refused to play an extra half-hour, in their absence Chester kicked off – shades of Goldenhill – 'scored', and were, bizarrely but quite correctly, awarded the tie.

The spectre of that season's apparently vague on-the-day organisation followed the team into the Cheshire Cup. Drawn away against Northwich Victoria, the team missed their connecting train at Knutsford, and lost a 'very rough game' 0–4.

On the plus side, victories were recorded against Manchester (4–1) and Bollington (9–0). In the debit column, a 3–0 half-time lead against Denton, one of the teams soon to compete alongside Macclesfield in the Football Combination, was frittered away into a final 3–4 defeat. In the year of Preston North End's first ever League and Cup double, the Silkmen seemed destined to remain on the periphery of glory.

Yet it took but a few months for the real success story to begin.

Season 1889–90 saw a determined effort to 'keep the team together'. There is a good deal of evidence that around this time public and private sponsorship was one of the factors that helped the club to revert to professional status, and therefore to regain the right to register players for the season. The new mayor, one Alderman James Kershaw, made a lasting mark in his year of office. On his own admission this gentleman was, to coin a phrase, football daft. His enthusiasm was infectious, and used his position and persuasive skills to promote the two-way benefits of sponsorship. He had also spotted the role of football success in putting a town on the map. Fanatically opposed to player importations, he took great pride in the fact that the team that was about to sweep all before them was composed exclusively of local lads.

The contributions of the town's bigwigs and pub landlords to Macc.'s sudden – and long overdue – rise to prominence will be looked at later.

For the moment, the raw results tell their own tale: after losing 1–3 to Chester on the opening day of the season, the side recorded a phenomenal unbeaten run. Jewels in the crown were:

| | |
|---|---|
| Newton Heath | 7–2 |
| Sheffield Park Grange | 13–3 |
| Bollington | 6–0 |
| Hartford and Davenham | 3–0 |

The free-scoring forward line was led by Johnny Hall, who bagged six in the rout of Park Grange. He was ably assisted by Tom Burgess, new from the Juniors, and veteran Howarth. Another new acquisition was winger Tom Lea, a native of Southport who now worked as a tailor at Swanwick's in the Market Place. In defence George Millington, team captain and a former half-back, was a tower of strength. At 11 stone (70kg) he was, apart from Howarth, by far the biggest and heaviest of the team. This emphasises the skill which was the hallmark of the team, rather than the brute force which unfortunately still typified some of the opposition.

Millington was to be captain for several years to come. His partner was George Gaskell. The half-back line comprised Nathan Dixon, Joseph Birchenall, and William Bolton – 'the incomparable Billy Bolton' as John Earles termed him.

## Victory in the Cheshire Cup

The Cheshire Cup campaign opened with an away game with one of the previous year's semi-finalists: Chester St Oswald's. Here would surely be a touchstone by which to measure the team's chances. In front of 1,000 spectators Burgess drew first blood after a quarter of an hour's play. The score stayed the same until half-time, then immediately after the re-start the home side hit the equaliser. Towards the end of a dour, defensive game Ronson, a late inclusion from the reserves, snatched the winner for Macc.

The news from the other first round games was encouraging: Nantwich had beaten Davenham, and Crewe Alexandra – 'the Hornets' – had disposed of Northwich. So two of the three previous Cheshire Cup winners were no longer in contention. The team to watch, evidently, was the rapidly improving Nantwich side, relative newcomers to the Senior County scene.

The draw for the semi-final pitted Macc. against theoretically the weakest remaining contender: Over Wanderers, from Winsford. However, they were to give the Silkmen a rough ride, in more ways than one.

The tie was played once more at Northwich, on the Drill Field. Macc. attacked from the kick-off, but despite their array of fire-power, were unable to subdue Brittleton, the Over goalkeeper. Shot after shot was either held or fisted clear. The rest of the Over team seemed intent on rough-housing the lighter opposition. At one point the diminutive Kent received a bad kick, and was advised to leave the field. He did: for a matter of minutes, drawing a burst of loud cheering when he returned.

Over persisted in their intimidatory tactics, and had a spell of supremacy in the second half. In the end, though, the boxer defeated the slugger, and Tom Lea, running in from the left, hit the late winner.

The Winsford club lodged a protest, claiming that the referee had not played the full ninety minutes. But nothing came of it, and Macclesfield were through to the Cheshire Cup Final for the first time in their history.

The team went into special training, using the *Queen's Hotel* as their headquarters. John Allcock, licensee of the *Oxford Road* tavern, fitness buff and local character, had undertaken to supervise training. Alcohol and tobacco were out, and the team followed a strict regime involving diet, country walks, and Turkish baths.

The final, once again at Northwich, took place on 22 March 1890. An estimated 1,500 supporters trekked along the Saltway from Macclesfield, many availing themselves of the three special excursion trains. There was a 'visible effect on some businesses', said the *Courier*, dryly commenting on the semi-ghost town the exodus had left behind.

For those who could not make the journey, bulletins were wired to the *Courier* offices, outside which a fair-sized crowd gathered during the course of the afternoon.

At the Drill Field some 7,000 spectators had gathered. They were to be treated to what some

saw as 'the finest game which had taken place on Cheshire ground'.

The line-ups were:
*Macclesfield*: Kent; Millington (c), Gaskell; Dixon, Birchenall, Bolton; Burgess, Hindley, Hall, Lea, Howarth
*Nantwich*: Hassall; Shenton, Davies; Critchley, Bullock, Crawford; Hind, Prince, Bull, Hollowood, Cartwright

Macclesfield adopted their usual policy of immediate attack. They forced some early corners, with which Bolton, using the strong wind and his in-swinging technique, sought to test Hassall. Nothing came of this early pressure, despite shots from Howarth and Burgess.

Worryingly, though, Nantwich showed themselves fast and dangerous on the break, their forwards working well in the classic 'paired' attacking runs.

It was in one such breakaway that Nantwich obtained a free kick deep into their opponents' half, close to the touchline. Bull sent in a precise centre, from which Prince scored.

After that it was constant Macc. pressure, with Nantwich apparently hunkering down and conserving themselves for that next crucial break from defence. 'Thick and fast did Macclesfield shower shots at the Nantwich goal, but none of them were effectual,' wrote one reporter.

There were a few minutes to go to half-time when Bolton, taking a free kick from far out, chose to drop the ball close to Hassall. Under pressure, the goalie fisted clear – straight into the path of Howarth, who rolled back the years with a fine shot on the volley. It was the long-awaited equalising goal, and it was greeted by a deafening cheer, during which display of enthusiasm 'not a few

> John Allcock, trainer of the Cheshire Cup winning teams of 1890 and 1891, is also renowned for twice (1875 and 1902) walking backwards from Macclesfield to Buxton for a wager. The second time it was attempted Allcock was a 62-year-old suffering from a bronchial ailment, and walking against medical advice. Despite this, and the fact that his progress through Buxton was baulked by large crowds of spectators, Allcock accomplished the feat with ease.

dozen hats came to grief'.

Psychologically, it was the perfect time to score. Just before the end of the first half Millington sent in a thundering shot from fully half-way which skimmed the crossbar. By now the Silkmen were champing at the bit, hungry for the second half.

After the restart Macc. reaped the reward of all their training and preparation. Their attacks rolled forward relentlessly. 'Kent may have taken forty winks,' one observer commented. Hindley was moving in to score the second when he was held back by a Nantwich defender. Fifteen months later this would have earned a penalty, but at the time all free kicks were still indirect. Poetic justice prevailed, as Hindley followed up the kick and scored anyway, from close in.

By now Nantwich were being run ragged. Before long Lea hit the third, a well-struck shot from far out whose speed foiled Hassall. Soon afterwards it was Lea again who embarked on a run down the left. Defenders had moved across to intercept, but this left Hindley unmarked. Lea delivered an accurate pass to his fellow forward, and Hindley scored number four.

On the final whistle a great cheer greeted a popular victory. Macc. players were lifted onto shoulders and borne to the enclosure, where C. J. Hughes, secretary of the Cheshire Association, presented the cup to Millington. Alderman Kershaw was naturally in attendance, and he had cleverly persuaded other town dignitaries – W. F. Taylor, Town Clerk, and succeeding mayor John Staniforth – to join the entourage.

On their return home the team was met by a huge crowd, through which the brass band had to struggle. From the Hibel Road station wagonettes bore the players and trophy on a tour of the town, finishing at the *Queen's Hotel* where an evening of speeches and celebration ensued.

George Millington elicited vigorous applause when he stated that, now that the coveted cup was in the hands of the Silkmen at last, he for one was determined they should hang onto it for the foreseeable future.

The immediate future would be bright indeed: within a year the club was on the verge of winning its first ever league, was in the Cheshire Senior Final once more, and was making plans for moving into a new home.

# 4

# New Ground, New Faces

'There were several thousand spectators present, from Magistrates, ex-Mayors, and Aldermen down to the humblest workers in our mills and third and fourth standard boys at our elementary schools. There was also a sprinkling of working men accompanied by their wives, sons and daughters ... the vast multitude of people ...'

William Laycock at the Moss Rose (1891)

## The Combination

After their first Cheshire Cup win, Macclesfield finished the 1889–90 season with a flourish.

They had a busy and profitable Easter. On Good Friday Stoke Swifts were entertained, and a 1–1 draw resulted. The next day a combined team from Northwich, Davenham and Hartford came to Victoria Road. Evidence that the balance of power had swung away from the Saltite band, Macc. won easily, 5–0. Easter Monday saw the arrival of Bollington, who were beaten 3–0. A total of £70 was taken over the three days.

The club's finances were by now in a cheerful state once more. A combination of healthy gate receipts and the interest shown by a good number of the town's élite was swelling the coffers. Town Clerk W. F. Taylor, for whom the trip to the Drill Field had had a 'road to Damascus' effect, was to state that 'Macclesfield could travel another road to prosperity than through the silk trade'. It did not harm matters, of course, that a famous ex-player, the popular William Bromley-Davenport, was now the MP for the town.

Mr W. Greaves, manager of the Globe spinning Company at Lower Heyes Mill and one of the vice-presidents of the club, was one of those quick to nail his colours to the Cheshire Cup bandwagon. The week after the win at Northwich, before the friendly with Chester, he presented a silk scarf to each member of the team. This was, incidentally, the occasion of the first ever recorded team photo.

Mr B. R. Leech, another sponsor, took the pictures, of the Cup holders clad in their Final kit of red, yellow and blue stripes. (The blue and white would appear the next season, quite possibly a happy switch for any onlookers suffering from migraine.)

In September 1890 the club entered its first league competition. The Combination, like professionalism, suited the Silkmen. As the club had discovered to its frequent cost, the trouble with a season composed of friendlies and the odd cup tie was that too often last-minute cancellations left teams without a match, and therefore that week's staple income.

They would meet some familiar adversaries: Leek, Chester, and Northwich Victoria. Strong contenders, besides Macc., were Gorton Villa and Burton Swifts. Twelve teams started the season, but only nine would finish it: Staffs. County, Witton, and Derby St Luke's withdrew before the following spring. In future years, each club would have to tender a deposit of £10, returnable only when all fixtures were completed. These withdrawals, as it turned out, were crucial in deciding where the first Combination championship ended up.

The campaign began well. Macc. were league leaders until late November, when they lost the top of the table clash with Chester, 2–3 away. Thereafter the championship was a three-way battle between the two Cheshire sides and Gorton Villa.

## Silkmen sail to Ireland

In the meantime Macclesfield were back in the FA Cup, after a year's absence. Their opponents in the Midland qualifying division, at first glance somewhat oddly, were Cliftonville of Belfast. The Silkmen made the rough crossing to Ireland on 3 October, the day before Wakes Saturday.

The opposition was a strong outfit comprising no less than ten Irish internationals. Nevertheless in an open, exciting tussle Macc. came close to making a nonsense of the form book. Cliftonville scored first after half an hour, but Burgess equalised a few minutes later. It was 1–1 at change of ends. In the second half the home side regained the lead twice, only for the visitors to pull back each time. Hindley made it 3–3 with a few minutes to go, so into extra time it went. Macc. held out for a further twenty-five minutes, before a Cliftonville forward hit his side's fourth, decisive, goal. The Belfast match report generously conceded that 'Macclesfield had the best of the game'.

As had often happened, the Silkmen got the defeat out of their system by returning home and taking it out on their next opponents. This time it was Leek in the Combination, beaten 4–1, with Johnny Hall scoring all four goals.

In the Cheshire Cup Macc. were drawn in the first round against Nantwich, the previous year's beaten finalists. For obvious reasons the tie attracted great interest, and a crowd of over 2,000 congregated on the Victoria Road field. It was another high-scoring spectacular, with two goals in the first two minutes.

First it was Hall, latching onto a pass from Howarth. Then Bullock equalised with a long shot from midfield. Before half-time Hall had restored the lead, only to see Nantwich draw level again. The West Cheshire side were proving to be tougher nuts to crack than in the previous meeting. However, as the second half progressed, once again it was Macc.'s superior fitness that won the day. Hall scored twice more, and with Burgess and Hindley contributing, the final tally was a convincing 6–2 to the Silkmen.

## Time to move on?

The race for the Combination was really hotting up. Joint leaders Gorton Villa were played twice in a week in January. The first encounter, on the Abbey Hey ground, took place on the Monday morning, the original game having been postponed through fog. The result was a 2–2 draw, which gave Macc. some confidence for the return game the following Saturday.

On the day, the Victoria Road pitch was performing its frequent midwinter trick of doubling as an ice-rink. The morning saw men working at the ice with sledgehammers and carting it away in barrows. Six bags of salt were distributed over the ground, and 'a quantity of refuse' was scattered in front of both goals in an attempt to improve grip. Most of these efforts seem to have been to no avail, as the players still 'tumbled like skittles', much to the amusement of sections of the 3,000 crowd. The home side won the somewhat farcical, but in results terms crucial, match 3–1. This victory put Macc. back on the top of the Combination, although Chester, looming ominously, had games in hand.

In February the following front-page notice – perhaps ironic, but fundamentally heartfelt – appeared in the *Courier*:

### MACCLESFIELD CRICKET CLUB

### WANTED, A GROUND, IMMEDIATELY

Constant winter wear of the Victoria Road pitch surface (or what was left of it) had taken its toll. It was becoming evident that it was time for Macclesfield Football Club to move on, for their own good as well as for others'. (Interestingly, it would take the MCC just one more year to reach the same decision on the hallowed turf of the Kennington Oval, and insist the football fraternity play their Cup and international matches elsewhere.)

Macc. FC took the hint, and by next season had moved to a field adjoining the *Moss Rose* – which pub was much later renamed *Silklands* (see Chapter 19), then *Bonkers*, then *The Bramble*, and finally *The Silkman*. The cricket club's premises remain on Victoria Road until this day.

Cheshire Cup semi-final adversaries were again Over Wanderers. In another close game, but notably less physical than the previous year's battle, Hall scored the only goal of the game late in the second half. The winners would meet Crewe Alexandra Hornets in the final the following month.

Macc. now had their eyes on a tremendous double. Gorton Villa and Chester fought out a 3–3 draw, which left the top of the Combination table thus:

|              | P  | W | D | L | F  | A  | Pts |
|--------------|----|---|---|---|----|----|-----|
| Gorton Villa | 15 | 9 | 3 | 3 | 43 | 27 | 21  |
| Macclesfield | 14 | 9 | 2 | 3 | 43 | 23 | 20  |
| Chester      | 13 | 8 | 2 | 3 | 35 | 22 | 18  |

In some versions of the league published at the same time, Macc. were clear leaders, and seeming a good bet for the title. However, these calculations included the results involving the three teams who had withdrawn, against whom Macc. had registered high-scoring wins. In the official interpretation of events, these matches 'never took place', at least not for the purposes of compiling the statistics. Now, with nine teams remaining, the east Cheshire club had two games left in which to try and rectify matters, whilst hoping that their rivals did not pick up too many more points.

## Another final

Easter Monday saw the Silkmen contest the 1891 Cheshire Cup Final against Crewe. The match took place at Stockport in front of 11,000 fans, some of whom had travelled from Manchester, Liverpool, and Sheffield. The team had changed somewhat from the previous year's: Gaskell and Lea had left for Stockport County, 'Mush' Howarth had deemed it time to hang up his boots, and Dixon had departed for an undisclosed destination. Their replacements – Braddock, Wheeldon, Nolan and Heath respectively, had acquitted themselves well over the season, but the Hornets were considered doughtier opponents than Nantwich, and a closer game was anticipated.

Once again John Allcock had been in charge of training, and it was in buoyant mood – 'with whistle and song' – that the Silkmen made the short journey to Stockport.

The crowd's loyalties were seen to be largely with Macclesfield, as every attack by them was cheered and applauded. Midway through the first half Birchenall's run set up Heath, who scored. It was to be the game's only goal, Millington subsequently marshalling a resolute defence against the formidable Crewe counterattacks. At the final whistle, amidst 'a scene of indescribable confusion', the Macc. captain made his way through the throng to the grandstand, where he received the trophy once more. One section of his speech may be of interest to the historian of local tradition:

> We have today been doing battle against the Crewe Hornets, but their stings do not seem to be strong enough to penetrate the silk of Macclesfield, or they have not been able to get through the treacle.

Again a large celebratory crowd greeted their return, and another convivial evening was spent at the *Queen's Hotel*.

The winning goal was commemorated in a song that went the rounds for a time, as recalled by John Earles:

*Heath, he passed to Wheeldon,*
    *And Wheeldon passed to Hall*
*Good old Lukie Nolan*
    *Had his eye upon the ball;*
*Birchenall he had a try*
    *And cheers rang out again,*
*For Billy Heath he banged the ball*
    *Right beneath the bar.*

*Fifty Years of Football*

The combination title, having looked a distinct possibility for so long, slipped away at the end. The week before the victory at Stockport the team had suffered an implausible 0–3 home reverse against Burton Swifts. The players had sported 'silk jerseys and caps' for the first time on that day, but sartorial splendour had seemed to detract from footballing skills. Now everything depended on the last game: Gorton Villa beat local rivals Denton 4–1, putting them of reach of their pursuers, whilst Macc. could only draw 2–2 at Northwich. The final top of the table read as follows:

|              | P  | W  | D | L | F  | A  | Pts |
|--------------|----|----|---|---|----|----|-----|
| Gorton Villa | 16 | 10 | 3 | 3 | 47 | 28 | 23  |
| Macclesfield | 16 | 9  | 3 | 4 | 44 | 27 | 21  |
| Chester      | 16 | 8  | 4 | 4 | 42 | 30 | 20  |

The season ended with a 'past *v.* present' exhibition match, appropriately the last football played by the club on the Victoria Road pitch. The heroes of yesteryear – who were allowed to field eleven men against their opponents' nine! – were:

J. Morton, F. Lees, A. Bancroft, W. Goodfellow, G. Robinson, J. Chambers, J. Howarth, Walton, Moulds, Hall, P. Wright

The younger legs outran the old, and the current first team albeit depleted, won 5–2.

In May, at the Drill Hall, the new mayor, Cllr. John Staniforth, presented medals to the Cheshire Cup victors. He said that he had been impressed by the skills displayed by the team in the final, and their ability to outwit the more robust play from Crewe 'who were ahead in strength and muscle'. The town players had 'kept their tempers and minded their work'. Cllr. Staniforth, having by now well and truly caught the footballing bug from his predecessor, proposed a Charity Cup for the borough's teams, which would replace the long-defunct Silver Medal Competition.

The next season saw the introduction of the penalty kick, and the replacement of umpires by linesmen – the modern-day referee's assistants. Goal nets had made their first appearance earlier in the year.

Great changes were afoot locally, too. The Combination was back to twelve members: Macclesfield, Gorton Villa, Chester, Denton, Wrexham, Northwich Victoria, Leek, Everton Reserves, Chirk, Stoke Swifts, Stockport County, and Buxton. Stockport had flatteringly asked for their opening fixture to be against the Silkmen, as that way they were certain of a large gate. The return was to be at Macclesfield on Christmas Day.

## The Moss Rose

The club moved into the Moss Rose for the new season. The first game ever played there was on 12 September 1891, in sweltering heat. The opponents were Hyde.

The field was on the north-eastern corner of Dane's Moss, close to the London Road a mile or so south of the town centre. There was no grandstand at first, but a knoll at the south end, and 'a fine range of hills to the east' afforded vantage points. Also on the east was a small tree plantation, useful in sheltering the otherwise open terrain from the cold winter winds from the Peaks. Close by there was 'a small rustic arbour' which however 'needs a coat of paint'.

Initially, controversy dogged the change of venue. There were those who doubted whether the fans would make the journey from town in sufficient numbers to render the move profitable.

On the day of the match with Hyde these detractors were proven gloriously wrong, as fully 3,000 came along to the house-warming party. The stewards had difficulty in marshalling such unexpectedly high numbers, so that an estimated 1,000 missed the start of the match. The crowd had plenty to cheer: Hyde were trounced 6–1, with Heath especially revelling in the improved conditions.

Before the end of the season the Moss Rose was the cause of another war of words, in its way every bit as heated as the battles fought out on the pitch. One signing himself 'A Well-wisher to the Club' wrote a letter to the *Courier* expressing concern about the influence of public houses in the running of Macclesfield FC. The landlord of the *Albion* on London Road was quick to respond, echoing the sentiments of fellow publicans from the Sutton end of the town: basically, they were delighted with the extra business the football crowds brought along!

Mr Freeston, leading light of the town's temperance campaign, joined the fray. He noted 'the very unsatisfactory condition of the club', and, not allowing a little thing like the truth to get in the way of a good soap-box harangue, went on:

The club is so infested with public-house interests that it seems it only exists for their benefit ...

... all the possible results of this noble game may be, and often are, not only counteracted but converted into a terrible curse by the demon intoxication. *Courier* Correspondence (16/1/92)

The crucial influence of public houses in furthering the cause of the Association game had obviously eluded Mr Freeston's attention. The role of the *Pack Horse*, the *Spread Eagle*, the *Oxford Road*, and the *Queen's Hotel* has been documented in this history, and need not be brought forward in evidence here.

Once again, it was a spokesman for the club who was allowed the final word. William Laycock, writing under the transparent *nom de plume* of

'Layhen' described the 'vast multitude of well-behaved people' at a recent match at the Moss Rose. He confessed himself at a loss as to what 'these goody-goody people want'. The gist of his response was: go and see for yourselves. There the matter seemed to rest, and Mr Freeston and his platoon went on to tilt at other more justifiable targets.

The league season had started with a famous win at Stockport County. Johnny Hall bagged two of the goals: one with his head, and the other a tap-in after some attractive close-passing approach work from the other forwards. The final score was 3–0.

An unlucky 2–3 defeat at the hands of Everton Reserves – who were widely tipped to run away with the title that year – was followed by a gratifying 4–0 win over reigning champions Gorton Villa.

> The record attendance for any match at the Moss Rose is 10,041 at the 1948 Cheshire Senior Cup semi-final between Witton Albion and Northwich Victoria

On the Tuesday of Wakes week Preston North End paid a visit to the Moss Rose. Despite the torrential rain, 3,000 spectators turned up to watch the Silkmen take on 'The Invincibles'. The Lancashire side had just finished runners-up to the Everton first team in the Football League, and as expected, ran out 4–1 winners. Macc. were nevertheless worthy opposition, and contributed to an open, entertaining game for the holiday crowd. Wheeldon, at 5ft 2 ins (1m 59) easily the smallest on the pitch, hit the home side's goal.

Macclesfield were unable to achieve a hat-trick of Cheshire Cup successes, losing 1–3 to a resurgent Northwich Victoria in the semi-final.

In the FA Cup Macc. sent a reserve side to meet the same team for their Third Qualifying Round match, as the first team was due to meet Combination leaders Everton on the same day. Ample evidence of what would surely happen if the club's resources were so stretched, both games were lost.

By March of the 1891–92 season, Everton were twelve points clear at the head of the Combination. Northwich Vics., with convincing wins over Denton (13–0) and Stoke Swifts (6–0) overtook Macclesfield into runners-up position. So it was at the end, with the Silkmen being pipped into third place by a single point.

To compensate, the Swifts won the Cheshire Junior Cup, as well as the inaugural Charity Cup. Warrington, top scorer, would soon be appearing as centre-forward on the first team.

The final match of the season at the Moss Rose was a friendly with the great Blackburn Rovers, who the previous year had won the FA Cup for a record-equalling fifth time. Macc. put up a fight, narrowly losing 2–3. The occasion was another financial success, the gate money received being a ground record of £70.

1892–93 was a further transition stage. The team was now studded with players who had shown promise in the reserves:

Kent, Braddock, Hindley; Burgess, Nolan, Heapy, Allman, Heath, Warrington, Potter, Hall

This was the side that lost 0–4 to Northwich Victoria in that year's FA Cup. The Vics., struggling in their first year in the new Second Division of the Football League, would have their own problems by the end of the season, when a loss of £300 would be disclosed at the general meeting. Their solution was to hold a bazaar and sports day to raise the necessary capital. By now, even the most die-hard of the amateur school of thought was having to accept the marriage, for better or worse, of football and finance.

Macc. finished in the lower half of the Combination – won easily again by Everton – and went out of the Cheshire Cup at the semi-final stage once more, 1–3 at the hands of Crewe Alexandra. It was becoming clear that, to keep pace with other clubs, Macc. would have to cast its net wider in a search for players.

## *Professionals*

Thus it was that, at the beginning of 1893–94, five newcomers registered with the Silkmen. Three of them came from Staffordshire: full-back Dick Ray, later to move to Manchester City; forward Danny Hollinshead from Leek; and winger Sol Riley. From Middlesbrough Ironopolis there was centre-forward McCabe; and 'Augustus' Brown, a Stockport man, joined Heapy and Billy Bolton in the half-back line. These new arrivals were hailed as 'the veritable champions of the team'. Perhaps unsurprisingly, though, the new line-up took some time to jell, as it was well into October before the first win was registered. It was achieved in memorable circumstances.

In the opening round of the FA Cup Macclesfield fought out a thrilling 5–5 draw at the Moss Rose with Shropshire club Newtown, who were to win the Welsh Cup the following year. In the replay the Silkmen sustained an early goal, before

Bullock equalised close to half-time. Thereafter the away team took control, and goals from McCabe, Hollinshead (2) and Burgess brought matters to a happy conclusion.

In the next round Chester were beaten 6–1. The forward line, dubbed 'the quintette' by the *Courier* reporter, by now had obviously found their shooting boots.

It was Crewe Alexandra, again, who were the thorn in Macc.'s side. An unexpected 2–3 reverse against the Railwaymen put an end to the dreams of an FA Cup run that season. Bad luck struck again within a month, when Bullock and Brown were laid low with the 'flu. Combination defeats against Everton and Stockport County added to the midwinter misery.

A chance to make amends arrived in March. The club was drawn against Crewe Alexandra in the semi-final of the Cheshire Cup.

By now the squad had been further boosted by the arrival of several more fresh faces, notably John McVickers the ex-Irish international who had recently played for Ardwick. He was a tall, no-nonsense full-back who was to be a major factor in stemming the flow of adversaries' goals that had temporarily threatened to engulf the Silkmen. Other newcomers were: Joe Rogers, who had replaced the unhappy McCabe at centre-forward; and forwards Caton and Edge from Stoke. Edge was later to take over the proprietorship of the *Moss Rose* pub – just one example among many of an ex-footballer who went into the licensing trade upon his retirement from the game.

Macclesfield took revenge for the FA Cup defeat by disposing of Crewe 2–0 at Cale Green, Stockport. Bolton and Caton were the scorers. In the other semi-final Chester knocked out Northwich.

The 1894 Cheshire Cup Final took place at the Drill Field. Heath, who had injured his shoulder, was replaced on the right wing by the reserve player Gosling. The teams were:

*Macclesfield*: Kent; McVickers, Ray; B. Hall, Burgess, Bolton (c); Gosling, Bullock, Rogers, Edge, Caton

*Chester*: Moore; Thompson, Wilson; Turner, Farrall, Astbury; Bull, Fleming, Lewis, Hayes, Grewcock

In a close game, Hayes opened the scoring for Chester, but a second half goal from Rogers cancelled this out. 1–1 it remained, and the teams shaped up for the replay the following Saturday at Crewe.

The usual special train was laid on, with a saloon car for the players and their entourage. Altogether 1,000 faithful made the journey from Macclesfield, on a day of brilliant April sunshine.

The teams were the same as in the first match, except that Pickering replaced Fleming, and Heath, now recovered, returned to the Silkmen's line-up. The popular Johnny Hall replaced Edge.

For a while the pattern was the same as at Northwich: Chester took the lead with a goal from Grewcock, then in the second half Billy Bolton hit a penalty after Caton had been impeded by Turner. Late in the game Bullock struck the winner from a Heath cross.

It was Macclesfield's third Cheshire Cup triumph in five years. Their next target would be the Combination Championship.

The roller-coaster ride had begun.

# 5

# *The Moss Rose Bubble*

'To carry on the business of a Football and Athletic Club in all its branches, and to lay out and prepare any lands for the playing thereon of games of football, cricket, bowls, rounders, curling, lawn-tennis, polo, running races, steeplechases or any other kind of amusement, sport or entertainment, and to construct any stands, booths, refreshment and other erections, buildings and conveniences ... and to arrange ... agricultural, horse, flower shows and exhibitions ... and to contribute toward prizes and other rewards ...'
*From the prospectus of the* 'Macclesfield Football and Athletic Co., Ltd' (May 1895)

'In beautiful weather, the Macclesfield 'amateurs' – with no intent to flatter – left their home by wagonettes, and had an exceedingly pleasant drive to Northwich, arriving at that salubrious town of salt and rickety houses at around half past two o'clock.'
*Courier* (6/3/97)

## *The Limited Company*

Any enterprise with a history – and that, of course, includes football clubs – can point back to peaks and troughs in its career. What was about to happen to Macclesfield FC, as we follow the jolting trajectory of the next three years, was an extreme example of the 'boom – bust' cycle that can afflict a new business venture at the mercy of market forces.

There were those who had been convinced from the start that sport and finance were poor bedfellows, and any attempt to associate them was bound to come to grief sooner or later. But in these days of huge sporting conglomerates and universal sponsorship, we have the wisdom of over a century at our backs, and can come to different conclusions.

Besides, the idea of turning a football club into a limited company was nothing new. Small Heath (later Birmingham City) had taken the plunge in 1888, and within five years had won the inaugural Second Division title. More recently, and of more obvious significance, Ardwick had followed suit, becoming Manchester City in 1894. Enough cash had been generated to lure the promising nineteen-year-old winger Billy Meredith from

Northwich. The switch to 'Ltd Co.' appeared to make sense.

It was against this backdrop that the drama of 1894–97 began to unfold.

By the end of November Macc. were once more in the semi-finals of the Cheshire Cup, having defeated Crewe Alexandra 2–1. Kent injured his wrist during the game and was out of action for several weeks, but his place was ably taken by Jack Leather, the reserve goalie. Leather was to assume first team status permanently, when Kent left for Congleton the following year.

Then, within a week, came the first indication that all was not well. The Secretary, Mr J. E. Smith, resigned, amidst (totally unfounded) rumours of financial impropriety. Despite the vote of confidence from the committee – an audit had found the club accounts correct 'to a farthing' – Mr Smith stuck by his decision to stand down. The reason seems to have been more curiously personal than anything else: the ex-Secretary claimed that there were 'false rumours got abroad concerning his character'. This was greeted with a good deal of puzzlement on the part of the committee.

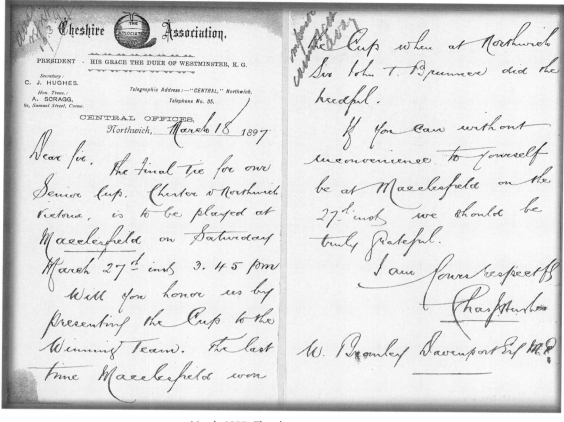

March 1897. The show must go on …
Whereas the 'Limited Comapny' was on its last legs the Moss Rose was still being used for that year's Cheshire Cup Final. (From the Bromley-Davenport archives, John Rylands Library, Manchester)

On the pitch, life went on: the Silkmen celebrated Christmas Day by inviting Bolton Wanderers (FA Cup finalists that year) to the Moss Rose. The 3,000 spectators warmed to a nine-goal thriller, the Lancastrians shading a 5–4 win. Surely another great season was in prospect?

Not so: within a month the first team were out on strike. The reserves took the field for the friendly against Heywood Central,

… owing to the refusal of the first team to conform to the reduced financial remuneration offered by the committee in the present straitened circumstances of the club. *Courier* (19/1/95)

As was often the case in late nineteenth century industrial relations, it was the management that held most of the trump cards. Footballers were even worse off than most, as so far they had not been mobilised into any sort of effective union. Within a few weeks the first team players had begun to drift grudgingly back, without any increase in their pay. Reading between the lines, one can guess that the committee had got their heads together and come up with what seemed the perfect solution. The money was not there – yet; but financial backing in abundance was only as far away as the next season. In promising 'jam tomorrow' the club's backers had more or less committed themselves to the 'limited liability company' option.

Some of the newly acquired players decided not to wait that long. On the day of the 1895 Cheshire Cup Final against Chester, not a single one of the much-trumpeted importations of 1893 made an appearance:

Kent, Hindley, Gaskell, Hall, Heapy, Bolton, Bullock, Wheeldon, J. Hall, Burton, Oldham

Chester had been beaten finalists for the past three years, and had not experienced too much joy in recent encounters with the Silkmen. This time, though, the usual agenda was reversed, in that Macclesfield scored the opening goal, through Heapy after twenty minutes. The lead was enjoyed for just two minutes, when Spencer enabled Chester to draw level.

In the second half, despite constant attacking from Macc., it was Chester that stole the winner. Brown sent in a long shot from the touchline, and the flight of the ball appeared to deceive Kent. This was the first time that Macclesfield had ever lost in the final of any knock-out competition.

In the Combination, the troubled season ended with the Silkmen slipping to sixth position.

The fateful AGM was held on 10 May 1895.

The balance in hand was reported as £24 12s. 2d. (£24.61). This was down on the previous season's £49 13s. 4d. (£49.67). Gate money showed a decrease of £300.

On the plus side, the club was clearly already a thriving concern, with assets estimated at £150.

After the preamble, it was recommended that the limited liability company be launched. 500 shares at £1 each would be offered, with no one person allowed to hold more than five. It was stated that 300 of these had already been provisionally taken up.

Macclesfield Football and Athletic Company officially came into being on the last day of July 1895. Within a month one half of the available shares had been snapped up, and as another successful season got under way, the rest were soon bought. It seems clear that those who took up the shares were genuine supporters of the club, and not carpetbaggers seeking a quick 'killing'. (The maximum annual dividend had been fixed by law at five per cent, so the chances of rapidly acquiring a fortune this way were slim.)

The sudden influx of cash attracted more soldiers of fortune: from Derby came Shannon and Sawyer. W. Ray (Dick's brother) joined the attack, as three Scotsmen: Murray, a Dundee man, was centre-forward for a while, and Drinkwater and McKenzie, natives of the tiny Grampian village of Braemar, formed a left wing partnership.

## A great season

The Combination was down to eight teams, but Everton Reserves were back. This time, though, there would be no runaway win: Macc. would see to that.

The early season found the forward line in lively form. Leek were beaten 7–0, then Oldham County succumbed 5–0. In November Bury of the First Division came to the Moss Rose and were trounced 5–2.

By December the top of the Combination table read as follows:

| | P | W | D | L | F | A | Pts |
|---|---|---|---|---|---|---|---|
| Everton | 9 | 8 | 1 | 0 | 41 | 8 | 17 |
| Macclesfield | 7 | 5 | 2 | 0 | 17 | 5 | 12 |
| Glossop NE | 6 | 4 | 2 | 0 | 12 | 3 | 10 |

The success story continued: Welsh Champions Druids were beaten 5–0 on Christmas Day. Macc. travelled to Liverpool early in the New Year to lock horns with Everton, in what was widely seen to be the virtual battle for the title. The Merseysiders won 3–0, but that was the last match the Silkmen were to lose for the rest of the season.

The semi-final of the 1896 Cheshire Cup pitted Macc. against Congleton Hornets, whose line-up included exile Jack Kent in goal. In the first match at the Moss Rose, Kent, evidently with something to prove, kept all the home attacks at bay. The goalless draw necessitated a replay at Willow

Street, Congleton. Here the Silkmen made amends, hitting five goals to the Hornets' one, in a very one-sided game. The home player Beresford walked off the pitch in disgust after Mr Dale, the Manchester referee, had disallowed a goal for offside. The high jinks did not end here: at the end of the game the match official was chased by an irate mob the mile or so to the railway station, where he was able to call upon police protection.

The final was at Northwich, and the opponents Crewe Alexandra. One of the thousand or so Macc. supporters who made the journey was William Bromley-Davenport, who motored up from Capesthorne in his new-fangled 'horseless carriage'. (The Red Flag Act had just been repealed.)

The Macclesfield team had no less than eight players from the town:

Leather; Gaskell, Ray; Reddish, Heapy, Bolton (c); Hall, Potter, Murray, Wheeldon, Drinkwater

The game was as good as decided within one minute half-way through the first period, when first Ray, then Murray, scored. Late Crewe pressure was cancelled by a defence well marshalled by Gaskell. So for the fourth time in seven years the Cheshire Cup came home to Macclesfield.

The usual celebratory tour of the town with brass band took place on the team's return that evening. Hallefield, winners of the Charity Cup the same day, followed in the wagonette behind. Within another twelve months the aptness of this would become plain.

The Combination went right down to the wire. Everton, having lost at Glossop, needed just one point from their last home game – again versus Glossop – to be certain of the title. The away team scored first, then a late Everton goal had the Merseysiders breathing a huge sigh of relief.

In the end goal average decided matters:

|  | P | W | D | L | F | A | Pts |
|---|---|---|---|---|---|---|---|
| Everton | 14 | 11 | 2 | 1 | 54 | 12 | 24 |
| Macclesfield | 14 | 11 | 2 | 1 | 37 | 13 | 24 |

On the surface, then, all seemed well. The season had been the most successful in the club's twenty-odd year history. Football League teams had been challenged and beaten. Would the Silkmen now follow Northwich and try their hand at the English Second Division?

Alas! The Limited Company was already in financial difficulties. The expected income had not materialised; the planned money-spinning non-football events – with one exception – were not happening. Patronage from the influential appears to have declined. Crowd numbers were erratic, some said because of the distance of the Moss Rose from the centre of town. Matches were sometimes very late starting, which cannot have helped gates.

Players were seeking their fortune elsewhere. Jack Leather joined the up and coming Woolwich Arsenal; Gaskell left for Oldham, his place taken by the ever-faithful McVickers. One by one the Scotsmen and the Midlands contingent left for pastures new, as the club's dwindling resources took their toll.

Despite these departures the enterprise in general put on a brave face. In August 1896 the Company organised an 'Amateur Athletics Sports' at Victoria Road. Several dignitaries were in attendance, and ex-Mayor J. Kershaw presented the prizes. Over 2,000 spectators lent their support, during an afternoon enlivened by the Volunteer Riflemen's band. It looks like a conscious effort on the part of the organisers to bind the business venture into tradition.

## Collapse

The Company, however, was already locked into a tailspin. This had a knock-on effect on the pitch, since, as the next season progressed, Macc.

eventually fielded what was mostly a reserve side. Of the old guard, only Wheeldon, McVickers and Bolton remained. The team was constantly chopped and changed by the committee – their selection policy was likened to 'a game of shuttlecock' – and after a reasonable start, defeat followed defeat. One spark of encouragement was visible on Christmas Day, when Northwich were beaten 2–1 on the Moss Rose. Then by March the players had agreed to play without wages; at least this way the club could keep going until the end of the season.

Thanks to this gesture, and to a draw which showed a profit of £60, a £210 deficit was cut to a mere £10. Unfortunately, hydra-like, the debts kept on materialising, and ideas, income and capital were by now well-nigh exhausted.

Of the last few games, the less said the better. As the town of Macclesfield prepared its contributions to Queen Victoria's Diamond Jubilee celebrations, the football club agonised quietly in the wings. The last match was a 1–6 defeat at Chester, for which only nine Macc. men turned up.

As the club's assets were sold to make good the Limited Company's debts, the first Macclesfield FC folded at the end of the 1896–97 season.

> The inevitable has happened ... all that now remains of the once popular Silk team is a pair of goalposts, a few old shoes, and a number of unsettled bills. *Staffordshire Sentinel* (4/9/97)

The shareholders received a commemorative silver sixpence (2½p) each, and that was that.

Appropriately, it was Hallefield FC who now adopted the Moss Rose as their home ground.

# 6

# *Re-birth*

'Red Riding Hood kicked the ball off.'
*Courier* (8/1/98)

'In the yard of the dressing room an enterprising photographer expressed a desire to take my photograph posing with the Cheshire Cup alongside, but natural modesty forbade it. I suggested he might take a group of our team along with that trophy and publish it as a "Study in Futures" but as he wanted cash in advance we did not trade.'
Walter Addy (Treasurer) *Staffordshire Sentinel* (23/1/04)

## *Hallefield fill the breach*

It was not, of course, a definitive full stop. There was some measure of continuity, in that some of the amateur players switched allegiance to the new town representatives. Reece, Upton and Hooley, who had figured in the reserves, appeared in the forward line for Hallefield's opening game of the 1897–98 season. It was a friendly against Middlewich, members of the newly formed Cheshire League.

The result was an inspiring omen: Hallefield ran out 7–1 winners. They now set about the task of restoring some pride to the town. It was in the arena of the Stockport and District League that the team gave notice that the footballing flame of the Silk town was burning as bright as ever. Hallefield were clearly out of their class. High-scoring victories were accumulated, so that by January, when they had completed their games in hand and hit the top of the league for the first time, they were still undefeated. In the year of the Klondike, the side had hit its own version of pay dirt: after eleven matches their goal tally was 43, against 7.

There was continuity, too, in the official and administrative domain. Josh Whittaker and Peter Wright had joined the Cheshire FA executive committee, and Wright, Jos. Chambers and McVickers (back from a brief stay at Port Vale)

were refereeing. Former player and club Secretary Alfred Sadler had tried his hand at this latter activity, but upon angering a section of the Chester crowd who had threatened to 'pull his whiskers off' he had decided to ply his considerable skills elsewhere.

As the success and fame of the amateur side grew, so there was a gradual drift back into the fold. First it was Gosling, winger in the 1894 Cheshire Cup Final; then Tommy Bullock, Wheeldon, Joe Heapy, and perhaps the biggest surprise, Jack Kent in goal. By Christmas Murray had forsaken his native Dundee for Macclesfield once more.

One of the most popular returns of those days was Billy Bolton, back from a cup-winning stint at Stockport County. Without quite the sharpness of old, he was still a solid half-back, and one of the reasons why, for a while, the crowds seemed to be showing signs of returning to the Moss Rose.

One long-term concern, nonetheless, would be the number of spectators, for obvious reasons down on previous years. The steam tramline that in halcyon days had reached as far as the football ground now lay idle. In turn-of-the-century Macclesfield, there were many other leisure distractions: cycling was the new craze, its column in the *Courier* dwarfing the football entries. When

Hallefield demolished Sandbach 10–1 in the Cheshire Amateur Cup during Wakes week 1898, there was a scant crowd, partly due to the arrival of the Barnum circus in town!

Hallefield, then, were runaway winners of the Stockport and District League, winning fifteen of their eighteen matches, drawing the rest, and amassing sixty-four goals in the process. Their only defeat that season was in a New Year exhibition game against members of the local theatre group dressed up as pantomime characters. The winning goal was scored by The Old Woman Who Lived in a Shoe.

Pre-grandstand days at the Moss Rose, *c.* 1900. In the early years, ladies were admitted free.

1897–98 was a happy time, a necessary healing process; but there were sterner challenges ahead.

Despite the return of some of the old players, the next decade is not notable for trophies won or famous opponents sent packing. Rather, beyond that first all-conquering season of Hallefield, that time will be remembered for the tenacious spirit that kept the club alive at all. Walter Addy recalls:

> It was suggested to me by a gentleman highly connected with the club that it might be advisable to allow the town team to fall through. The utter absurdity of such an idea admits of little comment …
>
> The executive are not built that way.
> *Staffordshire Sentinel* (31/3/00)

Several personalities, on both playing and administrative sides of the game, are prominent in carrying the Silkman torch through those years.

Alderman Savage, President of the club, devoted his energies to successfully enlisting support from the town's influential. Mr Bennett, Secretary until 1901, was instrumental in launching the Factories' and Workshops' Medal Competition, concrete evidence of the cross-fertilisation of sponsorship. And might not the factory and mill floor bring to light players of first-team calibre?

Walter Addy, writing in his column in the *Staffordshire Sentinel*, helped spread far and wide the awareness that the football team of Macclesfield was still alive and kicking. He wrote with relentless good humour (which occasionally shifted into steely satire) and never lost the belief that one day the Silkmen would rise again.

This faith was especially needed during the two torrid years spent in the North Staffs. and District League. The records (see Appendix) look worse than they really were, as some teams dropped out before the end of the season, taking a fair slice of Hallefield's points and goals tally with them.

At least the lesson of 1897 had been learned:

the finances of the club were sound, and would remain so. 'Expenditure beyond capital' was recognised as a criminal folly, and every penny was now scrupulously watched. Hallefield had inherited, along with the Moss Rose ground, a debt of £15. This was cleared before the end of the first season.

The Cheshire FA had decided that it would be in order for amateur clubs to pay general expenses and overheads out of their share of the gate money, then divide what remained between the players. In this way, amateur status was not threatened.

(This was fairly common practice: Newton Heath had resorted to this so as to survive the 1901–02 season, before re-emerging as the Limited Company 'Manchester United' the following September.)

After toying with a double-barrelled name for a year or two, by the turn of the century 'Hallefield' had reverted to 'Macclesfield' plain and simple. In September 1900 the club joined the Manchester League, and found they had old adversaries on the agenda.

## Return journey

Amongst co-members of the Manchester League were Hyde, Oldham Athletic, Buxton, Lymm, and Northwich Victoria. Macc. would do well enough, finishing ninth out of fifteen teams. High-scoring victories, in front of the newly white-washed Moss Rose stand, were 8–0 against Prestwich, 5–1 against Lymm, and a 7–3 defeat of Oldham Athletic. Such displays must have been well worth the threepence (1½p) entrance fee. Overall, though, results were too erratic for there to be any serious challenge to the leaders.

In 1901 the committee was disbanded and another formed. The list of those attending reads like a Who's Who of the club, past and present:

Chairman: Tom Sheldon
Treasurer: Walter Addy
Secretary: George Hall
Assistant Secretary: John McVickers
Also present: Alfred Sadler, George Burgess, William Bolton, James Sheldon, Dick Ray, Peter Wright, etc., etc.,

Alderman Savage was re-elected President. William Fitchett was re-appointed trainer, and the line-up for the first team that autumn was:

Hawley; Yates, Turner (or Stevenson); Rose, Laycock (or Bolton), Vigrass; Bullock (c), Reece, Bloor, Livesey, Moores

These were all local players, it not being financially viable – as yet – to import foreigners.

One exception was Tom Lloyd who came 'with excellent credentials' from Crewe, to take over the goalkeeping by the New Year.

Before the end of the season Lloyd himself was to be supplanted by one of the great characters of that time: the mountainous Frank Smith. Celebrated in a rhyme by Walter Addy was a last-minute penalty save in a league match:

SMITH, M. B. (*Macclesfield's Best*)

Smith, M. B. advanced yards three
Away from front of goal.
Centre shot could not pot,
Far too small that hole.
Great delight, left and right,
Many had left, poor dears!
Quoth Lowe to me: 'That's one to thee',
Cheers! Cheers!! Cheers!!!

Full-back Stanley Turner also played cricket for the County. George Laycock was the son of the Rev. William Laycock who had supported the club against attacks from Temperance a decade before.

It was a time of staunch parochial support: would-be poachers from other clubs, notably Oldham, Poynton and Stockport, went away empty-handed. The foundations for future success were being laid, both on the pitch and off it. Season tickets were now available at 7s. 6d. (37½p) and were usually snapped up within days of issue. The hoarding around the ground was

Macclesfield A.F.C. 1906. Postcard

repaired, frustrating those who had been able to peer through the holes in the woodwork and watch the games for free. The Borough Reed Band entertained the crowd during half-time – and they would receive the proceeds from a benefit match. By 1902 the subscribers had broken the £100 barrier; a member of the committee wagered that he could drum up support from fifty more within two weeks. He won his bet.

There was a thoughtful arrangement of fixtures. The season now traditionally began with a 'Salt v. Silk' match with popular rivals Northwich. As many home games as possible would be crammed into the more clement months of September and April. The result was at last a significant increase in gates: 3,000 at the Moss Rose was now the rule rather than the exception.

The atmosphere of gathering momentum – plus well-publicised healthy finances – helped attract a clutch of new players in September 1903. The bulk of these came from Langley, but the vanguard of a migration from Crewe was composed of two skilful forwards: Clewes and Jack Williams.

Williams, who was later to be controversially transferred to Manchester United – helping that club achieve promotion to the First Division in 1906 – was to be a prolific scorer for the Silkmen in his two years' stay.

By 1905 the club had an impressive 73 players on its books. In the Manchester League only Buxton, with 85, could boast more. The first team before the departure of Williams was:

W. Humphries; W. Yates, J. Poulson;

J. Sutton, F. Warham, A. Byrne (c); T. Reece,

D. Barnett, M. Goodwin, J. Williams,

H. Holland (or J. Clewes)

That season, which saw Macc. finish mid-table again in the Manchester League, nonetheless gave some hint of the glories to come. By mid-October they were fifth, a mere three points behind leaders Denton. On Boxing Day North-wich were beaten 3–0, in what was described as 'one of the best games ever seen on the Moss Rose ground'.

This win helped sweeten the pill of the exit from that year's Cheshire Senior Cup. Bollington St John's had, against all expectations, drawn their first round tie at the Moss Rose. (Macc. had already drubbed them 4–1 earlier in the season.) The replay, on a pitch which was 'like running up Church Wallgate' saw an unusually lethargic Macclesfield lose 3–4. Yates missed a last-minute penalty. So inexplicably sluggish was the Silkmen's performance that a rumour circulated to the effect that Bollington had employed the services of a hypnotist to influence their opponents!

Nonsense it may have been ('Professor Knoc-kout, specialities rheumatism and football,' was an aside from Addy) but it reflects the growing expectation of Macc. success.

The following season (1905–06) a stirring run of five consecutive away victories early in the New Year lifted the team into sixth posi-tion. A new committee had been formed, and whilst some of their decisions did not meet with universal approval (for example Williams' transfer) it was difficult to argue with hard results.

The position in the league is very creditable, and says a good deal not only for the unity of the players but as well for the discernment of the committee. *Courier* (3/2/06)

In the summer of 1906 the forward line was strengthened by four new arrivals, chief among whom were the resourceful striker Tom Case from Chester, and inside-left Tommy Nolan, a diminutive but tricky Bollington player. Wood-house, a fast orthodox winger from Worksworth in the Midland League, completed the left-sided attacking partnership.

Alongside Yates in defence was the deceptively obese-looking Jess Robinson, possessor of a kick like a mule, but unfortunately with a moodiness to match. (And as we shall see, thereby hangs a tale ...) Goalkeeper was now the small but ef-fective John Wilkinson, who, along with half-backs Vic Hall (son of club Chairman Fred) and Albert Byrne would soon be representing Cheshire.

It was almost like old times. Now for the loyal Silkmen supporters the years of waiting were about to be rewarded.

# 7

# In Pursuit of the Double

'Never say die, and the end shall be wagonette, bugles and cup!'
*Courier* (29/9/06)

## The new stand

There was an upbeat start to the season. The opening game was at Northwich on a bakingly hot day, the adjacent River Dane swarming with swimmers. The Silkmen came away with a creditable point in a 2–2 draw, the visitors' goals being scored by Case and Nolan.

The new attack settled in quickly. At the first home game, against north Manchester outfit Berry's, a record 8–0 defeat was inflicted. Case netted two in the first three minutes, and went on to score two more before retiring injured.

The one early season defeat was at the hands of Altrincham, thanks to a highly controversial penalty award. Wilkinson appeared to be the object of a dangerously high kick from an opposing forward; great surprise was expressed on all sides when the goalkeeper was penalised for impeding! The 2–1 result would be looked back on ruefully by the end of the campaign, when Altrincham would pip Macclesfield to the Championship by a single point.

The following week such quibbles were far from the club's mind. The new grandstand was opened on 6 October 1906. It had been erected in just a fortnight, having cost £77, most of which had been rapidly raised through donations. It could seat 300, was 58 ft (17 metres) long, and was to remain the centrepiece of the ground for another 62 years. The new changing rooms soon followed, situated in the pub corner, on the site of the present snack bar.

The mayor-elect, Dr Somerville, officially opened the stand. Also present were faces from the club's past: founder Walter Thorp, now a colonel, and Alderman Savage, who praised the Moss Rose as 'one of the finest grounds in the Manchester League'.

In front of what was estimated as the 'biggest crowd for twelve years' Macc. beat Heywood Utd 2–0, Case scoring twice.

After several lean years in the Cheshire Senior Cup, the Silkmen now embarked on a run which would take them back to the final. In the first round at Congleton, a neutral observer might have been forgiven for supposing that the game was at the Moss Rose, such was the numerical strength and vocal power of the Macclesfield support. (Indeed, the club's away following has remained a proud tradition down the years.) Urged on by the visiting hordes, the team registered a 2–0 win. Their reward was a bye into round three, where they would meet Bollington.

In the meantime, the club was continuing its challenge for the Manchester League. They were leaders briefly in December, after a 1–0 victory over Tonge. It was a dour, rough game, in which it took a flash of genius from Case after 78 minutes to break the deadlock. He headed clear from a knot of players, then followed the ball at speed to create his own scoring chance, hitting an unstoppable shot on the half-volley.

Case was by no means the only striker to grab the limelight. In the 6–0 rout of Newton Heath, Tommy Nolan bagged all six – and he missed a penalty! It was about this time that the word was Port Vale were on the prowl for his services.

8  MACCLESFIELD TIMES AND CHRONICLE, FRIDAY, APRIL 21, 1911.

WATCH THE FOOTBALLERS CLIMB THE MANCHESTER LEAGUE LADDERS.

THE GRADUAL PROGRESS OF THE TEAMS AT A GLANCE.

WHICH TEAM WILL REACH THE TOP FIRST?

For the present Football Season we are producing for the third time, as will be seen from the above, an interesting feature which we introduced two years ago, and which will, no doubt, be watched with keen interest by all football enthusiasts. Above are 16 ladders, representing the 16 teams in the Manchester League, with which Macclesfield Town Club is connected. The number attached to each football ladder indicates the particular club, the name of which will be found in the list given herewith. As the points are made the Footballers will climb the ladders, their right-hand being opposite the figure on the ladder giving the number of points gained, so that the position of the various Clubs will be seen at a glance. The following is the list of the Clubs in the League, the numbers indicating the footballer on the above ladders —

1—MACCLESFIELD.
2—ALTRINCHAM.
3—NORTHWICH VICTORIA.
4—CREWE ALEXANDRA RESERVE
5—WITTON ALBION.
6—NANTWICH.
7—TONGE.
8—BUXTON.
9—SALFORD UNITED.
10—HOOLEY HILL
11—HAZEL GROVE.
12—NEW MILLS
13—TYLDESLEY ALBION.
14—BERRY'S
15—BUSHOLME.
16—HURST

Just after Easter, 1911, and Macc. are about to claim the Manchester League title for the second time.
(*Macclesfield Express*)

Whether this was true or not, Nolan was not about to move anywhere.

Bollington having been disposed of 6–0, Macc. now prepared to take on championship rivals Altrincham at home. The circumstances of the previous meeting, plus the teams' proximity at the top of the league table, ensured a phenomenal interest. Over 6,000 crowded into the Moss Rose, and the takings were a ground record.

Altrincham scraped home 1–0, seemingly scotching Macc.'s hopes. However, a late run in the league would maintain Silk involvement to the end.

Lostock Gralam were the next opponents in the Cheshire Cup, and they were duly dispatched 2–1. The semi-final necessitated a journey across the county to Port Sunlight to take on the team financed by Lord Lever, and thus with a sprinkling of Liverpool players. On a day of pouring rain the home side had the edge and scored first, albeit with a lucky shot that squirmed through Wilkinson's grasp, the ball greasy with the mud. Tommy Nolan equalised.

The replay took place at the Moss Rose a fortnight later. On a day on which 'all roads led to the ground', once again the takings record was overhauled. Macclesfield won by the single goal, and so were through to the Cheshire Cup final for the first time in over a decade. By a quirk of fate their opponents were the same as last time: Crewe Alexandra.

## Bridesmaids

So there was the by now familiar trip to the Drill Field, with what was theoretically a strong team:

Wilkinson; Yates, Robinson; Pickford,
Warham (c), Hall; Mitchell, Nolan, Case,
Maybury, Woodhouse

They were wearing their red and white strip – such had been the first team choice since the Hallefield days. The Drill Field enclosure and touchline were awash with the red silk kerchieves sported by the usual enthusiastic band from back home. One supporter accompanied Macc.'s attacks (of which there were many) with a blast on his trumpet.

In a fast, flowing game the Silkmen had most of the play, but strangely, given the fire power in the forwards, could not score. Mitchell hit the crossbar, Nolan inexplicably put wide of an open goal; ex-Macc. full-back Poulson foiled a late Nolan run, executing a well-timed tackle and scrambling the ball out for a corner.

Crewe scored twice, both goals coming against the run of play. So, as in the Manchester League, Macc. had to be content with runners-up.

The following season (1907–08) saw the Silkmen back in the FA Cup, after an eleven-year absence. First there was a superb 4–1 win over Lancashire Combination team Wigan Town. Case shared the

Silkmen stars of the pre-First World War era. (*Staffordshire Sentinel*)

Macclesfield F.C. 1907–08.

goals with Howard, a new acquisition from Buxton.

The Second Round was a gristly series of struggles with Buxton themselves, in which both hero and villain was the inimitable Jess Robinson.

Robinson was a native of Rusholme, Manchester. The previous year he had been guilty of an unexplained absence from a crucial match, and his sullen and apparently off-hand manner when questioned by the committee seems to have provoked them into dropping him for the next game. Too good a full-back to be sidelined for long, though, he was soon forgiven.

The first match with Buxton was a goalless draw. In the replay the following Wednesday evening at the Moss Rose Robinson scored the first goal with a thundering shot from far out, the sheer force of which unbalanced the goalkeeper and caused him to stagger backwards over the line. Buxton drew level, and during extra time Robinson showed the darker side to his nature,

head-butting an opposing forward in the penalty area. Buxton scored from the kick, but the gods were truly on Macc.'s side that evening, as the match was abandoned as darkness descended.

The Silkmen finally won through 3–2 the following Monday at Stockport, in a thrilling game in which Swindells, the reserve goalkeeper, saved a penalty. The best joke of that evening, fittingly, revolves around Jess Robinson. A local lady, observing the defender's physical appearance and style of play, referred to him as 'that great bulldog'. Up piped a lad from Macclesfield: 'Aye, and he's fed on treacle too, Mrs'.

The FA Cup run of that year came to an end in the next round. Macc. went to Atherton and were outplayed, losing 0–5. But once more, it was a defeat from which the team were to learn much.

Another positive note: the FA Cup ties had brought in £50 profit.

In the Cheshire Cup they were drawn against

crack amateurs, the Manchester-based Northern Nomads. Considered by some to be the north's answer to the Corinthians, they were to reach the Amateur Cup Final in 1914. Non-professional members of Liverpool, Sunderland, Sheffield Wednesday and Port Vale figured in their line-up.

Macc. won through at the third attempt, by a whisker: 1–0 at home. All three encounters had been notable for almost total absence of fouls and gamesmanship: impressive advertisements for pure football.

After beating Tranmere Rovers – another Combination team – 2–0 in the next round, they were drawn against Altrincham in the semi-final. Without Howard and Nolan, they succumbed 1–3.

But the very next week saw a significant, talismanic victory: Macc. played Altrincham again, this time in the league, and won 2–0. It was the first time they had beaten the north Cheshire side. The victory lifted them into fourth position; their first Manchester League championship was now just twelve months away.

## Race for the title

The 1908–09 season could not have asked for a more sensational start. Macc. kicked off in their opening match at the Drill Field, and immediately set off Hulme, the new right winger, on a run which took him to the corner flag. Here, he gave his full-back the slip and sent in a precise centre. Upton, the other Northwich back, panicked and handled the ball on the goal line. Nolan took the penalty, and the Silkmen were a goal to the good after thirty seconds. By half-time it was 3–0, and though the Vics. rallied in the second half to make the final score 3–2, the game had seemed to set the optimistic tone for the coming year.

There was a surprisingly early exit from the FA Cup at the hands of St Helens Town, but thereafter defeats were a rare phenomenon. League leaders New Mills were to beat them 5–2 in October, when they lost Yates early on through a recurrence of his knee injury. Denton, the previous year's champions, were the only other team to overcome them in the first half of the season, by 4–3. The leading positions by Christmas were:

|  | P | W | D | L | F | A | Pts |
|---|---|---|---|---|---|---|---|
| New Mills | 13 | 7 | 4 | 2 | 39 | 18 | 18 |
| Sale Holmfield | 12 | 8 | 1 | 3 | 31 | 18 | 17 |
| Macclesfield | 11 | 7 | 2 | 2 | 30 | 18 | 16 |
| Northwich Vics. | 13 | 7 | 2 | 4 | 40 | 23 | 16 |
| Tonge | 12 | 7 | 2 | 3 | 20 | 11 | 16 |

On Christmas Day Buxton were beaten 2–0, then the following day Northwich – perhaps having wassailed too keenly – lost 0–5 at the Moss Rose. At New Year New Mills, Macc. and Tonge were joint leaders on 20 points, but the Silkmen had played one game less.

January was the pivotal month. As their rivals faltered, Macc. collected a series of wins and worthy away draws. The return match with New Mills, seen by many as the decider, was watched by more than 6,000 at the Moss Rose. The home side found it impossible to unpick a stubborn, skilful New Mills defence. The game was goalless until well into the second half, when came the hour, came the man. A corner to Macc. was cleared to midfield, where Robinson was lurking. He unleashed a special which flew like a rocket into the net. This provoked

> … a continued shout of triumph, which, carried by the wind, was distinctly heard in the hills as faraway as Walker Barn. Robinson had scored, and whatever his burly faults, that one kick has forever wiped them out. *Courier* (23/1/09)

They were now leaders, with a cushion of three points.

Having lost another Cheshire Cup semi, this time to eventual winners Chester, the Silkmen could now devote all their attention to the league. On Easter Saturday Sale Holmfield were the visitors, and after a 2–0 win the club awaited news from Salford, where New Mills had to win to stay in contention. The result was a cause for celebration: their rivals had lost 0–2, and Macc. were Manchester League Champions with two games to spare. The *Manchester Guardian* (24/4/09) asserted that 'Macclesfield won the race with ease, and deserve their prominence'.

## Summit

Thoughts now turned to the double of Cheshire Cup and Manchester League. It had been achieved only once before, by the Altrincham side of 1904–05.

As usual the club had attracted some new faces by the start of the season: chief protagonists in the drama to come were Joe Bentley, a forward who had started out as a Knutsford full-back, but who had since been a goalscorer for Crewe and Chester; Cranna, a winger from Manchester United; and Hayes, an alert and skilful centre-half from Hazel Grove. Robinson had left, his place taken by Pickford, a local player. Pickford had represented Macclesfield Modern School, showing such promise that Liverpool and Derby County had made bids for him. He had declined because of business commitments, but had done good service as captain of Stockport County.

In goal was now Burbidge, ex-Newton Heath. He had performed well in the closing stages in the run for the championship, and was automatic first choice. Unfortunately he was to meet a tragic end within the year, through a severe form of aggravated influenza.

Such darker days seemed impossibly distant as the season got under way, with Macc. apparently sweeping all before them. They opened with seven consecutive victories, scoring twenty-eight goals against six. After the 3–1 win over Witton Albion, an opposing supporter was heard to ask: 'Are Macclesfield invincible?'

It took two defeats in November for the question to be temporarily answered. The pack started to close in, notably Salford United, Denton, and Altrincham. Another winning spell steadied the boat, but then in March Burbidge took ill.

Whenever morale sagged, the inspirational role of club Chairman Fred Hall came into play. His half-time pep-talks gained him a well-earned reputation, and Macc.'s second half rallies were a frequent and stirring sight.

Typical was the fourth round Cheshire Cup tie at Altrincham. The home side were a goal up inside twelve minutes. On sale outside the ground were mock 'funeral cards' – a popular idea for a while – whose verses cried crocodile tears for the Silkmen's imminent demise. This time, though, the card vendors went home out of pocket, as the visitors hit back with three late goals. Their semi-final opponents would be Stockport County.

A 6–0 win over Newton Heath replaced Macc. on top of the Manchester League, but other teams had games in hand. Allen, the reserve goalkeeper, had been playing brilliantly: the defence let in just six goals after Burbidge's departure. However, too many drawn games, and a 1–2 home defeat to Altrincham, saw the title slip away. The club could console itself with the highest goal tally – 86 – although goal average, unusually, was not taken into consideration under Manchester League rules. The final top of the table was:

> When Fred Smith died in 1958, at his request his ashes were scattered over the Moss Rose pitch.

|  | P | W | D | L | F | A | Pts |
|---|---|---|---|---|---|---|---|
| Salford United | 34 | 20 | 6 | 8 | 79 | 44 | 46 |
| Hurst | 34 | 19 | 8 | 7 | 70 | 39 | 46 |
| Altrincham | 34 | 20 | 5 | 9 | 82 | 41 | 45 |
| Macclesfield | 34 | 18 | 6 | 10 | 86 | 45 | 42 |

In the Cheshire Cup, the final was reached yet again, with a creditable 2–1 semi defeat of Stockport County, despite conceding an early goal.

The final – history repeating itself, or at least playing a variation on a familiar theme – was against Crewe Alexandra. The venue was the

Racecourse Ground, Chester. The pitch had been criticised for its sodden, unresponsive turf, and the result, a 0–0 draw, seems to reflect this. Certainly Macc. had a poor first half, especially since Bentley had to retire injured after just five minutes.

The second half, no doubt partly due to Mr Hall's ministrations, was a livelier affair, with the Silkmen doing most of the attacking. Cranna hit the ball over the bar when it had seemed easier to score; in partial mitigation Crewe were awarded a penalty which they missed.

The replay, on the Wednesday of the following week at Edgeley Park, Stockport, saw the Railwaymen win 1–0. It was another penalty, awarded after Pickford had appeared to knock the ball down with his hand. Thus the season which had promised so much ended barren.

Joe Bentley left for Manchester City. A far-seeing committee replaced him with Richard Best, a Preston North End man with a range of skills. One of the few criticisms of Bentley had been that his service to his wing men was not always what it should have been. Best, playing as a deep-lying centre-forward, was now to prove the perfect linkman. His passes were precise, defence-splitting; he had the speed and supreme reading of the game to get among the goals as well.

The team for that momentous 1910–11 season was:

Allen; Johnson, Smith; Warham (or
Pickford), Hayes (c), Warrington (or Taylor);
Winnington, Nolan, Best, Brogden, Cranna

Full-back Fred Smith, ex-Derby County and Buxton, a whisper short of six feet (1m 83) was to prove another inspired acquisition. This year Macc. ran a waiting, positional race in the league, giving away few goals and not hitting the leading position until the final months. By February Altrincham were six points clear – but the Silkmen had three games in hand. The scene was set for a barnstorming finish.

In the meantime there was another FA Cup defeat at St Helens. This time there was not even the compensation of a cut of a substantial gate. Macclesfield actually sustained a financial loss on the trip to Lancashire. The meagre crowd was due to the fact that local allegiance had just switched to Rugby League, the result of the arrival in town of five New Zealanders!

The Cheshire Cup was a succession of potentially tough ties. They were exempt until round three, where the opposition was Combination high flyers Hyde. Rubbishing the form book, Macc. ran out convincing 4–1 winners. They then disposed of Stockport County 2–0 in a replay. The receipts from this game were a Moss Rose record of £92 9s. 10d. (£92.49).

Into the semi-final once more, where they met Northern Nomads, hungry for revenge. A fast and determined Nomads team, which contained ex-Silkman Vic Hall, scored an early goal. Outplayed for most of the match, Macc. lived on by the skin of their teeth, thanks to a fluky 87th minute equaliser, a mishit drive from Warham. So another replay, this time at Altrincham. A purple patch early in the second half, during which Best and Taylor scored a goal apiece, was enough to clinch the tie.

Their opponents in the final were Chester, winners of the trophy twice in the past three years. The venue was the Crewe Alexandra ground at Gresty road.

McAngus, a versatile forward fresh from the Lancashire Combination, was given the inside left spot alongside Cranna. Brogden, who had performed well deputising for Nolan, was switched to right wing.

Macc. scored in their first attack. Nolan dispossessed a Chester forward and ran deep into the opposing half. Reversing the usual process, he then set up Best with an accurate pass.

The goal had a devastating effect on the Chester morale, and for a while it looked as if Macclesfield could win as they pleased. No further goals were forthcoming, however, and gradually the opposition worked their way back into the game.

Hero of the day was Allen, as time after time he beat away or held some forceful shots, always placing himself for the best. A Crewe observer was to comment: 'I never saw a custodian who kept goal more cleverly'.

The fort was held until the final minutes. For-tune, which had seemingly deserted the Silkmen the previous year, now dealt them a large favour. Allen punched clear, but for once was in an irrelevant position as Smith of Chester found himself in front of an open goal. Incredibly, the forward snapped at his shot and the ball flew over the crossbar.

So Macc. scraped home 1–0. It was their fifth Cheshire Cup win; only Crewe (9) and Northwich (7) had won more, and Macc. were to overtake them both as the century progressed.

'W. J. L.' was inspired to compose the following:

> Hurrah, hurrah, hurrah, my boys,
>   At last the battle's done.
> The final tie has now been played,
>   The Cheshire Cup we've won;
> So loudly cheer with three times three
> For such a famous victory.
>
> We had to meet the Chester men
>   Who played with zeal and zest.
> Their forwards were a splendid lot
>   But hadn't got a 'Best'.
> How Macclesfield's supporters roared
> To see the lovely goal he scored.

> The Chester men fought gallantly
>   To neutralise that goal;
> Their combination was superb
>   They played with heart and soul,
> And sent in many a stinging shot
> But 'Allen' bravely saved the lot . . .

*Courier (15/4/11)*

Now for the Manchester League.

As was often the case, it was the Easter pro-gramme which virtually decided matters. On Good Friday, after a parade of the Cheshire cup around the Moss Rose perimeter, Altrincham were beaten 2–1. A point at Crewe (1–1) the following day, and a victory against Buxton on Easter Monday, left Macc. poised to take the title. To be mathe-matically certain, they had to beat Tonge on the Thursday evening. Nolan scored the necessary single goal, and the Silkmen had achieved the second half of a fantastic double. They eventually finished six points clear of their nearest chal-lengers.

Now, like Altrincham, Macclesfield would be seeking to leave the comparative mediocrity of the Manchester League. The next rung up the ladder was seen as the two divisions of the prestigious Lancashire Combination.

# 8

# *A Sterner Struggle*

'Clubs are requested to place their grounds at the services of the local Recruiting Agencies
and to arrange for addresses to be given out at the commencement of matches and also at
the interval with a view to encouraging the enlistment of His Majesty's forces. Clubs are
also requested to make collections at all matches and to arrange for special matches to be
played on behalf of this fund.'
*Cheshire FA Committee meeting (6/9/14)*

## *Two first teams*

There were voices of caution on the new threshold: notably Secretary G. Sumner, who spoke of previous winners of the Manchester League who had gone on to higher things, then, because of increased expenditure, had 'slid into bankruptcy and extinction'.

This was possibly a touch of scare-mongering. Sumner was a member of the Manchester League committee, who were well aware that they needed the support of the successful clubs such as Macclesfield in order to survive. However, the style of play of the recent champions was clearly superior to the 'hustling game' of the majority of such company.

The Macclesfield committee decided to hedge their bets, and put out two first teams: one for the Manchester League, and one for the second division of the Lancashire Combination ... This way, it was reasoned, they would always have the old league to fall back on if ambition over-reached itself.

The dual campaign started ambitiously enough, with a 3–2 Combination win over South Liverpool. One of the goals was a headed effort from H. Coid, a half-back recently acquired from Altrincham. The midfields were further strengthened by the arrival in December of Gaskell, a Bollington-born man who had just completed a useful stint at Bolton Wanderers.

He was noted for his subtle contributions to approach play – 'the expert at work' as one report had it.

Such intelligent half-back play was to be the secret of much of the Silkmen's success as they made their way up the leagues. Of stalwart Warham it was said: 'He uses his head in many ways, and the brains are quite as much used as the bones.' (*Staffordshire Sentinel* 14/10/11)

On a fixture-free day in November the two teams played one another:

*Manchester League*: Allen; Pickford, Smith; Warham, Hayes, Coid; Hallworth, McAngus, Butterworth, Barnett, Craven

*Lancs. Combination*: Marshall; Johnson, Beresford; Daniels, McMahon, Lomas; Blackburn, Hodgson, Worthington, Brogden, Ogden

The result was 1–1. There was 'not the difference of one acorn between the teams'.

As was perhaps to be expected, though, such division of resources diluted the season's achievements. Results were erratic, also due to the constant shuffling of line-ups. A first team pool of just fifteen players was all that had been required to reach the heights of the previous season. The lesson was obvious.

For a while there was a rumour – given further credibility by a couple of newspaper reports – that the club was about to decamp to Wright's Field off the Buxton Road, using the *Puss in Boots* as a base. In the event, this was to prove just another in the long line of such unfounded tales which seemed to have dogged the club since its move out to the Moss Rose in 1891.

The crowds still came: the entrance fee was still just 2*d*. (1p), or 3*d*. (1½p) for the grandstand. A season ticket at 10*s*. 6*d*. (53p) remained a popular option, despite the increasing number of possible alternative demands on leisure time and finances. For example, the town could now boast three purpose-built 'electric cinemas', and the 'Macclesfield and District Motor Club' would soon be in existence.

By the end of the season the problem of the two teams solved itself, as the reactionary and increasingly unpopular Manchester League folded. Macc. had finished fourth, and a late run in the Lancashire Combination (using the more dependable League team) had lifted them to a reasonable sixth position.

But for a town that had come to expect success, and considering the early exit from Cheshire and FA Cups that year, it was clear that changes had to be made.

## Promotion

A squadron of Cheshire clubs accompanied Macc. into the Combination: Nantwich, Witton Albion, and old rivals Northwich Victoria. They were all to make their mark, with the Vics. winning the race to be first promoted to the Lancs. First Division. The Silkmen would be hot on their heels.

The 1912–13 season was barely a month old when the whole town was shocked to hear of the sudden death of ex-mayor Colonel W. J. Thorp. Walter Thorp, it will be remembered, had been instrumental in the founding of the Macclesfield Football Club forty years previously, although he had severed his links with the Association club upon the arrival of professionalism. Ironically he had been on his way to London to plead the pro-amateur case to the Rugby Union when he was struck by a 'seizure'.

Just four years previously another of the enthusiastic old guard, Alderman Savage, had passed away. The club, of course, was not short of a new generation of supporters and patrons.

Now, in football terms, the Silkmen were determined to put the immediate past behind them. They reverted to a single first team, with the reserves playing in the North Staffs. League.

Notable in that season was a spectacular run of seven consecutive league victories, which eased them into top position by Christmas:

| | P | W | D | L | F | A | Pts |
|---|---|---|---|---|---|---|---|
| Macclesfield | 14 | 9 | 2 | 3 | 35 | 17 | 20 |
| Atherton | 14 | 9 | 2 | 3 | 43 | 27 | 20 |

It will be noticed that the team's strength was in its defence. The preferred line-up was the experienced Allen in goal, and the equally battle-proven Pickford and Smith at full-backs.

By March, following three more landmark wins (Darwen 2–0, Lancaster 4–0, Bacup 8–0) 'Weaver' wrote in the *Staffordshire Sentinel*:

Macclesfield are virtually certain to pass into the First Division of the Lancashire Combination.

Unfortunately this was to prove a case of chicken-counting, as Macc. suffered puzzling reverses towards the end of the season, eventually finishing sixth once more. They had, however, almost doubled their goal tally from the previous year, and had dealt out enough drubbings to serve notice of their intent.

By Christmas of the last season before the outbreak of war, Macc. were hovering mid-table. This was despite the return of Bentley from Manchester City, and of Gaskell from a coaching stint with a Moscow team. Gaskell was not to stay long, disappearing by mid-December to a Football League club. Priceless new acquisitions that autumn were Tom Greaves, an ex-Stoke City centre forward and prolific goalscorer; Lingard, a skilful winger from Tranmere; and possibly the pick of the crop, the subtly effective inside forward Bithell (hat-tricks a speciality).

In goal was now the 'smart and nippy' Birds, initially chosen to replace the injured Allen in November. Partnering Pickford at full-back was Harry Pearson, and the half-back line eventually comprised Gilfinnan ('the penalty king'), Stanfast and Johnson.

It was potentially a powerful team, which, once into its stride, launched into another cavalry charge up the league. In the twenty games after Christmas just five points were dropped, and on the 18 April, when a solitary Greaves goal gained the points at Newton Heath, promotion was clinched. The final position was runners-up, three points behind Witton Albion.

There was one shadow over that year: the death of club president Bradley Smale. He was one of the two guarantors of the club (the other was succeeding president J. G. Frost), and a good deal of financial support was lost with him. The end-of-season debt of £150 would plague the club until the end.

## Heroes

Upon the outbreak of war, Macclesfield FC, amidst a good deal of controversy, decided to emulate the majority of Association clubs and embark on the new season. There was a very persuasive push for recruits, both locally and nationally. Against those who rebuked the foot-ballers for apparently ignoring the 'greater game', there were those who saw the football grounds as a rich source of recruits. (Certainly players could not be accused of unpatriotic behaviour: several of the Macclesfield club joined up before conscription came into force in January 1916, and the final tally of Association players nation-wide to support the war effort was a staggering 500,000. No other section of English society was to supply such numbers.)

The proceeds from the pre-season practice games on the Moss Rose were divided between the Infirmary and the War Fund.

Some clubs were not to last the season. Macc. managed to do so, albeit with a deficit, through a combination of stringency, doggedness, and quality play. The harshest economy was to disband the reserve side in October. The first team agreed to take a 25% cut in wages in November – and then a further 25% a month later! The club reached the final of the lucrative North Staffs. Infirmary Cup, in which they gave Central League side Port Vale a run for their money – see below.

In return, the team provided football which was 'a treat to watch'. A thrilling tussle with North-wich Victoria on the Moss Rose on Boxing Day was typical. Outplayed and losing 0–2 at half-time, the Silkmen turned the game on its head in the second half and ran out 3–2 winners. Greaves (2) and Spooner (a winger from Brighton) were the scorers.

One episode of low drama just before Christmas illustrates as well as anything the fact that the team was a clear cut above some of the other members of the Combination. Barrow – who soon after the war were to be admitted to the Football League – were the visitors. One weapon in the Barrow armoury appeared to be the free use of boot and fist upon their

Advert from 1913. (*Macclesfield Express*)

opponents. Towards the end of an ugly game Pickford cleverly dispossessed Robertson, the Barrow forward, whose response was to floor the local man with a haymaker. (A matter of minutes before this, Pearson had been struck by the winger Bond, a blow which was to necessitate minor nasal surgery.) Robertson was ordered off the field, but was reluctant to go. A section of the crowd then rushed onto the pitch, trying to make a grab for the apparent villain of the piece. At this point Robertson decided it might be a sensible idea to head for the dressing rooms, outside which a few dozen furious fans waited at the end of the match. Fortunately for all concerned, the intended quarry eluded his pursuers by climbing unseen over the streetside hoarding and taking a specially hired car to the station. For the record, Macclesfield won 3–1, and the two Barrow players were fined and suspended by the Combination committee.

Chester, the early runaway leaders, were soon to drop out. Macc. won ten of their last thirteen games, drawing the rest. So in their first (and only) season in the Lancashire First Division, they would finish an excellent fourth, three points adrift of champions Eccles Borough.

The same week the FA announced it would no longer permit organised football competitions until after the war.

The last game before the curtain fell was at Altrincham. Macc. finished in full flight, scotching their old adversaries 3–1. The *Staffordshire Sentinel* commented:

> So closes one of the most remarkable seasons in the history of the club ... one of which both players and committee can be proud. (1/5/15)

It may seem insensitive and irrelevant in the context of wartime, but it is difficult not to indulge in a bit of speculation here: how high would that gutsy and skilful Silkmen outfit

have risen, had events not overtaken them?

One level above the Lancashire Combination was the Central League; and above *that*, the Football League itself. Some indication of how the team might have fared against Central League opposition can be gleaned from the fact that several such teams had been encountered, in friendlies or Cup matches, in the year or so before the cessation of the game in 1915.

Manchester City Reserves had been held 1–1 in a home friendly. Rochdale had been met in a qualifying round of the FA Cup, and had been rocked by three late goals in a 3–5 defeat. Port Vale (pushing for promotion to the Football League themselves) were the opponents in the final of the North Staffs. Infirmary Cup. Losing 0–2 with twelve minutes remaining, Macc. hit back with a goal from Greaves, then equalised with a Spooner penalty, the last kick of the match. In the replay Port Vale decided to treat the Cheshire upstarts with more respect, and won 3–0.

And what of the Lancashire Combination

Advert from 1914. (*Macclesfield Express*)

games against those clubs with Central League aspirations? Hurst, Eccles Borough, and Stalybridge Celtic were in the forefront of such applications for betterment – and Macc. had beaten them all at one time or another in the couple of year before the end.

So – would they have held their own if they had risen to the Central League? The evidence suggests that if footballing skills had been the only criteria, then they would certainly have performed at least as well as their fellow Lancashire Combination adventurers.

## Last act

Macclesfield FC carried on in name only until March 1916, when the Moss Rose lease ran out. Rent was a wartime £10 a year, money was owed for repairs, the 1915 deficit had been reduced but not cleared; and obviously, with no games, there could be no income.

The previous year, the Cheshire FA had been asked if they could contribute help to individual clubs. Elder statesman Peter Wright suggested £100 from the Association coffers divided among the 35 members, most of whom were in a similar situation. The motion was defeated 13–12. The clubs were on their own.

The Moss Rose was put up for sale in February 1916. The landlords, the North Cheshire Brewery Ltd, were indifference personified. One Walter Brown, councillor and owner of a Mill St hardware store, bought the grandstand. This saved it from being dismantled and the precious timber sold off.

Despite the immediate outlook of gloom, the scene was set for the phoenix to rise once more.

**For Sale.**

**EXPIRATION OF LEASE.**
**MOSS ROSE FOOTBALL GROUNDS.**
**TWO SUBSTANTIALLY BUILT STANDS FOR SALE.**

No. 1.—Grand Stand with seating accommodation for over 300, built of substantial tongued and grooved boards, corrugated iron roofing, etc.

No. 2.—Stand or Shelter, 70 yards long; built of substantial deal battens, 7 x 3, usual lengths, built in tiers and in good condition.

No. 3.—Partition and Fencing round the playing pitch, together with a dressing-room.

Permission to view may be obtained from the Tenant, Moss Rose Hotel, London Road, Macclesfield, adjoining the Football Ground.

Offers to be in writing to Geo. Sumner, 39, Church Side, Macclesfield.

February 1916: the stands go up for sale. They were bought (and saved from likely demolition) by Walter Brown, a local shopkeeper. (*Macclesfield Express*)

# 9

# *Mixed Fortunes*

'King Football entered his kingdom again.'
*Courier* (6/9/19)

## *Business as usual*

A new president and committee; the debt wiped out through public and private subscriptions; new nets and goalposts, and a facelift to the neglected stands and hoardings. A clutch of keen local players, and a band of useful professionals from elsewhere, attracted by the advertisements in *Athletic News* in which they were asked to 'name their terms'. So the renascent Macclesfield Football Club (having briefly considered the name 'United') set out their stall in late summer 1919.

The football-starved public came to the Moss Rose in droves. The takings for the match with Crewe (a 3–1 win) on 6 September were £120, easily a new ground record.

Tom Greaves and Sam Marshall wrote to the club, asking for to be considered for selection. Otherwise the only survivor from the pre-war team was Harry Pearson at left back.

The committee had a few dozen players to choose from, but little pre-season time in which to assess them. Events had been threatening to leave Macc. behind. A skeletal Cheshire Cup competition held earlier in the year had been won by Tranmere. A Cheshire League had been formed in May. A dozen clubs had put their names forward, including Chester, Northwich Vics., Altrincham, Crewe Alexandra, and Stalybridge Celtic. From Macclesfield, however – silence. The old committee had been dragging its feet, muttering that resuscitating the Silkmen was an impossibility. It was not until late June, at a packed meeting at Park Green School, that the club had been finally re-launched.

Two sides withdrew from the new Cheshire League; within a week Macc.'s fixture list had been printed and circulated.

In July negotiations with the North Cheshire Brewery concerning the ground rent and repairs had been embarked upon. The brewery's response, in marked contrast to their unhelpful caution of 1916, was in keeping with the post-war mood of optimism and co-operation. Firstly, they agreed to repair the hoarding of one half of the ground, provided the club found the money to do the rest. At a cost of £50, the club erected a length of corrugated iron, fulfilling their part of the bargain.

Secondly, the Brewery pointed out that they had let the ground, along with the *Moss Rose* pub, to Joseph Harrison, proprietor. Under the terms of the agreement with the Brewery, Mr Harrison was able to sub-let the ground, so it was to him that the committee was referred. The result of this was an unexpected windfall: 'the tenant was prepared to make no charge for the ground, and also lend them a horse with which to roll it'. (*Courier* 2/8/19)

That same month, Joseph Harrison made another canny move. Afternoon licensing hours had been severely curtailed during the war so as not to offer a distraction to munitions workers. (This law, of course, was not to be relaxed in England for another eighty years.) Mr Harrison, seeing by now that the club was on the march again, applied to sell alcohol on Saturday afternoons. The application was granted, provided (a) he sold his wares from a back window facing onto the ground, and to *bona fide* supporters only (b) he kept the front door shut (c) he informed the Chief Constable there was a match on!

Within a matter of weeks, £200 from voluntary contributions alone had rolled into the club coffers. (The price of a brand new top- of-the-range motor car at the time was £220.) As far away as Paterson, New Jersey, where Peter Wright had formed his team of émigré Silkmen back in 1884, the call was answered. A donation of 35 dollars – £7 3s. 6d. (£7.17) at the 1919 rate of exchange – was received.

> When Macclesfield played Runcorn in February 1921, Furn, the Runcorn inside right, had walked from his home town to the Moss Rose. He had covered the 35 miles in 5 hours. He then had lunch, a bath and a rest before turning out to play! Macc. won 3–0.

As for the grandstand, Walter Brown – 'a man of shrewd common sense and business ability' – was willing to shelve his vested interest until the club was thriving once more. He was to decline the invitation to be club President, the honour going instead to Harry Turner

On 31 August, in front of a crowd of over 2,000, Macc. – in their new kit of black and white stripes – opened their League campaign on the Moss Rose, defeating Crighton's Athletic from Chester 2–1.

So, within the space of two months, the new club had grown from an idea to a vigorous reality.

There was, however, the inevitable result of a glut of players combined with little time: to give everyone a trial, team line-ups were chopped and changed to a degree that for most of the season was counter-productive. In the first ever Cheshire League, Macc. finished ninth out of twelve teams.

There was a welcome and deserved silver lining. In the Altrincham Senior Cup, after disposing of Northern Nomads 3–0, then Stalybridge Celtic 4–1, Macc. met Winsford Utd. (Cheshire Cup finalists and League Champions the following year) in the final at Altrincham. The team, greatly changed from the beginning of the season, was:

> Osbaldeston; Bayley, Pearson; Lyons, Rourke, Birtles; Bushby, Swain, Donbavand, Twemlow (c), Daley

It was an engrossing, ding-dong game, and with a good deal of skill on display despite the glutinous pitch. Macc. were trailing 0–1 at the interval, then a Twemlow goal, after a brilliant solo run, took matters into extra time. Swain notched a second for the Silkmen, then, in the last minute, Winsford were awarded a penalty. Osbaldeston, drafted in from the reserves, faced up:

> Corbett took the kick and sent in a hard, low drive, but Osbaldeston got well down to the ball and turned it high into the air ... it was a very fine save. *Macclesfield Times* (7/5/20)

The Silkmen held on to their lead for the remaining minute. The usual reception and festive crowds awaited the team on their return.

## Celebrated players

The received wisdom on the 'twenties is that Macclesfield FC had a hard time of it: no major trophies won, and a yo-yo performance in the league. John Earles, in *Fifty Years of Football*, virtually ends the tale at the Great War, reducing the remaining years to 1925 – the year of publication – to a couple of paragraphs praising a half-dozen individuals. Nevertheless, up until mid-decade (after which things went temporarily haywire with the change of the offside law) there was much to admire in the battling Silkmen side.

Of course individuals stand out. Harry Pearson – also a professional sprinter – continued to give great service. During the war he had been a Royal Navy PT instructor, so had lost none of his pre-war

verve. He was a clever exponent of the offside trap,
disagreeing with fellow full-
back Fred Smith as to the
fairness in spirit of such tactics. According to Smith, the
policy of deliberately aiming
to catch out opposing forwards this way was 'akin to
potting your opponent's ball
in billiards'.

From the Potteries came
Enoch Collinson. Despite his
comparative lack of height he
was a mobile, dominating
presence in midfield, as
near to the perfect old-style
centre-half as the Moss Rose
had ever seen. Never shy of

Macclesfield F.C. 1920–21.

joining the attack, his raking shots troubled many
a goalkeeper. A snippet from the Macclesfield
Times speaks volumes:

A correspondent writes asking us whether
Collinson works during the week. We forget,
but we are certain he works on Saturday
afternoons. (23/12/21)

Right-half J. Lyons, a 5ft 6ins (1m 67) power-
house from Manchester, had spent most of the
war working as a POW in an iron mine. His wiry
frame thus toughened, he was also a part-time
professional boxer of no mean skill. When moved
into the forward line his response was typically
spirited. In the 4–1 rout of Crewe he netted twice,
and had a hand in the other two goals.

Captain Chester Twemlow left for Congleton,
then Stoke, but returned to Macclesfield within
a year or so. Liverpool had expressed an interest
in the inside-forward, but Twemlow (ex-Macc.
Modern School) preferred to return home. A
wing-half in later years, he was one of the
'formidable trio' that also comprised Collinson and
Frank Simpson (ex-Leeds United), an accurate
distributor of the ball.

W. Osbaldeston carried on the tradition of
quality Silkmen goalkeepers. Originally from

Southport, he had been living locally for ten years
or more. His secret in saving penalties – for which
he had something of a reputation – was in trying
to 'read the kicker's thoughts'. He was to be succeeded between the sticks by Blackburn, a local
lad who had performed well in the reserves; then
Joseph Anderton, a native of Horwich who had
had a season or two at Manchester United; then
John Lee, whose forte was taking penalties as well
as saving them!

Captain for 1923–24 was W. E. Peake, a teacher
whose ports of call had been Northern Nomads,
Eccles Borough, and Tottenham Hotspur. A former centre-forward, he took on the role of
centre-half for Macclesfield. Highly respected
throughout the game, he was the subject of a
potted biography in *Football Chronicle* in February
1924. (Peter Wright was to be accorded the same
honour later that same year.) Peake left for Manchester North End at the end of the season. This
move set the scene for a climactic confrontation
with his former club the following year, in the
final of the League Challenge Cup.

Itchy feet were often an occupational hazard of
the Silkmen of those years. This was certainly true
of centre-forwards.

First there was the famous Bob Whittingham, who in pre-war days had been acquired by Chelsea at a then astronomical £2,000. A veteran of FA Cup matches with Crewe, he had come to Macc. via South Shields. Although his best days were behind him – injury curtailed his appearances – he nonetheless helped to bring the crowds to the Moss Rose. He had a hand in the high-scoring autumn of 1921 (Nantwich 5–1, Witton 3–0, Ashton National 3–0) when the story was put about that the Moss Rose goalposts were in need of repair 'due to the deadly shooting'.

The next season Whittingham was replaced by Reg Forrester, a 'rare bustler' from Stoke, whose career had included a year at Manchester City. Forrester's goalscoring feats of that one year with the Silkmen are the stuff of legends. The quantity is a matter of record: top league scorer, with twenty in five games over Christmas and New Year. The quality was something to savour too. In the 6–0 bonanza against Congleton on Christmas Day, Forrester notched a cheekily brilliant solo goal, wriggling and side-stepping his way around the defenders – including the goalkeeper – and sliding the ball into an empty net. So impressed were his team-mates that they forgot their English reserve and actually hugged him.

Candidate for goal of the season 1923–24 involved two home-grown players. Eli Bullock's quick reaction to Ingleson's cross was a low hard drive into the corner, and both crowd and reporters reacted with great enthusiasm.

Harold Kelly (ex-Stalybridge) continued the line of imported centre-forwards. This one, though, was to stay somewhat longer. In 1924–25, like Forrester before him, he was the league's top scorer. And as we shall see, he was to save the best for last.

## 'A team of moods'

There was a string of Cheshire Cup semi-finals. The first of these was in March 1921, against Congleton Town at Crewe. The North Cheshire Railways ran special trains at reduced fare from Macclesfield, and supporters were asked to 'form an orderly queue at the Buxton Road entrance' of the station. A crowd of 10,000 watched the match.

Congleton had employed the services of a professional masseur – one Jack Harvey – from Stoke. His ministrations appeared to work, as the Silkmen were beaten 2–0. In mitigation Fred Smith sustained an injury during the game – which took place in teeming rain and splattering mud – and Chester Twemlow had recently switched allegiance to the Town. Even so, the result ran contrary to form, especially as Macc. were to demolish the same opponents 4–1 six days later in a Good Friday league match.

There were to be four Senior Cup semis in

> During a Macc. match at Connah's Quay in the 'twenties a weasel ran onto the pitch. Play was suspended whilst both teams, the referee and a spectator gave chase.

seven years. The next one, against Altrincham in 1923, came after a stirring run that had seen the following victories: Hyde 6–3, Middlewich 6–1, and Stockport County 7–1. Most of the goals had been scored by Forrester, but the semi, a 2–3 defeat, was to be his nemesis. After netting both Macc. goals, the forward was sent off after a fracas with the opposing 'keeper. Once in the lead, Altrincham were content to boot the ball into touch. In the final they were to be overwhelmed by the double-winning Crewe Alexandra.

Unbeaten at home until the final match that year, Macc. finished fourth in the league. So once more, despite the many hefty wins (Nantwich 7–1, Winsford 5–0, Altrincham 6–3 away, Witton 5–1, Congleton Town 6–0 and 4–0) no trophies came to the Moss Rose that season.

The Cheshire League had grown from a dozen clubs in the first post-war season to twenty-two within four years. County boundaries for football purposes having always been flexible, the popular competition came to include the likes of Manchester North End and Port Vale.

Macc.'s most promising league season of the decade was probably 1924–25. Victories over Manchester North End (5–2 away), Winsford (4–1) and Port Vale (a 4–3 thriller) helped lift the Silkmen into the position of early leaders.

In December a 1–2 home defeat at the hands of Tranmere had provoked a demonstration from the crowd in the form of a pitch invasion. Nonetheless, by Christmas the Silkmen were still at the head of the league, albeit somewhat precariously:

|  | P | W | D | L | F | A | Pts |
|---|---|---|---|---|---|---|---|
| Macclesfield | 21 | 12 | 4 | 5 | 39 | 29 | 28 |
| Port Vale | 20 | 11 | 5 | 4 | 45 | 25 | 27 |
| Hurst | 19 | 11 | 4 | 4 | 48 | 24 | 26 |
| Stalybridge Celtic | 18 | 12 | 2 | 4 | 31 | 17 | 26 |

Unfortunately Macc. found it impossible to fend off the challenge from the pursuing clubs. Too many defeats in the last dozen or so games pulled them down to a final sixth position.

That season, though, was to have its compensations.

## The Supporters' Club

The early 'twenties saw important developments off the pitch as well. The first official match programmes were printed in 1921, and June 1922 saw the formation of the Supporters' Club.

This was to prove an invaluable money-spinner, as it was becoming increasingly clear that a club of Macclesfield's ambitions could not live by the clicking of turnstiles alone.

Now there was a regular, formal income from subscriptions. Finances were also generated by concerts, draws, whist drives and a 'shilling fund'. The benefits bestowed by the Supporters' Club were seen almost immediately. New changing rooms – complete with bath! – were built under the main stand (August 1922). The 'popular side' was repaired and extended.

Season tickets were now 17s. 6d. (87½p) for the stand, or ten shillings (50p) on the popular side. One of the more expensive subscriptions was taken up by a 67-year-old lady.

Whilst Chaplin and Valentino packed them in at the *Picturedrome* and the *Majestic*, the Moss Rose on Saturday afternoon was a crowd magnet of even greater potency. On Boxing Day 1921 the Silkmen played the league leaders Congleton, and beat them 2–0. One report's estimate of the crowd was 9,000. Although unofficial (the committee had yet to implement an accurate method of counting paying customers), this figure, if anything like correct, would at least challenge the official Moss Rose record of 9,003 for a Macc. game. (See Chapter 13.) The takings – £270 – were certainly a record.

Frank Hodkinson, a nippy Silkman forward of the 'twenties, retained a fair degree of fitness to a ripe old age. In 1964, aged 71, Frank challenged Stanley Matthews to a 100-yard sprint race, with a £100 side bet. Sir Stan declined. In 1978, now aged 85, the ex-Macc. player repeated the challenge to anyone over 75 – 'I'll give 'em a ten-year start,' said the octogenarian. Again, there were no takers.

## The League Challenge Cup

It had started life as a subsidiary league in 1919, to fill up the threadbare fixture list. It switched to a cup format the following year, but its rationale was still much the same: it was for those Cheshire

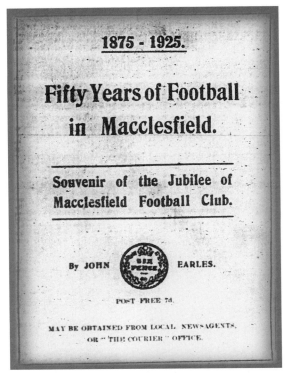

**1875 - 1925.**

# Fifty Years of Football in Macclesfield.

## Souvenir of the Jubilee of Macclesfield Football Club.

By JOHN        EARLES.

POST FREE 7d.

MAY BE OBTAINED FROM LOCAL NEWSAGENTS,
OR " THE COURIER " OFFICE.

For many years the definitive history of the Silkmen. A very readable collection of personal reminiscences – available in Macclesfield Library Reference Section.

clubs who were able to fit the competition into their schedule. So the 'Cheshire League Challenge Cup' or 'Subsidiary Cup' was never to have the prestige of the Senior trophy.

Still, a Cup Final is a Cup Final, especially when the likes of Northwich Victoria have been removed *en route*.

The opponents in May 1925 were Manchester North End, who included the recently-departed Peake. His place had been taken by the commanding figure of Jack Vigrass. Macc. were fortunate to enjoy home advantage, but for most of the match this factor seemed to be of small significance.

Their team was:

H. Wood; Burgess, Whalley; Collinson, Vigrass, Twemlow; Findlow, Wainwright, Kelly, Millett, Forrest

Manchester took the lead after ten minutes, and held onto it until well into the second half. Kelly the goal machine rarely got into his stride, either through poor feeds from his wings and half-backs, or from the skilful breaking up of moves by Peake, who was reading the game well. With twenty minutes to go the North End increased their lead.

Twemlow now moved into the forward line, changing places with the out-of-form Millett. Five minutes after the second Manchester goal Peake committed a rare error, fouling Vigrass in the area. Burgess scored from the penalty. From now on it was all Macclesfield, with the visitors defending frenetically. There was a minute of normal time remaining when Kelly ran in to meet a cross from the wing, and bundled the ball into the net. The North End protested, claiming that the Macc. forward had handled. The referee consulted his linesman, and awarded the goal.

Into extra time: Twemlow, relishing his old position of forward, sent in a searching through ball to Kelly. The striker, although by now closely marked by two defenders, managed to squeeze in a shot which flew 'fast and true into the rigging'. The same forward finished the job a few minutes later, meeting a Findlow corner with his head to notch a hat-trick and his team's fourth. A trophy at last!

Celebrations continued that evening in the appropriately named Victory café on Chestergate. The future seemed to hold much promise.

However, within a month, at a meeting of FIFA in Paris, a decision was taken which would change the nature of the Association game forever. It was a development for which the Macclesfield team, amongst many others, would find itself unprepared.

# I O

# *A Flood of Goals*

'I think it is time the management had a walk round the parks and crofts on a Saturday afternoon. They can find better talent than they have got now.
At present I am coaching a team known as "Macclesfield West End Juniors", and I can say with all sincerity that they would give the Macclesfield team a good, hard fight and perhaps a beating. Anyway, they would not lose by 9 or 10 goals to nothing.'
'DISGUSTED' *Times* Correspondence (26/3/26)

'We could not have seen a better tussle had we been watching a First Division match.'
A spectator at Bower Fold, Boxing Day 1929
(Match result: Stalybridge Celtic 2, Macclesfield 4)

## *Jubilee*

Before all the commotion, the Football Club celebrated the first fifty years of its existence.

The event got the full treatment in the *Times*, with a two-page spread comprising brief history and photographs of the 1911 and 1924 sides. Pride of place went to three interviews: William Fitchett, still the first team trainer after 27 years and nearly 1,000 matches; and indomitable veterans Billy Bolton and 'Mush' Howarth, the latter now 65 years old.

Fitchett recalled the mudflat pitches of the Manchester League, in particular at Newton Heath, where Bill Vigrass, trapping the ball, caused it to disappear into the slutch. It had to be dug out before the game could continue. In the same match the referee dropped his whistle, which sank without trace. The good-humoured and popular trainer was of the opinion that the modern game was 'much more scientific, and demanded greater intelligence'.

Billy Bolton agreed, remarking on the 'gentlemanly spirit' of the contemporary game. He had a nostalgia for the great dribbling days of yore, noting a current over-emphasis on the passing game. Another change he noted was an increase in players' wages: in his day ten shillings (50p) was the ceiling for a week's football. 'Mush' Howarth could go even further back, when 2s. 6d. (12½p) was the most he could expect. Howarth remembered the Neanderthal days of heavy, steel-rimmed boots and huge shinguards.

So, with many a backward glance, the jubilee season of 1925–26 began.

## *Change in the offside law*

The life and soul of football has always been the getting of goals and fluid, purposeful movement. Defences, however, have had one spoiling weapon in their legal armoury: that of the offside trap. Under the old rule, an attacker had to have at least three defenders between himself and the goal when the ball was played forward to him. It was becoming too easy for a well-marshalled defence, one man moving upfield at the crucial moment, to throttle many a promising attack. Ten men – we are still well before the arrival of substitutes – could even be at an advantage, through

Macclesfield F.C. 1924–25
*standing*: W. Fitchett (trainer), Dalton, referee, linesmen, C. Burgess, H. Wood, J. Vigrass, C. Twemlow, Barnett.
*seated*: F. Wood, J. Morris, V. Foweather, H. Kelly, E. Collinson (capt.), S. Mellor, A. Forrest. (*Macclesfield Express*)

playing the 'one-back game'. There could be as many as thirty or forty stoppages in one match, just for offside infringements.

In June 1925 the International Board met in Paris and decided to reduce the number of defenders in the offside equation to two. It seemed a simple enough solution to a problem which was threatening to stifle the game, but the repercussions were enormous.

At all levels of football there was a dramatic increase in the number of goals scored, as forwards now revelled in the new freedom. In the season before the change, the total number of goals scored in Cheshire League matches was 3442. In the next season, it was 4200.

Unfortunately, 142 of these found their way into Macclesfield's net.

It is a simple enough task – again, with the privilege of hindsight – to analyse the reasons behind the freakishly high scores. Under the old rule, attacks were intricate, circumspect, with a

touch of the cat-and-mouse. Suddenly, all that had changed. Now, speed was of the essence.

Time and again this shortcoming of the Macc. side of 1925–26 is brought out by contemporary analyses of the game. 'Onlooker', writing in the *Macclesfield Times*, repeatedly hit the nail on the head:

Nantwich 5, Macc. 1: 'The homesters are yards faster than the Silkmen.' (12/9/25)

Macc. 3 Port Vale 9: 'The two defenders ... were too prone to lie up the field, and gave the fast Vale forwards too much scope.' (3/10/25)

Stalybridge Celtic 10, Macc. 1: 'Several of the goals were not the result of combined play, but of breakaways, when the Macclesfield defence was completely out of position.' (Boxing Day 1925)

Manchester North End 7, Macc. 3: 'The defences were not prepared for these lightning raids.' (30/1/26)

Enough of the bad news; the Silkmen had enough self-belief to realise that the nightmare tallies conceded were mainly due to the new conditions of play, and not to some inherent defects in the team. (Although there were those who disagreed.) Therefore there had to be a solution to the problem.

Famously, Herbert Chapman's Arsenal were to pull back the centre-half behind the defence, to act as 'stopper': the extra man whose role was to foil the deadly through ball. Many clubs were to follow suit.

> Macc.'s record defeat is usually given as 1–13 against 'Tranmere Rovers Reserves' on 3 May 1930. However, the Silkmen lost two players through injury, and had to play a significant part of the game with nine men (this was before substitutes). Also, nine of the Tranmere side had been drafted in from their Football League team, so on the day 'Reserves' was a scarcely accurate title.

In the meantime, in typically cavalier fashion, the Silkmen's attitude seemed to be: no matter how many goals are scored against us, we will go out and try and score more!

They had the forwards to do it. Kelly was still in rampant form, despite the tribulations of the team as a whole. In 1926–27 he was joined by ex-Corinthian Morris, and the penalty-taker *par excellence*, Frost.

High-scoring draws became common: 3–3 (Hurst – twice, – Altrincham, Congleton, Ellesmere Port); 4–4 with Altrincham, in which 'the speed of the game was delightful', and certainly an improvement on the previous year's 2–8 defeat.

There was a veritable spree over Christmas 1926. On Christmas Day Congleton came to the Moss Rose, and honours were shared in one of the 3–3 thrillers. The following day Macc. travelled to Bower Fold to take on the free-scoring Stalybridge Celtic. Trailing 1–6 at half-time, the Silkmen threw themselves into the second half like men possessed. Three quick goals took the score to 6–4, and there arose the brief possibility of the greatest come-back since Lazarus. Then the home side recovered, and scored three themselves. Macc. had the last word through winger Jones, making the final score an outlandish 9–5. Twenty goals in two games! – and there were many more to come.

## A brace of semis

The team of that mercurial 1926–27 was commemorated in rhyme:
*When we see our Eleven turn out in grand style,*
*Each looks like a winner, each one has a smile.*
*With Bossons as goalie, he's great 'twixt the sticks,*
*It's surprising how seldom he misses the kicks;*
*There's Rutledge and Newton, a grand pair of backs,*
*In footwork and judgement, neither one lacks.*
*We have Knowles, and Plant, and good ol' Chest.,*
*A trio of halves, they're all of the best;*
*Now Wainwright, Kelly, Frost, Morris and Jones,*
*They get 'shut' of the ball and score us the goals;*
*Here's luck to the lads of 'Treacle Town' fame,*
*May they bring back the Cup, by playing the game.*
'S. M. L.' *Courier (19/3/27)*

But the Cup was once more, tantalisingly, just beyond their reach. The previous year they had reached the semi-final, going down 1–4 to Winsford after a 3–3 draw. This year, hopes were high, after wins against Poulton Rovers (6–0), Hyde United away (3–1), and a frenzied quarter-final victory at Chester.

A blow-by-blow account of the fisticuffs and subsequent pitch invasion at Sealand Road may be found in contemporary newspapers. Suffice it to say that the referee's report exonerates the Macc. team and supporters of all blame. Chester had allowed a two-goal lead to be overtaken, and this had obviously added fuel to the fire. The Cheshire FA allowed the result to stand, and

Standing on the far left is W. Fitchett, trainer for nearly thirty years.
Seated on either side of W. Holmes (chairman) are captain Chester Twemlow, and prolific goalscorer Harold Kelly.

Chester were ordered to close their ground for a fortnight.

After the blood-and-thunder, the semi was something of an anti-climax, Macc. being overrun 4–0 by eventual winners Tranmere Rovers.

The following year there was to be a pitch encroachment of a different sort at the Moss Rose, during the league game with Tranmere. The *Courier* reported:

> There was an amusing diversion when a flock of sheep invaded the playing pitch and caused a brief stoppage. The referee waved them back, but they ambled in front of goal before being driven off. (8/10/27)

There was always a touch of the surreal at the Moss Rose during the 'twenties.

## Rally to the call

The week after a 1–5 home defeat to Port Vale, one signing himself 'Subscriber of 45 years' felt compelled to air his exasperation:

> Sometimes I wish the old club would go smash. Then we would have a limited company, or else be taken over by a first league club as a nursery for them. *Times* Correspondence (14/10/27)

Surrendering to one of the powerful clubs must have seemed a periodically tempting option. It was the time when amateur dressing rooms would be invaded by a chequebook-waving posse of agents or committee men from the professional outfits. Scouts from First Division clubs would make the odd appearance in the non-league grandstands. (Walker, the Macc. full-back, was asked

Macclesfield A.F.C. 1928–29. *Standing*: Cheetham, Parkes, Mace, Jones, Walker, Gascoign, Fitchett (trainer), *seated*: Massey, Kelly, Williams, Mr Bullock (president), Woods, Cox. (*Macclesfield Express*)

to play a half-dozen games at centre-forward so he could be assessed by the Arsenal.)

Moreover, as the decade progressed, Macclesfield FC once more found itself in financial difficulties. The Supporters' Club had done a sterling job, supplying most of the wherewithal for further ground improvements: ladies' toilets, two turnstiles, and a new entrance in Moss Lane (summer 1926). However, costs had continued to rise. Chief among these was players' wages, which passed the annual £1,000 mark for the first time in 1926–27. At the end of that season, there were two expensive undertakings: the pitch was re-turfed, and a new covered area on the popular side was constructed. The club's debts were by now in four figures.

By spring 1928, at the AGM, the circumstances were made public knowledge. The *Times* under the headline 'Football Club's Dilemma' reported the call for a public meeting. Did the people of Macclesfield want the club to continue in its present form?

'Subscriber' and those of his mind-set were no doubt nodding sagely at all this, but such pessimists had clearly underestimated the by now inseverable links between football club and community.

The public meeting was

> In the 1930s players' boots were identified by the owner's initials depicted in tin-tacks stuck into the soles. It was the job of the groundsman, Percy Swindells, to look after them for away games. It was Swindells, of course, who was also responsible for the continuing high standard of pitch surface at the Moss Rose.

At half-time during the 1926 Cheshire Cup semi against Winsford Utd., with Macc. leading 3–0, two members of the committee came to the Silkmen dressing room bearing bottles of champagne. Each player was urged to take a glass, so the tale was told in later years, persuaded by the committee members that this would give them the necessary lift for the second half. The final score was 3–3, and Macc. lost the replay. Apparently the two worst players in that second half were the two abstainers on the team!

held on 5 May 1928 at Lord Street Sunday School. There was a 'large gathering'. Worthy of note is the fact that the idea of selling out to a Football League outfit was not even considered.

First things first: the new landlords, Messrs. Adshead, who had bought the *Moss Rose* and the adjoining pitch from the North Cheshire Brewery, made another generous gesture. They would overlook rent and rates for the next two years, and take care of any upkeep and repairs. There was a proviso:

> ... at the end of two seasons they were prepared to review the position. If they then considered an honest endeavour was being made to give the public good football they were going to help in every possible way.

*Times* (8/5/28)

Some changes were suggested. One of the more interestingly prophetic proposals was put forward by a Mr F. Parkinson, who thought the next step forward would be the appointment of a manager, who would assist the committee and be responsible for the day-to-day running of the team. The cult of the manager was still some years off, though, and the gap between players and directors, for better or worse, would remain for some time yet.

An appeal was launched, target £1,000. Over one-third of this amount was collected within

the next three weeks. When the appeal was closed the following January, two of the more eye-catching contributions had been recorded as:

Whippet Association – eight guineas (£8.40)
The Hazel Grove Twins' Carnival Effort – £33 12s. 7d. (£33.63)

The Hazel Grove Twins were a well-known fun-day turn. Dressed in outrageous garb and presenting faces of stoney seriousness, they challenged members of the public – for a nominal fee – to make them break into a smile. Successful punters were promised a pound.

By then the club was thriving once more: an FA Cup run under its belt, and on the threshold of the greatest half-decade in its history so far.

1928–29 saw them get within an ace of the FA Cup proper, for the first time since preliminaries and qualifiers had been introduced forty years before. The *Times* boldly tempted fate with its headline 'Wembley in the Distance'.

The run saw off Welsh clubs Colwyn Bay (3–1 after 2–2), Flint Town (2–1 away) and Connah's Quay (2–1). Their nemesis was Rhyl Athletic – whom they were to beat the following year – in the last of three closely-fought games (2–2, 0–0, then 0–2).

In the league they finished tenth, albeit with a couple of six-goal wins over Nantwich and Crewe.

It was in December of 1928 that the Moss Rose roar was immortalised on a 'broadcasting record'. Mr A. C. Crosby, the manager of the Macclesfield Opera House, wanted a sound effect of a cheering

After the Cheshire Cup Final victory in 1930, the veterans of the 1890 win were asked by a *Macclesfield Times* reporter how the match had compared with the one of forty years before. 'Not half as good,' growled one. Added another: 'When we won, the score was 4–1, and Nantwich scored the first.' The reporter 'beat a hasty retreat'.

Cheshire Senior Cup Final April 1930. Caption in the *Courier*. 'MACCLESFIELD'S FIRST GOAL. Johnston (right) running forward after his shot had passed through Astley's [actually Sewell's] legs into the net. Stanton and Taylor are seen on the left.' Final score: Macclesfield 5, Nantwich 4. (*Macclesfield Express*)

racecourse crowd for his production of *The Sport of Kings*. The crowd duly obliged at the Tranmere Rovers game, and the making of the recording was pronounced 'a signal success'.

## The nine-goal final

In 1929 the club suffered the death of two crucial members: half-back William Bailey, tragically young at 26, of a heart attack after a tough match; and president Harry Bullock, 61. The Cheshire League would donate £20 to Bailey's widow, which sum would be augmented by the proceeds from a special match that summer with the Cheshire Cup holders, Northwich Victoria.

In mere football terms, though, the omens were good. Macc. won all five of their Christmas and New Year fixtures of 1929–30. The goal record for these matches was 24 for, 7 against. The sweetest plum of the bunch was the 4–2 Boxing Day win at Stalybridge. In the return at the Moss Rose on New Year's Day Macc. won by a similar score, in a match which was Kelly's 'day out'. It was 2–2

after 87 minutes, then the centre-forward scored two quick goals and was carried shoulder-high by his team-mates. As this was his benefit match, he could not have chosen a more timely showcase for his skills.

The team had been boosted by the arrival of several new faces. In goal was Harold Compston, a local lad who had just completed a successful spell at Ashton National. The backs were Walker and Eyre; the half-back line, after many re-shuffles, now contained Unwin, Martin, and Holt. Clifford Unwin, who had signed professional with Bury before coming to Macclesfield, had played in all three right-sided outfield positions. John C. Martin at centre-half had tasted League football with Bradford; his speciality was the long, probing pass into space for his forwards. Stanley Holt completed the trio: an all-purpose outfield player 'of stalwart build' he had appeared for Arsenal, Manchester City and Altrincham before donning the Silkmen colours.

But it was the forward line that provided the real dazzle. Kelly was now flanked by associates of proven pedigree: right wing Stanton from Stockport, where he had played centre-forward and been a prolific goalscorer; the clever and incisive inside-right Taylor, dubbed 'Happy' by the fans; the ex-Scottish international William Johnston; and on the left wing the diminutive but speedy Joseph Laws, whose previous clubs included Grimsby and Notts. Forest. This attack was to score a total of 182 goals in all competitions that season.

In the first round of the Cheshire Senior Cup the opponents were Barnton Victoria, theoretically easy meat from the Manchester League. Macc., perhaps understandably, made the near-fatal error of underestimating their visitors. The Victoria shrugged off an early goal and swept into a 4–1 half-time lead. At 5–2, with twenty minutes left, the shock result of the season seemed to be looming. Then late goals from Stanton (2) and Kelly (2) made the final score a delirious 6–5 to the Silkmen.

Round two was a relatively sane and straightforward 4–1 win over Witton Albion, again at the Moss Rose.

This was the team's ninth successive victory – a club record. Unfortunately the very next game was a sensational home league defeat at the hands of Northwich Victoria. The *Courier* noted that this was the thirteenth consecutive time the same forward line had played together. Thankfully, good sense won out over superstition, and the line-up was retained!

The luck of the draw again favoured Macc. in the third round of the Senior Cup, when they were pitted against Runcorn at home. The Merseysiders were accompanied by around a thousand fans, noisy and colourful with their bugles, rattles and flags.

Also at the match were representatives from Huddersfield Town. They had come to watch O'Neill, the high-scoring Runcorn centre-forward (49 goals in the last 26 games). O'Neill obliged by scoring a hat-trick, but a late rally from the visitors was not quite enough: Macc. won 4–3, with Taylor himself notching three.

The semi, against Winsford United, was a Baron Munchausen of a match. It took place at Edgeley Park, Stockport. One of the 9,000 supporters carried a placard which predicted:

RESULT: MACCLESFIELD 3, WINSFORD
CAN'T SCORE

How wrong he was.

Winsford attacked from the kick-off, repeatedly exploiting their nippy forwards. For most of the first half Macc. were overrun, and their opponents were three goals to the good within twenty-eight minutes. Was the semi-final bogey about to strike again?

Stanton pulled one back before half-time, and this clearly gave his team some heart. The second half was a rout. After five minutes Laws went on one of his scampering runs down the left and centred to Stanton. A quick pass to Johnston, and the captain had the ball in the net. 3–2. Two minutes later, Stanton scored the equalising goal which seemingly knocked the stuffing out of Winsford. His overhead kick, helped a little by the wind, eluded the opposing 'keeper.

It was now becoming increasingly clear that Johnston's team could win as they pleased. Taylor bagged the fourth, a thundering shot from twenty yards. ('Good old Happy' was the general shout.) Three more goals in the last twenty minutes completed the job.

> William Johnston, Captain of the 1930 Cheshire Cup-winning team, scored three goals for Manchester United in their 1927–28 FA Cup run. After two seasons with the Silkmen, Johnston returned to United's colours, but retained ownership of his tobacconist's and sweet shop at 15b Mill Lane Macclesfield.

In the other semi, Nantwich beat Tranmere 2–1, thus setting up a repeat of the first of Macc.'s Cheshire Cup finals, all of forty years before.

The 1930 final took place at Crewe on the 12 April. In the 14,000 crowd, the majority from Macclesfield:

> ... club favours were much in evidence, umbrellas, top hats, coloured caps, rattles and 'musical' instruments, all helped to add gaiety to the otherwise drab surroundings, whilst the Macclesfield Jazz Band played a large part in the preliminary proceedings. *Courier* (19/4/30)

Six of the victorious 1890 team were in the grandstand: Joe Birchenall, George Gaskell, Nathan Dixon, Billy Bolton, 'Mush' Howarth (now 70!) and Tommy Lea.

The teams were:

*Macclesfield*: Compston; Walker, Eyre; Unwin, Martin, Holt; Stanton, Taylor, Kelly, Johnston, Laws

*Nantwich*: T. Thompson; C. Thompson, Astley; E. Davies, Blake, Sewell; Mason, F. Davies, Harris, Slight, Robinson

The first exchanges were beset by nerves, typified by Laws, in front of an empty goal, lifting his shot over the bar. Most of the first half belonged to Nantwich, but on the quarter-hour, and against the run of play, Kelly and Johnston executed some fast inter- passing down the inside-left channel which led to the Macclesfield captain opening the scoring.

Nantwich now began to use their left wing: Robinson sent in many a pin-point centre that repeatedly troubled the Silkmen defence. It was from such a cross that Harris equalised with a header. Before half-time Harris fired Nantwich into the lead with a fast drive just inside the foot of the post. The same forward had a chance to put the 'Wychers' even further ahead, but he directed his header straight at Compston.

The second half opened with a series of thrilling end-to-end attacks. Kelly had a goal disallowed for hand-ball. Then, on 54 minutes, Johnston scored his second, chesting the ball down and running it over the line. Nantwich attacked all the harder, forcing a full-length save from Compston, and an equally vital tackle by Martin on the ever-dangerous F. Davies.

Matters remained evenly balanced until Johnston fastened onto a twenty-yarder to put Macc. back into the lead. Now the Silkmen started to turn it on in familiar fashion. Attack after attack rolled forward, and soon Stanton and Johnston – again – made the score 5–2. With six minutes left, Nantwich's cause seemed lost, but then F. Davies surprised everyone by scoring with an overhead kick. Three minutes later he reduced the arrears still further, driving the ball though a massed but tiring defence. At 5–4, with Nantwich suddenly displaying a remarkable second wind, the Macclesfield contingent were understandably nervous. With seconds remaining, Nantwich were awarded a corner. Robinson sent over one of his crosses, but this time it was cleared. The final whistle sounded, and Macc. had won their first Cheshire Senior Cup for nearly twenty years.

After an exuberant return journey by special bus, during which intervening Cheshire towns and villages were treated to glimpses of the trophy and 'the singing of snatches of popular airs and melodies', the team arrived at the *Rising Sun* in Congleton Road, where

> ... cyclists and motorcyclists were assembled, together with the Macclesfield Town Silver Band, who were ready in a bus to lead the triumphant march into the town of treacle fame. *Times* (18/4/30)

The bringing home of the Cup was to open the door to an unprecedented run of success.

# Years of Plenty

'Butt is acknowledged to be one of the cleverest inside-forwards in the Cheshire League ...
He is probably the finest individual player
Macclesfield have had for some seasons and most popular with the crowd.'
*Times (2/6/33)*

## Three great players

They were the years when the records tumbled. Unequalled by the club until the 1950's, and unsurpassed until the climactic 1960's, it was the time when the Silkmen bestrode the Cheshire soccer scene like a colossus. In seven years they were League Champions twice, runners-up once; Senior Cup winners twice, beaten finalists once; Challenge Cup winners once.

It was the style of the wins, too, that lingered gratefully in the memory. The Silkmen were a fearsome attacking force. Goals were plentiful, and many of them thrillingly executed. In each of the seven years at least 100 League goals were scored, with the high water mark of 142 reached in 1933–34. H. H. Taylor, of arch-rivals Altrincham, opined: 'Macclesfield's football is the best I have ever seen in the Cheshire League.'

The winning formula was individual skill, allied to attacking ingenuity and a shared self-belief, all three attributes in abundant evidence. A team would come together in August, and within a few weeks were showing a unity of purpose that belied the brief time-scale.

Individual players jostle for prominence. For the moment, a closer look at just three will capture much of the essence of those years.

There was Leonard Butt, a mazey dribbler with an explosive shot which once laid out Heywood, the Altrincham right back. Memorable, too, was his spectacular diving header against Manchester North End. Then there was his dribble from the half-way line in the match with Congleton, culminating in a successful shot at goal from 20 yards. Inside forward Butt replaced Billy Johnston, who returned to Manchester United. (Johnston continued to live in Macclesfield, owner of the tobacconist's on Mill Lane.)

For just one season (1933–34) though, even Butt was outshone in attack by Albert Valentine, a centre-forward of extraordinary ability *en route* for League Football at Halifax Town. He notched a phenomenal 84 goals that year (including 15 hat-tricks), and his brief and dazzling career at the Moss Rose was studded with strikes of high quality. Against Rhyl in the FA Cup he spotted goalkeeper Fairhurst off his line, and unleashed a dipping thirty-yard volley to score the only goal of the game. Against Nantwich he was entrusted with a penalty – full-back Harris being the usual incumbent – and scored, breaking the net in the process. His athleticism was aided by his vision and speed of thought: outwitting defences that committed themselves too early was a major element of his attacking style.

Richard Williams was an agile and dependable goalkeeper. He had several notable penalty saves to his credit, including one heart-stopping sequence in the 1933 League match with Nantwich. With the score 1–0 to Macc., Johnson, the Nantwich centre-forward, struck a fine spot kick, hard and low into the corner. Williams dived and managed to parry the ball – straight into Johnson's path.

The forward immediately cracked in another shot, which Williams turned round a post.

There were many others, of course, who would have integral roles to play in the ensuing run. In the relatively barren first season after the 1930 Senior Cup win, however, the major talking point was the moving of Macclesfield FC to a more central location.

## Windmill Street

Just beyond where the Silk Road joins the London Road, less than a kilometre south of Macclesfield centre, Windmill Street shoots off at right angles up the first of the town's eastern slopes. Climb the street past its first kink, and nearly opposite St Peter's Church there is a recreation area, with football pitch, children's playpark, and that relic of the 1980's, a BMX track. It is a well-kept expanse of several acres set in a shallow grassy bowl, and it does not take too much of a stretch of imagination to mentally superimpose a stadium. The FC committee certainly thought so, in 1930 when the future playing fields were still a derelict storage space put up for sale by a local brickworks. It was to this more central venue that the club's premises were to be moved.

As in the case of the supposed decamping to Wright's Field off the Buxton Road in 1911, the move was presented as a *fait accompli* in the newspaper reports. The lease on the Moss Rose would run out in four years' time, it was argued, and the shift to Windmill Street was just a formality.

At the same time, other interests had their eyes on the space. The Council, awaiting the completion of a Town Planning report, were considering a recreation area. By 1934 the flattened central portion was being used as a home pitch by amateur side Sutton Athletic. A Stockport-based consortium built a greyhound stadium on the site, despite the fact that the council had informed them they would have to clear out, without compensation, as soon as the recreation area plans were ready. The controversial and ill-fated dog track was defunct within a year, the makeshift stand having collapsed, and the owners bankrupt.

By then Macc.'s involvement had long since ceased. Several factors had combined to persuade the club to stay put. Firstly, the cost of the move would have been huge: one estimate was that it would have taken twenty years to pay off the expense. Secondly the hoary old argument that the Moss Rose was too far out of town was becoming increasingly unconvincing. In January 1931 a new bus service to the Moss Estate was introduced. (Single fare 3d. – 1p) Later in the decade, special match-day buses were laid on.

The Moss Rose greensward, praised to the skies by visitors, many of whom were used to uneven or muddy conditions, was another factor. The *Macclesfield Times* published a letter from a visiting Bradford fan, in which he spoke warmly of:

> … a fine playing pitch, in my opinion far better than the one I understand they are contemplating taking. (8/4/32)

At the club AGM in June 1934 it was recorded:

> The Windmill Street Ground Account has now been finally closed and the income and expenditure in connection therewith are shown in the statements of accounts. To clear off the deficit the club have paid the sum of £50 4s. 6d. [£50.22] out of the general account. *Times* (22/6/34)

Within a couple of years the open space was filled in, turfed, and officially opened as the King George V Playing Fields.

Meanwhile the Moss Rose had undergone further improvements. The extension to the covered section of the popular side was officially opened in November 1934. Cushions were now available for hire – at threepence (1p) each – for those who had been braving the hard wooden seats of the main stand. A loudspeaker was erected, firstly on top of a car, later on the roof of the old snack bar, from which half-time music was broadcast. Support was as staunch as ever, despite the increase of entertainment tax – one of the lingering legacies of the war years – to 16½%. On Carnival Saturday in August 1931 over 1,000 spectators preferred to attend the Moss Rose: and that was just to watch a trial match!

## Crescendo

The season in 1930–31 was relatively indifferent: early exits from all three trophies competed for, and a slip to ninth in the league. One high spot was the visit of Everton in May, the proceeds of which went to the Infirmary fund. Dixie Dean was not present, but the 5–5 draw sent everyone home happy; the great Billy Meredith, now a doughty 56-year-old, was the referee. Both teams were entertained at the Alexandra café afterwards, and the Everton team were presented with silk ties. It was Johnston's penultimate match.

The 1931–32 team was reinforced by several new acquisitions: Eddie Chesters, from Crewe, was a winger with an impressive goalscoring record; and Bert Burridge, a centre-half with Football League experience with Sheffield Wednesday and Oldham Athletic. He had also helped Darlington to their recent Third Division Championship. James Dickie, ex-Chester, was a fast and skilful left wing. John Jepson, another former Football League player with Wigan Borough, filled the centre-forward spot from January 1932, and thereafter scored in every game but one until the end of the season. Jack Shirley, ex-Stoke City, was a clever and industrious inside-forward. And of course, there was the 21-year-old Lennie Butt.

Macc. started that season at a gallop. Unbeaten in the league until late November, the sequence included a win and a draw with champions Port Vale. The only defeat sustained in that time was the FA Cup Third Qualifying Round match at Altrincham, who were to dismiss the Silkmen from this competition three years in succession. The score was 6–4 to the Robins, but Macc. had the satisfaction of knowing they were a party to a record gate of £245, paid by a crowd of 7,800.

By early January the top of the table gave cause for optimism:

|                  | P  | W  | D | L | F  | A  | Pts |
|------------------|----|----|---|---|----|----|-----|
| Macclesfield     | 22 | 15 | 5 | 2 | 67 | 38 | 35  |
| Congleton Town   | 22 | 14 | 3 | 5 | 73 | 37 | 31  |
| Hyde United      | 23 | 14 | 3 | 6 | 54 | 30 | 31  |
| Stalybridge Celtic | 20 | 13 | 4 | 3 | 72 | 32 | 30  |

As the season progressed, however, it became clear that the principal rivals would be Altrincham, who were winning their games in hand in February and March. The Easter matches, for once, resolved nothing. Macc. could only gather three points from as many games, whilst Altrincham, with 100% over the holiday, edged into a two-point lead, still with a match in hand. Macc. lost 1–2 at Whitchurch in early April, but that was the last time they were to taste defeat that season.

The Silkmen gained revenge for their league and FA Cup reversals by beating Altrincham 5–1 the following week. Left half Bob Morrison scored the fifth goal, which brought the league total to exactly 100.

The title race was now wide open once more.

> Lennie Butt was also adept at crown green bowling. He reached the quarter-final of an all-Macclesfield competition in 1936.
> After his Football League seasons with Huddersfield, Blackburn Rovers and a war-time Manchester United, Butt had successful managerial spells at Mossley and Wilmslow Albion. He then returned to the Moss Rose in 1960, to take charge of the reserves.
> Lennie Butt died in 1994 at the age of 83.

Macclesfield F.C., Cheshire League Champions 1932–33, Lennie Butt is seated, second from the left. (*Maccselfield Express*)

Macc. disposed of Hurst (6–0), then Witton Albion (5–0 away), whilst the Robins crashed 1–5 at Chester. A 5–2 win over Hurst (also beaten in the semi-final of the Challenge Cup) left the Silkmen needing to win their final game of the season, against Sandbach on the following Monday night, to be certain of the Cheshire League title for the first time in their history.

It was soon evident that Sandbach, despite their lowly league position, were not going to play the routine fall guys. The score was 1–1 until well into the second half. Stockton, the Macc. right half, missed a penalty. Bourne, in the Sandbach goal, was living up to his reputation as the best 'keeper in the county. Eventually – and inevitably – Jepson took a pass from Stockton and steered the ball at speed round the advancing Bourne. This was the goal which clinched the championship.

Later that week Port vale were beaten 1–0 in the final of the Challenge Cup.

It was traditional for the new title-holders to play a select XI from the rest of the league. Macc. won the match 3–2, with Jepson signing off from his four and a half month Moss Rose career with a hat-trick. The teams were:

*Macclesfield*: Williams; Scott, Sharples; Stockton, Burridge, McGrae; Chesters, Butt, Jepson, Shirley, Dickie

*Rest of the League*: Bourne (Sandbach); Heywood (Altrincham), Wootton (Port Vale); Littlehales (Tranmere), White (Congleton), Kellard (Mossley); Clifford (Stalybridge), Mayers (Mossley), Broadhurst (Manchester North End), Drinkwater (Ashton National), Trotter (Manchester Central)

The next season saw another successful league campaign. The Silkmen eventually finished six points clear of their nearest challengers – at the time another Cheshire League record. Nine successive away wins – a club record – in mid-season was a major boost. Top scorers were

Roscoe (36) and Butt (28). (Jack Roscoe was a centre-forward from Chester. He had replaced Jepson who, to the fans' incomprehension, had been transferred to Altrincham along with Chesters.)

The final top of the table was:

|  | P | W | D | L | F | A | Pts |
|---|---|---|---|---|---|---|---|
| Macclesfield | 42 | 29 | 5 | 8 | 121 | 64 | 63 |
| Port Vale | 42 | 26 | 5 | 11 | 112 | 57 | 57 |
| Manchester North End | 42 | 24 | 7 | 11 | 124 | 78 | 55 |

The match with the Rest of the League was this year won 8–5, with the usually deeper-lying schemer Jack Shirley notching six. A half-dozen in a single match was considered to be another club record, until John Earles recalled Tommy Nolan's second-half six against Newton Heath in 1907 (see Chapter 7). The achievement was to be equalled again within a year.

Memorable for quite different reasons was Macc.'s exit from the 1932–33 Senior Cup, in its way every bit as cataclysmic as Arsenal's FA Cup defeat by Walsall the previous month.

The Cheshire FA had barred reserve teams of Football League clubs from the Senior Cup – although they would be back by 1935 – as the playing of first team ringers was becoming too common a trend. It would have made more sense, perhaps, to have tightened up the rules on eligibility, nonetheless for two years the competition was bereft of the likes of Crewe, Chester, and Tranmere Rovers. Obviously, in these circumstances, Macc. fancied their chances.

In the first round Witton Albion were beaten 3–0 away, with Butt netting a corker from 25 yards. They were then drawn, again away, against amateur works team ICI Alkali, average age 21. Secretary Harry Oldfield, usually a shrewd negotiator, was unable to persuade the opponents to switch the venue to the Moss Rose, arguing the bigger potential gate. ICI, coached by ex-Manchester City centre-half Sydney Scott, stuck to their guns, and the Silkmen travelled to Winnington.

Profiting, then, from home advantage, a strong wind, goalkeeper W. Lees in outstanding form, and

an unusually feeble forward display from their illustrious opposition, ICI provided the shock of the round by winning 2–1. They were to progress to the final, where they lost narrowly (0–1) to Nantwich.

Still, with two successive championships under their belt, Macc. embarked on the 1933–34 season determined to make it three in a row. In early September the Silkmen travelled to Stockport to take on the County. Valentine notched the first of his fifteen hat-tricks in the 8–1 win. Another high-scoring win was against Altrincham, 7–2. This was the occasion on which Valentine equalled the club record of six goals in a match.

And no narrative of that year would be complete without mention of the scintillating strike against Runcorn, dubbed 'wonder goal' by the headline writers. Owen, an outside-left who was later to impress on Manchester United's first team, started the move with a dribble into the centre circle, drawing his full-back and unbalancing the Runcorn defence. He delivered a reverse pass to Butt, who was now unmarked out on the wing. Butt laid off to Valentine, who rounded his marker and from thirty yards 'sent the ball soaring like a rocket' into the net.

Despite the riot of scoring, though, and looking likely winners for most of the season, Macc. had to relinquish the championship to new boys Wigan Athletic. They finished runners-up, five points adrift.

One of the contributory factors to Macc.'s loss of league form towards the end was a titanic series of struggles with Stalybridge Celtic in the quarter-finals of the Challenge Cup. It took three replays to decide the issue. In the fourth game, at Bower Fold, the Silkmen, reduced to ten men, were trailing 1–3 with twenty minutes left. Two late goals forced the tie into extra time, and Valentine grabbed the winner with the last kick of the match. Stirring stuff – but the extra games were ultimately unwelcome in the long, tough campaign. Macc. lost the semi, again in a replay, to Stockport County.

At H. Oldfield's suggestion, the Champions *v.* Rest of the League match was replaced by a Champions *v.* Runners-up. Another canny move, this ensured that Macc. could reap the same gate profits as when they had been title-holders themselves. The Silkmen regained some pride by defeating the Lancastrians 2–1.

There was another minor compensation: Macclesfield won their section of the 1933–34 Subsidiary League. This was a relatively meaningless experiment which compiled two separate tables based on the results of Cheshire League games already played. More of an academic exercise than anything else, the idea was dropped after one year.

## Another Cup win

Valentine was a hard act to follow, but for the next season Macc. engaged the services of Oswald Jones, a 24-year-old from Oswestry. Another major catch was Thomas Thornley, a right-back who had just completed a stint as captain of Stalybridge Celtic. (Football for the Thornleys was a family affair: Thomas' wife was a centre-forward for Preston Ladies and England, and his brother Jesse was later to play for the Silkmen.)

In the league, the goal feast continued, but it was not always Macc. who had sole rights to the lion's share. In October a home match with Stalybridge Celtic was lost by the odd goal in eleven. The visit of champions Wigan saw a ferociously competitive 4–4 draw, with the Silkmen leading 4–1 at one stage. Nevertheless Macc. were for a long time the league's top scorers, with a string of emphatic wins to their credit:

| | | | |
|---|---|---|---|
| Runcorn | H | W | 6–1 |
| Crewe Alex. | H | W | 8–0 |
| Congleton | A | W | 5–1 |
| Congleton | H | W | 7–1 |
| Prescot Cables | H | W | 9–0 |
| Northwich Vics. | H | W | 7–1 |
| Winsford Utd. | H | W | 9–1 |

But too many away points dropped, and a poor end to the season, dragged them down to a final eighth position.

In the Senior Cup of 1934–35, though, it was a different story.

In the first round they were drawn away to village side Moulton Verdin. Once again the minnows refused to shift the venue to the Moss Rose, no doubt inspired by the example of ICI

Alkali. So the Silkmen made their way to Moulton, a hamlet mid-way between Northwich and Winsford, just down the lane from the once-great Davenham.

The *Times* report tells of the teams getting changed in the billiard room of the village institute. As one of the Macc. players said: 'That's the first time I've ever seen a bar in a dressing room!' This amenity, of course, was sportingly kept closed until after the match.

The players then walked 300 yards down the main street, through a gauntlet of cheering mothers and children, to where a crowd of just 700 was waiting. (Northwich Vics. and Winsford Utd. were contesting the local derby on the same day.) The pitch had to be prepared first, though: the groundsman chased off a flock of sheep, then diligently shovelled off the droppings. Harry Bruce, the Macc. centre-half and captain, booted the ball onto the pitch – scattering a bevy of hens that had taken a fancy to one of the goalmouths.

Once the match got under way the visitors were determined that history should not repeat itself. Macc. overcame the bumpy pitch and the opponents' spirited resistance and ran out 5–1 winners. This was Moulton's first home defeat in the first two and a half years of their existence.

The club lost out financially with this poorly-attended match, and were hoping for a better deal in the next round. Their prayers were answered with a home tie against Chester, who were dispatched 4–1.

The luck of the draw held out: the third round tie was with Northwich Victoria, once again at the Moss Rose. The Vics. found the Silkmen attack at the height of its powers, and finished on the wrong end of an 8–1 drubbing.

Into another semi-final, the adversaries the redoubtable Altrincham, Senior Cup holders, current league leaders, and making no secret of the fact that they were aiming for the double.

Recent form gave no clue as to the likely outcome. The Robins had ended Macc.'s FA Cup runs with depressing frequency in the past few years; the last league match at the Moss Rose had produced that rare bird of the 'thirties, a goalless draw. The previous season, of course, had been the day of Valentine's six-hit. Could Jones produce anything like his predecessor's form?

The Macclesfield team was:

Williams; Thornley, Hartshorne; Swann,
Bruce (c), Naylor; Eaton, Butt, Jones, Ward,
Davies

The match, played in torrential rain at Edgeley Park, Stockport, was probably Macc.'s finest team effort of the whole season. Jones notched a hat-trick, one a glorious flying header, and a quick-thinking Davies ran in for the fourth. The 4–1 result did not flatter the Silkmen.

The final against Crewe Alexandra, three weeks later, was held at Moss Lane, Altrincham. Macc. were not at their fullest strength: Naylor was out with a septic knee, and Williams was suffering from a bad cold. Sproson took Naylor's place at left half, otherwise the team was the same as in the semi. Crewe's line-up was:

Johnson; Spencer, Slicer; Gilchrist, McHale,
Major; Rosson, Hills, Merrie, Rogers, Dyer

In a nervy, physical first half – partly due to the hard pitch and lively ball, partly to the pressure of the occasion – there was little to celebrate, apart from the cohesive play of Butt and Eaton. Macc.'s first goal owed a lot to good fortune. Davies' shot seemed well covered by Spencer, but the luckless full-back, in attempting to clear, sliced the ball into his own net. The same player made amends on the stroke of half-time, lifting a free kick into the Macc. goal from fully forty-five yards.

The second half was a much more eventful affair. Both teams at last settled, and end-to-end attacks were the order of the day. Macclesfield threw men forward, despite the gaps that this left in defence. Within two minutes of the re-start the gamble paid off. From Eaton's cross, Jones raced in to make it 2–1. Five minutes later Crewe were back on level terms, Merrie sprinting onto a through ball.

Now the excitement really began: first Rosson missed a couple of chances for Crewe, then Hartshorne sent a free kick skimming over the bar. Attacks swung back and forth, in a manner that one reporter likened to the rallies of a basketball match.

It was Lennie Butt on the hour, in what was to be one of his last matches for the Silkmen, who scored the vital third goal, timing his run and shot on to a loose, bounding ball to perfection. He was the recipient of 'a fusillade of handshakes, shoulder pats and hugs'.

Crewe were not finished: Merrie was unlucky not to be awarded a penalty when he was brought down by Thornley. But with Eaton in outstanding form, it was Macc. who finished the game with a flourish. Ward scored twice in the last ten minutes, making the final score a slightly flattering 5–2.

On Good Friday the team and officials were invited to the *Majestic* cinema, where there was a special showing of the film of the final. This was certainly a contrast to the bill of fare on offer at the town's other cinemas that week: Shirley Temple, Jean Harlow, and Harold Lloyd.

# Twilight

'Before the start of Macclesfield's FA cup-tie at Bangor on Saturday, the players and officials lined up in the centre of the field and joined with the crowd in singing *Land of My Fathers* the Welsh national song, and the National Anthem as a tribute to the maintenance of peace.'
*Times* (7/10/38)

## Losing finalists

In the words of Arsène Wenger: 'When you have tasted caviar, it is difficult to go back to sausage.'

The four seasons before the outbreak of war brought mostly plain fare to the Silkman table. There were changes aplenty, the two most crucial of which were the departure of Lennie Butt to Huddersfield Town, and the standing down of Secretary Harry Oldfield. Butt would go on to even greater things at Blackburn Rovers, scoring four goals in that team's 1938–39 FA Cup run. Oldfield's change of office to club Chairman meant the weakening of links forged with nearby Football League clubs, which had been a crucial ingredient of the years of success.

Macclesfield had exploited the transfer system to perfection. If a League player was placed on the transfer list, and was therefore ineligible to play for another League team until bought, it followed that to keep match fit and to have an opportunity to display his skills to the travelling scouts, it would be to his benefit to find a non-league club. The top-class players acquired free by Macc. this way during the 'thirties included: Billy Johnston, Bert Burridge, Albert Valentine, and of course Lennie Butt, five years 'on the list' with Stockport County.

It had been a fruitful symbiosis. Now the uncertainty brought about by too many changes was to divert and dilute the winning formula.

1935–36 saw a new club committee, and a new training staff.

John Minshull, a local man, was now chief trainer. His assistant was strong man Jim Evans, trained masseur and qualified in first aid. He was well known to the crowds at the Moss Rose, having once enlivened a half-time by challenging any three of those present to a tug-of-war, a battle which he convincingly won. His other claim to fame was his magic elixir which he used to revive flagging players. The pungent ammonia-based brew was reported to reduce its recipients to tears.

That season was a chequered affair. In the league the record by the end of February was a striking display of even-handedness:

| P | W | D | L | F | A | Pts |
|----|----|---|----|----|----|-----|
| 30 | 13 | 4 | 13 | 73 | 72 | 30 |

They would rally slightly towards the end, finishing ninth.

Yet another financial crisis reared its head, exacerbated by the closing of the ground by the Cheshire FA for a fortnight in March. There had been a crowd disturbance at the end of the match with Manchester North End in January, during which a spectator was seen to throw a snowball at the referee. (This, incidentally, was not the first time that the decisions of this official, one G. Fletcher, had incensed a crowd.) With no revenue from home games and no cash in hand, the club could not even afford to send a team to a midweek league game at Nantwich. On the spot contributions raised the wherewithal within a matter of hours, and the club was saved from a sticky end. Macc. won the game 3–2.

Another public appeal, and an acceptance of a 12½% wage cut for the rest of the season by the players, enabled the finances to return to an even keel.

It should not be thought, of course, that Macc. were the only club to suffer such crises. Buxton FC ran up debts of over £1,000 in the 'thirties, and a number of Cheshire League outfits – Connah's Quay, Prescot Cables – went to the wall during the same period. What is noteworthy about Macc.'s problems is the stead-fastness of local support, which could be relied upon to keep the club running in times of need.

And there was another lucrative Cheshire Cup run, which would take the Silkmen back to the final.

After a bye in the first round, Macc. then disposed of Chester (3–0), and Hyde United (3–1). The opponents in the semi were Winsford, who had fought with the Silkmen in that wild ten-goal match at the same stage six years before. This time – at Witton Albion's ground – there were fewer goals, but no shortage of thrills. An exciting game was won 4–1 in extra time, despite Winsford taking an early lead.

Runcorn were the opposition in the final. The teams were:

*Macclesfield*: Thiemicke; Manifould, Rawlinson; McMain, Bruce, Thornley; Titley, Eaton, Jones, Rigby, Smallwood
*Runcorn*: Williams; Peacock, Long; Houghton, Foxley, Gilmour; Chedgzoy, Rogers, Search, Fitton, Ascroft
Richard Williams had transferred allegiance; he

Peter Wright's son, Harold, carried on the family tradition by becoming a highly respected referee. He officiated at many First Division and FA Cup matches in the 1930's, and was entrusted with the 1937 Cheshire Cup Final between Northwich Vics. and Witton Albion. He was also proprietor of a shop on Chestergate.
He became Chairman of Macclesfield and District Football League during 1940, and was a tireless campaigner for the launch of the new town club in 1946.
He died in 1992, aged 88.

was thus to be awarded a winner's medal in two successive years with different clubs.

Thiemicke, the new goalie, was ex-Stoke City. Rawlinson had come from Halifax Town, Titley from Port Vale. Jesse Thornley was the younger brother of Thomas. Left wing Smallwood was a capable Welsh amateur, late of Chester.

Runcorn were the county's new footballing power, fin-anced by Merseyside businessmen and profiting from links with the two Liverpool giants. Chedgzoy, the right winger, was the son of the great Sam, the Everton forward. The team had re-cently changed its shirt colours from green to blue and white quarters, *à la* Blackburn Rovers, with a parallel switch in fortunes. They were current league leaders, having taken maxi-mum points off the Silkmen during the year. Macc. had gained partial revenge with a 3–2 win at Runcorn in the Challenge Cup a fortnight before, so a battle royal was forecast.

Thirty motor coaches, a fleet of private cars, and special trains took over 2,000 Macclesfield supporters to Crewe. The team arrived slightly later than expected, as their bus had stalled. (There were those who were later to cite this as an omen.)

The game was as close as predicted. After a goalless first half, Smallwood opened the scoring after ten minutes of the second, with a fine header from one of Titley's outswinging corners. It was a lead that was enjoyed for just three minutes. With Macc. committed to attack, the ball was cleared to an unmarked Fitton, who equalised matters. 1–1 it remained until the third minute of extra time, when Ascroft cleverly drew out Thiemicke from his goal before lobbing over his head. Chedgzoy swept in to supply the *coup de grâce*.

Runcorn were to go from strength to strength in those pre-war years. They reached the Third Round proper of the FA Cup in 1938–39, losing 2–4 at home to Preston North End. And as we will see, their golden age in Cheshire Cup terms would occur a half-century later.

## A *player-manager*

Macclesfield's first waged player-manager was introduced in the summer of 1936. James Stevenson, a Scots inside-forward from Stockport, pipped Harry Bruce for the job. Bruce, team captain until the end of the season, had just returned from coaching a Copenhagen club.

Stevenson received £3 10s. (£3.50) a week for his services, which included supervision of training: 'skipping, running, walking, ball control and heading practice', as well as implementation of a firmer team base:

> The players will not only report for training at the Moss Rose ground, but they are to live in the town where Stevenson will also reside. *Courier* (12/6/36)

As it turned out, the post lasted just the one season. By 1938 Stevenson was back at Stockport, where he remained as assistant trainer until the war.

The new committee made no secret of the fact that under discussion was an application to join the Third Division North of the Football League – the first time that the consideration of such a move had been publicly admitted. In the event, no application would be forthcoming, possibly because Wigan Athletic had knocked the year before, and found the door barred. It was the first version of the mutual back-scratching society that was to deny promotion to many a deserving non-league club for the next forty years, until a theoretical opening was created in the 1980's with the 'pyramid' arrangement.

> On 29 June 1938, the Moss Rose was chosen as the venue for a soccer match billed as the World Championship Final: England v. France. It was the Ladies' competition, with England's team mostly composed of members of the Preston Ladies' club. England won convincingly 5–0, in front of a crowd of well over six thousand.

Another item under discussion was the formation of a Limited Company. Scars of 1897 had long since healed, and the lessons assimilated. Once again, the idea was shelved, and it was not until after the war that it was reconsidered.

One popular innovation at the Moss Rose was the scoreboard, worked by members of the Supporters' Club. This facility first made its appearance in August 1936, displaying the half-time results of Football League games. The pools had become enormously popular – and in Macclesfield as much as anywhere, since a man from Cornbrook Road, a stone's-throw from the ground on the Moss Estate, had won over £10,000 the previous May.

The burgeoning Estate, incidentally, finally reached the ground the following summer, with houses being built on Moss Lane. An article in the *Courier* noted the change:

> The Moss Rose is no longer in the open country ... Soon the little country walk between the centre of town and the hamlet which used to be at the centre of the Moss Rose will be no more. (20/8/37)

The club, naturally, relished the arrival of large numbers of potential supporters on its doorstep.

Those years, alas, were trophy-less. A flirtation with the Welsh Senior Cup came to naught, with successive second round defeats at the hands of Shrewsbury Town and Rhyl Athletic.

There was a glimmer of hope in the 1936–37 Challenge Cup, which saw Macc. progress to the semi-final. Winsford United, however, ended the run with a 3–1 win.

The FA Cup put them into the hat with the likes of Linotype, Timperley, and Moulton Verdin in 'Preliminary' and 'Extra Preliminary' rounds – much to the club's annoyance. It was not a question of pride, simply of finances. It was a similar situation in the Cheshire Senior Cup: for two years in succession the Silkmen were drawn away against Wilmslow Albion. After one of these matches (won 5–0) the club was left with a net profit of just £11: in real terms, a significant loss. Their appeals for a fine-tuning of the seeding process fell on deaf ears.

With a team based on youth and local talent, Macc. performed well enough in patches, but the consistency essential for league prowess eluded them. The last three years before the outbreak of war saw them stuck in the lower reaches of the table.

Then by the beginnings of the 1939–40 season, of course, the world had other things on its mind.

# I 3

# *War and Peace*

'On Saturday Macclesfield entertain Wigan Athletic, kick-off 2.45 p.m. All spectators must
have their gas masks or admission will be refused.'
*Courier* (12/10/39)

'The meeting passed a resolution authorising Mr Harry Mottershead, solicitor, to proceed
with the formation and registration of a limited liability company, under the title of
MACCLESFIELD TOWN FOOTBALL CLUB LTD.'
*Times* (25/4/46)

### *The Cup won under war conditions*

Within a week or two of the opening of the new season, a full-scale soccer programme was evidently out of the question. At all levels, major competition ceased, and for a while a reduced, local programme supervened.

The town of Macclesfield braced itself once more for the strictures of war. Gas masks were mandatory in cinemas and at football matches. Black-out curtains, designated air-raid shelters (one of which was at the King George Playing Fields on Windmill Street), and severely restricted travel were to be part of everyday life for the next four-and-a-half years. With conscription necessitating the moving around of players, it was clear that, at Cheshire League level at least, soccer's days were numbered.

The Macclesfield Football Club would not survive the year. It had, nevertheless, one inspiring shot left in its locker. Northwich Victoria were the opponents in the final of the 1939–40 Cheshire Senior Trophy, a close-run affair which took place at Crewe. The Silkmen team was:

Pitt; Hamlett, Harrop; Hackney, Davies (c), Rosson; James, Crawshaw, Beswick, Daniels, Alcock

> Macclesfield have won the record number of Cheshire Senior Cups: twenty, not including the wartime trophy of 1940.

The final score was 3–2, with Daniels, James and Beswick supplying the Macc. goals. Rudd of Northwich served up a moment or two of high drama in the dying seconds, beating three defenders in the area and rifling in a low shot which was 'all the way a winner'. Pitt, however, proved himself equal to the task and flung himself full-length to fist the ball round the corner. This was all the more remarkable as Pitt was suffering from mild concussion sustained earlier in the match.

The game's other major talking point was the eccentric refereeing of Mr Heskine. Daniels was tripped in the Northwich penalty area, and great was the surprise when the official awarded an indirect free kick to Macc. inside the box. To restore the haphazard balance, Beswick was clearly seen to handle the ball on his way to scoring the winner. The referee, on the blind side so to speak, chose to award the goal.

So, a couple of months before the club officially folded, the prized Senior Cup came home once more. The Cheshire FA had not been able to afford winners' medals, but anonymous donors from the town ensured that the appropriate mementoes found their way to the winning eleven.

| P | W | D | L | F | A | Pts | Pos |
|---|---|---|---|---|---|-----|-----|
| 14 | 3 | 2 | 9 | 28 | 46 | 8 | 8 |

The League had been re-moulded into two competitions, named Series West and Series East, with respective winners playing off for the overall title. Somewhat oddly, Macc. found themselves in Series West for the first half of the 1939–40 season, finishing last out of eight teams:

– although they fared slightly better when they switched to Series East:

| P | W | D | L | F | A | Pts | Pos |
|---|---|---|---|---|---|-----|-----|
| 12 | 4 | 0 | 8 | 23 | 42 | 8 | 6 |

Runcorn were the eventual winners. Even this minimal arrangement, though, was to be scrapped after a year.

## The Moss Rose during war-time

The Chairman of one year's standing, Cllr. J. Sinnett, speaking at the Supporters' Club social in August 1940, was succinct on the matter: 'I have finished'.

The landlords of the Moss Rose, now Messrs. Lonsdale and Adshead, wisely gave their permission for the ground to be kept in use during the hostilities. Some recreation areas had been turned into crop or drill fields, but the Moss Rose was the venue for the occasional sporting contest put on for purposes of fund-raising or morale. There was a baseball game there during War Weapons Week in May 1941, an event which raised over £100. The following March, as part of Warships Week, there was a rugby match between a Military XV and a Macclesfield and District Select. That week the town raised an astonishing £750,000 to finance the building of a destroyer.

That same month the old warrior 'Mush' Howarth celebrated his 82nd birthday.

From December 1942 the Americans started to arrive in the neighbourhood. The following June, as part of the Barnaby Week festivities, a special match was arranged on the Moss Rose between the local Police and the US Army. Forty-five minutes' baseball was followed by a similar ration of football. The baseball, unsurprisingly, was convincingly won by the US: 22–2. Looking to redress the balance in the football, the Police were however beaten 1–0 by their 'younger and unorthodox' opponents. It was an eerie predictor of a similar upset

Winners of the War-time Senior Cup 1940, beating Northwich Victoria 3–2. Players pictured are: *standing*: Hackney, Daniels, Pitt, Hamlett, Rosson, Crawshaw, Harrop.
*seated*: James, Beswick, Davies (capt.), Cock, C. Barton (trainer).
*(Macclesfield Express)*

that was to befall the national team in seven years' time.

The Home Guard and the Fire Service also had teams, the latter even forming a league. Their possible grounds were the Moss Rose, Westminster Street (near the King's School) or at Wilmslow. Sometimes, especially if a team from the Military was involved, for obvious reasons the venue was not advertised. 'Somewhere in Macclesfield' would be the only specific.

## *Resurrection*

Within a week of D-Day, fourteen clubs met in Chester to discuss the re-creation of the Cheshire League, to begin in August of the following year. Macclesfield were not represented.

In April 1945 a meeting was held in the *Bate Hall*, Chestergate, at which it was decided not to re-form the Macclesfield club, at least until better times. Although the end of the war was in sight, it was felt that the town, for the moment, had more pressing concerns. The launching of a PLC, correctly seen as the only viable way forward, was considered beyond the finances and energies of the townspeople in that time of crippling austerity.

Besides, the town had 'done its bit' with conspicuous glory during the hostilities. Well over £2,000,000 had been raised – was still being raised – to sponsor Spitfires and the battleship HMS Teazer. No borough of comparable size or population in England had been as forthcoming.

So, whilst the Cheshire League season of 1945–46 got under way – participants included Buxton, Stockport County Reserves and Northwich Victoria – Macclesfield was to do without senior football for a year.

The Don Cossack Riders – 'The Fearless Russian Horsemen' – had used the Moss Rose as their showcase as part of VE celebrations in May 1945. The same month it became known that other interests were targeting the ground. The landlords turned down an offer from a dogtrack syndicate, then started negotiations with the Borough Education Advisory Committee, who were considering buying the land as a playing field 'for the young people of the town'. It was also suggested that the land be sold for housing or industrial purposes.

The Macclesfield and District Junior Football League, partly under the aegis of Harold Wright (Peter's son) was re-launched in 1945.

But what of the Senior club?

The *Times* was to play a major role in the rebirth. First, the seeds were judiciously planted. Jess Robinson (see Chapter 7), now the landlord of the *Spread Eagle* in Romiley, was interviewed. He 'expressed concern at the absence of senior football in Macclesfield'. Luke Nolan, member of that 1891 Cup-winning side and now living in Newark, was spotted watching a cricket match at Bollington:

He made many enquiries about old football friends, to whom he wishes to be remembered. *Times* (13/9/45)

From a letter written by Gunner W. H. Hicks, published the following week:

It would be a tragedy to me, and hundreds more, if the club became extinct. *Times* (20/9/45)

By February there was a 'now or never' tone to the campaign. The *Times* generously offered to bear the cost of a public meeting, provided that the proposed club received promises from at least 500 townspeople to take up as total of £1,500 in shares. The deadline was the end of March.

On the 28 March 1946 the total was published: 619 people had promised a total of £1,587. The Football Club was alive – if not as yet kicking – once more.

## Macclesfield Town PLC

There was, of course, still much work to be done. There was an inspection of the Moss Rose ground and stands in April, attended by the architect R. A. Riseley, directors of Lonsdale and Adshead, and representatives from the *Times* and the newly-formed club committee. The pitch was declared 'in excellent condition', but Mr Riseley – let it be remembered, less than a month after the Burnden Park disaster – expressed concern about the wooden supports on the main stand. This would be remedied by cutting off every main support about a foot above the ground, and inserting steel anchor plates embedded in concrete.

SUPPORTERS' SELF-APPOINTED TASK

SCOUTS AND GUIDES HELD SWIMMING GALA

The annual swimming gala of Macclesfield and Congleton Boy Scouts' Association and Maccles- field Girl Guides' Association was held at the Macclesfield swimming

YOUNG TORIES' TENNIS

BEFORE re-laying the turf on half of the Moss Rose football ground, Macclesfield, the members of the Macclesfield Sup- porters' Club are attending to the drainage system. This photo- graph shows them busily en- gaged on their self-appointed task.

There is still a tremendous amount of work to be done, and the Supporters' Club would welcome assistance from outsiders. They are at the ground every night

Volunteers digging drainage ditches on the Moss Rose summer 1946, in preparation for the re-birth of Macclesfield Town F.C.
(*Macclesfield Express*)

Another recommendation was the rebuilding of the changing rooms, at an estimated cost of £632.

Later that month, in a 'cup-tie atmosphere' at the public meeting at the Town Hall, the future of the club was mapped out. A three-year lease had been obtained from Lonsdale and Adshead, so the use of the ground had been preserved. It was decided to co-opt the Central School Old Boys' team as the reserves, to play in the Manchester League. A place had been made available for the first team in the next season's Cheshire League, thanks mainly to the efforts of county FA committee man Edward Case, Tommy's brother.

A resolution was passed that the name of the club would be Macclesfield Town. This was seen as a fitting tribute to the communal energies that had brought the new club into being.

An appeal was launched for clothing coupons, so that the kitting out of the team could be completed. Five coupons bought a pair of boots, and the remainder of the outfit could be had at the following rate: shorts, 5; shirts, 4; socks, 2 per pair.

Jos. Stevenson (no relation to James) was invited to take up the post of team manager. To him fell the unenviable task of rebuilding the team from scratch. By the start of the season twenty players would have signed, four of them professionals. These numbers were to swell encouragingly during the course of the season.

Other innovations were: the first appearance of adverts inside the ground; the use of the front of the *Moss Rose* as a car parking space; ambulances converted into mobile snack bars; and, by November, the installa- tion of a loudspeaker system, a gift from the Radio Relay Company.

The long-awaited day came on 31 August 1946. Buxton were the visitors in the opening league game. The Moss Rose entrance fees were: stand two shillings (10p); reserve side one and sixpence (7½p); ground one shilling (5p). There was a good crowd of over 4,000.

The team was:

Foxcroft; Gosling, Harris; Bardsley, Needham (c), Davies; Taylor, James, Williams, Ryan, Craven

Reserves: Burke, Garfoot

Frederick Needham, a professional, had come from Stockport County, on Lennie Butt's recommendation. The £100 transfer fee had been waived by the County. Other professionals in the team were William Bardsley, ex-captain of the Royal Navy team at Lowestoft; G. Foxcroft the 'keeper from Burnley; and J. H. Ryan, an inside-right who had appeared for Stockport and Raith Rovers. The one link with the pre-war team was forward C. F. James, who had played right wing in the 1940 Cheshire Cup final.

Buxton, who had finished third in the Cheshire League the previous season and who were fielding virtually the same side, profited from more combined play to win 2–0.

This would be the keynote of Macc.'s year: individual skills undermined by a lack of team cohesion. The line-up changed from week to week as new players were brought in and given a trial run, there being no opportunity to test them thoroughly in a non-competitive context. Jos Stevenson preferred to let the committee select the team. Then after three months Stevenson opted to stand down.

The role of manager had still not been crystalised. Theo Kelly, the Everton team boss, offered advice in selection procedure and the drawing up of a job description. By January 1947, from a short list of five, the club appointed Bill Edwards, one of Kelly's protégés. Edwards was to have 'wide powers in the signing of players', and would be 'in charge of the ground and staff'.

The *entente cordiale* with Everton was to bring inside-left John Lyons to the Moss Rose. His wing partnership with Ken Speak, an acquisition from Portsmouth, was one of the following season's choicer aspects, as the Silkmen worked towards another winning blend.

## Challenge and Gilgryst Cups

Summer 1947 saw further improvements to the ground. The embankment was raised on the stand and popular sides, terraces of concrete slabs being laid down on mounds of cinders. The stands and new dressing rooms were painted in black and white (although the new dark blue team strip would make its appearance by Christmas). In November, for the home match with Runcorn, the Silkmen at last bowed to fashion by numbering their shirts for the first time.

There was a dispiriting start to the season: five successive defeats, and elimination from the FA Cup 6–1 by Buxton. There were glimpses of better things. Trailing 1–5 at Chester, Macc. threw caution to the winds and, using full-backs Prescot and Bardsley as extra attackers, created a rousing second-half fight-back. The final score was a narrow 5–6 defeat.

It was not until the New Year that they really got into their stride. Although the league form remained largely indifferent – they finished in eighteenth place – two trophies were to make their way to the Moss Rose that year.

On Valentine's Day the visitors were Winsford United in the second round of the Senior Cup. A big crowd was expected, as the word was an armada of coaches was on its way from mid-Cheshire. So it proved: the gate of 9,003 is still the official Moss Rose record for a game involving the Silkmen. Unfortunately the day was marred by a 2–3 defeat, especially galling as a 2–0 half-time lead had been overtaken.

In the Challenge Cup, however, it was a different story. The regional pairing system meant that Macc. had their usual first round game with Congleton Town. A 2–0 win saw them progress to a much more challenging prospect: away against Wellington Town, unbeaten at home in the league, and Cheshire League champions in both years since the war.

No respecter of reputations, the Silkmen ran out 2–1 winners. The semi-final pitted them

Nat McKinstry, Silkmen goalkeeper in the immediate post-war period. (Nat McKinstry)

time. Brown, a reserve replacing the injured Speak, scored the first. Prescott's penalty rebounded from the crossbar into Lomax's path, and the centre-forward notched the second. An own goal completed the Macc. tally.

The replay took place at Stalybridge Celtic's ground. Once again the Silkmen confounded the sceptics by winning 3–2. The final would be against Altrincham, away.

That same week, the reserves contested the final of the Gilgryst Trophy, the knock-out competition based on the Manchester League. Bert Swindells, first team centre-forward until the arrival of Lomax, was their inspirational player-coach. Playing at Newton Heath, the reserves drew 2–2 with Hazel Grove Celtic. In the replay, at the Moss Rose, they were convincing 5–1 winners.

The following week the first team endeavoured to follow suit. Leading 3–1 with five minutes left, and having survived a tidal wave of sustained Altrincham pressure for most of the second half, Macc. succumbed at last: two late goals took the tie to a replay on the Friday evening.

The Macclesfield team was:
McKinstry; Bardsley, Edwards; Stott, McWilliam, Warren; Owen, Davies, Lomax, Lyon, Speak

This time there was a clear gap in class and purpose between the two teams, reflected in the 3–1 scoreline. Speak and Lyon cleverly drew the defence with a typical display of inter-passing, before the winger centred for the unmarked Lomax to open the scoring. Davies made it two by half-time, with a partially mishit shot which bounded awkwardly into the net. Lomax added the third on 87 minutes.

The press photos show Edwards brandishing the hourglass trophy, surrounded by a crush of team-mates and ecstatic fans.

against Mossley at the Moss Rose. The two attack-minded teams finished on 3–3, after extra

## Swindells takes the wheel

On the Monday after the first of the Altrincham games the guests at the Moss Rose were Zeeburgia FC, a Dutch touring side. Ver-

hagen, the international, was at inside-right. Macc. acquitted themselves well with a 2–2 draw.'Keeper Liddell, soon to be transferred to

Team for the Final of the 1948 Challenge Cup, won vs. Altrincham 3–1 after a 3–3 draw. (Nat McKinstry)

Wellington, gave an impressive display.

First choice for goalkeeper in 1948–49 was Nat McKinstry, who like second string Arnold had come to prominence in the reserves. The Lyon-Speak partnership was left intact, and Owen and Lomax remained in the largely unchanged attack. With Edwards shifting between centre-half and 'third back', and the midfield boosted by the addition of Patrick Quinn an ex-Scottish Junior international, the team approached the new season with some optimism.

Once again, though, the start was disastrous. After a 1–0 victory over Buxton on the opening day, there followed eight successive league defeats – the club's worst ever run at any level. In mid-October they were propping up the table, and had been knocked out of the FA Cup by Northwich Vics., 0–3 at home. At this point there was a breathtaking transformation, beginning with a thoroughly unexpected 2–0 win at Runcorn, of all places.

The trip to Mossley the following Saturday was

regarded with great interest, not least because the player-manager of the Tame Valley side was none other than former Moss Rose favourite Lennie Butt. He scored one against his old club, but could not prevent Macc. winning 5–3. It was 5–1 with six minutes left – a better indication of the Silk-men's superiority.

The run continued, with a 6–2 drubbing of Altrincham, then victories over Tranmere Rovers

In 1949, the town of Macclesfield had a contribution to make to three major finals: FA Cup, Scottish Cup, and Rugby League Challenge Cup. Humphreys Bros. of Lower Heys Mill made the kit for Wolves, Glasgow Rangers, and Bradford Northern. All three teams won.
The same firm also supplied the kit for Manchester United's European Cup-winning team of 1968.

The team takes the field against Buxton in the opening game of 1948–49. Note that the changing rooms were in the corner of the ground, on the site of the present offices. (Nat McKinstry)

and Droylsden. With 11 points from 6 games, Macc. rose to mid-table, eventually finishing eleventh out of twenty-two teams.

Player-manager Bill Edwards had worked a minor miracle. However, there were whispers of an overbearing, or at least over-attentive, committee. The team that lost to Northwich in the FA Cup, for example, was rumoured not to have been wholly Edwards' selection.

There was a telling comment from 'Silkman' (Clifford Rathbone), the *Times* football columnist:

Macclesfield do not seem to have got the right idea of the duties of a player-manager. If you pay a man for this job, for goodness' sake let him do it. *Times* (10/3/49)

Edwards' resignation in the final week of the season nevertheless came as a shock. The official reason given was that he was upset by a number of townspeople persistently barracking him for a defensive lapse which had allowed South Liverpool to score the winning goal in a recent league game. Whatever the motive for his standing down, the majority of the crowd were in no doubt about the value of his two-and-a-half year contribution to the club. He was chaired off the pitch in his final game.

Within a week, reserve manager Bert Swindells was appointed as his successor. Edwards had done a lot of the groundwork. Now Swindells was to lead the club into another golden era.

# I 4

# *Four Years, Four Trophies*

'To be returned to Macclesfield after midnight.'
*Note found inside the Cheshire Senior Trophy,*
*before the 1952 Final at Crewe.*

'Your players have put class into football in Cheshire.'
J. R. Stockbridge, Cheshire League Secretary (8/5/53)

## *Threshold*

In those two energetic and fruitful years, manager Bert Swindells took the Silkmen to two Senior Cup Finals, and one Challenge Cup Final. In 1950–51 Macc. finished in fifth position in the league. Moreover, invaluable foundations were being laid for the further glories achieved by Swindells' successor, Jack Smith.

The most important development off the pitch was the re-launch of the Supporters' Club, which had folded along with the parent organisation at the onset of war. The assets of the pre-war club were transferred, and a healthy membership of 500 set the ball rolling by financing the refreshment huts, in place for that August's trial matches.

The nucleus of the 1948–49 team had stayed on: McKinstry, Bardsley, Prescott, Davies, Marsh and Speak were the pick of the professionals. In August 1949 the club brought off an astute move by persuading Eric Barber, a 23-year-old forward late of Stockport County and Sheffield United, to sign. He was to stay but six months before being lured back to the Football League, but as we shall see, his contribution was ultimately considerable.

Ernest Tagg came from Carlisle United. He formed the right-sided attack with Kenneth Jowett, a winger lately of Halifax Town. James Cardno, an ex-Rhyl player, partnered either Prescott or Bardsley at full-back. Finney, a St Helens man, was the first inside-left to replace Lyon, who had moved to Wigan Athletic.

The first match was a convincing 7–1 win over Buxton. Macc.'s attacking strategy, which involved a quick and bewildering inter-changing of forward positions – perhaps an early version of 'total football' – time and again caught the Buxton defence on the hop. Barber scored in the first minute, after a quick-thinking assist from the industrious, ginger-haired Finney, who was for a short while the crowd's favourite.

Yet the following Wednesday, in the return league match, Buxton were prepared. Close man-to-man marking and fierce tackling kept the score down to 1–1. A home defeat at the hands of South Liverpool led to changes in the attack, and the initial impetus was lost.

There were nonetheless to be many reasons for celebration in the coming months: Chester were beaten 3–0 away, then 5–1 at home; the arrival of Vincent Pritchard from Wrexham was a significant fillip to the forward line, as was fellow inside forward Jimmy Lovery from Hyde. The Silkmen attack, on its day, was a force to be reckoned with. Droylsden were disposed of 5–2, then Wrexham 5–4 away. Stalybridge Celtic (4–0) and Mossley (5–0) were other memorable league wins that year.

The home match with Wrexham in November was notable for being Ken Speak's 'day out' in more ways than one. Speak had got married in the morning, and turned out to play in the afternoon, en route for his honeymoon at Blackpool!

The winger celebrated in style by scoring a goal after a rousing solo run. To cap a perfect day, Macc. won 3–1.

The real excitement of those Swindells years was to be found in two Senior Cup runs. The first ended in a 0–1 defeat in the final against Northwich Vics. (incidentally the first time these two old rivals had ever met in a peace-time Senior final). This was a disappointment following the heroics of earlier rounds, in which Macc. had overcome three severe tests, against the odds and most neutrals' expectations. First there had been Runcorn, beaten 3–1. After trailing 0–1, the injury-hit Silkmen gave a powerful second half display, culminating in a smoothly executed final goal: Barber cleverly drew the defence before slipping the ball to an unmarked Triner.

Donald Triner had been signed from Port Vale to help boost the forward line, weakened through an unlucky spate of injuries. Another addition of that time was future manager Jack Smith, ex-Congleton inside-right of some experience.

The attack was now clicking into gear. In round two, against Crewe Alexandra, after a goalless draw at home, a seven-goal thriller ensued at Gresty Road. The Macclesfield team was:

McKinstry; Bardsley, Cardno; Jones, Marsh, Davies; Triner, Smith, Barber, Pritchard, Speak

It was 3–3 with a minute of normal time remaining. Triner took a free kick from near the corner flag. Bardsley – one of the backs who had a penchant for joining the attack – continued the move with a glancing header, and Barber settled matters by heading strongly into the net.

It was a fitting signing-off from the 6ft. 1½in. (1m 87) forward. The next week he joined Bolton Wanderers for £1,500, then a club record. (Macc.

When Walter Owen sold a dummy to half the Wellington Town defence to score a vital goal in a 1949 league match, such was the enthusiasm displayed in one section of the crowd that one gentleman parted company with his false teeth. A sharp-eyed reporter spotted him still looking for them long after the match had finished.

were promised a further £500 should Barber decide to stay on with Bolton for a further season, which he did.)

His replacement was Albert Mycock, a tough bustler who nonetheless was capable of subtle distribution and approach work besides knocking in the goals.

The semi-final, at Witton, pitted Macc. against Winsford United, who had beaten Altrincham 6–0 in a previous round. Finalists in 1949, the mid-Cheshire side looked the better bet on form, but once again the Silkmen attack carried the day. This was despite the fact that Lovery and Davies were unable to play because of 'flu.

At the end of ninety minutes it was 1–1. Barely thirty seconds into extra time Speak, in a typical run, rounded his marker and sent in a searching cross. Ray Jones, hobbling from an earlier injury, donned the hero's mantle by heading a goal. This was a body-blow from which Winsford never recovered. Ten minutes later Pritchard made it 3–1, and Triner notched the fourth. The final score was 4–2.

To watch the final 6,000 travelled from Macclesfield to Crewe. The crowd that day was a phenomenal 15,400: at the time a record for the ground, including Football League and FA Cup games.

The teams were:

*Macclesfield*: McKinstry; Bardsley, Cardno; Hackney, Marsh, Davies; Triner, Lovery, Mycock, Pritchard, Speak

*Northwich Victoria*: Humphreys; Bateman, Bossons; Booth, Hobson, Blunt; Johnson, Basnett, Yearsley, Heaselgrove, Gould

Hopes were high for a Silkmen victory. Much was made of a dream McKinstry had had on the night before the first round match with Runcorn: Macc. had reached the final at Crewe, and were

The Silkmen take the field against Northwich Victoria in the Cheshire Senior Cup Final of 1950. In front of a ground record crowd of 15,400 at Gresty Road, Crewe, Macc. lost a close-fought game 0–1. They would gain their revenge. (Nat McKinstry)

leading 2–1 with two minutes left. At which point, said the 'keeper: 'I woke up'.

The reality was a cruel anti-climax.

Macc. had most of the play, but a combination of feeble finishing, bad luck, and clever positioning by Humphreys ensured Northwich kept a clean sheet. The only goal of the game was due to an uncharacteristic error by McKinstry. Instead of holding or punching out a cross, he palmed the ball into the path of the unmarked Gould, who netted.

The two teams were to meet again in the final the following year. This match would be as different from the first as it is possible to get.

## Goslings

Arthur Harding, club Secretary, called it 'the greatest soccer news we have ever had'.

It was a once-in-a-lifetime windfall: the Goslings club, formed by Abe Gosling and his two brothers ten years previously, perennial winners of the Manchester League, were folding because they were unable to obtain their own ground. The players were insistent that whatever happened to them, they were to stick together. They were therefore open to offers to a club to take them en bloc, without transfer fees.

Albert Mycock, who trained with them at the Newton Heath Loco ground, was one of the factors which swayed the semi-professional outfit towards the Moss Rose. Another was Macclesfield's approach: whereas the other two clubs in the running – Stalybridge and Northwich – sent just their respective team manager to do the wooing, Macc. sent a delegation of six.

Each club was given thirty minutes to present its case to the ten players present. After a brief deliberation the decision was unanimous: the Goslings would be starting the new season at the Moss Rose.

Those who were to play a major part in the ensuing success story were: Norman Gillott, a left back who, like Bardsley, liked to go on the offensive; right-half Clifford Freer; Walter Shepherd, an England amateur international left-half; and the inside-forward Dave Casey, small but hard as nails, soon to rejoice in the nickname 'Cast-iron Casey'.

This last, who was never able to command a regular first team spot, ousted first by ex-Manchester City Bill Murray and then by the free-scoring Frank Monaghan, was nonetheless a favourite with the crowd. He was possessed of a great sense of humour and immense spirit. The tale is told of a match with Northwich Victoria at the Moss Rose in January 1953 – a match which Macc. had to win to stay in contention for the Championship.

Approaching half-time, with the Vics. stubbornly holding on to their 1–0 lead, Casey clashed with a defender and had to retire from the game, blood pouring from a gash in his forehead. After having the wound stitched at a nearby doctor's, he decided he was well enough to rejoin the match, returning to the pitch, to a huge ovation, seventeen minutes into the second half. The score was still 1–0 to the Vics., but within two minutes of Casey's return, Macc. had equalised. The final score was 3–1 to the Silkmen, and it was the inside-forward's run that set up the third goal.

Bill Murray, on Manchester City's list at a respectable £4,000, was a 1950 close-season signing. He was to stay a year, before moving to Ashton United.

Two more acquisitions helped complete the jigsaw. From Hyde came centre-half Jimmy Richardson, soon to be captain, and linchpin of the formidable Freer-Richardson-Shepherd half-back line.

Then, continuing the tradition of 'character' goalkeepers at the Moss Rose, Jack Hacking arrived from Accrington Stanley. Son of the England international goalie John, he nevertheless had a style of keeping net that was quite different from that of his father. Whereas Hacking Senior had been renowned for his sound and workmanlike approach, the son seemed to prefer the flamboyant, the eye-catching. Acrobatic penalty saves were his speciality.

## Revenge

Once again the route to the Cheshire Senior Cup Final was far from easy. At least there was the early good fortune of two home draws: first Crewe were dismissed 3–1, then in round two reigning League Champions Witton Albion were beaten 1–0. The only goal in this close, fierce tussle was scored by Jack Smith, squeezing the ball home from an acute angle.

The semi-final, on the 'Moss Lane mudflats' at Altrincham, was another narrow squeak, this time against Tranmere Rovers. Again a single goal sep-

arated the teams. It was scored by Bernard Jones, usually a reserve half-back but drafted into the attack to replace the injured Smith.

So, without the glorious progress of the previous year, Macc. returned to Crewe to face Northwich Vics. once more. The team had changed significantly from twelve months before:

Hacking; A. Jones, Gillott; Freer, Bardsley, Shepherd; B. Jones, Murray, Smith, Lovery, Davies

The attack scored ninety goals in the league

that year, but they were up against a resourceful and ambitious Northwich side who would be applying for Football League status within the year.

Their line-up was:

Jepson; Booth, Bateman; Johnson, Hobson, Hawshall; Burkhill, Basnett, Neilson, Hanlon, Middleham

It was Macclesfield who scored first, after nineteen minutes. Hobson, in an attempt to contain the ebullient Smith, handled the ball in the Northwich area. Murray took the penalty. He had spent some time in training practising spot kicks, and the effort paid off: 1–0. Towards half-time Freer passed forward to his winger Bernard Jones. Davies had switched to inside-right, leaving his marker in limbo. Jones laid off into Davies' stride, and the native Maxfeldian thumped the ball home.

The second half was a vastly different affair. Northwich attacked from the off: forty seconds had elapsed when Basnett's shot whacked against the Macc. crossbar, and Hanlon netted the rebound. The Vics. now began to roll forward, and the Silkmen were reduced to wild clearances. With fourteen minutes left Burkhill embarked on a bewilderingly fast solo run which took him into the area. His hard and low shot beat the advancing Hacking. 2–2.

In the last moments of the game Burkhill all but grabbed the winner, but Hacking, not for the first time, showed he fully deserved his team-mates' accolade of player of the season. The shot was speeding for the far corner of the net, with the goalie apparently out of position. Hacking flung himself full-length and finger-tipped the ball round the post.

Extra time was three minutes old when Murray settled things with a touch of class that befitted a Cup Final winning goal. He dummied a pass out to the wing, wrong-footing the defence, then belted in a twenty-yard shot. Murray was 'lifted off his feet by his delighted colleagues'.

The following week was eventful too. On the Monday, with the Cup on display, a testimonial match was held on the Moss Rose to mark the five years' service of Cyril Davies and Bill Bardsley. Bury were the visiting team. Two days later Macc. contested the final of the Challenge Cup, against Altrincham at Northwich. The post-trophy doldrums kicked in, the Silkmen having to be content with the runners-up spot, losing 0–1.

They would be back in the Senior final the next year, making it three in a row. By then they would have a new manager.

A scene from the 1950 Cheshire Cup Final. McKinstry repels a Vics. attack. Full-back Cardno covers on the goal-line. (Nat McKinstry)

## Jack Smith takes charge

A matter of weeks into the new season, Bert Swindells resigned. The major issue seems to have been the club's withdrawal of the reserve side, on financial grounds and with scant consultation.

In October, Jack Smith took the reins. He was promised an 'absolutely free hand in regard to team selection'. And, the penny finally dropping, the committee kept to their word. Smith marked the complete transition from the old-style team manager as administrative official or enhanced captain, to the more influential figure in the Herbert Chapman mould. He would even get his way in the reformation of the reserves, used as an invaluable nursery for his Cheshire League side.

The 1951–52 campaign was contested with largely the same team. Only the spearhead was changed, with three inspired buys: inside men Frank Monaghan from Winsford, and Bob MacMorran from Northwich; and centre-forward Malcolm Glazzard, a tall, sturdy and good-humoured 20-year-old geology student, on Liverpool's books. It was to develop into a fearsome goalscoring partnership.

Macc. were destined to hover mid-table throughout the season, but once again it was the Senior Cup that cheered.

Understandably tense in their first round tie at Hyde – where a 1–6 defeat had been sustained some weeks previously – the Silkmen made matters secure with three goals in eight minutes mid-way through the second half. Goalscorers were Monaghan (2), Smith himself playing at centre-forward, and Davies. The final score was 4–1.

Glazzard now signed on for the rest of the season after his month's trial.

Despite the fact that Macc. were now fielding their strongest team for several years, the visitors in the second round, Manchester League side Lostock Gralam, proved an unexpectedly tough nut to crack. Lostock left-back Higginson broke his leg after just seven minutes, but the ten men put up a heroic resistance. The home side scraped a

2–1 win, with goals from Monaghan and Glazzard. 'Victory without honour' was the headline.

The semi-final was a true test of Silkman grit. Winsford United, who had left the Moss Rose happy with a 2–0 win in the league match three weeks previously, were the pundits' choice to progress. Their attack contained ex-Macc. players Speak and Neilson (a brief tenant of the centre-forward spot earlier in the season). This last, a native of Aberdeen, had scored a hundred goals in two seasons whilst at Northwich.

In the event, it was Macclesfield who dominated the tie, but without any definitive result. A 1–1 draw meant the teams returned to Altrincham. Again it was 1–1, after extra time. 'Cast-iron' Casey got the goal, and Hacking kept hopes alive with a late penalty save from Neilson.

The second replay, at Crewe, broke the deadlock. Richardson scored from the spot, then Bernard Jones, back from injury, bagged the second.

It was back to Gresty Road for the final, the opponents Witton Albion. Once again there appeared to be a clear favourite: Witton were ten points ahead of the Town in the league, and had won the rehearsal match 1–0 three weeks earlier.

But Jack Smith had done his homework. Witton's defence seemed to rely on the offside trap, still a useful resource in a well-drilled team. Smith, however, had reasoned that his speedy forwards would foil such tactics, and so it proved.

The teams were:

*Macclesfield*: Hacking; A. Jones, Gillott; Freer, Richardson, Shepherd; B. Jones, MacMorran, Glazzard, Monaghan, Davies

*Witton Albion*: Radcliffe; Chew, Battrick; Ashley, Robinson, Cowden; Thomson, Tilley, Christopher, Hyde, Johnson

Towards half-time Glazzard delivered a precise pass into Monaghan's path. The inside-forward's pace beat the defence, and his shot sped past Radcliffe to open the scoring.

Witton countered swiftly. Within a minute

## CHESHIRE COUNTY LEAGUE
# MACCLESFIELD v. STOCKPORT COUNTY
Saturday, 29th December, 1951     Kick-off 2-30 p.m.
Official Programme    -    Twopence

Match Programme 1951. (David Jones)

Silkmen 1952. *Back row*: Gillott, Freer, Richardson, Shepherd, D. Jones, J. A. Jones, Hacking, Glazzard. *Front row*: MacMorran, Walton, Monagham, B. Jones. (David Jones)

Gillott was adjudged to have fouled Tilley as both jumped for the ball. Hyde took a textbook penalty, hitting it hard and low to Hacking's right. Almost inevitably, the 'keeper flung himself down to turn the ball out for a corner. This, it was felt, was the turning point.

On the hour it was the tactic of inter-changing forward positions which helped secure the second goal. Glazzard had drifted to the left wing, and set up Davies who had moved inside. Once again the full-back was left marking fresh air as Davies found himself in front of goal with just the 'keeper to beat. A dummy sent Radcliffe the wrong way, and the putative winger shot into an empty net.

After a brief tour of the town, the victorious team repaired to the Savoy restaurant. They also appeared to an appreciative audience at the Majestic cinema, but on the stage this time, rather than on the screen.

## Contributions from the Supporters' Club

Parallelling the stylish performances on the pitch, the Moss Rose underwent a major refurbishment.

The new £600 stand on the popular side was opened before the Senior Cup match with Crewe in February 1951. Terracing and a rear wall were added within the year. In the close season 1952 the playing surface underwent a thorough overhaul. The Moss Lane end was completely returfed, and the old wooden goalposts were replaced with tubular metal ones. The dressing rooms and the structures were re-painted.

Most of this work was undertaken by the volunteers from the Supporters' Club, who supplied a large slice of the finances as well.

The Spion Kop (the present Star Lane end), still little more than a glorified mound of earth, had the top pushed back and levelled out. The slope was thus rendered gentler, providing room for an estimated 'several hundred more spectators'.

When the Supporters' Club put on sale special blue and white rosettes for the 1952 Senior Cup Final, it seemed emblematic of the ambition and style of the football club.

## Coronation Year

The borough of Macclesfield has always been proud of its connections with Royalty. It was perhaps fitting, then, that the football team should serve up something special in the Coronation Year of 1953.

Jack Smith made no secret of the fact that his real target was the Cheshire League Championship, absent from the Moss Rose for twenty years. The Silkmen had the players and the will; all that was needed was consistency, and perhaps a little luck.

The race for the title was one to savour, featuring high scoring, several switches of leadership, and in doubt until the penultimate match.

For once Macc. were able to retain the bulk of the same squad, enriched by the return of Eric Barber from Bolton Wanderers. With Glazzard and Monaghan again prolific, the attack averaged three goals per game. Witton Albion (6–1), Chester (5–2 away), Rhyl (6–2), and Northwich (5–1 away) were noteworthy victories in the first half of the season. So, despite surprising reverses at Wrexham (1–7) and Bangor (0–4), by the New Year the leaders were:

| | P | W | D | L | F | A | Pts |
|---|---|---|---|---|---|---|---|
| Macclesfield Town | 23 | 16 | 4 | 3 | 65 | 41 | 36 |
| Stockport County | 22 | 15 | 2 | 5 | 48 | 24 | 32 |
| Wellington Town | 22 | 14 | 3 | 5 | 44 | 19 | 31 |
| Rhyl Athletic | 22 | 12 | 6 | 4 | 53 | 41 | 30 |

Here Macc.'s challenge began to falter. After the 1–4 defeat at Witton in January, one of the opposing team's committee stated publicly that Stockport County would win the Championship 'by at least five points'. In the top of the table clash the next month, Macc. relinquished the lead by going down 2–3 in the snow at Edgeley Park. When they were knocked out of the Senior Cup 4–2 by Tranmere one week later, it looked as though the Witton man's prediction would not

be far wrong.

However, one of the now famous Silkmen grandstand finishes was on the cards. Of the remaining thirteen league matches, nine were won and three drawn. With two games remaining, they were two points clear, but with a greatly inferior goal average. A 3–0 win against Port Vale gave cause for cautious optimism, which became more positive when the news arrived from Bangor: Stockport had lost 1–3. This meant that a win at Crewe the following Monday would bring the championship trophy and flag to the Moss Rose. The Alexandra, though, had been unbeaten at home throughout the season.

It was a polished goal from Barber that eventually breached the Crewe defences. Davies crossed, Barber tipped the ball away from his marker and lifted a strong shot into the net.

The team was in a celebratory mood for the last game, at home against Hyde United. They had scored ninety-seven league goals; would they make it a round hundred?

During the 3–0 win over Stalybridge Celtic on Boxing Day 1953 goalkeeper David Jones – 'hero of the day' – sustained a broken finger. Unbowed, he turned out for the reserves the following day at inside-left, and scored a goal. For good measure, he ran the line in the New Year's Day Cheshire League match at Stockport.

Incidentally, Dave Jones was the only person since the nineteenth century to have represented Macclesfield at both cricket and football.

Early on the crowd was treated to the unique sight of Jack Hacking running up to take a penalty. He had jokingly criticised Richardson's spot kick technique, so it seemed reasonable to allow him a crack himself. Hacking, for whom little had seemed to go wrong that year, duly scored. Shortly before half-time it was Glazzard who netted the Silkmen's third, and a storm of cheering greeted the season's century. The final score was 6–1.

There can be few better examples of the infuriating – or exhilarating – illogicality of football than the game between the same two sides two days later, in the final of the Challenge Cup. Hyde United, albeit having won the toss to play the game at their ground, confounded nearly everyone by winning 2–1. The Silkmen would have to wait another ten years for their next double of league and cup.

## Tenth Senior Cup win

Most of the class of '53 signed on again that summer, but a rash of mid-season injuries was to blight the next league campaign. Even so, Macc. finished a reasonable fifth, scoring 97 goals.

Ample compensation came in the form of yet another Senior Cup win – the third in four years, and the tenth overall. Other cup sorties had not been anything like as successful: performances in the Challenge Cup had been hit-and-miss, and in the recent FA Cup there had been a sequence of early exits. For the moment, the Silkmen were content to leave the giant-killing to the Yeovils and the Peterboroughs of the world, and concentrate on attainable targets.

And at least the injuries gave the young reserves an opportunity to show their mettle. David Jones, a lively and mad-keen goalie in the Hacking mould, stepped into the breach for several crucial mid-winter games. One report dubbed him 'hero of the day' after his clean sheet against Stalybridge Celtic on Boxing Day. Reserve right-half Allan Senior replaced Freer, and held on to the spot for the Senior Cup semi and final.

After two narrow wins (Hyde United 2–1, Runcorn 3–2) Macc. faced up to Witton Albion in the semi-final at Stockport. Jack Smith's plan was to nullify the dangerous opposition half-back line, through close marking from the Silkmen's own midfield. For a while Witton's advance was thus contained, and the Town, once more employing the tactic of switching attacking roles, swept into a two-goal lead. The second was a marvellous diving header from Arthur Jones, yet another reserve who was playing instead of the injured Monaghan. The last fifteen minutes saw a thrilling series of offensives from the Albion, inspiring the newly returned Hacking to many spectacular saves. Witton scored the one goal, but Macc. held on to win 2–1.

The final, again at Crewe, was against Winsford United. The same team was fielded as in the semi:

Hacking; Alan Jones, Smith; Senior, Richardson, Shepherd; Barber, Arthur Jones, Glazzard, Wood, Davies

Winsford had had the better of that season's earlier encounter, winning 3–0 in the Christmas Day league match. A strong wind making cohesive play in the final difficult, Barber nonetheless cashed in on the conditions by scoring the first goal direct from a corner. Winsford's late rally made it 2–2.

The replay took place the following Wednesday. This time a single late goal from Arthur Jones returned the Cup to the Moss Rose. Bowles, the Winsford 'keeper, booted out, and Barber half-intercepted. The wildly spinning ball arrived at the feet of the unmarked Jones, whose task was easy once he had killed the spin.

Earlier that month, Jack Smith had signed a contract for a further two years.

# I 5

# *Interlude*

'Silkmen hit rock bottom.'
*Times and Courier* headline (10/11/55)

'Macclesfield, the "team that hadn't a chance", won the Cheshire Senior Cup at Crewe on Saturday, through a goal scored by Gordon following a brilliant run by Goalen in the third minute of extra time.'
*County Express* (28/4/60)

## The bad news

On 20 January 1957 the top of the Cheshire League read as follows:

|                   | P  | W  | D | L | F  | A  | Pts |
|-------------------|----|----|---|---|----|----|-----|
| Northwich Vics.   | 28 | 16 | 4 | 8 | 91 | 51 | 36  |
| Stockport County  | 29 | 14 | 8 | 7 | 70 | 51 | 36  |
| Chester           | 28 | 15 | 6 | 7 | 69 | 58 | 36  |
| Macclesfield Town | 26 | 14 | 7 | 5 | 74 | 35 | 35  |

The Silkmen had just beaten the Vics. 4–2 on the Drill Field. The *Times and Courier* hailed 'the play of champions'. It was a rare respite from that infamous half-decade: a catalogue of misfortune that at times threatened to take on biblical proportions, and that would have finished off a lesser club.

Jack Smith stepped down in November 1955, his ostensible reason being that this way the club would save money by not having to pay his salary. Bert Swindells returned, for the moment agreeing to do the job on a voluntary basis. Peter Robinson took over the manager's post in late September 1958. When the results had still not significantly improved by the following September, Robinson was sacked by the board, and the team continued managerless until the end of the 1959–60 season.

At least by then the dark days of 1957–58 were long gone. During that winter of discontent a Silkman team ravaged by injuries and the 'flu epidemic sustained the worst series of defeats for over thirty years: Tranmere Rovers hit nine past them, Bangor City and Stalybridge notched eight, and Stafford Rangers and Winsford hit seven apiece.

There was more in-fighting in the boardroom, the main issues being the perennial one of the inclusion of a reserve side, and the modern one of commercial sponsorship from the town's firms. The tussles culminated in an *en bloc* resignation of the club's directorship at Easter 1958.

League performances reached a nadir. The club finished second from bottom on two occasions, and twice had to suffer the smart of application for re-election. Cheshire League attendances habitually sank to three figures, for one of the very rare times in the club's long history.

---

Macclesfield Town's first ever game under floodlights was against Stalybridge Celtic at Ashton United on 1 November 1954. The Silkmen won 2–0, with goals from Glazzard and Monaghan.
The match started 100 minutes late, as the Macc. coach had been stranded in the fog at Stockport. The final whistle sounded at 10–20 pm., by which time a lot of the crowd had left in time for last orders.

The Moss Rose ground 1955. In the north-east corner of the ground, between the pub and the main London Road, are the old changing rooms. The snack bar was in the middle of the building, on the site of the present offices. Note the absence of terracing at north and south ends. The main stand, erected in 1906 and severely damaged by a gale in 1957, is on the right. The present main stand dates from 1968. New dressing rooms were built in 1979. The Estate side – the Alfred McAlpine Stand – was officially opened in March 2001. (Aerofilms)

Cup results were no better. Things had to improve, though, after 'black March' of 1955, which saw exits from three trophies: Senior Cup (0–1 at Northwich), Challenge Cup (0–2 to Mossley), and a 1–4 defeat at the hands of Wigan Athletic in the semi-final of the Ashton United Floodlight Cup.

Macc. entered this latter competition twice, but without too much success, and sustaining injuries and an ultimate financial loss in the process.

To cap it all, in the early hours of Sunday 8 December 1957, a gale tore down part of the main stand, scattering parts of the roof across the London Road and the railway line. The damage was estimated at £1,000.

That the club weathered the storm – in more ways than one – was due to the accumulated reputation of the past as well as the initiatives of the present. J. Roach, the capable Secretary, twice argued, and won, the case for re-election to the league. There had been enough of the positive to persuade that dramatically better days could not be far away.

## The good news

A few players stand out. In summer 1956 David Jones returned from National Service and took over the goalkeeper's role, emerging at last from Hacking's shadow. The success of the defence he anchored can be measured from the 'goals against' column in the table given at the beginning of this chapter. Memorable was a 6–0 drubbing of reigning champions Hyde United in October. Jones lost his place just once that season, to Alan Lindsay in the match with Bangor. Some surprise was expressed when Bert Swindells played Jones at centre-forward that day. But the 'keeper, who had played outfield for the Army, silenced the doubters by scoring the Silkmen's only goal. And a cracker it was, larruped in from an implausible spot out on the wing.

The evergreen Cyril Davies chalked up his 400th appearance for the club in February 1955. He was made captain for the day, and the team celebrated with a 5–4 win over Stockport County. Upon retirement from playing the following year he became coach, but retained enough fitness to be in the frame for first team selection!

Malcolm Glazzard stayed until summer 1955, when he took up a teaching post in the USA. He became a member of the Los Angeles Scottish FC, one of only three Sassenachs in the team. He commented, interestingly, on the different style of play adhered to by the ex-pat continentals on the other teams: close-passing as against the British long-ball approach. There as here, football was once again nearing a crossroads.

A succession of centre-forwards replaced him, notably John Clowes from Stoke. He was later to be shifted to a deeper midfield role, but was a keen marksman during that mini-revival of 1956–57, when a typical team would be:

Jones; Newbery, Monks; Leyfield (c), Spence, Lockton; Bevans, Bainbridge, Clowes, Ridgway, Wood

Outside-left Roger Wood was another forward who would re-invent himself as a half-back, reaching a peak in the Senior Cup run of 1960.

By then his place on the wing had been taken by one Keith Goalen, an ex-Stockport County first team player who made his debut for the Silkmen in October 1957. After nearly a year's lay-off recovering from an operation, Goalen returned to weave his cultured skills into the 'sixties bonanza.

David Jones left for Congleton Town, and for some years the goalkeeper's spot was something of a hot potato. After many changes – partly due to the injury bogey – Gordon Cuddeford was the principal incumbent by the end of the decade. One temporary choice (1958–59) had been Tony Waiters, a 22-year-old from Loughborough College, before he signed amateur, then professional, forms for Blackpool. He was to gain five England caps in the mid-sixties. Although not obliged to do so, the Seasiders, recognising their good fortune in signing up such talent for free, sent Macclesfield a 'grant' of £200 as soon as Waiters joined the professional staff.

The club's finances, incidentally, were generally in a healthy state in those years of sparse success on the field. Once again we must look to the vital work of the Supporters' Club, which raised an impressive £7,300 for the parent organisation in four years.

Entertainment tax, that dinosaur legacy from the First World War, was finally killed off in 1957. Keeping the entrance fees the same meant that the extra monies could now be directed into clubs' coffers.

> The winner of the 1955 Supporters' Club Beauty Queen Competition was a Miss Margaret Hill. She thus qualified for the all-Cheshire final held at Winsford. Her prize was a ticket to the FA Cup Final. (The past is indeed another country!)

NORTHWICH WERE GOAL RHYTHM BOYS

As Bill Haley returned to the charts, the cartoonist cast a rueful eye over the Senior Cup result of February, 1957. Two weeks previously, Macc. had beaten the Vics. 4–2 at the Drill Field.
(*Macclesfield Express*)

Another welcome money-spinner came through a mini-run in the FA Cup of 1956–57. After defeats of Altrincham (3–1 away), and Winsford United (2–2, then 4–2), there ensued a series of exciting, high-scoring ties with Hyde United. The first match at the Moss Rose finished 4–4, with Bainbridge and Clowes cancelling a two-goal deficit in the last ten minutes. The reply went into extra time, as Macc. let slip a 2–0 lead to finish 3–3. Finally, under the floodlights at Edgeley Park in front of over 11,000 spectators, Hyde emerged 5–3 victors. From all six matches Macclesfield made a profit of £500.

Thus it was that by the end of the decade the Moss Rose could boast new bathing facilities, an improved playing surface, and a generally smartened appearance.

The damage caused by the December 1957 gale was soon repaired, thanks to a contribution from the town's Parks Committee. This was yet more evidence of the traditionally strong bond between club and community.

The links with the past were brought more sharply into focus by the *Times and Courier*'s search for the oldest living Silkman supporter. Three octogenarians made themselves known. There was W. Hackney, of Barton Street, '70 years a supporter'; and C. M. Howard, at the time (1954) residing in Buxton. Both could remember the Boughey Lane/Victoria Road ground, and seeing Bromley-Davenport play. And there was James Adams, 86 in 1958, who was one of those who had helped prepare the Moss Rose ground for the switch of venue in 1891!

Evidence of the resurgent popularity of the club may be seen in the exhibition game with Stoke City in April 1959. With a touch of the razzamatazz, twenty-two of the new-style plastic footballs were kicked into the crowd by the players before the game. At half-time a Morris Minor, first prize in the Supporters' Club lottery, was driven onto the pitch and presented to the winner, a Mrs Hall of Garden Street, Hurdsfield. The great Stanley Matthews, although unable to play, kicked off.

The teams were:
*Macclesfield Town*: Waiters; Hodkinson, Clowes; Tomkinson, Massey, Fenton[1]; Jones, Downie[2], Charnley, Snowden[1], Goalen
*Stoke City*: Robertson; Andrews, McCue; Astbury, Thomson, Cairns; Hewitt, Bowyer, Bullock, Ward, King
[1] Blackpool
[2] Manchester United
It will be noted that Frank Bowyer, playing at inside-right for Stoke, made his first appearance at the Moss Rose that day.

## Transition

On paper Peter Robinson was ideal managerial material: aged 34, with a playing career that include spells at Chesterfield, Notts. County, and Manchester City, he was a fitness fanatic who demanded unwavering dedication from his men. His playing strategy was innovatory, perhaps too much so, as he stubbornly advocated a style of play that needed too many adjustments, given the habitual approach and particular skills available at the time. In the 2–3–5 days of Jack Smith and Bert Swindells the vigorous long ball, *à la* the Wolves of Stan Cullis, culminating in the frequent crack at goal, had been the norm. Now Robinson urged the so-called continental style, based on the deep-lying centre-forward system that would later be termed 4–2–4, of finding the closest man in space, and thus working a painstaking route forward. Possession was all.

Unfortunately, patience on the terraces ('Get rid of it, man!' was an oft-heard cry) and in the boardroom, worn thin by a continued dearth of success, reached breaking point after five consecutive defeats at the opening of the 1959–60 season. Robinson was dismissed, and the Silkmen completed the season without a manager.

## Vindication

Suddenly, though, they were a changed team. Whether Robinson's ideas had finally – and perversely – found fertile ground, or whether the side were giving expression to a new-found freedom, of the fourteen league games immediately after the manager's departure, twelve were won

With many a reference to the Congleton emblem, a cartoonist celebrated a narrow win by Macc. in the Challenge Cup, March 1957. (*Macclesfield Express*)

and one drawn. The goal record for this spell was 46–14.

Chief marksman was Bill Gordon, originally acquired by Robinson from Stockport as a half-back, but now shifted to centre-forward. Also in the attack were Bill Finney, on Rochdale's list at £2,000; Eric Anderson, inside-left from Barnsley; and Will Sowden, another ex-Stockport player. Derek Tomkinson, who had started his career as a 15-year-old with Port Vale, was an attacking right-half who, like Sowden, had been signed the previous season.

The run could not be sustained, however, and by February ambition had realistically turned to the Senior and Challenge Cups.

In the first round of the Senior Cup Macc. were drawn against Ellesmere Port Town at home. The Silkmen reversed the usual trend of Port cup victories over them by scraping a 2–1 win, Anderson and Sowden scoring second half goals.

Opponents in round two were the battling amateur side Runcorn Athletic, reigning mid-Cheshire League Champions, and unlikely conquerors of Stalybridge Celtic in the previous round. Complacency would have proven fatal. The Athletic pulled off a 2–2 draw, on the Moss Rose if you please, recovering from a third minute strike by Finney. Macc. secured the replay 3–1, thanks to late goals courtesy once more of Sowden and Anderson.

Onto the semi-final at Bower Fold, Stalybridge, the opponents old rivals Altrincham. In the tradition of Silkmen semis, this was another feast.

Jones, the Robins' centre-forward, opened the scoring after 12 minutes. Gordon, picking up the rebound from Finney's ferocious shot, equalised soon after. Jones scored twice more before the interval, Anderson pulling one back – a header form Tomkinson's searching cross.

2–3 down at half-time; and then but 45 seconds after the re-start Macc. sustained a blow which would have knocked the stuffing out of most teams. It was Jones yet again, heading his fourth from a corner.

Altrincham now relied on the big clearance kick, whilst Macc. retaliated with more combinative play. This paid off mid-way through the second half, as Finney swept the ball home after some clever approach work from Goalen and Sowden. On 70 minutes Gordon headed another equaliser, and with ten minutes left the same player executed an opportunist one-two in the area with Anderson, flicking the return past Allen.

The teams were:

*Macclesfield*: Cuddeford; Hodkinson, Bannister (c); Tomkinson, Wood, Fleming; Finney, Sowden, Gordon, Anderson, Goalen
*Altrincham*: Allen; Ravenscroft, Gillespie; Cunningham, Reed, Dewar; Bardsley, Kay, Jones, Brooks, Pike

Macc. kept the same eleven for the final against Hyde United, at Crewe.

Ominously, Hyde had already beaten the Silkmen three times that season, most recently in the semi-final of the Challenge Cup. They were currently second in the league, with four players with Football League experience. Unsurprisingly, then, Macc. were not fancied to win.

Hyde's team was:

Capewell; Taylor, Popland; Ashton, Saunders, McLoughlin; Cook, Evison, Drake, Grey, Lansley

Hyde had the better of the first half, exploiting the long ball tactic to keep the Macc. goal under almost constant pressure. It was a surprise, then, when a Sowden body-swerve – of which, it was said, Matthews himself would have been proud –

> Keith Goalen had been to a friend's wedding before the 1960 Senior Cup semi with Altrincham at Bower Fold, Stalybridge. He was rushed to the ground, arriving just twenty minutes before kick-off, still wearing top hat and tails. Unrecognised by stewards, he was refused entry until a Macc. official came to the rescue.
> Goalen, a solicitor by profession, is also an accomplished musician.

set up Anderson, whose accurate shot foiled Capewell. This was shortly before half-time.

The second half continued much the same. On sixty-six minutes Cook equalised, his shot somehow finding its way through a crowded penalty area. The favourites now went all-out for the winner, but Macclesfield's packed defence anchored by Roger Wood, quick tackling and the alert goalkeeping of Cuddeford kept the scores level until the end of normal time.

Three minutes into extra time, a clearance found Goalen on the left. His wing run, shaking off tackles as he went, took him to the corner of the Hyde area. Here he delivered a perfectly weighted pass into the stride of Gordon, the only other Macc. player to have kept up with the devastatingly fast counter-attack. Gordon's coruscating shot hit the bar, then a defender. The centre-forward, following up, was able to bundle the ball over the line.

It was the winning goal. It was significant that the Silkmen had out-manoeuvred one of the prime exponents of the long ball game. They were clearly ready to take the new decade by storm.

Goalen scores with a diving header in the FA Cup win over Nelson in October, 1960. (See Chapter 16) (Keith Goalen)

# 16

## Swinging Sixties (1)

'This is grand.
The best exhibition of constructive football I have ever seen on the Moss Rose.'
Supporters' comments after Macc. 5, Rhyl 0 (21/1/61)

'Tonight I want to pay tribute to Albert Leake, our Player-Manager, who has fulfilled all the
confidence we had in him when we gave him the appointment.
… he demanded only two things from his players – 90 minutes of all-out football and a
feeling of pride to be wearing the colours of the town team.'
Club Chairman Frank Bullock, at the Civic Reception for the team (13/5/64)

### Quantum leap

In Roger Wood's benefit match in May 1960 (in which Macclesfield beat Accrington Stanley 7–2) Frank Bowyer guested for the Silkmen. The attendant rumours proved true: within a week Bowyer came from Stoke City to the Moss Rose as player-manager, and proceeded to turn the world on its head. Within a matter of months he took a pedestrian, intermittently successful side and transformed it into the Rolls Royce of the non-league world. Or to quote a committee member of a rival club: 'the Tottenham of the Cheshire League'.

Although unable to pull off the double in the same season as the Spurs, the Blues nonetheless celebrated the 700th anniversary of the granting of the Royal Charter to the borough by carrying off the league title in style.

The key was the ambition of Bowyer to cram his team with players of proven class. This process was accelerated in 1961 with the abolition of the maximum wage, as many Football League clubs took the financially necessary step of off-loading a number of their professional players. Macclesfield Town were in the perfect position to profit from such a development.

The 1960–61 forward line, cited by club website historian Mike Griffiths as 'perhaps the most

famous ever at the Moss Rose', was Jack 'Dickie' Cunliffe, Bowyer, Stan Smith, Rex Grey and Keith Goalen. Continuing the theme of 4–2–4, Bowyer played himself as deep-lying forward. The system would employ two orthodox wingers (Cunliffe and Goalen) and two central strikers (Smith and Grey).

Grey, who had opposed Macc. in the 1960 Senior Cup Final, was Bowyer's first signing. A free-scoring forward with Hyde, he had also had Central League experience with Manchester City.

Next to arrive, in early September, was Bowyer's former clubmate Jack Cunliffe. A member of the famous giant-killing Port Vale side of 1953–54, Cunliffe had lost none of his speed, nor of his ability to cut in from the wing and crack in shots at goal.

Completing the picture was Stan Smith, scorer of 60 goals in 92 appearances for Witton Albion.

The first major test was the FA Cup.

The First Qualifying Round was against Northwich Victoria, at the Drill Field. The Vics. had won 2–1 on the Moss Rose the previous week, but this time the tables were turned, the Town winning 3–0. Linotype, surprise conquerors of Buxton, were the next opponents. The amateurs drew 1–1 on the Moss Rose, but in the replay found

1959–60. All but one (Finney) of the Senior Cup-winning side of 1960 are here.
*Back row*: Tomkinson, Bannister, Cuddeford, Hodkinson, Anderson, Goalen.
*Front row*: Birkett, Wood, Gordon, Sowden, Hunter. (Keith Goalen)

the Silkmen clicking into gear. Again the margin was 3–0.

The same score was registered against Congleton, again away, in the next round. Cunliffe notched two, one of them direct from a corner.

Then came the history-making match with the powerful Nelson side, currently undefeated leaders of the Lancashire Combination. Once more drawn away, Macc. travelled with a fair degree of confidence, despite the fact that the newly-acquired Smith was injured, his place taken by Sowden. Victory would put them into the First Round proper of the competition for the first time in the club's history.

In the town, cup fever was taking hold. The day before the game, 21 October, a wag came out with the nice one-liner: 'Today is Trafalgar Day, but tomorrow will see the death of Nelson'. A supporter sent four-leaf clovers to Sowden, Grey and Cunliffe.

In a tough, nervy game Sowden justified his inclusion by heading the opener after 24 minutes. Nelson, led by Everton's Alan Shackleton, equalised on the half-hour. Just one minute later Grey netted from thirty yards. Soon after the interval Goalen scored with a spectacular diving header from a Cunliffe cross, and although the Lancastrians pulled one back, Macc. held onto their lead.

The reward was an away tie with Third Division Southport in the First Round. Another 'first' was registered: Macclesfield Town appeared on the football pools coupons for Saturday, 5 November 1960.

Almost at the dawn of the decade in which, so they say, dreaming was permissible, Macc. journeyed to Southport and had the effrontery to take the early game to their Football League opponents. In the third minute Goalen ran onto a through ball and was fouled just outside the Southport area. Bowyer chipped in the free kick, and Harris, the opposing goalkeeper, dropped the ball. Grey's instinctive shot hit Harris and rebounded to Goalen, whose attempt struck a full-back on the line before being scrambled away for a corner.

It was a rare moment of encouragement. The home side proceeded to dominate the midfield and rubbed in their clear superiority, scoring two quick goals. A penalty from Bowyer on 20 minutes brought the score back to 2–1, but ultimately no one but the most partisan was fooled. The final score was 7–2 to the Lancashire seasiders, and the Silkmen returned home to think again, and to count the handy £900 profit from the run.

The League was a different matter.

A series of high-scoring wins, which included a 6–0 against Winsford and a 9–3 against Wigan Rovers, and maximum points from the Christmas matches, presented mouth-watering possibilities by the end of the year:

|  | P | W | D | L | F | A | Pts |
|---|---|---|---|---|---|---|---|
| Ellesmere Port Town | 22 | 14 | 2 | 6 | 60 | 32 | 30 |
| Hyde United | 24 | 12 | 6 | 6 | 57 | 36 | 30 |
| Buxton | 24 | 12 | 6 | 6 | 61 | 47 | 30 |
| Macclesfield Town | 20 | 13 | 3 | 4 | 64 | 33 | 29 |

In January Bowyer made arguably his shrewdest acquisition: the great Albert Leake, like Cunliffe a veteran of Port Vale's epic FA Cup run of some years before, arrived at the Moss Rose. A glance at the record books will reveal Leake's steady stream of goals – seven in all – in the Vale's run of '54. More of a midfield schemer than a striker

by the time he joined the Silkmen, he would become a nationally recognised player-manager within a couple of years.

A typical team that season would be:
Dixon (or Dave Jones or Cuddeford);
Tomkinson, Potts; Leake, Wood, Dickie
Jones; Cunliffe, Bowyer, Smith, Grey, Goalen

The Silkmen finally hit the top of the league in March, after a 4–1 win over Oswestry. Leake scored the 100th goal during the 7–1 drubbing of Sankey's. Easter brought maximum points, thereby leaving Macc. needing seven points from the remaining six games to be sure of the championship.

In the event they needed only five, the other teams obligingly dropping points. The title was sewn up at Bangor, where, on a hard and bumpy pitch, the Blues demonstrated an array of scoring skills. Grey dribbled past four defenders to net the first; the same player lobbed over the advancing 'keeper to increase the lead; and then, fittingly, Bowyer made matters secure by blasting in a thirty-yard free kick. It was the same month as the Charter Year Celebrations, of which the Town FC was naturally proud to be a part. For good measure, the reserves, coached by Lennie Butt in the year before his move to Knutsford, won the Gilgryst Cup.

Of the 133 league goals scored that season, Smith hit 39, Grey 34, and Bowyer 29. Smith notched seven hat-tricks, and Grey five.

And all this from a club who just three seasons before had had to seek re-election!

## Getting and spending

As often, energising this meteoric rise was a bouncingly healthy balance sheet. Once more we must acknowledge the contributions from the Supporters' Club. Immediately after the Betting and Gaming Act of December 1960 Bob Tomkinson and his committee added the latest craze of bingo to the list of moneymaking schemes. Membership rose to 14,800 within a couple of years, and by mid-decade around £10,000 a year was being generated for the good of the football club.

The only problem with such an embarrassment of riches was how to spend the money. Acquiring and keeping quality players was justifiably the first priority – although eyebrows were raised when forward Pat Connolly was bought from Crewe in April 1963 for a Cheshire League record fee of £1,000. As we shall see, though, it was money well spent.

Once the transfer fees and wage bill had been covered, there remained the question of what to do with the surplus. Floodlights were first suggested (and costed) in 1961, but as one cynic put it, might not the lights merely show up the short-comings of the ground? The pro-floodlights faction claimed that the amenity would bring in an extra £800 per year, thus paying for itself, they calculated, within eight seasons.

This time around the consolidators won, and by summer 1963 the money had been spent on terracing the pub end of the ground, widening the pitch, some new turnstiles for the Moss Lane entrance, and the creation of a cinder practice pitch at the rear of the Spion Kop – the Star Lane end.

## Inter-League Cup

The relatively unpopular Challenge Cup was shelved for two years, and was replaced by the Inter-League Challenge Cup. This was a knock-out tournament involving clubs from the Cheshire League and Lancashire Combination.

Macc. began well, winning their first round tie against Prescot Cables 7–1. Colin Davies, a close season signing from Port Vale, was nominally a half-back, but was to prove himself a utility forward with a scoring knack. He hit the first of several hat-tricks that day.

> The Silkmen were Cheshire League Champions a total of six times, a record. In 1963–64 they finished thirteen points ahead of the runners-up, the joint highest ever winning margin.

Round two brought Earlestown to the Moss Rose, where the Blues ran out 6–3 winners. This was the limit of their progress that year, as they suffered an unexpected reverse at the hands of part-timers Marine Crosby in round three. The first match took place under the lights at Crewe, and Macc. were held 1–1. Marine won the replay 3–0 at Southport.

The second and final year in which this competition was held brought happier results.

The semi-final was reached, after wins over Darwen (6–0), Fleetwood (1–0), and Netherfield of Kendal (3–0).

Wigan Athletic, playing at home, ended the run. 0–2 down, the Town threw nine men into a prolonged, frenzied attack. Bowyer reduced the deficit with a header, but further goals were not forthcoming.

At least the Silkmen's involvement in the Inter-League Cup had lasted longer than in that year's Senior Cup. The terrible winter of 1962–63 – frost on the Moss Rose pitch was 36 inches (90 cm) deep in January – which saw so many matches postponed, relented just enough for the first round tie with Stalybridge on Bower Fold. Macc. lost 1–2. (This was on the same day, incidentally, that four hopeful young musicians calling themselves the Beatles struggled through the snow-covered roads to perform a gig at Macclesfield's *El Rio* dance hall. Both pop group and football club, of course, were on the threshold of a phenomenal run of success.)

## Annus mirabilis

After winning the Cheshire League in 1961, Macc. were runners-up and thus winners of the Case Trophy the following year. Bowyer continued with his policy of putting the accent on attack: the Town were top scorers with 109 goals. Davies continued with his hat-trick habit, heading three in the 5–2 win at Rhyl.

Uniquely, all seven goals in this match were headers.

Keith Goalen received his benefit match in May 1962, in which the Silkmen drew 3–3 with an All-Star XI:

Fleet (Man. City); Gratrex (Blackpool), Martin (Blackpool); Murray (Stockport Co.),

Franklin (Sankey's/England), Crawford (Blackpool); Edge (Port Vale), Pearson (Man. Utd.), Charnley (Blackpool), Parry (Blackpool), Mullington (Macc.)

Johnnie Mullington was to hit the headlines the following May. Drafted in from the reserves in place of the injured Connolly for the league match with Witton Albion, he highlighted the folly of allowing an opportunist centre-forward room to manoeuvre. Macclesfield won 8–0, Mullington bagging the lot. This was, and still is, a club record.

At the end of 1962–63 Bowyer opted not to renew his contract, leaving for Cornwall due to family commitments. The reins were handed over to Albert Leake, and seldom can there have been a smoother transition. Leake, like his predecessor, was a firm disciplinarian, and was the possessor of a chess-like ability to pre-empt and outfox an opponent's strategy. Bowyer's last two signings, along with Bill Guttridge, a rugged full-back from Walsall, were to be the defensive rock on which the victories were built. There was Wilf Hall – 'that grinning, defiant bulk of a man' – who had played in goal for Ipswich's first team. And partnering Guttridge was Peter Ford, formerly a wing-half, and on Port Vale's list at £2,500. The raw figures tell the story: only 38 goals conceded in 42 games that season, a club record in a league of that size until 1997.

The team for the opening game against Buxton was:

Hall; Ford, Guttridge; Donaldson, Leake, Goalen; Bazley, Hutchinson, Connolly, Wilson, Massey

> On several occasions during the 'fifties and 'sixties, generally on a Sunday in August, the football club played a charity cricket match against the town cricket club. The FC usually gave as good as they got, even winning on a couple of occasions. From 1964, a cup was presented to the victorious team.

The early games gave little clue to what was to come. A 1–0 home win was scraped over Buxton; the midweek return was lost 3–4. It was only by November, with Derek Edge (ex-Crewe) taking over the right wing spot, and Connolly and Wilson switching roles, that the Silkmen got into their stride.

Reigning champions Runcorn were beaten 6–2, in a fast-paced, classy game. Typical of the team's style of rapid switching from defence to attack was Connolly's goal: Leake pounced on a moment of hesitancy in Runcorn's midfield, delivered a finely-judged pass into the forward's path, and Connolly netted from thirty yards. Warren Bradley, a two-footed, quick-thinking right winger and ex-England full international who was a temporary replacement for Edge, scored a hat-trick.

Once again by Christmas the Blues were poised to take over the leadership:

|              | P  | W  | D | L | F  | A  | Pts |
|--------------|----|----|---|---|----|----|-----|
| Buxton       | 24 | 14 | 6 | 4 | 61 | 38 | 34  |
| Macclesfield | 21 | 14 | 5 | 2 | 60 | 20 | 33  |
| Sankey's     | 21 | 13 | 4 | 4 | 53 | 25 | 30  |

Come New Year 1964, Brian Wilson was revelling in his centre-forward role. Averaging a goal a game, with Connolly making most of the bullets, the ex-Walsall man would display the striker's knack of popping up in the right place at the right time.

Macclesfield now proceeded to build up a formidable unbeaten sequence, stretching their lead at the top. Major scalps were Ellesmere Port Town (7–1), Chester (4–0), and Mossley (4–1 away).

A measure of light relief was available on the Moss Rose a week or so before Easter, when the Showbiz XI played a charity game against a selection of TV luminaries. Amongst those on view were Emile Ford, Bill Grundy, Mike Yarwood, Stan Stennett, 'diddy' David Hamilton, and boxer Brian London. Despite excited rumours, Sean Connery was not in evidence. The Showbiz side won 6–2, with a youthful Jimmy Tarbuck helping himself to a hat-trick. Albert Quixall refereed, and Leake and Connolly ran the line.

Back in the real world, Macc. took their unbeaten run to 26 games by early April. Now a massive thirteen points ahead of the following pack, they needed just two more to make sure of the title. A 3–0 win against Stalybridge Celtic did the necessary.

The Celtic were then beaten 2–1 in the semi of the restored county Challenge Cup. At this stage the Silkmen had reached the Senior final as well, after eliminating Congleton (5–1), Runcorn (4–0 after 2–2), and Tranmere Rovers (3–2 at Chester).

The Rovers' side contained two lively wingers: Sinclair and an 18-year-old Tony Coleman, who was to go on to greater fame at Manchester City. He was also to make a brief return to the Moss Rose some twelve years later.

So the talk was of an unprecedented treble. Even the double of Senior Cup and Cheshire League had not been achieved since Crewe Alexandra in 1923.

The final of the Senior Cup pitted Macc. against Northwich Victoria. Excluding the 1940 wartime trophy, the tally of wins before the 1964 final read: Macclesfield 11, Northwich 11.

The teams were:
*Macclesfield*: Hall; Bailey, Guttridge; Donaldson, Leake, Goalen; Ringstead, Connolly, Wilson, Hutchinson, McKay
*Northwich Victoria*: Kelly; Edwards, Jones; Dolbell, Cope, Wann; Brown, Angell, Gorrie, Haspell, McLoughlin

The Blues won an uninspired, defensive game 1–0. The goal was something of a gift: Kelly dropped Connolly's cross, and the hovering Wilson struck.

Still – the second leg of the treble had been

---

**CHESHIRE SENIOR CUP FINAL**

SATURDAY, 18th APRIL, 1964

On the Ground of Crewe Alexandra Football Club

**MACCLESFIELD T. v. NORTHWICH V.**

Kick-off 3 p.m.

To-day we are once again hosts at Gresty Road to the finalists in the Cheshire Senior Cup Competition, Macclesfield Town and Northwich Victoria, teams who both have an identical record so far as this competition is concerned.

Macclesfield Town come today as Champions of the Cheshire County League and are no doubt anxious to complete the "double." This will be their 17th appearance in the final, their first recorded victory was in 1890 and their last appearance was in 1960 and in both these appearances they were successful. In all they have secured the cup on 11 occasions and been runners-up on five occasions.

Northwich Victoria are also making their 17th appearance in the final. From 1880 to 1886 they won six finals in succession, this being the period prior to professionalism starting. One must go back to 1955 to find their last appearance in the final but this was another successful appearance. Their full record is 16 appearances, 11 wins, and 5 defeats.

To reach today's Final Tie, Macclesfield have defeated Congleton, Runcorn and Tranmere Rovers. Northwich have defeated West Kirby, Stalybridge and Altrincham.

Twice before has the Final Tie seen these two teams in opposition, in 1950 Northwich Victoria defeated Macclesfield 1–0 and in the following year the position was reversed Macclesfield defeating Northwich 3–2. As a single goal has decided the two previous encounters, no doubt a tense encounter will be witnessed once again before the coveted trophy is handed over to the successful team.

**Official 3d. Programme**

---

achieved. The final of the Challenge Cup (a home and away affair, at Macclesfield's suggestion) would take place on the following Thursday and Monday. The opponents were Altrincham, whom Macc. had beaten 7–1 less than a month before.

Everything was going to plan: the famed Silkmen defence kept a clean sheet in the first leg. 0–0 was the score, apparently setting things up for a field day back at the Moss Rose.

Freddie Pye's Altrincham, however, had other ideas.

The Robins cast caution to the winds and attacked from the off. They were 2–0 in the lead before the Town finally shook themselves and started to play. Connolly pulled one back before half-time, but on the day Altrincham were unstoppable. The final score was 4–2 to the North Cheshire team, and the Blues had to be content with two out of three.

## 'Lucky Wrexham'

The next season (1964–65), handicapped by a poor start, the Silkmen were league runners-up, relinquishing the title to Wigan Athletic. The FA Cup, however, brought another stirring run.

Johnnie Mullington scored both goals in the 2–0 defeat of Oswestry in the Preliminary. Then

Fred Arrowsmith, landlord of the *Flower Pot Inn*, Congleton Road, pours champagne into the Cheshire Senior Cup, 1964. On the coach steps are Hutchinson, Goalen, McKay and holding the trophy, player-manager Albert Leake. (Keith Goalen)

Northwich Victoria succumbed to a convincing 4–1 on the Moss Rose. The *Express* reporter could not resist a spot of hand-rubbing:

They demolished the Victoria just as effectively as the later 'blowing-up' of the old railway bridge near the ground to make way for another bridge. (24/9/64)

This win was especially gratifying at the time, as up to this point the Vics. had scored twenty league goals to Macc.'s four.

The next round involved a trip to Rhyl. The Silkmen progressed, thanks to a 2–0 win. Both goals were credited to Wilson, who had been recalled from his honeymoon to take part in the match! A subsequent pair of 2–1 home wins, over Witton and Ellesmere Port (albeit thanks to a disputed penalty in the latter) saw Macc. enter the hat for the First Round – the second time in five years.

This time they were granted a home tie against Fourth Division Wrexham, led by player-manager Ken Barnes, late of Manchester City.

By now the Town's line-up had changed – though not drastically – from the previous year. Up front Warren Bradley had returned from injury; he was partnered on the right wing by new signing David Latham. (Pat Connolly had been transferred to Colchester, Macclesfield making a sizeable profit on the deal.) On the left, the speedy McKay now had alongside him Bill Myerscough, ex-Aston Villa first team, and on Wrexham's books himself until the summer.

On a day of strong wind, roared on by a crowd of nearly 6,000, Macc. opted for a strategy of containment and denial, at least while the visitors had the wind behind them. It was a policy which worked until the final seconds of the first half, when Wrexham right winger McMillan broke away and scored.

Shaken but unbowed, the Blues switched to attack in the second half. Before long Bradley's sinuous run took him past three defenders and left him with just goalie Fleet to beat. When it may have seemed more productive to try a chip or lob, Bradley chose a ground-level shot. Fleet anticipated correctly, and saved.

At the other end, Hall saved a Barnes penalty. Then, with two minutes left, Wilson equalised, to a tumultuous cheer.

The drama was far from finished: McMillan scored again for Wrexham. Then in the dying seconds Goalen embarked on a heroic run which took him deep into the opponents' area, where he was clearly seen to be brought down. To everyone's – including Wrexham's – astonishment, the referee waved play on. Seconds later, the final whistle blew.

Later Barnes magnanimously admitted his team's good fortune, adding: 'The standard of Macclesfield's play surprised me. They are a very good side'.

That vintage Silkmen decade was only half over – and there was even better wine to follow.

# I 7

# *Swinging Sixties (2)*

*Silkmen went to London*
*Took the pride of their town;*
*The team which played at Fulham*
*For ever will know renown.*
*Thousands followed the Silkmen*
*Cheering and chanting the game;*
*Fulham will always remember*
*The day the Silkmen came . . .*
Margaret Leigh (8/2/68)

## *Floodlights*

The long-cherished ambition became a reality in the summer of 1965.

The original estimate of 'eight seasons' to make good the expenditure was shortened to just one, thanks to civic and public interest and contributions, and Albert Leake's brainwave of a floodlit tournament based at the Moss Rose.

The Mayor launched the 'raise a pound' appeal in February, and over £2,000 had been accumulated by the time construction began in June. Leake himself lent a hand in laying the bricks for the switching-gear building. The lights were atop eight pylons, each 55 feet (16.8 metres) tall. They were first illuminated in August, and first used for a match on 1 September, when Northwich were beaten 4–1.

The official switch-on in October was originally to have been effected by comedian Tommy Trinder – no doubt to the accompaniment of his catch-phrase 'You lucky people!' – but happily for posterity it was Malcolm Allison and Sir Stanley Matthews who did the honours. Fourth Division Port Vale provided the opposition, and won a hard-fought game 3–2.

The Macclesfield FC Floodlit Cup attracted eight teams. The arrangement was that 20% of the gate, whoever was playing, would go to the host club. The seven games played were watched by a total of 13,126 spectators, so the competition was a financial success. Unfortunately Macc. were put out of their own competition in the semi-final by Stalybridge Celtic. Eventual winners were Altrincham, their attack now boasting the itinerant ex-Silkman Pat Connolly. The Robins were already well into their mid-decade purple patch: Cheshire League Champions 1966, the double the following year, and an FA Cup Third Round against Wolves in January 1966, albeit losing this tie 0–5.

For winter 1966 the Macc. tournament was absorbed by the new North West Floodlit Cup.

> During their English tour, Israeli champions Maccabi from Tel Aviv played a friendly against Macclesfield Town at the Moss Rose in August 1966. They won by the same score they had beaten Everton, the FA Cup holders: 1–0. When asked why they had found Macc. such a tough nut to crack, the Maccabi captain claimed that 'the grass was too long'.

This contained sixteen clubs from Lancashire and Cheshire, and matches took place at the Moss Rose and Moss Lane, Altrincham. The Town would fare better this time, although losing 2–5 on aggregate in the two-legged final with Northwich Victoria.

## *Arrivals*

There were several important signings in the mid-sixties, as the Silkmen worked towards another all-conquering side. First there came goalkeeper John Cooke from Port Vale, a 14 stone (89 kg.) giant who was eventually to oust Wilf Hall. Cooke demonstrated a rare combination of strength and agility, and became the mainstay of Macclesfield's outstanding defence in their last years in the Cheshire League: an average of just over a goal a game conceded in three seasons.

At about the same time Leake signed David Latham, a forward one time of Manchester United. Latham was to enter the record books with a hat-trick in an astonishing two minutes, five seconds in the 9–0 demolition of Witton Albion in an FA Cup match in September 1965. From Bollington came the young centre-forward Derek Rogers. There were five crucial acquisitions the following summer: David Goodwin, the blond winger, ex-Manchester Youth; the Scot George Sievwright, late of the Rochdale club, originally a wing-half but transformed into a no-nonsense defender; fellow full-back George Forrester, a member of the famous Altrincham FA Cup run the previous year; John Collins the 22-year-old defender from Blackburn Rovers; and Frank Beaumont, an attacking midfield player, later the manager who would preside over the enormously successful switch to the Northern Premier League.

**TVrental** the best in town *Parkers*
70 MILL STREET · 25 CHESTERGATE
1 PARK STREET · MACCLESFIELD

*Macclesfield Express*
Thursday, December 14, 1967

A night to remember at the Moss Rose

# CROWD MOB TEAM AFTER BRILLIANT VICTORY

## MACCLESFIELD 2 - STOCKPORT COUNTY 1

Macclesfield are immaculate. They can certainly claim that after last night's brilliant victory over Stockport County in the F.A. Cup, 1st round replay. They now have a home game in the second round against the winners of the Goole Town–Spennymoor tie. This is the first time the Silkmen have reached the second round.

There were remarkable scenes at the close of the game, thousands of excited Macclesfield supporters mobbing the Macclesfield team. This was indeed one of the most glorious nights in the history of the club. Police moved in to assist the players to get to the dressing room...

**Goal earned second chance**

... Calder races through a surprising gap in the County defence to head for goal.

The World Cup came and went, sowing seeds of change. Ramsey's wingless wonders seemed to set the template for future achievement at all levels. Suddenly the vogue was for 4–4–2 or 4–3–3. Leake, typically, stuck to his guns: his first signing after the World Cup victory was a winger!

Most colourful arrival at the Moss Rose (late September '66) was probably prolific goalscorer Brian Fidler. Fast, and possessor of a range of skills, he had been top marksman at Heanor Town of the Midland League. Whereas Wilson had been the hovering, predatory type of striker, Fidler was

> In the summer of 1967 a slogan competition was held amongst Macclesfield supporters. The winning entry, closely beating 'We are in-MACC-ulate', was the terse 'Smacc 'em in MACC'. Several thousand car stickers bearing the legend were produced and sold.

a return to the combative style of old. His goals were often followed by his trademark 'lap of honour'; ever the showman, his antics off the pitch sometimes veered toward the prima donna-esque. At one point in mid-season he announced his intention to emigrate to America to work in his brother's firm, then changed his mind within a few days.

On the pitch, though, Fidler could rarely be faulted. Along with Fred Taberner, he was to become one half of the formidable double act of strikers that would reach its peak in the next couple of seasons.

## Challenge Cup fireworks

Before the Cheshire League changed out of all recognition in 1968, its corollary competition, the Challenge Cup, had ceased to be looked upon as the poor relation to the Senior Cup. The County League of the mid-sixties was considered to be so strong by non-league standards (and often beyond) that any trophy based solely on its clientèle was a most sought-after prize.

Certainly, the Silkmen encountered many a battle royal in those years. First there was the episode at Ellesmere Port, where the match was abandoned six minutes from time by the referee, since the dismissed Port player-manager Dave Hickson refused to leave the pitch. In the heated atmosphere 'blows were exchanged in scuffles' amongst the two sets of supporters. The tie was awarded to Macc., who progressed to the semi-finals, where they lost by a single goal to Wigan Athletic.

The following season it took six and a half hours to dismiss Frickley Colliery. After a 3–3 draw at the Moss Rose, Macclesfield 'won' the return at South Elmsall. It was then pointed out by a Frickley official that Macc. had included

Fidler, who had not played in the first match, and who was therefore ineligible. This time, the League decided against the Town, and ordered the game to be replayed on Frickley's ground. The result of this 'second replay' was 0–0, after extra time.

Finally, at Altrincham, nearly two months after the original match, Macc. won through against the doughty Yorkshiremen 4–1.

That year (1966–67) the Silkmen reached the final, winning the two-legged tie with Runcorn, 3–0 on aggregate.

The win was achieved without a manager, as the previous month Albert Leake had been 'relieved of his duties' by the committee. The circumstances were – and remain – something of a mystery. Possibly it was felt that the intransigent Leake was not receptive to the new ideas that were in the air. After a few weeks of muffled legal sabre-rattling Leake accepted the severance settlement, and Keith Goalen stepped in as player-coach for the new season.

Goalen showed himself to be flexible and innovative. In order to make training enjoyable *per se*, he introduced accompanying music played over the loudspeakers, and a points system for the exercises. ('They drew the line at ballet, though,' he recalls.) He experimented with 4–3–3 in the trial matches, but in the end wisely decided to stick with the tried-and-tested 4–2–4, which had been honed to perfection under Leake. Acquisi-tions during the summer of 1967 were Fred Taber-ner, scorer of sixty-five goals with Witton Albion; Dick Young, an inside-forward from Stockport County; and Bill Calder, ex-Rochdale centre-for-ward.

Another dazzling season ensued.

## FA Cup runs 1966–68

*We never get to Wembley*
*Nor win the FA Cup.*
*In fact against the big dogs*
*We're just a little pup.*
*Now in lesser limelights*
*We are a shining light,*
*And every game we play in*
*We play with all our might.*
*And other Cheshire League clubs*
*Who know the Moss Rose roar*
*And see the football we dish up*
*It makes them feel real sore.*
*So let us Macc. supporters*
*To every lad and lass,*
*Continue to support our team*
*Right in to Super Class.*
*Anon.*

This was penned by a supporter in October 1967. It took just two and a half years to disprove the first line; and a matter of weeks for the pup to show that it, too, had teeth.

The writing had been on the wall for some years. In the autumn of 1965, during striker Carl Davenport's high-scoring year with the Blues, Winsford United and Witton Albion were scotched in the FA Cup Qualifying Rounds, 7–0 and 9–0 respectively. Davenport hit a hat-trick in each match. The run ended at Oswestry, where on a mudbath of a pitch Macc. succumbed 2–3.

For the next campaign Macclesfield were in-cluded in the Derbyshire regional division. They went one stage further, eliminating Alfreton Town (2–1), Matlock Town (6–1 after 2–2), and Work-sop (3–1). This time the nemesis came in the shape of a well-drilled Nuneaton Borough, who kept the score to 1–1 on the Moss Rose, and won the replay 3–1.

Something exceptional was being threatened. The breakthrough finally occurred in that festive season of 1967–68.

The First Qualifying Round saw off Bacup Bo-rough, 7–0. All the goals were scored in a thirty-minute second half spree. Next to go were Witton Albion and Hyde United, both beaten 2–0, and both played away. The final barrier to the competition proper was the seasoned cup fighters of Wigan Athletic. Again drawn away, Macc. survived 1–1, partially thanks to a Taberner penalty, and partially to Cooke and his defence who withstood an almighty second half battering. In the replay the Town were clear 3–0 winners. Fidler, having retracted his transfer request of earlier in the season, returned to the side to score the first. Two late counter-punches from Taberner and Rogers completed the job.

The First Round again, then: would fortune be favourable in the draw?

Apparently not: their opponents would be Stockport County, mid-table in the old Third Division, away. Thoughts naturally returned to the Senior Cup match of two years before, when the County had fielded a team which was mostly their Football League side: an unsporting, if not exactly illegal, measure. The Cheshire League si-de's response had been to take their illustrious neighbours to a fighting replay, eventually losing 0–2 at the Moss Rose. This time County were taking the upstarts seriously, spending two days at Southport before the tie.

On an Edgeley Park pitch with its icy sheen of snow, Stockport opted for aerial bombardment, reasoning that ground skills would be difficult to maintain in the conditions. For the most part such a strategy suited the visitors perfectly: the two tall, dominating Macc. centre backs Berry and Forrester dealt adequately with every hopeful cross. The defence was breached just once throughout the first half, when Atkins headed the County into the lead. Midway through the second half Calder equalised, ghosting in to meet a Goodwin corner with his head. The Blues then spent the rest of the match keeping possession and slowing the pace, understandably aiming for the replay. It worked, and the teams met again the following Wednesday.

The team spent the afternoon relaxing as guests of the Macclesfield Golf Club. No doubt on their mind was the responsibility of being the eleven players who, should they win, would take the club further than ever before in the FA Cup.

The magnitude of the task was emphasised in the third minute of the game, when Kevan opened the scoring for Stockport. Refusing to bow to what seemed like the inevitable, the Silkmen hit back soon after: Goodwin's centre was met by Taberner,

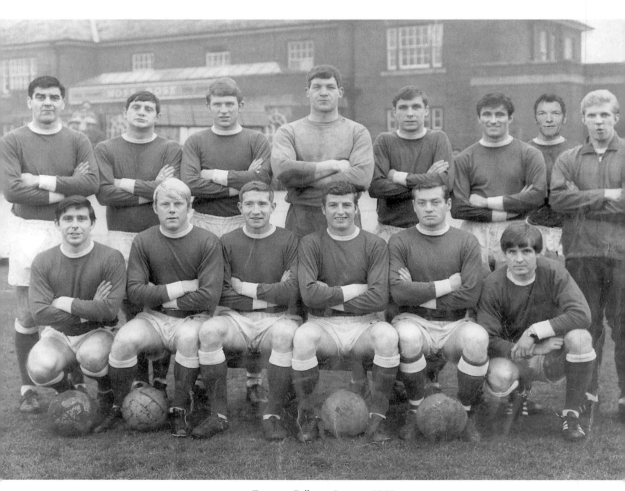

Team *v.* Fulham, January 1968
*back row*: Forrester, Collins, Berry, Cooke, Beaumont, Goalen, Sievwright, Latham
*front row*: Young, Goodwin, Taberner, Fidler, Calder, Rogers. (Keith Goalen)

whose powerful half-volley crashed into the roof of the net. After twenty-five minutes Macc. went into the lead. Taberner took a penalty, awarded for a foul on the irrepressible Goodwin. Ogley, the County 'keeper, saved; then the referee ordered the kick to be retaken because of an infringement. This time Fidler took the kick, and put it away.

The expected second half storm was weathered by the Silkmen, mainly thanks to Cooke who was in dominant form. It was Macc. who had the last word, with Calder's run and thundering shot that flew inches wide.

The draw for the Second Round was kinder. They were to play host to the Northern League team Spennymoor United. Confidence lifted by their side's impressive away form, the Geordie fans were in little doubt of the outcome, singing the praises of their goalie and top scorer:

> *Aye, aye, aye, aye!*
> *Crompton is better than Yashin.*
> *Tobin is better than Eusebio*
> *And we will give Macclesfield a thrashin'!*

Mere enthusiasm was not enough, though: Macc. progressed 2–0, the scorers once more Taberner and Fidler.

The town came to a standstill the following Monday at 12.45 p.m., when the draw for the Third Round was broadcast on the radio. To add to the tension, Macclesfield Town were third last out of the bag. They were to play Fulham, of the old First Division, away.

## The battle of Craven Cottage

Suddenly the club was the centre of national media attention. For the Senior Cup tie with Lostock Gralam the Saturday before the FA Cup match, the Moss Rose spectators were treated to the sight of BBC cameras behind the pub end goal! Much was made of Goalen's academic background, one report referring to his use of psychology to motivate the players. (Perhaps it was felt that the presence of a non-league team in the Third Round had to be explained somehow …)

Fulham, meanwhile, were having their share of tribulation. Struggling in the First Division, they sacked their manager Vic Buckingham days before the tie, replacing him with the 33-year-old Bobby Robson.

Their side was a cosmopolitan mix of the proven and the up-and-coming. Johnny Haynes, the original Brylcreem Boy and the first one hundred pounds-a-week footballer, was nearing the end of his career, but was still a force to be reckoned with. Goalkeeper Tony Macedo was on the fringes of international selection; and the attack contained a 21-year-old Allan Clarke, before his moves to Leicester and then Leeds, as part of Revie's successful side of the early 'seventies.

Macc. travelled down to London on the Friday, having made a send-off tour of the town beforehand. They were quoted at 20–1 to beat Fulham, and 2,000–1 to win the Cup. No London bookmaker could be found, however, who would accept a bet on Macclesfield winning the trophy! The capital was nervous.

Not so the Silkmen. They indulged in a gentle spot of tourism – Buckingham Palace, Hyde Park – apparently unfazed by the occasion. Brian Fidler came out with the much-quoted: 'This is the one match I am least worried about, and if we don't all come off the field with the blood running out

> The 1968 FA Cup team came close to earning free haircuts. Clifford the Barber's on Park Lane, Macclesfield, offered such a service if the Silkmen beat Fulham in the Third Round tie.
> The barber's shop still exists, although now a hairdresser's.

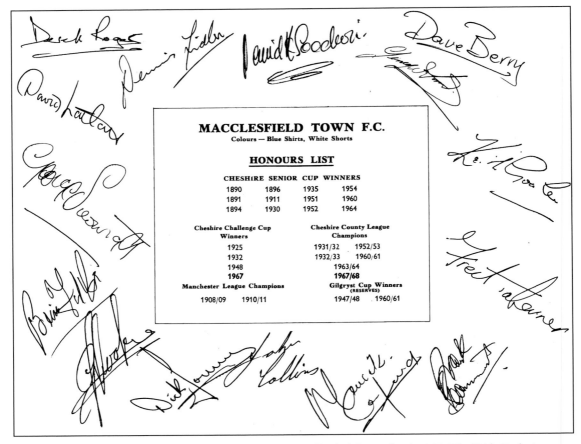

### MACCLESFIELD TOWN F.C.
Colours — Blue Shirts, White Shorts

#### HONOURS LIST

CHESHIRE SENIOR CUP WINNERS

| 1890 | 1896 | 1935 | 1954 |
|------|------|------|------|
| 1891 | 1911 | 1951 | 1960 |
| 1894 | 1930 | 1952 | 1964 |

| Cheshire Challenge Cup Winners | Cheshire County League Champions |
|---|---|
| 1925 | 1931/32    1952/53 |
| 1932 | 1932/33    1960/61 |
| 1948 | 1963/64 |
| **1967** | **1967/68** |

| Manchester League Champions | Gilgryst Cup Winners (RESERVES) |
|---|---|
| 1908/09    1910/11 | 1947/48    1960/61 |

Collected autographs of the heroes of Fulham 1968. (*Official Club Handbook 1967–68*). (Keith Goalen)

of us from the effort we'll want whipping'.

Goalen delayed his final team selection until the Saturday morning, after examining the state of the ground. The respective line-ups were:

*Fulham*: Macedo; Ryan, Dempsey; Brown, Callaghan, Conway; Haynes, Earle, Clarke, Gilroy, Barrett (Sub. for Callaghan – Parmenter)

*Macclesfield Town*: Cooke; Sievwright, Forrester; Beaumont, Collins, Goalen; Goodwin, Taberner, Fidler, Young, Latham (Sub. not used – Calder)

In a crowd of 23,642 an estimated 9,500 had made the journey south. (Macclesfield petrol stations had reported 'absolutely fantastic' sales over the previous twenty-four hours.)

The crowd did not have to wait long for the excitement to begin. In the second minute Haynes took a corner on the Macc. right. Beaumont cleared with a diving header, to Goodwin who passed on to Fidler, in space in midfield. The quick-thinking forward found Taberner with a perfectly-weighted through ball. Fulham were caught square, and Taberner, having galloped through an ineffectual tackle, bore down on goal, steadied himself, and hooked a fierce left-foot shot beyond Macedo's plunge into the far corner of the net.

It was an advantage Macc. enjoyed for just two minutes. Clarke, capitalising on a moment's hesitancy, cracked one in from fifteen yards.

On seventeen minutes the Blues took the lead again. Cooke sent a massive sixty-yard clearance down the middle, to where Fidler was waiting. The harassed Dempsey, the Eire international, underestimating the no. 9's pace and tenacity, headed into his path. Fidler ran on, stabbing in a shot high to Macedo's left. There was the usual triumphal run, the forward blowing two-handed kisses to the supporters and the *Match of the Day* cameras.

Macc. kept their lead until half-time, relying on their resolute defence and the quick break. For the second half Fulham changed their deployment: Haynes became a deeper-lying link man, and Parmenter, replacing Callaghan, was used as an extra defender to cover the breaks. The pivotal moment of the match came after ten minutes. Cooke rose to collect a high cross, and the referee blew for a foul on Clarke. This was to everyone's puzzlement – Fulham's included – as no foul appeared to have been committed. The London-based *News of the World* called the decision 'highly arguable'. Goalen the diplomat calmed his players; Clarke took the penalty and scored.

There was worse to come: Macc. were denied two apparently justifiable penalty claims at the other end, then, with just thirteen minutes left, disaster struck. Haynes, following up behind his front line, won back a loose ball in the area and scored in the corner. One or two of the Macclesfield men sank to their knees.

Two minutes later it was effectively over: Gilroy netted Fulham's fourth, after a neat right-wing move.

So it ended, 4–2 to Fulham, but praise for the Silkmen rang loud across the land:

This was so nearly, and on the run of play, so justly, the shock result of the round. *Observer* (28/1/68)

They have carved their little niche on the cup as indelibly as if they had their names engraved on it. Matt Busby, in the *Daily Express* (29/1/68)

## Aftermath

There were, besides, many favourable outcomes to the defeat.

Keith Goalen received the *Evening Standard*'s 'Footballer of the Month' award – the first non-league player to do so. Fulham agreed to send a team to the Moss Rose for Goalen's end-of-season testimonial (when a grand time would be had by all present, in an 8–5 win for the Londoners).

Macclesfield Town had made many friends: they had also made a pot of money (£6,344 to be exact) from the Cup run as a whole. At last the new cantilever main stand was more than just an item on the agenda.

First there was the question of Macc.'s last ever Cheshire League competition. The Blues were many games in arrears because of their FA Cup matches, but important wins were recorded over closest rivals Northwich (1–0 away) and Altrincham (2–0).

It was in this latter match that Fidler's goal-scoring celebrations so irritated Freddie Pye that the Altrincham manager emptied a bucket of water over the forward. Further unpleasantness was avoided by Pye coming to the Macc. changing room later to apologise. Fidler kept his own counsel for the moment.

The Silkmen won the championship with a point earned in a downbeat home game against Oswestry at the end of April. By then a vital addition to the attack was Dennis Fidler (no relation to Brian) a speedy left winger, Stockport-born, and fresh from a notable stint at Fourth Division Darlington.

There remained the two-legged final of that year's North West Floodlit Cup. Opponents were Altrincham, who now had ex-Silkman Wilf Hall in goal. The first leg at Moss Lane resulted in a hard-fought 1–1 draw, a late Robins goal by sub. Reilly cancelling out Dick Young's second half strike.

In the second leg Altrincham scored first, and hung on to their lead until fifteen minutes from time. Then, almost inevitably, Brian Fidler grabbed the equaliser – and promptly set off on his trademark celebratory run. He made straight for the Altrincham bench, where, in front of Freddie Pye, he picked up the trainer's bucket of water. Pye flinched ... and Fidler poured the water over himself, to the huge delight of the crowd. The referee, his sense of propriety taking precedence over his sense of humour, booked the Macc. forward.

But what did it matter? Reserve Merrick Corfield

scored the second within a couple of minutes, and yet another piece of silverware was on its way to the Moss Rose cabinet.

The Northern Premier League was about to be launched: and thus would begin Macclesfield Town's thirty-year battle to rise to the Football League. In the short term, the decade was to finish in a blaze of glory.

After his one unforgettable year as player-coach, Keith Goalen stepped down to take charge of the reserves. The week before the building of the new stand began, Frank Beaumont was appointed player-manager.

Cover of programme for Keith Goalen testimonial match
May 1968. Photo shows Taberner scoring first goal
against Fulham. (Keith Goalen)

# 18

# Northern Premier League

'We have to play away at Wembley, so we will just have to get used to the idea and accept it.'
Player-manager Frank Beaumont, when asked for his comments on a tough FA Trophy
quarter-final draw away at Burton Albion. (26/2/70)

## A fresh challenge

The new main stand was completed during the summer of 1968, at a cost of £14,000. Still an imposing structure, its royal blue cantilever is visible from a fair way down the London Road as the visitor makes his or her way south to the ground from the town centre.

A dramatic new look to the Moss Rose was only fitting. Macclesfield Town had been elected to the Northern Premier League, intended for the 'best non-league clubs between Newcastle-on-Tyne and Derby', according to NPL committee member Peter Swales. Five clubs each from the Cheshire League and the Lancashire Combination had gained entry, by the following method: positions for the past three years were scrutinised, with champions being awarded five points, runners-up four, and so on. A glance at Macc.'s records for 1965–68 will highlight the comparative ease with which the club qualified for the inaugural Super League. The remaining ten places were made up with the cream of the Northern and Midland Leagues, plus some 'wild card' entries.

The Silkmen would be joined by long-time Cheshire stablemates Northwich Victoria, Altrincham, Bangor City, Hyde United, Wigan Athletic, and Runcorn. From further north there was Scarborough, Goole Town, Gateshead, and South Shields. From the Lancashire Combination: South Liverpool, Chorley, Morecambe, and Netherfield of Kendal. The southernmost outfits were Worksop, Gainsborough Trinity, and the reigning Midland League Champions Boston United.

It was this latter team who were Macc.'s first ever Northern Premier League opponents, at Boston, in mid-August. The Lincolnshire side won an ill-tempered, bruising match 2–1, the away side's goal supplied by ex-England centre-forward Derek Kevan, during his two months' stay at the Moss Rose.

The return game with Boston took place in October, in much the same atmosphere. On this occasion, though, Macc. were 2–0 winners, thanks to a brace of penalties from close-season signing John Clay, an ex-Manchester City inside forward. By then the Silkmen were pushing for the leadership of the league.

It was after another rumbustious, physical affair – this time against Bangor City (with Brian Fidler being sent off) – that Beaumont defended his men: 'Who wants to watch a team of gentlemen, struggling half-way down the league?' It was a clear enough message: if circumstances demanded it, the team's usually classy style could be augmented by a fiercely competitive approach. Thankfully, not many more such chest-thumping proofs were needed, and the competition settled down to trials of skill. Given the talent available at the Moss Rose at the time, this suited the Cheshire Champions perfectly. By Christmas the contenders for the inaugural NPL title had been realistically whittled down to two:

| | P | W | D | L | F | A | Pts |
|---|---|---|---|---|---|---|---|
| Macclesfield Town | 23 | 16 | 4 | 3 | 52 | 17 | 36 |
| Wigan Athletic | 23 | 14 | 7 | 2 | 40 | 19 | 35 |

The new main stand, built 1968. (*Macclesfield Express*)

After the defeat at Goole in late January Macc. embarked on a long unbeaten sequence, as their rivals' challenge stuttered. A goalless draw at Wigan in March – in which the Blues had much the better of the play, despite a penalty miss – was just the tonic needed. By Easter Monday it was all over. Needing to win at Netherfield to be sure of the title, Macc. rubbed out an early goal with a sixteenth minute penalty from Young. Then Brian Fidler, haring after and retrieving an apparently lost ball, centred for Sievwright to crash in the winner. The Silkmen were champions with five weeks to spare. They eventually finished twelve points ahead of the runner-up.

That was the year that five trophies were gathered in. Three of them were won by Goalen's reserves: Manchester League, the Gilgryst Cup, and the Macclesfield FA Cup. The first team brought back yet another Cheshire Senior Cup – the thirteenth – although not without a couple of hiccups *en route*. The semi-final against a

> The first ever Macc. match to be decided by penalties was the pre-season Inter-Town Football Cup against Buxton in August 1970. After a 1–1 draw, Macclesfield won the tie 5–4 in a penalty shoot-out.

Witton Albion reinforced by the presence of the great Dennis Viollet, late of Manchester United, went to a replay. Macc. eventually won through 3–1, both matches taking place at the Drill Field, Northwich.

In the third and last year in which the Senior Cup Final was played to a two-legged home-and-away format, Northwich Victoria were the opponents. The Town returned from the Drill Field with a single goal advantage, courtesy of Dave Lyon, a teenage forward recently signed from Mossley. It should have been plain sailing back at the Moss Rose in the second leg, but the fighting Vics. took the game to extra time, thanks to an equalising goal from Powell. Two late goals from Dennis Fidler settled matters.

About the only downside of those years was the football club's ill-fated venture into the licensing trade. The *Moss Rose* pub was bought from Ind Coope in May 1968, only to be sold back, at a substantial loss, the following year. Recorded philosophically at the 1969 AGM as 'a bold venture which failed', the sortie brought home the fact that, once more, high up on the list of priorities should be the wooing and keeping of quality professional players. The 1969–70 season was an especially satisfying vindication of this policy.

### *FA Cup First Round ties*

Macc. were to reach the First Round proper of the FA Cup in four consecutive seasons. This feat, it must be admitted, was rendered easier by the FA's decision to exempt the Silkmen until the Fourth Qualifying Round in 1968–70, and then the First Round proper the following year. They were the only non-league team to be so honoured, which is signal proof of the success of Frank Beaumont's side.

The First Round, however, was to prove an insurmountable obstacle. Lincoln City came to the Moss Rose in November 1968, and this time the Football League team were clear winners, with little in the way of heroics or arguments from the home side. The Imps were two goals to the good within ten minutes of the start. A John Clay penalty gave a veneer of respectability to the scoreline, but Lincoln were well worth their 3–1 win. At least the crowd was a highly estimable 6,834.

The next year Altrincham were disposed of 3–0 in the Qualifying Round, George Sievwright blotting out the much-publicised threat from a 19-year-old Frank Carrodus, just days before the *wunderkind*'s move to Manchester City. Beaumont and Lyons (2) supplied the goals, all scored in the first 35 minutes.

The opposition in the First Round were Fourth Division Scunthorpe United, a young and ambitious team that included another teenager with a bright future: one Kevin Keegan.

The match on the Moss Rose was a defence-dominated affair, with Sievwright once more quelling the aspiring youngster. Keegan showed some of the less likeable turns in his professional repertoire by rolling on the ground as if in agony whenever getting the worse of one of Sievwright's tackles, then showing remarkable powers of recovery once the stretcher-bearers had been waved

away. Heath opened the scoring for the visitors after 14 minutes; Lyon hit the equaliser just before half-time.

The replay, though, was a Keegan showcase. Scunthorpe won 4–2, the future England manager scoring two and having a hand in the others. Even though Young scored for Macc. in the first few minutes, and Sievwright blasted in a forty-yard free kick to regain the lead midway through the first half, in the end the pace of the Football League team decided the tie.

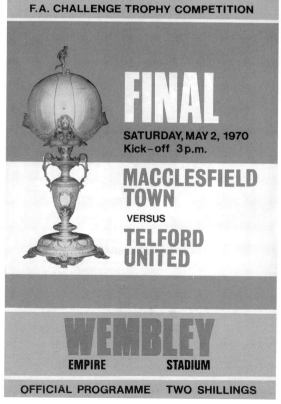

F.A. CHALLENGE TROPHY COMPETITION

FINAL

SATURDAY, MAY 2, 1970
Kick-off 3 p.m.

MACCLESFIELD TOWN

VERSUS

TELFORD UNITED

WEMBLEY

EMPIRE        STADIUM

OFFICIAL PROGRAMME    TWO SHILLINGS

Programme for the 1970 FA Trophy Final at Wembley.
(Keith Goalen)

Ron Flowers (left), captain of Telford, and Frank Beaumont, before the first ever FA Trophy Final. Wembley 1970.
(*Macclesfield Express*)

Bradford City, also of Division Four, supplied the First Round opposition in 1970–71. Here, at least, the Silkmen recaptured some of the fire of Fulham.

At Valley Parade, after early Macc. pressure, the visitors went behind to yet another controversial penalty. Equality was restored with a Brian Fidler second half strike; two minutes later, Bradford went ahead again. With less than ten minutes remaining, Lyon hit another equaliser. Macc.

could have been excused for having thoughts of a replay. Then a most uncharacteristic error by Sievwright, stumbling over a simple trap, allowed O'Neill to dart in and set up Corner, whose wickedly swerving shot sneaked in under Cooke's dive.

It was the last taste of the FA Cup proper for a number of years. But by then the Silkmen had joined the select band of teams that had played at Wembley.

## A trip to the Twin Towers

The germ of the idea behind the FA Challenge Trophy had been planted as long ago as 1950. Originally floated as an 'Intermediate FA Cup', the rationale of a nationwide knockout competition for non-league clubs remained when the tournament was finally launched in 1969–70. Given their recent history, Macclesfield Town were expecting to make an impact.

The beginning was less than auspicious: with nine men injured or laid low with the 'flu, Macc. requested a postponement of the First Round tie with Burscough. This was granted, and the Blues were given a reprieve of just four days. They squeezed home 1–0.

Round two was another home match, with Gainsborough Trinity. Once more the forwards were contained, allowing half-back Dave Roberts to bag the two goals which took his side into the last sixteen. Here they met Bangor City, eventually despatched by a single goal in a replay. A spy from Burton Albion, who were to be Macc.'s opponents, away, in the next round, was heard to say: 'Albion's semi-final place should be safe'.

Canny cup veterans Macclesfield, however, went about their task in typically level-headed fashion. Once Brian Fidler had secured an equaliser (compensating for an earlier howler of a miss from four yards out) the Blues brought on Sievwright to bolster the defence, weathering the siege and surviving until the replay. Here the Silkmen cast care and doubt aside, sweeping into a 3–0 lead after thirty minutes. The Albion had no answer to Dennis Fidler's forays, the winger's runs and centres causing continual embarrassment to the opposition defence. Lyon, B. Fidler (2) and Young were the scorers in the emphatic 4–2 win.

The semi-final, at the Victoria Ground, Stoke, was against Barnet, at the time a top Southern League club. Yet again just one goal separated the two teams: a memorable, fulminating strike from

Lap of honour after the 2–0 win. Fidler holds the trophy. (*Macclesfield Express*)

Dick Young seven minutes before half-time.

In the Wembley final Macc. would meet Telford United, also of the Southern League. Their daunting line-up included player-coach Ron Flowers, a member of the 1966 England World Cup squad; his ex-Wolves team-mate Jimmy Murray; and Northern Ireland international goalkeeper Bobby Irvine.

On the Wednesday afternoon preceding the Final, having once more made a tour of the town beforehand, Macc. set out for the south. Their intention was to spend a couple of days relaxing in Brighton, and then travel to London on the eve of the match. The *Express* had had printed 1,500 car stickers proclaiming 'Silkmen – Wembley bound'. They were snapped up in less than an hour.

Fully 10,000 Macc. supporters made the journey to the capital on that May Saturday. 'The day we painted London blue and white', would be the headline. It was almost as if a whole community wished to lay the ghosts of the team's last visit to London, just over two years before.

The teams were:

*Macclesfield Town*: Cooke; Sievwright, Bennett; Beaumont, Collins, Roberts; Lyon, B. Fidler, Young, Corfield, D. Fidler (Sub.: Berry)

*Telford United*: Irvine; Harris, Croft; Flowers, Coton, Ray; Fudge, Hart, Bentley, Murray, Jogger (Sub.: Ball)

---

During the 4–1 win over Goole Town at the Moss Rose in October 1970, Goole full back Jackson, sprinting back in an attempt to forestall Brian Fidler, hurtled into the Star Lane end net and broke the rear stanchion. The goals collapsed, and Dave Berry essayed a makeshift repair job, hammering in a few nails with a policeman's truncheon. 'Silkman' reckoned the result 'looked about as safe as a giraffe on roller-skates.' The game was completed, however, without further ado.

---

The Silkmen's confidence was high, despite the powerful opposition and the soft and strength-sapping Wembley pitch. They had opted for the potentially suicidal strategy of allowing Flowers the freedom of midfield, banking on solid defence and the quick break.

On twenty-five minutes the game plan paid off. Dave Lyon takes up the story: 'Dick Young pushed a short pass to me and screamed "Hit it!".'

And hit it Lyon did, firing in a hard low shot past three defenders and the unsighted Irvine. The diminutive Lyon, who according to one onlooker appeared 'petrified with joy', later said: 'I felt like rushing out of the ground to tell my mother at home. I had actually scored at Wembley!'

As the second half progressed, the wisdom of Macc.'s retreating defence tactics – the football equivalent of 'rope-a-dope' – became clear. The Telford attack, repeatedly frustrated by a defence, and especially Cooke, in unbeatable form, began to tire. The heavy turf was taking its toll. On the hour Brian Fidler broke free into space some thirty yards from the Telford goal. As the defenders converged and Irvine advanced, the striker coolly lobbed over the 'keeper into the unguarded net.

Even by Fidler standards, his subsequent run was a bit special. He sprinted eighty yards and vaulted the perimeter fence to acknowledge the cheers of the Macclesfield thousands. ('I was on my way up to collect my medal', he later quipped.)

Telford, of course, were far from finished. However the defence remained firm, and man of the match Cooke turned away or held every shot sent his way.

So it remained, 2–0 to a deserving Macc. team. Frank Beaumont led his team up the famous 39 steps to receive the first ever FA Challenge Trophy.

Two days later, the team had another final to contend: against Witton Albion in the North-West Floodlit Cup. Macc. would have been excused a lacklustre performance so soon after Wembley; nonetheless after a seven-goal thriller another trophy was added, the Blues shading a 4–3 win.

Victory tour of Macclesfield after the FA Trophy win 1970. (*Macclesfield Express*)

The following Saturday, in the penultimate Northern Premier League match, the away opponents were Scarborough, level on points (50) with Macclesfield, but with a superior goal average. A victory for the Yorkshire side would almost certainly give them the championship. Wigan, expected to win their last game, and Boston United, who had the best goal average of the leaders, were both also on fifty points.

The Silkmen lifted themselves above the tangle by defeating Scarborough by a single goal: Dave Lyon, unmarked, with a simple close-range header. Although losing 1–3 in the last match with South Shields, Macc. won possibly the closest league title race ever – at any level – by 0.006 of a goal!

| | P | W | D | L | F | A | Pts |
|---|---|---|---|---|---|---|---|
| Macclesfield Town | 38 | 22 | 8 | 8 | 72 | 41 | 52 |
| Wigan Athletic | 38 | 20 | 12 | 6 | 56 | 32 | 52 |
| Boston United | 38 | 21 | 8 | 9 | 65 | 33 | 50 |
| Scarborough | 38 | 20 | 10 | 8 | 74 | 39 | 50 |

The playing of sixty-eight competitive matches in a season, however, was proving a drain on the energies and appetite. The campaign wound up with the two legs of the NPL Challenge Cup against Altrincham.

It was to be a case of *déjà vu*: after holding the Robins to 1–1 at Moss Lane, the return home game was a match too far, Altrincham winning 2–1. The attendance – 6,833 – was a Northern Premier League record.

Percy Vickerstaff the long-serving groundsman also departed in 1970. Percy's claim to lasting fame, besides his considerable turf-nurturing skills, was his tea: 'the elixir on which so many Macclesfield players based their training', and still spoken of by players of the 'sixties in hushed and reverential tones.

The following season the FA Trophy campaign ended in the quarter-final, as Hereford United – no mean Cup giant-killers themselves, and elected

The 1970 team. (*Macclesfield Express*)

to the Fourth Division within a year – were the pacey, skilful 2–0 victors. Telford United were the eventual winners.

The Cheshire Senior Cup was regained in 1970–71. Northwich held Macc. 1–1 in the first game of the final at Stockport, but in the replay at Crewe Broadhead and Brian Fidler scored in the 2–1 win. Fidler's goal was his 150th for the club, easily a post-war record.

There was an embarrassing exit from the same trophy the next year, as Sandbach Ramblers, supposedly easy pickings from the Cheshire League, won 2–0 in a first round replay at the Moss Rose.

Another Senior Cup victory was to follow in 1973, but by then the long, slow decline had begun. It was to take four games in the final, all held at Crewe, to dispose of Cheshire League side Winsford United. Macc. finally won through 2–1. It was to be their last trophy for ten years.

## A changing world

Some onlookers did not take too kindly to the comparative lack of success. Unusually for the Moss Rose, there were some minority crowd disturbances. A pint pot was thrown from the terraces after one defeat, the first missile to be so despatched since the snowball of 1936. Happily no one was injured, and the quick-reacting FA threatened a large fine and ground closure if the club did not put its house in order.

Players were not innocent of misdemeanours. Beaumont himself was suspended for fourteen days and fined £250; and his team seemed to receive a hefty quota of bookings – often, admittedly, fully justified – in the first few years of the NPL.

To some extent game circumstances led to an aggressive response. There were teams who, wary of the side's reputation, came to the Moss Rose with strategies designed solely to frustrate and negate. More objectionable than most were Bradford Park Avenue (defunct by 1974) with their ugly big-boot rationale of foul and clear the lines; and the seven-man defensive phalanx deployed by NPL leaders Boston United (which, depressingly, worked: 0–1).

The crowd trouble – such as it was – was perhaps a symptom of a deeper malaise in late-century Western society; certainly, compared to the shenanigans of supporters of clubs with higher profiles elsewhere in the country at the time, the antics of the Silk followers were distinctly small beer.

Worse, in a way, were the largely uninformed armchair critics who reached for the green biro and hurled their vitriol at the club from afar; or the ungrateful and amnesiac barrackers who, from the anonymity of the terraces, would single out a player for abuse.

Incredibly, Brian Fidler, suffering a temporary loss of his galvanic form, was the target for a while. Then, after a 3–0 drubbing of Burton Albion in the FA Trophy in February 1972, 'Silkman' pointedly wrote:

Three superbly taken goals and the sight of Brian Fidler racing to the touchline after scoring the first with arms raised high in a 'Harvey Smith' salute to his critics will be a glorious memory for the loyal supporters.
*Express* (17/2/72)

Those years also saw the beginnings of industrial sponsorship, at local and national level. Already Burton's had supplied the team's suits, Bukta – via Tyldsley and Holbrook's – the kit. By 1971

Watney were sponsoring the NPL. Later, continuing the hop-based theme, Greenall, then John Smith's, then Bass, would grant their name and some of the financing to the competition. Closer to home, Harry Williamson, a Chester Road wine merchant (and later club chairman), contributed a bottle of malt whisky for the 'player of the month' award. The first winner, in August 1972, was John Turner, the tall and commanding centreback.

The first ever sponsors of a single match were Ernest Scragg and Sons, a textile machinery firm based on Sunderland Street. This was the game with Morecambe on 24 August 1974.

The departure of Frank Beaumont in April 1972 had opened the door for the ex-Stockport full-back Billy Haydock to take over as manager. He had just returned from a successful year coaching the South African side Port Elizabeth. Intent on making his presence felt from the off, he put the players through a training session which was declared 'the toughest for several weeks'. Haydock was a fan of orthodox wingers, supposedly a dying breed, and to this end he used Dave Lyon on the right, and Dennis Fidler, back from his year at Altrincham, on the left. A typical team of 1972–73 would have been:

Mailey; Dover, Turner, Corfield, Collins, Shawcross, Lyon, Hartle, Morris, Wilcockson, D. Fidler

Willie Mailey, the comparatively small but effective goalie, had arrived from Altrincham; which was where Johnnie Cooke finished up.

This line-up was augmented in December by the Fleetwood striker Geoff Collier, a bargain at £400. A series of wins the next month, including a pleasing 4–1 rectification against Sandbach Ramblers in the Cheshire Cup, owed a lot to the newcomer's eye-catching scoring and lay-off skills.

> Macclesfield Ladies' FC (nicknamed the Silkgirls) performed well in their first competitive season (1971–72). They drew twice (2–2 and 4–4) with the powerful Preston Ladies' team, and recorded wins of 20–0 and 35–0! Longest-serving member was Veronica Bailey.

Before long scouts from Everton, Spurs and Walsall came to assess the forward. Haydock priced his star asset at £10,000, adding: 'Start the bidding at £7,000'. Most of the clubs having been frightened off by this optimistic ante, Collier eventually went to Notts. County in the close season for £2,500.

It was a financial *coup* for the club, especially as the striker was to return to the Moss Rose on a free transfer the following year.

However, as the club approached its centenary, there were signs of unrest. Billy Haydock resigned in January 1974, in the same season as the departures of Dennis Fidler (i/c the reserves), George Sievwright (trainer) and the former goalie Wilf Hall, who had been doing a sterling job as groundsman. Fidler's letter of resignation gave evidence of a sad harking-back to an old, old problem:

I can no longer operate effectively against the weight of uninformed interference ...

Macclesfield will never again have a successful team until the Board leave team management and coaching decisions to the professionals who are appointed to do the job. *Express* (22/10/73)

Ironically, the rich harvest of the previous dozen years was now becoming a burden, adding to the pressure on successive teams and staff. Macc. finished eighth in the NPL in 1974; for the next five seasons they would be unable to rise above fifteenth.

As the English non-league soccer scene moved towards the National Premier competition – theoretically the 'Fifth Division' of the Football League – the Silkmen had begun to drift in the opposite direction. There were dark days ahead.

# 19

# *The Seventies Slump*

'It is important to the town that the football club is successful in the future.'
The Mayor, Cllr. Crossley, at the Macclesfield FC centenary dinner. (19/4/75)

'Shouts of "rubbish!" and "give over!" came from the audience at last Wednesday's annual meeting of Macclesfield Town FC when a shareholder criticised the club's move to join the proposed Alliance and urged that, instead, it should rejoin the Cheshire League.'
*Express* (1/2/79)

## *False dawn*

Under caretaker-manager Eddie Brown there was a rush of goals, and signs (ultimately, alas, illusory) that the corner had been turned. Brown's watchword was 'Attack!', and with the twin strike force of Birtwistle and Wilcockson in top form, notable victories were achieved. Worksop Town were dismissed 4–0 from the FA Trophy, and a week or so later Wigan Athletic were beaten 4–2 away. This latter game included a Birtwistle goal from an acrobatic scissor-kick, doubly satisfying as it was against his old club.

The FA Trophy of 1974 saw Macc. progress to the semis, where they lost a two-legged tie with Dartford (1–2 at the Moss Rose, 0–0 away). 0–2 down in the first leg, the Silkmen overwhelmed their opponents in the last ten minutes, but had just the one goal to show for it: a John Collins strike from a rebound from the bar.

The previous week they had contested another semi, this time against Poulton, at Witton, in the Cheshire Cup. Amazingly, the amateur side were leading 1–0 until the second minute of injury time, when Birtwistle saved the tie and sundry blushes by equalising. In extra time substitute Malcolm Woodward – a speedy winger acquired from Skelmersdale – left his marker for dead, raced on and scored.

The final took place at Crewe. The opponents were Runcorn, at the time a couple of points ahead of Macc. in the NPL. Partially due to the fixture congestion (they would play nearly seventy games that season), the Blues gave an unusually flaccid performance, Runcorn winning by the single goal. The teams were:

*Runcorn*: Rawlinson; Baker, Rutter, Bailey, Duff, King, Hipwell, Wilson, Worth, Howard, Whitbread (Sub.: Foreshaw)
*Macclesfield Town*: Mailey; Eccleshare, Mobley, Goodwin, Collins, Turner, Morris, Woodward, Birtwistle, Bradshaw, Hartle (Sub.: Jones)

Willie Stevenson, of the great Liverpool 'sixties side, took over the role of player-manager in August of that year, but would step down in December. The reasons given show a constructive honesty:

I cannot concentrate on playing and managing. My own form has deteriorated ... It is very difficult for me to criticise other players when I have not been playing well myself. *Express* (19/12/74)

John Collins, along with John Turner, had been in charge of team selection under Eddie Brown. Collins now led the Silkmen in a minor revival, which culminated in an FA Cup run the following season. Once again, after victories over four clubs from the Midland Counties League, the First Round proper was reached. The opponents were

133

Keith Eccleshare's 25–yard cracker against Sheffield Wednesday.
FA Cup First Round, November 1975. (*Macclesfield Express*)

after the re-start – one of them a heart-breaking own goal from newcomer Tony Coleman – swung the tie, and the League outfit progressed.

The Town line-up was: Mailey; Eccleshare, Mobley, Fish, Collins, Heys, Morris, Lloyd, Collier, O'Connor, Coleman (Sub.: Brennan)

Collins, still a redoubtable centre-back, was the only survivor from the heroes of Fulham; ('John Collins for Minister of Defence', as the Market Street banner, memorably, had read). Collier had returned from Notts. County,

Sheffield Wednesday, at the time in the old Third Division. The venue was Hillsborough.

After conceding a clumsily-struck goal midway through the first half, Macc. raised the hopes of the travelling thousands with an invigorating equaliser. Eccleshare fastened on to a Wednesday clearance and sent a half-volley rocketing into the top corner. The next fifteen minutes saw the best of Macc., as the clearly rattled home side fell back on defence. However, two quick Wednesday goals

where his performances, mainly in the reserves, had been sound, with a steady stream of goals to his credit. Alan Fish, ex-Fleetwood, had replaced John Turner at centre-back. Tony Coleman, erstwhile Maine Road idol, was caretaker-manager for a couple of months early in 1976.

John Collins resigned in January of that year. His departure was seen by many to symbolise the last severance of the links with the glory years.

## The tangerine and blacks

The perennial issue of finances provided yet more evidence of the ingenuity and will of a supportive community. Despite the club's slide from grace on the pitch, public and private contributions in those years were legion.

Sponsorship grew apace. FMK, under the aegis of Harry Kearns, bought 3000 shares, as well as supplying £600 towards a pre-season tournament in August 1975. For that season the team wore the firm's colours of tangerine and black. Kearns also bought the *Moss Rose* pub, re-inventing it as the upmarket restaurant-cabaret venue *Silklands*. Comedian George Roper was present at the official opening in December.

Peripheral money-spinners were bingo, social events, sponsored walks and swims, and once, during that blazing summer of 1976, a Sunday bout of wrestling at the ground.

A couple of King's School pupils started a 'sponsored goals' scheme, where individuals and firms promised a cash sum for every goal the Silkmen scored. In return, the firms would receive free publicity via the Moss Rose loudspeakers during the games. Advertising hoardings around the pitch first made their appearance in 1979.

An attempt to hold a Sunday morning market outside the ground – such a venture had proven successful at Leek Town – fell foul of the council's ruling which adhered to the still extant Sunday Trading Act. After a first session which saw the market handing over a cash contribution to the club, the traders arrived at the spot adjacent to the London Road the following week to find that several council refuse wagons had blockaded the site. What ensued was a diversionary manoeuvre worthy of the master tacticians on the pitch. The traders moved *en bloc* to the railway station car park, where they gave the appearance of going their separate ways. As arranged, they waited an hour for the coast to clear, then reconvened at the ground, where the market enjoyed another lucrative half-day.

Despite the influx of cash, cost-cutting measures in those parsimonious 'seventies were still necessary. Thus began the club's Youth policy, whereby a stream of talented reserves were co-opted into the first team. Wilf Hall, by then a director, presented the rationale with the same lack of prevarication which had typified his goalkeeping:

> The policy I take is for youth pushing for the first team. Let's build our youth up … and save some money. (Club AGM February 1976)

Dave Connor, manager from 1976 until January 1978, did not spend a penny on transfer fees. The youngsters and non-contract players succeeded in reaching the Senior Cup final in 1977, but were no match for the powerful Northwich Victoria side of the time. On a day of wind and high rain at Gresty Road, Crewe, Macc. were comprehensively beaten 4–1.

The teams were:

*Northwich Victoria*: Hancock; Eccleshare, P. Jones, Wain, Nieman, K. Jones, Morry, Corrigan, Williams, King, Smith (Sub.: Collier)

*Macclesfield Town*: Lownds; Jukes, Booth, Green, Mobley, Gannon, Baber, Brennan, Heys, Boulton, Connor (Sub.: Crompton)

Of the Vics.' team Eccleshare and Collier were both ex-Silkmen. Mick Brennan was to follow them the next season. Graham Heys went to Altrincham, making the total amount accrued through transfer fees some £3,000.

Thus it was that by the end of the decade the board could boast that a deficit of £12,600 had been wiped clean. Moreover, in contrast to the decline and fall on the pitch, the razzle-dazzle peripherals reached new heights. Well-rehearsed cheer-leaders and a professional DJ were employed on match days. A lottery – first prize £1,000 – was launched, its objective to raise the cash for a projected £40,000 ground development. (The social club under the stand was finally opened in November 1978.)

Unfortunately in the short term the team, weakened by the stringent policies and off-loading of players, was to reach one of its lowest points of the century.

> Manager Dave Connor took part in the Macclesfield to Buxton and back sponsored run/walk in November 1977. He completed the 24-mile round trip in a highly creditable 2 hrs 40 mins.

## Annus horribilis

The extrovert Derek Partridge was manager for just six months, his tenure straddling the summer of 1978. A disastrous opening three weeks of the new season led the board into the arguably premature decision to dismiss him by mid-September.

Mossley had swamped Macc. 7–1 in the first round of the NPL Cup; one week later Marine came to the Moss Rose and ended any FA Cup run hopes, 4–2. That same week Runcorn inflicted a 6–0 humiliation in the league. Macc. would finish in bottom position, but avoided having to apply for re-election, ironically because in this of all seasons clubs were being selected for promotion to the long-awaited Alliance Premier League.

Macclesfield had applied, but it was no great surprise when they were turned down. History had wrong-footed the Silkmen: imagine the ease with which they would have been accepted had the creation of the Alliance been ten years earlier! The Northern Premier clubs creamed off for the inaugural APL were: Altrincham, Scarborough, Boston United, Stafford Rangers, Northwich Victoria, Bangor City, and Barrow. Runcorn were turned down because their ground did not meet the League standards (which disappointment was to have an echo closer to home some fifteen years later ...)

It was Altrincham who knocked out Macc. from that year's Cheshire Cup, 3–0, again in the first round. There was an exit at the same stage in the FA Trophy, more difficult to swallow as the victorious side was Witton Albion from the Cheshire League, the same team who had put them out of the Senior Cup the previous year. Manager of Witton was Brian Booth, whose brother Bob was on the Silkmen books. The Albion, who had won the Senior Cup that year, were about to be promoted into the NPL. (An attempt to bring Brian to the Moss Rose after Partridge's sacking had fallen through.)

At least the club was financially solvent once more. At the end of the season manager of eight months Phil Staley received a vote of confidence from the board. It was a firm enough foundation from which to rebuild.

# 2 0

# *The Brian Booth Effect*

'The board, Mr Booth and the players desperately need supporters to stop living in the past, and drawing comparisons with the "golden years". Judge them on what they've done in the five years since Macclesfield finished bottom of the Northern Premier League.'
*Express Advertiser* (5/1/84)

## *The £800 team*

Staley now set about rebuilding, basing what was to become a 15-strong first team squad on a 4–4–2 formation, with two attacking midfielders ready to break forward into orthodox wing positions. Notable acquisitions were Phil Marsden from Stafford Rangers – soon to be captain – Geoff Gay from Exeter City, Mike Sherlock, a 'keeper from Altrincham, and the striker Tibor Szabo, late of Bradford City. Sherlock and Marsden had cost £400 each; the rest were obtained on free transfers, or as non-contract players. It was Staley's boast that a team which had cost him £800 was worth £30,000 in real terms.

For a while the boast seemed justified. New Brighton were dismissed 7–1 away in the FA Cup. Here was proof positive, in case anybody still needed convincing, that Macc.'s Cheshire League days were firmly ensconced in the past. Szabo, instantly recognisable with his mop of dark hair and D'Artagnan beard, notched a hat-trick that day.

Geoff Gay scored one of his trademark forty-yarders in the 3–1 FA Trophy defeat of Witton Albion, at the time NPL leaders. The game was marred by crowd scuffles, a recurring and worsening theme over the next few years, until the clubs involved took measures to ensure segregation of fans.

In 1979–80 early league victories were overshadowed by a poor mid-season run, so that the final position was eighth, a comparative disappointment

given the early promise, and the diluted nature of that year's NPL.

In May 1980, to celebrate the tenth anniversary of the trip to Wembley, Beaumont's side was re-mustered to play the current first team. The youngsters won 4–2, but not without some inspiring memories from the veterans. The teams were:

*1980*: Simpson, Lucas, Nelson, Wardle, Higham, Mason, McClure, Markland, Szabo, Bradley, Perry (Sub.: Goodwin)
*1970*: Cooke, Berry, Bennett, Beaumont, Goalen, Roberts, Latham, B. Fidler, Young, Corfield, D. Fidler

The 1980 team were 3–0 up before Brian Fidler shook off the cobwebs and hit a couple, one of them a penalty. Scorers for the present side were Szabo, Perry, Bradley, and Goodwin.

Football being the cruel business that it is, Phil Staley's managership did not survive the first month of the following season. Already out of the FA Cup, losing 2–6 at Stalybridge, and with just one win in seven league games, the club decided it could wait no longer. Staley's second in command Jimmy Williams took over as coach/caretaker-manager, with a promise from the board that the permanent post awaited him if results justified it.

In the event by the following March chairman Alan Brocklehurst had fulfilled a long-cherished ambition by persuading the successful Witton

Albion manager, Brian Booth, to take up the reins at the Moss Rose. In the long term, it was to be an appointment every bit as significant as that of Frank Bowyer, twenty years before.

## *The plundering of Albion*

There was a happy omen in the first month of Booth's tenure. On the 24 March 1981 the all-weather 5-a-side pitch was officially opened by Manchester United manager Dave Sexton. Former Old Trafford star Alex Stepney kept goal for the local youngsters' penalty competition. Later on the atmosphere of 'Gala Night' continued with a 1–0 league victory over Burton Albion, the first win under the new manager.

Booth was a native Maxonian who had played for the Silkmen reserves back in the early ' seventies. Tenacious and forthright of character, he was quick to target the two areas that needed work: defence and fitness. Improvement in the first of these was soon targeted and implemented: in the final six matches of '80–'81, ten points were accrued, and only four goals conceded. By then Macc. had risen from the depths to a position in mid-table.

Fitness could be worked on over the summer. In the meantime Booth began bringing fancied players to the Moss Rose. For the new manager, and in the context of the NPL, this meant transferring the nucleus of his former club Witton Albion, who had been in the hunt for the championship the previous year.

Thus the defence was further strengthened by the arrival of Albion players David Moss and the returning Mick Brennan. Other Wincham Park *émigrés* were midfielder Mark Tansey, and the quick-turning forward Brian Griffin. By October they were joined by the 30-year-old Johnnie Walker, another forward; and the following September by John 'Chalkie' White, striker, for £750.

There had been a profit of over £1,700 from the previous season, largely thanks to Phil Staley's stringency. Thus it was possible for Booth to attract a clutch of players from across the APL and NPL. Kevin Keelan was brought from Mossley; Graham Tobin, the Altrincham defender, and Ben Seddon, the bearded centre-back from APL champions Runcorn, arrived within the year. Right-back Ian Elsby, who was to maintain a 100% appearance record, and receive the Player of the Year award for '81-'82, was another Booth acquisition.

As the *Express Advertiser* wryly observed:

Mr Booth is getting a better reputation for 'getting his man' than the Canadian Mounted Police. (15/7/82)

However, the cost of ground improvements – the 5-a-side area, the new changing rooms, and the injuries treatment clinic – meant that by mid-October 1981 the board had to instruct Booth to tighten his belt. Besides, results on the pitch had been worryingly erratic. (Embarrassingly, it was Witton who had knocked out Macc. from that year's FA Cup, 3–1 in the Preliminary Round.) The manager's reaction, potentially highly risky but with hindsight something of a master stroke, was to transfer list the entire first team squad. This showed the board his willingness to co-operate in cutting expenditure; it also appeared to be the short sharp shock the team needed.

Between October and March the analysis of all results, in cup and league competitions, reads as follows:

| P | W | D | L | F | A |
|---|---|---|---|---|---|
| 27 | 17 | 5 | 5 | 61 | 27 |

One of the five defeats was in the semi-final of the 1982 Cheshire Cup, 1–2 against Altrincham. It should be remembered, though, that the Robins were on the crest of a wave at the time. They

> The first ever sponsor's name to appear on Macc.'s playing strip was Sachs Dolmar UK, a firm based in Offerton, Stockport. This was in August 1981.

had been APL Champions for the past two years, and desperately unlucky not to be voted into the Football league. They had reached the Third Round proper of the FA Cup four years on the run – a record for a non-league club – collecting a string of Football League scalps on the way. In the circumstances the Silkmen acquitted themselves well.

The match took place at Witton, and the line-ups were:

*Altrincham*: Connaughton, Gardner, Davieson, Bailey, Cuddy, King, Allam, Heathcote, Johnson, Rogers, Howard (Sub.: Round)

*Macclesfield Town*: Simpson, Elsby, Fairclough, Wardle, Tobin, Marsden, Long, Gay, Griffin, Keelan, Walker (Sub.: Tansey)

Attacking midfielder Nigel Long put Macc. into the lead on 21 minutes. It took a flukey deflection off Rogers' shoulder to put Altrincham back in contention. Then, with ten minutes left, Wardle committed a rare error of hesitation enabling Johnson to steal the ball, run on and score. Altrincham won the final, beating Runcorn 1–0.

The Silkmen, with some justification now, began to set their sights on the Alliance.

Unfortunately their ambitions were to suffer a severe knock-back before the year was out.

## Storm and silver lining

In the '82–'83 FA Cup, after Bangor City had been dismissed 3–1 in the First Qualifying Round, the next opponents were Hyde United, away. It was a pulsating, high-scoring game, reminiscent of the classic confrontations between the two clubs. 1–2 down with fifteen minutes left, Hyde threw everything into attack. This left gaps at the back, which the visitors joyously exploited. Three goals in seven minutes, courtesy of Kersley, Keelan and Gay, ensured Macc.'s progress.

Next, Ashton United were beaten 2–0, again away. Kersley netted once more, with an impressive demonstration of speedy skills. From his own area, Griffin hefted a high ball upfield. In a continuous movement Kersley brought the lively ball under control by heading it down into his path, then darted in from the left to slide his shot past Senior, the Ashton 'keeper.

Two late Nigel Long goals in two minutes put paid to Stafford Rangers (3–1). Thus the club went on to play host to Worcester City of the APL in the First Round proper. It was the first time in seven years that the Silkmen had reached this stage.

What should have been a positive occasion, and a chance to assess the club's potential for the Alliance, turned out to be a black day indeed. Overcrowding in the main stand led to a low

peripheral wall collapsing, and running battles between rival groups of fans – again unsegregated. The folly spread to the players. A minute before half-time, with Macc. trailing 0–1, captain Phil Marsden was entrusted with a penalty. He hit the post, having sent the 'keeper the wrong way, and in the ensuing scrimmage appeared to give vent to his frustration by attacking the goalie. He was immediately sent off. Bereft of their captain for all of the second half, the home side conceded four more goals.

The club needed something to lift the spirits. The fillip was provided by a close-run race for the NPL Championship, and that season's League and Cheshire Cups.

There were now three points for a win, a bonus intended to stimulate attacking football. The Silkmen certainly responded: the 24 league wins was the highest since 1969, and the goal tally of 71 the healthiest for twelve years. The final position was fifth, albeit a long way behind runaway winners Gateshead.

The NPL Cup, now sponsored by Bass, never a source of much joy, at last stirred the imagination. The Town reached the final, played at Maine Road, Manchester, where they lost 1–2 in a tight struggle with Burton Albion. The Blues' equalising goal came four minutes into the second half: Kersley, after a typically vivid run over half the length of the pitch, centred for Keelan to head in. With just five minutes remaining, Fisher scored the winner for Albion, with another header. Immediately afterwards there was a further blow as Urquhart was stretchered off following a collision with the Burton goalkeeper.

Urquhart's replacement for the next week's Cheshire Cup Final at Crewe was 'Chalkie' White.

The Cheshire Cup run had accounted for Nantwich (2–0), and then, in round two, there had been a magnificent 2–1 away win over reigning APL Champions Runcorn. Then it was back to Runcorn for the semi, when Witton Albion were beaten 3–1.

The opponents in the final were Congleton Town, then in the North-West Counties League. Theoretically a cakewalk for the Silkmen, the tie with a spirited Congleton side was however a struggle from start to finish. A goal behind after three minutes, it took well over an hour for the equaliser to be scored by substitute Goodwin. Then, with barely seconds left, the quick-thinking White headed a half-cleared ball back over the Congleton defence and stranded 'keeper. It sneaked in just under the bar for the winning goal.

The teams were:

*Macclesfield Town*: Eales, Elsby, Fairclough, Tobin, Seddon, Marsden, Long, White, Griffin, Keelan, Kersley (Sub.: Goodwin – for Griffin 70)

*Congleton Town*: Ryder, Price, Bossens, Clack, Scholes, Drew, Moran, Shaw, Biddle, Jennings, Vickers (Sub.: Jepson)

It was the first trophy for ten years. Here was palpable evidence that the corner had been turned at last.

## 'Macc. will go places'

There followed two more FA Cup runs as far as the First Round proper. Although the Blues were eliminated on both occasions, the manner of the two defeats was as different as could be.

In 1983–84, the attack ran riot in the qualifying rounds, demolishing Tamworth (6–1 away, with Keelan scoring four), Marine (3–0 away), Congleton (6–0), and Horwich (4–3 after a 0–0 draw). In the First Round they were drawn at home against York City, who were already disappearing into the distance at the top of the Fourth Division.

In front of a Moss Rose crowd of 4,300 the Football League side were subjected to early sustained pressure, but they weathered the storm and kept the score goalless. Back at Bootham Crescent York demonstrated their superiority by winning 2–0. The *Express Advertiser* declared the Yorkshire team 'well worth their win'.

No such sentiments would be expressed by anyone connected with Macclesfield the following year, when the opponents in the First Round were Port Vale, at home.

The Potteries side, who would finish mid-table in that season's Fourth Division, brought with them a couple of thousand of their notorious supporters. Mindful of this reputation, the club had extra police drafted in for the match. All to no avail: after White had put Macc. in front with a third minute penalty, and the home team had kept this lead until the interval, the visiting fans decided to put their oar in. Just after the restart they gathered to form a crush behind the pub end goal, which Macclesfield were defending. Before too long the wall collapsed, and the game had to be stopped for nearly a quarter of an hour whilst injured spectators were stretchered away. It was almost like a macabre rehearsal for another similar, but larger scale and ultimately far graver, disaster in Brussels six months later. On that November day at the Moss Rose, happily there were no serious injuries. It was possibly an attempt to get the match abandoned; if so, it failed, but it was noteworthy that when play was resumed much of the Silkmen's concentration had evaporated. Despite a late spirited rally from the home side, Port Vale went on to score twice and win the tie.

The President's Cup – played for on a two-legged knock-out basis by the top eight teams in the NPL – once more brought the Blues to the brink of success. Although dismissed in the first round by Hyde in 1983–84, the next season saw Macc. progress to the final with Rhyl. A 0–0 at the Moss was followed by a 2–0 victory for the Welshmen.

In January 1984 Brian Booth – after finishing runner-up on innumerable occasions – was finally awarded the NPL manager of the month title. Macc.'s twelve-goal 100% spree throughout the four weeks had settled matters.

There were four important signings during the summer of '84. From Stafford Rangers came striker Steve Burr, and from the same club the experienced midfielder Stewart Chapman, team captain before long. Goalkeeper Alan Zelem was given a trial in the pre-season friendlies, and impressed enough to command a first team place for the subsequent campaign. Ex-England Universities player Bob Askey, son of the Colin who was on Leake's squad in the early 'sixties, partnered Burr. Completing a family affair reminiscent of the Thornleys in the 1930's (see Chapter 11), Bob's brother John would be a regular first team choice within a year or two. It was Bob who scored a hat-trick in the season's first game, a 4–2 win at Buxton.

1984–85 was the year of the scramble for the NPL title, with a gaggle of teams in contention throughout the season. Just before Easter the top of the table looked like this:

|  | P | W | D | L | F | A | Pts |
|---|---|---|---|---|---|---|---|
| Witton Albion | 29 | 17 | 5 | 7 | 47 | 27 | 56 |
| Macclesfield Town | 28 | 15 | 10 | 3 | 43 | 24 | 55 |
| Hyde United | 32 | 16 | 7 | 9 | 51 | 38 | 55 |
| Stafford Rangers | 27 | 16 | 5 | 6 | 53 | 28 | 53 |

On Good Friday Macc. beat Workington 3–1, an occasion on which West Ham scout Stuart Diamond gave his opinion that 'Macclesfield Town would go places'. This was followed by a nerve-shredding 1–0 away win over major rivals Stafford, Steve Burr hitting the vital goal. Goalkeeper Zelem gave a brilliant display that day,

crowning the achievement with a one-handed save in the fourth minute of injury time. The Blues were back in the hunt.

But nothing could stop Stafford's finishing burst. The Silkmen lost at Bangor, then could only draw 2–2 at home with Southport. (It was to be the high number of Macc. draws – thirteen in all – that would swing the title the Rangers' way.) On the Tuesday of the final week of the season hopes were raised by a 3–2 home win over Morecambe. Then the news came from Goole: Stafford had clung onto a 2–1 lead, gaining them the three points that put them out of reach. Runners-up was the Town's best position for fifteen years; promotion to the APL was surely only a matter of time.

It was in the dressing room after the final match of the season – a 1–0 win at Worksop – that Booth dropped the bombshell: he would be quitting the game, on doctor's orders. He had already suffered a mild heart attack in February 1983, forcing him to stay away from the Moss Rose until that summer.

His parting comment for the benefit of the press looks now like a beacon of sanity, at the very onset of the darkest half-decade in the history of the English game:

I've lived, loved and breathed football for the past twenty years or so I've been a manager, but the game's not worth dying for. *Express Advertiser* (9/5/85)

His time at the club shows evidence of a distinctive, often empirical style of managership. His use of psychology – both kid glove and iron fist variety – was little short of sustained genius. Bob Askey, writing in a match programme in February 2000, recalled how Booth suggested he be more demonstrative after scoring a goal: 'maybe taking off his shirt and throwing it to the fans'. There was a touching testament to the players' loyalty when the manager announced his retirement from the game after the Worksop win: their first reaction was to ask what they had done wrong. The well-spring of this response was Booth's initial loyalty *to* his squad.

It was this balanced working relationship with his players that went a long way towards the achievement of an exemplary disciplinary record, one of the factors which led to Booth receiving the NPL Manager of the Year award for 1984–85.

At first glance his legacy to the club appears to pale beside the more arresting achievements of Wragg and McIlroy. Indeed, in terms of trophies won, the four years have a threadbare look. But look beyond the mere collection of silverware to the more intangible concerns of spirit and self-belief. Most crucially of all, under Booth the mind-set that had habitually funnelled back to the 'golden age', to the detriment of present endeavours, was at long last consigned to history. A club that six years before had considered, however briefly, returning to the Cheshire League was now knocking on the door of the Alliance (soon to be renamed the GM Vauxhall Conference). From now on, the club was dealing in futures.

# Climbing the Pyramid

'I can't wait for August to arrive. I just feel it's going to be a great year for us.'
Steve Burr, Macc. striker (May 1986)

## Peter Wragg arrives

Booth, as successor Neil Griffiths discovered, was a hard act to follow. Griffiths was a back four player of considerable ability, and he would often include himself in the starting line-up. He displayed energy, enthusiasm and a thorough knowledge of the game. In the area of man-management, however, at which his predecessor had excelled, there is evidence that he still had something to learn.

The 1985–86 season had started with much promise. The Blues set an early hot pace at the top of the NPL, now termed the Multipart League. Two whirlwind 7–2 victories within a week or so of each other (against Caernarfon and Horwich RMI) strengthened the position. In the First Round proper of the FA Cup Hartlepool of the Fourth Division were run ragged, but were able to cling on to a 2–1 lead. The Macc. goal was scored by John Askey, standing in for injured brother Bob.

Then the rot set in. A string of flaccid home defeats saw the league lead seep away. There was an unexpected exit from the FA Trophy at the hands of Leek Town (1–2), although on that soggily depressing January day, as *Express Advertiser* reporter Mike Woods pointed out, the pitch curtailed much in the way of proper football:

> ... a mammoth bed of pâté, add to that a skimming of treacle, a few generous heaps of Christmas pudding, topped off with a thick coating of porridge. (23/1/86)

Not even the treacle helped.

Within a month, as tales of dressing room arguments filtered through to the press, and after a 1–5 reverse at Morecambe, the club directorate, as ever impatient for the breakthrough everyone felt was imminent, dismissed Neil Griffiths. Caretaker manager for a couple of weeks was secretary Roy Campbell. Then, the club's second brilliant managerial *coup* within five years: Peter Wragg, Hyde United's boss, was persuaded to up sticks and take over at the Moss Rose.

The new manager was an effervescent, talkative individual, but never one to allow the sizzle to supplant the steak. He had a deep understanding of the game's tactical needs, for example – to consolidate a lead – switching from a 4–3–3 line-up to a 4–4–2 during a match with a perceptive use of substitutes. He was approachable too: he launched a 'fans' forum' held in the Moss Rose social club, at which he invited supporters to come and air their views. He also wrote a weekly column for the local newspaper: 'Wragg Time', later re-titled, with the requisite touch of *gravitas*, 'From the Manager's Desk'.

He was to spend just £1,500 in transfer fees during his first two years. His acquisitions, though few, were exactly right: Mike Lake, a young midfielder from Curzon Ashton; Trevor Brissett, a Witton Albion back four player; and, canniest move of the lot, Elfyn Edwards – 'Mr Reliable' – from Wrexham. Edwards had played sweeper, but Wragg, in another shrewd strategic ploy, now used him, as captain, as a mobile midfield man.

In his first full season in charge, Wragg led the Silkmen to an unprecedented treble of NPL trophies.

## High noon at Hyde

The season that was eventually to lift into the stratosphere spent a long time on the runway. The club sustained a severe blow before a pre-season match when the car carrying four first team members was involved in a serious smash. Ian Elsby, Nigel Shaw, Steve Waddington and Trevor Brissett fortunately survived the collision, but their injuries were such that a large proportion of the squad was effectively lost for the foreseeable future. Shaw (broken arm) and Waddington (cracked ribs) were to return to match fitness before the end of the season. Elsby and Brissett (back and leg injuries) were hospitalised for longer, and would not play again for a considerable time.

In the short term, dismissals from the FA Cup, the FA trophy and the Cheshire Cup, each at the first hurdle, did not bode well. The Cheshire Cup defeat was inflicted by Runcorn (0–2 away), which side was well into its five-in-a-row spree in this competition. Macc. would meet them in the final, twice, very soon.

The 1986–87 Multipart League showed the Town theoretically in contention by the end of February:

|                  | P  | W  | D | L | F  | A  | Pts |
|------------------|----|----|---|---|----|----|-----|
| Bangor City      | 30 | 20 | 6 | 4 | 58 | 24 | 66  |
| Marine           | 28 | 16 | 6 | 6 | 57 | 29 | 54  |
| Macclesfield Town| 29 | 15 | 8 | 6 | 50 | 34 | 53  |
| Caernarfon       | 27 | 14 | 9 | 4 | 45 | 24 | 51  |

It was at this stage that Macc. started to put together a remarkable unbeaten sequence, as their rivals' charge began to waver.

A 4–0 win over Hyde United in the quarter-finals of the NPL Challenge Cup (scorers Burr, Shaw, Hardman and Lake) set them up for a two-legged semi with Caernarfon. A 5–2 aggregate win set the scene for an intriguing final at Maine Road with Burton Albion (now managed by Brian

Graham Tobin (left, arms up) cannons in a last minute header against Hartlepool. FA Cup First Round 1985–86. The ball hits the bar and the League team scrape a 2–1 win. (*Macclesfield Express*)

Fidler), the club who had beaten them the last time they had reached this stage.

Another two-legged semi victory, this time against Worksop in the President's Cup, meant that, with their thrilling late run in the league, the club found itself with possibly the most crucial week's fixtures in its history:

Friday 24 April: NPL Cup Final *v.* Burton Albion

Sunday 26 April: Final, President's Cup, first leg (A) *v.* Marine

Tuesday 28 April: final home league game *v.* Burton Albion

Thursday 30 April: Final, President's Cup, second leg (H) *v.* Marine

Saturday 2 May: final league game *v.* Hyde United (A)

After everything that had happened that season, the climax was sheer *Roy of the Rovers.*

The team, unchanged for the week: Zelem, Roberts, Shaw, Edwards, Tobin, Hardman, Lake, Waddington, J. Askey, Burr, Hanlon

First, the NPL Final. After a nondescript first half Elfyn Edwards, in one of his best games ever for the club, took firm control of the midfield. It was a breakaway goal via a well-flighted clearance from Hardman which opened the scoring. The pass found John Askey with a modicum of space deep in enemy territory. The striker evaded a clumsy tackle, ran on a few yards and cracked one in from the edge of the box. With two minutes left it was Askey again, from sixteen yards. Thus the NPL Cup came to Macclesfield for the first (and as it transpired, only) time. Edwards and coach Dave Denby went through their 'gimme ten' routine, and Wragg danced in the middle of the Maine Road pitch. Chairman Alan Brocklehurst's jubilant prediction: 'This is only the beginning.'

Two days later the Silkmen travelled to Crosby to contest the first leg of the final of the President's Cup. A disciplined defence did the necessary, keeping the score to 0–0. So far, so good.

Next it was Burton Albion again, in the

Steve Burr, John Askey, Nigel Shaw and (front) Elfyn Edwards celebrate the year of the treble (1986–87). (*Macclesfield Express*)

penultimate league match. Interest was kept alive with another 2–0 win.

Now Bangor City and Macclesfield had one game each left to play. The Silkmen had a lead of just one point, but Bangor's last game was at home against South Liverpool, one the Welsh side were expected to win. So, on the Thursday of that unforgettable week, as the Town faced Marine in the second leg of the President's Cup final, there was many a worried glance at the subtext of the game over at Bangor.

Macc. went behind early on to a penalty. Despite an equaliser on the night from Nigel Shaw, as away goals counted double it looked as though Marine were about to steal a march. Then, with seconds remaining, John Askey netted a crisp

NPL Cup winners 1987 at Maine Road, Manchester. Macc. 2, Burton Albion 0. (*Macclesfield Express*)

twenty-yarder, and the second trophy in six days was Moss Rose-bound.

The only downside to the evening was the news from Bangor: the City had won, restoring their lead to two points. Nothing less than a win at Hyde would now do.

Hyde United were a mid-table side, but with the best attack in the league. Major threat was Simon Rudge, and it was from this striker that Alan Zelem made two typically brave saves early on. After that first dicey ten minutes, though, the Silkmen took charge. A tactic introduced and honed by Wragg was Edwards' heading-on from corners and set pieces, shifting the focus of the attack. Midway through the first half just such a manoeuvre forced Hyde 'keeper into an error: he palmed the ball away, straight into the path of Burr, whose low shot found the net.

On 64 minutes it was Edwards himself who headed his side further into the lead. Close to the end Lake set off John Askey on a classic wing run and bewilderingly fast cross into Burr's stride, and the striker scored the third from close range. A last-minute penalty converted by Hyde was an irrelevance. Macc. were Multipart League Champions, and so promoted to the Vauxhall Conference. Hyde's artificial pitch was the scene of an impromptu party.

## *Giant-killers*

The very same season ('86–'87) the Football League had decreed that winning the Conference would mean automatic promotion to the Fourth Division, subject to ground conditions. At long last the re-election farce had been brought to an end, and the club path from non-league obscurity to the higher echelons was, at least in theory, clear-cut.

In the meantime, Macclesfield Town FC were addressing the problem of the increased expenditure that their promotion would necessitate. There would be further to travel, some matches requiring an overnight stop. Ground improvements were on the agenda: during the next year the Spion Kop would slowly disappear beneath row after row of terracing. An enhanced playing squad would be a further drain on the coffers. That summer saw the arrival of defender David Grant, 133-game veteran of Sheffield Wednesday. The following year leading Conference goalscorer Phil Derbyshire, at a club record fee of £6,000, came from Stafford Rangers.

As usual, the club met the challenge. A draw organised during the close season, based on house-to-house calls, showed a healthy profit. Ex-Manchester United star Gordon Hill, who now ran a sports shop in the town, presented the winner's cheque.

Sponsorship was further developed. The financial support of individual matches, introduced on an occasional basis some years before, now became a more regular feature. Macclesfield Tile Centre backed the first ever Conference game, against Maidstone in August. Match ball and player sponsorship was also launched that year.

The bulk of the money, though, came from another stirring FA Cup run, roughly echoing the one of twenty years before. Macc. reached the Third Round again, demolishing two Football League teams *en route*. The total of goals scored in the competition was 24, the most by any team that year.

The First Qualifying Round saw the Town defeat Kevin Keelan's Stalybridge Celtic 5–1 in a replay. The Silkmen then again hit five in disposing of North-West Counties side Chadderton. The gallop was halted in the next round as they could only draw at home against Marine. Then in the replay, in the rain and wind of seaside Crosby, they progressed 2–1, courtesy of goals from Keith Mountford (one of Booth's last signings) and Burr.

Peter Wragg, manager 1986–93. (*Macclesfield Express*)

Then the final obstacle to the competition proper was Whitby, at home. The visitors took the lead early on, then Mountford equalised before half-time. Late in the match Grant thumped in a free kick which the goalkeeper could only parry into the net. With three minutes left Burr delivered a perfectly-weighted through ball to Askey, who after a typically powerful run, cracked in a

Steve Burr scores Macc.'s first ever Conference goal, against Maidstone, 22 August 1987. (*Macclesfield Express*)

fierce shot to make it 3–1.

Opponents in the First Round were Carlisle United of the Fourth Division. The 3,000 crowd at the Moss Rose were treated to a game of almost non-stop attacks from both sides. The Town were 0–1 down after a quarter of an hour, then fell further behind early in the second half. Within three minutes Hardman had reduced the arrears; six minutes later Burr set up Askey who levelled the scores; and after that the home side exploited their clear superiority. Mountford's cross found Tobin, who headed Macc. into the lead, and in the final minutes Burr made it four.

Norman Hunter's Rotherham – also of the Fourth Division – were the Second Round opposition, again at the Moss Rose. It was a Sunday game, and the first one at which a video camera was used, in anticipation of crowd trouble. Extra barriers at a cost of £2,000 had been erected; money well spent, as the match passed off peaceably enough. On the pitch, there was an interesting reversal of supposed roles: the unimaginative, physical Football League outfit succumbed to a Conference side displaying a degree of subtlety quite beyond the visitors. The Blues finished 4–0 winners, with Steve Burr running through his range of skills to grab a hat-trick. A bemused Hunter conceded: 'There was only one team in it. Macclesfield were a different class.'

The draw for the Third Round was a disappointment to Wragg, as there was to be no glamour fixture with one of the high rollers. Third Division Port Vale, away, was the tie. It was another Sunday match, in front of a Vale Park crowd of 10,800 of whom it was estimated over a third had made the short trip south from Macclesfield. In a tense, parsimonious game the Town held out until five minutes from time. Then thoughts of a replay were dashed when Darren Hughes crossed from the wing, and the 18-year-old Finney dived forward full-length and met the ball brilliantly with his head (or flukily with his shoulder, depending on where your allegiance lay) and for the first time Zelem was beaten.

The teams were:

*Port Vale*: Grew; Steggles, Hughes, Walker, Banks, Sproson, Ford, Finney, Riley, Beckford, Hamson (Subs: Earle, Maguire)
*Macclesfield Town*: Zelem; Roberts, Grant, Edwards, Tobin, Hanlon, J. Askey, Shaw, Lake, Burr, Mountford (Subs: B. Askey, Hardman)

As a footnote, the Vale were then drawn against Tottenham Hotspur in the next round, a tie which the Potteries team won 2–1!

## Five Cheshire Cup finals

Conference teams from the county were exempt from the Senior Cup until the quarter-final stage, which partly explains why the nine finals of 1984–92 were contested by just six clubs:

John Askey (no. 7) scores with a glancing header against Lincoln in the Conference. (*Macclesfield Express*)

*Above* Elfyn Edwards lifts the Cheshire Cup 1991. (This was win no. 16). (*Macclesfield Express*)
*Below* Cheshire Cup Winners 1992. (John Rooney)

Runcorn, the Vics., Altrincham, Witton Albion, Macc., and the one interloper from a lower league, Hyde United. After losing the '84 final to Northwich, Runcorn then strung together five wins in a row. It was Macclesfield who were on the receiving end of the last two: 1–2 at Crewe, then 1–3 at the Drill Field.

The following year (1990) the Blues reached the final again, when it was felt that the omens were in their favour. It was exactly one hundred years since the first Senior Cup win, that glorious 4–1 scotching of Nantwich. Even the venue of the Drill Field was the same. Opposition in the final were Hyde United of the HFS Loans League, which was what the NPL was now called. Surely the Cheshire Cup was as good as in the Moss rose cabinet?

Alas, no: Hyde adapted well to the dusty, rockhard pitch and scored the game's only goal. It came after thirteen minutes, and to rub it in the scorer was Joe Connor, brother of Macc. defender Jim.

The next year, after a superb extra-time victory over Altrincham in a two-legged semi, the Silkmen met Witton Albion in the final. Witton were no slouches themselves, having just stormed away with the HFS Loans League title, and put the wind up Kidderminster in two close FA Trophy semis.

This time the match took place at Crewe, and with the change of venue came a welcome change of fortune: Macc. won 2–0, with goals by supporters' Player of the Year John Askey, and Graham Tobin. Both strikes came from precisely-placed free kicks: Askey volleying home from Heesom, and Tobin with a header from Shepherd.

Then the opponents in the '92 final were Witton again. After a 1–1 draw at Tranmere, the

Figurehead of the early Conference years, Steve Burr notched 65 league goals in four seasons.
(*Macclesfield Express*)

Blues won 2–0 in the replay at Northwich. Goalscorers were Askey again, this time with a header, and Hanlon who stabbed in a close-range shot.

But we are getting ahead of the main story. We must now go back a few seasons to pick up the Conference thread, and follow the Silkmen to another Wembley appearance.

# 22

# A Foothold in the Conference

'How can we be letting the fans down after the four years we have had? Anywhere else and
the achievements of this team would go down in folk lore.'
Peter Wragg (4/4/90)

## Wembley again

The FA Trophy, barren territory for several years, at last came good in 1988–89. The beginning was none too auspicious, Macc. being held to 2–2 with Marine. Then in the replay at the Moss Rose a clear 4–1 win, with Graham Tobin heading two, saw the Blues progress. Teesside outfit South Bank were next, beaten 3–0 away.

Gravesend and Northfleet, conquerors of both Barnet and Kettering in earlier rounds, were the visitors in round three. At the time the Town were riding high at the top of the Conference, and a well-nigh perfect February (for which Wragg was to win the Manager of the Month award for the third time) was garnished with a 2–0 win over the Kent team. Scorers were Paul Kendall, and Burr with a powerful header. In the quarter-final a single goal from new signing John Timmons was enough to dismiss Welling United.

It was around this time that the vogue for inflatable bananas hit north-west football grounds. Whilst reaching epidemic proportions at Manchester City, the fad was soon supplanted by regional variations (pink panthers, black puddings, rainbow trout, and see below). Macclesfield, of course, rose magnificently to the occasion with inflatable royal blue silkworms (£5 each).

Local musician Arthur Wakefield composed a song – *We're On Our Way To Wembley* – which was recorded by the squad involved in the FA Trophy Final of 1989. It was released as a single on cassette by 'The Silkmen', but failed to chart nationally.

Thus it was that the Moss Rose was treated to the sight of brandished banks of oversized silkworms and penguins when Dartford came for the second leg of the semi-final. The first leg had produced no goals, and naturally there were worrying memories of the last semi meeting of the two teams, when Dartford had won their away leg. Indeed, the Southern League side scored first, but within a few minutes Burr equalised with a diving header. This was the first goal the visitors had conceded in the whole of that season's FA Trophy competition. In the second half the Silkmen put on a virtuoso performance, scoring three more without reply. John Askey hit in a rebound, then it was Burr again in one of those fast-reaction close-in situations he relished. Finally John Timmons, with a cleverly-glanced looping header that dropped beyond the goalkeeper into the net, made it 4–1. Impromptu community singing, led and conducted by Wragg, greeted the win.

That date – 15 April 1989 – has other connotations in football history, of course. Suffice it to say that, as elsewhere in the country, whatever celebrations there might have been turned cold as there filtered through on the media that evening the full horror of the Hillsborough disaster.

Silkmen 1991. (*Macclesfield Express*)

That afternoon's lasting, nationwide, seismic shock, which was eventually to polarise into litigation and resolutions, was to have repercussions at the Moss Rose too. Throughout the renovation of the ground during the following decade, safety concerns were to be highest on the agenda. After the publication of the Taylor Report, criteria for the upgrading of grounds were to become more stringent; and this would have a crucial knock-on effect for the ambitions of Macclesfield Town in the mid-nineties.

More immediately, the Silkmen shaped up for a Wembley FA Trophy Final against Telford United, the opponents of nineteen years before. The Blues travelled to London with some optimism: Edwards was back after injury, the United had lost both league matches with Macc. that season, and the bookies had made the Cheshire side firm favourites.

The line-ups were:

*Macclesfield Town*: Zelem; Roberts, Hardman, Edwards, Tobin, Hanlon, J. Askey (Derbyshire 51), Timmons, Lake, Burr, Imrie (Kendall 85)

*Telford United*: Charlton; Lee, Wiggins, Mayman (Crawley 65), Brindley, Hancock, Joseph, Granger, Lloyd, Stringer (Griffiths 105), Nelson

Telford, canny veterans of a record five trophy Finals including this one, and with the stingiest defence in the Conference, set about hunkering down and nullifying the strong Silkmen attack. Macc. had most of the play, but the United held out until the end of normal time. Then, on 96 minutes, Zelem made the crucial, and wholly untypical, error. An optimistic long ball had been hefted from deep, and with no apparent immediate danger Zelem left his line to collect. But the 'keeper had misread the flight of the ball, which bounced cruelly beyond him. Crawley with his fresh substitute's legs raced in ahead of Tobin and scored. It was the winning goal.

## Ground-share with Chester

Assuming the role of beaten finalists was becoming a habit: the Cheshire Cup (see last Chapter), and the 1990 Staffs. Senior Trophy, eventually conceded 2–3 in extra time to the Vics., were events of programme-wringing frustration.

At least the club finances were healthy. In the early 'nineties cash flowed in from several sources. The Star Lane practice pitch was sold off to the Templar Housing Association for £200,000, to make way for the present flats. Mike Lake went to Sheffield United for £40,000, – a club record – with another £20,000 promised should the midfield man chalk up 50 first team appearances. (He did.) The United rose from the Third Division to the old First in successive years, owing a lot to Lake's contribution. Steve Burr left for Hednesford

(£12,000), and a number of Football League scouts came to watch John Askey and 6ft 6ins (1m 95) goalkeeper Steve Farrelly. Wragg priced Askey at £100,000 and Farrelly at £80,000. The fairly unsubtly-coded message was: 'Hands off!'

Satellite TV was beginning to make its appearance in the Conference. Runcorn and Macc. shared the £2,500 from their match in April 1991.

Another major windfall occurred from the fact that Chester City, at the time in the old Third Division, whilst waiting for their new Deva stadium to be built, would be without a ground for two seasons. The Cestrians were panicking, as one by one their contingency plans for the two limbo years fell through. Then Macclesfield came forward at the eleventh hour to offer the Moss Rose.

Elfyn Edwards with mascot, and an arch of inflatable silkworms. Conference 1988–89. (*Macclesfield Express*)

Perks would be a rent of £40,000 per year, and a package of seating and ground safety improvements, to be installed at Chester's expense. The process was seen as the laying of a firmer foundation to support the Silkmen's advance towards Football League status.

The downside was that once more Macc. had to postpone the re-launch of their reserve side, and that for the next two years access to the pitch for training purposes was of necessity restricted.

But so far the tide had not turned for Wragg and his team: fourth in the Conference 1989–90 after leading for some time, and a brace of Cheshire Senior Cups, kept optimism alive.

'The Blues' social club, opened late 1980s. (*Macclesfield Express*)

## Thrust and parry

Wragg continued to rule in lively, volatile style. There was the occasional fine or banishment to the stands for his outbursts to match officials, but he was never one to wear his heart anywhere other than on his sleeve. Intransigently supportive of his players, and yet prone to the odd touchline burst of invective, he seemed for a while to thrive on criticism. After the ignominious exit from the FA Cup at the hands of supposed donkeys Gretna, a section of the crowd set up a chant of 'Wragg – out!' The manager's typically irrepressible response was to stand in the centre circle and applaud the fans. For the next home match he took his place on the bench wearing a safety helmet.

The fans' forums continued, as did the newspaper column. One item unique to Wragg was the annual list of jokey Christmas presents to players and fans, which ranged from the obscure to the risqué. To the supporters in '89 he wished: 'long memories, good times, and something shiny'. The following year for captain Elfyn Edwards he proposed a bra: 'He wants to get used to handling cups again'.

Most important signings of the later Wragg years were: George Shepherd, a back four player from Hyde; the 20-year-old Darren Heesom, another defender, formerly of Altrincham; and the talented left-back Stuart Bimson from Southport. Filling the striker's gap left by Burr's departure was proving difficult, but the manager made an inspired buy in the summer of '92 by acquiring the 18-year-old Richie Mitchell from Port Vale. Stuart Leicester, a left-sided attacker, arrived from Stalybridge Celtic; John Timmons dropped back into midfield, from where he launched many a dangerous attack. He was partnered by the precise and quietly effective Colin Lambert. Neil Sorvel made his debut in '92–'93, initially released from Crewe for Macc.'s FA Cup games.

Yet the Conference situation deteriorated. In 1991–92 the Town sank to thirteenth, scoring a

Alan Zelem (top) and Graham Tobin deal with an
Altrincham attack. Christmas week, 1988.
(*Macclesfield Express*)

Mike Lake chats with supporters at Wembley, FA Trophy
Final 1989. (*Macclesfield Express*)

public his belief that:

> This club is years away from the Football
> League. Your expectations are too high.
> *Express Advertiser* (18/3/92)

Towards the end there was a mounting tide of
criticism from the public, some of it veiled, some
more confrontational. At the outset of '92–'93,
Wragg himself admitted to a certain degree of
'lethargy'.

Nonetheless, his final year in charge of Macclesfield Town was the football equivalent of a ride
on Blackpool's Big One.

mere fifty goals, their lowest since the mid-seven-
ties doldrums. It was possibly at one of the fans'
forums, in March 1992, that Wragg inadvertently
implied that henceforth his days at the Moss Rose
were numbered. In his unequivocal way he made

Mark Dempsey, first team player of
the early 1990's, had been a child
TV star, appearing in *Potter's Picture
Palace.*

Burr, Hanlon and Timmons attack the Telford goal. FA Trophy Final 1989. Result: Macc. 0, Telford United 1. (*Macclesfield Express*)

Steve Hanlon, attack-minded midfielder, scores the winner vs. Northwich Vics. Cheshire Senior Cup semi, First Leg, at the Drill Field, 1988. (*Macclesfield Express*)

## Swan song

It started with one of Macc.'s last great FA Cup runs as a non-league club. The overture was quiet enough, with a couple of 1–0 wins over Glossop and Horwich. It was in the Fourth Qualifying Round that things began to liven up: Netherfield were brought back from their muddy Kendal home (1–1) to be eclipsed 5–0 at the Moss Rose. With a run of eight wins and three draws Wragg received – for the last time – the Conference Manager of the Month award.

Opponents in the First Round were Chesterfield of the new DivisionThree, at home. The Silkmen laid siege to the Chesterfield goal, but the League side survived in a goalless draw. Lee Turnbull, the Derbyshire team's forward, admitted: 'We've had a roasting'.

Back at the Recreation Ground, though, things would surely be different? Not so: with sublime impertinence, Macc. took the game to their op-

ponents. After just four minutes a probing pass from Timmons found Richie Mitchell, who swept a close-range shot into the net. Turnbull hit back for the Spireites mid-way through the half with an acrobatic bicycle kick which found the top corner. The score remained the same until the end of normal time.

Then a Timmons-Lambert manoeuvre found the unmarked Mitchell, who restored the Silkmen's lead. Unfortunately the 'golden goal' concept was still some years in the future, and the home side were able to scrape an equaliser through a Steve Williams back-header.

And so to penalties. Mitchell took the first, and netted with the minimum of fuss. Chesterfield scored theirs, then Lambert missed his. The home side then went 2–1 up, and although Bimson made it 2–2, the odds were clearly now in the Football League team's favour.

Recording *We're on our Way to Wembley* 1989. Peter Wragg tests the mike for Steve Burr. (It is reported that Jive Bunny had no fear of being upstaged.). (*Macclesfield Express*)

Andy Green, striker. 9 Conference goals 1991–92.
(*Macclesfield Express*)

What ensued must go down as one of the finest individual performances of any Silkman ever. The giant Steve Farrelly made three consecutive, brilliantly anticipatory saves, rendering the last kick irrelevant, and ensuring that his side progressed to a home Round Two tie with Stockport County. The team at Chesterfield was:

S. Farrelly; Shepherd, Bimson, Edwards, Kendall, McMahon, Askey, Timmons (M. Farrelly 120), Lambert, Mitchell, Leicester (Sub.: Sorvel)

The same team was kept for the game with County, who at the time were pushing for promotion from DivisionTwo. The result was a 0–2 defeat, despite the Town once more having much of the play. Stockport scored from a counter-attack on just two minutes, and thereafter a clinical defence stifled all Macc.'s endeavours.

Meanwhile the Conference performances were sliding rapidly downhill. After losing 0–1 to Stafford Rangers in February, the Blues were actually

Singular local poet William Arthur Magee (1908–92), as reported in the *Express Advertiser* of 1/4/92, was moved to pen the following on the occasion of the Silkmen's return from Fulham:

No hero ever earned (or reaped)
A richer accolade,
Nor needed they
A ceremonial sword
To dub them worthy.

For thousands came
To pay them homage
And respect,
Their fluttering expressive
Arms upraised,
Their lusty chant and cheer
Planting a township's honour
Firmly, square, upon their shoulders:
Shoulders unbowed
In moment of defeat.

Their dignity superb
In crisis, ne'er left them
When proud lady luck
Deserted them,
But left their conquerors
With the knowledge in their hearts
That they themselves were hollow victors.

Play on then
'Lads of Silk'
Your prowess shall remain,
And you shall be heard of,
After you are gone;
When Sportsmen of the Town
Shall tell of Silktown's
Moral victory.

One unusual detail given by the newspaper was that Mr Magee passed away on the very day of publication.

bottom, for the first time since their promotion in 1987. A series of 1–1 draws gave them a lifeline, which appeared to be severed as they went down 0–2 to Bromsgrove in April. Now they needed seven points from the last three games to be certain of survival. The next two results – a win and a draw – would have given some hope, were it not for the fact that the last game was away against Champions-elect Wycombe. The Wanderers were leading the Conference by a record fifteen points, and they were about to add the FA Trophy to their collection in this their final non-league year. Macc. had to beat them to avoid the drop. Surely not even Wragg could pull this one off?

The result: 1–0 to Macclesfield. The only goal of the game was a solo effort from the Town's Roy Green, an ex-Wolves striker brought to the club two months previously in an attempt to beef up the attack.

Phil Power in full flight. (*Macclesfield Express*)

An obviously relieved Wragg said afterwards: I'm going to have a pint and enjoy the result. What happens next is anybody's guess.

Richie Mitchell, Conference sharpshooter. A dozen goals in the first half of 1992–93. (*Macclesfield Express*)

Stuart Leicester – 7 Conference goals in 1992–93. (*Macclesfield Express*)

Stuart Bimson (right). Defensive stalwart – 137 starts between 1991–95. (*Macclesfield Express*)

Colin Lambert (left) on the overlap against Wycombe Wanderers. (*Macclesfield Express*)

# 23

# *Enter Mr McIlroy*

'We have a vibrant town, with many new and future prospects on the agenda. Why not a
League football team?'
Geoff Griffiths (*Express Advertiser* Correspondence 26/10/94)

'I simply don't see Macclesfield as an on-going Conference club.'
Sammy McIlroy (16/11/94)

## *Two finals: 4–1 and 14–1*

What happened next was that, despite the Great Escape and the '92–'93 FA Cup run, Wragg's contract was terminated, There was a general feeling that the working relationship had achieved all it was going to, and new blood was needed.

In the frame for the successor were Mike Pejic, ex-Chester manager Harry McNally, and Mike McKenzie of Winsford. There was even some speculation as to whether Brian Booth might take up the reins again. By the end of May, however, the new appointment had been made: Sammy McIlroy, fresh from short-lived tenures at Northwich and Ashton United, was the new Macclesfield Town team manager.

McIlroy had had a lustrous playing career as an inventive attacking midfielder. As a seventeen-year-old he scored in his debut for Manchester United in the 1971 derby match at Maine Road,

symbolically whipping the ball off countryman George Best's toe to hit the opening goal. One of the Old Trafford stars of the 'seventies and early 'eighties, he also amassed a total of 88 international caps, featuring in Billy Bingham's World Cup Finals teams in Spain '82 and Mexico '86.

His managerial initiation, though, had so far been undistinguished: he had been dismissed from Northwich, and had walked out of the job at Ashton after five months. What was remarkable, once his career at the Moss Rose got into its stride, was the speed with which the tyro became the master.

Transitions are seldom easy: a patchy performance in the league, not helped by the three defeats out of four games, conceding twelve goals in the process, at the opening of '93–'94, led to a final Conference position of seventh. Wragg, now at Halifax Town, had almost immediately persuaded Colin Lambert, John Timmons and Elfyn Edwards to join him. To regain some stability, McIlroy brought midfielder Steve Wood from Ashton, and Neil Howarth on a month's loan from Burnley. At the same time striker Carl Alford arrived from Witton. He was to score 24 Conference goals in the coming season.

Coach Gil Prescott had accompanied McIlroy from Ashton. Wayne Porter, an ex-Manchester United junior, was appointed manager of the renascent reserve side. The new foundations were

> In John Askey's testimonial in August 1994, the visiting Manchester United XI included a couple of youngsters by the name of David Beckham and Gary Neville. Sammy McIlroy played for Macc., before being substituted by his son, Sammy Junior. Both McIlroys turned out for the reserves in mid-decade.

strong enough to support a quintet of useful cup runs that season.

The Bob Lord Trophy, otherwise known as the Drinkwise Cup, played for by Conference teams only, saw the Silkmen at their best. After eliminating Witton (6–2 on aggregate), Runcorn 4–0 away, Wragg's Halifax 2–1 away, and the Vics. (3–1 on aggregate), Macc. faced a potentially tough two-legged final against Yeovil Town. The Somerset side had already discomfited them to the tune of 4–0, in an ill-tempered game the previous September, and would win the return league match at the Moss Rose before the season was out. In the Bob Lord final, though, it was another story, the Blues building up a handy 4–1 cushion for the second leg. The team was:

Sammy McIlroy, Macc.'s most successful manager.

Farrelly; Shepherd, Bimson (Wood 45), Lillis, Howarth, Sorvel, Askey, McDonald, Alford, Lyons, Adams

Goal of the game was scored by Darren Lyons, acquired in February in a part-exchange deal for Richie Mitchell. From an acute angle near the right-hand touchline, Lyons belted in a cross-shot which eluded the advancing 'keeper and rebounded in off the far post.

The second leg finished 0–0, so the first of many cups made its way to the McIlroy war chest.

Lyons was both hero and unwitting villain in the Cheshire Cup tie with Colwyn Bay. The striker hit four in the 7–1 drubbing of the Welshmen; it was then discovered that he had been transferred too close to the original date set for the match –

even though the tie itself was postponed to what everyone had assumed was a later, 'safe' date. The pedants won the argument, and Macc. were disqualified.

The FA Trophy was looking promising until the home tie with 50–1 outsiders Billingham Synthonia in round three. The exotic name of the club had nothing to do with music, contrary to popular assumption. The compression of 'synthetic ammonia' indicated their links with ICI. So the shades of 1933 (see Chapter 11) returned: an unusually effete performance saw the Blues succumb 0–1.

In the FA Cup the competition proper was reached once more. There was a touch of romance in the stirring 2–0 victory over Division Two Hartlepool in Round One. Martin McDonald, substituting the injured Wood, scored the all-important second goal with a thumping volley just before half-time. McDonald was a Sunday League player, turning out for a Stockport pub with the happily coincidental name of the *Rifle Volunteer*. In Round Two the Town travelled to Crewe and were eliminated 1–2, despite a furious fightback from 0–2 down, and a dubiously disallowed effort from Askey in the final minutes.

The second success story of McIlroy's first year with the club was in the Staffordshire Senior Cup. Cheshire clubs tended to do their share of poaching what was nominally their neighbour's pot, and 1994 was Macclesfield's turn. Despite needing a replay to dispose of lowly Pelsall Villa in an earlier round, thereafter the road to the

Steve Wood takes on his marker. He scored in the 3–0 win over Stafford Rangers, October 1994. (*Macclesfield Express*)

final was reasonably straightforward. Because of fixture congestion the two-legged final with Wednesfield was postponed, to act as the curtain-raiser to the following season. So in August Macc. drove down the M6 and rounded off the holiday season with a 10–1 win. Lyons scored four – legitimately this time! The return leg result was 4–0 in the Blues' favour. This was an early indication that another of those rousing Silkmen eras was brewing.

## Shifting the goalposts

The year 1994–95 was schizophrenic at the Moss Rose.

On the one hand the league was dominated in unprecedented fashion. A Conference record of ten consecutive victories saw the club take over the top spot by early November. It was a position they were never to relinquish, leading at one point by an astonishing eighteen points. Their pre-season odds of 20–1 were cut to 2–5 by Christmas, and by February the bookies had stopped taking bets. McIlroy was awarded the Manager of the Month on three occasions. In January he became the first ever full time manager at the Moss Rose: a shrewd move from the club's directorate, as several Football League outfits had been eyeing him.

A solid defence, reinforced by Stalybridge's Stuart Locke, Steve Payne on loan from Huddersfield, and the return of Bimson, was the bedrock of the success. Upon Carl Alford's £25,000 departure to Kettering the strike force consisted of Phil Power, and the free-scoring reserve Steve Powell. Speedy wing work was a vital factor too: Darren Lyons and Graham Tobin did the damage here.

On the other hand, in marked contrast to the fluency on the pitch, efforts and negotiations that aimed to persuade the Football League to accept the likely Conference champions were beset by obstacles galore. Kidderminster Harriers, the previous year's champions, had been denied access because of the more demanding criteria imposed on Grade A – or Football League compatible – grounds. The fact that Chester had played League football on the Moss Rose less than three years before was therefore deemed an irrelevance. Macclesfield had been given until 31 December 1994 to upgrade their ground, a date from which the Football League refused to budge.

So the race was on to install £100,000 worth of improvements before the deadline. Public and private donations, plus a number of sponsored events, were to produce the wherewithal, but in November the building of the Star Lane end roof hit – literally – another snag. The foundation work cut into an underground water culvert which ran north-south from beneath one goalmouth to the other. This necessitated extra drainage work, which set the schedule back several weeks. Tireless campaigner

Carl Alford poised to score. (24 goals 1993–94.). (*Macclesfield Express*)

John Askey vs. Stafford Rangers, Oct. 1994. Macc. won the Conference title that year, only to be denied promotion to the Football League. (*Macclesfield Express*)

Darren Lyons – a speedy winger with 19 Conference goals to his credit 1994–96. (*Macclesfield Express*)

George Shepherd, a back four regular. Nearly 200 games 1989–95. (*Macclesfield Express*)

Chairman Arthur Jones, realising now that the deadline would never be met, asked for an extension. The League committee refused to grant one. Plan B was to ask for a temporary groundshare with Chester. In the circumstances, it was felt that it was impossible to deny this. The League came back with the ruling that teams had to play within 'their own conurbation'. Councillor Colin Farnworth joined the fray with some semantic sniping:

> Conurbations are a feature of large centres of population. They simply do not exist in rural areas and as such the rule is a nonsense. (January 1995)

MP Nicholas Winterton took the issue to the Minister of Sport Iain Sproat, and thus government backing for Macc.'s case was obtained. Despite all, the League still refused to change their mind. They even declined to send a representative to a discussion on BBC's *Football Focus*.

It is easy to nurture paranoia about all this, especially when you discover that the new tighter ground criteria had originally been drafted by a consortium of Chairmen from Third Division

clubs. Add to this the fact that the Football Trust was handing out £750,000 to *each* League club for ground development, whilst dividing the same amount between all 22 Conference clubs, and it will be seen how the odds were stacked against the non-league aspirants.

Meanwhile, the Moss Rose work continued. By May 1995 the ground had a 6,000 capacity with 1,000 seats. Money was still arriving: besides the silver Pyramid Trophy, the club received £8,000 for winning the Conference. The Borough donated another £5,000. Now all that remained was to await the League AGM on 3 June to see if Macclesfield's efforts had managed to persuade.

It was no real surprise, though, when the door to a 1995 promotion was finally slammed shut that day. The Silkmen had to do it all again.

*Above* The Silkmen do the town tour after winning the 1995 Conference title. (MTFC)
*Below* Steve Farrelly (GK) with the Conference Trophy 1995. (MTFC)

## Wembley '96

In the interim year of '95–'96 McIlroy bought wisely. In October Cec Edey, a reliable centre-back from Witton, came to the Moss. The defence was anchored the following month by the arrival of Ryan Price, a 6ft 6ins (1m 95) goalkeeper who had made several appearances on the Birmingham City first team. The fast and tricky left-sided attacker Tony Hemmings came from Wycombe Wanderers; and with the signing of Darren Tinson in February the jigsaw was complete.

a long-time supporter and tireless sponsor. It was a cruel irony that he had just sold his business so as to 'spend more time with his family and his club'.

That year the team to beat would be Stevenage Borough, whose linchpin was the Nigerian international Efetobore Sodje. It was he who had executed a spectacular goal-line clearance, with the 'keeper well beaten, during the Borough's 3–0 win at the Moss Rose at the end of the previous season. This year he went one better, scoring in his club's 4–0 rout of Macc. in December. So it was Stevenage who finished at the top of the Conference, with the Town fourth. The Borough too would find the door to the League closed, a decision they took to a legal tribunal, to no avail.

There would be ample consolation in the FA Trophy.

After an unremarkable early run – three home wins by a single goal – then a 2–0 away win over Gresley Rovers, the Blues faced up to Chorley in a two-legged semi. Macc. built up a 3–1 home advantage, despite the viscous state of the pitch, not conducive to the team's free-flowing style of football. For the second leg McIlroy promised: 'We'll go to win and not defend. It's not in the nature of my teams to sit back.' A Sorvel goal after 88 minutes cancelled out Chorley's first half opener, making the aggregate 4–2. The Silkmen were at Wembley again.

Supporters *en route* for Wembley 1996 – another FA Trophy Final. (*Macclesfield Express*)

But there was to be no respite from the slings and arrows of a perverse fortune. The services of three key players were lost before a ball was kicked: Steve Wood's foot was badly injured in an industrial accident; Neil Matthews was out for seven weeks with cartilage problems; and John Askey would not play that season, having sustained a broken leg in a late summer friendly.

In February the club suffered another body blow with the death of Vice-Chairman Bob Isherwood,

Fully 6,000 made the journey south, despite the final being broadcast live on Sky TV. Alistair Walker, a member of the town's under–15 side at the time, wrote:

Walking up Wembley Way, it could have been Mill Street on a Saturday afternoon. It seemed half of Macclesfield were there.
*Express Advertiser* (15/5/96)

Hemmings applies the *coup de grâce* to his brilliant solo run to score Macc.'s third goal *v.* the Vics. in the FA Trophy Final 1996. (*Macclesfield Express*)

The teams in the final were:
*Macclesfield Town*: Price; Edey, Gardiner, Payne, Howarth, Sorvel, Lyons, Wood (Hulme 84), Coates, Power, Hemmings (Cavell 90)
*Northwich Victoria*: Greygoose; Ward, Duffy, Burgess, Abel, Walters, Butler, Cook, Humphreys, Williams, Vicary (Subs: Steele, Simpson, Ball)

The Town were two up inside 28 minutes. The first was a Payne header from a Gardiner free kick; the second a Burgess own goal with Power ('the falcon') hovering.

There was now a spell of pressure from the Vics., which continued after the break when Carwyn Williams pulled one back. It took a strike of especial brilliance to finally scotch Northwich's challenge.

Macc.'s third goal, which many claim to be the best ever seen under the old Twin Towers, was scored by Hemmings. Collecting the ball in his own half, the winger set off on a jaw-dropping sixty-yard slalom which took him deep into the Northwich penalty area. No defender had dared to commit himself, and the forward crowned the achievement with a left-footed shot lashed in

from a dozen yards. It was the goal which at last broke the Vics. Two minutes later Ward, whose purgatorial assignment had been to police the quicksilver Hemmings, committed his second bookable foul on the winger and was duly red-carded. The Town drew the line under their superiority by concluding with a spate of attacks and near-misses.

It was an emotional Neil Howarth who climbed the steps to collect the trophy. It had taken twenty-six years for the club to regain this particular pinnacle. Now, as they went on to retain the Championship Shield – only the second time this feat had been achieved – there was a feeling that

When Steve Wood opened the scoring for Macc. in their 5–3 win over Southport in the Fourth Qualifying Round in October 1993, he had the honour of notching the club's 500th goal in the FA Cup. Kevin Hulme's first in the 7–0 rout of Halifax Town in March 1996 was Macc.'s 500th Conference goal.

Celebrations after the 1996 FA Trophy win. (*Macclesfield Express*)

the worst was over, and that the Silkmen, buoyed up by a new optimism, could plan for a very near future in the Football League.

And yet, hardly had the new season got under way when the club was rocked by the cruellest blow of all.

## Arthur Jones

Arthur Jones, a Liverpudlian by birth and a Macclesfield Town fanatic by inclination, made an inestimable contribution to the club in those years. A long-time sponsor (via his firm Crosland Metals) he became Chairman on the standing down of Alan Brocklehurst in December 1993. A man of tenacious persuasive skills, it was principally he who had argued long and hard for the League case in that bittersweet year of '94–'95. It was he who had the flexibility of vision to

sanction clauses in players' contracts that were instrumental in keeping them at the Moss Rose. ('Keeper Steve Farrelly, for example, received a bonus for every clean sheet.) It was he who had supervised the move to promote Sammy McIlroy to a full-time manager. When the German national team opted to use the Moss as their training headquarters during Euro '96, and it transpired that the visitors would refuse to allow Macc. to charge spectators entrance fees, it was he who negotiated the hefty lump sum that the club received from the German FA.

He appeared to enjoy the vocation and trappings of the role of club Chairman. With his cigars and liking for flash cars he received the players' nickname of Boycie, after the ostentatious character in *Only Fools and Horses*. It was a monicker he enjoyed, by all accounts.

So it was a deep shock when the news of 14 September 1996 broke. Arthur Jones had committed suicide in the offices of his firm on Duke Street.

The club was devastated. The eulogies were many, and moving. McIlroy's reaction was:

I've lost more than a chairman. I've lost a personal friend. I said after Matt Busby there would never be another man like him and there'll never be another man like Arthur Jones.

Club Secretary Colin Garlick:

I don't know why he decided to take himself from us, but he has made me a better person, and I have many treasured memories that will always stay with me.

For a while there was general mystification as to why Jones should have taken such a course of action. Then the accounts of Crosland metals were examined, and it became known that an apparently thriving firm was in reality struggling. The financial pressures, with no obvious short-term resolution, had simply become too much for one man to support.

Clearly all this had serious implications for Macclesfield Town FC. It was Arthur Jones who had virtually bankrolled the series of ground upgrades; the question the accountants and creditors were asking was: to what extent had the club been financed by Jones' personal donations, and to what extent by company loans?

The full analysis of this issue is beyond the scope of this book. It should be recorded that the club was brought back from the brink of extinction mainly by the dogged loyalty and sheer hard work of a small band of directors. Matters were eventually brought to a universally satisfactory conclusion, quietly and efficiently, under the aegis of succeeding Chairman Alan Cash.

In the short term Northwich striker Carwyn Williams, whom the club were now committed to buy, was brought to the Moss Rose mostly through communal contributions. Macc. Town gritted its teeth and set to work. Arthur Jones had literally given his all; in football terms there was only one tribute that would do: promotion to the Third Division.

McIlroy summed up the determination:

He [Arthur Jones] came to me and said let's go for it. And I said I'm going to do it for you.

## The long run for home

By mid-January 1997 the top of the Conference read as follows:

| | P | W | D | L | F | A | Pts |
|---|---|---|---|---|---|---|---|
| Kidderminster Harriers | 28 | 19 | 4 | 5 | 59 | 22 | 61 |
| Stevenage Borough | 23 | 14 | 4 | 5 | 50 | 28 | 46 |
| Macclesfield Town | 24 | 13 | 7 | 4 | 32 | 14 | 46 |

At the same time there was a surge of commercial activity. There was the Silkman 'Premier Club' which offered perks – including free entry to all home games – for a nominal weekly sum. A fresh share initiative was launched, with £8,000-worth snapped up within weeks. There was another drive for match- and ball-sponsorship.

Club T-shirts, whose legends included 'Moving on up – Macc. Town' and 'It's just like watching Brazil' proved popular purchases.

As the financial boat was steadied, so the team performed with growing confidence. Within a month the fifteen-point deficit had been reduced to just two. A 3–0 away win over Bath City, deploying an attack significantly boosted by Peter Davenport and Chris Byrne, saw the Silkmen pull into the lead for the first time.

Davenport, at age 35, had had a long and illustrious career, with spells at Manchester United and Notts. Forest, collecting an England cap on the way. Byrne, who set a club record with his goal after just thirteen seconds at Welling in March, also hit the injury-time winner in a late rally against Southport. The youngster had embarked on the meteoric career that would take him from Droylsden all the way to Peter Reid's Sunderland.

After the 3–0 win over Gateshead, Macc. travelled to Stevenage on a sunny Easter Saturday aiming at least to contain one of their two closest pursuers.

0–2 down, and reduced to ten men after John Askey had been sent off on receiving his second yellow card, there were just thirty minutes left when the fightback began. 19-year-old Demis Ohandjanian cracked in a shot which the Stevenage 'keeper could only parry, and the lurking Steve Wood stabbed in from close range. Shortly afterwards Carwyn Williams was brought down in the area. Eschewing discussion or delay, the striker placed the spot-kick and scored. In stoppage time the same player was floored just outside the box. Wood sent in a bold free kick that swerved neatly into the top corner of the net.

Two days later there was a sobering 1–4 defeat at Hednesford. Then after the five-goal second half deluge that disposed of Woking, the top of the Conference table looking like this:

|  | P | W | D | L | F | A | Pts |
|---|---|---|---|---|---|---|---|
| Macclesfield Town | 39 | 25 | 8 | 6 | 69 | 26 | 83 |
| Kidderminster Harriers | 40 | 25 | 7 | 8 | 80 | 39 | 82 |
| Stevenage Borough | 38 | 23 | 8 | 7 | 80 | 45 | 77 |

In an understandable, if premature, carnival atmosphere in the final home game, the Moss Rose was treated to the spectacle of a streaker and a fancy dress conga as Bromsgrove were eclipsed 4–0. It was just like watching Brazil.

Now three points from the penultimate match, away at Halifax, would put the Silkmen out of reach, and set for the Nationwide Football League.

Fiction could scarcely have enhanced the scenario. It was as if an epic tale, after a century and a quarter of innumerable twists and turns, was gathering to a supreme climax.

# 24

# *The League at Last*

'I've played in World Cups and FA Cup Finals at Wembley but this has to be my greatest success and proudest moment.'

Sammy McIlroy (*News of the World Football Annual* 1997–98)

## *Lift-off*

And still there was a wriggle or two left in the plot.

At Halifax Macc. opened the scoring after three minutes. Chris Byrne set up Phil Power on a lively left wing run; the return ball was delivered perfectly into Byrne's stride, and 1–0 it was. On twenty-six minutes the same player laid off a free kick for Sorvel to increase the lead. The Silkmen and travelling support were exultant.

There was a warning note just before half-time, when Halifax pulled one back. Then, when Davenport restored the two-goal lead with a dozen minutes left, the promised land drew appreciably closer. But there was to be a further, unexpected cliffhanger: the home side scored two late goals to finish on 3–3. It was scant consolation that it was ex-Silkman Kevin Hulme who hit the last one, with Macclesfield five minutes away from their dream.

So it all depended on the last Saturday of the season. Macc. were away at Kettering, and Kidderminster, by now the only team who could overtake them, were at Gateshead.

The team at Kettering was:
Price; Tinson, Edey, Bradshaw (Gee), Howarth, Sorvel, Askey, Wood, Davenport, Power, Byrne

The home side were a goal to the good after seven minutes, but Davenport equalised a couple of minutes later. The rest of the half was a Chris Byrne showpiece, with a gaggle of football scouts watching from the stands. Within another two minutes he had headed his team into the lead, from a Davenport corner. His second was a

The best Silkman defence ever: (left to right) Darren Tinson, Steve Payne, Neil Howarth and Cec Edey. Front: Ryan Price. (See p. 175 for stats.).
(John Rooney)

First Football League squad 1997–98. (John Rooney)

mesmerising 40-yard dribble, culminating in a penalty area chicane which wrong-footed two defenders; profiting from the sudden space, he whacked the ball into the top corner. For his hat-trick he dropped a craftily-placed header beyond the Kettering goalie.

4–1 up at half-time – and the news from Gateshead was that Kidderminster were losing.

There were no more goals at Kettering. The Town turned the second half into a cruise, albeit alert to the final score from Tyneside. Since the Kettering match had started fifteen minutes late, it was possible to relay the Gateshead result to the players well before the final whistle. Kidderminster had lost 1–3, and Conference

> In a poll conducted by *Total Football* magazine in January 1998, the cheese and onion pies on sale at the Moss Rose snack bar were voted tastiest in the Football League.

representative Peter Wragg was seen to walk along the touchline to present the long-anticipated bottle of bubbly to Sammy McIlroy.

A poignant detail which speaks volumes of the Macc. supporters: as Neil Howarth brandished the Pyramid Trophy, hardly had the first wave of cheers subsided when the travelling contingent broke into a spontaneous chant of 'Arthur Jones, Arthur Jones …'

Back home in Macclesfield the celebrations went on long into the night. One joke going the rounds was that the Silkmen could be playing Manchester City (just relegated from the Premiership) in the League the season after next. But surely the giddy stuff of fantasy, that.

First Football League Team sheet August 1997. (MTFC)

Neil Howarth's role in the promotion to Football League status in May 1997 was commemorated by a piece of doggerel penned by goalkeeper Ryan Price:

Neil Howarth is our Captain Marvel
He stands tall and podgy
He writes a weekly column
Slags US off for being dodgy
You never read of his mistakes
Or his rubber gum shields
He takes them out to have a moan
On many northern fields …
His nickname is that of 'Beckenbauer'
Some are puzzled why
Especially chummy Philly Power
'Cause most shots hit the sky!
He's put a few past Ryan Price
Who features in his column
He tells us that he didn't slice
Then leaves the field quite solemn
I've told you of some good and bad
But this part is so really sad
Lads' night out he's raving mad
He sinks two pints then wants his dad.
But where would we be
Without this man?
Certainly not Division Three
I must confess I am his fan.
(*Macclesfield Express* 14/5/97)

The *Express Advertiser* devoted a front page to a full colour dressing-room post-Kettering shot of the jubilant team. (In the rush for publication, though, the editors had overlooked the appearance of an unwarranted appendage. A detailed, not to say convoluted, apologia followed in the next week's issue, sports editor David Lafferty referring to the club's 'finest tackle of the season'.)

The foundation of the success of that year was the defence. Goalkeeper Ryan Price and back four Darren Tinson, Cec Edey, Steve Payne and Neil Howarth had conceded just 30 league goals. For a better defensive record by the club we have to go back an astonishing 99 years, to when Hallefield were winning the Stockport and District League by a country mile. In terms of goals per game conceded (0.71) the 1996–97 record was

the best ever.

Almost unnoticed in all the euphoria was the fact that Macc. had reached the final of two County Cups. Beaten by Hyde United 3–0 in the Cheshire Senior final at the Drill Field, they made amends by pilfering the Staffordshire Cup for the second time in four years, defeating Bilston 4–3 on aggregate. They also won the Championship Shield for a record-equalling third consecutive time. They were bidding farewell to the non-league world with a flourish.

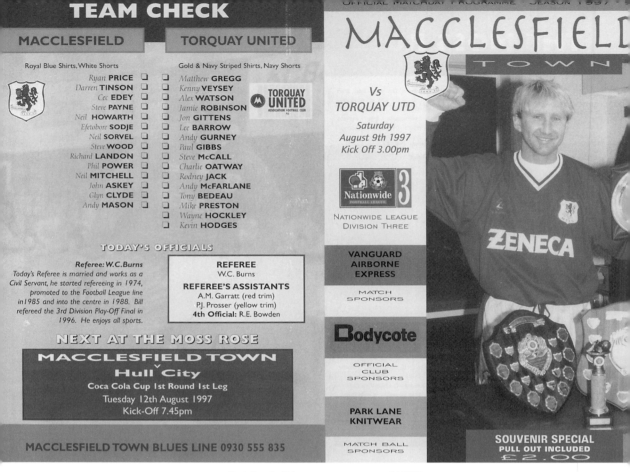

First Football League programme. (MTFC)

## Blue shift

Then there were the last preparations for the entry to the Football League. Part-time players who had been postmen or construction workers now became full-time professionals. A mandatory segregation of fans was introduced at the Moss Rose. An appeal for double the number of match-day stewards was launched. There was to be a lion mascot, the competition for the best name yielding 'Roary'.

There was the usual crop of close season signings. Lee Martin, originally a deputy goalie for Price, arrived. Major *coup* was Nigerian international Efetobore Sodje, who had been the mainstay of the Stevenage defence. He made his impressive debut for the Silkmen in the pre-season friendly with Manchester City, whose eleven that Friday evening included Uwe Rosler, Nigel Clough, and a classy young left-back by the name of Rae Ingram.

Sodje, with his trademark bandana, rapidly became an icon. The *Express Advertiser* reported:

Efe Sodje has already amassed a cult following with his performances and appearances in pre-season friendlies, and it took less than ten minutes for his fan club to grow as he scored the club's first league goal. (20/8/97)

Seven minutes, to be exact. The opponents at the Moss Rose for the first ever Football League game were Torquay United. Colin Rose took the corner, and Sodje lifted himself above the penalty area melee to thump a firm header into the net.

The Blues went on to win 2–1. A mixed bag of results followed, although a couple of 3–0 wins

(Doncaster Rovers and Swansea City) gave some cause for optimism. They would be unbeaten at home throughout the season – the only Football League team to enjoy that honour in 1997–98 – and, as the results started to swing Macc.'s way, by Christmas a play-off place was a distinct possibility. (The top three teams are promoted by right, then the subsequent four play a knock-out mini-tournament to determine the fourth promotion spot.)

League leaders Lincoln were held 1–1 away in December. Then second placed Peterborough were beaten 1–0, also away, in February, with John Askey the scorer. With six games left, the scenario looked very promising:

The Silkmen bench 1998. (John Rooney)

|  | P | W | D | L | F | A | Pts |
|---|---|---|---|---|---|---|---|
| Notts County | 40 | 26 | 10 | 4 | 68 | 35 | 88 |
| Torquay United | 40 | 20 | 9 | 11 | 61 | 49 | 69 |
| Macclesfield Town | 40 | 18 | 13 | 9 | 52 | 39 | 67 |
| Barnet | 40 | 18 | 12 | 10 | 55 | 41 | 66 |

Three points behind Macc. were Lincoln City. So when the Imps visited the Moss Rose for the next League match, the situation was already potentially volatile. Mad March overflowed into early April that year: first there was a brief pitch invasion by Lincoln fans; then Roary was escorted off by police, after a provocative half-time gesture with his tail in front of the away crowd at the pub end; then shortly into the second half the powderkeg exploded. Martin McDonald mistimed a lunge at Lincoln 'keeper Richardson, and apparently the boot made contact. Richardson's OTT reaction was to kick out at the grounded McDonald, seemingly striking the forward. Other Lincoln players arrived on the scene to add their two-penn'orths, and from there an escalation to a full-scale brawl was a matter of moments. Every player on

the pitch, whether in the role of aggressor or would-be pacifier, was soon involved. It took the match officials five minutes, and two red cards, to restore order. It was somewhat in the style of poetic justice when Steve Wood struck the winner on 88 minutes. It was possibly this match that prompted Wood to assert, later in the season, that Third Division sides were 'just a bunch of pub teams'.

Before the month was out the Town met Chester at home, needing three points to assure themselves of an automatic promotion place. The crowd was queuing round the block with over an hour to kick-off. A few fans had commandeered the pub balcony in order to display a makeshift score update for the Lincoln and Torquay games. A huge Nigerian flag was unfurled at the front of the packed Star Lane end, and several rows back a Union Jack displayed the single word 'Woody'.

It was indeed Steve Wood who opened the scoring just before the quarter-hour. Stuart Whittaker pulled a corner way back, and Woody's header found the net. It was another header, this time close-range, from Neil Sorvel which increased the lead shortly after the interval. The final score was 3–2, Phil Power capitalising on a defensive

Efe Sodje surveys the defence (1998). (John Rooney)

blunder to hit the third. A late 30-yarder from visiting striker Rod Thomas caused a nervy last few minutes as Chester pushed for an equaliser, but the home defences were not breached again. (Both Lincoln and Torquay had lost anyway, so promotion would have been assured no matter what the result!) The final whistle blew, and McIlroy and Prescott sprinted onto the pitch to join in the general jubilation. A bewigged Ryan Price swung on the Star Lane crossbar and saluted the crowd celebrating on the site of the old Spion Kop.

History was in the making once more: it was 125 years, give or take a few weeks, since that band of Rifle Volunteers had trotted out onto their drill field across town to take on the Grammar School at the new Association game. The Silkmen had reached the high point of their long history: Division Two of the Football League. And one of their opponents would be Manchester City.

The team against Chester was:

Price; Tinson, McDonald, Payne, Ingram, Sodje, Askey (Chambers), Wood, Sorvel, Power, Whittaker (Durkan) (Sub.: Howarth)

For good measure, '97–'98 saw yet another Cheshire Cup win, the nineteenth overall. After a close two-legged semi tussle with the Vics., which Macc. won by virtue of the away goals rule, a 1–0 victory over Runcorn at the Drill Field did the business in the final.

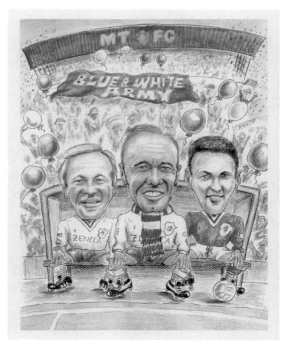

'Three Wise Men' (MTFC)

## Division Two

Pedro Matias, a midfield player lately of the Spanish First Division, arrived during the summer. Ingram's initial two-month loan spell was upgraded to a full contract. Otherwise the line-up was much the same as the previous season.

The Moss Rose capacity was increased to 6,500. Seating was purchased from Stoke's Victoria ground, as that club was moving to its new Britannia stadium.

1998–99 was the club's League high water mark, at least this time around. The Blues struggled to make any headway in Division Two, never lifting free of the relegation zone. There were many close-run games, but time and again a crucial goal, often conceded in the last four or five minutes of a match, would result in a loss of two points. A heroic run in the last month was not quite enough.

So, painfully, unluckily, Macc. returned to Division Three after just one season. A few scalps had been gathered, though. York City had been eclipsed 2–0 away, as had Northampton Town. Among the established League teams toppled during the year had been Oldham Athletic, Burnley, Reading, Chesterfield, and Preston North End.

Both the games with Manchester City were lost (0–1, 0–2) but without there being noticeable any dramatic difference between the teams.

The FA Cup that year ended in Round Three. Macc. travelled to Highfield Road to find Coventry City in general, and Darren Huckerby in particular, at the mid-season height of their powers. A crushing 0–7 defeat nonetheless flattered the Premiership side.

At least the Worthington Cup brought some joy: a long-awaited victory over Stoke City (3–1, and 3–2 on aggregate). Then hopes of further progress were emphatically scotched by Birmingham City in Round Two.

> To celebrate the Silkmen's promotion to Division Two in May 1998 the Potteries-based Titanic Brewery brought out a special beer for the concurrent Macclesfield Beer Festival. Name of the brew: 'Mad Macc.'s Two'.

In the summer of '99 Sodje's contract expired, and no agreement could be reached over a renewal. A partial replacement was found in the young George Abbey; and by now 'Razor' Ingram with his positional sense and precise tackles had developed into a formidable component of the defence. Other new arrivals were striker Richard Barker from Brighton, and attack-minded wing-back Greg Rioch, son of Scottish international Bruce. Defender Simon Collins and midfielder Chris Priest completed the outfield picture. As Ryan Price left for Telford, the 'keeper spot was filled by Lee Martin, who had impressed in the reserves.

Star Lane optimists 1998–99. (John Rooney)

Striker Damien White-head, scorer of 52 goals for Warrington, was initially de-ployed in the reserves, with the odd appearance on the first team bench. Then a flurry of joyously executed Football League goals in March and April 2000 assured his regular place. The theo-rists immediately partnered him with Barker, who had hit 11 League goals by November of the same season. It was certainly a twin strike force to be reckoned with.

Richie Barker with his eye on the ball. John Askey in support. *v.* Rotherham February 2000. Barker scored a total of 27 goals for the Silkmen. (John Rooney)

## Farewell to McIlroy

Over the years, the list of clubs that had been supposedly moving in to poach Sammy McIl-roy reads like a north-west and Potteries League Directory. Each time, though, he had preferred to stay put.

> Sammy McIlroy's daughter Faye was short-listed for the role of George Best's girlfriend Miss World Mary Stavin in the 1999 film *Best*.

Then the managership of the Northern Ireland national team became available, and less than a week into the new millennium, the rumours were proven true: McIlroy was leaving the Moss Rose, after six and a half glorious years.

His record with the club is one of unrivalled lustre:

1993–94:  Bob Lord Trophy
            Staffs. Senior Cup
1994–95:  Vauxhall Conference
            Championship Shield

1995–96:  FA Challenge Trophy
            Championship Shield
            Bob Lord Trophy Finalists
1996–97:  Vauxhall Conference
            Championship Shield
            Staffs. Senior Cup
            Cheshire Senior Cup Finalists
            Bob Lord Trophy Finalists
1997–98:  Runners-up Division Three
            (promoted)
            Cheshire Senior Cup

The farewell salutes, unsurprisingly, were legion:

Neil Howarth: 'He's a very good manager. He encourages you to express yourself.'

Richard Barker: 'One of the reasons I came to Macclesfield was because I thought I would improve as a player under Sammy and Peter Davenport.'

Steve Wood: 'I've been with Sam for around seven years, since our days together at Ashton … Without doubt he's made me a better player. He's a quality coach.'

Phil Power: 'His brand of passing football

suited me. He always stuck by his principles.'

Rae Ingram: 'He knows his players very well and has a knack of getting the best out of them.'

Eddie Furlong, club director, and later Chairman: 'He's built this club into a force in the last six and a half years and his achievements will never be forgotten.'

Alan Cash, then club Chairman: 'He has been at the cutting edge of our success but has left us with a good squad of players, a solid position in the Football League and a professional backroom staff with the skills to build for the future.'

(All quotations from *Macclesfield Express* 12/1/00)

Assistant coach Peter Davenport now took over. Macc. finished the season mid-table in Division Three, a handful of points shy of the play-offs. Richard Barker was chosen by the PFA to be a member of their divisional Team of the Season.

Year 2K also saw yet another triumph in the final of the Cheshire cup: win number twenty in this competition was a 2–1 win over Altrincham at Witton's ground. Ben Sedgemore hit both goals for the Blues.

Steve Payne, captain *v.* Preston North End in the Division Two match (1998–99). (John Rooney)

Chris Byrne takes on the Hull City defence August 1999. (John Rooney)

The highest attendance for a match involving Macclesfield Town, home or away, including Wembley appearances, is the 31,086 at the Division Two game with Manchester City at Maine Road on 20 February 1999.

*Opposite top*:Team 1999–2000

MANCHESTER CITY F.C. ★★★
WHERE APPROPRIATE, THIS TICKET IS FOR THE SEAT STATED ONLY.
PLEASE TAKE UP YOUR POSITION AT LEAST 45 MINUTES PRIOR TO KICK-OFF
THE NATIONWIDE FOOTBALL LEAGUE
M.C.F.C. v MACCLESFIELD TOWN
SAT 20 FEB 1999 KICK OFF 03:00 P.M.

NORTH STAND - T
ROW      SEAT      PRICE
10       142       £11.00

MACCLESFIELD TOWN F.C.    110299 BULK

DIAL-A-SEAT ★ RETAIN THIS PORTION OF TICKET ★ CITY CLUB CALL
0161 227 9229 ★ FOR FUTURE APPLICATIONS ★ 0891 12 11 91

Macclesfield Town Football Club Ltd.

v
**MIDDLESBROUGH**
Moss Rose Ground, Macclesfield
**Worthington Cup 2nd Round – 2nd Leg**
Tuesday 26 Sept 2000      ko 7.45pm
**ADULT £12.00    JRN/SNR £7.00**
**STAR LANE SEATING**
Row C  Seat 73

50018

*Opposite bottom*: Macclesfield Town FC August 2000.
*Back row*: Steve Wood, George Abbey, Damien Whitehead, Shaun Came, Paul O'Neill, Danny Whittaker
*Middle row*: Frank Peate (kit man), Mark Bamber, Simon Collins, Chris Preist, Tony Bullock, Lee Martin, Simon Davies, Ben Sedgemore, Lee Glover, Eric Campbell (assistant physio)
*Front row*: Allan Preston (assistant manager), Darren TInson, Rae Ingram, Steve Hitchen, Richard Barker, Peter Davenport (manager), Kieron Durkan, John Askey, Karl Munroe, Gregor Rioch, Ewan Simpson (physio)

# New Millennium

Macclesfield prides itself on being a family club and trouble is extremely rare.
*Nationwide Football Fans' Guide*

Credit to Macclesfield, they battled throughout and gave everything to their cause.
*Middlesbrough FC website (26/9/00)*

## A trip to the Moss Rose

If you seek their monument, look about you.
Start with the official website, widely regarded as one of the most polished of Football League club sites: www.mtfc.co.uk. The home page in smart-as-paint Silkman blue displays a menu of match reports, diary and daily updates on club news, on-line shopping, the Football in the Community venture, a database of players past and present, access to the SilkChat forum, and so on. The site is now run by Premium TV, and one popular state-of-the-art feature is live audio commentary on matches.

Due praise should be given here to the 'old' (pre-July 2001) official site, orchestrated for five years by indefatigable webmaster Mike Griffiths. Also worth a look is the independent site on www.thesilkweb.com.

The SilkChat facility has around 450 members – although anyone may contribute as a guest – from directors and club officials to die-hard supporters to casual browsers. Topics have included the fans' choice of Player of the Season, the best ever Silkmen XI, the long and tortuous tale of the supposed new stadium, and a regular item for which contributors are asked to predict score, scorers and crowd for an upcoming match. Travelling supporters often give a brief report on an away game, sometimes within minutes of returning home!

Football in the Community (FITC) quite rightly has a section to itself. Originally set in motion by Gil Prescott, and subsequently in the capable hands of John Clubb, FITC is sponsored by the PFA, the Borough Council, and local firms. The scheme, whose aim is to promote youth football throughout the borough, has combined the club's Junior Blues with Macclesfield Town Ladies (U–16, U–14, U–12, and U–10 teams) under the same FITC umbrella. Events have been coaching sessions and playing tours.

Popular items in the shop (cyber or real) are videos of games. The Worthington Cup win over Bolton (September 2000) for some time held pride of place. (It is also possible to download the three home leg goals onto the hard drive of your computer.) And here would be another appropriate place for a plug for the book *Against All Odds* – see bibliography.

Fans hail from all over the world, from Uruguay to Australia, and from Serbia to Canada. There is a strong faction based in Norway, thanks to some employees from that country who spent some time at the Zeneca plant a few years ago.

The interested outsider may now be tempted to make a trip to the Moss Rose, to experience at first hand the hub of all this activity.

The ground retains much of its rural setting, with the range of hills over towards Blakelow and Sutton forming a backdrop to the east. It is just over a mile from the centre of town, and on match days as kick-off time approaches we see a pilgrimage of supporters, on foot or in cars, strung along

London Road or making their way through the estates to the north and west.

The *Silkman* pub, that bastion of tradition tucked for over a century into one corner of the Moss Rose, is alas no more. But the ground beckons: we see the jutting royal blue cantilever stand, and join the steady stream of fans clicking through the turnstiles.

The match is the midweek Worthington Cup second leg against Premiership Middlesbrough. It is the first time a top-flight team has played a competitive match against Macc. at the Moss Rose.

We make our way round to the Star Lane End, the old Spion Kop, where the fans are, we are told, more vociferous than those who frequent the traditionally staider main stand.

Gil Prescott, manager from early 2001. (MTFC)

We take our place, under the brilliant web of the floodlights.

Those used to Premiership matches will not fail to notice the many differences: everything is on a smaller scale, and everyone seems to know everyone else. We discover the prevalence of voluntary jobs: from stewards, programme sellers and snack bar assistants to the PA announcer, David Westbury. (We recall Mr Westbury's contribution to the presentation of the Sky TV match with Darlington the previous Friday, not least the on-the-pitch interview with mascot seven-year-old Jimmy Read. The South Cheshire Pipe Band were in evidence too. Unfortunately Sky chose to show neither activity on their main camera.)

In tonight's cup tie, the situation is finely balanced. Boro have a 2–1 lead from the first leg at the Riverside Stadium, scoring twice in the last five minutes to scrape home. That precious away goal means that a 1–0 win will see Macc. through.

A look at the programme shows that Bryan Robson's Middlesbrough are taking no chances this time. The line-up bristles with international players: Curtis Fleming (Republic of Ireland), Gianluca Festa (Italy), Colin Cooper and Paul Ince (England), Noel Whelan (England U–21), Paul Okon (Australia), and Hamilton Ricard (Colombia). Alan Boksic, crack Croatian striker and one of the highest-paid players in the world, is one of the subs.

David Westbury on the PA extends a warm welcome to the Teesside contingent who 'have come a long way down the A1 to get here tonight'. (Topical comment from the Star Lane chorus: '*What a waste of petrol . . .*')

The home starting line-up is:
Bullock; Abbey, Adams, Tinson, Ingram, Sedgemore, Wood, Twynham, Munroe, Keen, Barker (Subs.: Askey, Whitehead, Bamber, Glover, Durkan)

Macc. start well, keeping possession and inflicting some pressure, but on seventeen minutes Ricard exploits the penalty area confusion following a free kick and stabs the ball home. Now there is a mountain to climb, but the home side set

Ben Sedgemore. Over 100 Football League starts
1998–2001. (John Rooney)

about their task with a will. Davenport's 4–5–1 system, linked by rapid inter-passing, takes the game back to the illustrious opponents. As half-time approaches, team and crowd alike seem to sense that something has to give. It does: Whelan floors Kevin Keen the ex-Wolves player, and Macc. are awarded a penalty.

Up steps Ben Sedgemore, who tucks it away to tumultuous cheers (which, we learn later, can be heard on the other side of town). It remains at 1–1 until half-time. Can the Blues pull off an unlikely victory?

In the crowd the veterans reminisce. Someone recalls the 4–0 FA Cup drubbing of Rotherham; another the defeat of Chesterfield on penalties. One gentleman tops the lot: he was at Craven Cottage, on that glorious day in January 1968.

Tonight, though, the dreams are smashed by two quick second half goals, both struck by Ricard. Now Macc. have to score four in thirty-eight minutes. For a while Boro give a stress-free display of possession football, confidently stroking the ball from man to man across the midfield. The Town are now playing for pride alone. The Star Lane choir belts out a series of insults of varying inventiveness to the visitors. On comes Whitehead, to an expectant burst of cheering. Some late fire is thus injected up front. Askey, then Bamber, are also summoned to duty.

Indeed, 'Mo' Whitehead almost gives the home side the last word, as in the final minute he whips a shot against the upright, with the Boro 'keeper standing watching.

So it ends, 2–5 on aggregate. As the fans file out, exchanging views and commiserating, the PA plays *Always Look on the Bright Side of Life*. And as someone points out, how far the Town have come, since the last time they took on a moneyed Premiership side!

## A study in futures

In the final week of 2000, Davenport's contract was terminated by the board. Director of Football Gil Prescott, who had been McIlroy's right arm since the Ashton United days, seemed the perfect replacement. Despite the departures of Richie Barker and Ben Sedgemore, the 'yin and yang' attacking partnership of Whitehead and Askey (or, Glover and Bermudan international Kyle Lightbourne) now swung into action. And a firm foundation to all the Football League activity, the club's Centre of Excellence was beginning to produce the goods.

Almost since the beginnings of the professional game the general trend has been for useful local footballers to be snapped up by the big clubs. Occasionally, for example with the demise of the maximum wage in the early 'sixties, the traffic moved in the opposite direction, and Macc. were able to lure a quota of players off-loaded from their more affluent neighbours. Now, with YTS

Kieron Durkan, another Silkmen League centurion. (John Rooney)

Damien 'Mo' Whitehead. Six goals in five games, March–April 2000. (John Rooney)

Richard Tracey, scoring against Blackpool. March, 2001. (John Rooney)

signings from the Centre of Excellence, there are signs that decent players born in the borough may remain loyal to their roots.

For a time there was some expectation that a new stadium would figure in the club's future, its venue part of the Lyme Green development area just along the London Road.

It would be a fruitless exercise here to itemise the claims and counter-claims of what was or was not said by the interested parties. The council preferred Shepherd Developments to other hot favourites McAlpine; and both proposals may or may not have included the plans for a new stadium.

The advantages of a change to a new venue for Macclesfield Town FC and its attendant activities seemed obvious. Most saliently, the club stood to harvest around a million pounds from the sale of the Moss Rose, and to quote FITC officer John Clubb:

The stadium plan wasn't just about providing

a pitch for the first team; it went much deeper than that. The plans were there for the whole community to use.

The Red Card Day protest at the Town Hall was called off at the eleventh hour. Supreme irony, it was due to take place on the same day that the council were to have sponsored the match with Chester City. The council withdrew its support, and the bill was footed by the Stadium Action Group (SAG), later given the less contentious name, and wider purpose, of the Silkman Alliance.

However, there were benefits in staying put, too. The estate side has been reconstructed: the smart new McAlpine stand (due to include bar, function room, superstore and communal-access IT room) was declared open for business on 11 March 2001. Sammy McIlroy returned to make an on-the-pitch speech and release the swarm of multi-coloured balloons, and the Silkmen toasted the occasion with a 3–0 destruction of Barnet.

Plans for cover for the north end, where the away fans have had to provide their own shelter in inclement weather, are on the table. There are those who cite the lack of atmosphere at all-seater stadia. And there are the romantics, loath to abandon the scene of so many past successes.

This football club history has become, in part, the history of the community in which Macclesfield Town FC is rooted. It has reflected the Maxonian character too: the loyalty, ingenuity and resilience which have seen the club through the grim times, and a capacity for celebration in style whenever the team has triumphed. We have noted that special brand of humour too: knowing, wry, with the occasional satirical bite.

Time and again this theme of community has underpinned the club's progress, a dynamic driven by a successful blend of the traditional and the new, of consolidation and reasoned ambition.

If history tells us anything at all, it gives us a sound basis on which to predict the future. It seems unlikely that Macc. will emulate for example Wimbledon's relentless gallop up through the Leagues. That is not, and never has been, the Silkman way. However, their place in the Football League seems assured for many seasons to come.

Whatever fate has waiting in the wings for the Town club in the next few years, we can be certain of one more thing: there will always be those willing to continue this tale, and record and celebrate the on-going, and perennially fascinating, saga of the Silkmen.

'Flag Day'! 5 May 2001: day of the official opening of the new stand. (GPP)

Party on the pitch, after the last home game of the 2000–01 season: 5 May.
*Above*: A view of the new stand. *Below*: The cantilever stand in the background. (GPP)

# Silkmen Honours

**Cheshire Senior Cup:**

Winners 1890, 1891, 1894, 1896, 1911, 1930, 1935, 1951, 1952, 1954, 1960, 1964, 1969, 1971, 1973, 1983, 1991, 1992, 1998, 2000

Finalists: 1895, 1907, 1910, 1936, 1950, 1974, 1977, 1988, 1989, 1990, 1997

**Manchester League:**

Champions 1909, 1911

Runners-up 1907

**Stockport and District League:**

(as Hallefield) Champions 1898

**Cheshire County League:**

Champions 1932, 1933, 1953, 1961, 1964, 1968

Runners-up 1934, 1962, 1965

**Northern Premier League:**

Champions 1969, 1970, 1987

Runners-up 1985

**GM Vauxhall Conference:**

Champions 1995, 1997

**Cheshire League Challenge Cup:**

Winners 1925, 1932, 1948, 1967

Finalists: 1926, 1951, 1953, 1964

**FA Challenge Trophy:**

Winners 1970, 1996

Finalists: 1989

**Championship Shield:**

Winners 1995, 1996, 1997

**NPL Challenge Cup:**

Winners: 1987

Finalists: 1970, 1971, 1983

**Nationwide Football League:**

Runners-up, Division Three, 1997–98

**Staffordshire Senior Cup:**

Winners 1994, 1997

# APPENDIX 2

# *Managers*

| | |
|---|---|
| James Stevenson | 1936–37 (player-manager) |
| Jos Stevenson | 1946 (player-manager) |
| William Edwards | 1947–49 (player-manager) |
| Bert Swindells | 1949–51 |
| Jack Smith | 1951–55 (player-manager) |
| Bert Swindells | 1955–58 |
| Peter Robinson | 1958–59 (player-manager) |
| Frank Bowyer | 1960–63 (player-manager) |
| Albert Leake | 1963–67 (player-manager) |
| Keith Goalen | 1967–68 (player-coach) |
| Frank Beaumont | 1968–72 (player-manager) |
| Billy Haydock | 1972–74 |
| Eddie Brown | 1974 |
| Willie Stevenson | 1974 (player-manager) |
| John Collins | 1974–76 (player-manager) |
| Tony Coleman | 1976 (caretaker-manager) |
| John Barnes | 1976 |
| Brian Taylor | 1976 |
| Dave Connor | 1976–78 |
| Derek Partridge | 1978 |
| Phil Staley | 1978–80 |
| Jimmy Williams | 1980–81 |
| Brian Booth | 1981–85 |
| Neil Griffiths | 1985–86 (player-manager) |
| Roy Campbell | 1986 (caretaker-manager) |
| Peter Wragg | 1986–93 |
| Sammy McIlroy | 1993–2000 |
| Peter Davenport | 2000 |
| Gil Prescott | 2001 |
| Kevin Keen | 2001– |

# APPENDIX 3

# League Tables, 1890–1987

## League Tables, 1890–1915

### 1890–91: THE COMBINATION

| | P | W | D | L | F | A | Pts |
|---|---|---|---|---|---|---|---|
| Gorton Villa | 16 | 10 | 2 | 4 | 47 | 26 | 22 |
| Macclesfield | 16 | 9 | 3 | 4 | 44 | 27 | 21 |
| Chester | 16 | 8 | 4 | 4 | 42 | 30 | 20 |
| Burton Swifts | 14 | 9 | 0 | 5 | 55 | 28 | 18 |
| Denton | 16 | 8 | 1 | 7 | 39 | 32 | 17 |
| Northwich Victoria | 16 | 5 | 7 | 4 | 28 | 30 | 17 |
| Hyde | 14 | 3 | 4 | 7 | 25 | 39 | 10 |
| *Wrexham | 16 | 4 | 4 | 8 | 25 | 47 | 10 |
| Leek | 16 | 1 | 1 | 14 | 18 | 60 | 3 |

* 2 points deducted
Some teams did not complete their fixtures

### 1891–92: THE COMBINATION

| | P | W | D | L | F | A | Pts |
|---|---|---|---|---|---|---|---|
| Everton Reserves | 22 | 17 | 2 | 3 | 99 | 20 | 36 |
| Northwich Victoria | 22 | 15 | 1 | 6 | 84 | 25 | 31 |
| Macclesfield | 22 | 15 | 0 | 7 | 52 | 38 | 30 |
| Stoke Swifts | 22 | 13 | 1 | 8 | 49 | 29 | 27 |
| Buxton | 22 | 11 | 3 | 8 | 35 | 30 | 25 |
| Wrexham | 22 | 9 | 2 | 11 | 45 | 65 | 20 |
| Chirk | 22 | 7 | 5 | 10 | 48 | 56 | 19 |
| Chester | 22 | 8 | 3 | 11 | 52 | 61 | 19 |
| Gorton Villa | 22 | 8 | 3 | 11 | 41 | 51 | 19 |
| Leek | 22 | 8 | 0 | 14 | 46 | 62 | 16 |
| Stockport County | 22 | 7 | 2 | 13 | 29 | 44 | 16 |
| Denton | 22 | 2 | 2 | 18 | 25 | 124 | 6 |

### 1892–93: THE COMBINATION

| | P | W | D | L | F | A | Pts |
|---|---|---|---|---|---|---|---|
| Everton Reserves | 22 | 18 | 2 | 2 | 107 | 13 | 38 |
| Stoke Swifts | 22 | 14 | 4 | 4 | 48 | 23 | 32 |
| Chester | 22 | 12 | 2 | 8 | 52 | 41 | 26 |
| Chirk | 22 | 10 | 3 | 9 | 63 | 43 | 23 |
| Buxton | 22 | 8 | 7 | 7 | 36 | 29 | 23 |
| Stockport County | 22 | 8 | 6 | 8 | 38 | 35 | 22 |
| Wrexham | 22 | 9 | 1 | 12 | 41 | 66 | 19 |
| Dresden United | 22 | 8 | 3 | 11 | 34 | 43 | 17 |
| Macclesfield | 22 | 6 | 6 | 10 | 45 | 55 | 18 |
| Leek | 22 | 6 | 3 | 13 | 31 | 60 | 15 |
| Nantwich | 22 | 6 | 3 | 13 | 36 | 81 | 15 |
| Gorton Villa | 22 | 6 | 2 | 14 | 29 | 68 | 12 |

### 1893–94: THE COMBINATION

| | P | W | D | L | F | A | Pts |
|---|---|---|---|---|---|---|---|
| Everton Reserves | 18 | 15 | 2 | 1 | 77 | 19 | 31 |
| Stoke Swifts | 18 | 10 | 1 | 7 | 57 | 31 | 21 |
| Leek | 18 | 9 | 2 | 7 | 32 | 27 | 20 |
| Stockport County | 18 | 7 | 6 | 5 | 33 | 32 | 20 |
| Dresden United | 18 | 7 | 5 | 6 | 34 | 28 | 19 |
| Chester | 18 | 6 | 6 | 6 | 24 | 26 | 18 |
| Macclesfield | 18 | 5 | 7 | 6 | 36 | 35 | 17 |
| Wrexham | 18 | 5 | 6 | 7 | 36 | 46 | 16 |
| Buxton | 18 | 5 | 4 | 9 | 28 | 41 | 14 |
| Nantwich | 18 | 1 | 1 | 16 | 12 | 84 | 3 |

### 1894–95: THE COMBINATION

| | P | W | D | L | F | A | Pts |
|---|---|---|---|---|---|---|---|
| Ashton North End | 20 | 14 | 3 | 3 | 62 | 32 | 31 |
| Glossop North End | 20 | 14 | 2 | 4 | 49 | 19 | 30 |
| Chester | 20 | 12 | 2 | 6 | 53 | 35 | 26 |
| Dresden United | 20 | 9 | 7 | 4 | 52 | 25 | 25 |
| Stalybridge Rovers | 20 | 8 | 5 | 7 | 41 | 35 | 21 |
| Macclesfield | 20 | 8 | 3 | 9 | 44 | 38 | 19 |
| Leek | 20 | 7 | 4 | 9 | 36 | 47 | 18 |
| Hurst Ramblers | 20 | 7 | 1 | 12 | 35 | 61 | 15 |
| *Hanley Town | 20 | 6 | 2 | 12 | 37 | 62 | 12 |
| Buxton | 20 | 4 | 3 | 13 | 22 | 48 | 11 |
| Northwich Victoria | 20 | 4 | 2 | 14 | 26 | 55 | 10 |

* 2 points deducted for fielding ineligible players

### 1895–96: THE COMBINATION

| | P | W | D | L | F | A | Pts |
|---|---|---|---|---|---|---|---|
| Everton Reserves | 14 | 11 | 2 | 1 | 54 | 12 | 24 |
| Macclesfield | 14 | 11 | 2 | 1 | 37 | 13 | 24 |
| Glossop North End | 14 | 9 | 3 | 2 | 33 | 13 | 21 |
| Oldham | 14 | 5 | 1 | 8 | 24 | 39 | 11 |
| Chester | 14 | 4 | 2 | 8 | 27 | 29 | 10 |
| Northwich Victoria | 14 | 4 | 1 | 9 | 14 | 35 | 9 |
| *Leek | 14 | 3 | 3 | 8 | 15 | 35 | 7 |
| Buxton | 14 | 1 | 2 | 11 | 15 | 43 | 4 |

* 2 points deducted for fielding ineligible player

## 1896–97: The Combination

|                    | P  | W  | D | L  | F  | A  | Pts |
|--------------------|----|----|---|----|----|----|-----|
| Everton Reserves   | 18 | 14 | 3 | 1  | 61 | 14 | 31  |
| Rock Ferry         | 18 | 12 | 3 | 3  | 57 | 18 | 27  |
| Chester            | 17 | 10 | 3 | 4  | 37 | 25 | 23  |
| Northwich Victoria | 18 | 8  | 2 | 8  | 31 | 41 | 18  |
| Buxton             | 18 | 7  | 3 | 8  | 39 | 34 | 17  |
| Wrexham            | 18 | 7  | 2 | 9  | 41 | 40 | 16  |
| *Middleton         | 18 | 7  | 3 | 8  | 40 | 32 | 15  |
| Macclesfield       | 18 | 5  | 2 | 11 | 34 | 60 | 12  |
| *Crewe Alexandra   | 17 | 5  | 1 | 11 | 35 | 49 | 9   |
| *Barnton Rovers    | 18 | 2  | 2 | 14 | 18 | 80 | 4   |

* 2 points deducted for fielding ineligible players

## 1897–98: Stockport and District League

|                        | P  | W  | D | L  | F  | A  | Pts |
|------------------------|----|----|---|----|----|----|-----|
| Hallefield             | 18 | 15 | 3 | 0  | 64 | 17 | 33  |
| Heaton Norris Wanderers| 17 | 11 | 4 | 2  | 47 | 28 | 26  |
| Gorton Ramblers        | 17 | 10 | 2 | 5  | 34 | 22 | 22  |
| Christ Church          | 17 | 8  | 5 | 4  | 33 | 30 | 21  |
| Brabayns               | 18 | 8  | 2 | 8  | 51 | 42 | 18  |
| Norris Bank            | 17 | 4  | 4 | 9  | 21 | 25 | 12  |
| Brinksway              | 18 | 3  | 6 | 9  | 20 | 35 | 12  |
| Poynton                | 17 | 3  | 2 | 12 | 22 | 40 | 8   |
| Heaton Mersey          | 17 | 2  | 2 | 13 | 23 | 67 | 6   |

## 1898–99: North Staffs and District League

|                          | P  | W  | D | L  | F  | A  | Pts |
|--------------------------|----|----|---|----|----|----|-----|
| Stoke Reserves           | 22 | 17 | 1 | 4  | 84 | 25 | 35  |
| Congleton Hornets        | 22 | 14 | 5 | 3  | 56 | 26 | 33  |
| Port Vale Reserves       | 22 | 14 | 3 | 5  | 57 | 28 | 31  |
| Leek                     | 22 | 12 | 6 | 4  | 50 | 30 | 30  |
| Stafford Rangers         | 22 | 12 | 2 | 8  | 65 | 35 | 26  |
| Stone Town               | 22 | 10 | 4 | 8  | 56 | 27 | 24  |
| Nantwich                 | 22 | 9  | 4 | 9  | 50 | 55 | 22  |
| Crewe Alexandra Reserves | 22 | 9  | 3 | 10 | 34 | 36 | 21  |
| Market Drayton           | 22 | 5  | 2 | 15 | 28 | 78 | 12  |
| Hallefield               | 22 | 3  | 5 | 14 | 29 | 63 | 11  |
| Audley                   | 22 | 5  | 0 | 17 | 25 | 85 | 10  |
| Sandbach                 | 22 | 2  | 5 | 15 | 30 | 63 | 9   |

## 1899–1900: North Staffs and District League

|                          | P  | W  | D | L  | F  | A  | Pts |
|--------------------------|----|----|---|----|----|----|-----|
| Port Vale Reserves       | 16 | 13 | 1 | 2  | 33 | 11 | 27  |
| Stafford Rangers         | 16 | 11 | 1 | 4  | 48 | 20 | 23  |
| Stoke Reserves           | 16 | 9  | 1 | 6  | 50 | 27 | 19  |
| Crewe Alexandra Reserves | 16 | 9  | 1 | 6  | 37 | 25 | 19  |
| Congleton Hornets        | 15 | 8  | 2 | 5  | 34 | 23 | 18  |
| Hanley Swifts            | 15 | 7  | 2 | 6  | 36 | 31 | 16  |
| Nantwich                 | 16 | 5  | 0 | 11 | 37 | 37 | 10  |
| Stone Town               | 14 | 2  | 3 | 9  | 14 | 40 | 7   |
| Hallefield – Macclesfield| 14 | 1  | 3 | 10 | 21 | 67 | 5   |

## 1900–01: Manchester League

|                    | P  | W  | D | L  | F  | A   | Pts |
|--------------------|----|----|---|----|----|-----|-----|
| Tonge              | 28 | 23 | 2 | 3  | 94 | 32  | 48  |
| Northwich Victoria | 28 | 20 | 4 | 4  | 75 | 36  | 44  |
| Newton Heath       | 28 | 19 | 2 | 7  | 78 | 35  | 40  |
| Sale Holmfield     | 28 | 15 | 5 | 8  | 66 | 41  | 35  |
| Hyde               | 27 | 14 | 5 | 8  | 79 | 41  | 33  |
| Broadheath         | 27 | 13 | 4 | 10 | 75 | 59  | 30  |
| Manchester Talbot  | 28 | 12 | 6 | 10 | 48 | 44  | 30  |
| Buxton             | 28 | 12 | 4 | 12 | 54 | 46  | 28  |
| Macclesfield       | 28 | 10 | 3 | 15 | 60 | 75  | 23  |
| Oughtrington Park  | 28 | 8  | 6 | 14 | 46 | 64  | 22  |
| Lymm               | 28 | 7  | 6 | 15 | 42 | 64  | 20  |
| Oldham Athletic    | 28 | 8  | 4 | 16 | 40 | 68  | 20  |
| Stretford          | 28 | 7  | 6 | 15 | 36 | 66  | 20  |
| *Middleton         | 28 | 8  | 5 | 15 | 47 | 66  | 19  |
| Prestwich          | 28 | 1  | 1 | 26 | 18 | 128 | 3   |

* 2 points deducted for rule infringement

## 1901–02: Manchester League

|                       | P  | W  | D | L  | F  | A   | Pts |
|-----------------------|----|----|---|----|----|-----|-----|
| Newton Heath Athletic | 26 | 17 | 6 | 3  | 76 | 26  | 40  |
| Hyde                  | 26 | 17 | 6 | 3  | 74 | 27  | 40  |
| Northwich Victoria    | 26 | 16 | 2 | 8  | 61 | 53  | 34  |
| Sale Holmfield        | 26 | 13 | 7 | 6  | 61 | 37  | 33  |
| Tonge                 | 26 | 13 | 4 | 9  | 79 | 47  | 30  |
| Oldham Athletic       | 26 | 13 | 4 | 9  | 59 | 46  | 30  |
| Berry's               | 26 | 12 | 4 | 10 | 55 | 52  | 28  |
| Failsworth            | 26 | 10 | 4 | 12 | 64 | 54  | 24  |
| Manchester Talbot     | 26 | 11 | 2 | 13 | 47 | 50  | 24  |
| Heywood               | 25 | 8  | 4 | 13 | 59 | 66  | 20  |
| Buxton                | 25 | 7  | 6 | 12 | 43 | 70  | 20  |
| Broadheath            | 26 | 6  | 6 | 14 | 40 | 72  | 18  |
| Macclesfield          | 26 | 8  | 1 | 17 | 44 | 68  | 17  |
| Lymm                  | 26 | 2  | 2 | 22 | 24 | 118 | 8   |

## 1902–03: MANCHESTER LEAGUE

|  | P | W | D | L | F | A | Pts |
|---|---|---|---|---|---|---|---|
| Northwich Victoria | 26 | 20 | 4 | 2 | 59 | 22 | 44 |
| Failsworth | 26 | 16 | 3 | 7 | 87 | 42 | 35 |
| Newton Heath | 25 | 16 | 3 | 6 | 71 | 36 | 35 |
| Berry's | 26 | 14 | 3 | 9 | 68 | 41 | 31 |
| Hyde | 26 | 14 | 1 | 11 | 70 | 47 | 29 |
| Oldham Athletic | 24 | 12 | 5 | 7 | 47 | 30 | 29 |
| Buxton | 26 | 12 | 2 | 12 | 47 | 53 | 26 |
| Sale Holmfield | 25 | 9 | 6 | 10 | 46 | 59 | 24 |
| Broadheath | 26 | 9 | 5 | 12 | 43 | 55 | 23 |
| Denton | 24 | 8 | 4 | 12 | 41 | 53 | 20 |
| Macclesfield | 25 | 8 | 3 | 14 | 35 | 59 | 19 |
| Tonge | 26 | 6 | 7 | 13 | 25 | 68 | 19 |
| Hooley Hill | 25 | 5 | 2 | 18 | 40 | 62 | 12 |
| Manchester Talbot | 25 | 3 | 4 | 18 | 19 | 68 | 10 |

(Levenshulme resigned mid-season – their record was deleted.)

## 1903–04: MANCHESTER LEAGUE

|  | P | W | D | L | F | A | Pts |
|---|---|---|---|---|---|---|---|
| Berry's | 28 | 19 | 2 | 7 | 91 | 42 | 40 |
| Northwich Victoria | 28 | 17 | 4 | 7 | 69 | 40 | 38 |
| Oldham Athletic | 28 | 15 | 7 | 6 | 71 | 41 | 37 |
| Sale Holmfield | 28 | 15 | 3 | 10 | 75 | 50 | 33 |
| Denton | 28 | 13 | 7 | 8 | 72 | 47 | 33 |
| Newton Heath | 28 | 14 | 4 | 10 | 65 | 50 | 32 |
| Failsworth | 28 | 13 | 5 | 10 | 75 | 50 | 31 |
| Tonge | 28 | 15 | 1 | 12 | 57 | 54 | 31 |
| Hyde | 28 | 12 | 4 | 12 | 73 | 55 | 28 |
| Altrincham | 28 | 12 | 4 | 12 | 56 | 55 | 28 |
| Macclesfield | 28 | 9 | 8 | 11 | 49 | 57 | 26 |
| Glossop United | 28 | 9 | 3 | 16 | 40 | 74 | 21 |
| Hooley Hill | 28 | 8 | 4 | 16 | 52 | 72 | 20 |
| Buxton | 28 | 7 | 1 | 20 | 41 | 71 | 15 |
| Stretford | 28 | 4 | 1 | 23 | 21 | 135 | 9 |

## 1904–05: MANCHESTER LEAGUE

|  | P | W | D | L | F | A | Pts |
|---|---|---|---|---|---|---|---|
| Altrincham | 30 | 18 | 8 | 4 | 84 | 43 | 44 |
| Buxton | 30 | 16 | 6 | 8 | 68 | 42 | 38 |
| Denton | 30 | 16 | 5 | 9 | 63 | 49 | 37 |
| Sale Holmfield | 30 | 14 | 9 | 7 | 66 | 39 | 37 |
| Tonge | 30 | 11 | 14 | 5 | 60 | 33 | 36 |
| Failsworth | 30 | 14 | 8 | 8 | 63 | 41 | 36 |
| Northwich Victoria | 30 | 13 | 10 | 7 | 47 | 43 | 36 |
| Berry's | 30 | 13 | 6 | 11 | 51 | 43 | 32 |
| Witton Albion | 30 | 9 | 12 | 9 | 44 | 41 | 30 |
| Macclesfield | 30 | 7 | 11 | 12 | 44 | 55 | 25 |
| Hyde | 30 | 9 | 7 | 14 | 41 | 42 | 25 |
| Hooley Hill | 30 | 9 | 6 | 15 | 47 | 52 | 24 |
| Newton Heath | 30 | 8 | 6 | 16 | 57 | 72 | 22 |
| Stretford | 30 | 8 | 5 | 17 | 54 | 78 | 21 |
| Heywood United | 30 | 6 | 7 | 17 | 45 | 91 | 19 |
| Oughtrington Park | 30 | 8 | 2 | 20 | 47 | 101 | 18 |

## 1905–06: MANCHESTER LEAGUE

|  | P | W | D | L | F | A | Pts |
|---|---|---|---|---|---|---|---|
| Denton | 30 | 22 | 1 | 7 | 88 | 38 | 45 |
| Sale Holmfield | 30 | 15 | 10 | 5 | 53 | 30 | 40 |
| Altrincham | 30 | 16 | 5 | 9 | 81 | 51 | 37 |
| Northwich Victoria | 30 | 17 | 3 | 10 | 67 | 57 | 35 |
| Tonge | 30 | 15 | 5 | 10 | 67 | 57 | 35 |
| Macclesfield | 30 | 15 | 4 | 11 | 58 | 58 | 34 |
| Heywood United | 30 | 14 | 5 | 11 | 62 | 58 | 33 |
| Pendlebury | 30 | 10 | 10 | 10 | 74 | 53 | 30 |
| Witton Albion | 30 | 10 | 8 | 12 | 47 | 45 | 28 |
| Berry's | 30 | 10 | 6 | 14 | 53 | 71 | 26 |
| Buxton | 30 | 9 | 7 | 14 | 36 | 46 | 25 |
| Hyde | 30 | 10 | 4 | 16 | 48 | 81 | 24 |
| Hooley Hill | 30 | 9 | 4 | 17 | 57 | 65 | 22 |
| Salford United | 30 | 10 | 2 | 18 | 54 | 74 | 22 |
| Newton Heath | 30 | 9 | 4 | 17 | 45 | 73 | 22 |
| Stretford | 30 | 7 | 6 | 17 | 45 | 77 | 20 |

## 1906–07: MANCHESTER LEAGUE

|  | P | W | D | L | F | A | Pts |
|---|---|---|---|---|---|---|---|
| Altrincham | 28 | 18 | 7 | 3 | 70 | 30 | 43 |
| Macclesfield | 28 | 19 | 4 | 5 | 75 | 39 | 42 |
| Witton Albion | 28 | 18 | 5 | 5 | 49 | 30 | 41 |
| Sale Holmfield | 28 | 13 | 8 | 7 | 53 | 38 | 34 |
| Salford United | 28 | 10 | 10 | 8 | 61 | 39 | 30 |
| Northwich Victoria | 28 | 12 | 6 | 10 | 59 | 51 | 30 |
| Tonge | 28 | 12 | 6 | 10 | 51 | 45 | 30 |
| Denton | 28 | 12 | 5 | 11 | 52 | 44 | 29 |
| Pendlebury | 28 | 19 | 9 | 9 | 57 | 51 | 29 |
| Stretford | 28 | 11 | 4 | 13 | 39 | 55 | 26 |
| Berry's | 28 | 7 | 7 | 14 | 40 | 66 | 21 |
| Heywood United | 28 | 8 | 4 | 16 | 54 | 63 | 20 |
| Buxton | 28 | 7 | 5 | 16 | 39 | 57 | 19 |
| Hooley Hill | 28 | 4 | 7 | 17 | 35 | 68 | 15 |
| Newton Heath | 28 | 3 | 5 | 20 | 32 | 90 | 11 |

## 1907–08: MANCHESTER LEAGUE

|  | P | W | D | L | F | A | Pts |
|---|---|---|---|---|---|---|---|
| Denton | 30 | 21 | 5 | 4 | 108 | 48 | 47 |
| Northwich Victoria | 30 | 15 | 10 | 5 | 75 | 53 | 40 |
| Eccles Borough | 30 | 16 | 7 | 7 | 59 | 44 | 39 |
| Macclesfield | 30 | 16 | 5 | 9 | 63 | 39 | 37 |
| Tonge | 30 | 14 | 8 | 8 | 67 | 46 | 36 |
| Altrincham | 30 | 13 | 6 | 11 | 63 | 53 | 32 |
| Witton Albion | 30 | 12 | 8 | 10 | 52 | 54 | 32 |
| Sale Holmfield | 30 | 14 | 3 | 13 | 70 | 53 | 31 |
| Ramsbottom | 30 | 10 | 8 | 12 | 61 | 68 | 28 |
| Rochdale | 30 | 10 | 8 | 12 | 49 | 63 | 28 |
| Buxton | 30 | 10 | 7 | 13 | 35 | 52 | 27 |
| Hooley Hill | 30 | 8 | 9 | 13 | 56 | 59 | 25 |
| Salford United | 30 | 9 | 5 | 16 | 49 | 68 | 23 |
| Berry's | 30 | 9 | 5 | 16 | 46 | 66 | 23 |
| Stretford | 30 | 5 | 10 | 15 | 43 | 75 | 20 |
| Newton Heath | 30 | 3 | 6 | 21 | 33 | 88 | 12 |

1908–09: MANCHESTER LEAGUE

|  | P | W | D | L | F | A | Pts |
|---|---|---|---|---|---|---|---|
| Macclesfield | 30 | 18 | 6 | 6 | 78 | 43 | 42 |
| Northwich Victoria | 30 | 17 | 4 | 9 | 73 | 51 | 38 |
| Altrincham | 30 | 16 | 4 | 10 | 61 | 36 | 36 |
| New Mills | 30 | 13 | 8 | 9 | 73 | 45 | 34 |
| Hazel Grove | 30 | 13 | 8 | 9 | 62 | 48 | 34 |
| Tonge | 30 | 14 | 5 | 11 | 54 | 45 | 33 |
| Sale Holmfield | 29 | 15 | 3 | 11 | 65 | 56 | 33 |
| Salford United | 30 | 14 | 5 | 11 | 61 | 55 | 33 |
| Witton Albion | 30 | 13 | 5 | 12 | 67 | 59 | 31 |
| Tyldsley Albion | 30 | 12 | 6 | 12 | 74 | 67 | 30 |
| Denton | 30 | 11 | 7 | 12 | 70 | 67 | 29 |
| Ramsbottom | 30 | 12 | 5 | 13 | 61 | 51 | 29 |
| Hooley Hill | 30 | 11 | 6 | 13 | 57 | 64 | 28 |
| Berry's | 29 | 10 | 5 | 14 | 57 | 53 | 25 |
| Buxton | 30 | 7 | 4 | 19 | 39 | 74 | 18 |
| Newton Heath | 30 | 0 | 3 | 27 | 34 | 148 | 3 |

1910–11: MANCHESTER LEAGUE

|  | P | W | D | L | F | A | Pts |
|---|---|---|---|---|---|---|---|
| Macclesfield | 30 | 20 | 8 | 2 | 61 | 30 | 48 |
| Altrincham | 30 | 19 | 4 | 7 | 81 | 38 | 42 |
| Crewe Alexandra | 30 | 17 | 8 | 5 | 74 | 36 | 42 |
| Northwich Victoria | 30 | 16 | 5 | 9 | 75 | 41 | 37 |
| Tyldsley Albion | 30 | 15 | 5 | 10 | 62 | 55 | 35 |
| Hurst | 30 | 14 | 4 | 12 | 69 | 66 | 32 |
| Hazel Grove | 30 | 11 | 10 | 9 | 47 | 52 | 32 |
| Buxton | 30 | 13 | 5 | 12 | 57 | 56 | 31 |
| Witton Albion | 30 | 11 | 7 | 12 | 68 | 64 | 29 |
| Berry's | 30 | 11 | 6 | 13 | 62 | 72 | 28 |
| Rusholme | 30 | 11 | 4 | 15 | 67 | 76 | 26 |
| Hooley Hill | 30 | 7 | 11 | 12 | 41 | 56 | 25 |
| Nantwich | 30 | 8 | 6 | 16 | 60 | 83 | 22 |
| New Mills | 30 | 6 | 6 | 18 | 49 | 71 | 18 |
| Salford United | 30 | 7 | 3 | 20 | 43 | 85 | 17 |
| Tonge | 30 | 5 | 6 | 19 | 42 | 76 | 16 |

1909–10: MANCHESTER LEAGUE

|  | P | W | D | L | F | A | Pts |
|---|---|---|---|---|---|---|---|
| Salford United | 34 | 20 | 6 | 8 | 79 | 44 | 46 |
| Hurst | 34 | 19 | 8 | 7 | 70 | 39 | 46 |
| Altrincham | 34 | 20 | 5 | 9 | 82 | 41 | 45 |
| Macclesfield | 34 | 18 | 6 | 10 | 86 | 45 | 42 |
| Denton | 34 | 18 | 6 | 10 | 76 | 60 | 42 |
| Tonge | 34 | 20 | 2 | 12 | 66 | 42 | 42 |
| Northwich Victoria | 34 | 18 | 4 | 12 | 81 | 65 | 40 |
| Tyldsley Albion | 34 | 14 | 9 | 11 | 65 | 51 | 37 |
| Buxton | 34 | 15 | 5 | 14 | 61 | 51 | 35 |
| Hooley Hill | 34 | 11 | 13 | 10 | 67 | 62 | 35 |
| Berry's | 34 | 14 | 6 | 14 | 59 | 67 | 34 |
| Witton Albion | 34 | 13 | 6 | 15 | 73 | 67 | 32 |
| Hazel Grove | 34 | 11 | 9 | 14 | 58 | 69 | 31 |
| New Mills | 34 | 9 | 9 | 16 | 51 | 68 | 27 |
| Ramsbottom | 34 | 11 | 5 | 18 | 61 | 89 | 27 |
| Rusholme | 34 | 8 | 3 | 23 | 49 | 91 | 19 |
| Sale Holmfield | 34 | 4 | 6 | 24 | 27 | 90 | 14 |
| Newton Heath | 34 | 3 | 4 | 27 | 28 | 115 | 10 |

1911–12: MANCHESTER LEAGUE

|  | P | W | D | L | F | A | Pts |
|---|---|---|---|---|---|---|---|
| Hurst | 24 | 18 | 4 | 2 | 82 | 30 | 40 |
| Northwich Victoria | 24 | 14 | 5 | 5 | 51 | 32 | 33 |
| Witton Albion | 24 | 13 | 5 | 6 | 58 | 32 | 31 |
| Macclesfield | 24 | 12 | 5 | 7 | 51 | 34 | 29 |
| Eccles Borough | 24 | 11 | 3 | 10 | 48 | 39 | 25 |
| Stalybridge Celtic | 24 | 10 | 3 | 11 | 55 | 53 | 23 |
| Chester | 24 | 10 | 3 | 11 | 40 | 50 | 23 |
| Nantwich | 23 | 11 | 1 | 11 | 40 | 45 | 23 |
| Crewe Alexandra | 23 | 10 | 1 | 12 | 39 | 47 | 21 |
| Hooley Hill | 24 | 7 | 3 | 14 | 46 | 65 | 17 |
| Rochdale | 24 | 6 | 4 | 14 | 45 | 70 | 16 |
| Buxton | 22 | 5 | 4 | 13 | 30 | 66 | 14 |
| Hazel Grove | 24 | 5 | 3 | 16 | 48 | 70 | 13 |

## 1911–12: Lancashire Combination 2nd Division

|  | P | W | D | L | F | A | Pts |
|---|---|---|---|---|---|---|---|
| Stalybridge Celtic | 29 | 23 | 2 | 4 | 110 | 36 | 48 |
| Altrincham | 30 | 23 | 2 | 5 | 92 | 37 | 48 |
| Tranmere Rovers | 30 | 18 | 6 | 6 | 83 | 41 | 42 |
| Fleetwood | 30 | 16 | 4 | 10 | 64 | 31 | 36 |
| South Liverpool | 30 | 17 | 2 | 11 | 85 | 49 | 36 |
| Macclesfield | 30 | 14 | 6 | 10 | 39 | 40 | 34 |
| Padiham | 30 | 14 | 4 | 12 | 58 | 61 | 32 |
| Oswestry United | 29 | 12 | 5 | 12 | 73 | 63 | 29 |
| Tyldsley Albion | 30 | 11 | 5 | 14 | 61 | 66 | 27 |
| Hindley Central | 29 | 11 | 3 | 15 | 64 | 69 | 25 |
| Atherton | 30 | 11 | 3 | 16 | 49 | 77 | 25 |
| Barnoldswick | 30 | 11 | 5 | 15 | 53 | 79 | 25 |
| Darwen | 30 | 9 | 3 | 18 | 34 | 84 | 21 |
| Great Harwood | 30 | 7 | 5 | 18 | 49 | 62 | 19 |
| Portsmouth Rovers | 30 | 6 | 5 | 19 | 51 | 86 | 17 |
| Lancaster | 30 | 4 | 4 | 22 | 29 | 123 | 12 |

## 1912–13: Lancashire Combination 2nd Division

|  | P | W | D | L | F | A | Pts |
|---|---|---|---|---|---|---|---|
| South Liverpool | 34 | 24 | 5 | 5 | 94 | 24 | 53 |
| Stalybridge Celtic | 34 | 21 | 5 | 8 | 74 | 45 | 47 |
| Atherton | 34 | 20 | 7 | 7 | 87 | 59 | 47 |
| Northwich Victoria | 34 | 18 | 9 | 7 | 101 | 43 | 45 |
| Hurst | 34 | 19 | 6 | 9 | 93 | 62 | 44 |
| Macclesfield | 34 | 17 | 8 | 9 | 75 | 40 | 42 |
| Hindley Central | 34 | 17 | 6 | 11 | 89 | 56 | 40 |
| Witton Albion | 34 | 17 | 5 | 12 | 81 | 57 | 39 |
| Great Harwood | 34 | 16 | 7 | 11 | 62 | 62 | 39 |
| Oswestry United | 34 | 17 | 3 | 14 | 79 | 80 | 37 |
| Padiham | 34 | 14 | 4 | 16 | 61 | 76 | 32 |
| Nantwich | 34 | 12 | 7 | 15 | 64 | 70 | 31 |
| Rochdale | 34 | 10 | 5 | 19 | 52 | 63 | 25 |
| Darwen | 34 | 9 | 5 | 20 | 53 | 85 | 23 |
| Barnoldswick United | 34 | 7 | 6 | 21 | 50 | 99 | 20 |
| Portsmouth Rovers | 34 | 8 | 3 | 23 | 53 | 101 | 17 |
| Bacup | 34 | 8 | 1 | 25 | 43 | 116 | 17 |
| Lancaster Town | 34 | 3 | 6 | 25 | 27 | 100 | 12 |

## 1913–14: Lancashire Combination 2nd Division

|  | P | W | D | L | F | A | Pts |
|---|---|---|---|---|---|---|---|
| Witton Albion | 34 | 22 | 5 | 7 | 107 | 44 | 49 |
| Macclesfield | 34 | 21 | 4 | 9 | 79 | 39 | 46 |
| Rossendale | 33 | 19 | 4 | 10 | 83 | 40 | 42 |
| Denton | 34 | 18 | 4 | 12 | 62 | 56 | 40 |
| Great Harwood | 34 | 18 | 3 | 13 | 76 | 56 | 39 |
| Stalybridge Celtic | 34 | 17 | 4 | 13 | 77 | 47 | 38 |
| Lancaster Town | 34 | 16 | 6 | 12 | 70 | 54 | 38 |
| Darwen | 34 | 15 | 6 | 13 | 66 | 65 | 36 |
| Crewe Alexandra | 34 | 14 | 7 | 13 | 60 | 50 | 35 |
| Oswestry United | 34 | 14 | 4 | 16 | 47 | 60 | 32 |
| Barnoldswick United | 33 | 13 | 5 | 15 | 61 | 71 | 31 |
| Nantwich | 33 | 11 | 7 | 15 | 72 | 71 | 29 |
| Padiham | 32 | 11 | 7 | 14 | 58 | 87 | 29 |
| Hindley Central | 32 | 11 | 6 | 15 | 61 | 74 | 28 |
| Rochdale | 34 | 11 | 5 | 18 | 44 | 72 | 27 |
| Newton Heath | 34 | 10 | 5 | 19 | 44 | 89 | 25 |
| Portsmouth Rovers | 33 | 10 | 2 | 21 | 49 | 80 | 22 |
| Bacup | 34 | 5 | 5 | 24 | 40 | 112 | 15 |

## 1914–15: Lancashire Combination 1st Division

|  | P | W | D | L | F | A | Pts |
|---|---|---|---|---|---|---|---|
| Eccles Borough | 32 | 18 | 8 | 6 | 77 | 41 | 44 |
| Hurst | 32 | 17 | 8 | 7 | 76 | 48 | 42 |
| Tranmere Rovers | 32 | 19 | 3 | 10 | 84 | 52 | 41 |
| Macclesfield | 32 | 19 | 3 | 10 | 68 | 49 | 41 |
| Northwich Victoria | 32 | 16 | 6 | 10 | 71 | 50 | 38 |
| Accrington Stanley | 32 | 15 | 7 | 10 | 75 | 59 | 37 |
| Altrincham | 32 | 15 | 4 | 13 | 68 | 55 | 34 |
| Atherton | 32 | 15 | 4 | 13 | 69 | 59 | 34 |
| South Liverpool | 32 | 13 | 7 | 12 | 72 | 67 | 33 |
| Witton Albion | 32 | 13 | 6 | 13 | 61 | 63 | 32 |
| Nelson | 32 | 13 | 4 | 15 | 66 | 64 | 30 |
| Denton | 32 | 13 | 2 | 17 | 72 | 98 | 28 |
| Barrow | 32 | 11 | 6 | 15 | 59 | 89 | 28 |
| Fleetwood | 32 | 9 | 5 | 18 | 65 | 94 | 23 |
| Rossendale United | 32 | 11 | 0 | 21 | 42 | 64 | 22 |
| Hyde | 32 | 8 | 5 | 19 | 65 | 93 | 21 |
| Chorley | 32 | 6 | 4 | 22 | 46 | 91 | 16 |

# League Tables, 1919–1939

## 1919–20: CHESHIRE LEAGUE

|  | P | W | D | L | F | A | Pts |
|---|---|---|---|---|---|---|---|
| Runcorn | 22 | 17 | 2 | 3 | 57 | 19 | 36 |
| Mossley | 22 | 11 | 3 | 8 | 41 | 43 | 25 |
| Witton Albion | 22 | 10 | 4 | 8 | 41 | 38 | 24 |
| Crewe Alexandra | 22 | 10 | 3 | 9 | 45 | 45 | 23 |
| Crighton's Athletic | 22 | 9 | 4 | 99 | 48 | 38 | 22 |
| Chester | 22 | 9 | 4 | 9 | 55 | 55 | 22 |
| Winsford United | 22 | 10 | 1 | 11 | 45 | 34 | 21 |
| Altrincham | 22 | 7 | 6 | 9 | 38 | 47 | 20 |
| Macclesfield | 22 | 8 | 4 | 10 | 36 | 54 | 20 |
| Monk's Hall | 22 | 8 | 2 | 12 | 47 | 54 | 18 |
| Nantwich | 22 | 8 | 2 | 12 | 39 | 54 | 18 |
| Northwich Victoria | 22 | 5 | 5 | 12 | 33 | 44 | 15 |

## SUBSIDIARY COMPETITION: SECTION A

|  | P | W | D | L | F | A | Pts |
|---|---|---|---|---|---|---|---|
| Mossley | 10 | 6 | 2 | 2 | 24 | 14 | 14 |
| Altrincham | 10 | 3 | 5 | 2 | 15 | 13 | 11 |
| Northwich Victoria | 10 | 3 | 5 | 2 | 14 | 13 | 11 |
| Witton Albion | 10 | 3 | 2 | 5 | 15 | 15 | 8 |
| Winsford United | 10 | 2 | 4 | 4 | 15 | 16 | 8 |
| Macclesfield | 10 | 2 | 4 | 4 | 11 | 23 | 8 |

## 1920–21: CHESHIRE LEAGUE

|  | P | W | D | L | F | A | Pts |
|---|---|---|---|---|---|---|---|
| Winsford United | 34 | 19 | 6 | 9 | 67 | 48 | 44 |
| Congleton Town | 34 | 17 | 8 | 9 | 68 | 56 | 42 |
| Runcorn | 34 | 17 | 7 | 10 | 64 | 42 | 41 |
| Monk's Hall | 34 | 16 | 9 | 9 | 58 | 40 | 41 |
| Crewe Alexandra | 34 | 15 | 9 | 10 | 80 | 51 | 39 |
| Macclesfield | 34 | 16 | 7 | 11 | 67 | 50 | 39 |
| Crighton's Athletic | 34 | 16 | 6 | 12 | 72 | 62 | 38 |
| Mossley | 34 | 14 | 8 | 12 | 49 | 48 | 36 |
| Altrincham | 34 | 14 | 8 | 12 | 59 | 70 | 36 |
| Chester | 34 | 15 | 5 | 14 | 72 | 74 | 35 |
| Nantwich | 34 | 14 | 6 | 14 | 82 | 72 | 34 |
| Ashton National | 34 | 14 | 5 | 15 | 69 | 64 | 33 |
| Northwich Victoria | 34 | 12 | 5 | 17 | 53 | 60 | 29 |
| Tranmere Rovers | 34 | 13 | 3 | 18 | 52 | 69 | 29 |
| Stalybridge Celtic | 34 | 11 | 5 | 18 | 61 | 74 | 27 |
| Sandbach Ramblers | 34 | 8 | 9 | 17 | 42 | 68 | 25 |
| Witton Albion | 34 | 10 | 3 | 21 | 48 | 77 | 23 |
| Connah's Quay | 34 | 6 | 9 | 19 | 44 | 82 | 21 |

## 1921–22: CHESHIRE LEAGUE

|  | P | W | D | L | F | A | Pts |
|---|---|---|---|---|---|---|---|
| Chester | 38 | 25 | 3 | 10 | 78 | 50 | 53 |
| Congleton Town | 38 | 22 | 6 | 10 | 82 | 49 | 50 |
| Ashton National | 38 | 23 | 2 | 13 | 79 | 63 | 48 |
| Witton Albion | 38 | 20 | 7 | 11 | 77 | 54 | 47 |
| Stalybridge Celtic | 38 | 18 | 8 | 12 | 71 | 59 | 44 |
| Nantwich | 38 | 15 | 13 | 10 | 71 | 57 | 43 |
| Northwich Victoria | 38 | 15 | 10 | 13 | 62 | 40 | 40 |
| Macclesfield | 38 | 13 | 13 | 12 | 60 | 64 | 39 |
| Connah's Quay | 38 | 13 | 12 | 13 | 51 | 52 | 38 |
| Whitchurch | 38 | 16 | 6 | 16 | 65 | 71 | 38 |
| Winsford United | 38 | 13 | 12 | 13 | 53 | 64 | 38 |
| Altrincham | 38 | 13 | 9 | 16 | 75 | 70 | 35 |
| Sandbach Ramblers | 38 | 13 | 9 | 16 | 51 | 54 | 35 |
| Ellesmere Port Cement | 38 | 14 | 6 | 18 | 61 | 63 | 34 |
| Crewe Alexandra | 38 | 13 | 8 | 17 | 61 | 70 | 34 |
| Saltney Athletic | 38 | 9 | 15 | 14 | 65 | 75 | 33 |
| Mossley | 38 | 11 | 7 | 20 | 54 | 84 | 29 |
| Stockport County | 38 | 11 | 6 | 21 | 57 | 102 | 28 |
| Tranmere Rovers | 38 | 10 | 7 | 21 | 50 | 66 | 27 |
| Runcorn | 38 | 10 | 7 | 21 | 56 | 80 | 27 |

## 1922–23: CHESHIRE LEAGUE

|  | P | W | D | L | F | A | Pts |
|---|---|---|---|---|---|---|---|
| Crewe Alexandra | 38 | 27 | 6 | 5 | 102 | 42 | 60 |
| Stockport County | 38 | 20 | 8 | 10 | 89 | 58 | 48 |
| Altrincham | 38 | 19 | 10 | 9 | 86 | 60 | 48 |
| Macclesfield | 38 | 18 | 10 | 10 | 84 | 52 | 46 |
| Ellesmere Port Cement | 38 | 18 | 7 | 13 | 69 | 48 | 43 |
| Saltney Athletic | 38 | 20 | 3 | 15 | 75 | 83 | 43 |
| Winsford United | 38 | 17 | 7 | 14 | 51 | 52 | 41 |
| Tranmere Rovers | 38 | 16 | 9 | 13 | 69 | 71 | 41 |
| Mossley | 38 | 15 | 10 | 13 | 76 | 62 | 40 |
| Stalybridge Celtic | 38 | 15 | 9 | 14 | 56 | 49 | 39 |
| Ashton National | 38 | 14 | 10 | 14 | 75 | 57 | 38 |
| Whitchurch | 38 | 14 | 9 | 15 | 66 | 78 | 37 |
| Congleton Town | 38 | 14 | 8 | 16 | 64 | 71 | 36 |
| Nantwich | 38 | 15 | 5 | 18 | 61 | 84 | 35 |
| Chester | 38 | 13 | 8 | 17 | 59 | 60 | 34 |
| Sandbach Ramblers | 38 | 10 | 10 | 18 | 53 | 81 | 30 |
| Runcorn | 38 | 11 | 5 | 22 | 56 | 85 | 27 |
| Northwich Victoria | 38 | 8 | 10 | 20 | 47 | 75 | 26 |
| Witton Albion | 38 | 9 | 7 | 22 | 43 | 83 | 25 |
| Middlewich | 38 | 8 | 7 | 23 | 40 | 70 | 23 |

## 1923–24: Cheshire League

| | P | W | D | L | F | A | Pts |
|---|---|---|---|---|---|---|---|
| Crewe Alexandra | 42 | 28 | 5 | 9 | 96 | 62 | 61 |
| Port Vale | 42 | 24 | 10 | 8 | 109 | 60 | 58 |
| Whitchurch | 42 | 24 | 8 | 10 | 81 | 52 | 56 |
| Stalybridge Celtic | 42 | 24 | 6 | 12 | 93 | 50 | 54 |
| Stockport County | 42 | 21 | 12 | 9 | 92 | 56 | 54 |
| Northwich Victoria | 42 | 18 | 10 | 14 | 85 | 77 | 46 |
| Congleton Town | 42 | 18 | 9 | 15 | 86 | 59 | 45 |
| Hurst | 42 | 19 | 7 | 16 | 78 | 76 | 45 |
| Macclesfield | 42 | 18 | 6 | 18 | 82 | 67 | 42 |
| Altrincham | 42 | 19 | 4 | 19 | 69 | 75 | 42 |
| Ashton National | 42 | 15 | 11 | 16 | 59 | 60 | 41 |
| Ellesmere Port Cement | 42 | 14 | 12 | 16 | 66 | 64 | 40 |
| Mossley | 42 | 16 | 8 | 18 | 77 | 90 | 40 |
| Winsford United | 42 | 17 | 5 | 20 | 56 | 77 | 39 |
| Wallasey United | 42 | 13 | 12 | 17 | 50 | 71 | 38 |
| Chester | 42 | 11 | 15 | 16 | 59 | 66 | 37 |
| Witton Albion | 42 | 14 | 9 | 19 | 55 | 67 | 37 |
| Tranmere Rovers | 42 | 13 | 9 | 20 | 78 | 90 | 35 |
| Runcorn | 42 | 13 | 9 | 20 | 54 | 68 | 35 |
| Middlewich | 42 | 12 | 8 | 22 | 56 | 101 | 32 |
| Nantwich | 42 | 9 | 6 | 27 | 53 | 101 | 24 |
| Sandbach Ramblers | 42 | 7 | 9 | 26 | 41 | 85 | 23 |

## 1924–25: Cheshire League

| | P | W | D | L | F | A | Pts |
|---|---|---|---|---|---|---|---|
| Port Vale | 42 | 25 | 10 | 7 | 112 | 43 | 60 |
| Northwich Victoria | 42 | 25 | 6 | 11 | 94 | 58 | 56 |
| Stalybridge Celtic | 42 | 24 | 7 | 11 | 92 | 52 | 55 |
| Ashton National | 42 | 24 | 6 | 12 | 94 | 50 | 54 |
| Hurst | 42 | 22 | 10 | 10 | 101 | 61 | 54 |
| Macclesfield | 42 | 21 | 6 | 15 | 79 | 77 | 48 |
| Tranmere Rovers | 42 | 21 | 5 | 16 | 106 | 79 | 47 |
| Crewe Alexandra | 42 | 20 | 5 | 17 | 91 | 68 | 45 |
| Middlewich | 42 | 18 | 6 | 18 | 67 | 71 | 42 |
| Mossley | 42 | 17 | 8 | 17 | 85 | 83 | 42 |
| Winsford United | 42 | 18 | 6 | 18 | 83 | 87 | 42 |
| Altrincham | 42 | 16 | 7 | 19 | 70 | 93 | 39 |
| Manchester North End | 42 | 15 | 7 | 20 | 96 | 95 | 37 |
| Congleton Town | 42 | 14 | 8 | 20 | 77 | 93 | 36 |
| Whitchurch | 42 | 12 | 12 | 18 | 55 | 66 | 36 |
| Sandbach Ramblers | 42 | 12 | 11 | 19 | 57 | 81 | 35 |
| Chester | 42 | 14 | 7 | 21 | 59 | 103 | 35 |
| Witton Albion | 42 | 13 | 7 | 22 | 59 | 82 | 33 |
| Nantwich | 42 | 12 | 9 | 21 | 72 | 102 | 33 |
| Runcorn | 42 | 13 | 6 | 23 | 62 | 94 | 32 |
| Ellesmere Port Cement | 42 | 13 | 6 | 23 | 67 | 82 | 32 |
| Ellesmere Port Town | 42 | 12 | 6 | 24 | 56 | 88 | 30 |

## 1925–26: Cheshire League

| | P | W | D | L | F | A | Pts |
|---|---|---|---|---|---|---|---|
| Chester | 42 | 29 | 5 | 8 | 110 | 57 | 63 |
| Port Vale | 42 | 26 | 6 | 10 | 115 | 58 | 58 |
| Congleton Town | 42 | 25 | 9 | 11 | 125 | 74 | 56 |
| Stalybridge Celtic | 42 | 24 | 4 | 14 | 133 | 77 | 52 |
| Witton Albion | 42 | 21 | 8 | 13 | 121 | 85 | 50 |
| Ashton National | 42 | 20 | 8 | 14 | 98 | 84 | 48 |
| Winsford United | 42 | 22 | 3 | 17 | 96 | 87 | 47 |
| Nantwich | 42 | 19 | 9 | 14 | 90 | 90 | 47 |
| Tranmere Rovers | 42 | 17 | 11 | 14 | 104 | 97 | 45 |
| Manchester North End | 42 | 18 | 7 | 17 | 92 | 111 | 43 |
| Crewe Alexandra | 42 | 18 | 6 | 18 | 96 | 75 | 42 |
| Runcorn | 42 | 19 | 4 | 19 | 79 | 92 | 42 |
| Hurst | 42 | 16 | 9 | 17 | 114 | 95 | 41 |
| Mossley | 42 | 14 | 8 | 20 | 80 | 106 | 36 |
| Ellesmere Port | 42 | 16 | 4 | 22 | 73 | 107 | 36 |
| Altrincham | 42 | 15 | 4 | 23 | 85 | 94 | 34 |
| Sandbach Ramblers | 42 | 14 | 6 | 22 | 81 | 92 | 34 |
| Northwich Victoria | 42 | 14 | 5 | 23 | 75 | 101 | 33 |
| Whitchurch | 42 | 14 | 4 | 24 | 85 | 124 | 32 |
| Macclesfield | 42 | 12 | 8 | 22 | 88 | 142 | 32 |
| Middlewich | 42 | 13 | 4 | 25 | 76 | 120 | 30 |
| Eccles United | 42 | 9 | 5 | 28 | 84 | 132 | 23 |

## 1926–27: Cheshire League

| | P | W | D | L | F | A | Pts |
|---|---|---|---|---|---|---|---|
| Chester | 42 | 31 | 3 | 8 | 147 | 67 | 65 |
| Ashton National | 42 | 29 | 4 | 9 | 119 | 63 | 62 |
| Tranmere Rovers | 42 | 28 | 4 | 10 | 163 | 72 | 60 |
| Congleton Town | 42 | 27 | 5 | 10 | 125 | 59 | 59 |
| Stalybridge Celtic | 42 | 26 | 6 | 10 | 136 | 79 | 58 |
| Crewe Alexandra | 42 | 26 | 6 | 10 | 118 | 81 | 58 |
| Port Vale | 42 | 24 | 5 | 14 | 119 | 74 | 53 |
| Manchester North End | 42 | 24 | 3 | 15 | 156 | 90 | 51 |
| Altrincham | 42 | 20 | 7 | 15 | 129 | 108 | 47 |
| Runcorn | 42 | 19 | 7 | 16 | 94 | 101 | 45 |
| Macclesfield | 42 | 19 | 5 | 18 | 113 | 112 | 43 |
| Nantwich | 42 | 16 | 10 | 16 | 95 | 86 | 42 |
| Winsford United | 42 | 18 | 5 | 19 | 120 | 97 | 41 |
| Middlewich | 42 | 15 | 6 | 21 | 99 | 132 | 36 |
| Witton Albion | 42 | 13 | 6 | 23 | 79 | 108 | 32 |
| Eccles United | 42 | 10 | 9 | 23 | 84 | 127 | 29 |
| Mossley | 42 | 11 | 7 | 24 | 88 | 146 | 29 |
| Northwich Victoria | 42 | 11 | 4 | 27 | 70 | 141 | 26 |
| Whitchurch | 42 | 10 | 6 | 26 | 62 | 134 | 26 |
| Hurst | 42 | 8 | 6 | 28 | 65 | 119 | 22 |
| Sandbach Ramblers | 42 | 7 | 7 | 28 | 59 | 124 | 21 |
| Ellesmere Port | 42 | 8 | 3 | 31 | 77 | 196 | 19 |

## 1927–28: CHESHIRE LEAGUE

| | P | W | D | L | F | A | Pts |
|---|---|---|---|---|---|---|---|
| Port Vale | 42 | 31 | 5 | 6 | 147 | 48 | 67 |
| Stockport County | 42 | 26 | 9 | 7 | 158 | 81 | 61 |
| Ashton National | 42 | 28 | 5 | 9 | 145 | 78 | 61 |
| Congleton Town | 42 | 26 | 7 | 9 | 105 | 60 | 59 |
| Chester | 42 | 23 | 6 | 13 | 120 | 73 | 52 |
| Winsford United | 42 | 21 | 9 | 12 | 122 | 101 | 51 |
| Stalybridge Celtic | 42 | 21 | 6 | 15 | 120 | 93 | 48 |
| Runcorn | 42 | 19 | 10 | 13 | 86 | 81 | 48 |
| Manchester North End | 42 | 20 | 7 | 15 | 133 | 101 | 47 |
| Hurst | 42 | 19 | 7 | 16 | 105 | 101 | 45 |
| Tranmere Rovers | 42 | 21 | 3 | 18 | 104 | 101 | 45 |
| Crewe Alexandra | 42 | 17 | 9 | 16 | 112 | 98 | 43 |
| Witton Albion | 42 | 18 | 7 | 17 | 89 | 98 | 43 |
| Middlewich | 42 | 15 | 8 | 19 | 87 | 102 | 38 |
| Sandbach Ramblers | 42 | 13 | 8 | 21 | 89 | 101 | 34 |
| Nantwich | 42 | 15 | 3 | 24 | 103 | 133 | 33 |
| Macclesfield | 42 | 13 | 5 | 24 | 75 | 117 | 31 |
| Northwich Victoria | 42 | 10 | 9 | 23 | 88 | 136 | 29 |
| Mossley | 42 | 12 | 5 | 25 | 86 | 138 | 29 |
| Altrincham | 42 | 10 | 4 | 28 | 77 | 146 | 24 |
| Whitchurch | 42 | 8 | 3 | 32 | 77 | 166 | 18 |
| Eccles United | 42 | 7 | 4 | 31 | 64 | 153 | 18 |

## 1929–30: CHESHIRE LEAGUE

| | P | W | D | L | F | A | Pts |
|---|---|---|---|---|---|---|---|
| Port Vale | 42 | 29 | 6 | 7 | 146 | 49 | 64 |
| Connah's Quay | 42 | 30 | 3 | 9 | 148 | 59 | 63 |
| Tranmere Rovers | 42 | 26 | 6 | 10 | 154 | 90 | 58 |
| Macclesfield | 42 | 24 | 7 | 11 | 139 | 109 | 55 |
| Ashton National | 42 | 24 | 4 | 14 | 118 | 70 | 52 |
| Stalybridge Celtic | 42 | 25 | 2 | 15 | 136 | 109 | 52 |
| Runcorn | 42 | 23 | 5 | 14 | 123 | 98 | 51 |
| Sandbach Ramblers | 42 | 21 | 5 | 16 | 112 | 108 | 47 |
| Chester | 42 | 18 | 5 | 19 | 120 | 109 | 41 |
| Mossley | 42 | 18 | 5 | 19 | 99 | 126 | 41 |
| Crewe Alexandra | 42 | 15 | 10 | 17 | 99 | 115 | 40 |
| Northwich Victoria | 42 | 19 | 2 | 21 | 95 | 111 | 40 |
| Witton Albion | 42 | 15 | 8 | 19 | 105 | 120 | 38 |
| Winsford United | 42 | 16 | 5 | 21 | 105 | 129 | 37 |
| Manchester Central | 42 | 15 | 4 | 23 | 92 | 125 | 34 |
| Manchester North End | 42 | 14 | 4 | 24 | 115 | 130 | 32 |
| Congleton Town | 42 | 11 | 10 | 21 | 69 | 92 | 32 |
| Whitchurch | 42 | 14 | 4 | 24 | 86 | 122 | 32 |
| Hurst | 42 | 14 | 2 | 26 | 96 | 130 | 30 |
| Nantwich | 42 | 12 | 5 | 25 | 69 | 112 | 29 |
| Middlewich | 42 | 12 | 5 | 25 | 70 | 125 | 29 |
| Altrincham | 42 | 12 | 3 | 27 | 81 | 140 | 27 |

## 1928–29: CHESHIRE LEAGUE

| | P | W | D | L | F | A | Pts |
|---|---|---|---|---|---|---|---|
| Port Vale | 38 | 24 | 6 | 8 | 121 | 64 | 54 |
| Ashton National | 38 | 23 | 5 | 10 | 115 | 70 | 51 |
| Winsford United | 38 | 22 | 7 | 9 | 109 | 74 | 51 |
| Congleton Town | 38 | 21 | 7 | 10 | 97 | 76 | 49 |
| Manchester North End | 38 | 20 | 8 | 10 | 122 | 81 | 48 |
| Tranmere Rovers | 38 | 18 | 8 | 12 | 128 | 88 | 44 |
| Stalybridge Celtic | 38 | 19 | 6 | 13 | 92 | 75 | 44 |
| Chester | 38 | 19 | 5 | 14 | 99 | 75 | 43 |
| Crewe Alexandra | 38 | 18 | 5 | 15 | 92 | 84 | 41 |
| Macclesfield | 38 | 17 | 3 | 18 | 94 | 93 | 37 |
| Runcorn | 38 | 13 | 11 | 14 | 86 | 94 | 37 |
| Hurst | 38 | 14 | 8 | 16 | 126 | 119 | 36 |
| Mossley | 38 | 14 | 8 | 16 | 89 | 93 | 36 |
| Northwich Victoria | 38 | 13 | 7 | 18 | 85 | 90 | 33 |
| Sandbach Ramblers | 38 | 14 | 2 | 22 | 101 | 116 | 30 |
| Whitchurch | 38 | 13 | 4 | 21 | 96 | 115 | 30 |
| Witton Albion | 38 | 9 | 12 | 17 | 62 | 82 | 30 |
| Middlewich | 38 | 11 | 4 | 23 | 51 | 125 | 26 |
| Altrincham | 38 | 8 | 7 | 23 | 74 | 128 | 23 |
| Nantwich | 38 | 8 | 1 | 29 | 62 | 159 | 17 |

## 1930–31: CHESHIRE LEAGUE

| | P | W | D | L | F | A | Pts |
|---|---|---|---|---|---|---|---|
| Port Vale | 42 | 33 | 5 | 4 | 163 | 48 | 71 |
| Chester | 42 | 31 | 6 | 5 | 170 | 59 | 68 |
| Hyde United | 42 | 25 | 6 | 11 | 133 | 84 | 56 |
| Altrincham | 42 | 22 | 8 | 12 | 123 | 96 | 52 |
| Runcorn | 42 | 20 | 9 | 13 | 129 | 83 | 49 |
| Stalybridge Celtic | 42 | 21 | 6 | 15 | 122 | 114 | 48 |
| Crewe Alexandra | 42 | 19 | 8 | 15 | 132 | 104 | 46 |
| Ashton National | 42 | 18 | 8 | 16 | 114 | 90 | 44 |
| Macclesfield | 42 | 20 | 4 | 18 | 112 | 101 | 44 |
| Sandbach Ramblers | 42 | 19 | 4 | 19 | 123 | 124 | 42 |
| Witton Albion | 42 | 18 | 6 | 18 | 97 | 105 | 42 |
| Tranmere Rovers | 42 | 18 | 6 | 18 | 105 | 120 | 42 |
| Manchester North End | 42 | 19 | 4 | 19 | 97 | 119 | 42 |
| Hurst | 42 | 18 | 5 | 19 | 132 | 115 | 41 |
| Congleton Town | 42 | 14 | 8 | 20 | 68 | 112 | 36 |
| Mossley | 42 | 12 | 10 | 20 | 104 | 124 | 34 |
| Northwich Victoria | 42 | 15 | 3 | 24 | 105 | 135 | 33 |
| Connah's Quay | 42 | 15 | 2 | 25 | 96 | 122 | 32 |
| Winsford United | 42 | 13 | 4 | 25 | 98 | 151 | 30 |
| Whitchurch | 42 | 10 | 7 | 25 | 79 | 160 | 27 |
| Nantwich | 42 | 9 | 8 | 25 | 83 | 132 | 26 |
| Manchester Central | 42 | 7 | 5 | 30 | 51 | 140 | 19 |

## 1931-32: CHESHIRE LEAGUE

| | P | W | D | L | F | A | Pts |
|---|---|---|---|---|---|---|---|
| Macclesfield | 40 | 25 | 8 | 7 | 119 | 65 | 58 |
| Port Vale | 40 | 25 | 5 | 10 | 110 | 50 | 55 |
| Stalybridge Celtic | 40 | 25 | 5 | 10 | 124 | 71 | 55 |
| Altrincham | 40 | 25 | 5 | 10 | 94 | 69 | 55 |
| Manchester Central | 40 | 23 | 7 | 10 | 108 | 68 | 53 |
| Hyde United | 40 | 22 | 7 | 11 | 98 | 56 | 51 |
| Tranmere Rovers | 40 | 22 | 4 | 14 | 116 | 80 | 48 |
| Congleton Town | 40 | 20 | 6 | 14 | 105 | 81 | 46 |
| Chester | 40 | 17 | 10 | 13 | 82 | 73 | 44 |
| Crewe Alexandra | 40 | 19 | 6 | 15 | 89 | 107 | 44 |
| Runcorn | 40 | 18 | 5 | 17 | 104 | 97 | 41 |
| Manchester North End | 40 | 18 | 4 | 18 | 106 | 103 | 40 |
| Hurst | 40 | 16 | 6 | 18 | 98 | 108 | 38 |
| Ashton National | 40 | 16 | 3 | 21 | 110 | 92 | 35 |
| Mossley | 40 | 13 | 7 | 20 | 71 | 104 | 33 |
| Winsford United | 40 | 12 | 4 | 24 | 70 | 99 | 28 |
| Whitchurch | 40 | 10 | 8 | 22 | 74 | 109 | 28 |
| Witton Albion | 40 | 10 | 7 | 23 | 73 | 116 | 27 |
| Northwich Victoria | 40 | 10 | 7 | 23 | 76 | 122 | 27 |
| Sandbach Ramblers | 40 | 8 | 5 | 27 | 68 | 120 | 21 |
| Nantwich | 40 | 1 | 11 | 28 | 60 | 155 | 13 |

## 1932-33: CHESHIRE LEAGUE

| | P | W | D | L | F | A | Pts |
|---|---|---|---|---|---|---|---|
| Macclesfield | 42 | 29 | 5 | 8 | 121 | 64 | 63 |
| Port Vale | 42 | 26 | 5 | 11 | 112 | 57 | 57 |
| Manchester North End | 42 | 24 | 7 | 11 | 124 | 78 | 55 |
| Hurst | 42 | 25 | 4 | 13 | 129 | 98 | 54 |
| Wigan Athletic | 42 | 21 | 11 | 10 | 121 | 54 | 53 |
| Ashton National | 42 | 23 | 7 | 12 | 130 | 83 | 53 |
| Congleton Town | 42 | 22 | 6 | 14 | 105 | 103 | 50 |
| Hyde United | 42 | 22 | 5 | 15 | 105 | 93 | 49 |
| Crewe Alexandra | 42 | 19 | 8 | 15 | 110 | 77 | 46 |
| Stalybridge Celtic | 42 | 19 | 8 | 15 | 132 | 100 | 46 |
| Chester | 42 | 21 | 2 | 19 | 118 | 109 | 44 |
| Altrincham | 42 | 17 | 9 | 16 | 108 | 95 | 43 |
| Mossley | 42 | 19 | 4 | 19 | 96 | 101 | 42 |
| Tranmere Rovers | 42 | 18 | 5 | 19 | 108 | 118 | 41 |
| Northwich Victoria | 42 | 17 | 6 | 19 | 100 | 123 | 40 |
| Buxton | 42 | 16 | 5 | 21 | 81 | 92 | 37 |
| Runcorn | 42 | 15 | 6 | 21 | 88 | 109 | 36 |
| Nantwich | 42 | 12 | 7 | 23 | 84 | 133 | 31 |
| Witton Albion | 42 | 9 | 7 | 26 | 71 | 119 | 25 |
| Winsford United | 42 | 8 | 6 | 28 | 65 | 143 | 22 |
| Sandbach Ramblers | 42 | 6 | 7 | 29 | 63 | 146 | 19 |
| Whitchurch | 42 | 6 | 6 | 30 | 70 | 146 | 18 |

## 1933-34: CHESHIRE LEAGUE

| | P | W | D | L | F | A | Pts |
|---|---|---|---|---|---|---|---|
| Wigan Athletic | 42 | 30 | 6 | 6 | 111 | 46 | 66 |
| Macclesfield | 42 | 29 | 3 | 10 | 142 | 71 | 61 |
| Witton Albion | 42 | 21 | 9 | 12 | 85 | 75 | 51 |
| Stockport County | 42 | 23 | 3 | 16 | 104 | 77 | 49 |
| Prescot Cables | 42 | 21 | 7 | 14 | 93 | 78 | 49 |
| Altrincham | 42 | 19 | 9 | 14 | 99 | 72 | 47 |
| Tranmere Rovers | 42 | 22 | 3 | 17 | 110 | 95 | 47 |
| Manchester North End | 42 | 21 | 4 | 17 | 132 | 105 | 46 |
| Stalybridge Celtic | 42 | 18 | 9 | 15 | 100 | 84 | 45 |
| Ashton National | 42 | 21 | 3 | 18 | 89 | 85 | 45 |
| Hyde United | 42 | 19 | 6 | 17 | 99 | 84 | 44 |
| Mossley | 42 | 15 | 12 | 15 | 91 | 87 | 42 |
| Runcorn | 42 | 19 | 2 | 21 | 91 | 104 | 40 |
| Chester | 42 | 16 | 7 | 19 | 84 | 97 | 39 |
| Buxton | 42 | 14 | 11 | 17 | 81 | 95 | 39 |
| Hurst | 42 | 17 | 3 | 22 | 103 | 111 | 37 |
| Nantwich | 42 | 15 | 4 | 23 | 77 | 112 | 34 |
| Crewe Alexandra | 42 | 16 | 2 | 24 | 71 | 111 | 34 |
| Congleton Town | 42 | 11 | 8 | 23 | 84 | 97 | 30 |
| Northwich Victoria | 42 | 14 | 2 | 26 | 63 | 87 | 30 |
| Winsford United | 42 | 11 | 6 | 25 | 70 | 118 | 28 |
| Sandbach Ramblers | 42 | 8 | 5 | 29 | 57 | 142 | 21 |

## 1934-35: CHESHIRE LEAGUE

| | P | W | D | L | F | A | Pts |
|---|---|---|---|---|---|---|---|
| Wigan Athletic | 42 | 27 | 9 | 6 | 153 | 59 | 63 |
| Altrincham | 42 | 26 | 11 | 5 | 118 | 57 | 63 |
| Stalybridge Celtic | 42 | 28 | 7 | 7 | 136 | 74 | 63 |
| Port Vale | 42 | 23 | 6 | 13 | 113 | 69 | 52 |
| Hyde United | 42 | 21 | 6 | 15 | 89 | 73 | 48 |
| Stockport County | 42 | 21 | 5 | 16 | 94 | 88 | 47 |
| Chester | 42 | 22 | 2 | 18 | 116 | 98 | 46 |
| Macclesfield | 42 | 19 | 7 | 16 | 137 | 83 | 45 |
| Buxton | 42 | 19 | 5 | 18 | 95 | 95 | 43 |
| Manchester North End | 42 | 15 | 9 | 18 | 112 | 110 | 39 |
| Congleton Town | 42 | 17 | 5 | 20 | 93 | 113 | 39 |
| Mossley | 42 | 17 | 5 | 20 | 97 | 119 | 39 |
| Ashton National | 42 | 15 | 7 | 20 | 68 | 86 | 37 |
| Witton Albion | 42 | 16 | 5 | 21 | 60 | 106 | 37 |
| Hurst | 42 | 13 | 10 | 19 | 82 | 101 | 36 |
| Northwich Victoria | 42 | 14 | 7 | 21 | 83 | 95 | 35 |
| Prescot Cables | 42 | 13 | 9 | 20 | 70 | 100 | 35 |
| Winsford United | 42 | 12 | 9 | 21 | 68 | 104 | 33 |
| Tranmere Rovers | 42 | 14 | 4 | 24 | 82 | 110 | 32 |
| Runcorn | 42 | 14 | 3 | 25 | 95 | 147 | 31 |
| Nantwich | 42 | 11 | 9 | 22 | 71 | 121 | 31 |
| Crewe Alexandra | 42 | 12 | 6 | 24 | 72 | 105 | 30 |

## 1935–36: Cheshire League

| | P | W | D | L | F | A | Pts |
|---|---|---|---|---|---|---|---|
| Wigan Athletic | 42 | 31 | 6 | 5 | 136 | 46 | 68 |
| Altrincham | 42 | 22 | 11 | 9 | 88 | 51 | 55 |
| Stockport County | 42 | 23 | 8 | 11 | 103 | 57 | 54 |
| Chester | 42 | 22 | 9 | 11 | 104 | 85 | 53 |
| Stalybridge Celtic | 42 | 23 | 6 | 13 | 112 | 64 | 52 |
| Runcorn | 42 | 21 | 8 | 13 | 129 | 88 | 50 |
| Northwich Victoria | 42 | 20 | 10 | 12 | 98 | 74 | 50 |
| Crewe Alexandra | 42 | 21 | 6 | 15 | 113 | 84 | 48 |
| Macclesfield | 42 | 21 | 4 | 17 | 105 | 106 | 46 |
| Port Vale | 42 | 17 | 10 | 15 | 69 | 72 | 44 |
| Buxton | 42 | 18 | 7 | 17 | 95 | 90 | 43 |
| Hurst | 42 | 16 | 10 | 16 | 89 | 106 | 42 |
| Tranmere Rovers | 42 | 16 | 9 | 17 | 113 | 120 | 41 |
| Manchester North End | 42 | 17 | 6 | 19 | 94 | 107 | 40 |
| Hyde United | 42 | 17 | 5 | 20 | 107 | 108 | 39 |
| Mossley | 42 | 16 | 4 | 22 | 90 | 113 | 36 |
| Congleton Town | 42 | 15 | 4 | 23 | 95 | 114 | 34 |
| Prescot Cables | 42 | 15 | 4 | 23 | 59 | 94 | 34 |
| Nantwich | 42 | 13 | 7 | 22 | 74 | 115 | 33 |
| Witton Albion | 42 | 11 | 5 | 26 | 58 | 96 | 27 |
| Ashton National | 42 | 7 | 8 | 27 | 64 | 114 | 22 |
| Winsford United | 42 | 4 | 5 | 33 | 44 | 135 | 13 |

## 1937–38: Cheshire League

| | P | W | D | L | F | A | Pts |
|---|---|---|---|---|---|---|---|
| Tranmere Rovers | 42 | 30 | 6 | 6 | 148 | 45 | 66 |
| Runcorn | 42 | 30 | 3 | 9 | 123 | 54 | 63 |
| Stockport County | 42 | 29 | 4 | 9 | 104 | 48 | 62 |
| Hyde United | 42 | 24 | 8 | 10 | 105 | 67 | 56 |
| Crewe Alexandra | 42 | 21 | 11 | 10 | 99 | 61 | 53 |
| Witton Albion | 42 | 20 | 7 | 15 | 104 | 68 | 47 |
| Mossley | 42 | 19 | 9 | 14 | 86 | 76 | 47 |
| Northwich Victoria | 42 | 19 | 6 | 17 | 86 | 79 | 44 |
| Altrincham | 42 | 17 | 10 | 15 | 77 | 80 | 44 |
| Stalybridge Celtic | 42 | 18 | 6 | 18 | 96 | 86 | 42 |
| Wigan Athletic | 42 | 19 | 4 | 19 | 95 | 89 | 42 |
| Port Vale | 42 | 16 | 7 | 19 | 77 | 76 | 39 |
| Chester | 42 | 17 | 4 | 21 | 84 | 92 | 38 |
| Manchester North End | 42 | 18 | 2 | 22 | 112 | 131 | 38 |
| Macclesfield | 42 | 14 | 10 | 18 | 96 | 115 | 38 |
| Congleton Town | 42 | 16 | 6 | 20 | 74 | 122 | 38 |
| Ashton National | 42 | 16 | 5 | 21 | 78 | 92 | 37 |
| Buxton | 42 | 14 | 5 | 23 | 87 | 108 | 33 |
| Winsford United | 42 | 12 | 6 | 24 | 71 | 98 | 30 |
| Rhyl | 42 | 11 | 7 | 24 | 74 | 117 | 29 |
| Nantwich | 42 | 8 | 4 | 30 | 59 | 140 | 20 |
| Hurst | 42 | 7 | 4 | 31 | 63 | 145 | 18 |

## 1936–37: Cheshire League

| | P | W | D | L | F | A | Pts |
|---|---|---|---|---|---|---|---|
| Runcorn | 42 | 30 | 6 | 6 | 156 | 60 | 66 |
| Stockport County | 42 | 23 | 11 | 8 | 105 | 55 | 57 |
| Northwich Victoria | 42 | 27 | 3 | 12 | 92 | 52 | 57 |
| Witton Albion | 42 | 24 | 8 | 10 | 107 | 56 | 56 |
| Port Vale | 42 | 22 | 8 | 12 | 97 | 91 | 52 |
| Buxton | 42 | 22 | 6 | 14 | 107 | 89 | 50 |
| Ashton National | 42 | 18 | 9 | 15 | 97 | 96 | 45 |
| Wigan Athletic | 42 | 19 | 6 | 17 | 94 | 73 | 44 |
| Stalybridge Celtic | 42 | 19 | 6 | 17 | 96 | 81 | 44 |
| Rhyl | 42 | 17 | 9 | 16 | 75 | 71 | 43 |
| Crewe Alexandra | 42 | 18 | 5 | 19 | 77 | 88 | 41 |
| Chester | 42 | 14 | 9 | 19 | 79 | 93 | 37 |
| Altrincham | 42 | 14 | 8 | 20 | 91 | 94 | 36 |
| Winsford United | 42 | 14 | 8 | 20 | 75 | 94 | 36 |
| Congleton Town | 42 | 15 | 6 | 21 | 83 | 104 | 36 |
| Tranmere Rovers | 42 | 15 | 6 | 21 | 74 | 100 | 36 |
| Mossley | 42 | 11 | 13 | 18 | 84 | 108 | 35 |
| Manchester North End | 42 | 15 | 5 | 22 | 85 | 113 | 35 |
| Macclesfield | 42 | 14 | 6 | 22 | 74 | 96 | 34 |
| Hyde United | 42 | 13 | 7 | 22 | 97 | 114 | 33 |
| Nantwich | 42 | 11 | 6 | 25 | 78 | 146 | 28 |
| Hurst | 42 | 9 | 5 | 28 | 76 | 125 | 23 |

## 1938–39: Cheshire League

| | P | W | D | L | F | A | Pts |
|---|---|---|---|---|---|---|---|
| Runcorn | 42 | 28 | 6 | 8 | 134 | 60 | 62 |
| Tranmere Rovers | 42 | 29 | 2 | 11 | 136 | 63 | 60 |
| Ashton National | 42 | 25 | 7 | 10 | 131 | 90 | 57 |
| Crewe Alexandra | 42 | 26 | 4 | 12 | 132 | 74 | 56 |
| Wellington Town | 42 | 23 | 8 | 11 | 108 | 68 | 54 |
| Chester | 42 | 22 | 8 | 12 | 111 | 74 | 52 |
| Wigan Athletic | 42 | 21 | 5 | 16 | 104 | 84 | 47 |
| Northwich Victoria | 42 | 20 | 7 | 15 | 88 | 87 | 47 |
| Witton Albion | 42 | 17 | 9 | 16 | 94 | 78 | 43 |
| Hyde United | 42 | 20 | 3 | 19 | 84 | 91 | 43 |
| Congleton Town | 42 | 16 | 10 | 16 | 80 | 89 | 42 |
| Mossley | 42 | 14 | 12 | 16 | 77 | 78 | 40 |
| Port Vale | 42 | 18 | 4 | 20 | 84 | 86 | 40 |
| Hurst | 42 | 15 | 10 | 17 | 86 | 113 | 40 |
| Stockport County | 42 | 18 | 3 | 21 | 86 | 90 | 39 |
| Buxton | 42 | 12 | 11 | 19 | 71 | 93 | 35 |
| Macclesfield | 42 | 14 | 7 | 21 | 55 | 90 | 35 |
| Stalybridge Celtic | 42 | 13 | 8 | 21 | 87 | 108 | 34 |
| Rhyl | 42 | 12 | 9 | 21 | 94 | 117 | 33 |
| Altrincham | 42 | 9 | 7 | 26 | 72 | 119 | 25 |
| Winsford United | 42 | 8 | 6 | 28 | 57 | 134 | 22 |
| Manchester North End | 42 | 7 | 4 | 31 | 57 | 142 | 18 |

WAR-TIME LEAGUES
## 1939: CHESHIRE LEAGUE, SERIES WEST

| | P | W | D | L | F | A | Pts |
|---|---|---|---|---|---|---|---|
| Runcorn | 14 | 7 | 6 | 1 | 46 | 28 | 20 |
| Altrincham | 14 | 7 | 3 | 4 | 45 | 29 | 17 |
| Witton Albion | 14 | 5 | 5 | 4 | 32 | 28 | 15 |
| Winsford United | 14 | 6 | 3 | 5 | 25 | 25 | 15 |
| Northwich Victoria | 13 | 6 | 3 | 4 | 23 | 26 | 15 |
| Chester | 13 | 5 | 1 | 7 | 32 | 40 | 11 |
| Wigan Athletic | 14 | 3 | 3 | 8 | 37 | 46 | 9 |
| Macclesfield | 14 | 3 | 2 | 9 | 28 | 46 | 8 |

## 1940: CHESHIRE LEAGUE, SERIES EAST

| | P | W | D | L | F | A | Pts |
|---|---|---|---|---|---|---|---|
| Hyde United | 12 | 8 | 2 | 2 | 40 | 21 | 18 |
| Droylsden | 12 | 7 | 1 | 4 | 35 | 25 | 15 |
| Ashton National | 12 | 6 | 1 | 5 | 36 | 31 | 13 |
| Mossley | 12 | 5 | 3 | 4 | 24 | 27 | 13 |
| Hurst | 12 | 4 | 3 | 5 | 29 | 33 | 11 |
| Macclesfield | 12 | 4 | 0 | 8 | 23 | 42 | 8 |
| Stalybridge Celtic | 12 | 1 | 4 | 7 | 26 | 36 | 6 |

# League Tables, 1946-1968

## 1946–47: CHESHIRE LEAGUE

| | P | W | D | L | F | A | Pts |
|---|---|---|---|---|---|---|---|
| Wellington Town | 42 | 25 | 7 | 10 | 113 | 69 | 57 |
| Buxton | 42 | 24 | 8 | 10 | 117 | 79 | 56 |
| South Liverpool | 42 | 23 | 9 | 10 | 92 | 62 | 55 |
| Port Vale | 42 | 24 | 6 | 12 | 100 | 58 | 54 |
| Northwich Victoria | 42 | 21 | 11 | 10 | 95 | 69 | 53 |
| Stalybridge Celtic | 42 | 24 | 5 | 13 | 108 | 89 | 53 |
| Witton Albion | 42 | 20 | 7 | 15 | 96 | 84 | 47 |
| Droylsden | 42 | 22 | 1 | 19 | 108 | 101 | 45 |
| Mossley | 42 | 17 | 10 | 15 | 94 | 90 | 44 |
| Altrincham | 42 | 17 | 8 | 17 | 85 | 83 | 42 |
| Hyde United | 42 | 19 | 3 | 20 | 108 | 100 | 41 |
| Runcorn | 42 | 13 | 13 | 16 | 80 | 89 | 39 |
| Wrexham | 42 | 17 | 4 | 21 | 81 | 80 | 38 |
| Rhyl | 42 | 16 | 6 | 20 | 96 | 106 | 38 |
| Macclesfield Town | 42 | 16 | 6 | 20 | 77 | 89 | 38 |
| Chester | 42 | 16 | 4 | 22 | 70 | 91 | 36 |
| Congleton Town | 42 | 15 | 5 | 22 | 83 | 100 | 35 |
| Tranmere Rovers | 42 | 14 | 7 | 21 | 70 | 89 | 35 |
| Stockport County | 42 | 14 | 7 | 21 | 79 | 104 | 35 |
| Crewe Alexandra | 42 | 13 | 6 | 23 | 90 | 120 | 32 |
| Ashton United | 42 | 8 | 10 | 24 | 65 | 107 | 26 |
| Wigan Athletic | 42 | 9 | 7 | 26 | 66 | 114 | 25 |

## 1947–48: CHESHIRE LEAGUE

| | P | W | D | L | F | A | Pts |
|---|---|---|---|---|---|---|---|
| Rhyl | 42 | 30 | 8 | 4 | 121 | 54 | 68 |
| Northwich Victoria | 42 | 24 | 9 | 9 | 109 | 58 | 57 |
| Witton Albion | 42 | 24 | 8 | 10 | 104 | 59 | 56 |
| Wellington Town | 42 | 23 | 8 | 11 | 111 | 65 | 54 |
| Stalybridge Celtic | 42 | 18 | 11 | 13 | 85 | 87 | 47 |
| Tranmere Rovers | 42 | 18 | 9 | 15 | 76 | 62 | 45 |
| Winsford United | 42 | 22 | 1 | 19 | 90 | 83 | 45 |
| Crewe Alexandra | 42 | 19 | 7 | 16 | 80 | 80 | 45 |
| South Liverpool | 42 | 18 | 7 | 17 | 81 | 81 | 43 |
| Chester | 42 | 18 | 6 | 18 | 83 | 92 | 42 |
| Stockport County | 42 | 16 | 9 | 17 | 87 | 84 | 41 |
| Hyde United | 42 | 18 | 4 | 20 | 88 | 83 | 40 |
| Wrexham | 42 | 17 | 5 | 20 | 85 | 71 | 39 |
| Runcorn | 42 | 15 | 9 | 18 | 79 | 88 | 39 |
| Altrincham | 42 | 17 | 5 | 20 | 100 | 115 | 39 |
| Port Vale | 42 | 16 | 7 | 19 | 53 | 69 | 39 |
| Droylsden | 42 | 13 | 11 | 18 | 80 | 82 | 37 |
| Macclesfield Town | 42 | 13 | 11 | 18 | 78 | 83 | 37 |
| Buxton | 42 | 13 | 6 | 23 | 89 | 113 | 32 |
| Mossley | 42 | 14 | 4 | 24 | 66 | 99 | 32 |
| Ashton United | 42 | 11 | 3 | 28 | 74 | 143 | 25 |
| Congleton Town | 42 | 9 | 4 | 29 | 50 | 118 | 22 |

## 1948–49: CHESHIRE LEAGUE

|                    | P  | W  | D  | L  | F   | A   | Pts |
|--------------------|----|----|----|----|-----|-----|-----|
| Witton Albion      | 42 | 29 | 6  | 7  | 106 | 39  | 64  |
| Rhyl               | 42 | 27 | 7  | 8  | 110 | 53  | 61  |
| Northwich Victoria | 42 | 26 | 9  | 7  | 118 | 67  | 61  |
| Winsford United    | 42 | 25 | 8  | 9  | 95  | 59  | 58  |
| Mossley            | 42 | 21 | 9  | 12 | 97  | 74  | 51  |
| Wellington Town    | 42 | 20 | 10 | 12 | 91  | 68  | 50  |
| South Liverpool    | 42 | 18 | 9  | 15 | 94  | 91  | 45  |
| Wrexham            | 42 | 17 | 10 | 15 | 81  | 77  | 44  |
| Stalybridge Celtic | 42 | 18 | 7  | 17 | 79  | 90  | 43  |
| Altrincham         | 42 | 18 | 6  | 18 | 91  | 95  | 42  |
| Macclesfield Town  | 42 | 16 | 9  | 17 | 82  | 80  | 41  |
| Runcorn            | 42 | 17 | 7  | 18 | 76  | 79  | 41  |
| Chester            | 42 | 17 | 4  | 21 | 78  | 88  | 38  |
| Hyde United        | 42 | 14 | 9  | 19 | 80  | 87  | 37  |
| Port Vale          | 42 | 13 | 10 | 19 | 65  | 79  | 36  |
| Ellesmere Port Town| 42 | 14 | 8  | 20 | 80  | 96  | 36  |
| Buxton             | 42 | 15 | 6  | 21 | 77  | 104 | 36  |
| Crewe Alexandra    | 42 | 13 | 7  | 22 | 74  | 88  | 33  |
| Stockport County   | 42 | 10 | 12 | 20 | 65  | 81  | 32  |
| Congleton Town     | 42 | 11 | 7  | 24 | 78  | 113 | 29  |
| Tranmere Rovers    | 42 | 11 | 4  | 27 | 57  | 101 | 26  |
| Droylsden          | 42 | 7  | 6  | 29 | 59  | 124 | 20  |

## 1949–50: CHESHIRE LEAGUE

|                    | P  | W  | D  | L  | F   | A   | Pts |
|--------------------|----|----|----|----|-----|-----|-----|
| Witton Albion      | 42 | 25 | 13 | 4  | 101 | 42  | 63  |
| Rhyl               | 42 | 28 | 6  | 8  | 116 | 42  | 62  |
| Stockport County   | 42 | 21 | 14 | 7  | 78  | 46  | 56  |
| Northwich Victoria | 42 | 22 | 7  | 13 | 101 | 61  | 51  |
| Winsford United    | 42 | 16 | 18 | 8  | 78  | 56  | 50  |
| Altrincham         | 42 | 20 | 10 | 12 | 79  | 64  | 50  |
| Runcorn            | 42 | 18 | 11 | 13 | 70  | 52  | 47  |
| Macclesfield Town  | 42 | 21 | 5  | 16 | 88  | 76  | 47  |
| Wellington Town    | 42 | 17 | 13 | 12 | 70  | 67  | 47  |
| Crewe Alexandra    | 42 | 16 | 10 | 16 | 86  | 78  | 42  |
| Hyde United        | 42 | 16 | 10 | 16 | 81  | 83  | 42  |
| Ellesmere Port Town| 42 | 16 | 10 | 16 | 69  | 79  | 42  |
| Buxton             | 42 | 11 | 16 | 15 | 78  | 88  | 38  |
| Tranmere Rovers    | 42 | 15 | 8  | 19 | 62  | 80  | 38  |
| Congleton Town     | 42 | 15 | 5  | 22 | 65  | 99  | 35  |
| Chester            | 42 | 12 | 11 | 19 | 56  | 89  | 35  |
| Port Vale          | 42 | 9  | 15 | 18 | 51  | 62  | 33  |
| South Liverpool    | 42 | 12 | 9  | 21 | 65  | 78  | 33  |
| Mossley            | 42 | 8  | 16 | 18 | 53  | 92  | 32  |
| Stalybridge Celtic | 42 | 9  | 11 | 22 | 57  | 85  | 29  |
| Droylsden          | 42 | 9  | 9  | 24 | 69  | 114 | 27  |
| Wrexham            | 42 | 9  | 7  | 26 | 54  | 94  | 25  |

## 1950–51: CHESHIRE LEAGUE

|                    | P  | W  | D  | L  | F   | A   | Pts |
|--------------------|----|----|----|----|-----|-----|-----|
| Rhyl               | 42 | 31 | 6  | 5  | 99  | 36  | 68  |
| Witton Albion      | 42 | 28 | 4  | 10 | 116 | 56  | 60  |
| Northwich Victoria | 42 | 27 | 5  | 10 | 116 | 58  | 59  |
| Tranmere Rovers    | 42 | 23 | 5  | 14 | 73  | 52  | 51  |
| Macclesfield Town  | 42 | 20 | 11 | 11 | 90  | 67  | 51  |
| Wellington Town    | 42 | 20 | 9  | 13 | 80  | 55  | 49  |
| Bangor City        | 42 | 20 | 8  | 14 | 85  | 70  | 48  |
| Port Vale          | 42 | 19 | 10 | 13 | 71  | 66  | 48  |
| Winsford United    | 42 | 19 | 9  | 14 | 84  | 67  | 47  |
| Altrincham         | 42 | 19 | 8  | 15 | 77  | 63  | 46  |
| Wrexham            | 42 | 19 | 6  | 17 | 88  | 68  | 44  |
| Ellesmere Port Town| 42 | 17 | 6  | 19 | 73  | 78  | 40  |
| Stockport County   | 42 | 15 | 9  | 18 | 52  | 50  | 39  |
| Runcorn            | 42 | 15 | 8  | 19 | 81  | 89  | 38  |
| Buxton             | 42 | 14 | 9  | 19 | 55  | 69  | 37  |
| Crewe Alexandra    | 42 | 15 | 6  | 21 | 88  | 102 | 36  |
| South Liverpool    | 42 | 13 | 6  | 23 | 65  | 101 | 32  |
| Hyde United        | 42 | 11 | 6  | 25 | 51  | 90  | 28  |
| Stalybridge Celtic | 42 | 12 | 4  | 26 | 55  | 125 | 28  |
| Mossley            | 42 | 11 | 5  | 26 | 51  | 91  | 27  |
| Congleton Town     | 42 | 9  | 9  | 24 | 54  | 102 | 27  |
| Chester            | 42 | 6  | 9  | 27 | 65  | 114 | 21  |

## 1951–52: CHESHIRE LEAGUE

|                    | P  | W  | D  | L  | F   | A   | Pts |
|--------------------|----|----|----|----|-----|-----|-----|
| Wellington Town    | 42 | 26 | 9  | 7  | 85  | 44  | 61  |
| Rhyl               | 42 | 25 | 8  | 9  | 101 | 58  | 58  |
| Port Vale          | 42 | 21 | 11 | 10 | 72  | 41  | 53  |
| Witton Albion      | 42 | 22 | 7  | 13 | 77  | 46  | 51  |
| Tranmere Rovers    | 42 | 20 | 9  | 13 | 79  | 57  | 49  |
| Northwich Victoria | 42 | 21 | 6  | 15 | 78  | 70  | 48  |
| Mossley            | 42 | 22 | 4  | 16 | 90  | 89  | 48  |
| Altrincham         | 42 | 19 | 9  | 14 | 78  | 72  | 47  |
| Crewe Alexandra    | 42 | 19 | 8  | 15 | 114 | 83  | 46  |
| Stockport County   | 42 | 16 | 12 | 14 | 66  | 61  | 44  |
| Bangor City        | 42 | 17 | 9  | 16 | 79  | 68  | 43  |
| Wrexham            | 42 | 16 | 10 | 16 | 88  | 83  | 42  |
| Runcorn            | 42 | 16 | 10 | 16 | 75  | 76  | 42  |
| Macclesfield Town  | 42 | 15 | 12 | 15 | 62  | 69  | 42  |
| Winsford United    | 42 | 17 | 6  | 19 | 72  | 84  | 40  |
| Congleton Town     | 42 | 17 | 5  | 20 | 66  | 93  | 39  |
| Chester            | 42 | 15 | 7  | 20 | 65  | 79  | 37  |
| Stalybridge Celtic | 42 | 13 | 7  | 22 | 56  | 83  | 33  |
| Buxton             | 42 | 10 | 11 | 21 | 73  | 84  | 31  |
| Ellesmere Port Town| 42 | 11 | 4  | 27 | 70  | 104 | 26  |
| South Liverpool    | 42 | 7  | 10 | 25 | 45  | 98  | 24  |
| Hyde United        | 42 | 7  | 6  | 29 | 66  | 120 | 20  |

## 1952-53: CHESHIRE LEAGUE

| | P | W | D | L | F | A | Pts |
|---|---|---|---|---|---|---|---|
| Macclesfield Town | 42 | 27 | 8 | 7 | 103 | 63 | 62 |
| Wellington Town | 42 | 25 | 9 | 8 | 89 | 44 | 59 |
| Stockport County | 42 | 24 | 9 | 9 | 85 | 52 | 57 |
| Rhyl | 42 | 20 | 14 | 8 | 104 | 76 | 54 |
| Bangor City | 42 | 23 | 7 | 12 | 87 | 68 | 53 |
| Tranmere Rovers | 42 | 18 | 14 | 10 | 95 | 71 | 50 |
| Port Vale | 42 | 17 | 14 | 11 | 77 | 65 | 48 |
| Witton Albion | 42 | 18 | 9 | 15 | 107 | 100 | 45 |
| Buxton | 42 | 17 | 10 | 15 | 76 | 81 | 44 |
| Crewe Alexandra | 42 | 18 | 5 | 19 | 72 | 75 | 41 |
| Stalybridge Celtic | 42 | 16 | 9 | 17 | 84 | 88 | 41 |
| Runcorn | 42 | 18 | 3 | 21 | 83 | 97 | 39 |
| Chester | 42 | 12 | 13 | 17 | 78 | 78 | 37 |
| Wrexham | 42 | 15 | 7 | 20 | 69 | 78 | 37 |
| Ellesmere Port Town | 42 | 16 | 5 | 21 | 70 | 81 | 37 |
| Northwich Victoria | 42 | 13 | 8 | 21 | 61 | 82 | 34 |
| Winsford United | 42 | 13 | 7 | 22 | 70 | 82 | 33 |
| Mossley | 42 | 13 | 6 | 23 | 57 | 86 | 32 |
| Hyde United | 42 | 11 | 10 | 21 | 71 | 108 | 32 |
| Stafford Rangers | 42 | 11 | 9 | 22 | 67 | 73 | 31 |
| Congleton Town | 42 | 11 | 8 | 23 | 64 | 91 | 30 |
| Altrincham | 42 | 8 | 12 | 22 | 54 | 84 | 28 |

## 1954-55: CHESHIRE LEAGUE

| | P | W | D | L | F | A | Pts |
|---|---|---|---|---|---|---|---|
| Hyde United | 42 | 25 | 10 | 7 | 125 | 64 | 60 |
| Wellington Town | 42 | 24 | 7 | 11 | 91 | 59 | 55 |
| Stafford Rangers | 42 | 19 | 14 | 9 | 74 | 50 | 52 |
| Wrexham | 42 | 20 | 11 | 11 | 105 | 68 | 51 |
| Stockport County | 42 | 22 | 6 | 14 | 96 | 65 | 50 |
| Stalybridge Celtic | 42 | 21 | 8 | 13 | 73 | 68 | 50 |
| Macclesfield Town | 42 | 20 | 7 | 15 | 103 | 82 | 47 |
| Ellesmere Port Town | 42 | 18 | 9 | 15 | 62 | 63 | 45 |
| Runcorn | 42 | 20 | 4 | 18 | 86 | 74 | 44 |
| Tranmere Rovers | 42 | 19 | 5 | 18 | 82 | 85 | 43 |
| Port Vale | 42 | 17 | 8 | 17 | 71 | 71 | 42 |
| Altrincham | 42 | 15 | 11 | 16 | 71 | 77 | 41 |
| Witton Albion | 42 | 17 | 5 | 20 | 98 | 95 | 39 |
| Chester | 42 | 13 | 13 | 16 | 76 | 86 | 39 |
| Bangor City | 42 | 16 | 7 | 19 | 78 | 96 | 39 |
| Rhyl | 42 | 14 | 9 | 19 | 66 | 75 | 37 |
| Winsford United | 42 | 16 | 5 | 21 | 68 | 78 | 37 |
| Mossley | 42 | 11 | 13 | 18 | 65 | 75 | 35 |
| Crewe Alexandra | 42 | 11 | 12 | 19 | 75 | 97 | 34 |
| Congleton Town | 42 | 12 | 8 | 22 | 65 | 88 | 32 |
| Northwich Victoria | 42 | 11 | 6 | 25 | 68 | 117 | 28 |
| Buxton | 42 | 7 | 10 | 25 | 59 | 124 | 24 |

## 1953-54: CHESHIRE LEAGUE

| | P | W | D | L | F | A | Pts |
|---|---|---|---|---|---|---|---|
| Witton Albion | 42 | 27 | 7 | 8 | 117 | 62 | 61 |
| Bangor City | 42 | 23 | 7 | 12 | 104 | 83 | 53 |
| Stockport County | 42 | 22 | 7 | 13 | 93 | 75 | 51 |
| Hyde United | 42 | 19 | 12 | 11 | 86 | 73 | 50 |
| Macclesfield Town | 42 | 20 | 9 | 13 | 97 | 78 | 49 |
| Altrincham | 42 | 21 | 7 | 14 | 75 | 67 | 49 |
| Crewe Alexandra | 42 | 19 | 10 | 13 | 87 | 65 | 48 |
| Tranmere Rovers | 42 | 18 | 11 | 13 | 79 | 62 | 47 |
| Wrexham | 42 | 21 | 5 | 16 | 85 | 69 | 47 |
| Wellington Town | 42 | 21 | 5 | 16 | 80 | 66 | 47 |
| Rhyl | 42 | 19 | 9 | 14 | 70 | 61 | 47 |
| Chester | 42 | 16 | 8 | 18 | 67 | 70 | 40 |
| Port Vale | 42 | 17 | 6 | 19 | 69 | 75 | 40 |
| Winsford United | 42 | 15 | 8 | 19 | 70 | 76 | 38 |
| Ellesmere Port Town | 42 | 13 | 9 | 20 | 54 | 75 | 35 |
| Stalybridge Celtic | 42 | 14 | 7 | 21 | 62 | 88 | 35 |
| Mossley | 42 | 11 | 12 | 19 | 66 | 89 | 34 |
| Runcorn | 42 | 13 | 8 | 21 | 63 | 86 | 34 |
| Northwich Victoria | 42 | 13 | 7 | 22 | 72 | 97 | 33 |
| Stafford Rangers | 42 | 11 | 10 | 21 | 73 | 89 | 32 |
| Congleton Town | 42 | 11 | 5 | 26 | 66 | 109 | 27 |
| Buxton | 42 | 10 | 7 | 25 | 58 | 98 | 27 |

## 1955-56: CHESHIRE LEAGUE

| | P | W | D | L | F | A | Pts |
|---|---|---|---|---|---|---|---|
| Hyde United | 42 | 27 | 7 | 8 | 138 | 78 | 61 |
| Rhyl | 42 | 22 | 12 | 8 | 93 | 68 | 56 |
| Wellington Town | 42 | 22 | 10 | 10 | 112 | 59 | 54 |
| Northwich Victoria | 42 | 22 | 10 | 10 | 99 | 70 | 54 |
| Ellesmere Port Town | 42 | 20 | 13 | 9 | 81 | 51 | 53 |
| Port Vale | 42 | 21 | 8 | 13 | 94 | 80 | 50 |
| Witton Albion | 42 | 16 | 16 | 10 | 91 | 80 | 48 |
| Wrexham | 42 | 19 | 8 | 15 | 109 | 88 | 46 |
| Chester | 42 | 16 | 13 | 13 | 90 | 74 | 45 |
| Runcorn | 42 | 20 | 5 | 17 | 93 | 88 | 45 |
| Buxton | 42 | 19 | 6 | 17 | 94 | 78 | 44 |
| Winsford United | 42 | 16 | 11 | 15 | 73 | 76 | 43 |
| Stockport County | 42 | 17 | 8 | 17 | 82 | 76 | 42 |
| Altrincham | 42 | 15 | 8 | 19 | 74 | 78 | 38 |
| Tranmere Rovers | 42 | 13 | 12 | 17 | 59 | 74 | 38 |
| Stalybridge Celtic | 42 | 13 | 10 | 19 | 64 | 82 | 36 |
| Bangor City | 42 | 13 | 7 | 22 | 71 | 107 | 33 |
| Stafford Rangers | 42 | 12 | 9 | 21 | 52 | 80 | 33 |
| Mossley | 42 | 10 | 13 | 19 | 68 | 114 | 33 |
| Congleton Town | 42 | 10 | 6 | 26 | 68 | 104 | 26 |
| Macclesfield Town | 42 | 10 | 6 | 26 | 70 | 115 | 26 |
| Crewe Alexandra | 42 | 8 | 4 | 30 | 55 | 110 | 20 |

## 1956–57: Cheshire League

|  | P | W | D | L | F | A | Pts |
|---|---|---|---|---|---|---|---|
| Northwich Victoria | 42 | 25 | 7 | 10 | 139 | 72 | 57 |
| Hyde United | 42 | 25 | 5 | 12 | 129 | 102 | 55 |
| Wellington Town | 42 | 22 | 10 | 10 | 92 | 58 | 54 |
| Witton Albion | 42 | 22 | 9 | 11 | 84 | 66 | 53 |
| Rhyl | 42 | 22 | 6 | 14 | 111 | 71 | 50 |
| Stockport County | 42 | 19 | 12 | 11 | 105 | 73 | 50 |
| Chester | 42 | 20 | 8 | 14 | 86 | 87 | 48 |
| Winsford United | 42 | 20 | 6 | 16 | 92 | 77 | 46 |
| Buxton | 42 | 19 | 7 | 16 | 79 | 86 | 45 |
| Macclesfield Town | 42 | 17 | 10 | 15 | 102 | 73 | 44 |
| Ellesmere Port Town | 42 | 17 | 10 | 15 | 86 | 77 | 44 |
| Wrexham | 42 | 15 | 10 | 17 | 98 | 101 | 40 |
| Runcorn | 42 | 13 | 13 | 16 | 67 | 88 | 39 |
| Stalybridge Celtic | 42 | 15 | 9 | 18 | 86 | 111 | 39 |
| Tranmere Rovers | 42 | 16 | 6 | 20 | 99 | 95 | 38 |
| Altrincham | 42 | 14 | 7 | 21 | 94 | 102 | 35 |
| Port Vale | 42 | 13 | 9 | 20 | 78 | 96 | 35 |
| Mossley | 42 | 10 | 15 | 17 | 62 | 96 | 35 |
| Congleton Town | 42 | 12 | 10 | 20 | 79 | 111 | 34 |
| Stafford Rangers | 42 | 12 | 9 | 21 | 57 | 74 | 33 |
| Bangor City | 42 | 10 | 8 | 24 | 73 | 115 | 28 |
| Crewe Alexandra | 42 | 9 | 4 | 29 | 72 | 139 | 22 |

## 1957–58: Cheshire League

|  | P | W | D | L | F | A | Pts |
|---|---|---|---|---|---|---|---|
| Ellesmere Port Town | 42 | 24 | 10 | 8 | 91 | 53 | 58 |
| Hyde United | 42 | 26 | 6 | 10 | 106 | 68 | 58 |
| Northwich Victoria | 42 | 22 | 10 | 10 | 91 | 66 | 54 |
| Port Vale | 42 | 22 | 8 | 12 | 80 | 51 | 52 |
| Chester | 42 | 22 | 7 | 13 | 91 | 63 | 51 |
| Tranmere Rovers | 42 | 21 | 7 | 14 | 103 | 72 | 49 |
| Buxton | 42 | 20 | 9 | 13 | 86 | 66 | 49 |
| Bangor City | 42 | 19 | 11 | 12 | 81 | 68 | 49 |
| Rhyl | 42 | 22 | 4 | 16 | 94 | 76 | 48 |
| Witton Albion | 42 | 19 | 8 | 15 | 91 | 84 | 46 |
| Wrexham | 42 | 19 | 8 | 15 | 71 | 67 | 46 |
| Wellington Town | 42 | 19 | 8 | 15 | 89 | 88 | 46 |
| Winsford United | 42 | 17 | 8 | 17 | 87 | 83 | 42 |
| Runcorn | 42 | 15 | 10 | 17 | 71 | 74 | 40 |
| Altrincham | 42 | 14 | 10 | 18 | 70 | 78 | 38 |
| Stafford Rangers | 42 | 14 | 8 | 20 | 68 | 104 | 36 |
| Crewe Alexandra | 42 | 12 | 11 | 19 | 86 | 95 | 35 |
| Congleton Town | 42 | 13 | 8 | 21 | 52 | 76 | 34 |
| Stockport County | 42 | 11 | 10 | 21 | 67 | 84 | 32 |
| Stalybridge Celtic | 42 | 7 | 7 | 28 | 57 | 96 | 21 |
| Macclesfield Town | 42 | 6 | 9 | 27 | 71 | 136 | 21 |
| Mossley | 42 | 7 | 5 | 30 | 57 | 112 | 19 |

## 1958–59: Cheshire League

|  | P | W | D | L | F | A | Pts |
|---|---|---|---|---|---|---|---|
| Ellesmere Port Town | 38 | 25 | 7 | 6 | 106 | 41 | 57 |
| Bangor City | 38 | 22 | 5 | 11 | 85 | 61 | 49 |
| Tranmere Rovers | 38 | 21 | 5 | 12 | 90 | 58 | 47 |
| Port Vale | 38 | 20 | 6 | 12 | 90 | 51 | 46 |
| Chester | 38 | 20 | 6 | 12 | 73 | 63 | 46 |
| Wrexham | 38 | 20 | 3 | 15 | 85 | 75 | 43 |
| Rhyl | 38 | 15 | 12 | 11 | 72 | 76 | 42 |
| Hyde United | 38 | 19 | 3 | 16 | 73 | 69 | 41 |
| Buxton | 38 | 16 | 8 | 14 | 87 | 71 | 40 |
| Northwich Victoria | 38 | 16 | 7 | 15 | 96 | 74 | 39 |
| Winsford United | 38 | 15 | 9 | 14 | 80 | 69 | 39 |
| Runcorn | 38 | 13 | 11 | 14 | 67 | 57 | 37 |
| Altrincham | 38 | 14 | 6 | 18 | 57 | 64 | 34 |
| Crewe Alexandra | 38 | 13 | 8 | 17 | 73 | 94 | 34 |
| Mossley | 38 | 13 | 5 | 20 | 78 | 97 | 31 |
| Witton Albion | 38 | 12 | 6 | 20 | 71 | 90 | 30 |
| Stafford Rangers | 38 | 11 | 8 | 19 | 60 | 98 | 30 |
| Macclesfield Town | 38 | 11 | 5 | 22 | 67 | 99 | 27 |
| Congleton Town | 38 | 12 | 3 | 23 | 60 | 104 | 27 |
| Stalybridge Celtic | 38 | 8 | 5 | 25 | 60 | 122 | 21 |

## 1959–60: Cheshire League

|  | P | W | D | L | F | A | Pts |
|---|---|---|---|---|---|---|---|
| Ellesmere Port Town | 38 | 25 | 6 | 7 | 80 | 46 | 56 |
| Hyde United | 38 | 22 | 8 | 8 | 100 | 56 | 52 |
| Winsford United | 38 | 19 | 11 | 8 | 85 | 48 | 49 |
| Buxton | 38 | 21 | 7 | 10 | 85 | 56 | 49 |
| Runcorn | 38 | 21 | 5 | 12 | 87 | 70 | 47 |
| Northwich Victoria | 38 | 17 | 11 | 10 | 70 | 44 | 45 |
| Bangor City | 38 | 18 | 6 | 14 | 86 | 58 | 42 |
| Mossley | 38 | 18 | 6 | 14 | 77 | 70 | 42 |
| Altrincham | 38 | 14 | 11 | 13 | 65 | 73 | 39 |
| Oswestry Town | 38 | 15 | 8 | 15 | 82 | 84 | 38 |
| Tranmere Rovers | 38 | 16 | 5 | 17 | 72 | 73 | 37 |
| Rhyl | 38 | 15 | 7 | 16 | 50 | 58 | 37 |
| Macclesfield Town | 38 | 15 | 6 | 17 | 83 | 81 | 36 |
| Wrexham | 38 | 14 | 7 | 17 | 70 | 83 | 35 |
| Stalybridge Celtic | 38 | 13 | 6 | 19 | 65 | 85 | 32 |
| Witton Albion | 38 | 13 | 4 | 21 | 86 | 96 | 30 |
| Chester | 38 | 12 | 6 | 20 | 57 | 83 | 30 |
| Congleton Town | 38 | 9 | 8 | 21 | 59 | 87 | 26 |
| Stafford Rangers | 38 | 11 | 4 | 23 | 54 | 83 | 26 |
| Wigan Rovers | 38 | 4 | 4 | 30 | 41 | 119 | 12 |

## 1960–61: CHESHIRE LEAGUE

| | P | W | D | L | F | A | Pts |
|---|---|---|---|---|---|---|---|
| Macclesfield Town | 42 | 26 | 9 | 7 | 133 | 69 | 61 |
| Ellesmere Port Town | 42 | 25 | 6 | 11 | 111 | 61 | 56 |
| Frickley Colliery | 42 | 24 | 8 | 10 | 103 | 65 | 56 |
| Mossley | 42 | 23 | 7 | 12 | 93 | 66 | 53 |
| Oswestry Town | 42 | 23 | 7 | 12 | 113 | 84 | 53 |
| Bangor City | 42 | 22 | 8 | 12 | 103 | 65 | 52 |
| Wrexham | 42 | 22 | 6 | 14 | 109 | 83 | 50 |
| Buxton | 42 | 21 | 7 | 14 | 96 | 76 | 49 |
| Hyde United | 42 | 19 | 10 | 13 | 91 | 60 | 48 |
| Runcorn | 42 | 18 | 10 | 14 | 89 | 77 | 46 |
| Witton Albion | 42 | 16 | 14 | 12 | 89 | 78 | 46 |
| Northwich Victoria | 42 | 20 | 6 | 16 | 93 | 84 | 46 |
| Tranmere Rovers | 42 | 19 | 5 | 18 | 93 | 90 | 43 |
| Winsford United | 42 | 14 | 9 | 19 | 76 | 101 | 27 |
| Chester | 42 | 14 | 8 | 20 | 67 | 85 | 36 |
| Sankeys | 42 | 13 | 10 | 19 | 77 | 98 | 36 |
| Congleton Town | 42 | 14 | 7 | 21 | 67 | 91 | 35 |
| Rhyl | 42 | 11 | 7 | 24 | 65 | 85 | 29 |
| Stalybridge Celtic | 42 | 11 | 5 | 26 | 85 | 123 | 27 |
| Stafford Rangers | 42 | 8 | 10 | 24 | 54 | 84 | 26 |
| Altrincham | 42 | 8 | 6 | 28 | 68 | 125 | 22 |
| Wigan Rovers | 42 | 7 | 3 | 32 | 44 | 169 | 17 |

## 1962–63: CHESHIRE LEAGUE

| | P | W | D | L | F | A | Pts |
|---|---|---|---|---|---|---|---|
| Runcorn | 42 | 26 | 13 | 3 | 95 | 43 | 65 |
| Buxton | 42 | 24 | 7 | 11 | 104 | 71 | 55 |
| Tranmere Rovers | 42 | 19 | 15 | 8 | 88 | 57 | 53 |
| Stalybridge Celtic | 42 | 22 | 9 | 11 | 98 | 71 | 53 |
| Macclesfield Town | 42 | 20 | 12 | 10 | 87 | 59 | 52 |
| Ellesmere Port Town | 42 | 19 | 14 | 9 | 78 | 57 | 52 |
| Wigan Athletic | 42 | 22 | 6 | 14 | 70 | 54 | 50 |
| Altrincham | 42 | 19 | 8 | 15 | 90 | 68 | 46 |
| Northwich Victoria | 42 | 15 | 15 | 12 | 77 | 68 | 45 |
| Winsford United | 42 | 16 | 11 | 15 | 69 | 73 | 43 |
| Frickley Colliery | 42 | 16 | 11 | 15 | 66 | 79 | 43 |
| Hyde United | 42 | 14 | 14 | 14 | 81 | 74 | 42 |
| Bangor City | 42 | 13 | 16 | 13 | 71 | 68 | 42 |
| Witton Albion | 42 | 16 | 10 | 16 | 84 | 86 | 42 |
| Wrexham | 42 | 18 | 4 | 20 | 72 | 86 | 40 |
| Congleton Town | 42 | 16 | 7 | 19 | 73 | 80 | 39 |
| Rhyl | 42 | 12 | 10 | 20 | 64 | 86 | 34 |
| Sankeys | 42 | 10 | 13 | 19 | 64 | 76 | 33 |
| Mossley | 42 | 10 | 9 | 23 | 55 | 81 | 29 |
| Stafford Rangers | 42 | 9 | 10 | 23 | 50 | 90 | 28 |
| Chester | 42 | 7 | 7 | 28 | 62 | 105 | 21 |
| Oswestry Town | 42 | 6 | 5 | 31 | 53 | 119 | 17 |

## 1961–62: CHESHIRE LEAGUE

| | P | W | D | L | F | A | Pts |
|---|---|---|---|---|---|---|---|
| Ellesmere Port Town | 42 | 25 | 13 | 4 | 103 | 52 | 63 |
| Macclesfield Town | 42 | 25 | 10 | 7 | 109 | 61 | 60 |
| Runcorn | 42 | 27 | 3 | 12 | 108 | 60 | 57 |
| Northwich Victoria | 42 | 25 | 5 | 12 | 103 | 56 | 55 |
| Wigan Athletic | 42 | 24 | 7 | 11 | 86 | 51 | 55 |
| Hyde United | 42 | 24 | 4 | 14 | 81 | 65 | 52 |
| Buxton | 42 | 21 | 6 | 15 | 98 | 79 | 48 |
| Mossley | 42 | 20 | 7 | 15 | 87 | 78 | 47 |
| Stalybridge Celtic | 42 | 17 | 7 | 18 | 79 | 74 | 41 |
| Bangor City | 42 | 15 | 11 | 16 | 86 | 86 | 41 |
| Altrincham | 42 | 15 | 10 | 17 | 58 | 64 | 40 |
| Sankeys | 42 | 16 | 7 | 19 | 76 | 74 | 39 |
| Stafford Rangers | 42 | 12 | 13 | 17 | 72 | 84 | 37 |
| Rhyl | 42 | 12 | 11 | 19 | 52 | 63 | 35 |
| Congleton Town | 42 | 12 | 11 | 19 | 57 | 78 | 35 |
| Wrexham | 42 | 12 | 11 | 19 | 53 | 79 | 35 |
| Oswestry Town | 42 | 13 | 8 | 21 | 76 | 103 | 34 |
| Winsford United | 42 | 12 | 8 | 22 | 73 | 100 | 32 |
| Chester | 42 | 11 | 10 | 21 | 66 | 106 | 32 |
| Tranmere Rovers | 42 | 10 | 9 | 23 | 73 | 111 | 29 |
| Frickley Colliery | 42 | 10 | 9 | 23 | 65 | 108 | 29 |
| Witton Albion | 42 | 11 | 6 | 25 | 70 | 99 | 28 |

## 1963–64: CHESHIRE LEAGUE

| | P | W | D | L | F | A | Pts |
|---|---|---|---|---|---|---|---|
| Macclesfield Town | 42 | 30 | 9 | 3 | 112 | 38 | 69 |
| Sankeys | 42 | 23 | 10 | 9 | 98 | 57 | 56 |
| Altrincham | 42 | 22 | 8 | 12 | 94 | 68 | 52 |
| Bangor City | 42 | 21 | 9 | 12 | 75 | 55 | 51 |
| Witton Albion | 42 | 22 | 7 | 13 | 67 | 64 | 51 |
| Tranmere Rovers | 42 | 19 | 10 | 13 | 108 | 71 | 48 |
| Runcorn | 42 | 19 | 10 | 13 | 81 | 71 | 48 |
| Ellesmere Port Town | 42 | 20 | 8 | 14 | 77 | 76 | 48 |
| Buxton | 42 | 18 | 11 | 13 | 92 | 77 | 47 |
| Hyde United | 42 | 18 | 11 | 13 | 64 | 60 | 47 |
| Frickley Colliery | 42 | 18 | 9 | 15 | 65 | 57 | 45 |
| Wigan Athletic | 42 | 18 | 7 | 17 | 94 | 82 | 43 |
| Mossley | 42 | 16 | 7 | 19 | 66 | 77 | 39 |
| Rhyl | 42 | 13 | 12 | 17 | 73 | 88 | 38 |
| Oswestry Town | 42 | 13 | 10 | 19 | 85 | 94 | 36 |
| Stafford Rangers | 42 | 15 | 6 | 21 | 66 | 89 | 36 |
| Chester | 42 | 15 | 5 | 22 | 70 | 82 | 35 |
| Stalybridge Celtic | 42 | 14 | 6 | 22 | 66 | 80 | 34 |
| Northwich Victoria | 42 | 13 | 6 | 23 | 64 | 87 | 32 |
| Winsford United | 42 | 9 | 11 | 22 | 61 | 98 | 29 |
| Congleton Town | 42 | 4 | 13 | 25 | 43 | 95 | 21 |
| Wrexham | 42 | 7 | 5 | 30 | 58 | 113 | 19 |

## 1964–65: CHESHIRE LEAGUE

| | P | W | D | L | F | A | Pts |
|---|---|---|---|---|---|---|---|
| Wigan Athletic | 42 | 32 | 3 | 7 | 121 | 46 | 67 |
| Macclesfield Town | 42 | 28 | 6 | 8 | 115 | 45 | 62 |
| Runcorn | 42 | 27 | 5 | 10 | 121 | 60 | 59 |
| Bangor City | 42 | 25 | 4 | 13 | 94 | 58 | 54 |
| Tranmere Rovers | 42 | 22 | 6 | 14 | 93 | 70 | 50 |
| Hyde United | 42 | 22 | 6 | 14 | 96 | 76 | 50 |
| Frickley Colliery | 42 | 21 | 8 | 13 | 79 | 74 | 50 |
| Altrincham | 42 | 18 | 12 | 12 | 74 | 55 | 48 |
| Stalybridge Celtic | 42 | 17 | 11 | 14 | 78 | 74 | 45 |
| Ellesmere Port Town | 42 | 19 | 6 | 17 | 79 | 60 | 44 |
| Northwich Victoria | 42 | 18 | 6 | 18 | 100 | 87 | 42 |
| Rhyl | 42 | 17 | 6 | 19 | 69 | 79 | 40 |
| Oswestry Town | 42 | 17 | 5 | 20 | 100 | 100 | 39 |
| Mossley | 42 | 13 | 12 | 17 | 57 | 62 | 38 |
| Buxton | 42 | 15 | 7 | 20 | 77 | 99 | 37 |
| Witton Albion | 42 | 14 | 8 | 20 | 79 | 90 | 36 |
| Winsford United | 42 | 15 | 5 | 22 | 66 | 96 | 35 |
| Wrexham | 42 | 13 | 9 | 20 | 58 | 99 | 35 |
| Sankeys | 42 | 10 | 13 | 19 | 70 | 87 | 33 |
| Chester | 42 | 11 | 8 | 23 | 65 | 99 | 30 |
| Stafford Rangers | 42 | 6 | 5 | 31 | 44 | 120 | 17 |
| Congleton Town | 42 | 3 | 7 | 32 | 46 | 145 | 13 |

## 1966–67: CHESHIRE LEAGUE

| | P | W | D | L | F | A | Pts |
|---|---|---|---|---|---|---|---|
| Altrincham | 42 | 31 | 5 | 6 | 123 | 45 | 67 |
| Wigan Athletic | 42 | 26 | 8 | 8 | 101 | 61 | 60 |
| Northwich Victoria | 42 | 22 | 13 | 7 | 91 | 55 | 57 |
| Hyde United | 42 | 24 | 8 | 100 | 101 | 56 | 56 |
| Macclesfield | 42 | 24 | 8 | 10 | 78 | 47 | 56 |
| Witton Albion | 42 | 21 | 9 | 12 | 74 | 56 | 51 |
| Bangor City | 42 | 20 | 8 | 14 | 90 | 77 | 48 |
| Frickley Colliery | 42 | 18 | 10 | 14 | 71 | 69 | 46 |
| Runcorn | 42 | 16 | 11 | 15 | 75 | 75 | 43 |
| New Brighton | 42 | 16 | 7 | 19 | 69 | 73 | 39 |
| Mossley | 42 | 15 | 9 | 18 | 66 | 71 | 38 |
| Chester | 42 | 13 | 12 | 17 | 72 | 71 | 38 |
| Oswestry Town | 42 | 15 | 8 | 19 | 64 | 89 | 38 |
| Ellesmere Port Town | 42 | 11 | 15 | 16 | 61 | 70 | 37 |
| Stafford Rangers | 42 | 12 | 12 | 18 | 59 | 66 | 36 |
| Buxton | 42 | 13 | 10 | 19 | 69 | 78 | 36 |
| Tranmere Rovers | 42 | 14 | 8 | 20 | 66 | 84 | 36 |
| Stockport County | 42 | 12 | 9 | 21 | 58 | 76 | 33 |
| Rhyl | 42 | 11 | 9 | 22 | 59 | 86 | 31 |
| Stalybridge Celtic | 42 | 11 | 8 | 23 | 53 | 85 | 30 |
| Wrexham | 42 | 11 | 3 | 28 | 66 | 114 | 25 |
| Winsford United | 42 | 8 | 6 | 28 | 46 | 107 | 22 |

## 1965–66: CHESHIRE LEAGUE

| | P | W | D | L | F | A | Pts |
|---|---|---|---|---|---|---|---|
| Altrincham | 42 | 33 | 7 | 2 | 132 | 49 | 73 |
| Wigan Athletic | 42 | 32 | 8 | 2 | 133 | 40 | 72 |
| Macclesfield Town | 42 | 26 | 8 | 8 | 102 | 48 | 60 |
| Bangor City | 42 | 24 | 6 | 12 | 91 | 67 | 54 |
| Runcorn | 42 | 22 | 7 | 13 | 105 | 77 | 51 |
| Stalybridge Celtic | 42 | 21 | 8 | 13 | 98 | 84 | 50 |
| Northwich Victoria | 42 | 20 | 6 | 16 | 93 | 77 | 46 |
| Hyde United | 42 | 16 | 11 | 15 | 74 | 72 | 43 |
| Ellesmere Port Town | 42 | 16 | 10 | 16 | 97 | 80 | 42 |
| Stockport County | 42 | 14 | 13 | 15 | 61 | 65 | 41 |
| New Brighton | 42 | 17 | 6 | 19 | 76 | 86 | 40 |
| Buxton | 42 | 15 | 8 | 19 | 74 | 82 | 38 |
| Tranmere Rovers | 42 | 13 | 11 | 18 | 85 | 88 | 37 |
| Frickley Colliery | 42 | 13 | 11 | 18 | 76 | 102 | 37 |
| Mossley | 42 | 13 | 10 | 19 | 66 | 72 | 36 |
| Oswestry Town | 42 | 15 | 6 | 21 | 78 | 102 | 36 |
| Witton Albion | 42 | 14 | 7 | 21 | 93 | 107 | 35 |
| Wrexham | 42 | 15 | 5 | 22 | 92 | 107 | 35 |
| Stafford Rangers | 42 | 9 | 10 | 23 | 60 | 109 | 28 |
| Rhyl | 42 | 8 | 10 | 24 | 57 | 104 | 26 |
| Chester | 42 | 9 | 7 | 26 | 52 | 116 | 25 |
| Winsford United | 42 | 6 | 7 | 29 | 55 | 127 | 19 |

## 1967–68: CHESHIRE LEAGUE

| | P | W | D | L | F | A | Pts |
|---|---|---|---|---|---|---|---|
| Macclesfield Town | 42 | 28 | 10 | 4 | 96 | 39 | 66 |
| Altrincham | 42 | 28 | 7 | 7 | 108 | 64 | 63 |
| Bangor City | 42 | 24 | 9 | 9 | 99 | 61 | 57 |
| Witton Albion | 42 | 21 | 12 | 9 | 90 | 65 | 54 |
| Mossley | 42 | 20 | 13 | 9 | 90 | 62 | 53 |
| Tranmere Rovers | 42 | 22 | 6 | 14 | 71 | 50 | 50 |
| Northwich Victoria | 42 | 22 | 6 | 14 | 82 | 64 | 50 |
| Wigan Athletic | 42 | 18 | 12 | 12 | 62 | 48 | 48 |
| Stafford Rangers | 42 | 18 | 11 | 13 | 88 | 58 | 47 |
| Hyde United | 42 | 17 | 12 | 13 | 97 | 74 | 46 |
| New Brighton | 42 | 16 | 10 | 16 | 60 | 69 | 42 |
| Ellesmere Port Town | 42 | 15 | 11 | 16 | 68 | 67 | 41 |
| Runcorn | 42 | 16 | 8 | 18 | 99 | 95 | 40 |
| Wrexham | 42 | 16 | 8 | 18 | 72 | 77 | 40 |
| Buxton | 42 | 14 | 8 | 20 | 71 | 86 | 36 |
| Rhyl | 42 | 12 | 10 | 20 | 63 | 78 | 34 |
| Winsford United | 42 | 13 | 7 | 22 | 50 | 82 | 33 |
| Oswestry Town | 42 | 13 | 6 | 23 | 63 | 106 | 32 |
| Frickley Colliery | 42 | 10 | 10 | 22 | 61 | 83 | 30 |
| Stockport County | 42 | 10 | 7 | 25 | 55 | 92 | 27 |
| Stalybridge Celtic | 42 | 6 | 14 | 22 | 54 | 93 | 28 |
| Chester | 42 | 2 | 5 | 35 | 48 | 134 | 9 |

# League Tables, 1968-1987

## 1968–69: NORTHERN PREMIER LEAGUE

| | P | W | D | L | F | A | Pts |
|---|---|---|---|---|---|---|---|
| Macclesfield Town | 38 | 27 | 6 | 5 | 82 | 38 | 60 |
| Wigan Athletic | 38 | 18 | 12 | 8 | 59 | 41 | 48 |
| Morecambe | 38 | 16 | 14 | 8 | 64 | 37 | 46 |
| Gainsborough Trinity | 38 | 19 | 8 | 11 | 64 | 43 | 46 |
| South Shields | 38 | 19 | 8 | 11 | 78 | 56 | 46 |
| Bangor City | 38 | 18 | 9 | 11 | 102 | 64 | 45 |
| Hyde United | 38 | 16 | 10 | 12 | 71 | 65 | 42 |
| Goole Town | 38 | 15 | 10 | 13 | 80 | 78 | 40 |
| Altrincham | 38 | 14 | 10 | 14 | 69 | 52 | 38 |
| Fleetwood | 38 | 16 | 6 | 16 | 58 | 58 | 38 |
| Gateshead | 38 | 14 | 9 | 15 | 42 | 48 | 37 |
| South Liverpool | 38 | 12 | 13 | 13 | 56 | 66 | 37 |
| Northwich Victoria | 38 | 16 | 5 | 17 | 59 | 82 | 37 |
| Boston United | 38 | 14 | 8 | 16 | 59 | 65 | 36 |
| Runcorn | 38 | 12 | 11 | 15 | 59 | 63 | 35 |
| Netherfield | 38 | 12 | 4 | 22 | 51 | 69 | 28 |
| Scarborough | 38 | 9 | 10 | 19 | 49 | 68 | 28 |
| Ashington | 38 | 10 | 8 | 20 | 48 | 74 | 28 |
| Chorley | 38 | 8 | 9 | 21 | 46 | 75 | 25 |
| Worksop Town | 38 | 6 | 8 | 24 | 34 | 88 | 20 |

## 1969–70: NORTHERN PREMIER LEAGUE

| | P | W | D | L | F | A | Pts |
|---|---|---|---|---|---|---|---|
| Macclesfield Town | 38 | 22 | 8 | 8 | 72 | 41 | 52 |
| Wigan Athletic | 38 | 20 | 12 | 6 | 56 | 32 | 52 |
| Boston United | 38 | 21 | 8 | 9 | 65 | 33 | 50 |
| Scarborough | 38 | 20 | 10 | 8 | 74 | 39 | 50 |
| South Shields | 38 | 19 | 7 | 12 | 66 | 43 | 45 |
| Gainsborough Trinity | 38 | 16 | 11 | 11 | 64 | 49 | 43 |
| Stafford Rangers | 38 | 16 | 7 | 15 | 59 | 52 | 39 |
| Bangor City | 38 | 15 | 9 | 14 | 68 | 63 | 39 |
| Northwich Victoria | 38 | 15 | 8 | 15 | 60 | 66 | 38 |
| Netherfield | 38 | 14 | 9 | 15 | 56 | 54 | 37 |
| Hyde United | 38 | 15 | 7 | 16 | 59 | 59 | 37 |
| Altrincham | 38 | 14 | 8 | 16 | 62 | 65 | 36 |
| Fleetwood | 38 | 13 | 10 | 15 | 53 | 60 | 36 |
| Runcorn | 38 | 11 | 13 | 14 | 57 | 72 | 35 |
| Morecambe | 38 | 10 | 13 | 15 | 41 | 51 | 33 |
| South Liverpool | 38 | 11 | 11 | 16 | 44 | 55 | 33 |
| Great Harwood | 38 | 10 | 9 | 19 | 63 | 92 | 29 |
| Matlock Town | 38 | 8 | 12 | 18 | 52 | 67 | 28 |
| Goole Town | 38 | 10 | 6 | 22 | 50 | 71 | 26 |
| Gateshead | 38 | 5 | 12 | 21 | 37 | 94 | 22 |

## 1970–71: NORTHERN PREMIER LEAGUE

| | P | W | D | L | F | A | Pts |
|---|---|---|---|---|---|---|---|
| Wigan Athletic | 42 | 27 | 13 | 2 | 91 | 32 | 67 |
| Stafford Rangers | 42 | 27 | 7 | 8 | 87 | 51 | 61 |
| Scarborough | 42 | 23 | 12 | 7 | 83 | 40 | 58 |
| Boston United | 42 | 22 | 12 | 8 | 69 | 31 | 56 |
| Macclesfield Town | 42 | 23 | 10 | 9 | 84 | 45 | 56 |
| Northwich Victoria | 42 | 22 | 5 | 15 | 71 | 55 | 49 |
| Bangor City | 42 | 19 | 11 | 13 | 72 | 61 | 48 |
| Altrincham | 42 | 19 | 10 | 13 | 80 | 76 | 48 |
| South Liverpool | 42 | 15 | 15 | 12 | 67 | 57 | 45 |
| Chorley | 42 | 14 | 14 | 14 | 58 | 61 | 42 |
| Gainsborough Trinity | 42 | 15 | 11 | 16 | 65 | 63 | 41 |
| Morecambe | 42 | 14 | 11 | 17 | 67 | 79 | 39 |
| South Shields | 42 | 12 | 14 | 16 | 67 | 66 | 38 |
| Bradford Park Avenue | 42 | 15 | 8 | 19 | 54 | 73 | 38 |
| Lancaster City | 42 | 12 | 12 | 18 | 53 | 76 | 36 |
| Netherfield | 42 | 13 | 9 | 20 | 59 | 57 | 35 |
| Matlock Town | 42 | 10 | 13 | 19 | 58 | 80 | 33 |
| Fleetwood | 42 | 10 | 11 | 21 | 56 | 90 | 31 |
| Great Harwood | 42 | 8 | 13 | 21 | 66 | 98 | 29 |
| Runcorn | 42 | 10 | 5 | 27 | 58 | 84 | 25 |
| Kirkby Town | 42 | 6 | 13 | 23 | 57 | 93 | 25 |
| Goole Town | 42 | 10 | 4 | 28 | 44 | 98 | 24 |

## 1971–72: NORTHERN PREMIER LEAGUE

| | P | W | D | L | F | A | Pts |
|---|---|---|---|---|---|---|---|
| Stafford Rangers | 46 | 30 | 11 | 5 | 91 | 32 | 71 |
| Boston United | 46 | 28 | 13 | 5 | 87 | 37 | 69 |
| Wigan Athletic | 46 | 27 | 10 | 9 | 70 | 43 | 64 |
| Scarborough | 46 | 21 | 15 | 10 | 75 | 46 | 57 |
| Northwich Victoria | 46 | 20 | 14 | 12 | 65 | 59 | 54 |
| Macclesfield Town | 46 | 18 | 15 | 13 | 61 | 50 | 51 |
| Gainsborough Trinity | 46 | 21 | 9 | 16 | 93 | 79 | 51 |
| South Shields | 46 | 18 | 14 | 14 | 75 | 57 | 50 |
| Bangor City | 46 | 20 | 8 | 18 | 93 | 74 | 48 |
| Altrincham | 46 | 18 | 11 | 17 | 72 | 58 | 47 |
| Skelmersdale United | 46 | 19 | 9 | 18 | 61 | 58 | 47 |
| Matlock Town | 46 | 20 | 7 | 19 | 67 | 75 | 47 |
| Chorley | 46 | 17 | 12 | 17 | 66 | 59 | 46 |
| Lancaster City | 46 | 15 | 14 | 17 | 85 | 84 | 44 |
| Great Harwood | 46 | 15 | 14 | 17 | 60 | 74 | 44 |
| Ellesmere Port Town | 46 | 17 | 9 | 20 | 67 | 71 | 43 |
| Morecambe | 46 | 15 | 10 | 21 | 51 | 64 | 40 |
| Bradford Park Avenue | 46 | 13 | 13 | 20 | 54 | 71 | 39 |
| Netherfield | 46 | 16 | 5 | 25 | 51 | 73 | 37 |
| Fleetwood | 46 | 11 | 15 | 20 | 43 | 67 | 37 |
| South Liverpool | 46 | 12 | 2 | 22 | 61 | 73 | 36 |
| Runcorn | 46 | 8 | 14 | 24 | 48 | 80 | 30 |
| Goole Town | 46 | 9 | 10 | 27 | 51 | 97 | 28 |
| Kirkby Town | 46 | 6 | 12 | 28 | 38 | 104 | 24 |

## 1972–73: Northern Premier League

|                        | P  | W  | D  | L  | F  | A   | Pts |
|------------------------|----|----|----|----|----|-----|-----|
| Boston United          | 46 | 27 | 16 | 3  | 88 | 34  | 70  |
| Scarborough            | 46 | 26 | 9  | 11 | 72 | 39  | 61  |
| Wigan Athletic         | 46 | 23 | 14 | 9  | 69 | 38  | 60  |
| Altrincham             | 46 | 22 | 16 | 8  | 75 | 55  | 60  |
| Bradford Park Avenue   | 46 | 19 | 17 | 10 | 63 | 50  | 55  |
| Stafford Rangers       | 46 | 20 | 11 | 15 | 63 | 46  | 51  |
| Gainsborough Trinity   | 46 | 18 | 13 | 15 | 70 | 50  | 49  |
| Northwich Victoria     | 46 | 17 | 15 | 14 | 74 | 62  | 49  |
| Netherfield            | 46 | 20 | 9  | 17 | 68 | 65  | 49  |
| Macclesfield Town      | 46 | 16 | 16 | 14 | 58 | 47  | 48  |
| Ellesmere Port Town    | 46 | 18 | 11 | 17 | 52 | 56  | 47  |
| Skelmersdale United    | 46 | 15 | 16 | 15 | 58 | 59  | 46  |
| Bangor City            | 46 | 16 | 13 | 17 | 70 | 60  | 45  |
| Mossley                | 46 | 17 | 11 | 18 | 70 | 73  | 45  |
| Morecambe              | 46 | 17 | 11 | 18 | 62 | 70  | 45  |
| Great Harwood          | 46 | 14 | 15 | 17 | 63 | 74  | 43  |
| South Liverpool        | 46 | 12 | 19 | 15 | 47 | 57  | 43  |
| Runcorn                | 46 | 15 | 12 | 19 | 75 | 78  | 42  |
| Goole Town             | 46 | 13 | 13 | 20 | 64 | 73  | 39  |
| South Shields          | 46 | 17 | 4  | 25 | 64 | 81  | 38  |
| Matlock Town           | 46 | 11 | 11 | 24 | 42 | 80  | 33  |
| Lancaster City         | 46 | 10 | 11 | 25 | 53 | 78  | 31  |
| Barrow                 | 46 | 12 | 6  | 28 | 52 | 101 | 30  |
| Fleetwood              | 46 | 5  | 15 | 26 | 31 | 77  | 25  |

## 1973–74: Northern Premier League

|                        | P  | W  | D  | L  | F   | A  | Pts |
|------------------------|----|----|----|----|-----|----|-----|
| Boston United          | 46 | 27 | 11 | 8  | 69  | 32 | 65  |
| Wigan Athletic         | 46 | 28 | 8  | 10 | 96  | 39 | 64  |
| Altrincham             | 46 | 26 | 11 | 9  | 77  | 34 | 63  |
| Stafford Rangers       | 46 | 27 | 9  | 10 | 101 | 45 | 63  |
| Scarborough            | 46 | 22 | 14 | 10 | 62  | 43 | 58  |
| South Shields          | 46 | 25 | 6  | 15 | 87  | 48 | 56  |
| Runcorn                | 46 | 21 | 14 | 11 | 72  | 47 | 56  |
| Macclesfield Town      | 46 | 18 | 15 | 13 | 48  | 47 | 51  |
| Bangor City            | 46 | 19 | 11 | 16 | 65  | 56 | 49  |
| Gainsborough Trinity   | 46 | 18 | 11 | 17 | 77  | 64 | 47  |
| South Liverpool        | 46 | 16 | 15 | 15 | 55  | 47 | 47  |
| Skelmersdale United    | 46 | 16 | 13 | 17 | 50  | 59 | 45  |
| Goole Town             | 46 | 14 | 15 | 17 | 60  | 69 | 43  |
| Fleetwood              | 46 | 14 | 15 | 17 | 48  | 68 | 43  |
| Mossley                | 46 | 15 | 11 | 20 | 53  | 65 | 41  |
| Northwich Victoria     | 46 | 14 | 13 | 19 | 68  | 75 | 41  |
| Morecambe              | 46 | 13 | 13 | 20 | 62  | 84 | 39  |
| Buxton                 | 46 | 14 | 10 | 22 | 45  | 71 | 38  |
| Matlock Town           | 46 | 11 | 14 | 21 | 50  | 79 | 36  |
| Great Harwood          | 46 | 10 | 14 | 22 | 52  | 74 | 34  |
| Bradford Park Avenue   | 46 | 9  | 15 | 22 | 42  | 84 | 33  |
| Barrow                 | 46 | 13 | 7  | 26 | 46  | 94 | 33  |
| Lancaster City         | 46 | 10 | 12 | 24 | 52  | 67 | 32  |
| Netherfield            | 46 | 11 | 5  | 30 | 42  | 88 | 27  |

## 1974–75: Northern Premier League

|                        | P  | W  | D  | L  | F   | A  | Pts |
|------------------------|----|----|----|----|-----|----|-----|
| Wigan Athletic         | 46 | 33 | 6  | 7  | 94  | 38 | 72  |
| Runcorn                | 46 | 30 | 8  | 8  | 102 | 42 | 68  |
| Altrincham             | 46 | 26 | 12 | 8  | 87  | 43 | 64  |
| Stafford Rangers       | 46 | 25 | 13 | 8  | 81  | 39 | 63  |
| Scarborough            | 46 | 24 | 12 | 10 | 75  | 45 | 60  |
| Mossley                | 46 | 23 | 11 | 12 | 78  | 52 | 57  |
| Gateshead United       | 46 | 22 | 12 | 12 | 74  | 48 | 56  |
| Goole Town             | 46 | 19 | 12 | 15 | 75  | 71 | 50  |
| Northwich Victoria     | 46 | 18 | 12 | 16 | 83  | 71 | 48  |
| Great Harwood          | 46 | 17 | 14 | 15 | 69  | 66 | 48  |
| Matlock Town           | 46 | 19 | 8  | 19 | 87  | 79 | 46  |
| Boston United          | 46 | 16 | 14 | 16 | 64  | 63 | 46  |
| Morecambe              | 46 | 14 | 15 | 17 | 71  | 87 | 43  |
| Worksop Town           | 46 | 14 | 14 | 18 | 69  | 66 | 42  |
| South Liverpool        | 46 | 14 | 14 | 18 | 59  | 71 | 42  |
| Buxton                 | 46 | 11 | 17 | 18 | 50  | 77 | 39  |
| Macclesfield Town      | 46 | 11 | 14 | 21 | 46  | 62 | 36  |
| Lancaster City         | 46 | 13 | 10 | 23 | 53  | 76 | 36  |
| Bangor City            | 46 | 13 | 9  | 24 | 56  | 67 | 35  |
| Gainsborough Trinity   | 46 | 10 | 15 | 21 | 46  | 79 | 35  |
| Skelmersdale United    | 46 | 13 | 7  | 26 | 63  | 93 | 33  |
| Barrow                 | 46 | 9  | 15 | 22 | 45  | 72 | 33  |
| Netherfield            | 46 | 12 | 8  | 26 | 42  | 91 | 32  |
| Fleetwood              | 46 | 5  | 10 | 31 | 26  | 97 | 20  |

## 1975–76: Northern Premier League

|                        | P  | W  | D  | L  | F  | A   | Pts |
|------------------------|----|----|----|----|----|-----|-----|
| Runcorn                | 46 | 29 | 10 | 7  | 95 | 42  | 68  |
| Stafford Rangers       | 46 | 26 | 15 | 5  | 81 | 41  | 67  |
| Scarborough            | 46 | 26 | 10 | 10 | 84 | 43  | 62  |
| Matlock Town           | 46 | 26 | 9  | 11 | 96 | 63  | 61  |
| Boston United          | 46 | 27 | 6  | 13 | 95 | 58  | 60  |
| Wigan Athletic         | 46 | 21 | 15 | 10 | 81 | 42  | 57  |
| Altrincham             | 46 | 20 | 14 | 12 | 77 | 57  | 54  |
| Bangor City            | 46 | 21 | 12 | 13 | 80 | 70  | 54  |
| Mossley                | 46 | 21 | 11 | 14 | 70 | 58  | 53  |
| Goole Town             | 46 | 20 | 13 | 13 | 58 | 49  | 53  |
| Northwich Victoria     | 46 | 17 | 17 | 12 | 79 | 59  | 51  |
| Lancaster City         | 46 | 18 | 9  | 19 | 61 | 70  | 45  |
| Worksop Town           | 46 | 17 | 10 | 19 | 63 | 56  | 44  |
| Gainsborough Trinity   | 46 | 13 | 17 | 16 | 58 | 69  | 43  |
| Macclesfield Town      | 46 | 15 | 12 | 19 | 50 | 64  | 42  |
| Gateshead United       | 46 | 17 | 7  | 22 | 64 | 63  | 41  |
| Buxton                 | 46 | 11 | 13 | 22 | 37 | 62  | 35  |
| Skelmersdale United    | 46 | 12 | 10 | 24 | 45 | 74  | 34  |
| Netherfield            | 46 | 11 | 11 | 24 | 55 | 76  | 33  |
| Morecambe              | 46 | 11 | 11 | 24 | 47 | 67  | 33  |
| Great Harwood          | 46 | 13 | 7  | 26 | 58 | 86  | 33  |
| South Liverpool        | 46 | 12 | 9  | 25 | 45 | 78  | 33  |
| Barrow                 | 46 | 12 | 9  | 25 | 47 | 84  | 33  |
| Fleetwood              | 46 | 3  | 9  | 34 | 36 | 131 | 15  |

## 1976–77: Northern Premier League

| | P | W | D | L | F | A | Pts |
|---|---|---|---|---|---|---|---|
| Boston United | 44 | 27 | 11 | 6 | 82 | 35 | 65 |
| Northwich Victoria | 44 | 27 | 11 | 6 | 85 | 43 | 65 |
| Matlock Town | 44 | 26 | 11 | 7 | 108 | 57 | 63 |
| Bangor City | 44 | 22 | 11 | 11 | 87 | 52 | 55 |
| Scarborough | 44 | 21 | 12 | 11 | 77 | 66 | 54 |
| Goole Town | 44 | 23 | 6 | 15 | 64 | 50 | 52 |
| Lancaster City | 44 | 21 | 9 | 14 | 71 | 58 | 51 |
| Gateshead United | 44 | 18 | 12 | 14 | 80 | 64 | 48 |
| Mossley | 44 | 17 | 14 | 13 | 74 | 59 | 48 |
| Altrincham | 44 | 19 | 9 | 16 | 60 | 53 | 47 |
| Stafford Rangers | 44 | 16 | 14 | 14 | 60 | 55 | 46 |
| Runcorn | 44 | 15 | 14 | 15 | 58 | 50 | 44 |
| Worksop Town | 44 | 16 | 12 | 16 | 50 | 58 | 44 |
| Wigan Athletic | 44 | 14 | 15 | 15 | 62 | 54 | 43 |
| Morecambe | 44 | 13 | 11 | 20 | 59 | 75 | 37 |
| Gainsborough Trinity | 44 | 13 | 10 | 21 | 58 | 74 | 36 |
| Great Harwood | 44 | 11 | 14 | 19 | 63 | 84 | 36 |
| Buxton | 44 | 11 | 13 | 20 | 48 | 63 | 35 |
| Macclesfield Town | 44 | 8 | 15 | 21 | 41 | 68 | 31 |
| Frickley Athletic | 44 | 11 | 8 | 25 | 53 | 93 | 30 |
| Barrow | 44 | 11 | 6 | 27 | 56 | 87 | 28 |
| South Liverpool | 44 | 10 | 8 | 26 | 51 | 104 | 28 |
| Netherfield | 44 | 9 | 8 | 27 | 47 | 92 | 26 |

## 1977–78: Northern Premier League

| | P | W | D | L | F | A | Pts |
|---|---|---|---|---|---|---|---|
| Boston United | 46 | 31 | 9 | 6 | 85 | 35 | 71 |
| Wigan Athletic | 46 | 25 | 15 | 6 | 83 | 45 | 65 |
| Bangor City | 46 | 26 | 10 | 10 | 92 | 50 | 62 |
| Scarborough | 46 | 26 | 10 | 10 | 80 | 39 | 62 |
| Altrincham | 46 | 22 | 15 | 9 | 84 | 49 | 59 |
| Northwich Victoria | 46 | 22 | 14 | 10 | 83 | 55 | 58 |
| Stafford Rangers | 46 | 22 | 13 | 11 | 71 | 41 | 57 |
| Runcorn | 46 | 19 | 18 | 9 | 70 | 44 | 56 |
| Mossley | 46 | 22 | 11 | 13 | 85 | 73 | 55 |
| Matlock | 46 | 21 | 12 | 13 | 79 | 60 | 54 |
| Lancaster City | 46 | 15 | 14 | 17 | 66 | 82 | 44 |
| Frickley Athletic | 46 | 15 | 12 | 19 | 77 | 81 | 42 |
| Barrow | 46 | 14 | 12 | 20 | 58 | 61 | 40 |
| Goole Town | 46 | 15 | 9 | 22 | 60 | 68 | 39 |
| Great Harwood | 46 | 13 | 13 | 20 | 66 | 83 | 39 |
| Gainsborough Trinity | 46 | 14 | 10 | 22 | 61 | 74 | 38 |
| Gateshead | 46 | 16 | 5 | 25 | 65 | 74 | 38 |
| Netherfield | 46 | 11 | 13 | 22 | 50 | 80 | 35 |
| Workington | 46 | 13 | 8 | 25 | 48 | 80 | 34 |
| Worksop Town | 46 | 12 | 10 | 24 | 45 | 84 | 34 |
| Morecambe | 46 | 11 | 11 | 24 | 67 | 92 | 33 |
| Macclesfield Town | 46 | 12 | 9 | 25 | 60 | 92 | 33 |
| Buxton | 46 | 13 | 6 | 27 | 60 | 95 | 32 |
| South Liverpool | 46 | 9 | 7 | 30 | 53 | 111 | 25 |

## 1978–79: Northern Premier League

| | P | W | D | L | F | A | Pts |
|---|---|---|---|---|---|---|---|
| Mossley | 44 | 32 | 5 | 7 | 117 | 48 | 69 |
| Altrincham | 44 | 25 | 11 | 8 | 93 | 39 | 61 |
| Matlock Town | 44 | 24 | 8 | 12 | 100 | 59 | 56 |
| Scarborough | 44 | 19 | 14 | 11 | 61 | 44 | 52 |
| Southport | 44 | 19 | 14 | 11 | 62 | 49 | 52 |
| Boston United | 44 | 17 | 18 | 9 | 40 | 33 | 52 |
| Runcorn | 44 | 21 | 9 | 14 | 79 | 54 | 51 |
| Stafford Rangers | 44 | 18 | 14 | 12 | 67 | 41 | 50 |
| Goole Town | 44 | 17 | 15 | 12 | 56 | 61 | 49 |
| Northwich Victoria | 44 | 18 | 11 | 15 | 64 | 52 | 47 |
| Lancaster City | 44 | 17 | 12 | 15 | 62 | 54 | 46 |
| Bangor City | 44 | 15 | 14 | 15 | 65 | 66 | 44 |
| Worksop Town | 44 | 13 | 14 | 17 | 55 | 67 | 40 |
| Workington | 44 | 16 | 7 | 21 | 62 | 74 | 39 |
| Netherfield | 44 | 13 | 11 | 20 | 39 | 69 | 37 |
| Barrow | 44 | 14 | 9 | 21 | 47 | 78 | 37 |
| Gainsborough Trinity | 44 | 12 | 12 | 20 | 52 | 67 | 36 |
| Morecambe | 44 | 11 | 13 | 20 | 55 | 65 | 35 |
| Frickley Athletic | 44 | 13 | 9 | 22 | 58 | 70 | 35 |
| South Liverpool | 44 | 12 | 10 | 22 | 48 | 85 | 34 |
| Gateshead | 44 | 11 | 11 | 22 | 42 | 63 | 33 |
| Buxton | 44 | 11 | 9 | 24 | 50 | 84 | 31 |
| Macclesfield Town | 44 | 8 | 10 | 26 | 40 | 92 | 26 |

## 1979–80: Northern Premier League

| | P | W | D | L | F | A | Pts |
|---|---|---|---|---|---|---|---|
| Mossley | 42 | 28 | 9 | 5 | 96 | 41 | 65 |
| Witton Albion | 42 | 28 | 8 | 6 | 89 | 30 | 64 |
| Frickley Athletic | 42 | 24 | 13 | 5 | 93 | 48 | 61 |
| Burton Albion | 42 | 25 | 6 | 11 | 83 | 42 | 56 |
| Matlock Town | 42 | 18 | 17 | 7 | 87 | 53 | 53 |
| Buxton | 42 | 21 | 9 | 12 | 61 | 48 | 51 |
| Worksop Town | 42 | 20 | 10 | 12 | 65 | 52 | 50 |
| Macclesfield Town | 42 | 18 | 11 | 13 | 67 | 53 | 47 |
| Grantham | 42 | 18 | 8 | 16 | 71 | 65 | 44 |
| Marine | 42 | 16 | 10 | 16 | 65 | 57 | 42 |
| Goole Town | 42 | 14 | 13 | 15 | 61 | 63 | 41 |
| Lancaster City | 42 | 13 | 13 | 16 | 74 | 77 | 39 |
| Oswestry Town | 42 | 12 | 14 | 16 | 44 | 60 | 38 |
| Gainsborough Trinity | 42 | 14 | 8 | 20 | 64 | 75 | 36 |
| Runcorn | 42 | 11 | 11 | 20 | 46 | 63 | 33 |
| Gateshead | 42 | 11 | 11 | 20 | 50 | 77 | 33 |
| Morecambe | 42 | 10 | 12 | 20 | 40 | 59 | 32 |
| Netherfield | 42 | 7 | 15 | 20 | 37 | 66 | 29 |
| Southport | 42 | 8 | 13 | 21 | 30 | 75 | 29 |
| South Liverpool | 42 | 7 | 14 | 21 | 51 | 84 | 28 |
| Workington | 42 | 8 | 12 | 22 | 50 | 85 | 28 |
| Tamworth | 42 | 8 | 9 | 25 | 26 | 77 | 25 |

## 1980–81: Northern Premier League

|  | P | W | D | L | F | A | Pts |
|---|---|---|---|---|---|---|---|
| Runcorn | 42 | 32 | 7 | 3 | 99 | 22 | 71 |
| Mossley | 42 | 24 | 7 | 11 | 95 | 55 | 55 |
| Marine | 42 | 22 | 10 | 10 | 66 | 41 | 54 |
| Buxton | 42 | 21 | 7 | 14 | 64 | 50 | 49 |
| Gainsborough Trinity | 42 | 17 | 13 | 12 | 80 | 57 | 47 |
| Burton Albion | 42 | 19 | 8 | 15 | 63 | 54 | 46 |
| Witton Albion | 42 | 19 | 8 | 15 | 70 | 62 | 46 |
| Goole Town | 42 | 14 | 16 | 12 | 56 | 50 | 44 |
| South Liverpool | 42 | 19 | 6 | 17 | 59 | 64 | 44 |
| Workington | 42 | 15 | 13 | 14 | 57 | 48 | 43 |
| Gateshead | 42 | 12 | 18 | 12 | 65 | 61 | 42 |
| Worksop Town | 42 | 15 | 11 | 16 | 66 | 61 | 41 |
| Macclesfield Town | 42 | 13 | 13 | 16 | 52 | 69 | 39 |
| Grantham | 42 | 14 | 9 | 19 | 57 | 74 | 37 |
| Matlock Town | 42 | 12 | 12 | 18 | 57 | 80 | 36 |
| Lancaster City | 42 | 13 | 9 | 20 | 48 | 70 | 35 |
| Netherfield | 42 | 11 | 12 | 19 | 73 | 81 | 34 |
| Oswestry Town | 42 | 13 | 8 | 21 | 54 | 67 | 34 |
| King's Lynn | 42 | 8 | 18 | 16 | 46 | 65 | 34 |
| Southport | 42 | 11 | 11 | 20 | 42 | 68 | 33 |
| Morecambe | 42 | 11 | 8 | 23 | 42 | 74 | 30 |
| Tamworth | 42 | 9 | 12 | 21 | 38 | 76 | 30 |

## 1981–82: Northern Premier League

|  | P | W | D | L | F | A | Pts |
|---|---|---|---|---|---|---|---|
| Bangor City | 42 | 27 | 8 | 7 | 108 | 60 | 62 |
| Mossley | 42 | 24 | 11 | 7 | 76 | 43 | 59 |
| Witton Albion | 42 | 22 | 10 | 10 | 75 | 42 | 54 |
| Gateshead | 42 | 19 | 14 | 9 | 65 | 49 | 52 |
| King's Lynn | 42 | 19 | 12 | 11 | 61 | 36 | 50 |
| Grantham | 42 | 18 | 13 | 11 | 65 | 53 | 49 |
| Burton Albion | 42 | 19 | 9 | 14 | 71 | 62 | 47 |
| Southport | 42 | 16 | 14 | 12 | 63 | 55 | 46 |
| Marine | 42 | 17 | 12 | 13 | 64 | 57 | 46 |
| Macclesfield Town | 42 | 17 | 9 | 16 | 67 | 58 | 43 |
| Workington | 42 | 18 | 7 | 17 | 62 | 60 | 43 |
| Worksop Town | 42 | 15 | 13 | 14 | 52 | 60 | 43 |
| South Liverpool | 42 | 13 | 13 | 16 | 55 | 57 | 39 |
| Goole Town | 42 | 13 | 13 | 16 | 56 | 60 | 39 |
| Oswestry Town | 42 | 14 | 11 | 17 | 55 | 59 | 39 |
| Buxton | 42 | 14 | 11 | 17 | 48 | 56 | 39 |
| Lancaster City | 42 | 13 | 12 | 17 | 47 | 50 | 38 |
| Gainsborough Trinity | 42 | 10 | 13 | 19 | 60 | 69 | 33 |
| Tamworth | 42 | 10 | 9 | 23 | 31 | 56 | 29 |
| Morecambe | 42 | 9 | 11 | 22 | 43 | 86 | 29 |
| Matlock Town | 42 | 7 | 12 | 23 | 38 | 72 | 26 |
| Netherfield | 42 | 5 | 9 | 28 | 31 | 91 | 19 |

## 1982–83: Northern Premier League

|  | P | W | D | L | F | A | Pts |
|---|---|---|---|---|---|---|---|
| Gateshead | 42 | 32 | 4 | 6 | 114 | 43 | 100 |
| Mossley | 42 | 25 | 9 | 8 | 77 | 42 | 84 |
| Burton Albion | 42 | 24 | 9 | 9 | 81 | 53 | 81 |
| Chorley | 42 | 23 | 11 | 8 | 77 | 49 | 80 |
| Macclesfield Town | 42 | 24 | 8 | 10 | 71 | 49 | 80 |
| Marine | 42 | 17 | 17 | 8 | 81 | 57 | 68 |
| Workington | 42 | 19 | 10 | 13 | 71 | 55 | 67 |
| Hyde United | 42 | 18 | 12 | 12 | 91 | 63 | 66 |
| King's Lynn | 42 | 17 | 13 | 12 | 62 | 44 | 64 |
| Matlock Town | 42 | 18 | 10 | 14 | 70 | 65 | 64 |
| Witton Albion | 42 | 17 | 12 | 13 | 82 | 52 | 63 |
| Buxton | 42 | 17 | 9 | 16 | 60 | 62 | 60 |
| Morecambe | 42 | 16 | 11 | 15 | 75 | 66 | 59 |
| Grantham | 42 | 15 | 13 | 14 | 49 | 50 | 58 |
| Southport | 42 | 11 | 14 | 17 | 58 | 65 | 47 |
| Goole Town | 42 | 13 | 7 | 22 | 52 | 66 | 46 |
| Gainsborough Trinity | 42 | 11 | 9 | 22 | 60 | 71 | 42 |
| Oswestry Town | 42 | 10 | 8 | 24 | 56 | 99 | 38 |
| South Liverpool | 42 | 7 | 15 | 20 | 57 | 91 | 36 |
| Tamworth | 42 | 7 | 8 | 27 | 44 | 97 | 29 |
| Worksop Town | 42 | 5 | 10 | 27 | 50 | 98 | 25 |
| Netherfield | 42 | 2 | 9 | 31 | 28 | 129 | 15 |

## 1983–84: Northern Premier League

|  | P | W | D | L | F | A | Pts |
|---|---|---|---|---|---|---|---|
| Barrow | 42 | 29 | 10 | 3 | 92 | 38 | 97 |
| Matlock Town | 42 | 23 | 8 | 11 | 72 | 48 | 77 |
| South Liverpool | 42 | 22 | 11 | 9 | 55 | 44 | 77 |
| Grantham | 42 | 20 | 8 | 14 | 64 | 51 | 68 |
| Burton Albion | 42 | 17 | 13 | 12 | 61 | 47 | 64 |
| Macclesfield Town | 42 | 18 | 10 | 14 | 65 | 55 | 64 |
| Rhyl | 42 | 19 | 6 | 17 | 64 | 52 | 63 |
| Horwich RMI | 42 | 18 | 9 | 15 | 64 | 59 | 63 |
| Gainsborough Trinity | 42 | 17 | 11 | 14 | 82 | 50 | 62 |
| Stafford Rangers | 42 | 15 | 17 | 10 | 65 | 52 | 62 |
| Hyde United | 42 | 17 | 8 | 17 | 61 | 63 | 59 |
| Marine | 42 | 16 | 10 | 16 | 63 | 68 | 58 |
| Witton Albion | 42 | 14 | 14 | 14 | 64 | 57 | 56 |
| Chorley | 42 | 14 | 11 | 17 | 68 | 65 | 53 |
| Workington | 42 | 14 | 9 | 19 | 53 | 57 | 51 |
| Southport | 42 | 14 | 8 | 20 | 57 | 34 | 50 |
| Worksop Town | 42 | 13 | 8 | 21 | 57 | 74 | 47 |
| Goole Town | 42 | 12 | 10 | 20 | 59 | 80 | 46 |
| Morecambe | 42 | 11 | 12 | 19 | 59 | 75 | 45 |
| Oswestry Town | 42 | 11 | 8 | 23 | 66 | 97 | 41 |
| Buxton | 42 | 11 | 6 | 25 | 52 | 91 | 39 |
| *Mossley | 42 | 9 | 9 | 24 | 47 | 74 | 33 |

*3 points deducted for fielding ineligible player

## 1984–85: Northern Premier League

| | P | W | D | L | F | A | Pts |
|---|---|---|---|---|---|---|---|
| Stafford Rangers | 42 | 26 | 8 | 8 | 81 | 40 | 86 |
| Macclesfield Town | 42 | 23 | 13 | 6 | 67 | 39 | 82 |
| Witton Albion | 42 | 22 | 8 | 12 | 57 | 39 | 74 |
| Hyde United | 42 | 21 | 8 | 13 | 68 | 52 | 71 |
| Marine | 42 | 18 | 15 | 9 | 59 | 34 | 69 |
| Burton Albion | 42 | 18 | 15 | 9 | 70 | 49 | 69 |
| Worksop Town | 42 | 19 | 10 | 13 | 68 | 56 | 67 |
| Workington | 42 | 18 | 9 | 15 | 59 | 53 | 63 |
| Horwich RMI | 42 | 16 | 14 | 12 | 67 | 50 | 62 |
| Bangor City | 42 | 17 | 9 | 16 | 70 | 61 | 60 |
| Gainsborough Trinity | 42 | 14 | 14 | 14 | 72 | 73 | 56 |
| Southport | 42 | 15 | 9 | 18 | 65 | 66 | 54 |
| Matlock Town | 42 | 14 | 9 | 19 | 56 | 66 | 51 |
| Oswestry Town | 42 | 14 | 9 | 19 | 59 | 75 | 51 |
| Mossley | 42 | 14 | 9 | 19 | 45 | 65 | 51 |
| Goole Town | 42 | 13 | 11 | 18 | 60 | 65 | 50 |
| Rhyl | 42 | 11 | 14 | 17 | 52 | 63 | 47 |
| Morecambe | 42 | 11 | 14 | 17 | 51 | 67 | 47 |
| Chorley | 42 | 12 | 10 | 20 | 47 | 65 | 46 |
| South Liverpool | 42 | 9 | 15 | 18 | 43 | 71 | 42 |
| *Grantham | 42 | 8 | 13 | 21 | 41 | 69 | 36 |
| Buxton | 42 | 8 | 6 | 28 | 38 | 79 | 30 |

* 1 point deducted for fielding ineligible player

## 1985–86: Northern Premier League

| | P | W | D | L | F | A | Pts |
|---|---|---|---|---|---|---|---|
| Gateshead | 42 | 24 | 10 | 8 | 85 | 51 | 82 |
| Marine | 42 | 23 | 11 | 8 | 63 | 35 | 80 |
| Morecambe | 42 | 17 | 17 | 8 | 59 | 39 | 68 |
| Gainsborough Trinity | 42 | 18 | 14 | 10 | 66 | 52 | 68 |
| Burton Albion | 42 | 18 | 12 | 12 | 64 | 47 | 66 |
| Southport | 42 | 17 | 11 | 14 | 70 | 66 | 62 |
| Worksop Town | 42 | 17 | 10 | 15 | 51 | 48 | 61 |
| *Workington | 42 | 14 | 18 | 10 | 54 | 46 | 59 |
| Macclesfield Town | 42 | 17 | 8 | 17 | 67 | 65 | 59 |
| Hyde United | 42 | 14 | 15 | 13 | 63 | 62 | 57 |
| *Witton Albion | 42 | 15 | 13 | 14 | 56 | 59 | 57 |
| Mossley | 42 | 13 | 16 | 13 | 56 | 60 | 55 |
| Bangor City | 42 | 14 | 15 | 14 | 51 | 51 | 54 |
| Rhyl | 42 | 14 | 10 | 18 | 65 | 71 | 52 |
| South Liverpool | 42 | 11 | 17 | 14 | 43 | 44 | 50 |
| *Horwich RMI | 42 | 15 | 6 | 21 | 53 | 63 | 50 |
| Caernarfon Town | 42 | 11 | 17 | 14 | 51 | 63 | 50 |
| Oswestry Town | 42 | 12 | 13 | 17 | 51 | 60 | 49 |
| Buxton | 42 | 11 | 12 | 19 | 55 | 76 | 45 |
| Chorley | 42 | 9 | 15 | 18 | 56 | 64 | 42 |
| Matlock Town | 42 | 9 | 15 | 18 | 59 | 75 | 42 |
| *Goole Town | 42 | 7 | 11 | 24 | 37 | 78 | 31 |

* 1 point deducted for rule infringement

## 1986–87: Northern Premier League

| | P | W | D | L | F | A | Pts |
|---|---|---|---|---|---|---|---|
| Macclesfield Town | 42 | 26 | 10 | 6 | 80 | 47 | 88 |
| Bangor City | 42 | 25 | 12 | 5 | 74 | 35 | 87 |
| Caernarfon Town | 42 | 20 | 16 | 6 | 67 | 40 | 76 |
| Marine | 42 | 21 | 10 | 11 | 70 | 43 | 73 |
| South Liverpool | 42 | 21 | 10 | 11 | 58 | 40 | 73 |
| Morecambe | 42 | 20 | 12 | 10 | 66 | 49 | 72 |
| Matlock Town | 42 | 20 | 10 | 12 | 81 | 67 | 70 |
| Southport | 42 | 19 | 11 | 12 | 67 | 49 | 68 |
| Chorley | 42 | 16 | 12 | 14 | 58 | 59 | 60 |
| Mossley | 42 | 15 | 12 | 15 | 47 | 42 | 57 |
| Hyde United | 42 | 15 | 10 | 17 | 81 | 70 | 55 |
| Burton Albion | 42 | 16 | 6 | 20 | 56 | 68 | 54 |
| Buxton | 42 | 13 | 14 | 15 | 71 | 68 | 53 |
| Witton Albion | 42 | 15 | 8 | 19 | 68 | 79 | 53 |
| Barrow | 42 | 15 | 7 | 20 | 42 | 57 | 52 |
| Goole Town | 42 | 13 | 12 | 17 | 58 | 62 | 51 |
| Oswestry Town | 42 | 14 | 8 | 20 | 55 | 83 | 50 |
| Rhyl | 42 | 10 | 15 | 17 | 56 | 74 | 45 |
| Worksop Town | 42 | 9 | 13 | 20 | 56 | 74 | 40 |
| Gainsborough Trinity | 42 | 9 | 10 | 23 | 53 | 77 | 37 |
| *Workington | 42 | 5 | 14 | 23 | 38 | 70 | 28 |
| *Horwich RMI | 42 | 3 | 12 | 27 | 36 | 85 | 20 |

*1 point deducted for rule infringement

# APPENDIX 4

# *Conference Match by Match*

Home games are in capitals; (p) = penalty; names of subs used in brackets

## 1987–88: GM VAUXHALL CONFERENCE

| Comp | Date | Opponents | Result | Scorers | Gate | Team |
|------|------|-----------|--------|---------|------|------|
| Lg 1 | Aug 22 | MAIDSTONE U | W 1–0 | Burr | 850 | Zelem, Roberts, Grant, Edwards, Tobin, Hanlon, J Askey, Shaw, Lake (Esser), Burr, Glendon (Hardman) |
| Lg 2 | Aug 25 | Runcorn | W 2–1 | Burr J Askey | 1000 | Zelem, Roberts, Grant, Edwards, Tobin, Hanlon, J Askey, Shaw, Lake, Burr, Glendon |
| Lg 3 | Aug 29 | BARNET | D 2–2 | Edwards Lake | 1311 | Zelem, Roberts, Grant, Edwards, Tobin, Hardman, Hanlon, J Askey, Shaw, Lake, Burr, Glendon (Mountford) |
| Lg 4 | Aug 31 | KIDDERMINSTER H | L 1–2 | Lake | 1332 | Zelem, Roberts, Grant, Edwards, Hardman (R Askey), Hanlon, J Askey, Shaw, Lake, Burr, Glendon (Mountford) |
| Lg 5 | Sep 05 | Dagenham | D 0–0 | | 401 | Zelem, Roberts, Grant, Edwards, Tobin, Hanlon, J Askey, Shaw, Lake, Burr, Glendon (Mountford) |
| Lg 6 | Sep 08 | NORTHWICH V | W 5–0 | J Askey(2) Tobin Burr Edwards | 1265 | Zelem, Roberts, Grant, Edwards, Tobin, Hanlon, J Askey (Hardman), Shaw, Lake, Burr, Mountford (Glendon) |
| FAC 1Q | Sep 12 | Stalybridge Celtic | D 1–1 | J Askey | 750 | Zelem, Roberts, Grant, Edwards, Tobin, Hanlon, J Askey, Shaw, Lake, Burr, Mountford (Esser) |
| FAC 1Q r | Sep 15 | STALYBRIDGE CELTIC | W 5–1 | Burr(3) Tobin Mather(og) | 1000 | Zelem, Roberts, Grant, Edwards, Tobin, Hanlon, J Askey, Esser (Glendon), Lake, Burr (Mountford), Shaw |
| Lg 7 | Sep 19 | Wealdstone | D 1–1 | Burr | 865 | Zelem, Roberts, Grant, Edwards, Tobin, Hanlon, J Askey, Shaw, Lake, Burr, Glendon (Hardman) |
| Lg 8 | Sep 22 | STAFFORD R | L 2–3 | Edwards Esser | 1682 | Zelem, Roberts, Grant, Edwards, Tobin, Hanlon, J Askey, Shaw (Esser), Lake, Burr, Glendon |
| FAC 2Q | Sep 26 | CHADDERTON | W 5–0 | Shaw(2) Hanlon Burr J Askey | 759 | Zelem, Roberts (Brissett), Grant, Hardman, Tobin, Hanlon (Esser), J Askey, Shaw, Lake, Burr, Glendon |
| Lg 9 | Sep 28 | Kidderminster H | L 2–3 | Lake Tobin | 1317 | Zelem, Roberts, Grant (Hardman), Edwards, Tobin, Hanlon, J Askey, Glendon (Esser), Lake, Burr, Shaw |
| Lg 10 | Oct 03 | SUTTON U | D 1–1 | Esser | 1056 | Zelem, Roberts, Grant, Edwards, Tobin, Connor, J Askey, Esser, Lake, Burr, Shaw |
| GMAC 1 | Oct 05 | Hyde United | W 4–3 | Shaw J Askey Esser Hanlon | 818 | Zelem, Roberts, Shaw (Glendon), Edwards, Tobin, Hardman, J Askey, Esser (Mountford), Lake, Burr, Hanlon |
| FAC 3Q | Oct 13 | MARINE | D 0–0 | | 805 | Zelem, Roberts, Shaw (Hardman), Edwards, Tobin, Grant, J Askey, Esser (Mountford), Lake, Burr, Hanlon |
| Lg 11 | Oct 17 | ENFIELD | L 0–3 | | 1046 | McKearnan, Roberts, Grant, Edwards, Tobin, Hardman (Esser), J Askey, Connor (Glendon), Lake, Burr, Shaw |
| FAC 3Q r | Oct 19 | Marine | W 2–1 | Burr Mountford | 650 | McKearnan, Roberts, Grant, Lake, Tobin, Hardman, J Askey, Hanlon, Mountford, Burr, Shaw |
| FAC 4Q | Oct 24 | WHITBY TOWN | W 3–1 | J Askey Mountford Grant | 942 | Zelem, Roberts, Grant, Lake, Tobin, Hardman, J Askey, Shaw, Mountford (Esser), Burr, Glendon (Edwards) |
| Lg 12 | Oct 27 | Telford U | D 0–0 | | 1284 | Zelem, Roberts, Grant, Edwards, Tobin, Hardman, J Askey, Lake, Mountford, Burr, Shaw |
| Lg 13 | Oct 31 | Bath C | W 4–3 | Burr(2) Neatis Hanlon | 593 | Zelem, Roberts, Grant, Edwards, Tobin (Hanlon), Hardman, J Askey, Neatis, Lake, Burr, Shaw |
| GMAC 2 | Nov 02 | ALTRINCHAM | L 0–1 | | 1628 | Zelem, Roberts, Grant (R Askey), Edwards, Tobin, Hardman, Mountford, Hanlon, Lake, Burr, Shaw |

| Comp | Date | Opponents | Result | Scorers | Gate | Team |
|---|---|---|---|---|---|---|
| Lg 14 | Nov 07 | WELLING U | W 3–2 | J Askey Hardman Lake | 893 | Zelem, Roberts, Shaw (Glendon), Edwards, Tobin, Hardman, J Askey, Hanlon, Lake, Burr, Mountford |
| FAC 1 | Nov 14 | CARLISLE UNITED | W 4–2 | Burr J Askey Tobin Hardman | 3500 | Zelem, Roberts, Shaw, Edwards, Tobin, Hardman, J Askey, Hanlon, Lake, Burr, Mountford |
| Lg 15 | Nov 17 | Stafford R | W 1–0 | J Askey | 1392 | Zelem, Roberts, Shaw, Edwards, Tobin, Hardman, J Askey, Connor, Lake, Burr, Hanlon |
| Lg 16 | Nov 21 | Fisher A | W 2–1 | Burr Edwards | 453 | Zelem, Roberts, Shaw, Edwards, Tobin, Hardman, J Askey, Connor, Lake, Burr (Neatis), Hanlon |
| Lg 17 | Nov 25 | Lincoln C | L 0–3 | | 2544 | Zelem, Roberts, Shaw, Edwards, Tobin, Hardman, J Askey, Connor, Lake, Burr (Neatis), Hanlon (Glendon) |
| Lg 18 | Nov 28 | CHELTENHAM T | W 1–0 | Grant | 1257 | Zelem, Roberts, Grant, Edwards, Tobin, Hanlon, J Askey, Shaw, Lake, Burr, Glendon |
| FAC 2 | Dec 06 | ROTHERHAM UNITED | W 4–0 | Burr(3) Grant | 4500 | Zelem, Roberts, Grant, Edwards, Tobin, Hanlon, J Askey (Glendon), Shaw, Lake, Burr, Mountford |
| Lg 19 | Dec 12 | Cheltenham T | L 0–1 | | 1038 | Zelem, Roberts, Grant (Neatis), Connor, Tobin, Hanlon, J Askey, Shaw, Lake, Burr, Mountford |
| FAT 1 | Dec 19 | BISHOP AUCKLAND | W 2–1 | J Askey Burr | 805 | Zelem, Roberts, Grant, Connor, Tobin, Hanlon, J Askey, Shaw, Lake, Burr, Mountford |
| Lg 20 | Dec 26 | Altrincham | W 3–1 | Burr(3) | 2640 | Zelem, Roberts, Grant, Edwards, Tobin, Connor, J Askey, Shaw, Lake, Burr, Hanlon |
| Lg 21 | Dec 28 | RUNCORN | W 4–0 | Burr(2) Lake Connor | 1789 | Zelem, Roberts, Grant, Edwards, Tobin, Connor, J Askey (Hardman), Shaw, Lake, Burr (Mountford), Hanlon |
| Lg 22 | Jan 02 | Kettering T | L 2–3 | Burr Grant | 1319 | Zelem, Roberts (Moutford), Grant, Edwards, Tobin, Connor, J Askey, Shaw, Lake, Burr, Hanlon |
| FAC 3 | Jan 10 | Port Vale | L 0–1 | | 10808 | Zelem, Roberts, Grant, Edwards, Tobin, Hanlon, J Askey, Shaw, Lake, Burr, Mountford (R Askey) |
| Lg 23 | Jan 16 | ALTRINCHAM | W 1–0 | J Askey | 1720 | Zelem, Roberts, Hardman, Edwards, Tobin, Connor, J Askey, Shaw (Mountford), Lake, Burr, Hanlon |
| FAT 2 | Jan 23 | Rhyl | W 2–0 | Burr(2) | 886 | Zelem, Roberts, Hardman, Edwards, Tobin, Connor, J Askey, Shaw, Lake, Burr, Hanlon |
| Lg 24 | Jan 30 | Enfield | W 2–1 | Burr J Askey | 818 | Zelem, Roberts, Shaw, Connor, Tobin, Hardman, J Askey, Lodge, Lake, Burr, Hanlon |
| Lg 25 | Feb 06 | Boston U | W 2–0 | Burr Hanlon | 1526 | Zelem, Roberts, Shaw, Connor, Tobin, Hardman, J Askey, Edwards (Mountford), Lake, Burr, Hanlon |
| FAT 3 | Feb 13 | Leyton – Wingate | W 2–1 | Burr J Askey | 572 | Zelem, Roberts, Shaw, Connor, Tobin, Hardman, J Askey, Edwards, Lake, Burr, Hanlon |
| Lg 26 | Feb 23 | KETTERING T | D 0–0 | | 1502 | Zelem, Roberts (Mountford), Shaw, Edwards, Tobin, Hardman, J Askey, Lodge, Lake, Burr, Hanlon |
| Lg 27 | Feb 27 | Wycombe W | L 0–5 | | 1492 | Zelem, Roberts, Shaw, Edwards, Hardman, Lodge, J Askey, Coleman, Lake, Burr, Hanlon |
| Lg 28 | Feb 29 | Northwich V | L 1–2 | Lake | 913 | Zelem, Roberts (Coleman), Shaw, Edwards, Hardman, Connor, J Askey, Mountford, Lake, Burr, Hanlon |
| FAT 4 | Mar 05 | Wokingham Town | L 0–2 | | 1300 | Zelem, Roberts (Neatis), Shaw, Connor, Tobin, Hardman, J Askey, Edwards, Lake, Burr, Hanlon |
| Lg 29 | Mar 12 | Barnet | L 1–2 | Hanlon | 2312 | Zelem, Roberts (Mountford), Shaw (Coleman), Connor, Tobin, Hardman, J Askey, Edwards, Lake, Burr, Hanlon |
| Lg 30 | Mar 19 | Weymouth | D 1–1 | Connor | 1061 | Zelem, Roberts, Hardman, Edwards, Connor, Hanlon, J Askey, Shaw, Lake, Burr, Mountford (Coleman) |
| Lg 31 | Mar 22 | WEALDSTONE | W 3–2 | Connor Burr Roberts | 753 | Zelem, Roberts, Shaw, Edwards, Hardman, Connor, J Askey, Hanlon, Coleman (Tobin), Burr, Mountford (Grant) |
| Lg 32 | Mar 26 | BOSTON U | W 2–1 | Hanlon Lake | 1002 | Zelem, Roberts, Shaw, Edwards, Tobin, Connor, J Askey, Hanlon, Lake, Burr, Hardman |
| Lg 33 | Mar 29 | WEYMOUTH | L 1–2 | Edwards | 1104 | Zelem, Roberts (Coleman), Shaw (Grant), Edwards, Tobin, Connor, J Askey, Hanlon, Lake, Burr, Hardman |
| Lg 34 | Apr 02 | WYCOMBE W | D 1–1 | J Askey | 1163 | Zelem, Roberts (Grant), Hardman, Connor, Tobin, Hanlon, J Askey, Coleman (Lodge), Lake, Burr, Shaw |
| Lg 35 | Apr 04 | Welling U | L 1–3 | Connor | 772 | Zelem, Roberts (Coleman), Hardman, Connor, Tobin, Hanlon, J Askey, Lodge, Lake (Mountford), Burr, Shaw |
| Lg 36 | Apr 09 | FISHER A | L 2–4 | Hanlon Coleman(p) | 808 | Zelem, Roberts, Hardman (Coleman), Connor, Tobin, Hanlon, J Askey, Lodge (Mountford), Lake, Burr, Shaw |

| Comp | Date | Opponents | Result | Scorers | Gate | Team |
|------|------|-----------|--------|---------|------|------|
| Lg 37 | Apr 12 | LINCOLN C | W 2–0 | J Askey Mountford | 2050 | Zelem, Roberts, Shaw (Coleman), Connor, Tobin, Edwards, J Askey, Hanlon, Lake, Burr (Lodge), Mountford |
| Lg 38 | Apr 16 | Maidstone U | L 0–2 | | 745 | Zelem, Roberts, Shaw, Connor, Tobin, Edwards, J Askey, Hanlon, Lake (Coleman), Burr, Lodge |
| Lg 39 | Apr 18 | TELFORD U | D 1–1 | Hanlon | 950 | Zelem, Roberts, Shaw, Edwards, Tobin, Connor, J Askey, Hanlon, Lodge, Burr, Mountford |
| Lg 40 | Apr 23 | DAGENHAM | W 3–1 | Burr Mountford J Askey | 802 | Zelem, Roberts, Hardman (Lodge), Edwards, Tobin, Connor, J Askey, Hanlon, Shaw, Burr, Mountford |
| Lg 41 | Apr 26 | BATH C | L 0–2 | | 866 | Zelem, Roberts, Shaw, Edwards, Tobin, Connor, Lodge, Glendon, Hanlon, Burr, Mountford |
| Lg 42 | Apr 30 | Sutton U | W 3–2 | Burr(2) Lake | 609 | Zelem, Roberts, Shaw (Hardman), Edwards, Tobin, Connor, J Askey, Hanlon, Lake, Burr, Lodge |

## 1988–89: GM Vauxhall Conference

| Comp | Date | Opponents | Result | Scorers | Gate | Team |
|------|------|-----------|--------|---------|------|------|
| Lg 1 | Aug 20 | Enfield | L 1–2 | Burr | 1203 | Zelem, Roberts, Hardman, Edwards, Tobin, Kendall, Lodge, Hanlon, Lake, Burr, Shaw (Connor) |
| Lg 2 | Aug 24 | Boston U | L 2–3 | Burr(p) Kendall | 2332 | Zelem, Connor, Roberts, Edwards, Tobin, Kendall, Derbyshire, Hanlon, Lake (Parlane), Burr, Lodge |
| Lg 3 | Aug 27 | WELLING U | W 3–0 | Askey Hanlon Derbyshire | 945 | Zelem, Roberts (Shaw), Grant, Edwards, Tobin, Kendall, Askey( Parlane), Derbyshire, Lake, Burr, Hanlon |
| Lg 4 | Aug 29 | NEWPORT C | W 3–0 | Derbyshire(2) Burr | 1172 | Zelem, Roberts (Parlane), Shaw, Edwards, Tobin, Kendall, Askey (Hardman), Derbyshire, Lake, Burr, Hanlon |
| Lg 4 | Sep 03 | Sutton U | W 2–1 | Burr(2) | 721 | Zelem, Roberts, Shaw, Edwards, Tobin, Kendall, Askey, Derbyshire, Lake, Burr, Hanlon |
| Lg 5 | Sep 06 | KIDDERMINSTER H | D 1–1 | Derbyshire | 1383 | Zelem, Roberts, Shaw, Edwards, Tobin, Kendall, Askey, Derbyshire, Lake, Burr, Hanlon |
| Lg 6 | Sep 10 | WEYMOUTH | W 2–0 | Derbyshire Burr | 1132 | Zelem, Roberts (Connor), Shaw, Edwards, Tobin, Kendall, Askey (Hardman), Derbyshire, Lake, Burr, Hanlon |
| Lg 7 | Sep 13 | Runcorn | D 2–2 | Burr Askey | 1155 | Zelem, Roberts, Shaw, Edwards, Tobin, Kendall, Askey (Connor), Derbyshire, Lake, Burr, Hanlon |
| Lg 8 | Sep 17 | MAIDSTONE U | W 4–3 | Burr(3) Derbyshire | 1342 | Zelem, Connor, Hardman, Edwards, Tobin, Kendall, Shaw (Mountford), Derbyshire, Lake, Burr, Hanlon |
| Lg 9 | Sep 24 | Barnet | W 4–1 | Burr(2) Tobin Gormley(og) | 2035 | Zelem, Connor, Grant, Edwards (Parlane), Tobin, Kendall, Roberts (Mountford), Derbyshire, Lake, Burr, Hanlon |
| Lg 10 | Sep 26 | Northwich V | L 2–3 | Derbyshire Burr | 1568 | Zelem, Connor, Grant, Roberts, Tobin, Kendall, Askey (Parlane), Derbyshire, Lake, Burr, Hanlon |
| Lg 11 | Oct 01 | CHORLEY | W 3–2 | Askey(2) Burr | 1760 | Zelem, Connor, Roberts, Hanlon, Tobin, Kendall, Askey, Derbyshire (Parlane), Lake, Burr, Mountford |
| Lg 12 | Oct 08 | YEOVIL T | L 2–3 | Burr Lake | 1616 | Zelem, Connor, Roberts, Hanlon, Tobin, Kendall (Mountford), Askey, Parlane, Lake, Burr, Shaw |
| Lg 13 | Oct 15 | Aylesbury U | W 2–1 | Burr Askey | 1039 | Zelem, Connor, Hardman, Hanlon, Tobin, Kendall, Askey, Derbyshire (Shaw), Lake, Burr (Parlane), Roberts |
| CCC 1 | Oct 18 | Witton Albion | L 0–2 | | 733 | Zelem, Connor, Hardman, Hanlon, Tobin, Kendall, Askey, Parlane, Lake, Burr, Shaw |
| Lg 14 | Oct 22 | CHELTENHAM T | D 0–0 | | 1402 | Zelem, Connor, Hardman (Imrie), Hanlon, Tobin, Kendall (Edwards), Askey, Derbyshire, Lake, Burr, Roberts |
| FAC 4Q | Oct 29 | ALTRINCHAM | D 0–0 | | 3014 | Zelem, Connor (Mountford), Hardman, Edwards, Tobin, Hanlon (Parlane), Askey, Derbyshire, Lake, Burr, Roberts |
| FAC 4Q r | Nov 01 | Altrincham | L 0–4 | | 2834 | Zelem, Connor (Mountford), Roberts, Edwards, Tobin, Shaw, Askey, Derbyshire, Lake, Burr, Parlane |
| Lg 15 | Nov 05 | Telford U | W 3–1 | Derbyshire(p) Lake Burr | 1208 | Zelem, Connor, Hardman, Edwards (Imrie), Tobin, Hanlon, Askey, Derbyshire, Lake, Burr (Shaw), Roberts |
| Lg 16 | Nov 12 | KETTERING T | L 0–1 | | 2196 | Zelem, Connor (Imrie), Hardman (Parlane), Hanlon, Tobin, Kendall, Askey, Derbyshire, Lake, Shaw, Roberts |

| Comp | Date | Opponents | Result | Scorers | Gate | Team |
|------|------|-----------|--------|---------|------|------|
| Lg 17 | Nov 19 | Chorley | W 1–0 | Derbyshire | 1012 | Zelem, Roberts, Shaw, Edwards, Tobin, Kendall, Askey, Derbyshire, Lake, Imrie, Hanlon |
| Lg 18 | Nov 26 | Fisher A | D 2–2 | Derbyshire Askey | 504 | Zelem, Connor (Imrie), Hardman (Parlane), Edwards, Tobin, Kendall, Askey, Derbyshire, Lake, Hanlon, Shaw |
| Lg 19 | Dec 03 | STAFFORD R | W 2–1 | Hanlon Shaw | 1344 | Zelem, Roberts, Shaw, Edwards, Tobin, Kendall, Askey, Derbyshire, Lake, Hanlon, Imrie (Mountford) |
| Lg 20 | Dec 10 | Kidderminster H | W 1–0 | Askey | 2841 | Zelem, Connor, Hardman, Edwards, Tobin, Kendall, Askey, Derbyshire (Parlane), Lake, Shaw (Imrie), Hanlon |
| Lg 21 | Dec 17 | Welling U | L 0–2 | | 1121 | Zelem, Connor, Hardman, Edwards (Parlane), Tobin, Kendall, Askey, Derbyshire, Lake, Hanlon, Imrie |
| Lg 22 | Dec 26 | ALTRINCHAM | W 1–0 | Lake | 2045 | Zelem, Roberts (Parlane), Shaw, Edwards, Tobin, Kendall, Askey, Derbyshire, Lake, Burr (Imrie), Hanlon |
| Lg 23 | Dec 31 | BOSTON U | L 0–1 | | 1865 | Zelem, Connor, Roberts (Hardman), Edwards, Tobin, Kendall, Mountford, Parlane, Lake, Hanlon, Shaw |
| Lg 24 | Jan 02 | Altrincham | W 3–1 | Hanlon(2) Parlane | 2139 | Zelem, Connor, Shaw, Edwards, Tobin, Kendall, Askey, Parlane, Lake, Hanlon, Mountford (Imrie) |
| Lg 25 | Jan 07 | BARNET | D 1–1 | Parlane | 1612 | Zelem, Connor, Hardman, Edwards, Tobin, Kendall, Askey, Parlane, Lake, Timmons, Hanlon |
| FAT 1 | Jan 14 | Marine | D 2–2 | Edwards Askey | 752 | Zelem, Connor, Hardman, Edwards, Tobin, Kendall (Roberts), Askey, Derbyshire, Hanlon, Timmons (Parlane), Imrie |
| FAT 1 r | Jan 17 | MARINE | W 4–1 | Tobin(2) Hanlon Timmons | 1350 | Zelem, Connor, Hardman (Roberts), Edwards, Tobin, Kendall (Parlane), Askey, Derbyshire, Hanlon, Timmons, Imrie |
| Lg 26 | Jan 21 | Maidstone U | D 3–3 | Askey(2) Derbyshire | 768 | Zelem, Connor (Parlane), Hardman, Edwards, Tobin, Kendall, Askey, Derbyshire, Lake, Timmons (Burr), Hanlon |
| Lg 27 | Jan 28 | NORTHWICH V | L 0–2 | | 1961 | Zelem (Roberts), Connor, Hardman, Edwards, Tobin, Hanlon, Askey (Parlane), Timmons, Lake, Burr, Derbyshire |
| FAT 2 | Feb 04 | South Bank | W 3–0 | Burr(2) Imrie | 632 | Zelem, Connor, Roberts, Edwards, Kendall, Hanlon, Askey, Derbyshire, Lake, Burr, Imrie |
| Lg 28 | Feb 11 | RUNCORN | W 3–2 | Burr(2) Askey | 1179 | Zelem, Connor, Roberts, Edwards, Kendall, Imrie, Askey, Derbyshire (Hardman), Lake, Burr, Timmons |
| Lg 29 | Feb 18 | AYLESBURY U | W 3–1 | Derbyshire(2) Imrie | 1309 | Zelem, Connor, Roberts, Edwards, Kendall, Imrie, Askey, Derbyshire, Lake, Burr (Parlane), Timmons |
| FAT 3 | Feb 28 | GRAVESEND & N | W 2–0 | Kendall Burr | 1344 | Zelem, Connor, Roberts, Edwards, Kendall, Imrie, Askey, Derbyshire, Lake, Burr, Timmons |
| Lg 30 | Mar 04 | ENFIELD | D 1–1 | Imrie | 1501 | Zelem, Connor, Hardman (Parlane), Edwards, Kendall, Roberts, Askey, Derbyshire, Timmons, Burr, Imrie |
| FAT 4 | Mar 11 | WELLING U | W 1–0 | Timmons | 2088 | Zelem, Roberts, Hardman, Edwards, Kendall, Hanlon, Askey, Timmons, Derbyshire, Burr, Imrie |
| Lg 31 | Mar 18 | TELFORD U | W 2–1 | Burr Timmons | 1076 | Zelem, Roberts, Hardman, Edwards, Tobin, Kendall, Askey, Timmons, Hanlon, Burr, Imrie (Blake) |
| Lg 32 | Mar 25 | Yeovil T | L 0–2 | | 2467 | Zelem, Roberts (Connor), Hardman, Edwards, Tobin, Kendall, Askey, Timmons (Derbyshire), Hanlon, Burr, Imrie |
| Lg 33 | Mar 27 | Wycombe W | D 1–1 | Derbyshire | 3873 | Zelem, Roberts, Hardman, Edwards, Tobin, Kendall (Connor), Askey (Parlane), Hanlon, Derbyshire, Timmons, Imrie |
| Lg 34 | Apr 01 | SUTTON U | L 1–3 | Burr | 1308 | Zelem, Connor, Blake (Humphries), Edwards, Hardman, Hanlon, Askey (Shenton), Derbyshire, Parlane, Burr, Imrie |
| FAT SF 1 | Apr 08 | Dartford | D 0–0 | | 4000 | Zelem, Roberts, Hardman, Edwards, Tobin, Hanlon, Askey, Timmons, Derbyshire (Connor), Burr (Kendall), Imrie |
| FAT SF 2 | Apr 15 | DARTFORD | W 4–1 | Burr(2) Timmons Askey | 4000 | Zelem, Roberts, Hardman, Edwards, Tobin, Hanlon, Askey, Timmons, Kendall, Burr, Imrie |
| Lg 35 | Apr 19 | Cheltenham T | L 0–3 | | 1279 | Zelem, Roberts, Kendall, Edwards, Parlane, Hanlon, Askey, Timmons, Lake, Burr, Imrie (Tobin) |
| Lg 36 | Apr 22 | Kettering T | L 0–1 | | 3253 | Zelem, Connor, Roberts, Hanlon, Hardman, Kendall, Askey, Timmons, Lake, Burr, Parlane |

| Comp | Date | Opponents | Result | Scorers | Gate | Team |
|------|------|-----------|--------|---------|------|------|
| Lg 37 | Apr 25 | FISHER A | D 2–2 | Timmons Shinners(og) | 733 | Zelem, Connor, Roberts, Kendall, Tobin, Hanlon, Askey, Timmons, Parlane, Burr, Humphries (Lake) |
| Lg 38 | Apr 27 | Stafford R | D 1–1 | Derbyshire | 1107 | Zelem, Connor, Kendall, Edwards, Tobin, Hanlon, Askey, Derbyshire, Lake, Burr, Parlane (Roberts) |
| Lg 39 | Apr 29 | WYCOMBE W | L 0–1 | | 1006 | Zelem, Connor (Hardman), Roberts (Askey), Edwards, Lake, Kendall, Timmons, Hanlon, Derbyshire, Burr, Imrie |
| Lg 40 | May 03 | Weymouth | W 2–1 | Askey Burr | 342 | Zelem, Roberts, Hardman, Kendall, Tobin, Hanlon, Askey, Derbyshire, Lake, Burr, Imrie |
| FAT F | May 13 | Telford U | L 0–1 | | 18106 | Zelem, Roberts, Hardman, Edwards, Tobin, Hanlon, Askey (Derbyshire), Timmons, Lake, Burr, Imrie (Kendall) |

## 1989–90: GM Vauxhall Conference

| Comp | Date | Opponents | Result | Scorers | Gate | Team |
|------|------|-----------|--------|---------|------|------|
| Lg 1 | Aug 26 | WELLING U | W 3–2 | Kendall Burr Worrall | 1153 | Zelem, Connor, Johnson, Edwards, Kendall, Hanlon, J Askey, Derbyshire (Hardman), Lake, Burr, Imrie (Worrall) |
| Lg 2 | Aug 28 | ENFIELD | W 4–0 | Lake(2) Burr J Askey | 1375 | Zelem, Connor, Johnson (Hardman), Edwards, Kendall, Hanlon, J Askey, Derbyshire, Lake, Burr (Worrall), Wilson |
| Lg 3 | Sep 02 | Fisher A | W 3–1 | Burr(2) Derbyshire | 908 | Zelem, Connor, Hardman, Edwards, Kendall, Hanlon, J Askey (Worrall), Derbyshire (Timmons), Lake, Burr, Wilson |
| Lg 4 | Sep 04 | Kidderminster H | D 2–2 | J Askey Derbyshire | 2040 | Zelem, Connor, Hardman, Edwards, Kendall (Worrall), Hanlon, J Askey, Derbyshire, Lake, Burr, Wilson |
| Lg 5 | Sep 09 | FARNBOROUGH T | D 0–0 | | 1507 | Zelem, Connor (Worrall), Hardman, Edwards, Kendall, Hanlon, J Askey, Derbyshire (Timmons), Lake, Burr, Wilson |
| Lg 6 | Sep 12 | NORTHWICH V | W 3–1 | J Askey Derbyshire Burr | 2005 | Zelem, Connor, Hardman, Kendall, Edwards, Hanlon, J Askey, Derbyshire, Lake, Burr, Wilson |
| Lg 7 | Sep 19 | Runcorn | L 0–2 | | 1374 | Zelem, Connor, Hardman (Worrall), Kendall, Tobin, Hanlon, J Askey, Derbyshire, Lake, Burr (Timmons), Wilson |
| Lg 8 | Sep 23 | SUTTON U | D 1–1 | Edwards | 1379 | Zelem, Connor, Hardman, Edwards, Tobin, Hanlon, Timmons (Derbyshire), Wilson, Lake, Burr, Worrall (Imrie) |
| Lg 9 | Sep 26 | CHELTENHAM T | W 3–0 | Burr(2) Hanlon | 1504 | Zelem, Shepherd, Hardman, Connor (Johnson), Tobin, Hanlon, Imrie, Timmons, Lake, Burr, Wilson |
| Lg 10 | Sep 30 | Merthyr T | W 3–2 | Burr(2) Wilson | 2756 | Zelem, Shepherd (Hardman), Johnson, Edwards, Tobin, Hanlon, J Askey (Imrie), Timmons, Lake, Burr, Wilson |
| Lg 11 | Oct 03 | Barrow | D 1–1 | J Askey | 1422 | Zelem, Shepherd, Johnson, Edwards, Tobin, Hanlon, J Askey (Imrie), Timmons, Lake, Burr, Wilson |
| Lg 12 | Oct 07 | YEOVIL T | L 1–2 | Derbyshire(p) | 1519 | Zelem, Shepherd, Johnson, Edwards, Tobin, Hanlon, Timmons, Wilson, Derbyshire, Burr (Hardman), Imrie |
| Lg 13 | Oct 21 | Barnet | D 0–0 | | 2309 | Zelem, Shepherd, Johnson, Edwards, Tobin, Kendall (Derbyshire), Timmons, Hanlon, Worrall (Roberts), Burr, Imrie |
| Lg 14 | Oct 28 | KETTERING T | W 3–1 | Burr(2) Lewis(og) | 1598 | Zelem, Farelly, Johnson, Edwards, Tobin, Hanlon, Timmons, Ellis, Derbyshire, Burr, Imrie |
| Lg 15 | Nov 04 | Yeovil T | D 0–0 | | 2361 | Zelem, Farelly, Johnson, Kendall, Tobin, Hanlon, Timmons, Ellis, Derbyshire, Burr (J Askey), Imrie |
| Lg 16 | Nov 11 | DARLINGTON | D 0–0 | | 3143 | Zelem, Connor, Hardman, Edwards, Tobin, Hanlon, J Askey, Farrelly (Derbyshire), Ellis, Burr, Imrie |
| FAC 1 | Nov 18 | CHESTER CITY | D 1–1 | Burr | 4200 | Zelem, Farelly, Johnson, Edwards, Tobin, Hanlon, J Askey, Timmons, Ellis, Burr, Wilson (Imrie) |
| FAC 1 r | Nov 21 | Chester City | L 2–3 | Burr(2) | 4202 | Zelem, Farelly, Johnson, Edwards, Tobin, Hanlon, J Askey, Timmons, Ellis (Connor), Burr, Imrie |
| Lg 17 | Nov 25 | Welling U | W 1–0 | Timmons | 1112 | Zelem, Farelly, Johnson, Edwards, Tobin, Hanlon, Imrie (Hardman), Wilson, J Askey, Burr, Timmons |
| Lg 18 | Dec 02 | TELFORD U | W 3–0 | Imrie Burr Timmons | 1311 | Zelem, Farelly (Connor), Johnson, Edwards, Tobin, Hanlon, Timmons, Wilson, J Askey, Burr, Imrie (Worrall) |

| Comp | Date | Opponents | Result | Scorers | Gate | Team |
|------|------|-----------|--------|---------|------|------|
| Lg 19 | Dec 09 | Stafford R | L 2–4 | J Askey Imrie | 1202 | Zelem, Farelly (Worrall), Hardman (Connor), Edwards, Tobin, Hanlon, Timmons, Wilson, J Askey, Burr, Imrie |
| Lg 20 | Dec 16 | MERTHYR T | W 3–2 | Burr(2) Timmons | 951 | Zelem, Connor, Johnson, Edwards, Tobin, Hanlon, Timmons (Ellis), Wilson, J Askey, Burr, Imrie (Kendall) |
| Lg 21 | Dec 26 | Altrincham | W 1–0 | Hanlon | 2023 | Zelem, Connor, Johnson, Edwards, Tobin, Hanlon, Timmons, Wilson, J Askey, Burr, Imrie |
| Lg 22 | Dec 30 | RUNCORN | W 4–0 | J Askey Hanlon Ellis(p) Burr | 1810 | Zelem, Connor, Johnson, Edwards, Tobin, Hanlon, J Askey, Timmons, Ellis (Worrall), Burr, Imrie |
| Lg 23 | Jan 01 | ALTRINCHAM | W 1–0 | Hanlon | 2009 | Zelem, Connor, Johnson, Edwards, Tobin, Hanlon, J Askey, Timmons, Ellis, Burr, Imrie |
| Lg 24 | Jan 06 | Chorley | D 0–0 | | 1069 | Zelem, Connor, Johnson, Edwards, Tobin, Hanlon, J Askey, Timmons, Ellis, Burr, Imrie |
| FAT 1 | Jan 13 | BOSTON U | D 0–0 | | 1924 | Zelem, Connor, Johnson, Edwards, Tobin, Hanlon, J Askey, Timmons, Ellis, Burr, Imrie |
| FAT 1 r | Jan 16 | Boston U | W 3–0 | Burr(2) Johnson | 1382 | Zelem, Connor, Johnson, Edwards, Tobin, Hanlon, J Askey, Timmons, Ellis (Worrall), Burr, Imrie |
| Lg 25 | Jan 20 | KIDDERMINSTER H | L 1–2 | Brazier(og) | 1651 | Zelem, Connor (Farrelly), Johnson, Edwards, Tobin, Hanlon, J Askey, Timmons, Ellis (Worrall), Burr, Imrie |
| BLT 2 | Jan 22 | Darlington | L 2–5 | Johnson Butler | 2125 | Zelem, Farelly, Johnson, Edwards, Tobin, Hardman, J Askey, Hanlon (Parlane), Kendall, Butler, Imrie (Worrall) |
| Lg 26 | Jan 27 | Wycombe W | D 1–1 | Edwards | 2002 | Zelem, Farelly, Johnson, Edwards, Tobin, Hanlon, J Askey, Imrie, Ellis, Burr, Worrall (Derbyshire) |
| FAT 2 | Feb 03 | Darlington | L 0–1 | | 3686 | Zelem, Farelly, Johnson, Edwards, Tobin, Hanlon, J Askey, Imrie, Ellis, Burr, Derbyshire (Lyons) |
| Lg 27 | Feb 10 | Enfield | D 1–1 | J Askey | 862 | Zelem, Kendall, Johnson, Edwards, Tobin, Hanlon, J Askey, Farrelly (Lyons), Ellis, Burr, Imrie |
| Lg 28 | Feb 17 | BARROW | W 2–1 | J Askey(2) | 1178 | Zelem, Farelly, Johnson, Edwards, Tobin, Hanlon, J Askey, Kendall, Ellis (Derbyshire), Imrie, Coyne |
| Lg 29 | Feb 21 | Boston U | L 0–3 | | 1698 | Zelem, Farelly (Lyons), Johnson, Edwards, Tobin, Hanlon, J Askey, Kendall, R Askey, Kirkham, Imrie |
| Lg 30 | Mar 03 | WYCOMBE W | W 1–0 | Imrie | 1210 | Zelem, Farelly, Johnson, Edwards, Tobin (Hardman), Hanlon, J Askey, Kendall, R Askey (Timmons), Derbyshire, Imrie |
| Lg 31 | Mar 10 | Cheltenham T | W 2–1 | Kendall R Askey | 1436 | Zelem, Connor, Johnson, Edwards, Tobin, Hanlon, J Askey (Farrelly), Kendall, R Askey (Timmons), Ellis, Imrie |
| Lg 32 | Mar 17 | Sutton U | L 1–2 | Ellis | 756 | Zelem, Connor, Johnson, Edwards, Tobin, Hanlon, J Askey, Kendall (Farrelly), Ellis, Timmons, Imrie (Worrall) |
| Lg 33 | Mar 24 | FISHER A | L 0–1 | | 1005 | Zelem, Farelly (Timmons), Johnson, Edwards, Tobin, Hanlon, J Askey, Kendall, Ellis, Glendon (Worrall), Imrie |
| Lg 34 | Mar 31 | Farnborough T | W 2–1 | Burr Edwards | 827 | Zelem, Kendall, Johnson, Edwards, Tobin, Hanlon, J Askey, Timmons, Ellis (Farrelly), Burr (Worrall), Imrie |
| Lg 35 | Apr 03 | Darlington | D 1–1 | Edwards | 4546 | Zelem, Farelly, Johnson, Edwards, Tobin, Hanlon, Timmons, Kendall, J Askey, Burr, Imrie |
| Lg 36 | Apr 07 | CHORLEY | D 0–0 | | 903 | Zelem, Farelly, Johnson, Edwards, Tobin, Hanlon, J Askey (R Askey), Kendall, Timmons, Burr, Imrie |
| Lg 37 | Apr 14 | Kettering T | D 0–0 | | 1550 | Zelem, Farelly, Johnson (Hardman), Edwards, Tobin, Hanlon, J Askey, Kendall, Timmons (R Askey), Burr, Imrie |
| Lg 38 | Apr 16 | Northwich V | L 0–2 | | 960 | Zelem, Farelly, Johnson, Edwards, Tobin, Hanlon, Coyne, Kendall, R Askey, Burr, Imrie |
| Lg 39 | Apr 24 | STAFFORD R | D 2–2 | Hanlon Hardman | 730 | Zelem, Kendall, Johnson (Hardman), Edwards, Tobin, Hanlon, J Askey, Coyne (Timmons), Ellis, Burr, Imrie |
| Lg 40 | Apr 28 | Telford U | L 0–1 | | 1016 | Zelem, Farelly, Johnson, Edwards, Tobin, Hanlon, Timmons, Kendall, Ellis, Burr (Lyons), Imrie (Hardman) |
| Lg 41 | May 01 | BARNET | L 0–1 | | 1180 | Zelem, Farelly (Worrall), Hardman, Edwards, Tobin, Hanlon, Ellis, Kendall, R Askey (Parlane), Timmons, Johnson |
| Lg 42 | May 05 | BOSTON U | D 0–0 | | 721 | Zelem, Kendall, Johnson, Hardman, Tobin, Hanlon, Lyons, Ellis, Parlane (R Askey), Timmons, Imrie (Worrall) |

## 1990–91: GM VAUXHALL CONFERENCE

| Comp | Date | Opponents | Result | Scorers | Gate | Team |
|------|------|-----------|--------|---------|------|------|
| Lg 1 | Aug 18 | BARNET | D 3–3 | Burr(2) Lambert | 1917 | Zelem, M Farrelly, Heesom, Edwards, Tobin, Hanlon, Askey, Kendall, Camden (Imrie), Burr, Lambert |
| Lg 2 | Aug 25 | WYCOMBE W | D 0–0 | | 1370 | Zelem, M Farrelly (Ellis), Heesom (Melrose), Edwards, Tobin, Hanlon, Askey, Kendall, Lambert, Burr, Imrie |
| Lg 3 | Aug 27 | GATESHEAD | W 4–0 | Burr(2) Camden Hanlon | 1306 | Zelem, Shepherd, Johnson, Edwards, Tobin, Hanlon, Askey (Melrose), Lambert (Kendall), Camden, Burr, Imrie |
| Lg 4 | Sep 01 | Kettering T | L 0–2 | | 1814 | Zelem, Shepherd, Johnson, Edwards, Tobin, Hanlon, Askey, Lambert, Camden (Kendall), Burr (Melrose), Imrie |
| Lg 5 | Sep 03 | Kidderminster H | D 0–0 | | 1448 | Ridler, Shepherd (M Farrelly), Johnson, Edwards, Tobin, Hanlon, Askey, Kendall, Ellis (Heesom), Camden, Imrie |
| Lg 6 | Sep 08 | MERTHYR T | L 0–1 | | 1314 | Ridler, Kendall, Johnson, Edwards, Tobin, Hanlon, Askey, Lambert, Ellis (Melrose), Camden, Imrie |
| Lg 7 | Sep 15 | Sutton U | L 1–3 | Askey | 751 | Ridler, Shepherd (Camden), Johnson (Kendall), Edwards, Tobin, Hanlon, Askey, Lambert, Ellis, Melrose, Imrie |
| Lg 8 | Sep 18 | Barrow | D 1–1 | Ellis | 1855 | Zelem, M Farrelly, Johnson, Edwards, Tobin, Hanlon, Imrie, Melrose (Lambert), Ellis, Camden, Heesom |
| Lg 9 | Sep 22 | SLOUGH T | L 1–2 | Hanlon | 1011 | Zelem, Shepherd, Johnson (Ellis), Edwards, Tobin, Hanlon, Askey, Lambert, Cutler, Burr, Imrie |
| Lg 10 | Sep 29 | Telford U | W 2–1 | Askey Burr | 1069 | Zelem, Shepherd, Heesom, Edwards, Tobin, Hanlon, Askey, Kendall, Ellis (Lambert), Burr, Imrie |
| Lg 11 | Oct 02 | Northwich V | L 1–4 | Young(og) | 1215 | Zelem, Shepherd, Heesom, Edwards, Tobin, Hanlon, Askey, Kendall, Ellis (Camden), Cutler, Imrie (M Farrelly) |
| Lg 12 | Oct 06 | COLCHESTER U | W 1–0 | Heesom | 1100 | Zelem, Shepherd, Heesom, Edwards, Tobin, Hanlon, Askey, Kendall, Lambert, Burr, Imrie |
| Lg 13 | Oct 13 | Stafford R | D 2–2 | Heesom(p) Cutler | 1639 | Zelem, Shepherd, Heesom, Edwards, Tobin, Hanlon, Askey, Kendall (Cutler), Lambert, Burr (M Farrelly), Imrie |
| Lg 14 | Oct 16 | KIDDERMINSTER H | D 0–0 | | 1072 | Zelem, Shepherd, Johnson, Edwards, Tobin, Hanlon, Askey, Kendall, Ellis, Lambert, Heesom (Camden) |
| Lg 15 | Oct 20 | Cheltenham T | D 2–2 | Askey(2) | 1021 | Zelem, Shepherd, Johnson, Edwards, Tobin, Hanlon, Askey, Kendall, M Farrelly, Lambert, Timmons (Camden) |
| FAC 4Q | Oct 27 | Altrincham | D 2–2 | Burr Lambert | 1843 | Zelem, Shepherd, Johnson, Edwards, Tobin, Hanlon, Askey, Timmons (Kendall), Lambert, Burr, Imrie (M Farrelly) |
| FAC 4Q r | Oct 30 | ALTRINCHAM | L 0–3 | | 2306 | Zelem, Shepherd, Johnson, Edwards, Tobin, Hanlon, Askey, Timmons (M Farrelly), Lambert, Burr, Kendall |
| Lg 16 | Nov 10 | Merthyr T | W 2–0 | Timmons(2) | 845 | Zelem, M Farrelly, Johnson, Edwards, Tobin, Hanlon, Askey (Ellis), Kendall, Lambert, Burr, Timmons (Heesom) |
| Lg 17 | Nov 17 | Slough T | W 1–0 | Askey | 991 | Zelem, M Farrelly, Johnson, Edwards, Tobin, Hanlon, Askey, Kendall, Lambert, Burr, Timmons (Ellis) |
| Lg 18 | Nov 24 | WELLING U | W 2–1 | Askey Hone(og) | 880 | Zelem, M Farrelly, Johnson, Edwards, Tobin, Hanlon, Askey, Kendall, Lambert, Burr (Ellis), Timmons |
| Lg 19 | Dec 15 | RUNCORN | W 2–1 | Timmons Burr | 1002 | Zelem, M Farrelly, Johnson, Edwards, Tobin, Hanlon, Askey, Kendall, Lambert, Burr, Timmons |
| BLT 2 | Dec 22 | Barrow | L 1–2 | Burr | 1011 | Zelem, M Farrelly (Ellis), Johnson (Heesom), Edwards, Tobin, Hanlon, Imrie, Kendall, Lambert, Burr, Timmons |
| Lg 20 | Dec 29 | TELFORD U | L 1–2 | Timmons | 1120 | Zelem, M Farrelly, Johnson (Imrie), Edwards, Tobin, Hanlon, Askey, Kendall (Ellis), Lambert, Burr, Timmons |
| Lg 21 | Jan 01 | Altrincham | L 3–5 | Hanlon Askey Wiggins(og) | 1398 | Zelem, M Farrelly (Ellis), Heesom (Lambert), Edwards, Tobin, Hanlon, Askey, Kendall, Imrie, Burr, Timmons |
| Lg 22 | Jan 05 | Boston U | D 1–1 | Timmons | 1239 | Pollitt, Shepherd, Johnson, Edwards, Tobin, Hanlon, Askey, Kendall, Imrie, Burr, Timmons (Ellis) |
| FAT 1 | Jan 12 | GRETNA | L 0–2 | | 1060 | Pollitt, Shepherd, Johnson, Edwards, Tobin, Hanlon, Askey, Kendall (Lambert), Imrie (Andrews), Burr, Timmons |
| Lg 23 | Jan 22 | STAFFORD R | W 2–1 | Askey Price(og) | 779 | Zelem, Shepherd, Johnson, Edwards, Tobin, Hanlon, Askey, Lambert, Ellis, Timmons, Imrie |
| Lg 24 | Feb 02 | SUTTON U | W 4–2 | Timmons Hanlon Ellis Lambert | 780 | Zelem, Shepherd, Johnson (Kendall), Edwards, Tobin, Hanlon, Askey, Lambert, Ellis (Heesom), Timmons, Imrie |

| Comp | Date | Opponents | Result | Scorers | Gate | Team |
|------|------|-----------|--------|---------|------|------|
| Lg 25 | Feb 16 | Wycombe W | D 0–0 | | 2616 | Zelem, Shepherd, Johnson, Edwards, Tobin, Hanlon, Askey, Lambert, Ellis, Timmons, Imrie |
| Lg 26 | Feb 23 | BOSTON U | W 2–0 | Askey Edwards | 778 | Zelem, Shepherd, Johnson, Edwards, Tobin, Hanlon, Askey, Lambert, Ellis, Timmons (Kendall), Imrie (Heesom) |
| Lg 27 | Mar 02 | CHELTENHAM T | W 5–1 | Hanlon(2) Edwards Lambert Imrie | 753 | Zelem, Shepherd, Johnson, Edwards (Kendall), Tobin, Hanlon, Askey, Lambert, Ellis, Imrie, Timmons (Burr) |
| Lg 28 | Mar 09 | Colchester U | L 0–1 | | 2735 | Zelem, Shepherd, Johnson, Edwards, Tobin, Hanlon, Askey, Lambert, Ellis (Burr), Imrie, Timmons (Tomlinson) |
| Lg 29 | Mar 16 | KETTERING T | L 1–2 | Burr | 1154 | S Farrelly, Connor, Johnson (Heesom), Edwards, Tobin, Hanlon, Askey, Tomlinson, Ellis, Burr, Imrie |
| Lg 30 | Mar 19 | ALTRINCHAM | L 0–1 | | 861 | S Farrelly, Connor, Heesom, Edwards, Kendall, Hanlon, Askey, Tomlinson, Ellis (Lambert), Burr, Imrie (M Farrelly) |
| Lg 31 | Mar 23 | Gateshead | D 1–1 | Heesom(p) | 604 | S Farrelly, Connor, Heesom, Edwards, Kendall, Hanlon, Askey, Lambert, Ellis, M Farrelly, Tomlinson (Kelsey) |
| Lg 32 | Mar 26 | BARROW | W 3–0 | Heesom Hanlon Lambert | 673 | S Farrelly, Connor, Heesom, Edwards, Kendall, Hanlon, Askey, Lambert (Edey), Ellis, Burr, Tomlinson (M Farrelly) |
| Lg 33 | Mar 30 | Fisher A | W 2–1 | Burr Askey | 363 | S Farrelly, Connor, Heesom, Edwards, Kendall, Hanlon (Tobin), Askey, M Farrelly, Ellis, Burr, Tomlinson |
| Lg 34 | Apr 01 | FISHER A | D 1–1 | Burr | 814 | S Farrelly, Connor, Heesom, Edwards, Kendall, Hanlon, Askey (Johnson), M Farrelly (Tobin), Ellis, Burr, Tomlinson |
| Lg 35 | Apr 06 | Welling U | D 0–0 | | 658 | S Farrelly, M Farrelly (Connor), Heesom, Edwards (Tomlinson), Tobin, Hanlon, Lambert, Kendall, Ellis, Burr, Johnson |
| Lg 36 | Apr 09 | BATH C | W 3–1 | Tobin Heesom(p) Askey | 608 | S Farrelly, Connor, Heesom, Kendall, Tobin, Hanlon, Askey, Lambert, Ellis, Burr (M Farrelly), Johnson (Edey) |
| Lg 37 | Apr 12 | Runcorn | W 2–1 | Ellis Johnson(p) | 994 | S Farrelly, Connor, Johnson, Kendall (Edey), Tobin, Hanlon, Askey, Lambert, Ellis, Burr, M Farrelly |
| Lg 38 | Apr 16 | Barnet | L 1–3 | Askey | 1315 | S Farrelly, Connor, Johnson (M Farrelly), Edey, Tobin, Hanlon, Askey, Lambert, Ellis, Burr, Heesom |
| Lg 39 | Apr 20 | NORTHWICH V | L 1–2 | Timmons | 880 | S Farrelly, Shepherd, Heesom, Connor, Tobin, Hanlon, Askey, Lambert, Ellis, Burr, Timmons (Edey) |
| Lg 40 | Apr 22 | YEOVIL T | W 2–1 | Askey(2) | 555 | S Farrelly, Shepherd, Heesom, Edwards, Tobin, Hanlon, Askey, Riddings, Lambert, Burr, Imrie |
| Lg 41 | Apr 27 | Yeovil T | L 1–2 | Timmons | 2582 | S Farrelly, Shepherd, Heesom, Connor, Tobin, Hanlon, Askey, Timmons (M Farrelly), Lambert, Burr, Imrie |
| Lg 42 | May 04 | Bath C | W 2–0 | Burr Ellis | 1010 | Zelem, Connor, Heesom, Edwards, Edey, Hanlon, Imrie (Lambert), M Farrelly, Ellis, Burr, Timmons |

## 1991–92: GM Vauxhall Conference

| Comp | Date | Opponents | Result | Scorers | Gate | Team |
|------|------|-----------|--------|---------|------|------|
| Lg 1 | Aug 17 | Colchester U | L 0–2 | | 2233 | S Farrelly, Shepherd, Johnson (M Farrelly), Edwards, Tobin, Hanlon, Askey, Lambert, Dempsey, Clayton, Imrie (Dawson) |
| Lg 2 | Aug 24 | SLOUGH T | L 0–1 | | 879 | S Farrelly, Shepherd (M Farrelly), Johnson, Edwards, Tobin, Hanlon, Askey, Dempsey, Lambert, Clayton, Dawson (Timmons) |
| Lg 3 | Aug 26 | CHELTENHAM T | D 3–3 | Lambert(2) Dempsey(p) | 834 | S Farrelly, M Farrelly, Johnson, Edwards, Tobin, Hanlon, Askey, Dempsey, Lambert, Clayton (Timmons), Dawson |
| Lg 4 | Aug 31 | Redbridge F | D 0–0 | | 472 | S Farrelly, Shepherd, Heesom (Timmons), Edwards, Tobin, Hanlon, Askey, M Farrelly, Lambert, Dempsey, Dawson (Ellis) |
| Lg 5 | Sep 03 | TELFORD U | W 2–1 | Timmons(2) | 838 | S Farrelly, Shepherd, Heesom, Edwards, Tobin, Hanlon, Askey, M Farrelly, Lambert, Dempsey, Dawson (Timmons) |

| Comp | Date | Opponents | Result | Scorers | Gate | Team |
|------|------|-----------|--------|---------|------|------|
| Lg 6 | Sep 07 | Yeovil T | W 1–0 | Lambert | 2110 | S Farrelly, Shepherd, Heesom, Edwards, Kendall, Hanlon, Askey, Dempsey, Lambert (Ellis), Timmons (Clayton), M Farrelly |
| FAC 1Q | Sep 14 | Skelmersdale United | W 4–0 | Askey Dawson Heesom Shepherd | 417 | S Farrelly, Shepherd, Heesom, Edwards, Kendall (Ellis), Hanlon, Askey (Clayton), Dawson, Lambert, Dempsey, M Farrelly |
| Lg 7 | Sep 17 | RUNCORN | W 3–0 | Edwards(2) Hanlon | 1065 | S Farrelly, Shepherd, Bimson, Edwards, Kendall, Hanlon, Askey (Dawson), Timmons (Ellis), Lambert, Dempsey, M Farrelly |
| Lg 8 | Sep 21 | Wycombe W | W 1–0 | Timmons | 3961 | S Farrelly, Shepherd, Johnson, Edwards, Kendall, Hanlon, Askey (Dawson), Timmons (Ellis), Lambert, Dempsey, M Farrelly |
| Lg 9 | Sep 23 | Kidderminster H | D 1–1 | Lambert | 1326 | S Farrelly, Shepherd, Johnson, Edwards, Kendall, Hanlon, Askey, Timmons (Ellis), Lambert, Dempsey, Heesom |
| FAC 2Q | Sep 28 | BORROWASH VICTORIA | L 1–2 | Timmons | 871 | S Farrelly, Shepherd, Bimson, Edwards, Johnson, Hanlon, Askey, Timmons, Lambert, Dempsey, Ellis (Dawson) |
| Lg 10 | Oct 01 | NORTHWICH V | D 0–0 | | 905 | S Farrelly, Shepherd, Heesom, Edwards, Johnson, Hanlon, Askey (Ellis), Timmons, Lambert, Dempsey, M Farrelly (Clayton) |
| BLT 2 | Oct 08 | Telford U | W 2–1 | Dawson Timmons | 597 | S Farrelly, Shepherd, Heesom, Edwards, Johnson, Hanlon, Dawson, Timmons, Lambert, Clayton (Miller), Ellis |
| Lg 11 | Oct 12 | BOSTON U | L 0–1 | | 869 | S Farrelly, Shepherd (Kendall), Bimson, Edwards, Johnson, Hanlon, Dawson, Ellis, Lambert, Timmons, Heesom (Clayton) |
| Lg 12 | Oct 19 | FARNBOROUGH T | L 1–2 | Dawson | 752 | S Farrelly, M Farrelly, Bimson, Edwards, Rutter, Hanlon, Askey (Clayton), Timmons (Dawson), Lambert, Ellis, Johnson |
| Lg 13 | Oct 26 | Bath C | D 1–1 | Askey | 532 | S Farrelly, M Farrelly, Heesom, Edwards, Johnson, Hanlon, Askey, Dempsey, Lambert, Timmons, Ellis (Dawson) |
| Lg 14 | Nov 02 | Welling U | L 1–2 | Brown(og) | 505 | S Farrelly, M Farrelly, Heesom, Edwards, Johnson, Hanlon, Askey, Green, Lambert, Timmons (Dawson), Dempsey |
| Lg 15 | Nov 05 | STAFFORD R | W 1–0 | Green | 522 | S Farrelly, M Farrelly, Heesom, Edwards, Johnson, Hanlon, Askey (Ellis), Green, Lambert, Timmons (Dawson), Dempsey |
| Lg 16 | Nov 09 | KETTERING T | L 0–2 | | 943 | S Farrelly, Shepherd (Dawson), Johnson, Edwards, M Farrelly, Hanlon, Ellis, Dempsey, Green, Clayton (Timmons), Lambert |
| Lg 17 | Nov 16 | Cheltenham T | W 3–2 | Green(2) Ellis | 783 | S Farrelly, Shepherd, Heesom (Ellis), Edwards, Johnson, Hanlon, Dempsey, Green, Lambert, Clayton, M Farrelly |
| Lg 18 | Nov 23 | Telford U | W 1–0 | Lambert | 1199 | S Farrelly, Shepherd, Johnson, Edwards, M Farrelly, Hanlon, Ellis (Bimson), Green, Timmons (Clayton), Lambert, Dempsey |
| Lg 19 | Nov 26 | Barrow | L 0–2 | | 1158 | S Farrelly, Shepherd, Johnson, Edwards, M Farrelly, Hanlon, Askey, Green, Lambert, Timmons, Dempsey |
| Lg 20 | Nov 30 | WITTON A | W 1–0 | M Farrelly(p) | 1015 | S Farrelly, Shepherd, Bimson, Edwards, M Farrelly, Hanlon, Askey, Green, Lambert, Timmons, Dempsey |
| Lg 21 | Dec 07 | KIDDERMINSTER H | D 0–0 | | 851 | S Farrelly, Shepherd, Heesom, Edwards, Johnson, Hanlon, Askey, Green, Lambert (Dawson), Timmons (Clayton), Dempsey |
| BLT 3 | Dec 17 | ALTRINCHAM | D 1–1 | Green | 447 | S Farrelly, Shepherd, Johnson, Edwards, M Farrelly, Hanlon, Askey, Green (Clayton), Dawson (Heesom), Timmons, Dempsey |
| Lg 22 | Dec 26 | ALTRINCHAM | D 1–1 | Askey | 1301 | S Farrelly, Shepherd, Bimson, Edwards, Johnson, Hanlon, Askey, Green (Clayton), Lambert, Timmons, Dempsey |
| Lg 23 | Jan 01 | Stafford R | D 1–1 | Green | 994 | S Farrelly, Shepherd, Bimson, Edwards, Johnson, Hanlon, Askey, Green, Lambert (Dawson), Timmons (Clayton), Dempsey |

| Comp | Date | Opponents | Result | Scorers | Gate | Team |
|---|---|---|---|---|---|---|
| FAT 1 | Jan 11 | BOSTON U | D 0–0 | | 833 | S Farrelly, Shepherd (Clayton), Bimson, Edwards, Johnson, Hanlon, Askey, M Farrelly, Lambert, Green (Timmons), Dempsey |
| FAT 1 r | Jan 15 | Boston U | W 2–0 | Lambert Edwards | 942 | S Farrelly, Shepherd, Bimson, Edwards, Johnson, Hanlon, Askey, M Farrelly, Lambert, Green, Dempsey |
| Lg 24 | Jan 18 | Boston U | W 5–1 | Askey(2) Lambert Clayton Timmons | 951 | S Farrelly, M Farrelly, Johnson, Edwards, Clayton, Hanlon, Askey, Green (Dawson), Lambert, Timmons, Dempsey |
| FAT 2 | Feb 04 | BANGOR CITY | W 1–0 | Hanlon | 631 | S Farrelly, Shepherd, Johnson, Edwards, M Farrelly, Hanlon, Timmons (Ellis), Green, Lambert, Dawson (Clayton), Dempsey |
| BLT 3 r | Feb 06 | Altrincham | L 1–3 | Askey | 524 | S Farrelly, Shepherd (Ellis), Johnson, Edwards, M Farrelly, Hanlon, Askey, Green, Lambert, Clayton, Dempsey |
| Lg 25 | Feb 08 | BATH C | D 0–0 | | 578 | S Farrelly, Lambert, Johnson, Edwards, M Farrelly, Hanlon, Askey, Green, Ellis (Hopley), Timmons, Dempsey |
| Lg 26 | Feb 15 | MERTHYR T | W 3–0 | Askey Hanlon Boyle(og) | 568 | S Farrelly, Shepherd, Johnson, Edwards, M Farrelly, Hanlon, Askey (Doherty), Green, Lambert, Timmons, Dempsey (Ellis) |
| FAT 3 | Feb 22 | Northwich V | W 1–0 | Hanlon | 1537 | S Farrelly, Shepherd, Johnson, Edwards, M Farrelly, Hanlon, Askey, Lambert, Green, Timmons, Dempsey |
| Lg 27 | Feb 29 | YEOVIL T | L 1–2 | Doherty | 701 | S Farrelly, Shepherd, Clayton, Edwards, Johnson, Hanlon, Askey, Doherty, Lambert, Timmons, Dempsey |
| Lg 28 | Mar 02 | Northwich V | L 1–2 | Doherty(p) | 802 | S Farrelly, Shepherd, Johnson, Lambert, Tobin, Hanlon, Askey, Doherty, Ellis, Timmons, Dempsey |
| Lg 29 | Mar 07 | Runcorn | D 0–0 | | 661 | S Farrelly, Shepherd, Johnson, Edwards, Lambert, Hanlon, Askey, Doherty, Green, Timmons, Dempsey |
| Lg 30 | Mar 10 | Farnborough T | L 2–4 | Hopley Wigmore(og) | 790 | Zelem, Lambert, Timmons, Kendall, Tobin, Hanlon, Hooley, Green, Clayton, Doherty, Ellis |
| FAT 4 | Mar 14 | Yeovil T | W 2–1 | Green Askey | 4269 | S Farrelly, Shepherd, Johnson, Edwards, M Farrelly, Hanlon, Askey, Lambert, Green, Timmons, Dempsey |
| Lg 31 | Mar 17 | BARROW | L 0–1 | | 502 | S Farrelly, Shepherd, Johnson, Edwards, Kendall, Hanlon (Hopley), Askey, Green, Lambert, Timmons, Doherty |
| Lg 32 | Mar 20 | Witton A | D 1–1 | Green | 1300 | S Farrelly, Lambert, Johnson, Edwards, M Farrelly, Hanlon, Askey (Hopley), Doherty, Green (Clayton), Timmons, Dempsey |
| Lg 33 | Mar 24 | Kettering T | L 0–2 | | 1367 | S Farrelly, Shepherd, Lambert, Edwards, M Farrelly, Hanlon, Askey, Doherty, Green (Clayton), Timmons, Dempsey |
| Lg 34 | Mar 28 | Gateshead | L 0–2 | | 250 | S Farrelly, Shepherd, Johnson, Edwards, M Farrelly (Boughey), Hanlon, Askey, Doherty, Lambert (Clayton), Timmons, Dempsey |
| FAT SF 1 | Apr 04 | Colchester U | L 0–3 | | 5443 | S Farrelly, Shepherd, Johnson, Edwards, M Farrelly, Hanlon, Askey, Green, Lambert, Timmons, Dempsey |
| Lg 35 | Apr 07 | Merthyr T | L 2–3 | Doherty(2) | 588 | Zelem, M Farrelly, Johnson, Kendall, Tobin, Hanlon, Askey, Ellis, Green, Doherty, Boughey |
| FAT SF 2 | Apr 10 | COLCHESTER U | D 1–1 | Timmons | 1650 | S Farrelly, Shepherd, Johnson, Edwards, M Farrelly, Hanlon, Askey, Green, Lambert, Timmons, Dempsey |
| Lg 36 | Apr 14 | WYCOMBE W | W 3–1 | Johnson(p) Green Lambert | 683 | Zelem, Shepherd, Johnson, Edwards, Kendall, Hanlon (Doherty), Askey, Green, Lambert, Timmons, Ellis (Boughey) |
| Lg 37 | Apr 18 | REDBRIDGE F | D 0–0 | | 460 | S Farrelly, Shepherd, Bimson, Edwards, Kendall, Ellis, Askey (Clayton), Green (Boughey), Lambert, Doherty, Timmons |
| Lg 38 | Apr 20 | Altrincham | L 1–3 | Green | 757 | S Farrelly, Shepherd, Bimson (Tobin), M Farrelly, Kendall, Hanlon, Timmons, Green, Lambert, Doherty, Ellis (Clayton) |
| Lg 39 | Apr 22 | WELLING U | L 1–2 | Ellis | 338 | S Farrelly, Johnson, Bimson, Edwards, Kendall, Ellis, Timmons (Clayton), Green, Lambert, Doherty, Dempsey |
| Lg 40 | Apr 25 | COLCHESTER U | D 4–4 | Lambert(2) Doherty Edwards | 896 | S Farrelly, Shepherd, Bimson, Edwards, Kendall, Johnson, Askey, Green, Lambert, Doherty, Dempsey (Ellis) |

| Comp | Date | Opponents | Result | Scorers | Gate | Team |
|------|------|-----------|--------|---------|------|------|
| Lg 41 | Apr 28 | GATESHEAD | W 1–0 | Hopley Wigmore(og) | 369 | Zelem, Shepherd, Bimson, Edwards, Kendall (Lambert), Johnson, Hopley, Green (Dempsey), Clayton, Doherty, Ellis |
| Lg 42 | May 02 | Slough T | W 3–0 | Bimson(2) Doherty | 588 | S Farrelly, Shepherd, Bimson, Edwards, Kendall, Hanlon (Zelem), M Farrelly, Clayton, Ellis, Doherty, Johnson |

## 1992–93: GM Vauxhall Conference

| Comp | Date | Opponents | Result | Scorers | Gate | Team |
|------|------|-----------|--------|---------|------|------|
| Lg 1 | Aug 22 | WYCOMBE W | D 1–1 | Lambert | 1397 | S Farrelly, Shepherd, Johnson, Edwards, O'Neill, Sorvel (Leicester), Askey, Timmons, Lambert, Doherty, Carberry |
| Lg 2 | Aug 25 | Runcorn | W 2–1 | Lambert M Farrelly | 780 | S Farrelly, Shepherd, Carberry, Edwards, O'Neill, Sorvel, Askey (A Green), M Farrelly, Lambert, Mitchell (Kendall), Leicester |
| Lg 3 | Aug 29 | Kettering T | L 0–1 | | 1209 | S Farrelly, Shepherd, Johnson, Edwards, O'Neill, Dempsey (Mitchell), Leicester (M Farrelly), Sorvel, Lambert, Timmons, Carberry |
| Lg 4 | Aug 31 | NORTHWICH V | L 1–2 | A Green | 1068 | S Farrelly, Shepherd, Johnson (Sorvel), M Farrelly, O'Neill, Dempsey, Timmons, A Green, Lambert, Doherty, Carberry |
| Lg 5 | Sep 05 | BATH C | W 1–0 | Sorvel | 651 | S Farrelly, Shepherd, Johnson, Edwards, M Farrelly, Dempsey (Carberry), Askey, Sorvel, Lambert, Timmons, Leicester (Mitchell) |
| DC 1–1 | Sep 08 | Altrincham | W 3–1 | Leicester M Farrelly Timmons | 621 | S Farrelly, Shepherd, Johnson, Edwards (Kendall), M Farrelly, Dempsey, Askey (Mitchell), Sorvel, Lambert, Timmons, Leicester |
| FAC 1Q | Sep 12 | Glossop North End | W 1–0 | Maunsell (og) | 805 | S Farrelly, M Farrelly, Johnson (Mitchell), Kendall, O'Neill, Dempsey, Askey, Timmons, Lambert, Carberry, Leicester |
| Lg 6 | Sep 15 | Bromsgrove R | L 0–3 | | 1045 | S Farrelly, Shepherd, Carberry (Kendall), Edwards, M Farrelly, Dempsey (Mitchell), Askey, Sorvel, Lambert, Timmons, Leicester |
| Lg 7 | Sep 19 | FARNBOROUGH T | L 1–2 | Lambert | 574 | S Farrelly, Shepherd, Johnson, Edwards, M Farrelly, Sorvel, Askey, Timmons, Lambert, Doherty, Leicester |
| DC 1–2 | Sep 22 | ALTRINCHAM | D 0–0 | | 449 | S Farrelly, M Farrelly, Bimson, Edwards, Kendall, Sorvel (Carberry), Askey, Timmons, Lambert, Doherty, Leicester |
| FAC 2Q | Sep 26 | Hucknall Town | D 1–1 | Thompson (og) | 1305 | S Farrelly, M Farrelly, Bimson, Edwards, Carberry, Johnson, Askey, Timmons, Lambert, Doherty, Leicester |
| FAC 2Q r | Sep 29 | HUCKNALL TOWN | W 3–1 | Timmons Askey Mitchell | 635 | S Farrelly, M Farrelly, Bimson, Edwards, Kendall, Dempsey (Mitchell), Askey, Timmons, Lambert, Doherty, Leicester |
| Lg 8 | Oct 03 | Merthyr T | W 2–1 | Lambert Askey | 554 | S Farrelly, M Farrelly (Sorvel), Johnson, Edwards, Kendall, Bimson, Askey, Timmons, Lambert, Doherty, Leicester (Sorvel) |
| FAC 3Q | Oct 10 | HORWICH RMI | W 1–0 | Leicester | 789 | S Farrelly, Shepherd, Bimson, Edwards, Kendall, M Farrelly, Askey, Dempsey, Lambert, Doherty, Leicester |
| Lg 9 | Oct 14 | Northwich V | W 3–1 | Sorvel Lambert Mitchell | 783 | S Farrelly, Shepherd (Dempsey), Bimson, Edwards, M Farrelly (Kendall), Sorvel, Askey, Timmons, Lambert, Mitchell, Leicester |
| Lg 10 | Oct 17 | Dagenham & R | W 2–1 | Timmons Mitchell | 1303 | S Farrelly, Shepherd, Bimson, Edwards, Kendall, Sorvel (Johnson), Askey, Timmons, Lambert, Mitchell, Leicester |
| DC 2 | Oct 20 | Witton A | W 1–0 | Leicester | 763 | S Farrelly, Shepherd, Bimson, Edwards, Kendall, McMahon, Askey, Timmons (Johnson), Lambert, Mitchell, Leicester |
| FAC 4Q | Oct 24 | Netherfield | D 1–1 | Leicester | 918 | S Farrelly, Shepherd, Bimson, Edwards, Kendall, McMahon, Doherty (Carberry), Timmons, Lambert, Mitchell, Leicester |
| Lg 11 | Oct 31 | KETTERING T | W 1–0 | Askey | 731 | S Farrelly, Shepherd, Bimson, Edwards, Kendall, Sorvel, Askey (Johnson), Timmons, Mitchell (Doherty), McMahon, Leicester |
| FAC 4Q r | Nov 02 | NETHERFIELD | W 5–0 | McMahon Mitchell Leicester Kendall Shepherd | 903 | S Farrelly, Shepherd, Bimson, Edwards, Kendall, Sorvel, Askey (Johnson), Timmons (Doherty), Mitchell, McMahon, Leicester |

| Comp | Date | Opponents | Result | Scorers | Gate | Team |
|---|---|---|---|---|---|---|
| Lg 12 | Nov 07 | Telford U | L 1–3 | Mitchell | 1175 | S Farrelly, Shepherd, Bimson, Edwards, Kendall, Sorvel, Askey, Timmons, Lambert (McMahon), Mitchell, Leicester |
| FAC 1 | Nov 14 | CHESTERFIELD | D 0–0 | | 3063 | S Farrelly, Shepherd, Bimson, Edwards, Kendall, Sorvel, Askey, Timmons, Lambert, Mitchell, Leicester |
| Lg 13 | Nov 17 | STAFFORD R | W 4–1 | Mitchell(2, 1p) Timmons Blain | 473 | S Farrelly, Shepherd, Bimson, Edwards, Kendall (McMahon), Sorvel, Askey (Blain), Timmons, Lambert, Mitchell, Leicester |
| Lg 14 | Nov 21 | SLOUGH T | L 1–2 | Mitchell | 651 | S Farrelly, Shepherd, Bimson, Edwards, Kendall, McMahon (M Farrelly), Blain, Timmons (Sorvel), Lambert, Mitchell, Leicester |
| FAC 1 r | Nov 25 | Chesterfield | D 2–2 | Mitchell(2) | 4143 | S Farrelly, Shepherd, Bimson, Edwards, Kendall, McMahon, Askey, Timmons (M Farrelly), Lambert, Mitchell, Leicester |
| Lg 15 | Nov 28 | Welling U | L 0–1 | | 959 | S Farrelly, Shepherd, Bimson, Edwards, Kendall, McMahon, Askey, Timmons (M Farrelly), Lambert, Mitchell (Doherty), Leicester |
| FAC 2 | Dec 05 | STOCKPORT COUNTY | L 0–2 | | 5700 | S Farrelly, Shepherd, Bimson, Edwards, Kendall, McMahon, Askey, Timmons (M Farrelly), Lambert, Mitchell (Sorvel), Leicester |
| Lg 16 | Dec 09 | Boston U | L 1–3 | Lambert | 818 | Sutton, Shepherd, Johnson (Mitchell), M Farrelly, Kendall, McMahon, Askey, Timmons, Lambert, Blain (Sorvel), Leicester |
| Lg 17 | Dec 12 | Slough T | L 1–2 | Pluckrose(og) | 930 | S Farrelly, Shepherd, Bimson, Edwards, Kendall (Doherty), M Farrelly (Blain), Askey, Sorvel, Lambert, Timmons, Mitchell |
| DC 3 | Dec 15 | KIDDERMINSTER H | W 3–1 | Mitchell(2) Lambert | 203 | S Farrelly, Shepherd, Bimson, Edwards, Kendall (Sorvel), McMahon, Askey, Timmons, Lambert, Mitchell, Leicester |
| Lg 18 | Dec 19 | Gateshead | L 0–1 | | 375 | S Farrelly, Shepherd, Bimson, Kendall, McMahon, Johnson (Doherty), Askey, Mitchell, Timmons, Blain, Leicester (Sorvel) |
| Lg 19 | Jan 02 | Witton A | D 1–1 | Mitchell | 1110 | S Farrelly, Shepherd, Bimson, Edwards, Kendall, McMahon, Askey, Timmons, Mitchell, Blain (Doherty), Leicester (Dempsey) |
| FAT 1 | Jan 09 | WITTON A | D 0–0 | | 590 | S Farrelly, Shepherd, Bimson, Edwards, Kendall, McMahon (Blain), Askey, Dempsey, Timmons, Mitchell, Leicester (Doherty) |
| FAT 1 r | Jan 12 | Witton A | D 0–0 | | 901 | S Farrelly, Shepherd, Bimson, Edwards, Sorvel, Timmons, Askey (Mitchell), Blain, Doherty, Dempsey (Leicester), McMahon |
| Lg 20 | Jan 16 | MERTHYR T | L 0–1 | | 490 | S Farrelly, Shepherd, Bimson, Edwards, Kendall, McMahon (Lambert), Blain, Sorvel, Mitchell (Pickering), Timmons, Leicester |
| FAT 1 2r | Jan 18 | Witton A | L 1–2 | Doherty | 907 | S Farrelly, McMahon, Bimson, Edwards, Kendall, Sorvel, Blain, Timmons, Lambert (Johnson), Doherty, Leicester |
| Lg 21 | Jan 23 | YEOVIL T | D 1–1 | Timmons | 431 | S Farrelly, Shepherd, Bimson, Edwards, Kendall (McMahon), Sorvel, Doherty, Timmons, Lambert, Mitchell, Leicester |
| Lg 22 | Jan 30 | Kidderminster H | L 1–2 | Dempsey | 1032 | S Farrelly, Shepherd, Bimson, Edwards, Sorvel, McMahon, Askey (Blain), Timmons, Lambert, Doherty (Mitchell), Dempsey |
| Lg 23 | Feb 06 | Stafford R | L 0–1 | | 1025 | S Farrelly, Shepherd, Bimson, Edwards, Kendall, Sorvel, Leicester (Doherty), Timmons, Lambert, Mitchell (Blain), Dempsey |
| Lg 24 | Feb 09 | BOSTON U | W 2–1 | Lambert Mitchell | 421 | S Farrelly, Shepherd, Bimson, Edwards, Kendall, Sorvel, Blain, Timmons, Lambert, Mitchell (Doherty), Dempsey |
| Lg 25 | Feb 13 | TELFORD U | D 1–1 | Leicester | 470 | S Farrelly, Shepherd, Bimson, Edwards, Kendall, Sorvel, Blain (McMahon), Mitchell, Lambert, Doherty (Leicester), Dempsey |
| Lg 26 | Feb 20 | Woking | L 0–4 | | 1868 | S Farrelly, Shepherd, Bimson, Edwards, Kendall (Blain), Sorvel, Leicester, Mulligan (McMahon), Lambert, Timmons, Dempsey |
| DC SF 1 | Feb 23 | Northwich V | L 0–2 | | 821 | S Farrelly, Shepherd, Bimson (Doherty), Edwards, Hardman, Sorvel, Leicester, Johnson, Lambert, Mitchell, Dempsey (McMahon) |

| Comp | Date | Opponents | Result | Scorers | Gate | Team |
|------|------|-----------|--------|---------|------|------|
| Lg 27 | Feb 27 | WELLING U | D 1–1 | Lambert | 437 | S Farrelly, Halliday, Johnson (Mitchell), Edwards, Kendall (Blain), Sorvel, Leicester, Bunter, Lambert, Timmons, Hardman |
| DC SF 2 | Mar 02 | NORTHWICH V | D 1–1 | McMahon(p) | 422 | S Farrelly, McMahon, Johnson, Edwards, Kendall, Hardman, Leicester, Sorvel, Lambert, Doherty, Timmons |
| Lg 28 | Mar 06 | Bath C | D 0–0 | | 478 | S Farrelly, Shepherd, Johnson (Leicester), Edwards, Kendall, Hardman, Sorvel, Timmons, Lambert, R Green, McMahon |
| Lg 29 | Mar 13 | ALTRINCHAM | D 1–1 | Askey | 875 | S Farrelly, McMahon, Bimson, Edwards (Hardman), Kendall, Sorvel, Askey, Timmons, Lambert (Johnson), R Green, Blain |
| Lg 30 | Mar 16 | DAGENHAM & R | D 1–1 | Askey | 387 | S Farrelly, Shepherd, Bimson, Edwards, Kendall, Hardman (Halliday), Askey, Sorvel, Timmons, R Green, McMahon |
| Lg 31 | Mar 20 | Stalybridge C | L 1–2 | Askey | 822 | S Farrelly, Shepherd, Bimson, Edwards, Kendall, Hardman (Blain), Askey, Sorvel, Timmons, R Green, McMahon |
| Lg 32 | Mar 23 | GATESHEAD | W 1–0 | Leicester | 473 | S Farrelly, Shepherd, Bimson, Edwards, Kendall, Leicester, Askey, Sorvel, Timmons, R Green, McMahon |
| Lg 33 | Mar 27 | WOKING | D 1–1 | Sorvel | 879 | S Farrelly, Shepherd, Bimson, Edwards, Kendall, Leicester (Doherty), Askey, Sorvel, Timmons, Blain, McMahon (Hardman) |
| Lg 34 | Mar 30 | KIDDERMINSTER H | D 1–1 | Askey | 593 | S Farrelly, Shepherd, Bimson, Edwards, Kendall, Leicester, Askey, Sorvel, Timmons, Doherty (Mitchell), McMahon |
| Lg 35 | Apr 03 | Yeovil T | D 1–1 | Blain | 2515 | S Farrelly, Shepherd, Bimson, Edwards, Kendall, Johnson, Askey, Sorvel, Timmons, McMahon (Blain), Leicester |
| Lg 36 | Apr 10 | STALYBRIDGE C | W 1–0 | Blain(p) | 844 | S Farrelly, Shepherd, Bimson, Edwards, Kendall, Sorvel, Blain, Timmons, Askey (Mitchell), Doherty (Hardman), Leicester |
| Lg 37 | Apr 12 | Altrincham | L 0–1 | | 1143 | S Farrelly, Shepherd, Bimson, Edwards, Kendall, Sorvel, Blain (Hardman), Timmons, Askey, Doherty (Mitchell), Leicester |
| Lg 38 | Apr 17 | BROMSGROVE R | L 0–2 | | 604 | S Farrelly, Shepherd, Bimson (R Green), Edwards, Kendall, Hardman, Blain, Sorvel, Askey, Timmons, McMahon (Leicester) |
| Lg 39 | Apr 20 | RUNCORN | D 1–1 | Timmons | 631 | S Farrelly, Shepherd, Bimson, Edwards, Kendall (Hardman), Sorvel, Askey, McMahon, R Green (Mitchell), Timmons, Leicester |
| Lg 40 | Apr 24 | Farnborough T | D 0–0 | | 676 | S Farrelly, Shepherd, Bimson, Edwards, Kendall, Sorvel, Askey, Timmons, McMahon, Leicester, R Green (Mitchell) |
| Lg 41 | Apr 27 | WITTON A | W 1–0 | Askey | 762 | S Farrelly, Shepherd, Bimson, Edwards, Kendall, Sorvel, Askey, Timmons (Mitchell), McMahon, Leicester, R Green |
| Lg 42 | May 01 | Wycombe W | W 1–0 | R Green | 5748 | S Farrelly, Shepherd, Bimson, Edwards, Kendall, Sorvel, Askey, Timmons, McMahon, Leicester (Hardman), R Green |

## 1993–94: GM Vauxhall Conference

| Comp | Date | Opponents | Result | Scorers | Gate | Team |
|------|------|-----------|--------|---------|------|------|
| Lg 1 | Aug 21 | Bath C | L 1–5 | Sharratt | 667 | Sutton, Shepherd, Bimson, Lillis, Allardyce (Sorvel), Dempsey, Leicester (Green), Wood, Alford, Roberts, Sharratt |
| Lg 2 | Aug 24 | BROMSGROVE R | W 4–3 | Green(2) Alford(2,1p) | 695 | Lennon, Shepherd, Bimson, Lillis, Alford, Dempsey (Sorvel), Leicester, Wood, Green, Roberts, Sharratt |
| Lg 3 | Aug 28 | DOVER A | L 0–2 | | 836 | Lennon, Shepherd, Bimson, Lillis, Alford, Dempsey, Leicester, Wood (Sorvel), Green (Mitchell), Roberts, Sharratt |
| Lg 4 | Aug 30 | Runcorn | L 1–2 | Alford | 737 | Lennon, Shepherd, Bimson, Lillis, Allardyce, Dempsey, Roberts (Leicester), Sorvel, Alford, Mitchell, Sharratt |

| Comp | Date | Opponents | Result | Scorers | Gate | Team |
|---|---|---|---|---|---|---|
| Lg 5 | Sep 04 | DAGENHAM & R | W 3–0 | Alford Sorvel Sharratt | 633 | Farrelly, Shepherd, Bimson, Lillis, Howarth, Dempsey, Roberts, Sorvel, Alford, Adams, Sharratt |
| DC 1–1 | Sep 07 | Witton A | W 2–1 | Roberts Alford | 826 | Farrelly, Shepherd, Bimson, Lillis, Howarth, Dempsey, Roberts, Sorvel, Alford, Adams, Sharratt |
| Lg 6 | Sep 11 | Woking | L 0–3 | | 1566 | Farrelly, Shepherd, Bimson, Lillis, Howarth, Dempsey, Roberts (Leicester), Sorvel, Alford, Adams, Sharratt (Mitchell) |
| Lg 7 | Sep 18 | KETTERING T | D 0–0 | | 933 | Walker, Shepherd, Bimson, Lillis, Howarth, Dempsey, Leicester (Askey), Sorvel, Alford, Adams, Sharratt |
| DC 1–2 | Sep 21 | WITTON A | W 4–1 | Askey(2) Alford(p) Sharratt | 466 | Walker, Shepherd, Bimson, Lillis, Howarth, Dempsey, Wood, Askey, Alford, Adams, Sharratt |
| Lg 8 | Sep 25 | Yeovil T | L 0–4 | | 2516 | Walker, Brown, Bimson, Kendall, Howarth, Dempsey, Wood (Sorvel), Askey, Alford (Mitchell), Adams, Sharratt |
| Lg 9 | Oct 02 | SOUTHPORT | L 0–1 | | 1002 | Walker, Shepherd, Bimson, Kendall, Alford, Dempsey, Sorvel, Askey, Roberts (Mitchell), Adams, Sharratt |
| Lg 10 | Oct 09 | Witton A | W 2–0 | Power Roberts | 1068 | Farrelly, Shepherd, Bimson, Kendall, Lillis, Roberts, Askey, Sorvel, Alford, Power (Mitchell), Adams |
| Lg 11 | Oct 11 | Kidderminster H | L 1–2 | Power | 1228 | Farrelly, Shepherd, Bimson, Kendall, Lillis, Roberts, Askey, Sorvel (Dempsey), Alford, Power (Mitchell), Heron |
| Lg 12 | Oct 16 | MERTHYR T | L 1–2 | Power | 835 | Farrelly, Shepherd, Bimson, Kendall (Green), Lillis, Roberts, Askey, Sorvel, Alford, Power, Adams (Wood) |
| FAC 4Q | Oct 23 | SOUTHPORT | W 5–3 | Wood Alford(3,1p) Sharratt | 1190 | Farrelly, Shepherd, Bimson, Kendall, Lillis, Roberts, Askey, Sorvel, Alford, Wood, Sharratt |
| Lg 13 | Oct 26 | TELFORD U | W 1–0 | Alford | 731 | Farrelly, Shepherd, Bimson, Kendall, Lillis, Sorvel, Askey, Wood, Alford, Roberts (Power), Sharratt |
| Lg 14 | Oct 30 | Stafford R | W 3–2 | Alford(3) | 1249 | Farrelly, Shepherd, Bimson, Kendall, Lillis, Sorvel, Askey, Wood, Alford, Power, Sharratt |
| DC 2 | Nov 02 | Runcorn | W 4–0 | Askey(2) Shepherd Wood | 471 | Farrelly, Shepherd, Bimson, Kendall, Lillis, Sorvel, Askey, Wood, Alford, Adams, Sharratt |
| Lg 15 | Nov 06 | GATESHEAD | W 6–1 | Askey(3) Wood Power Sharratt | 1033 | Farrelly, Shepherd (Heron), Bimson, Kendall, Lillis, Sorvel, Askey, Wood, Alford, Power, Sharratt |
| FAC 1 | Nov 13 | HARTLEPOOL UNITED | W 2–0 | Sorvel McDonald | 2747 | Farrelly, Shepherd, Bimson, Kendall, Lillis, Sorvel, Askey, Wood (McDonald), Alford, Adams, Sharratt |
| Lg 16 | Nov 20 | SLOUGH T | D 2–2 | Sharratt Alford | 1043 | Farrelly, Shepherd, Bimson, Kendall, Lillis, Sorvel, Askey, McDonald, Alford, Adams (Green), Sharratt |
| Lg 17 | Nov 27 | Welling U | W 1–0 | Sorvel | 773 | Farrelly, Shepherd, Bimson, Kendall, Lillis, Sorvel, Askey, McDonald, Alford, Power, Sharratt |
| FAC 2 | Dec 04 | Crewe Alexandra | L 1–2 | Askey | 6007 | Farrelly, Shepherd, Bimson, Kendall, Lillis, Sorvel, Askey, McDonald, Alford, Adams, Sharratt |
| Lg 18 | Dec 11 | STALYBRIDGE C | L 1–3 | Alford | 788 | Farrelly (Mitchell), Shepherd, Bimson, Kendall, Heron, Sorvel, Askey, McDonald, Alford, Power (Adams), Sharratt |
| Lg 19 | Dec 18 | Merthyr T | L 1–2 | Farrelly | 425 | Farrelly, Shepherd, Bimson, Kendall, Lillis, Sorvel, Askey, McDonald, Alford, Adams, Sharratt |
| DC 3 | Dec 21 | Halifax T | W 2–1 | Alford Lillis | 778 | Farrelly, Shepherd, Bimson, Kendall, Lillis, Sorvel, Askey, McDonald, Alford, Kinsey (Adams), Sharratt |
| Lg 20 | Jan 01 | Stalybridge C | W 2–0 | Power Sorvel | 1059 | Farrelly, Shepherd, Bimson, Kendall, Lillis, Sorvel, Askey, McDonald, Alford, Power, Adams |
| Lg 21 | Jan 05 | ALTRINCHAM | W 1–0 | Adams | 742 | Farrelly, Shepherd, Bimson, Kendall, Lillis, Sorvel, Askey, McDonald, Alford, Power (Thorpe), Adams |
| Lg 22 | Jan 15 | WOKING | D 1–1 | Power | 1053 | Farrelly, Shepherd, Bimson, Kendall (Thorpe), Lillis, Sorvel, Askey, McDonald, Alford, Power, Adams |
| FAT 1 | Jan 22 | Boston U | D 1–1 | Alford | 1559 | Farrelly, Shepherd (Wood), Bimson, Kendall, Lillis, Sorvel, Askey, McDonald, Alford, Power, Adams |
| FAT 1 r | Jan 25 | BOSTON U | W 1–0 | Alford | 590 | Farrelly, Thorpe, Bimson, Kendall, Lillis, Sorvel, Askey, McDonald, Alford, Power, Adams |
| Lg 23 | Jan 29 | Bromsgrove R | L 0–3 | | 1701 | Farrelly, Thorpe, Bimson, Kendall, Lillis, Sorvel, Askey, McDonald, Alford, Power, Lyons |

| Comp | Date | Opponents | Result | Scorers | Gate | Team |
|------|------|-----------|--------|---------|------|------|
| Lg 24 | Feb 05 | NORTHWICH V | D 0–0 | | 1141 | Farrelly, Shepherd, Bimson, Kendall, Howarth, Sorvel, Askey, McDonald, Alford (Wood), Power, Lyons |
| FAT 2 r | Feb 12 | Worcester City | D 0–0 | | 1587 | Farrelly, Shepherd, Bimson, Kendall, Howarth, Sorvel, Wood, McDonald, Lyons, Askey, Sharratt |
| Lg 25 | Feb 19 | RUNCORN | D 0–0 | | 1004 | Farrelly, Shepherd, Bimson, Kendall, Howarth, Sorvel, Askey, McDonald, Lyons (Adams), Power, Sharratt |
| FAT 2 r | Feb 21 | WORCESTER CITY | W 3–2 | Askey Power McGrath(og) | 704 | Farrelly, Shepherd (Lillis), Bimson, Kendall, Howarth, Sorvel, Askey, McDonald, Alford, Power (Lyons), Sharratt |
| Lg 26 | Feb 26 | Telford U | W 3–1 | Alford(2,1p) Sorvel | 1108 | Farrelly, Thorpe, Bimson, Kendall, Howarth, Sorvel, Askey, Lillis, Alford, Power (Lyons), Sharratt |
| Lg 27 | Mar 01 | Altrincham | W 1–0 | Power | 1030 | Farrelly, Thorpe, Bimson, Kendall, Howarth, Sorvel, Askey, Lillis, Alford, Power, Sharratt |
| FAT 3 | Mar 05 | BILLINGHAM SYNTHONIA | L 0–1 | | 909 | Farrelly, Shepherd, Bimson, Kendall, Howarth, Sorvel, Askey, McDonald, Alford, Power (Lyons), Sharratt (Thorpe) |
| DC SF 1 | Mar 08 | NORTHWICH V | W 2–1 | Alford Lyons | 578 | Farrelly, Shepherd, Bimson, Kendall, Howarth, Sorvel, Askey, McDonald, Alford, Lyons, Adams |
| Lg 28 | Mar 12 | BATH C | D 0–0 | | 757 | Farrelly, Shepherd, Bimson, Kendall, Howarth, Sorvel, Askey, McDonald, Adams, Lyons (Lillis), Sharratt |
| DC SF 2 | Mar 15 | Northwich V | W 1–0 | Lillis | 1008 | Farrelly, Shepherd, Bimson, Kendall, Howarth, Sorvel, Askey, McDonald, Alford (Lyons), Lillis, Sharratt (Adams) |
| Lg 29 | Mar 19 | HALIFAX T | L 0–1 | | 1115 | Farrelly, Shepherd, Bimson, Kendall, Howarth, Sorvel, Askey (Adams), McDonald, Lillis, Power (Lyons), Sharratt |
| Lg 30 | Mar 22 | Southport | L 0–1 | | 1012 | Farrelly, Locke, Bimson (Lyons), Kendall, Howarth, Sorvel, Askey, McDonald, Lillis, Power, Sharratt |
| Lg 31 | Mar 26 | Kettering T | W 1–0 | Howarth | 2158 | Farrelly, Locke, Lillis, Kendall (Adams), Howarth, Sorvel, Lyons, McDonald, Alford, Power (Wood), Sharratt |
| Lg 32 | Mar 30 | Gateshead | L 0–1 | | 306 | Farrelly, Locke, Lillis, Adams, Howarth, Sorvel, Askey (Lyons), McDonald, Alford, Power, Sharratt |
| Lg 33 | Apr 02 | Dover A | W 2–1 | Alford(2,1p) | 942 | Farrelly, Shepherd, Lillis, Locke, Howarth, Sorvel, Askey, McDonald, Alford, Power (Powell), Adams |
| Lg 34 | Apr 09 | Slough T | D 1–1 | Howarth | 584 | Farrelly, Shepherd, Lillis, Locke, Howarth, Sorvel, Askey, McDonald, Alford, Lyons, Adams |
| DC F 1 | Apr 12 | YEOVIL T | W 4–1 | Lyons(2) McDonald Alford | 651 | Farrelly, Shepherd, Bimson (Wood), Lillis, Howarth, Sorvel, Askey, McDonald, Alford, Lyons, Adams |
| Lg 35 | Apr 16 | KIDDERMINSTER H | D 0–0 | | 1128 | Farrelly, Shepherd, Lillis, Locke, Howarth, Sorvel, Askey, McDonald, Alford, Lyons, Adams (Wood) |
| DC F 2 | Apr 19 | Yeovil T | D 0–0 | | 1241 | Farrelly, Shepherd, Lillis, Wood, Howarth, Sorvel, Askey, McDonald, Alford (Powell), Lyons, Adams |
| Lg 36 | Apr 23 | WITTON A | W 2–0 | Sorvel Lyons | 720 | Farrelly, Shepherd, Lillis, Locke, Howarth, Sorvel, Askey (Power), Wood, Alford, Lyons, Adams |
| Lg 37 | Apr 24 | Dagenham & R | D 1–1 | McDonald | 829 | Farrelly, Shepherd, Bimson, Kendall, Howarth, Sorvel, Lyons (Wood), McDonald, Alford, Powell, Adams |
| Lg 38 | Apr 26 | Halifax T | W 2–1 | Power(2) | 732 | Farrelly, Shepherd, Bimson, Lillis, Howarth, Sorvel, Lyons, McDonald, Alford (Powell), Power, Adams |
| Lg 39 | Apr 30 | YEOVIL T | L 1–2 | Howarth | 817 | Farrelly, Shepherd, Bimson, Lillis, Howarth, Sorvel, Lyons (Wood), McDonald, Powell, Power, Adams |
| Lg 40 | May 02 | WELLING U | W 1–0 | Powell | 577 | Farrelly, Shepherd, Bimson, Lillis, Howarth, Sorvel, Lyons, McDonald, Powell, Power, Adams |
| Lg 41 | May 04 | STAFFORD R | D 0–0 | | 542 | Farrelly, Shepherd, Bimson, Lillis, Howarth, Sorvel, Lyons (Wood), McDonald, Powell, Power, Adams |
| Lg 42 | May 07 | Northwich V | D 1–1 | Powell | 1002 | Farrelly, Shepherd, Bimson, Lillis, Howarth, Sorvel, Askey, McDonald, Powell, Power, Adams |

## 1994–95: GM Vauxhall Conference

| Comp | Date | Opponents | Result | Scorers | Gate | Team |
|---|---|---|---|---|---|---|
| Lg 1 | Aug 20 | WELLING U | W 3–1 | Power Askey Sorvel | 757 | Farrelly, Locke, Murray, Kendall, Howarth, Sorvel, Askey, McDonald, Tobin, Power, Lyons (Wright) |
| Lg 2 | Aug 24 | Runcorn | D 2–2 | Tobin Power | 640 | Farrelly, Locke, Murray, Kendall, Howarth, Sorvel, Askey, McDonald, Tobin, Power, Lyons |
| Lg 3 | Aug 27 | Yeovil T | W 2–1 | Lyons Power | 1680 | Farrelly, Locke (Lillis), Murray, Kendall, Howarth, Sorvel, Askey, McDonald, Tobin (Crisp), Power, Lyons |
| Lg 4 | Aug 29 | BROMSGROVE R | D 2–2 | Power(2) | 933 | Farrelly, Shepherd, Murray, Kendall, Howarth, Sorvel, Askey (Wright), Crisp, Tobin, Power, Lyons |
| Lg 5 | Sep 03 | MERTHYR T | D 0–0 | | 801 | Farrelly, Shepherd, Murray, Kendall, Howarth, Sorvel, Askey, McDonald, Tobin, Crisp, Lyons (Wood) |
| Lg 6 | Sep 06 | Telford U | L 0–2 | | 763 | Farrelly, Shepherd, Murray, Kendall, Howarth, Sorvel, Askey, McDonald, Tobin (Wood), Power, Lyons (Crisp) |
| Lg 7 | Sep 10 | KETTERING T | W 1–0 | Askey | 947 | Farrelly, Shepherd, Bimson, Kendall, Howarth, Wood, Askey (Tobin), McDonald, Crisp, Power, Lyons |
| Lg 8 | Sep 13 | KIDDERMINSTER H | L 1–3 | Wood | 718 | Farrelly, Shepherd, Bimson, Kendall, Howarth, Wood (Sorvel), Tobin, McDonald, Crisp (Murray), Power, Lyons |
| Lg 9 | Sep 17 | Stevenage B | D 1–1 | Howarth | 1243 | Farrelly, Shepherd, Bimson, Payne, Howarth, Sorvel, Askey (Murray), McDonald, Wood, Power, Lyons |
| Lg 10 | Sep 20 | SOUTHPORT | W 3–0 | Wood Power McDonald | 792 | Farrelly, Shepherd, Bimson, Payne, Howarth, Sorvel, Tobin, McDonald, Wood, Power (Crisp), Lyons |
| Lg 11 | Sep 24 | HALIFAX T | D 1–1 | Tobin | 1010 | Farrelly, Shepherd (Kendall), Bimson, Payne, Howarth, Sorvel, Tobin, McDonald, Wood (Crisp), Power, Lyons |
| Lg 12 | Oct 01 | FARNBOROUGH T | W 4–1 | Askey Power Lyons Howarth | 779 | Farrelly, Shepherd (Kendall), Bimson, Payne, Howarth, Sorvel, Askey (Tobin), McDonald, Wood, Power, Lyons |
| Lg 13 | Oct 08 | Stafford R | W 3–0 | Power Shepherd Wood | 1072 | Farrelly, Shepherd, Bimson, Payne, Howarth, Sorvel, Askey, McDonald, Wood, Power (Tobin), Lyons |
| Lg 14 | Oct 11 | Altrincham | W 2–1 | Sorvel Askey | 2275 | Farrelly, Shepherd, Bimson, Payne, Howarth, Sorvel, Askey, McDonald, Wood, Power, Lyons |
| Lg 15 | Oct 15 | YEOVIL T | W 1–0 | Askey | 1102 | Farrelly, Shepherd, Bimson, Payne, Howarth, Sorvel, Askey (Tobin), McDonald, Wood, Power, Lyons |
| FAC 4Q | Oct 22 | Bishop Auckland | D 2–2 | Lyons Sorvel | 745 | Farrelly, Shepherd, Bimson, Payne, Howarth, Sorvel, Askey, McDonald, Wood (Tobin), Power, Lyons |
| FAC 4Q r | Oct 25 | BISHOP AUCKLAND | L 0–1 | | 1086 | Farrelly, Shepherd (Kendall), Bimson, Payne, Howarth, Sorvel, Askey, McDonald, Wood, Power, Lyons (Tobin) |
| Lg 16 | Oct 29 | Northwich V | W 3–1 | Power Sorvel Askey | 1593 | Farrelly, Locke, Bimson, Kendall, Howarth, Sorvel, Askey, McDonald, Wood, Power, Tobin |
| BLT 2 | Nov 01 | RUNCORN | W 4–2 | McDonald Askey Tobin Power | 441 | Farrelly, Locke, Bimson (Murray), Payne, Howarth, Sorvel, Askey, McDonald, Wood, Power, Tobin |
| Lg 17 | Nov 05 | BATH C | W 1–0 | Howarth | 868 | Farrelly, Locke, Bimson, Payne, Howarth, Sorvel (Monk), Lyons, McDonald, Wood, Power, Tobin |
| Lg 18 | Nov 19 | Dagenham & R | W 4–0 | Midwood(2) Wood Howarth | 882 | Farrelly, Locke, Bimson, Payne, Howarth, Sorvel, Midwood, McDonald, Wood, Power, Tobin (Monk) |
| Lg 19 | Nov 26 | GATESHEAD | W 2–1 | Power(2) | 1212 | Farrelly, Locke, Bimson, Payne, Howarth, Sorvel, Askey, McDonald, Wood (Tobin), Power, Midwood |
| Lg 20 | Dec 03 | Merthyr T | W 2–1 | Power Askey | 647 | Farrelly, Locke, Bimson, Payne, Howarth, Sorvel, Askey, McDonald, Wood, Power, Midwood |
| Lg 21 | Dec 10 | WOKING | W 2–0 | Payne Monk | 2186 | Farrelly, Locke, Bimson, Payne, Howarth, Sorvel, Askey, Monk, Wood, Power, Midwood |
| BLT 3 | Dec 13 | ALTRINCHAM | W 2–1 | Sorvel Midwood | 853 | Farrelly, Locke, Bimson, Payne, Howarth, Sorvel, Askey, Monk, Wood, Power (Wright), Midwood |
| Lg 22 | Dec 17 | Farnborough T | L 0–1 | | 724 | Farrelly, Locke, Bimson, Payne, Howarth, Sorvel, Askey, Monk, Wood, Power (Wright), Midwood (Tobin) |
| Lg 23 | Dec 26 | STALYBRIDGE C | W 3–0 | Howarth(2) Wood | 2010 | Farrelly, Locke, Bimson, Payne, Howarth, Sorvel, Askey, McDonald, Wood, Power, Monk |

| Comp | Date | Opponents | Result | Scorers | Gate | Team |
|------|------|-----------|--------|---------|------|------|
| Lg 24 | Dec 31 | STAFFORD R | L 1–2 | Power | 1432 | Farrelly, Locke, Bimson, Payne, Howarth, Sorvel, Askey, McDonald, Wood, Power, Monk (Allen) |
| Lg 25 | Jan 07 | Southport | W 3–2 | Monk Sorvel Howarth(p) | 2207 | Farrelly, Locke, Bimson, Payne, Howarth, Sorvel, Allen, McDonald, Wood, Power, Monk (Lyons) |
| Lg 26 | Jan 14 | DAGENHAM & R | W 2–0 | Howarth Lyons | 1179 | Farrelly, Locke, Bimson, Payne, Howarth, Sorvel, Allen (Lyons), McDonald, Wood, Power, Monk (Tobin) |
| FAT 1 | Jan 24 | West Auckland Town | W 2–1 | Power Lyons | 581 | Farrelly, Locke, Bimson (Norman), Payne, Howarth, Sorvel, Tobin (Askey), McDonald, Wood, Power, Lyons |
| Lg 27 | Feb 04 | TELFORD U | W 2–0 | Wood Power | 1083 | Farrelly, Locke, Bimson, Payne, Howarth, Sorvel, Askey, McDonald, Wood, Power (Norman), Monk (Lyons) |
| FAT 2 | Feb 13 | Ashton United | W 5–0 | Power(2) Sorvel(2) Lyons | 1045 | Farrelly, Locke (Murray), Norman, Payne, Howarth, Sorvel, Askey, McDonald, Wood (Tobin), Power, Lyons |
| Lg 28 | Feb 18 | DOVER A | W 3–0 | Wood(2) Howarth | 1034 | Farrelly, Norman (Locke), Bradshaw, Payne, Howarth, Sorvel, Askey, McDonald, Wood, Power (Lyons), Monk |
| Lg 29 | Feb 25 | ALTRINCHAM | W 4–2 | Power(2) McDonald Howarth | 2386 | Farrelly, Norman, Bradshaw, Payne, Howarth, Sorvel, Askey, McDonald, Wood, Power (Lyons), Monk |
| FAT 3 | Mar 04 | Gateshead | W 1–0 | Lyons | 2585 | Farrelly, Norman, Locke, Payne, Howarth, Sorvel, Askey, Lyons, Wood, Power, Tobin |
| Lg 30 | Mar 07 | Halifax T | W 1–0 | Lyons | 1002 | Farrelly, Norman (Tobin), Bradshaw, Payne, Howarth, Sorvel, Askey, Lyons, Wood, Power, Monk (Murray) |
| Lg 31 | Mar 11 | NORTHWICH V | W 3–1 | Power Monk Askey | 2025 | Farrelly, Norman, Bradshaw, Payne, Howarth, Sorvel, Askey (Lyons), McDonald, Wood, Power, Monk (Tobin) |
| BLT SF 1 | Mar 14 | BROMSGROVE R | W 2–1 | Power Lyons | 660 | Farrelly, Locke, Murray, Payne, Howarth, Sorvel, Askey (Tobin), McDonald, Wood, Power, Monk (Lyons) |
| Lg 32 | Mar 21 | Kettering T | L 0–1 | | 2130 | Farrelly, Norman, Bradshaw, Payne, Howarth, Sorvel, Midwood (Lyons), McDonald, Wood, Power, Monk |
| FAT 4 | Mar 25 | WOKING | L 0–1 | | 3019 | Farrelly, Norman, Locke (Midwood), Payne, Howarth, Sorvel, Askey, McDonald, Wood, Power, Tobin (Lyons) |
| BLT SF 2 | Mar 28 | Bromsgrove R | L 1–4 | Midwood | 1118 | Farrelly, Locke, Wood, Payne, Kendall, Sorvel, Midwood, McDonald, Tobin, Lyons, Monk (McKinley) |
| Lg 33 | Apr 01 | Bromsgrove R | D 2–2 | Askey Wood | 1233 | Farrelly, Norman, Bradshaw, Payne, Howarth, Sorvel, Askey, McDonald, Wood, Wright (Monk), Marginson |
| Lg 34 | Apr 04 | Gateshead | L 1–2 | McDonald | 937 | Farrelly, Norman, Bradshaw, Payne, Howarth, Sorvel, Askey (Monk), McDonald, Wood, Wright, Marginson |
| Lg 35 | Apr 08 | Welling U | W 1–0 | Power | 802 | Farrelly, Norman (Locke), Bradshaw, Payne, Howarth, Tobin, Monk, McDonald, Midwood, Power, Marginson |
| Lg 36 | Apr 15 | RUNCORN | L 0–1 | | 1148 | Farrelly, Norman, Bradshaw, Payne, Howarth, Sorvel, Askey, McDonald, Wood, Power, Marginson (Monk) |
| Lg 37 | Apr 18 | Kidderminster H | W 2–1 | Howarth Marginson | 2273 | Farrelly, Norman, Bradshaw, Payne, Howarth, Sorvel, Askey (Monk), McDonald, Wood, Power, Marginson |
| Lg 38 | Apr 25 | Woking | L 0–1 | | 2325 | Farrelly, Norman, Bradshaw, Payne, Howarth, Sorvel, Monk (Tobin), McDonald, Wood, Power, Marginson |
| Lg 39 | Apr 29 | Bath C | L 0–1 | | 779 | Farrelly, Norman, Bradshaw, Payne, Locke, Tobin (Sorvel), Askey, McDonald, Wood, Power, Marginson (Lyons) |
| Lg 40 | Apr 30 | Dover A | D 0–0 | | 884 | Farrelly, Wood, Bradshaw, Payne, Kendall, Sorvel, Monk, McDonald, Wright, Power, Lyons |
| Lg 41 | May 02 | Stalybridge C | D 2–2 | Sorvel Wright | 1319 | Farrelly, Wood, Bradshaw, Payne, Kendall, Sorvel, Monk, McDonald, Wright, Power, Lyons |
| Lg 42 | May 06 | STEVENAGE B | L 0–3 | | 2054 | Farrelly, Norman, Bradshaw, Payne, Howarth, Sorvel (Monk), Askey, McDonald, Wood, Power, Lyons (Wright) |

## 1995–96: GM Vauxhall Conference

| Comp | Date | Opponents | Result | Scorers | Gate | Team |
|------|------|-----------|--------|---------|------|------|
| Lg 1 | Aug 19 | WOKING | W 3–2 | Lyons Coates Marginson | 1370 | Williams, Locke, Bradshaw, Payne, Howarth, Sorvel, Lyons, McDonald, Coates, Power (Cavell), Marginson |
| Lg 2 | Aug 22 | Halifax T | L 0–1 | | 1169 | Williams, Locke, Bradshaw, Payne, Howarth, Sorvel, Lyons, McDonald, Coates (Cavell), Power, Marginson |
| Lg 3 | Aug 26 | Gateshead | W 1–0 | Power | 650 | Williams, Locke, Bradshaw, Payne, Howarth, Sorvel, Lyons (Clark), McDonald, Cavell, Power, Marginson (Clark) |
| Lg 4 | Aug 28 | DAGENHAM & R | W 3–1 | Bradshaw(2) McDonald(p) | 1172 | Williams, German (Locke), Bradshaw, Payne, Howarth, Sorvel, Lyons, McDonald, Cavell, Power, Marginson |
| Lg 5 | Sep 02 | BATH C | L 0–1 | | 1225 | Williams, German, Bradshaw, Middlemass, Howarth, Sorvel, Lyons, McDonald, Cavell (Coates), Power, Marginson (Clark) |
| Lg 6 | Sep 05 | Morecambe | W 4–2 | Cavell(2) Lyons Power | 1413 | Williams, German, Bradshaw, Payne, Middlemass, Sorvel, Lyons, McDonald, Cavell, Power, Marginson (Clark) |
| Lg 7 | Sep 09 | KETTERING T | D 1–1 | Cavell | 1320 | Williams, German, Bradshaw, Payne, Howarth, Sorvel, Lyons, McDonald, Cavell, Power (Coates), Marginson (Evans) |
| Lg 8 | Sep 12 | KIDDERMINSTER H | L 0–2 | | 1202 | Williams, German, Bradshaw, Payne, Howarth, Sorvel, Lyons, McDonald, Cavell, Coates, Clark (Tobin) |
| Lg 9 | Sep 16 | Dover A | W 3–2 | Cavell(2) Power | 822 | Williams, German, Bradshaw, Payne, Howarth, Sorvel, Lyons, McDonald, Cavell, Power, Marginson (Coates) |
| Lg 10 | Sep 23 | SOUTHPORT | W 3–1 | Cavell Power Sorvel | 1282 | Williams, Locke, Bradshaw, Payne, Howarth, Sorvel, Lyons, McDonald, Cavell (Coates), Power, Clark (Marginson) |
| Lg 11 | Sep 30 | Farnborough T | L 1–6 | Coates | 740 | Williams, Locke, Bradshaw, Payne, Howarth, Sorvel, Lyons, Clark, Cavell, Coates, Tobin (Marginson) |
| Lg 12 | Oct 07 | BROMSGROVE R | W 2–1 | Lyons Cavell | 1137 | Morgan, German, Locke, Payne, Howarth, Sorvel, Lyons, McDonald, Cavell, Coates, Marginson |
| Lg 13 | Oct 10 | MORECAMBE | W 2–0 | Sorvel Coates | 1034 | Morgan, German, Locke, Payne, Howarth, Sorvel, Lyons, McDonald, Cavell, Coates, Marginson (Clark) |
| Lg 14 | Oct 14 | Slough T | D 2–2 | Howarth Cavell | 1007 | Morgan, German, Locke, Payne, Howarth, Sorvel, Lyons, McDonald, Cavell, Coates (Edey), Marginson (Monk) |
| FAC 4Q | Oct 21 | NORTHWICH V | L 0–1 | | 1707 | Williams, Edey, Locke, Payne, Howarth, Sorvel, Lyons, McDonald, Cavell, Coates (Monk), Marginson (Bradshaw) |
| Lg 15 | Oct 24 | Runcorn | D 0–0 | | 600 | Morgan, German, Bradshaw, Payne, Howarth, Edey, Lyons, Gardiner, Cavell, Coates, Sorvel |
| Lg 16 | Oct 28 | WELLING U | W 2–1 | Coates Bradshaw | 988 | Morgan, German, Bradshaw, Payne, Howarth, Edey, Lyons, Gardiner, Cavell, Coates, Sorvel |
| Lg 17 | Oct 31 | Stalybridge C | W 2–1 | Cavell Sorvel | 884 | Morgan, Edey, Bradshaw, Payne, Howarth, Sorvel, Lyons, Gardiner, Cavell, Coates, Hemmings |
| Lg 18 | Nov 04 | Hednesford T | W 1–0 | Coates | 2019 | Price, Edey, Bradshaw, Payne, Howarth, Sorvel, Lyons, Gardiner, Cavell, Coates, Hemmings |
| Lg 19 | Nov 11 | STALYBRIDGE C | W 1–0 | Lyons(p) | 1457 | Price, Edey, Bradshaw, Payne, Howarth, Sorvel, Lyons, Gardiner, Cavell, Coates, Hemmings |
| Lg 20 | Nov 18 | Altrincham | W 4–0 | Lyons(2) Coates(2) | 1648 | Price, Edey, Bradshaw, Payne, Howarth, Sorvel, Lyons, Gardiner, Cavell, Coates, Hemmings |
| Lg 21 | Nov 25 | FARNBOROUGH T | W 1–0 | Sorvel | 1721 | Price, Edey, Bradshaw, Payne, Howarth, Sorvel, Lyons, Gardiner, Cavell (Marginson), Coates, Hemmings |
| SC 2 | Nov 28 | KIDDERMINSTER H | W 4–1 | Coates(2) Cavell Lyons(p) | 566 | Price, Edey, Bradshaw, Payne, Howarth, Sorvel, Lyons, Gardiner, Cavell, Coates (Hutchinson), Hemmings |
| Lg 22 | Dec 02 | Stevenage B | L 0–4 | | 2021 | Price, Edey, Bradshaw, Payne, Howarth, Sorvel, Lyons, Gardiner, Cavell (Hutchinson), Coates, Hemmings |
| Lg 23 | Dec 16 | GATESHEAD | W 1–0 | Howarth | 1161 | Price, Edey, Bradshaw, Payne, Howarth, Sorvel, Lyons (Hutchinson), Gardiner, Coates (Cavell), Power, Hemmings |
| Lg 24 | Jan 06 | STEVENAGE B | D 0–0 | | 2126 | Price, Edey, Bradshaw, Payne, Howarth, Sorvel, Hutchinson, Gardiner, Hulme, Power, Hemmings (Lyons) |

*Saga of the Silkmen*

| Comp | Date | Opponents | Result | Scorers | Gate | Team |
|------|------|-----------|--------|---------|------|------|
| Lg 25 | Jan 13 | Kidderminster H | W 4–0 | Power(3) Gardiner | 2703 | Price, Edey, Bradshaw, Payne, Howarth, Sorvel, Lyons, Gardiner, Hulme (Coates), Power, Hemmings |
| FAT 1 | Jan 20 | RUNCORN | W 1–0 | Power | 1401 | Price, Edey, Bradshaw, Payne, Howarth, Sorvel, Lyons, Gardiner, Hulme (Coates), Power, Hemmings |
| Lg 26 | Jan 30 | ALTRINCHAM | L 2–3 | Power Hemmings | 1301 | Price, Edey, Bradshaw, Payne, Howarth, Sorvel, Lyons, Gardiner (Hutchinson), Hulme, Power, Hemmings |
| FAT 2 | Feb 10 | PURFLEET | W 2–1 | Payne Bradshaw | 1003 | Price, Locke, Bradshaw, Payne, Edey, Sorvel, Lyons (Hutchinson), Gardiner (Wood), Hulme, Power (Coates), Hemmings |
| Lg 27 | Feb 13 | TELFORD U | W 1–0 | Lyons | 866 | Morgan, Locke, Bradshaw, Payne, Edey, Sorvel, Lyons, Wood (Gardiner), Hulme, Power, Hemmings |
| Lg 28 | Feb 17 | Bromsgrove R | L 0–1 | | 1481 | Morgan, Tinson, Bradshaw, Payne, Howarth, Sorvel (Coates), Lyons (Hutchinson), Wood, Hulme, Power, Hemmings |
| Lg 29 | Feb 24 | RUNCORN | W 1–0 | Hutchinson | 1410 | Morgan, Tinson, Bradshaw, Payne, Howarth, Sorvel, Hutchinson, Wood, Coates, Power, Hemmings |
| FAT 3 | Mar 02 | SUDBURY TOWN | W 1–0 | Coates | 1140 | Price, Edey, Bradshaw (Gardiner), Payne, Howarth, Sorvel, Hutchinson, Wood, Coates, Power (Cavell), Hemmings |
| SC 3 | Mar 05 | Morecambe | W 4–1 | Hulme(2) Payne Hemmings | 625 | Price, Edey, Bradshaw, Payne, Howarth, Sorvel, Wood (Norman), Hulme (Gardiner), Coates (Cavell), Power, Hemmings |
| Lg 30 | Mar 09 | HALIFAX T | W 7–0 | Power(2) Hulme(2) Hemmings Payne Lyons(p) | 1348 | Price, Tinson, Bradshaw, Payne (Edey), Howarth, Sorvel (Lyons), Wood, Hulme (Gardiner), Coates, Power, Hemmings |
| Lg 31 | Mar 16 | Kettering T | D 2–2 | Wood Power | 1433 | Price, Tinson, Bradshaw, Payne, Howarth, Sorvel, Wood, Hulme, Coates (Hutchinson), Power, Hemmings |
| SC SF 1 | Mar 19 | Southport | D 4–4 | Hemmings Power Sorvel Cochran(og) | 561 | Price, Norman, Bradshaw, Payne, Edey, Sorvel, Wood, Gardiner (Tobin), Cavell, Power, Hemmings |
| FAT 4 | Mar 23 | Gresley Rovers | W 2–0 | Bradshaw Power | 1727 | Price, Edey, Bradshaw, Payne, Howarth, Sorvel, Wood, Hulme (Hutchinson), Coates, Power, Hemmings |
| Lg 32 | Mar 26 | NORTHWICH V | D 0–0 | | 1117 | Price, Tinson (Edey), Bradshaw, Payne, Howarth, Sorvel (Hutchinson), Wood, Hulme, Coates (Cavell), Power, Hemmings |
| Lg 33 | Mar 30 | Telford U | W 2–1 | Coates(2) | 1015 | Price, Tinson, Gardiner, Edey, Howarth, Sorvel, Wood, Hutchinson (Lyons), Coates, Cavell, Hemmings |
| SC SF 2 | Apr 03 | SOUTHPORT | W 2–1 | Coates Power | 510 | Price, Edey, Gardiner, Payne, Howarth, Sorvel (Lyons), Wood, Hulme, Coates, Power, Hemmings |
| Lg 34 | Apr 06 | Woking | L 2–3 | Power(2) | 4583 | Price, Tinson, Gardiner, Payne, Howarth, Sorvel, Wood (Lyons), Hulme, Coates, Power, Hemmings |
| Lg 35 | Apr 08 | DOVER A | L 0–1 | | 1482 | Price, Edey, Gardiner, Payne, Tinson, Sorvel, Wood (Lyons), Hulme, Coates (Cavell), Power, Hemmings |
| FAT SF 1 | Apr 13 | CHORLEY | W 3–1 | Power Coates Thorpe(og) | 2260 | Price, Edey, Gardiner, Payne, Howarth, Sorvel, Lyons, Hulme, Coates, Power, Hemmings |
| Lg 36 | Apr 16 | Northwich V | W 2–1 | Tinson Wood | 936 | Price, Edey, Gardiner, Tinson, Howarth, Sorvel, Lyons (Burr), Hulme, Wood, Cavell, Hemmings (Hutchinson) |
| FAT SF 2 | Apr 20 | Chorley | D 1–1 | Sorvel | 3048 | Price, Edey, Gardiner, Payne, Howarth, Sorvel, Wood, Hulme, Coates, Power, Hemmings (Hutchinson) |
| Lg 37 | Apr 22 | Southport | L 1–2 | Lyons(p) | 736 | Price, Tinson, Edey, Payne, Howarth, Sorvel, Lyons, Wood, Cavell (Coates), Burr, Hemmings |
| SC F 1 | Apr 24 | BROMSGROVE R | D 1–1 | Coates | 547 | Price, Edey, Gardiner, Payne, Howarth, Sorvel, Lyons, Wood, Cavell, Coates, Hemmings |
| Lg 38 | Apr 27 | Dagenham & R | L 0–3 | | 660 | Price, Edey, Gardiner, Payne, Tinson, Sorvel, Hutchinson (Lyons), Hulme (Wood), Coates, Cavell (Burr), Hemmings |
| Lg 39 | Apr 28 | Welling U | W 2–1 | Hulme Wood | 558 | Price, Tinson, Gardiner, Payne, Howarth, Sorvel, Lyons, Hulme, Wood, Burr, Hemmings |
| Lg 40 | Apr 30 | Bath C | D 1–1 | Hulme | 361 | Price, Edey, Gardiner, Payne, Howarth, Sorvel, Tinson, Hulme, Cavell, Burr, Hemmings |

| Comp | Date | Opponents | Result | Scorers | Gate | Team |
|------|------|-----------|--------|---------|------|------|
| Lg 41 | May 02 | SLOUGH T | D 1–1 | Coates | 591 | Price, Edey, Gardiner, Tinson, Howarth, Sorvel, Lyons, Hulme, Cavell, Wood, Hemmings |
| Lg 42 | May 04 | HEDNESFORD T | D 1–1 | Coates | 1246 | Price, Tinson, Bradshaw, Payne, Howarth (Edey), Sorvel, Lyons, Hulme, Coates, Wood (Cavell), Hemmings |
| SC F 2 | May 06 | Bromsgrove R | L 1–3 | Sorvel(p) | 1341 | Price, Norman, Bradshaw (Lyons), Payne, Edey, Sorvel, Gardiner, Hulme (Tobin), Coates, Wood, Hemmings |
| FAT F | May 19 | Northwich V | W 3–1 | Payne Burgess(og) Hemmings | 8672 | Price, Edey, Gardiner, Payne, Howarth, Sorvel, Lyons, Wood (Hulme), Coates, Power, Hemmings (Cavell) |

## 1996–1997: GM Vauxhall Conference

| Comp | Date | Opponents | Result | Scorers | Gate | Team |
|------|------|-----------|--------|---------|------|------|
| Lg 1 | Aug 17 | KETTERING T | W 2–0 | Power Gardiner | 1250 | Price, Tinson, Gardiner, Payne, Howarth, Sorvel, Askey, Wood, Mitchell, Power, Hemmings |
| Lg 2 | Aug 21 | Morecambe | L 0–1 | | 1106 | Price, Tinson, Gardiner, Payne, Howarth, Sorvel, Askey, Wood, Mitchell, Power, Hemmings (Williams) |
| Lg 3 | Aug 24 | Farnborough T | W 1–0 | Wood | 647 | Price, Tinson, Gardiner, Payne, Howarth, Sorvel, Askey (Williams), Wood, Mitchell, Power, Hemmings |
| Lg 4 | Aug 26 | STEVENAGE B | W 2–1 | Power(2) | 1723 | Price, Tinson, Gardiner, Payne, Howarth, Sorvel, Askey, Wood, Mitchell (Edey), Power (Williams), Hemmings |
| Lg 5 | Aug 31 | DOVER A | W 1–0 | Sorvel | 1209 | Price, Tinson, Gardiner, Payne, Howarth, Sorvel, Askey (Williams), Wood, Mitchell, Power, Hemmings |
| Lg 6 | Sep 03 | Rushden & D | D 1–1 | Payne | 2242 | Price, Tinson, Gardiner, Payne, Howarth, Sorvel, Askey, Wood, Mitchell (Williams), Power, Hemmings (Edey) |
| Lg 7 | Sep 07 | Bromsgrove R | W 3–0 | Williams Askey Wood | 833 | Price, Tinson, Gardiner, Payne, Howarth, Sorvel, Askey, Wood, Mitchell, Williams (Mottram), Hemmings |
| Lg 8 | Sep 10 | MORECAMBE | D 0–0 | | 1161 | Price, Tinson, Gardiner, Payne, Edey, Sorvel, Askey, Wood, Mitchell (Mottram), Williams, Hemmings |
| Lg 9 | Sep 14 | Kidderminster H | D 0–0 | | 2331 | Price, Tinson, Gardiner (Bradshaw), Payne, Edey, Sorvel, Mitchell (Hulme), Wood, Williams, Power (Mottram), Hemmings |
| Lg 10 | Sep 21 | BATH C | D 2–2 | Power Williams | 1091 | Price, Tinson, Gardiner (Bradshaw), Payne, Edey, Sorvel, Mitchell, Wood, Williams, Power, Hemmings |
| Lg 11 | Sep 25 | Gateshead | D 0–0 | | 487 | Price, Tinson (Edey), Bradshaw, Payne, Howarth, Sorvel, Askey, Wood (Circuit), Williams (Mottram), Power, Hemmings |
| Lg 12 | Sep 28 | Northwich V | L 1–2 | Mottram | 1527 | Price, Edey, Bradshaw, Payne, Howarth, Sorvel, Askey (Mottram), Wood (Circuit), Williams, Power, Hemmings (Mitchell) |
| Lg 13 | Oct 01 | HALIFAX T | W 1–0 | Circuit | 951 | Price, Edey, Bradshaw, Payne, Howarth, Sorvel (Wood), Askey, Circuit, Mottram, Power, Mitchell (Hemmings) |
| Lg 14 | Oct 05 | Woking | W 3–2 | Wood(2) Williams | 2849 | Price, Edey, Bradshaw (Circuit), Payne, Howarth, Sorvel, Askey, Wood, Mottram, Williams (Power), Hemmings |
| Lg 15 | Oct 15 | STALYBRIDGE C | W 2–0 | Mottram(p) Hemmings | 792 | Price, Edey, Bradshaw, Payne, Howarth, Sorvel, Askey, Wood, Mottram (Coates), Williams, Hemmings |
| Lg 16 | Oct 19 | WELLING U | D 1–1 | Hemmings | 1102 | Price, Tinson, Bradshaw, Payne, Howarth, Sorvel, Askey, Wood (Circuit), Mottram, Williams (Power), Hemmings |
| Lg 17 | Oct 26 | NORTHWICH V | L 0–1 | | 1375 | Price, Tinson, Bradshaw, Payne, Howarth, Sorvel (Circuit), Williams, Wood, Mottram (Power), Coates, Hemmings |
| Lg 18 | Nov 02 | Telford U | W 3–0 | Mitchell(2) Power | 1015 | Price, Tinson, Edey, Payne, Howarth, Sorvel, Circuit, Wood, Coates, Power, Williams (Mitchell) |
| Lg 19 | Nov 09 | Southport | W 5–1 | Mitchell Power Wood Sorvel Bradshaw | 1546 | Price, Tinson (Bradshaw), Edey, Payne, Howarth, Sorvel, Circuit, Wood, Coates (Mottram), Power, Mitchell |
| FAC 1 | Nov 16 | ROCHDALE | L 0–2 | | 3134 | Oakes, Tinson, Edey, Payne, Howarth, Sorvel, Circuit (Bradshaw), Wood, Coates (Williams), Power, Mitchell |
| Lg 20 | Nov 23 | HAYES | W 1–0 | Askey | 909 | Morgan, Tinson, Edey, Payne, Howarth, Sorvel (Bradshaw), Circuit, Wood, Coates (Askey), Power, Mitchell |

| Comp | Date | Opponents | Result | Scorers | Gate | Team |
|------|------|-----------|--------|---------|------|------|
| Lg 21 | Nov 30 | Slough T | D 0–0 | | 1096 | Morgan, Tinson, Edey, Payne, Howarth, Sorvel, Askey, Wood, Circuit (Coates), Power, Mitchell (Williams) |
| SC 2 | Dec 07 | Altrincham | W 1–0 | Sorvel | 903 | Morgan, Tinson, Edey, Payne, Howarth, Sorvel, Askey, Wood, Coates, Power, Bradshaw (Circuit) |
| Lg 22 | Dec 10 | KIDDERMINSTER H | L 0–1 | | 1606 | Morgan, Tinson, Edey, Payne, Howarth, Sorvel, Askey, Wood, O'Reilly (Coates), Power, Mitchell |
| Lg 23 | Dec 14 | Stalybridge C | W 1–0 | Tinson | 887 | Morgan, Tinson, Edey, Payne, Howarth, Sorvel, Askey, Wood, O'Reilly, Power, Mitchell (Bradshaw) |
| SC 3 | Dec 17 | BROMSGROVE R | W 1–0 | Coates | 347 | Morgan, Tinson (Bradshaw), Edey, Payne, Howarth, Sorvel, Askey, Wood, O'Reilly (Coates), Power, Mitchell |
| Lg 24 | Dec 21 | TELFORD U | W 2–1 | Howarth Coates | 1054 | Morgan, Tinson, Edey (Gardiner), Payne, Howarth, Sorvel, Askey, Circuit, O'Reilly (Coates), Power, Mitchell |
| FAT 1 | Jan 18 | Kidderminster H | L 0–3 | | 2815 | Price, Tinson, Gardiner, Payne, Howarth, Sorvel, Askey, Wood, Mottram, Williams, Mitchell (Byrne) |
| Lg 25 | Jan 25 | SLOUGH T | W 2–0 | Wood Power | 1013 | Price, Tinson, Gardiner, Payne, Howarth, Sorvel, Askey, Wood, Landon, Power, Byrne |
| Lg 26 | Jan 28 | Altrincham | W 1–0 | Power | 1285 | Price, Tinson, Gardiner, Payne, Howarth, Sorvel, Askey, Wood, Landon, Power, Byrne (Bradshaw) |
| Lg 27 | Feb 01 | Hayes | W 2–0 | Landon(p) Howarth | 604 | Price, Bradshaw, Gardiner, Payne, Howarth, Sorvel, Askey, Wood, Landon, Power (Davenport), Byrne |
| Lg 28 | Feb 08 | Dover A | L 1–2 | Sorvel | 948 | Price, Tinson, Bradshaw, Payne, Howarth, Sorvel, Askey (Mitchell), Wood, Landon, Power (Davenport), Byrne |
| Lg 29 | Feb 11 | HEDNESFORD T | W 4–0 | Landon(2,1p) Wood Power | 1003 | Price, Tinson, Gardiner (Bradshaw), Payne, Howarth, Sorvel, Davenport (Askey), Wood, Landon, Power, Byrne |
| Lg 30 | Feb 15 | RUSHDEN & D | W 2–1 | Wood Byrne | 1304 | Price, Tinson, Bradshaw (Askey), Payne, Howarth, Sorvel, Davenport , Wood, Landon, Power (Williams), Byrne |
| Lg 31 | Feb 22 | Bath C | W 3–0 | Wood Byrne Askey | 955 | Price, Tinson (Gardiner), Edey, Payne, Howarth, Sorvel, Askey (Williams), Wood, Davenport, Mitchell, Byrne |
| Lg 32 | Mar 01 | FARNBOROUGH T | W 3–0 | Wood Mitchell Byrne | 1431 | Price, Tinson, Edey, Payne, Howarth, Sorvel, Askey, Wood (Gardiner), Davenport (Williams), Mitchell, Byrne |
| Lg 33 | Mar 08 | Welling U | W 3–0 | Davenport Askey Byrne | 874 | Price, Tinson, Edey, Payne, Howarth, Sorvel, Askey, Wood, Davenport, Power, Byrne |
| Lg 34 | Mar 15 | SOUTHPORT | W 3–2 | Byrne(2) Askey | 1601 | Price, Tinson, Edey, Payne, Howarth, Sorvel, Askey, Wood, Davenport, Power (Williams), Byrne |
| SC SF 1 | Mar 18 | Morecambe | W 2–0 | Byrne Ohandjanian | 513 | Price, Tinson, Edey, Payne, Howarth, Sorvel, Williams, Wood, Davenport (Levendis), Ohandjanian (Peel), Byrne (Bradshaw) |
| Lg 35 | Mar 22 | GATESHEAD | W 3–0 | Power Davenport Askey | 1763 | Price, Tinson, Edey, Payne, Howarth, Sorvel, Askey (Williams), Wood, Davenport, Power, Byrne |
| SC SF 2 | Mar 25 | MORECAMBE | W 4–1 | Sorvel(3,1p) Wood | 826 | Price, Tinson (Bradshaw), Edey, Payne, Howarth, Sorvel, Mitchell, Wood, Williams (Peel), Ohandjanian, Byrne (Levendis) |
| Lg 36 | Mar 29 | Stevenage B | W 3–2 | Wood(2) Williams(p) | 5760 | Price, Tinson, Edey, Payne, Howarth, Sorvel, Askey, Wood, Ohandjanian (Williams), Power, Byrne |
| Lg 37 | Mar 31 | Hednesford T | L 1–4 | Wood | 2177 | Price, Tinson, Edey (Bradshaw), Payne, Howarth, Sorvel, Askey, Wood, Davenport (Mitchell), Power (Williams), Byrne |
| Lg 38 | Apr 05 | ALTRINCHAM | D 1–1 | Wood | 2383 | Price, Tinson, Edey, Payne, Howarth, Sorvel, Askey, Wood, Davenport (Mitchell), Power, Byrne |
| SC F 1 | Apr 12 | KIDDERMINSTER H | D 1–1 | Davenport | 1320 | Price, Tinson (Levendis), Edey , Payne, Howarth, Bradshaw, Davenport, Wood, Williams, Power (Ohandjanian), Mitchell |
| Lg 39 | Apr 22 | WOKING | W 5–0 | Davenport Power Sorvel Askey Howarth | 1826 | Price, Edey, Bradshaw, Payne, Howarth, Sorvel, Askey (Williams), Wood, Davenport (Mitchell), Power (Peel), Byrne |
| Lg 40 | Apr 26 | BROMSGROVE R | W 4–0 | Williams(2) Davenport (p) Payne | 3004 | Price, Tinson, Edey, Payne, Howarth, Sorvel, Askey (Mitchell), Wood, Davenport (Peel), Williams, Byrne (Bradshaw) |

| Comp | Date | Opponents | Result | Scorers | Gate | Team |
|------|------|-----------|--------|---------|------|------|
| SC F 2 | Apr 28 | Kidderminster H | D 0–0 | | 2212 | Price, Tinson, Edey, Payne, Howarth, Sorvel (Gee), Mitchell (Ohandjanian), Levendis, Williams, Power, Bradshaw (Peel) |
| Lg 41 | Apr 30 | Halifax T | D 3–3 | Byrne Sorvel Davenport | 2191 | Price, Tinson, Edey, Payne, Howarth, Sorvel, Askey, Wood, Davenport, Power, Byrne |
| Lg 42 | May 03 | Kettering T | W 4–1 | Byrne(3) Davenport | 3461 | Price, Tinson, Edey, Bradshaw (Gee), Howarth, Sorvel, Askey, Wood, Davenport (Williams), Power, Byrne |

# APPENDIX 5

# *Conference League Tables, 1987–1997*

## 1987–88: GM VAUXHALL CONFERENCE

| | P | W | D | L | F | A | Pts |
|---|---|---|---|---|---|---|---|
| Lincoln City | 42 | 24 | 10 | 8 | 86 | 48 | 82 |
| Barnet | 42 | 23 | 11 | 8 | 93 | 45 | 80 |
| Kettering Town | 42 | 22 | 9 | 11 | 68 | 48 | 75 |
| Runcorn | 42 | 21 | 11 | 10 | 68 | 47 | 74 |
| Telford United | 42 | 20 | 10 | 12 | 65 | 50 | 70 |
| Stafford Rangers | 42 | 20 | 9 | 13 | 79 | 58 | 69 |
| Kidderminster Harriers | 42 | 18 | 15 | 9 | 75 | 66 | 69 |
| Sutton United | 42 | 16 | 18 | 8 | 77 | 54 | 66 |
| Maidstone United | 42 | 18 | 9 | 15 | 79 | 64 | 63 |
| Weymouth | 42 | 18 | 9 | 15 | 53 | 43 | 63 |
| Macclesfield Town | 42 | 18 | 9 | 15 | 64 | 62 | 63 |
| Enfield | 42 | 15 | 10 | 17 | 68 | 78 | 55 |
| Cheltenham Town | 42 | 11 | 20 | 11 | 64 | 67 | 53 |
| Altrincham | 42 | 14 | 10 | 18 | 59 | 59 | 52 |
| Fisher Athletic | 42 | 13 | 13 | 16 | 58 | 61 | 52 |
| Boston United | 42 | 14 | 7 | 21 | 60 | 75 | 49 |
| Northwich Victoria | 42 | 10 | 17 | 15 | 46 | 57 | 47 |
| Wycombe Wanderers | 42 | 11 | 13 | 18 | 50 | 76 | 46 |
| Welling United | 42 | 11 | 9 | 22 | 50 | 72 | 42 |
| Bath City | 42 | 9 | 10 | 23 | 48 | 76 | 37 |
| Wealdstone | 42 | 5 | 17 | 20 | 39 | 76 | 32 |
| Dagenham | 42 | 5 | 6 | 31 | 37 | 104 | 21 |

## 1988–89: GM VAUXHALL CONFERENCE

| | P | W | D | L | F | A | Pts |
|---|---|---|---|---|---|---|---|
| Maidstone United | 40 | 25 | 9 | 6 | 92 | 46 | 84 |
| Kettering Town | 40 | 23 | 7 | 10 | 56 | 39 | 76 |
| Boston United | 40 | 22 | 8 | 10 | 61 | 51 | 74 |
| Wycombe Wanderers | 40 | 20 | 11 | 9 | 68 | 52 | 71 |
| Kidderminster Harriers | 40 | 21 | 6 | 13 | 68 | 57 | 69 |
| Runcorn | 40 | 19 | 8 | 13 | 77 | 53 | 65 |
| Macclesfield Town | 40 | 17 | 10 | 13 | 63 | 57 | 61 |
| Barnet | 40 | 18 | 7 | 15 | 64 | 69 | 61 |
| Yeovil Town | 40 | 15 | 11 | 14 | 68 | 67 | 56 |
| Northwich Victoria | 40 | 14 | 11 | 15 | 64 | 65 | 53 |
| Welling United | 40 | 14 | 11 | 15 | 45 | 46 | 53 |
| Sutton United | 40 | 12 | 15 | 13 | 64 | 54 | 51 |
| Enfield | 40 | 14 | 8 | 18 | 62 | 65 | 50 |
| Altrincham | 40 | 13 | 10 | 17 | 51 | 61 | 49 |
| Cheltenham Town | 40 | 12 | 12 | 16 | 55 | 58 | 48 |
| Telford United | 40 | 13 | 9 | 18 | 37 | 43 | 48 |
| Chorley | 40 | 13 | 6 | 21 | 57 | 71 | 45 |
| Fisher Athletic | 40 | 10 | 11 | 19 | 55 | 65 | 41 |
| Stafford Rangers | 40 | 11 | 7 | 22 | 49 | 74 | 40 |
| Aylesbury United | 40 | 9 | 9 | 22 | 43 | 71 | 36 |
| Weymouth | 40 | 7 | 10 | 23 | 37 | 70 | 31 |

## 1989–90: GM VAUXHALL CONFERENCE

| | P | W | D | L | F | A | Pts |
|---|---|---|---|---|---|---|---|
| Darlington | 42 | 26 | 9 | 7 | 76 | 25 | 87 |
| Barnet | 42 | 26 | 7 | 9 | 81 | 41 | 85 |
| Runcorn | 42 | 19 | 13 | 10 | 79 | 62 | 70 |
| Macclesfield Town | 42 | 17 | 15 | 10 | 56 | 41 | 66 |
| Kettering Town | 42 | 18 | 12 | 12 | 66 | 53 | 66 |
| Welling United | 42 | 18 | 10 | 14 | 62 | 50 | 64 |
| Yeovil Town | 42 | 17 | 12 | 13 | 62 | 54 | 63 |
| Sutton United | 42 | 19 | 6 | 17 | 68 | 64 | 63 |
| Merthyr Tydfil | 42 | 16 | 14 | 12 | 67 | 63 | 62 |
| Wycombe Wanderers | 42 | 17 | 10 | 15 | 64 | 56 | 61 |
| Cheltenham Town | 42 | 16 | 11 | 15 | 58 | 60 | 59 |
| Telford United | 42 | 15 | 13 | 14 | 56 | 63 | 58 |
| Kidderminster Harriers | 42 | 15 | 9 | 18 | 64 | 67 | 54 |
| Barrow | 42 | 12 | 16 | 14 | 51 | 67 | 52 |
| Northwich Victoria | 42 | 15 | 5 | 22 | 51 | 67 | 50 |
| Altrincham | 42 | 12 | 13 | 17 | 49 | 48 | 49 |
| Stafford Rangers | 42 | 12 | 12 | 18 | 50 | 62 | 48 |
| Boston United | 42 | 13 | 8 | 21 | 48 | 67 | 47 |
| Fisher Athletic | 42 | 13 | 7 | 22 | 55 | 79 | 46 |
| Chorley | 42 | 13 | 6 | 23 | 42 | 67 | 45 |
| Farnborough Town | 42 | 10 | 12 | 20 | 60 | 73 | 42 |
| Enfield | 42 | 10 | 6 | 26 | 52 | 89 | 36 |

## 1990–91: GM Vauxhall Conference

| | P | W | D | L | F | A | Pts |
|---|---|---|---|---|---|---|---|
| Barnet | 42 | 26 | 9 | 7 | 103 | 52 | 87 |
| Colchester United | 42 | 25 | 10 | 7 | 68 | 35 | 85 |
| Altrincham | 42 | 23 | 13 | 6 | 87 | 46 | 82 |
| Kettering Town | 42 | 23 | 11 | 10 | 75 | 46 | 74 |
| Wycombe Wanderers | 42 | 21 | 11 | 10 | 75 | 46 | 74 |
| Telford United | 42 | 20 | 7 | 15 | 62 | 52 | 67 |
| Macclesfield Town | 42 | 17 | 12 | 13 | 63 | 52 | 63 |
| Runcorn | 42 | 16 | 10 | 16 | 69 | 67 | 58 |
| Merthyr Tydfil | 42 | 16 | 9 | 17 | 62 | 61 | 57 |
| Barrow | 42 | 15 | 12 | 15 | 59 | 65 | 57 |
| Welling United | 42 | 13 | 15 | 14 | 55 | 57 | 54 |
| Northwich Victoria | 42 | 13 | 13 | 16 | 65 | 75 | 52 |
| Kidderminster Harriers | 42 | 14 | 10 | 18 | 56 | 67 | 52 |
| Yeovil Town | 42 | 13 | 11 | 18 | 58 | 58 | 50 |
| Stafford Rangers | 42 | 12 | 14 | 16 | 48 | 51 | 50 |
| Cheltenham Town | 42 | 12 | 12 | 18 | 54 | 72 | 48 |
| Gateshead | 42 | 14 | 6 | 22 | 52 | 92 | 48 |
| Boston United | 42 | 12 | 11 | 19 | 55 | 69 | 47 |
| Slough Town | 42 | 13 | 6 | 23 | 51 | 80 | 45 |
| Bath City | 42 | 10 | 12 | 20 | 55 | 61 | 42 |
| Sutton United | 42 | 10 | 9 | 23 | 62 | 82 | 39 |
| Fisher Athletic | 42 | 5 | 15 | 22 | 38 | 79 | 30 |

## 1991–92: GM Vauxhall Conference

| | P | W | D | L | F | A | Pts |
|---|---|---|---|---|---|---|---|
| Colchester United | 42 | 18 | 10 | 4 | 98 | 40 | 94 |
| Wycombe Wanderers | 42 | 30 | 4 | 8 | 84 | 35 | 94 |
| Kettering Town | 42 | 20 | 13 | 9 | 72 | 50 | 73 |
| Merthyr Tydfil | 42 | 18 | 14 | 10 | 59 | 56 | 68 |
| Farnborough Town | 42 | 18 | 12 | 12 | 68 | 53 | 66 |
| Telford United | 42 | 19 | 7 | 16 | 62 | 66 | 64 |
| Redbridge Forest | 42 | 18 | 9 | 15 | 69 | 56 | 63 |
| Boston United | 42 | 16 | 9 | 15 | 71 | 66 | 63 |
| Bath City | 42 | 16 | 12 | 14 | 54 | 51 | 60 |
| Witton Albion | 42 | 16 | 10 | 16 | 63 | 60 | 58 |
| Northwich Victoria | 42 | 16 | 6 | 20 | 63 | 58 | 54 |
| Welling United | 42 | 14 | 12 | 16 | 69 | 79 | 54 |
| Macclesfield Town | 42 | 13 | 13 | 16 | 50 | 50 | 52 |
| Gateshead | 42 | 12 | 12 | 18 | 49 | 57 | 48 |
| Yeovil Town | 42 | 11 | 14 | 17 | 40 | 49 | 47 |
| Runcorn | 42 | 11 | 13 | 18 | 50 | 63 | 46 |
| Stafford Rangers | 42 | 10 | 16 | 16 | 41 | 59 | 46 |
| Altrincham | 42 | 11 | 12 | 19 | 61 | 82 | 45 |
| Kidderminster Harriers | 42 | 12 | 9 | 21 | 56 | 77 | 45 |
| Slough Town | 42 | 13 | 6 | 23 | 56 | 82 | 45 |
| Cheltenham Town | 42 | 10 | 13 | 19 | 56 | 82 | 43 |
| Barrow | 42 | 8 | 14 | 20 | 52 | 72 | 38 |

## 1992–93 GM Vauxhall Conference

| | P | W | D | L | F | A | Pts |
|---|---|---|---|---|---|---|---|
| Wycombe Wanderers | 42 | 24 | 11 | 7 | 84 | 37 | 83 |
| Bromsgrove Rovers | 42 | 18 | 14 | 10 | 67 | 49 | 68 |
| Dagenham & Redbridge | 42 | 19 | 11 | 12 | 75 | 47 | 67 |
| Yeovil Town | 42 | 18 | 12 | 12 | 59 | 49 | 66 |
| Slough Town | 42 | 18 | 11 | 13 | 60 | 55 | 65 |
| Stafford Rangers | 42 | 18 | 10 | 14 | 55 | 47 | 64 |
| Bath City | 42 | 15 | 14 | 13 | 53 | 46 | 59 |
| Woking | 42 | 17 | 8 | 17 | 58 | 62 | 59 |
| Kidderminster Harriers | 42 | 14 | 16 | 12 | 60 | 60 | 58 |
| Altrincham | 42 | 15 | 13 | 14 | 49 | 52 | 58 |
| Northwich Victoria | 42 | 16 | 8 | 18 | 68 | 55 | 56 |
| Stalybridge Celtic | 42 | 13 | 17 | 12 | 48 | 55 | 56 |
| Kettering Town | 42 | 14 | 13 | 15 | 61 | 63 | 55 |
| Gateshead | 42 | 14 | 10 | 18 | 53 | 56 | 52 |
| Telford United | 42 | 14 | 10 | 18 | 55 | 60 | 52 |
| Merthyr Tydfil | 42 | 14 | 10 | 18 | 51 | 79 | 52 |
| Witton Albion | 42 | 11 | 17 | 14 | 62 | 65 | 50 |
| Macclesfield Town | 42 | 12 | 13 | 17 | 40 | 50 | 49 |
| Runcorn | 42 | 13 | 10 | 19 | 58 | 76 | 49 |
| Welling United | 42 | 12 | 12 | 18 | 57 | 72 | 48 |
| Farnborough Town | 42 | 12 | 11 | 19 | 68 | 87 | 47 |
| Boston United | 42 | 9 | 13 | 20 | 50 | 69 | 40 |

## 1993–94: GM Vauxhall Conference

| | P | W | D | L | F | A | Pts |
|---|---|---|---|---|---|---|---|
| Kidderminster Harriers | 42 | 22 | 9 | 11 | 63 | 35 | 75 |
| Kettering Town | 42 | 19 | 15 | 8 | 46 | 24 | 72 |
| Woking | 42 | 18 | 13 | 11 | 58 | 58 | 67 |
| Southport | 42 | 18 | 12 | 12 | 57 | 51 | 66 |
| Runcorn | 42 | 14 | 19 | 9 | 63 | 57 | 61 |
| Dagenham & Redbridge | 42 | 15 | 14 | 13 | 62 | 54 | 59 |
| Macclesfield Town | 42 | 16 | 11 | 15 | 48 | 49 | 59 |
| Dover Athletic | 42 | 17 | 7 | 18 | 48 | 49 | 58 |
| Stafford Rangers | 42 | 14 | 15 | 13 | 56 | 52 | 57 |
| Altrincham | 42 | 16 | 9 | 17 | 41 | 42 | 57 |
| Gateshead | 42 | 15 | 12 | 15 | 45 | 53 | 57 |
| Bath City | 42 | 13 | 17 | 12 | 47 | 38 | 56 |
| Halifax Town | 42 | 13 | 16 | 13 | 55 | 49 | 55 |
| Stalybridge Celtic | 42 | 14 | 12 | 16 | 54 | 55 | 54 |
| Northwich Victoria | 42 | 11 | 19 | 12 | 44 | 45 | 52 |
| Welling United | 42 | 13 | 12 | 17 | 41 | 49 | 51 |
| Telford United | 42 | 13 | 12 | 17 | 41 | 49 | 51 |
| Bromsgrove Rovers | 42 | 12 | 15 | 15 | 54 | 66 | 51 |
| Yeovil Town | 42 | 14 | 9 | 19 | 49 | 62 | 51 |
| Merthyr Tydfil | 42 | 12 | 15 | 15 | 60 | 61 | 49 |
| Slough Town | 42 | 11 | 14 | 17 | 44 | 58 | 47 |
| Witton Albion | 42 | 7 | 13 | 22 | 37 | 63 | 34 |

## 1994–95: GM VAUXHALL CONFERENCE

| | P | W | D | L | F | A | Pts |
|---|---|---|---|---|---|---|---|
| Macclesfield Town | 42 | 24 | 8 | 10 | 70 | 40 | 80 |
| Woking | 42 | 21 | 12 | 9 | 76 | 44 | 75 |
| Southport | 42 | 21 | 9 | 12 | 68 | 50 | 72 |
| Altrincham | 42 | 20 | 8 | 14 | 77 | 60 | 68 |
| Stevenage Borough | 42 | 22 | 7 | 15 | 68 | 49 | 67 |
| Kettering Town | 42 | 19 | 10 | 13 | 73 | 56 | 67 |
| Gateshead | 42 | 18 | 10 | 14 | 61 | 53 | 64 |
| Halifax Town | 42 | 17 | 12 | 13 | 68 | 54 | 63 |
| Runcorn | 42 | 16 | 12 | 16 | 59 | 71 | 58 |
| Northwich Victoria | 42 | 14 | 15 | 13 | 77 | 66 | 57 |
| Kidderminster Harriers | 42 | 16 | 9 | 17 | 63 | 61 | 57 |
| Bath City | 42 | 15 | 12 | 15 | 55 | 56 | 57 |
| Bromsgrove Rovers | 42 | 14 | 13 | 15 | 66 | 79 | 55 |
| Farnborough Town | 42 | 15 | 10 | 17 | 55 | 64 | 55 |
| Dagenham & Redbridge | 42 | 13 | 13 | 16 | 56 | 69 | 52 |
| Dover Athletic | 42 | 11 | 16 | 15 | 48 | 55 | 49 |
| Welling United | 42 | 13 | 10 | 19 | 57 | 74 | 49 |
| Stalybridge Celtic | 42 | 11 | 14 | 17 | 52 | 72 | 47 |
| Telford United | 42 | 10 | 16 | 16 | 53 | 62 | 46 |
| Merthyr Tydfil | 42 | 11 | 11 | 20 | 53 | 63 | 44 |
| Stafford Rangers | 42 | 9 | 11 | 22 | 53 | 79 | 38 |
| Yeovil Town | 42 | 8 | 14 | 20 | 50 | 71 | 37 |

## 1996–97: GM VAUXHALL CONFERENCE

| | P | W | D | L | F | A | Pts |
|---|---|---|---|---|---|---|---|
| Macclesfield Town | 42 | 27 | 9 | 6 | 80 | 30 | 90 |
| Kidderminster Harriers | 42 | 26 | 7 | 9 | 84 | 42 | 85 |
| Stevenage Borough | 42 | 24 | 10 | 8 | 87 | 53 | 82 |
| Morecambe | 42 | 19 | 9 | 14 | 69 | 56 | 66 |
| Woking | 42 | 18 | 10 | 14 | 71 | 63 | 64 |
| Northwich Victoria | 42 | 17 | 12 | 13 | 61 | 54 | 63 |
| Farnborough Town | 42 | 16 | 13 | 13 | 58 | 53 | 61 |
| Hednesford Town | 42 | 16 | 12 | 14 | 52 | 50 | 60 |
| Telford United | 42 | 16 | 10 | 16 | 46 | 56 | 58 |
| Gateshead | 42 | 15 | 11 | 16 | 59 | 63 | 56 |
| Southport | 42 | 15 | 10 | 17 | 51 | 61 | 55 |
| Rushden & Diamonds | 42 | 14 | 11 | 17 | 61 | 63 | 53 |
| Stalybridge Celtic | 42 | 14 | 10 | 18 | 53 | 58 | 52 |
| Kettering Town | 42 | 14 | 9 | 19 | 53 | 62 | 51 |
| Hayes | 42 | 12 | 14 | 16 | 54 | 55 | 50 |
| Slough Town | 42 | 12 | 14 | 16 | 62 | 65 | 50 |
| Dover Athletic | 42 | 12 | 14 | 16 | 57 | 68 | 50 |
| Welling United | 42 | 13 | 9 | 20 | 50 | 60 | 48 |
| Halifax Town | 42 | 12 | 12 | 18 | 55 | 74 | 48 |
| Bath City | 42 | 12 | 11 | 19 | 53 | 80 | 47 |
| Bromsgrove Rovers | 42 | 12 | 5 | 25 | 41 | 67 | 41 |
| Altrincham | 42 | 9 | 12 | 21 | 49 | 73 | 39 |

## 1995–96: GM VAUXHALL CONFERENCE

| | P | W | D | L | F | A | Pts |
|---|---|---|---|---|---|---|---|
| Stevenage Borough | 42 | 27 | 10 | 5 | 101 | 44 | 91 |
| Woking | 42 | 25 | 8 | 9 | 83 | 54 | 83 |
| Hednesford Town | 42 | 23 | 7 | 12 | 71 | 46 | 76 |
| Macclesfield Town | 42 | 22 | 9 | 11 | 66 | 49 | 75 |
| Gateshead | 42 | 18 | 13 | 11 | 58 | 46 | 67 |
| Southport | 42 | 18 | 12 | 12 | 77 | 64 | 66 |
| Kidderminster Harriers | 42 | 18 | 10 | 14 | 78 | 66 | 64 |
| Northwich Victoria | 42 | 16 | 12 | 14 | 72 | 64 | 60 |
| Morecambe | 42 | 17 | 8 | 17 | 78 | 72 | 59 |
| Farnborough Town | 42 | 15 | 14 | 13 | 63 | 58 | 59 |
| Bromsgrove Rovers | 42 | 15 | 14 | 13 | 59 | 57 | 59 |
| Altrincham | 42 | 15 | 13 | 14 | 59 | 64 | 58 |
| Telford United | 42 | 15 | 10 | 17 | 51 | 56 | 55 |
| Stalybridge Celtic | 42 | 16 | 7 | 19 | 59 | 68 | 55 |
| Halifax Town | 42 | 13 | 13 | 16 | 49 | 63 | 52 |
| Kettering Town | 42 | 13 | 9 | 20 | 68 | 84 | 48 |
| Slough Town | 42 | 13 | 8 | 21 | 63 | 76 | 47 |
| Bath City | 42 | 13 | 7 | 22 | 45 | 66 | 46 |
| Welling United | 42 | 10 | 15 | 17 | 42 | 53 | 45 |
| Dover Athletic | 42 | 11 | 7 | 24 | 51 | 74 | 40 |
| Runcorn | 42 | 9 | 8 | 25 | 48 | 87 | 35 |
| Dagenham & Redbridge | 42 | 7 | 12 | 23 | 43 | 73 | 33 |

# APPENDIX 6

# *Match by Match – Football League*

Home games are in capitals; (p) = penalty; names of subs used in brackets

## 1997–98: NATIONWIDE DIVISION THREE

| Date | Opponents | Result | Scorers | Gate | Team |
|---|---|---|---|---|---|
| Aug 9 | TORQUAY | W 2–1 | Sodje, Landon | 3379 | Price, Tinson, Rose, Payne (Edey), Howarth, Sodje, Askey, Wood, Landon (Power), Mason, Sorvel |
| Aug 16 | Brighton | D 1–1 | Landon | 2249 | Price, Tinson, Rose, Payne, Howarth, Sodje, Askey, Wood, Landon, Mason, Sorvel |
| Aug 23 | DONCASTER | W 3–0 | Landon, Askey, Mason | 2336 | Price, Tinson, Rose, Payne, Howarth, Sodje, Askey (Mitchell), Wood, Landon, Mason (Power), Sorvel |
| Aug 30 | Hartlepool | D 0–0 | | 2635 | Price, Tinson, Rose, Payne, Howarth, Sodje, Askey (Mitchell), Wood, Landon, Mason (Power), Sorvel |
| Sep 2 | Rochdale | L 0–2 | | 2197 | Price, Tinson, Rose, Payne, Howarth, Sodje, Askey (Landon), Wood, Mason, Power, Sorvel (Mitchell) |
| Sep 6 | DARLINGTON | W 2–0 | Power 2 | 2459 | Price, Tinson, Rose, Payne, Howarth, Sodje, Mitchell, Wood (Askey), Peel (Mason), Power, Sorvel |
| Sep 13 | SWANSEA CITY | W 3–0 | Gardiner, Peel, Askey | 2479 | Price, Tinson, Rose, Payne (Hitchen), Howarth, Sodje, Mitchell (Askey), Gardiner, Peel, Power (Landon), Sorvel |
| Sep 20 | Scarborough | L 1–2 | Peel | 2256 | Price, Tinson, Rose, Hitchen (Mason), Howarth, Sodje, Askey, Gardiner, Peel (Davenport), Power (Landon), Sorvel |
| Sep 27 | PETERBOROUGH | D 1–1 | Landon (p) | 3079 | Price, Tinson, Rose, Gardiner, Howarth, Sodje, Askey, Cooper, Peel, Power (Landon), Sorvel |
| Oct 4 | Leyton Orient | D 1–1 | Landon | 4552 | Price, Tinson (Edey), Rose (Whittaker), Gardiner, Howarth, Sodje, Askey, Wood, Peel (Landon), Cooper, Sorvel |
| Oct 11 | Notts County | D 1–1 | Wood | 4871 | Price, Tinson, Edey, Cooper, Howarth, Sodje, Askey, Wood, Whittaker, Power, Sorvel |
| Oct 18 | MANSFIELD | W 1–0 | Cooper | 3277 | Price, Tinson, Edey, Cooper, Howarth, Sodje, Askey (Landon), Wood (Rose), Whittaker, Power (Irving), Sorvel |
| Oct 21 | EXETER CITY | D 2–2 | Whittaker, Cooper | 2286 | Price, Tinson, Edey, Cooper, Howarth, Sodje, Askey, Wood, Whittaker, Irving (Power), Sorvel |
| Oct 25 | Chester City | D 1–1 | Landon | 3245 | Price, Tinson, Cooper, Payne, Howarth, Sodje, Askey (Landon), Wood, Whittaker, Irving (Power), Sorvel |
| Nov 1 | Rotherham | L 0–1 | | 3649 | Price, Tinson, Rose, Payne, Howarth, Sodje, Cooper (Peel), Wood, Landon (Power), Irving, Sorvel |
| Nov 4 | COLCHESTER | D 0–0 | | 1577 | Price, Tinson, Gardiner, Payne, Whittaker, Sodje, Cooper, Wood, Landon (Peel), Irving (Power), Sorvel |
| Nov 8 | CAMBRIDGE U. | W 3–1 | Power 2, Gardiner | 2337 | Price, Tinson, Gardiner (Howarth), Payne, Rose, Sodje, Whittaker, Wood, Peel (Mason), Power, Sorvel |
| Nov 18 | Shrewsbury | L 3–4 | Wood, Power, o.g. | 2600 | Price, Tinson, Gardiner, Payne, Rose (Landon), Sodje, Whittaker, Wood, Peel (Irving), Power, Sorvel |
| Nov 22 | HULL CITY | W 2–0 | Peel, Landon | 2508 | Price, Tinson, Howarth, Payne, Rose, Sodje, Whittaker (Irving), Wood, Peel (Landon), Power, Sorvel |
| Nov 29 | Lincoln City | D 1–1 | Whittaker | 3402 | Price, Tinson, Howarth, Payne, Rose, Sodje, Whittaker, Wood (Mitchell), Peel (Landon), Power, Sorvel |
| Dec 13 | Barnet | L 1–3 | Wood | 1710 | Price, Tinson, Howarth, Payne, McDonald, Sodje, Askey, Wood, Peel (Landon), Power, Sorvel |
| Dec 20 | CARDIFF CITY | W 1–0 | Wood | 2392 | Price, Tinson, Edey, Payne, Howarth, McDonald, Askey, Wood (Rose), (Irving (Peel), Power, Sorvel |
| Dec 26 | Darlington | L 2–4 | o.g., Askey | 3042 | Price, Tinson (Rose), Edey, Payne, Howarth, McDonald, Askey, Wood, Irving (Peel), Power, Sorvel |

| Date | Opponents | Result | Scorers | Gate | Team |
|------|-----------|--------|---------|------|------|
| Dec 28 | ROCHDALE | W 1–0 | Howarth (p) | 2666 | Price, Edey, G. Brown, Payne, Howarth, McDonald, Askey, Wood, Davenport (Mason), Power, Sorvel |
| Jan 10 | Torquay | L 0–2 | | 2428 | Price, Edey, Brown, McDonald (Rose), Howarth, Sodje, Askey (Davenport), Wood, Chambers, Power (Landon), Sorvel |
| Jan 17 | HARTLEPOOL | W 2–1 | Chambers, Wood | 2334 | Price, Tinson, Howarth, Payne, McDonald, Sodje, Askey, Wood, Chambers, Sorvel, Whittaker |
| Jan 20 | SCUNTHORPE | W 2–0 | Chambers 2 | 1450 | Price, Tinson, Howarth, Payne, McDonald, Sodje, Askey (Power), Wood, Chambers, Sorvel, Whittaker |
| Jan 24 | Doncaster | W 3–0 | Wood 2, Sorvel | 1707 | Price, Tinson, Howarth (Edey), Payne, McDonald, Sodje, Askey (Power), Wood, Chambers, Sorvel, Whittaker |
| Jan 27 | BRIGHTON | W 1–0 | Whittaker | 2024 | Price, Tinson, Howarth, Payne, McDonald, Sodje, Askey, Wood, Chambers (Power), Sorvel, Whittaker |
| Jan 31 | SWANSEA C. | D 1–1 | Howarth | 3293 | Price, Tinson, Howarth, Payne, McDonald, Sodje, Askey, Wood, Chambers, Sorvel, Whittaker |
| Feb 7 | SCARBOROUGH | W 3–1 | Askey, Wood, Howarth | 2488 | Price, Tinson, Howarth, Payne, McDonald, Sodje, Askey (Power), Wood, Chambers, Sorvel, Whittaker |
| Feb 14 | LEYTON ORIENT | W 1–0 | McDonald | 2725 | Price, Tinson, McDonald, Payne, Howarth, Sodje, Askey (Philliskirk), Wood, Chambers, Sorvel, Whittaker (Power) |
| Feb 21 | Peterborough | W 1–0 | Askey | 6224 | Price, Tinson, McDonald, Payne, Howarth, Sodje, Askey, Wood, Chambers, Sorvel, Whittaker |
| Feb 24 | Mansfield | L 0–1 | | 2683 | Price, Tinson, Philliskirk, Payne, Howarth, Sodje, Askey, , Chambers (Power), Sorvel, Whittaker |
| Feb 28 | NOTTS CO. | W 2–0 | Wood, Askey | 5122 | Price, Tinson, Howarth, Payne, Power, Sodje, Askey, Wood, Chambers (Philliskirk), Sorvel, Whittaker |
| Mar 3 | Cambridge U. | D 0–0 | | 2012 | Price, Tinson, McDonald, Payne, Howarth, Sodje, Askey (Power), Wood, Chambers (Philliskirk), Sorvel, Whittaker |
| Mar 7 | ROTHERHAM | D 0–0 | | 3156 | Price, Tinson, McDonald, Payne, Howarth, Edey, Askey (Philliskirk), Wood, Chambers (Power), Sorvel, Whittaker |
| Mar 14 | Colchester Utd. | L 1–5 | Wood | 2760 | Price, Tinson, McDonald, Payne, Howarth, Edey, Askey, Wood, Chambers (Power), Sorvel, Whittaker (Philliskirk) |
| Mar 21 | SHREWSBURY | W 2–1 | Chambers, Wood | 3013 | Price, Tinson, McDonald, Payne, Ingram, Sodje, Askey, Wood, Chambers, Sedgemore, Whittaker (Philliskirk) |
| Mar 28 | Hull City | D 0–0 | | 3677 | Price, Tinson, Durkan (Sorvel), Payne, Ingram, Sodje, Askey, Wood, Chambers (Philliskirk), Sedgemore, Whittaker |
| Apr 4 | LINCOLN CITY | W 1–0 | Wood | 3278 | Price, Tinson, McDonald, Payne, Ingram, Sodje, Askey (Howarth), Wood, Mason (Chambers), Sedgemore, Whittaker (Sorvel) |
| Apr 11 | Scunthorpe | L 0–1 | | 2949 | Price, Tinson, McDonald, Payne, Ingram, Sodje, Chambers, Wood (Sorvel), Mason (Howarth), Sedgemore, Whittaker (Philliskirk) |
| Apr 13 | BARNET | W 2–0 | Sodje, Power | 4171 | Price, Tinson, McDonald, Payne, Howarth, Sodje, Askey (Chambers), Wood, Sedgemore, Power (Sorvel), Whittaker (Durkan) |
| Apr 18 | Cardiff City | W 2–1 | Sodje, Sorvel | 2497 | Price, Tinson, McDonald, Payne, Howarth, Sodje, Askey (Chambers), Wood, Sorvel, Power, Durkan (Whittaker) |
| Apr 25 | CHESTER CITY | W 3–2 | Wood, Sorvel, Power | 5982 | Price, Tinson, McDonald, Payne, Ingram, Sodje, Askey (Chambers), Wood, Sorvel, Power, Whittaker (Durkan) |
| May 2 | Exeter City | W 3–1 | Wood, Davenport, Philliskirk | 4499 | Price, Tinson (Edey), Davenport (Mason), Payne, Howarth, Sodje, Askey (Philliskirk), Wood, Sorvel, Power, Whittaker |

# FA Cup

| Date | Opponents | Result | Scorers | Gate | Team |
|------|-----------|--------|---------|------|------|
| 1: Nov 15 | Hartlepool | W 4–2 | Wood 2, Whittaker 2 | 3165 | Price, Tinson, Gardiner, Payne, Rose (Mitchell) Sodje, Whittaker, Wood, Peel (Irving, Landon), Power, Sorvel |
| 2: Dec 6 | WALSALL | L 0–7 | | 3566 | Price, Tinson, Payne, Howarth, Rose, Sodje, Sorvel, Power (Landon), Whittaker (Mason), Peel, Mitchell (Irving) |

## Coca-Cola Cup

| Date | Opponents | Result | Scorers | Gate | Team |
|------|-----------|--------|---------|------|------|
| 1 (1): Aug 12 | HULL CITY | D 0–0 | | 2249 | Price, Tinson, Payne, Rose, Howarth, Sodje, Askey, Wood, Landon, Mason, Sorvel |
| 1 (2): Aug 26 | Hull City | L 1–2 | Mason | 3300 | Price, Tinson, Payne, Rose, Howarth, Sodje, Askey, Wood (Mitchell), Landon (Power), Mason, Sorvel |

## AWS

| Date | Opponents | Result | Scorers | Gate | Team |
|------|-----------|--------|---------|------|------|
| 2: Jan 13 | PRESTON NE | L 0–1 | | 1618 | Price, Howarth, Edey, Payne, McDonald, Sodje, Askey (Sorvel), Wood, Chambers, Power (Landon), G. Brown |

## 1998–99: Nationwide Division Two

| Date | Opponents | Result | Scorers | Gate | Team |
|------|-----------|--------|---------|------|------|
| Aug 8 | FULHAM | L 0–1 | | 3933 | Price, Tinson, Ingram, Payne, McDonald, Sodje (Howarth), Askey, Wood, Landon (Barclay), Sedgemore, Whittaker |
| Aug 15 | Stoke City | L 0–2 | | 13981 | Price, Tinson, Ingram, Payne, McDonald, Sodje, Askey, Wood, Tomlinson (Barclay), Sedgemore, Whittaker |
| Aug 22 | LINCOLN CITY | D 0–0 | | 2794 | Price, Tinson, Ingram, Payne, McDonald, Sodje, Askey, Wood, Tomlinson (Barclay), Sorvel (Durkan), Whittaker |
| Aug 29 | Millwall | D 0–0 | | 5997 | Price, Tinson, Ingram, Payne, McDonald, Sodje, Askey (Whittaker), Wood, Tomlinson, S. Brown (Howarth), Durkan |
| Aug 31 | NOTTS COUNTY | L 0–1 | | 3148 | Price, Ingram, Tinson, Payne, McDonald, Sodje, Askey, Wood (Sorvel), Tomlinson (Howarth), Durkan (S. Brown), Whittaker |
| Sep 5 | Wrexham | L 1–2 | Wood | 3384 | Price, Tinson, Ingram, Payne (Howarth), McDonald, Sodje, Askey, Wood, Tomlinson (Barclay), Sorvel (Whittaker), Durkan |
| Sep 8 | Oldham Athletic | W 2–1 | Barclay, Wood (p) | 5401 | Price, Tinson, Ingram, Payne, McDonald, Sodje, Askey, Wood, Barclay, Sorvel, Durkan |
| Sep 12 | MAN. CITY | L 0–1 | | 6381 | Price, Tinson, Ingram (Howarth), Payne, McDonald, Sodje, Askey, Wood, Barclay, Sorvel (Sedgemore), Durkan (Whittaker) |
| Sep 19 | Wigan Athletic | L 0–2 | | 3893 | Price, Tinson, Ingram (Durkan), Payne, Howarth (Askey), Sodje, Sedgemore (Sorvel), Wood, Barclay, Hitchen, Whittaker |
| Sep 26 | READING | W 2–1 | Holt, Askey | 2920 | Price, Tinson, Hitchen, Howarth, McDonald, Sodje, Griffiths, Wood (Askey), Smith, Holt, Sedgemore |
| Oct 3 | Gillingham | D 2–2 | McDonald 2 | 6093 | Price, Tinson, Hitchen, Howarth, McDonald, Sodje, Griffiths (Whittaker), Wood, Smith, Holt, Sedgemore |
| Oct 10 | BOURNEMOUTH | D 2–2 | Smith, Whittaker | 2974 | Price, Tinson, Hitchen (Payne), Howarth, McDonald, Sodje, Askey, Wood, Smith, Holt (Whittaker), Sedgemore |
| Oct 17 | Wycombe Wand. | L 0–3 | | 4012 | Price, Tinson, Hitchen, Howarth (Payne), McDonald, Sodje, Askey, Wood (Sorvel), Smith, Sedgemore (Holt), Whittaker |
| Oct 20 | Preston NE | D 2–2 | Sodje, Smith | 10216 | Price, Tinson, Hitchen, Payne, McDonald, Sodje, Durkan, Sorvel, Smith (Askey), Sedgemore, Whittaker |
| Oct 24 | BURNLEY | W 2–1 | Smith, Sedgemore | 3995 | Price, Tinson, Hitchen, Payne, McDonald, Sodje, Durkan (Wood), Sorvel (Askey), Smith, Sedgemore, Whittaker |
| Oct 31 | NORTHAMPTON TOWN | L 0–1 | | 3201 | Price, Tinson, Hitchen, Howarth, McDonald, Sodje, Durkan, Sorvel, Smith, Sedgemore, Whittaker |
| Nov 6 | Colchester Utd. | D 1–1 | Griffiths | 4800 | Price, Tinson, Hitchen, Payne, McDonald, Sodje, Griffiths, Sorvel, Smith, Sedgemore, Whittaker |
| Nov 10 | York City | W 2–0 | Sorvel, Sedgemore | 2713 | Price, Tinson, Hitchen, Payne, McDonald, Sodje, Griffiths (Wood), Sorvel, Smith (Tomlinson), Sedgemore, Whittaker (Ingram) |
| Nov 21 | WALSALL | D 1–1 | Tomlinson | 3183 | Price, Hitchen, Ingram, Payne, Wood, Sodje (Howarth), Askey, Sorvel, Smith, Sedgemore (Tomlinson), Whittaker |
| Nov 28 | Chesterfield | L 0–2 | | 4788 | Price, Hitchen, Ingram, Payne, Wood (Tomlinson), Tinson, Askey, Sorvel, Smith, Sedgemore, Whittaker |
| Dec 12 | LUTON TOWN | D 2–2 | Sorvel, Tomlinson | 2905 | Price, Hitchen, Ingram, Howarth, McDonald, Sodje, Askey, Sorvel, Tomlinson, Wood, Whittaker (Sedgemore) |
| Dec 18 | Bristol Rovers | D 0–0 | | 5039 | Price, Hitchen, Ingram, Howarth, McDonald, Sodje, Davies, Sorvel, Tomlinson, Smith, Matias |

| Date | Opponents | Result | Scorers | Gate | Team |
|---|---|---|---|---|---|
| Dec 26 | Lincoln City | L 0–1 | | 3732 | Price, Hitchen, Ingram, Howarth, Wood, Sodje, Davies, Sorvel, Tomlinson, Matias, Whittaker |
| Dec 28 | BLACKPOOL | L 0–1 | | 3919 | Price, Hitchen, Ingram, Howarth, Wood, Sodje, Askey, Sorvel, Tomlinson, Davies, Whittaker |
| Jan 9 | Fulham | L 0–1 | | 10153 | Williams, Hitchen, Ingram, Payne, McDonald, Sodje, Askey (Whittaker), Sorvel, Wood, Tomlinson, Davies (Sedgemore) |
| Jan 26 | MILLWALL | L 0–2 | | 1998 | Williams, Howarth, Ingram, Payne (Tomlinson), Tinson, McDonald, Davies (Wood), Sorvel, Landon, Matias, Whittaker |
| Jan 30 | Blackpool | L 1–2 | Sodje | 4569 | Williams, Hitchen, Ingram, Payne, McDonald, Sodje (Payne), Askey, Sorvel (Whittaker), Matias, Bailey (Landon), Wood |
| Feb 6 | WREXHAM | L 0–2 | | 2578 | Williams, Hitchen, Ingram, Tinson, McDonald (Wood), Sodje, Askey, Sorvel, Matias, Bailey (Payne), Whittaker (Tomlinson) |
| Feb 13 | OLDHAM ATH. | W 1–0 | Sodje | 4038 | Price, Hitchen, Tinson (Howarth), Payne, Sedgemore, Sodje, Askey, Sorvel, Matias (Tomlinson), Bailey, Davies (Wood) |
| Feb 20 | Manchester City | L 0–2 | | 31086 | Price, Hitchen, Ingram, Payne, Sedgemore, Sodje, Askey (Barclay), Sorvel (Wood), Matias, Davies, Tomlinson |
| Feb 27 | WIGAN ATH. | L 0–1 | | 3706 | Price, Hitchen, Ingram, Payne, Sedgemore, Sodje, Askey, Sorvel (Tomlinson), Matias, Davies (Wood), Bailey (Barclay) |
| Mar 6 | Reading | L 0–1 | | 8085 | Price, Hitchen, Tinson, Payne, Sedgemore (Davies), Sodje, Durkan, Sorvel, Landon, Matias (Tomlinson), Wood |
| Mar 9 | GILLINGHAM | W 1–0 | Landon | 1868 | Price, Tinson (Ingram), Hitchen, Payne, Sedgemore, Sodje, Askey (Tomlinson), Sorvel, Landon, Matias, Durkan (Wood) |
| Mar 13 | COLCHESTER UTD. | W 2–0 | Landon, Bailey | 2796 | Price, Tinson, Hitchen, Payne, Sedgemore, Sodje, Askey (Bailey), Sorvel, Landon, Matias (Wood), Durkan |
| Mar 20 | Northampton T. | W 2–0 | Sorvel, Wood | 5790 | Price, Tinson, Hitchen, Payne, Sedgemore, Sodje, Askey, Sorvel, Landon, Wood (Bailey), Durkan (Ingram) |
| Mar 27 | Burnley | L 3–4 | Askey, Durkan 2 | 10500 | Price, Tinson (Ingram), Hitchen, Payne, Sedgemore, Sodje, Askey, Sorvel, Landon (Matias), Wood (Soley), Durkan |
| Apr 3 | WYCOMBE WANDS. | L 1–3 | Payne | 3183 | Price, Tinson, Hitchen, Payne, Sedgemore (Soley), Sodje, Askey, Sorvel, Bailey, Matias (Wood), Durkan |
| Apr 6 | Bournemouth | L 0–1 | | 8033 | Price, Tinson, Hitchen, Payne, Sodje, Askey, Sorvel, Landon (Bailey), Wood, Matias, Durkan |
| Apr 10 | PRESTON NE | W 3–2 | Askey, Durkan, Wood | 4325 | Price, Tinson, Hitchen (Ingram), Payne, Sodje, Askey, Sorvel (Sedgemore), Wood, Soley, Matias, Durkan |
| Apr 13 | CHESTERFIELD | W 2–0 | Payne 2 | 2216 | Price, Tinson, Hitchen, Payne (Ingram), Sodje, Askey (Bailey), Sorvel (Sedgemore), Wood, Soley, Matias, Durkan |
| Apr 17 | Walsall | L 0–2 | | 6256 | Price, Tinson, Hitchen, Ingram, Askey (Tomlinson), Sorvel, Wood (Sedgemore), Soley (Landon), Matias, Durkan, G. Brown |
| Apr 24 | YORK CITY | L 1–2 | Tomlinson | 3077 | Price, Tinson, Hitchen, Ingram (Tomlinson), Sorvel, Wood (Sedgemore), Soley (Askey), Landon, Matias, Durkan, G. Brown |
| Apr 27 | STOKE CITY | L 1–2 | Matias | 3825 | Price, Tinson, Hitchen, Sodje, Askey, Sorvel, Wood (Sedgemore), Tomlinson, Matias, Durkan (Bailey), G. Brown (Davies) |
| May 1 | Luton Town | W 2–1 | Sorvel, Davies | 5738 | Price, Tinson, Hitchen (Davies), Payne, Sedgemore, Sodje, Askey (Landon), Sorvel, Tomlinson (Soley), Matias, Durkan (Lomax) |
| May 4 | Notts County | D 1–1 | Matias | 3747 | Price, Tinson, Payne, Sedgemore, Sodje, Sorvel, Tomlinson, Landon, Matias, Durkan, G. Brown |
| May 8 | BRISTOL ROVERS | L 3–4 | Askey, Tomlinson (p), Davies | 3186 | Price, Davies, Payne, Sedgemore, Sodje, Askey, Sorvel, Tomlinson (Landon), Matias, Durkan (Lomax), G. Brown (Soley) |

## FA Cup

| Date | Opponents | Result | Scorers | Gate | Team |
|------|-----------|--------|---------|------|------|
| 1: Nov 14 | SLOUGH T. | D 2–2 | Sodje, Tomlinson | 2104 | Price, Hitchen, Ingram (Howarth), Payne, Wood, Sodje, Askey, Sorvel, Tomlinson, Sedgemore (Durkan), Whittaker |
| 1r: Nov 24 | Slough Town | D 1–1* | Sedgemore | 2010 | Price, Hitchen, Ingram, Tinson (Lonergan), Wood, Sodje, Askey, Sorvel, Tomlinson, Sedgemore (Griffiths), Whittaker (Howarth) |
| 2: Dec 5 | CAMBRIDGE U. | W 4–1 | Tomlinson 3, Askey | 2650 | Price, Tinson, Hitchen, Payne, Wood, Sodje (Ingram), Askey, Sorvel, Tomlinson, Sedgemore, Whittaker (Davenport) |
| 3: Jan 2 | Coventry City | L 0–7 | | 14197 | Price, Hitchen, Howarth, Payne, Sodje (Durkan), Wood (Lonergan), Askey, Sedgemore, Matias (Whittaker), Tomlinson, Davies |

* Macc. won 9–8 on pens.

## Worthington Cup

| Date | Opponents | Result | Scorers | Gate | Team |
|------|-----------|--------|---------|------|------|
| 1 (1): Aug 11 | STOKE CITY | W 3–1 | Askey 2, Wood | 2963 | Price, Tinson, Ingram, Payne, McDonald, Sodje, Askey, Wood (Sorvel), Tomlinson (Barclay), Sedgemore (Durkan), Whittaker |
| 1 (2): Aug 19 | Stoke City | L 0–1 | | 6152 | Price, Tinson, Ingram, Payne, McDonald, Sodje, Askey (Barclay), Wood, Durkan, Sorvel, Whittaker (Tomlinson) |
| 2 (1): Sep 15 | BIRMINGHAM C. | L 0–3 | | 2275 | Price, Tinson (Hitchen), Howarth, Payne, McDonald (Durkan), Sodje, Askey (S. Brown), Wood, Barclay, Sorvel, Whittaker |
| 2 (2): Sep 22 | Birmingham City | L 0–6 | | 3443 | Price, Tinson, Hitchen, Payne, McDonald, Sodje, Askey (Barclay), Wood, S. Brown, Sedgemore (Griffiths), Whittaker |

## AWS

| Date | Opponents | Result | Scorers | Gate | Team |
|------|-----------|--------|---------|------|------|
| 1: Dec 8 | WREXHAM | L 0–1 | | 804 | Price, Tinson, Ingram, Payne, Wood, Howarth, Griffiths, Tomlinson, Smith, Sedgemore, Whittaker |

## 1999–2000: Nationwide Division Three

| Date | Opponents | Result | Scorers | Gate | Team |
|------|-----------|--------|---------|------|------|
| Aug 7 | NORTHAMPTON TOWN | W 1–0 | Barker | 2694 | Price, Hitchen (Ingram), Collins, Tinson, Rioch, Wood, Barker, Durkan, Davies, Askey (Sedgemore), Priest |
| Aug 14 | Darlington | L 0–3 | | 5117 | Price, Ingram, Collins, Tinson, Rioch, Wood, Barker, Durkan (Tomlinson), Davies (Whitehead), Askey (Abbey), Priest |
| Aug 21 | SWANSEA CITY | L 1–2 | Askey | 2121 | Price, Collins (G. Brown), Tinson, Rioch, Wood, Barker Durkan (Whitehead), Askey, Priest, Whittaker (Tomlinson), Abbey |
| Aug 28 | Hull City | W 3–2 | Rioch 2 (1p) Ware | 6222 | Price, Ingram, Collins, Tinson, Rioch (Davies), Wood, Barker, Askey, Priest (Ware), Byrne, Abbey |
| Aug 30 | ROTHERHAM | D 1–1 | Barker | 2307 | Price, Ingram, Collins, Tinson, Rioch, Ware (Priest), Wood, Barker, Askey (Tomlinson), Byrne, Abbey |
| Sep 5 | Barnet | L 1–2 | Barker | 2426 | Price, Ingram (Priest), Collins, Tinson, Ware (Whitehead), Wood, Barker, Sedgemore, Askey (Durkan), Byrne, Abbey |
| Sep 11 | SOUTHEND U. | L 1–2 | Barker | 2059 | Price, Ingram, Collins, Tinson, Rioch (Whittaker), Barker, Durkan, Askey (Whitehead), Priest, Byrne, Abbey |
| Sep 18 | Lincoln City | D 1–1 | Barker | 2918 | Price, Ingram, Collins, Tinson, Ware, Barker, Durkan (Whitehead), Davies, Priest, G. Brown, Byrne (Whittaker) |
| Sep 25 | Exeter City | W 3–0 | Barker, Rioch, Durkan | 3202 | Price, Ingram, Collins, Tinson, Rioch, Wood, Barker, Durkan, Davies, Askey, Priest |
| Oct 2 | TORQUAY U. | L 1–2 | Collins | 2002 | Price, Ingram, Collins, Tinson, Rioch, Wood, Barker, Durkan, Davies, Priest (Sedgemore), Abbey (Whitehead) |
| Oct 9 | HALIFAX T. | L 0–2 | | 2185 | Price, Ingram, Collins, Tinson, Rioch, Wood, Barker, Durkan, Davies (Ware), Askey, Priest (Tomlinson) |
| Oct 16 | Chester City | W 2–1 | Barker, Collins | 2506 | Martin, Ingram, Collins, Tinson, Rioch, Wood (Ware), Barker, Durkan (Tomlinson), Davies (Sedgemore), Askey, Priest |

| Date | Opponents | Result | Scorers | Gate | Team |
|---|---|---|---|---|---|
| Oct 19 | Rochdale | W 1–0 | Askey | 2397 | Martin, Ingram, Collins, Tinson, Rioch, Barker, Sedgemore, Durkan, Davies, Askey, Priest |
| Oct 23 | EXETER CITY | W 1–0 | Barker | 1893 | Martin, Ingram, Collins, Tinson, Rioch, Barker (Tomlinson Sedgemore, Durkan, Davies, Askey, Priest |
| Nov 2 | MANSFIELD T. | W 5–2 | Priest, Barker 2, Sedgemore, Askey | 1541 | Martin, Ingram, Collins, Tinson, Rioch, Barker, Sedgemore, Durkan, Davies (Wood), Askey, Priest |
| Nov 6 | York City | W 2–0 | Barker, o.g. | 2469 | Martin, Ingram, Collins, Tinson, Rioch, Barker, Sedgemore, Durkan, Davies, Askey, Priest |
| Nov 14 | BRIGHTON | D 1–1 | Askey | 2920 | Martin, Ingram, Collins, Tinson, Rioch, Barker, Sedgemore, Durkan, Davies, Askey, Priest |
| Nov 20 | Peterborough | D 2–2 | Barker Askey | 5083 | Martin, Ingram, Collins, Tinson, Rioch, Barker, Sedgemore Askey, Durkan, Davies (Whittaker), Askey, Priest |
| Nov 27 | HARTLEPOOL | D 3–3 | Priest, Askey, Barker | 2351 | Martin (Price), Ingram, Collins, Tinson, Barker (Tomlinson), Sedgemore, Durkan, Davies (Wood), Askey, Priest, G. Brown |
| Dec 4 | Northampton T. | L 0–2 | | 5355 | Knight, Ingram (Abbey), Collins, Tinson, Rioch, Sedgemore, Durkan, Davies, Askey, Priest, Tomlinson (Whitehead) |
| Dec 11 | Cheltenham T. | D 1–1 | Durkan | 3107 | Knight, Collins, Tinson, Rioch, Wood, Barker, Sedgemore, Durkan, Askey, Priest, Moore |
| Dec 18 | LEYTON O. | W 1–0 | Davies | 2303 | Knight, Collins, Tinson, Rioch, Wood, Barker, Sedgemore, Durkan, Askey (Davies), Priest, Abbey |
| Dec 26 | Shrewsbury | W 1–0 | Durkan | 4302 | Martin, Tinson, Rioch, Wood, Barker, Sedgemore, Durkan, Davies (Askey), Priest, Abbey, Moore |
| Dec 28 | CARLISLE U. | W 2–1 | Priest 2 | 2826 | Martin, Tinson, Rioch, Wood, Barker (G. Brown), Sedgemore |
| Jan 3 | Plymouth A. | L 2–3 | Askey, Wood | 6128 | Martin, Tinson, Rioch, Wood, Barker, Sedgemore, (Whittaker), Davies, Askey, Abbey, Moore |
| Jan 8 | CHELTENHAM T. | L 1–2 | Rioch (p) | 3221 | Martin, Collins, Tinson, Rioch, Wood, Barker, Sedgemore (Whittaker), Durkan, Davies (Askey), Priest, Moore |
| Jan 15 | DARLINGTON | W 2–1 | Moore, Askey | 2399 | Martin, Ingram, Tinson, Rioch, Wood, Barker, Sedgemore, Durkan, Askey (Whitehead), Priest, Moore |
| Jan 22 | Swansea City | L 0–1 | | 6913 | Martin, Ingram (Abbey), Tinson, Rioch, Wood, Barker, Sedgemore, Durkan (Whittaker), Askey (Whitehead), Priest, Moore |
| Jan 29 | HULL CITY | L 0–2 | | 1900 | Williams, Ingram, Tinson, Rioch, Wood (Munroe), Barker, Sedgemore (Collins), Priest, Whittaker, Whitehead, Moore |
| Feb 5 | Rotherham U. | L 1–2 | Rioch | 4175 | Williams, Ingram, Collins, Tinson, Rioch, Wood, Barker, Sedgemore, Askey (Tomlinson), Priest (Davies), Moore |
| Feb 12 | BARNET | W 2–0 | Barker, Askey | 2114 | Williams, Ingram, Collins, Tinson, Rioch, Barker (Moore), Sedgemore (Wood), Durkan, Davies, Askey, Priest (Ware) |
| Feb 19 | Hartlepool U. | W 4–1 | Durkan, Barker 2, Askey | 2823 | Williams, Ingram, Collins, Tinson, Rioch, Barker, Sedgemore, Durkan (Ware), Davies, Askey (Whitehead) Priest |
| Feb 26 | LINCOLN CITY | D 1–1 | Askey | 2445 | Williams, Ingram, Collins, Tinson, Rioch, Barker, Sedgemore, Durkan (Ware), Davies, Askey, Priest |
| Mar 3 | Southend U. | L 0–1 | | 2372 | Williams, Ingram, Collins (Moore), Tinson, Rioch (Whitehead), Barker, Sedgemore (Wood), Durkan, Davies, Askey, Priest |
| Mar 7 | YORK CITY | D 1–1 | Durkan | 1581 | Williams, Ingram, Tinson, Rioch, Wood, Barker, Durkan (Ware), Davies, Askey (Sedgemore), Priest, Moore |
| Mar 11 | Mansfield T. | L 0–1 | | 2327 | Williams, Ingram, Tinson, Rioch, Wood, Barker (Collins) Durkan (Abbey), Davies, Askey (Whitehead), Priest, Moore |
| Mar 18 | PETERBOROUGH | D 1–1 | Moore | 2309 | Williams, Ingram (Moore), Collins (Whitehead), TinsonRioch, Wood, Durkan, Davies, Askey, Priest (Ware),Tomlinson |
| Mar 21 | Brighton | L 2–5 | Askey, Whitehead | 5596 | Williams, Tinson, Rioch, Ware, Wood, Sedgemore (O'Neill) Durkan, Askey, Tomlinson, Whitehead, Moore |
| Mar 25 | SHREWSBURY | W 4–2 | Collins, Whitehead 2, Tomlinson | 1931 | Williams, Ingram, Collins, Tinson, Rioch, Ware, Sedgemore (Munroe), Durkan (Wood), Askey (Abbey), Tomlinson,Whitehead |
| Apr 1 | Leyton Orient | D 0–0 | | 4302 | Martin, Ingram, Collins, Tinson, Ware (Munroe), Sedgemore, Durkan, Tomlinson (Hitchen), Whitehead, Abbey |

| Date | Opponents | Result | Scorers | Gate | Team |
|------|-----------|--------|---------|------|------|
| April 8 | PLYMOUTH A. | W 4–1 | Askey, Durkan, Whitehead 2 | 2231 | Martin, Ingram, Collins, Tinson, Rioch, Wood, Sedgemore, Durkan (Hitchen), Davies, Askey, Whitehead |
| April 15 | Carlisle U. | W 1–0 | Whitehead | 3047 | Martin, Ingram, Collins, Tinson, Rioch, Wood, Sedgemore, Durkan (Ware), Davies, Askey, Whitehead |
| April 22 | CHESTER CITY | D 1–1 | Askey | 3456 | Martin, Ingram (Hitchen), Collins, Tinson, Rioch, Wood, Sedgemore, Durkan, Davies (Tomlinson), Askey, Whitehead |
| Apr 24 | Torquay U. | L 2–3 | Askey, Ware | 2139 | Martin, Collins, Tinson, Rioch, Hitchen, Ware, Durkan, Davies (Wood), Askey (Tomlinson), Whitehead, Munroe |
| Apr 29 | ROCHDALE | L 1–2 | Tomlinson | 2202 | Martin, Collins, Tinson, Rioch, Ware (Bamber), Wood (Munroe), Sedgemore, Durkan, Tomlinson (Davies), Whitehead, Abbey |
| May 6 | Halifax T. | W 1–0 | Tinson | 2007 | Martin, Ingram (Abbey), Collins, Tinson, Rioch, Ware, Wood, Sedgemore, Durkan, Tomlinson (Davies), Whitehead |

## FA CUP

| Date | Opponents | Result | Scorers | Gate | Team |
|------|-----------|--------|---------|------|------|
| 1: Oct 30 | HULL CITY | D 0–0 | | 2401 | Martin, Ingram (Abbey), Collins, Tinson, Rioch, Barker, Sedgemore, Durkan, Davies, Askey (Tomlinson), Priest |
| 1r: Nov 9 | Hull City | L 0–4 | | 4844 | Martin, Ingram, Collins, Tinson, Rioch, Barker, Sedgemore, Durkan, Davies, Askey, Priest |

## WORTHINGTON CUP

| Date | Opponents | Result | Scorers | Gate | Team |
|------|-----------|--------|---------|------|------|
| 1 (1): Aug 10 | STOKE CITY | D 1–1 | Priest | 2551 | Price, Ingram, Collins, Tinson, Rioch, Barker, Sedgemore (Wood), Davies, Priest, Tomlinson (Askey), Whittaker (Durkan) |
| 1 (2): Aug 25 | Stoke City | L 0–3 | | 5003 | Price, Tinson, Rioch (G. Brown), Ware (Whittaker), Wood (Tomlinson), Barker, Sedgemore, Davies, Askey, Priest, Abbey |

## AWS

| Date | Opponents | Result | Scorers | Gate | Team |
|------|-----------|--------|---------|------|------|
| 2: Jan 11 | ROCHDALE | L 2–3 | Davies, Barker | 1123 | Martin, Collins (Ingram), Tinson, Rioch, Wood, Barker (Whittaker), Sedgemore, Durkan, Davies, Askey (Whitehead), Moore |

## 2000–01: NATIONWIDE DIVISION THREE

| Date | Opponents | Result | Scorers | Gate | Team |
|---|---|---|---|---|---|
| Aug 12 | SCUNTHORPE | L 0–1 | | 2561 | Bullock, Hitchen, Collins, Tinson, Ingram, Sedgemore (Twynham), Barker, Glover (Whitehead), Durkan (Bettney), Wood, Munroe |
| Aug 19 | Shrewsbury T. | D 2–2 | Sedgemore, Tinson | 2822 | Bullock, Hitchen, Collins, Tinson, Ingram, Sedgemore (Priest), Barker, Glover, Durkan, Wood, Twynham (Whitehead) |
| Aug 26 | HULL CITY | D 0–0 | | 1795 | Bullock, Hitchen, Collins, Tinson, Ingram, Barker, Glover (Askey), Wood, Abbey (Durkan), Twynham, Munroe (Sedgemore) |
| Aug 28 | Mansfield T. | D 4–4 | Askey, Sedgemore, Barker, Whitehead | 3360 | Bullock, Hitchen, Collins, Tinson, Ingram, Sedgemore (Bettney), Barker, Durkan (Whitehead), Askey, Wood, Twynham |
| Sep 2 | Plymouth A. | W 1–0 | Barker | 3888 | Bullock, Hitchen, Collins, Tinson, Ingram (Abbey), Sedgemore, Barker (Whitehead), Durkan, Askey, Wood, Twynham (Munroe) |
| Sep 9 | EXETER CITY | L 0–2 | | 1793 | Bullock, Hitchen, Collins (Ingram), Tinson, Sedgemore, Barker, Durkan, Askey (Whitehead), Wood (Adams), Abbey, Munroe |
| Sep 12 | LINCOLN CITY | W 2–0 | Whitehead 2 | 1349 | Bullock, Hitchen, Tinson, Ingram, Sedgemore, Barker, Askey, Wood (O'Neill), Adams, Munroe, Whitehead (Glover) |
| Sep 16 | Hartlepool U. | D 2–2 | Barker, Glover (p) | 2589 | Bullock, Hitchen, Tinson, Ingram, Sedgemore, Barker, Askey, Wood, Abbey, Munroe (Twynham, Durkan), Whitehead (Glover) |
| Sep 22 | DARLINGTON | D 1–1 | Sedgemore | 2389 | Bullock, Tinson, Ingram, Sedgemore, Barker, Durkan (Glover), Askey, Wood (Keen), Abbey, Adams, Munroe (Twynham) |
| Sep 30 | Chesterfield | L 1–4 | Barker | 4904 | Bullock, Tinson, Ingram, Sedgemore, Barker, Askey, Abbey (Whitehead), Adams, Twynham (Rioch), Munroe, Keen |
| Oct 8 | Barnet | W 2–0 | Glover 2 | 1841 | Bullock, Rioch, Tinson, Ingram, Sedgemore, Barker (Askey), Glover, Wood, Adams, Munroe (Woolley), Bamber |
| Oct 14 | CHELTENHAM T. | W 2–1 | Ingram, Wood | 2035 | Bullock, Rioch, Tinson, Ingram, Sedgemore, Barker, Glover, Askey (Whitehead), Wood, Adams, Bamber (Abbey) |
| Oct 17 | TORQUAY U. | W 2–1 | Tinson, Barker | 1681 | Bullock, Rioch, Tinson, Ingram, Sedgemore, Barker, Glover (Whitehead), Wood, Abbey (Twynham), Adams, Munroe |
| Oct 21 | Blackpool | L 1–2 | Whitehead | 3700 | Bullock, Rioch (Askey), Tinson, Ingram, Sedgemore, Barker, Glover, Wood, Adams, Munroe (Whitehead), Keen |
| Oct 24 | Rochdale | D 2–2 | Glover, Barker | 3608 | Bullock, Rioch, Tinson, Ingram, Sedgemore, Barker, Glover (Keen), Askey, Wood, Abbey, Adams |
| Oct 28 | HALIFAX TOWN | D 0–0 | | 1734 | Bullock, Rioch, Tinson, Ingram (O'Neill), Sedgemore (Whitehead), Barker, Glover (Munroe), Askey, Wood, Abbey, Adams |
| Nov 4 | Southend U. | L 1–3 | Munroe | 4190 | Bullock, Hitchen, Tinson, Sedgemore, Barker, Glover (Wood), Askey (Whitehead), Abbey, Adams, Munroe, O'Neill (Collins) |
| Nov 11 | BRIGHTON | D 0–0 | | 2654 | Bullock, Hitchen, Tinson, Ingram (O'Neill), Sedgemore, Barker, Glover, Askey (Durkan), Abbey, Adams, Munroe |
| Nov 25 | Leyton Orient | L 1–2 | Whitehead | 4013 | Martin, Hitchen, Collins, Tinson, Priest, Barker, Glover (Askey), Adams, Whitehead, O'Neill (Sedgemore), Keen (Durkan) |
| Dec 2 | Kidderminster H. | L 1–2 | Glover | 2638 | Martin, Hitchen, Collins, Tinson, Sedgemore (Munroe), Priest, Barker, Glover (Askey), Adams, Whitehead, Keen |
| Dec 16 | CARLISLE U. | W 1–0 | Barker | 1860 | Martin, Hitchen, Collins, Tinson, Sedgemore, Priest, Barker, Glover, Adams, Whitehead (Askey), Keen |
| Dec 23 | Cardiff C. | L 0–2 | | 8088 | Martin, Hitchen, Collins, Tinson, Sedgemore, Priest, Barker, Glover (Durkan), Adams, Whitehead (Askey), Keen |
| Dec 26 | YORK CITY | L 0–1 | | 2001 | Martin, Hitchen, Collins (Glover), Tinson, Sedgemore (Askey), Priest, Barker, Durkan, Adams, Whitehead, Keen |
| Jan 1 | Scunthorpe | D 2–2 | Durkan, Keen | 3168 | Bullock, Hitchen, Collins, Tinson, Sedgemore, Priest, Durkan, Askey, Wood, Adams, Keen |
| Jan 6 | Hull City | D 0–0 | | 6217 | Bullock, Hitchen, Collins (O'Neill), Tinson, Sedgemore (Munroe), Priest, Durkan, Askey, Wood, Adams, Keen |
| Jan 14 | MANSFIELD T. | L 0–1 | | 1893 | Bullock, Hitchen (Whitehead), Tinson, Priest, Glover, Durkan, Askey, Wood (Came), Adams, O'Neill, Keen |
| Jan 20 | York City | W 3–1 | Priest 2, Askey | 2287 | Bullock, Rioch, Tinson, Ingram (O'Neill), Priest, Durkan, Askey (Whitehead), Wood (Glover), Abbey, Adams, Keen |
| Jan 27 | CARDIFF C. | L 2–5 | Keen, Tracey | 2376 | Bullock, Hitchen, Rioch, Tinson, Ingram (O'Neill), Priest, Glover (Tracey), Durkan, Askey, Adams, Keen |
| Feb 3 | PLYMOUTH A. | W 3–1 | Priest 2, Whitehead | 1881 | Bullock, Hitchen (Collins), Rioch, Tinson, Ingram, Durkan, Priest, Askey (Whitehead), Tracey (Glover), Adams, Keen |

| Date | Opponents | Result | Scorers | Gate | Team |
|------|-----------|--------|---------|------|------|
| Feb 10 | Exeter City | D 0–0 | | 3458 | Martin, Hitchen, Rioch (Sedgemore), Tinson, Ingram, Durkan, Priest, Askey (Whitehead), Glover, Adams, Keen |
| Feb 13 | SHREWSBURY T. | W 2–1 | Whitehead 2 | 1430 | Martin, Hitchen, Rioch, Tinson, Ingram, Priest, Durkan, Askey (Tracey), Whitehead (Sedgemore), Adams, Keen |
| Feb 17 | HARTLEPOOL | L 0–1 | | 2176 | Martin, Hitchen, Rioch, Tinson, Ingram, Priest (Tereskinas), Durkan, Askey (Wood), Adams, Whitehead, Keen |
| Feb 20 | Lincoln City | W 2–1 | Tinson, Askey | 1853 | Martin, Hitchen, Rioch (Whitehead), Tinson, Ingram, Durkan, Askey (Connell), Wood, Adams, Munroe, Keen |
| Feb 24 | Darlington | D 1–1 | Durkan (p) | 3101 | Martin, Hitchen, Rioch (Abbey), Tinson, Ingram, Durkan, Askey (Whitehead), Wood, Adams, Munroe, Keen |
| Mar 3 | CHESTERFIELD | L 1–2 | Glover | 2740 | Martin, Hitchen, Rioch (Whitehead), Tinson, Ingram, Askey, Glover, Adams, Munroe (Bamber), Keen, Lambert |
| Mar 6 | Cheltenham T. | D 1–1 | Rioch | 3091 | Martin, Hitchen, Rioch, Tinson, Ingram, Durkan, Askey, Abbey (Glover), Adams, Munroe, Keen |
| Mar 11 | BARNET | W 3–0 | Durkan 2, Glover | 2060 | Martin, Hitchen, Tinson, Ingram, Durkan, Askey (Whitehead), Glover, Adams, Munroe (Abbey), Keen, Tracey (Lambert) |
| Mar 24 | BLACKPOOL | W 2–1 | Tracey, Askey | 3045 | Martin, Hitchen, Tinson, Ingram, Durkan, Askey (Lambert), Glover, Adams (O'Neill), Munroe, Keen, Tracey (Shuker) |
| Mar 31 | Carlisle U. | L 0–1 | | 3885 | Martin, Hitchen, Tinson, Ingram, Durkan, Shuker, Glover, Adams, Munroe, Keen, Tracey (Whitehead) |
| Apr 7 | KIDDERMINSTER H. | W 1–0 | Shuker | 1585 | Martin, Hitchen, Tinson (Came), O'Neill, Durkan, Wood, Glover, Adams (Abbey), Keen, Tracey (Whitehead), Shuker |
| Apr 10 | Torquay U. | L 0–2 | | 2911 | Martin, Hitchen, Abbey (Lambert), O'Neill, Came, Durkan, Wood, Glover, Keen, Tracey (Whitehead), Shuker |
| Apr 14 | ROCHDALE | D 0–0 | | 2255 | Martin, Hitchen, Collins, Tinson, Came, Wood, Glover, Keen, Tracey, Lambert, Shuker |
| Apr 16 | Halifax T. | L 0–3 | | 1945 | Martin, Hitchen, Collins, Tinson, Came, Glover, Keen, Tracey (Bamber), Lambert (Wood), Shuker, Woolley (Whitehead) |
| Apr 21 | SOUTHEND U. | W 1–0 | Glover (p) | 1597 | Wilson, Hitchen, Tinson, Ingram (Came), Wood, Glover, Adams, Keen, Tracey, Lambert (Bamber), Shuker |
| Apr 28 | Brighton | L 1–4 | Tracey | 6731 | Martin, Hitchen, Tinson, Ingram, Durkan, Askey, Wood, Glover (Whitehead), Adams, Keen (Shuker), Tracey (Lambert) |
| May 5 | LEYTON O. | L 0–2 | | 2527 | Martin, Hitchen, Tinson, Ingram (Came), Durkan, Askey (Shuker), Wood (Lambert), Glover, Adams, Keen, Tracey |

## FA CUP

| Date | Opponents | Result | Scorers | Gate | Team |
|------|-----------|--------|---------|------|------|
| 1: Nov 18 | OXFORD U. | L 0–1 | | 2141 | Martin, Hitchen, Tinson, Sedgemore, Barker, Glover, Askey (Whitehead), Abbey (Durkan), Adams, Munroe (Keen), O'Neill |

## WORTHINGTON CUP

| Date | Opponents | Result | Scorers | Gate | Team |
|------|-----------|--------|---------|------|------|
| 1 (1): Aug 22 | Bolton | L 0–1 | | 4957 | Bullock, Hitchen, Collins, Tinson, Ingram, Sedgemore, Barker (Askey), Durkan, Wood, Twynham, Munroe (Abbey) |
| 1 (2): Sep 5 | BOLTON | W 3–1 | Sedgemore, Barker, Munroe | 2235 | Bullock, Hitchen, Collins, Tinson, Sedgemore, Barker (Whitehead), Durkan, Askey (Adams), Wood, Abbey, Munroe |
| 2 (1): Sep 19 | Middlesbrough | L 1–2 | Barker | 5144 | Bullock, Hitchen (Glover), Tinson, Ingram, Sedgemore, Barker, Durkan, Askey (Keen), Wood, Abbey, Munroe |
| 2 (2): Sep 26 | MIDDLESBRO' | L 1–3 | Sedgemore (p) | 3153 | Bullock, Tinson, Ingram, Sedgemore (Askey), Barker, Wood (Whitehead), Abbey, Adams, Twynham (Bamber), Munroe, Keen |

## AWS

| Date | Opponents | Result | Scorers | Gate | Team |
|------|-----------|--------|---------|------|------|
| 2: Jan 9 | Chesterfield | L 2–4 | Glover 2 | 1839 | Bullock, Hitchen (Bamber), Rioch, Tinson, Priest, Glover, Whitehead (Askey), Munroe, Adams, O'Neill, Bentley (Cane) |

# APPENDIX 7

# *Nationwide Football League Tables, 1997–2001*

## 1997–98: NATIONWIDE DIVISION THREE

| | P | W | D | L | F | A | Pts |
|---|---|---|---|---|---|---|---|
| Notts County | 46 | 29 | 12 | 5 | 82 | 43 | 99 |
| Macclesfield Town | 46 | 23 | 13 | 10 | 63 | 44 | 82 |
| Lincoln City | 46 | 20 | 15 | 11 | 60 | 51 | 75 |
| Colchester United | 46 | 21 | 11 | 14 | 72 | 60 | 74 |
| Torquay United | 46 | 21 | 11 | 14 | 68 | 59 | 74 |
| Scarborough | 46 | 19 | 15 | 12 | 67 | 58 | 72 |
| Barnet | 46 | 19 | 13 | 14 | 61 | 51 | 70 |
| Scunthorpe United | 46 | 19 | 12 | 15 | 56 | 52 | 69 |
| Rotherham United | 46 | 16 | 19 | 11 | 67 | 61 | 67 |
| Peterborough United | 46 | 18 | 13 | 15 | 63 | 51 | 67 |
| Leyton Orient* | 46 | 19 | 12 | 15 | 62 | 47 | 66 |
| Mansfield Town | 46 | 16 | 17 | 13 | 64 | 55 | 65 |
| Shrewsbury Town | 46 | 16 | 13 | 17 | 61 | 62 | 61 |
| Chester City | 46 | 17 | 10 | 19 | 60 | 61 | 61 |
| Exeter City | 46 | 15 | 15 | 16 | 68 | 63 | 60 |
| Cambridge United | 46 | 14 | 18 | 14 | 63 | 57 | 60 |
| Hartlepool United | 46 | 12 | 23 | 11 | 61 | 53 | 59 |
| Rochdale | 46 | 17 | 7 | 22 | 56 | 55 | 58 |
| Darlington | 46 | 14 | 12 | 20 | 56 | 72 | 54 |
| Swansea City | 46 | 13 | 11 | 22 | 49 | 62 | 50 |
| Cardiff City | 46 | 9 | 23 | 14 | 48 | 52 | 50 |
| Hull City | 46 | 11 | 8 | 27 | 56 | 83 | 41 |
| Brighton and Hove Albion | 46 | 6 | 17 | 23 | 38 | 66 | 35 |
| Doncaster Rovers | 46 | 4 | 8 | 34 | 30 | 113 | 20 |

* Leyton Orient 3 points deducted for infringement

## 1998–99: NATIONWIDE DIVISION TWO

| | P | W | D | L | F | A | Pts |
|---|---|---|---|---|---|---|---|
| Fulham | 46 | 31 | 8 | 7 | 79 | 32 | 101 |
| Walsall | 46 | 26 | 9 | 11 | 63 | 47 | 87 |
| Manchester City | 46 | 22 | 16 | 8 | 69 | 33 | 82 |
| Gillingham | 46 | 22 | 14 | 10 | 75 | 44 | 80 |
| Preston North End | 46 | 22 | 13 | 11 | 78 | 50 | 79 |
| Wigan Athletic | 46 | 22 | 10 | 14 | 75 | 48 | 76 |
| Bournemouth | 46 | 21 | 13 | 12 | 63 | 41 | 76 |
| Stoke City | 46 | 21 | 6 | 19 | 59 | 63 | 69 |
| Chesterfield | 46 | 17 | 13 | 16 | 46 | 44 | 64 |
| Millwall | 46 | 17 | 11 | 18 | 52 | 59 | 62 |
| Reading | 46 | 16 | 13 | 17 | 54 | 63 | 61 |
| Luton Town | 46 | 16 | 10 | 20 | 51 | 60 | 58 |
| Bristol Rovers | 46 | 13 | 17 | 16 | 65 | 56 | 56 |
| Blackpool | 46 | 14 | 14 | 18 | 44 | 54 | 56 |
| Burnley | 46 | 13 | 16 | 17 | 54 | 73 | 55 |
| Notts County | 46 | 14 | 12 | 20 | 52 | 61 | 54 |
| Wrexham | 46 | 13 | 14 | 19 | 43 | 62 | 53 |
| Colchester United | 46 | 12 | 16 | 18 | 52 | 70 | 52 |
| Wycombe Wanderers | 46 | 13 | 12 | 21 | 52 | 58 | 51 |
| Oldham Athletic | 46 | 14 | 9 | 23 | 48 | 66 | 51 |
| York City | 46 | 13 | 11 | 22 | 56 | 80 | 50 |
| Northampton Town | 46 | 10 | 18 | 18 | 43 | 57 | 48 |
| Lincoln City | 46 | 13 | 7 | 26 | 42 | 74 | 46 |
| Macclesfield Town | 46 | 11 | 10 | 25 | 43 | 63 | 43 |

## 1999–2000: NATIONWIDE DIVISION THREE

| | P | W | D | L | F | A | Pts |
|---|---|---|---|---|---|---|---|
| Swansea City | 46 | 24 | 13 | 9 | 51 | 30 | 85 |
| Rotherham United | 46 | 24 | 12 | 10 | 72 | 36 | 84 |
| Northampton Town | 46 | 25 | 7 | 14 | 63 | 45 | 82 |
| Darlington | 46 | 21 | 16 | 9 | 66 | 36 | 79 |
| Peterborough United | 46 | 22 | 12 | 12 | 63 | 54 | 78 |
| Barnet | 46 | 21 | 12 | 13 | 59 | 53 | 75 |
| Hartlepool United | 46 | 21 | 9 | 16 | 60 | 49 | 72 |
| Cheltenham Town | 46 | 20 | 10 | 16 | 50 | 42 | 70 |
| Torquay United | 46 | 19 | 12 | 15 | 62 | 52 | 69 |
| Rochdale | 46 | 18 | 14 | 14 | 57 | 54 | 68 |
| Brighton and Hove Albion | 46 | 17 | 16 | 13 | 64 | 46 | 67 |
| Plymouth Argyle | 46 | 16 | 18 | 12 | 55 | 51 | 66 |
| Macclesfield Town | 46 | 18 | 11 | 17 | 66 | 61 | 65 |
| Hull City | 46 | 15 | 14 | 17 | 43 | 43 | 59 |
| Lincoln City | 46 | 15 | 14 | 17 | 67 | 69 | 59 |
| Southend United | 46 | 15 | 11 | 20 | 53 | 61 | 56 |
| Mansfield Town | 46 | 16 | 8 | 22 | 50 | 65 | 56 |
| Halifax Town | 46 | 15 | 9 | 22 | 44 | 58 | 54 |
| Leyton Orient | 46 | 13 | 13 | 20 | 47 | 52 | 52 |
| York City | 46 | 12 | 16 | 18 | 39 | 53 | 52 |
| Exeter City | 46 | 11 | 11 | 24 | 46 | 72 | 44 |
| Shrewsbury Town | 46 | 9 | 13 | 24 | 40 | 67 | 40 |
| Carlisle United | 46 | 9 | 12 | 25 | 42 | 75 | 39 |
| Chester City | 46 | 10 | 9 | 27 | 44 | 79 | 39 |

## 2000–01: NATIONWIDE DIVISION THREE

| | P | W | D | L | F | A | Pts |
|---|---|---|---|---|---|---|---|
| Brighton and Hove Albion | 46 | 28 | 8 | 10 | 73 | 35 | 92 |
| Cardiff City | 46 | 23 | 13 | 10 | 95 | 58 | 82 |
| Chesterfield* | 46 | 25 | 14 | 7 | 79 | 42 | 80 |
| Hartlepool United | 46 | 21 | 14 | 11 | 71 | 54 | 77 |
| Leyton Orient | 46 | 20 | 15 | 11 | 59 | 51 | 75 |
| Hull City | 46 | 19 | 17 | 10 | 47 | 39 | 74 |
| Blackpool | 46 | 22 | 6 | 18 | 74 | 58 | 72 |
| Rochdale | 46 | 18 | 17 | 11 | 59 | 48 | 71 |
| Cheltenham Town | 46 | 18 | 14 | 14 | 59 | 52 | 68 |
| Scunthorpe United | 46 | 18 | 11 | 17 | 62 | 52 | 65 |
| Southend United | 46 | 15 | 18 | 13 | 55 | 53 | 63 |
| Plymouth Argyle | 46 | 15 | 13 | 18 | 54 | 61 | 58 |
| Mansfield Town | 46 | 15 | 13 | 18 | 64 | 72 | 58 |
| Macclesfield Town | 46 | 14 | 14 | 18 | 51 | 62 | 56 |
| Shrewsbury Town | 46 | 15 | 10 | 21 | 49 | 65 | 55 |
| Kidderminster Harriers | 46 | 13 | 14 | 19 | 47 | 61 | 53 |
| York City | 46 | 13 | 13 | 20 | 42 | 63 | 52 |
| Lincoln City | 46 | 12 | 15 | 19 | 58 | 66 | 51 |
| Exeter City | 46 | 12 | 14 | 20 | 40 | 58 | 50 |
| Darlington | 46 | 12 | 13 | 21 | 44 | 56 | 49 |
| Torquay United | 46 | 12 | 13 | 21 | 52 | 77 | 49 |
| Carlisle United | 46 | 11 | 15 | 20 | 42 | 65 | 48 |
| Halifax Town | 46 | 12 | 11 | 23 | 54 | 68 | 47 |
| Barnet | 46 | 12 | 9 | 25 | 67 | 81 | 45 |

*Chesterfield 9 points deducted

# Football League Appearances, 1997–2001

*Appearances as substitute in brackets*

| | 1997-98 | 1998-99 | 1999-2000 | 2000-01 | | 1997-98 | 1998-99 | 1999-2000 | 2000-01 |
|---|---|---|---|---|---|---|---|---|---|
| G. Abbey | — | — | 12 (6) | 13 (5) | L. Martin | — | — | 21 | 21 |
| D. Adams | — | — | — | 36 (1) | A. Mason | 7 (5) | — | — | — |
| J. Askey | 37 (2) | 31 (7) | 37 (3) | 29 (8) | M. McDonald | 22 | 23 | — | — |
| A. Bailey | — | 5 (5) | — | — | P. Matias | — | 21 (1) | — | — |
| M. Bamber | — | — | - (1) | 2 (3) | N. Mitchell | 2 (4) | — | — | — |
| D. Barclay | — | 3 (6) | — | — | N. Moore | — | — | 12 (3) | — |
| R. Barker | — | — | 35 | 23 | K. Munroe | — | — | 1 (4) | 19 (4) |
| C. Bettney | — | — | — | - (2) | P. O'Neill | — | — | - (1) | 5 (7) |
| G. Brown | 2 | 5 | 2 (3) | — | S. Payne | 39 | 32 (6) | — | — |
| S. Brown | — | 1 (1) | — | — | N. Peel | 10 (4) | — | — | — |
| A. Bullock | — | — | — | 24 | A. Philliskirk | 1 (9) | — | — | — |
| C. Byrne | — | — | 5 | — | P. Power | 21 (17) | — | — | — |
| S. Came | — | — | — | 3 (4) | R. Price | 46 | 42 | 11 (1) | — |
| L. Chambers | 17 (4) | — | — | — | C. Priest | — | — | 34 (2) | 14 (1) |
| S. Collins | — | — | 37 (2) | 15 (2) | G. Rioch | — | — | 42 | 16 (1) |
| D. Connell | — | — | — | - (1) | C. Rose | 15 (4) | — | — | — |
| M. Cooper | 8 | — | — | — | B. Sedgemore | 5 | 25 (9) | 31 (4) | 23 (4) |
| P. Davenport | 2 (2) | - (1) | — | — | C. Shuker | — | — | — | 6 (3) |
| S. Davies | — | 9 (3) | 30 (6) | — | P. Smith | — | 12 | — | — |
| K. Durkan | 2 (2) | 23 (3) | 41 (1) | 26 (5) | E. Sodje | 41 | 42 | — | — |
| C. Edey | 9 (4) | — | — | — | S. Soley | — | 5 (5) | — | — |
| M. Gardiner | 7 | — | — | — | N. Sorvel | 41 (4) | 38 (3) | — | — |
| L. Glover | — | — | — | 29 (8) | A. Tereskinas | — | — | — | - (1) |
| P. Griffiths | — | 4 | — | — | D. Tinson | 44 | 37 | 46 | 45 |
| S. Hitchen | 1 (1) | 35 | 2 (3) | 37 | G. Tomlinson | — | 15 (13) | 7 (11) | — |
| M. Holt | — | 3 (1) | — | — | R. Tracey | — | — | — | 11 (2) |
| N. Howarth | 38 (3) | 11 (9) | — | — | G. Twynham | — | — | — | 5 (4) |
| R. Ingram | 5 | 23 (4) | 35 (1) | 32 (1) | P. Ware | — | — | 9 (9) | — |
| R. Irving | 6 (3) | — | — | — | D. Whitehead | — | — | 10 (13) | 9 (24) |
| K. Keen | — | — | — | 30 (2) | S. Whittaker | 29 (2) | 18 (9) | 2 (7) | — |
| R. Knight | — | — | 3 | — | A. Williams | — | 4 | 11 | — |
| R. Lambert | — | — | — | 4 (5) | S. Wilson | — | — | — | 1 |
| R. Landon | 6 (12) | 10 (4) | — | — | S. Wood | 43 | 29 (13) | 30 (6) | 27 (3) |
| M. Lomax | — | - (1) | — | — | M. Woolley | — | — | — | 1 (1) |

# Football League Hotshots, 1997–2001

**1997–98**

Wood 13, Landon 7, Power 7, Askey 6, Chambers 4, Whittaker 4, Howarth 3, Peel 3, Sodje 3, Sorvel 3, Cooper 2, Gardiner 2, Davenport 1, McDonald 1, Philliskirk 1, o.g. 3

**1998–99**

Askey 4, Sorvel 4, Tomlinson 4, Wood 4, Durkan 3, Payne 3, Smith 3, Sodje 3, Davies 2, Landon 2, McDonald 2, Matias 2, Sedgemore 2, Bailey 1, Barclay 1, Griffiths 1, Holt 1, Whittaker 1

**1999–2000**

Barker 16, Askey 15, Durkan 6, Whitehead 6, Rioch 5, Priest 4, Collins 3, Moore 2, Tomlinson 2, Ware 2, Davies 1, Sedgemore 1, Tinson 1, Wood 1, o.g. 1

**2000–01**

Glover 8, Whitehead 8, Barker 7, Askey 4, Durkan 4, Priest 4, Sedgemore 3, Tinson 3, Tracey 3, Keen 2, Ingram 1, Munroe 1, Rioch 1, Shuker 1, Wood 1

# Major Cup Records

## (a) Macclesfield Association Silver Medal Competition

1880–81: Rnd 1: Macc. 7, Hurdsfield 0
SF: Macc. 6, Bollington 2
F: Macc. 4, St George's Rangers 0　　Winners

1881–82: Rnd 1: Macc. 4, Macc. Res. 1
SF: King Edward's 2, Macc. 3
F: Macc. 3, Baptists 1　　Winners

## (b) Cheshire Senior Cup

### (For neutral semi and final venues, see text.)

1879–80: Rnd 1: Bowdon v. Macc. *No result recorded – see text.*

1880–81: Rnd 1: Northwich Vics. 2, Macc. 0

1881–82: Rnd 1: Chester Rovers 2, Macc. 2
Replay: Macc. 1, Chester Rovers 0
Rnd 2: Hartford St John's 2, Macc. 4
SF: Northwich Vics. 5, Macc. 1

1882–83: Rnd 1: Rainow 0, Macc. 6
Rnd 2: Macc. 10, Middlewich 2
SF: Crewe Alexandra 3, Macc. 1

1883–84: Rnd 1: Macc. 4, Over Wanderers 0
Rnd 2: Macc. 4, Chester St John's 0
Rnd 3: Crewe Alexandra 4, Macc. 2

1884–85: Rnd 1: Macc. 9, Crewe Olympic 0
Rnd 2: Macc. 2, Crewe Britannia 1
Rnd 3: Macc. 0, Northwich Vics. 2

1885–86: Rnd 1: Macc. 6, Marple 0
Rnd 2: *walkover – Middlewich scratched*
Rnd 3: Macc. 15, Chester St Mary's 0
SF: Davenham 4, Macc. 1

1886–87: Rnd 1: Crewe Alexandra 5, Macc. 2

1887–88: Rnd 1: Macc. 15, Barnton Rovers 0
SF: Crewe Alexandra 4, Macc. 2

1888–89: Rnd 1: Northwich Vics. 4, Macc. 0

1889–90: Rnd 1: Chester St Oswald's 1, Macc. 2
SF: Macc. 1, Over Wanderers 0
F: Macc. 4, Nantwich 1　　Winners

1890–91: Rnd 1: Macc. 6, Nantwich 2
SF: Over Wanderers 0, Macc. 1
F: Macc. 1, Crewe Alexandra 0　　Winners

1891–92: Rnd 1: Macc. 9, Saltney 2
SF: Northwich Vics. 3, Macc. 1

1892–93: Rnd 1: Macc. 7, Nantwich 0
SF: Crewe Alexandra 3, Macc. 1

1893–94: Rnd 1: bye
SF: Crewe Alexandra 0, Macc. 2
F: Macc. 1, Chester 1
*Replay*: Macc. 2, Chester 1　　Winners

1894–95: Rnd 1: Macc. 2, Crewe Alexandra 1
SF: Macc. 3, Chester Police 2
F: Chester 2, Macc. 1　　Finalists

1895–96: Rnd 1: Macc. 4, Crewe Carriage Works 1
Rnd 2: Chester 0, Macc. 0
*Replay*: Macc. 1, Chester 0
SF: Macc. 0, Congleton Hornets 0
*Replay*: Congleton Hornets 1, Macc. 5
F: Macc. 2, Crewe Alexandra 0　　Winners

1896–97: Rnd 1: Macc. 5, Barnton Rovers 0
Rnd 2: Macc. 1, Northwich Vics. 2

1897–98: *did not enter*

1898–99: Rnd 1: Crewe Alexandra 5, Macc./Hallefield 1

1899–1900: Rnd 1: Macc. 1, Congleton Hornets 3

1900–01: Rnd 1: Nantwich 4, Macc. 0

1901–02: Rnd 1: Broadheath 7, Macc. 1

1902–03: Rnd 1: *bye*
Rnd 2: Macc. 1, Northwich Vics. 0
Rnd 3: Sale Holmfield 2, Macc. 1

1903–04: Rnd 1: Congleton Town 0, Macc. 1
Rnd 2: Sale Holmfield 6, Macc. 1

1904–05: Rnd 1: Macc. 1, Bollington St John's 1
*Replay:* Bollington St John's 4, Macc. 3

1905–06: Rnd 1: Hyde St George's 2, Macc. 0

1906–07: Rnd 1: Congleton Town 2, Macc. 0
Rnd 2: *bye*
Rnd 3: Macc. 6, Bollington 0
Rnd 4: Macc. 2, Lostock Gralam 0
SF: Port Sunlight 1, Macc. 1
*Replay:* Macc. 1, Port Sunlight 0
F: Crewe Alexandra 2, Macc. 0          Finalists

1907–08: Rnds 1 and 2: *byes*
Rnd 3: Macc. 0, Northern Nomads 0
*Replay:* Northern Nomads 2, Macc. 2
*2nd replay:* Macc. 1, Northern Nomads 0
Rnd 4: Macc. 2, Tranmere Rovers 0
SF: Altrincham 3, Macc. 1

1908–09: Rnds 1 and 2: *byes*
Rnd 3: Sale Holmfield 0, Macc. 3
Rnd 4: Congleton Town 1, Macc. 2
SF: Chester 2, Macc. 0

1909–10: Rnds 1 and 2: *byes*
Rnd 3: Macc. 3, Alderley Edge 0
Rnd 4: Altrincham 1, Macc. 3
SF: Macc. 2, Stockport County 1
F: Macc. 0, Crewe Alexandra 0
*Replay:* Crewe Alexandra 1, Macc. 0      Finalists

1910–11: Rnds 1 and 2: *byes*
Rnd 3: Macc. 4, Hyde 1
Rnd 4: Macc. 0, Stockport County 0
*Replay:* Macc. 2, Stockport County 0
SF: Macc. 1, Northern Nomads 1
*Replay:* Northern Nomads 0, Macc. 2
F: Macc. 1, Chester 0                Winners

1911–12: Rnd 1: Macc. 0, Stalybridge Celtic 1

1912–13: Rnd 1: Macc. 2, Tranmere Rovers 1
Rnd 2: Stalybridge Celtic 3, Macc. 0

1913–14: Rnd 1: Macc. 2, Chester 3

1914–15: Rnd 1: Hyde 3, Macc. 2

1915–19: *no competition*

1919–20: Rnd 1: Crewe Alexandra 3, Macc. 0

1920–21: Rnd 1: Macc. 5, Tranmere Rovers 0
Rnd 2: Runcorn 1, Macc. 1
*Replay:* Macc. 3, Runcorn 0
SF: Congleton Town 2, Macc. 0

1921–22: Rnd 1: *bye*
Rnd 2: Macc. 0, Congleton Town 2
1922–23:
Rnd 1: Macc. 6, Hyde Utd. 3
Rnd 2: Macc. 6, Middlewich 1
Rnd 3: Macc. 7, Stockport County 1
SF: Altrincham 3, Macc. 2

1923–24: Rnd 1: Macc. 0, Stalybridge Celtic 0
*Replay:* Stalybridge Celtic 3, Macc. 1

1924–25: Rnd 1: Macc. 0, Crewe Alexandra 2

1925–26: Rnd 1: Macc. 2, Sandbach 1
Rnd 2: Macc. 4, Poulton Rovers 0
Rnd 3: Macc. 3, Middlewich 0
SF: Macc. 3, Winsford Utd. 3
*Replay:* Winsford Utd. 4, Macc. 1

1926–27: Rnd 1: Macc. 6, Poulton Rovers 0
Rnd 2: Hyde Utd. 1, Macc. 3
Rnd 3: Chester 2, Macc. 3
SF: Tranmere Rovers 4, Macc. 0

1927–28: Rnd 1: Macc. 5, Northwich Vics. 0
Rnd 2: Macc. 0, Middlewich 0
*Replay:* Middlewich 3, Macc. 2

1928–29: Rnd 1: Macc. 2, Tranmere Rovers 6

1929–30: Rnd 1: Macc. 6, Barnton Victoria 5
Rnd 2: Macc. 4, Witton Albion 1
Rnd 3: Macc. 4, Runcorn 3
SF: Winsford Utd. 3, Macc. 7
F: Macc. 5, Nantwich 4              Winners

1930–31: Rnd 1: Northwich Vics. 1, Macc. 3
Rnd 2: Northern Nomads 1, Macc. 1
*Replay:* Macc. 3, Northern Nomads 1
Rnd 3: Altrincham 2, Macc. 1

1931–32: Rnd 1: Macc. 6, Northern Nomads 1
Rnd 2: Macc. 1, Hyde Utd. 2

1932–33: Rnd 1: Witton Albion 0, Macc. 3
Rnd 2: ICI Alkali 2, Macc. 1

1933–34: Rnd 1: Congleton Town 5, Macc. 0

1934–35: Rnd 1: Moulton Verdin 1, Macc. 5
Rnd 2: Macc. 4, Chester 1
Rnd 3: Macc. 8, Northwich Vics. 1

SF: Altrincham 1, Macc. 4
F: Macc. 5, Crewe Alexandra 2          Winners

1935–36:  Rnd 1: *bye*
          Rnd 2: Macc. 3, Chester 0
          Rnd 3: Macc. 3, Hyde Utd. 1
          SF: Winsford Utd. 1, Macc. 4
          F: Runcorn 2, Macc. 1                Finalists

1936–37:  Rnd 1: Wilmslow Albion 0, Macc. 2
          Rnd 2: Hyde Utd. 0, Macc. 2
          Rnd 3: Macc. 2, Witton Albion 4

1937–38:  Rnd 1: Wilmslow Albion 0, Macc. 5
          Rnd 2: Macc. 3, Stockport County 1
          Rnd 3: Runcorn 3, Macc. 0

1938–39:  Rnd 1: *bye*
          Rnd 2: Congleton Town 2, Macc. 1

1939–40:  (*War conditions*)
          Rnd 1: *bye*
          Rnd 2: Macc. 3, Wilmslow Albion 1
          Rnd 3: Macc. 1, Rode Heath Rangers 0
          SF: Macc. 2, Hyde Utd. 1
          F: Macc. 3, Northwich Vics. 2        Winners

1940–45:  *no competition*

1945–46:  *did not compete*

1946–47:  Rnd 1: *bye*
          Rnd 2: Macc. 7, Fodens' Motors 2
          Rnd 3: Witton Albion 0, Macc. 3
          SF: Hyde Utd. 2, Macc. 0

1947–48:  Rnd 1: *bye*
          Rnd 2: Macc. 2, Winsford Utd. 3

1948–49:  Rnd 1: Macc. 0, Stockport County 2

1949–50:  Rnd 1: Macc. 3, Runcorn 1
          Rnd 2: Crewe Alexandra 0, Macc. 0
          *Replay*: Macc. 4, Crewe Alexandra 3
          SF: Macc. 4, Winsford Utd. 2
          F: Northwich Vics. 1, Macc. 0        Finalists

1950–51:  Rnd 1: Macc. 3, Crewe Alexandra 1
          Rnd 2: Macc. 1, Witton Albion 0
          SF: Macc. 1, Tranmere Rovers 0
          F: Macc. 3, Northwich Vics. 2        Winners

1951–52:  Rnd 1: Hyde Utd. 1, Macc. 4
          Rnd 2: Macc. 2, Lostock Gralam 1
          SF: Macc. 1, Winsford Utd. 1
          *Replay*: Winsford Utd. 1, Macc. 1
          *2nd replay*: Macc. 2, Winsford Utd. 0
          F: Macc. 2, Witton Albion 0          Winners

1952–53:  Rnd 1: Hyde Utd. 0, Macc. 1
          Rnd 2: Tranmere Rovers 4, Macc. 2

1953–54:  Rnd 1: Macc. 2, Hyde Utd. 1
          Rnd 2: Runcorn 2, Macc. 3
          SF: Macc. 2, Witton Albion 1
          F: Winsford Utd. 2, Macc. 2
          *Replay*: Macc. 1, Winsford Utd. 0    Winners

1954–55:  Rnd 1: Macc. 5, Linotype 1
          Rnd 2: Northwich Vics. 1, Macc. 0

1955–56:  Rnd 1: Macc. 3, Crewe Alexandra 2
          Rnd 2: Altrincham 5, Macc. 1

1956–57:  Rnd 1: Macc. 2, Northwich Vics. 6

1957–58:  Rnd 1: Stalybridge Celtic 2, Macc. 4
          Rnd 2: Macc. 2, Tranmere Rovers 4

1958–59:  Rnd 1: Witton Albion 3, Macc. 2

1959–60:  Rnd 1: Macc. 2, Ellesmere Port Town 1
          Rnd 2: Macc. 2, Runcorn Athletic 2
          *Replay*: Runcorn Athletic 1, Macc. 3
          SF: Altrincham 4, Macc. 5
          F: Macc. 2, Hyde Utd. 1              Winners

1960–61:  Rnd 1: Crewe Alexandra 1, Macc. 0

1961–62:  Rnd 1: Macc. 2, Northwich Vics. 1
          Rnd 2: Macc. 4, Chester 2
          SF: Runcorn 2, Macc. 0

1962–63:  Rnd 1: Stalybridge Celtic 2, Macc. 1

1963–64:  Rnd 1: Macc. 5, Congleton Town 1
          Rnd 2: Runcorn 2, Macc. 2
          *Replay*: Macc. 4, Runcorn 0
          SF: Tranmere Rovers 2, Macc. 3
          F: Macc. 1, Northwich Vics. 0        Winners

1964–65:  Rnd 1: Macc. 4, Chester 0
          Rnd 2: Macc. 1, Tranmere Rovers 1
          *Replay*: Tranmere Rovers 3, Macc. 2

1965–66:  Rnd 1: Stockport County 2, Macc. 2
          *Replay*: Macc. 0, Stockport County 2

1966–67:  Rnd 1: Tranmere Rovers 4, Macc. 2

1967–68:  Rnd 1: Macc. 3, Lostock Gralam 1
          Rnd 2: Runcorn 1, Macc. 1
          *Replay*: Macc. 0, Runcorn 0
          *2nd replay*: Runcorn 3, Macc. 2

1968–69:  Rnd 1: Crewe Alexandra 0, Macc. 3
          Rnd 2: Macc. 4, New Brighton 0
          SF: Witton Albion 1, Macc. 1

*Replay*: Macc. 3, Witton Albion 0
F: *First leg*: Northwich Vics. 0, Macc. 1
*Second leg*: Macc. 2, Northwich Vics. 1   Winners
(*Aggregate*: W 3–1)

1969–70: Rnd 1: Nantwich 2, Macc. 1

1970–71: Rnd 1: Macc. 3, Ellesmere Port Town 0
Rnd 2: Macc. 4, Altrincham 2
SF: Macc. 3, Witton Albion 1
F: Macc. 1, Northwich Vics. 1
*Replay*: Macc. 2, Northwich Vics. 1   Winners

1971–72: Rnd 1: Sandbach Ramblers 0, Macc. 0
*Replay*: Macc. 0, Sandbach Ramblers 2

1972–73: Rnd 1: Sandbach Ramblers 1, Macc. 4
Rnd 2: Macc. 3, Tranmere Rovers 2
SF: Macc. 3, Altrincham 2
F: Winsford Utd. 2, Macc. 2
*Replay*: Macc. 1, Winsford Utd. 1
*2nd replay*: Winsford Utd. 0, Macc. 0
*3rd replay*: Macc. 2, Winsford Utd. 1   Winners

1973–74: Rnd 1: Witton Albion 0, Macc. 0
*Replay*: Macc. 2, Witton Albion 0
Rnd 2: Macc. 2, Hyde Utd. 0
SF: Macc. 2, Poulton 1
F: Runcorn 1, Macc. 0   Finalists

1974–75: Rnd 1: Stockport County 0, Macc. 2
Rnd 2: Macc. 4, Chester 1
SF: Altrincham 3, Macc. 2

1975–76: Rnd 1: Macc. 2, Tranmere Rovers 1
Rnd 2: Hyde Utd. 0, Macc. 3
SF: Nantwich 2, Macc. 1

1976–77: Rnd 1: Stalybridge Celtic 0, Macc. 1
Rnd 2: Macc. 3, Poulton 0
SF: Macc. 3, Winsford Utd. 0
F: Northwich Vics. 4, Macc. 1   Finalists

1977–78: Rnd 1: Chester 1, Macc. 2
Rnd 2: Macc. 1, Witton Albion 2

1978–79: Rnd 1: Altrincham 3, Macc. 0

1979–80: Rnd 1: Macc. 1, Altrincham 1
*Replay*: Altrincham 1, Macc. 0

1980–81: Rnd 1: Macc. 1, Winsford Utd. 0
Rnd 2: Macc. 0, Stalybridge Celtic 1

1981–82: Rnd 1: Macc. 5, Alsager Town 0
Rnd 2: Macc. 3, Stockport County 0
SF: Altrincham 2, Macc. 1

1982–83: Rnd 1: Macc. 2, Nantwich 0

Rnd 2: Runcorn 1, Macc. 2
SF: Macc. 3, Witton Albion 1
F: Macc. 2, Congleton Town 1   Winners

1983–84: Rnd 1: Congleton Town 0, Macc. 1
Rnd 2: Runcorn 1, Macc. 0

1984–85: Rnd 1: Macc. 0, Northwich Vics. 2

1985–86: Rnd 1: Macc. 1, Bramhall 0
Rnd 2: Congleton Town 0, Macc. 0
*Replay*: Macc. 0, Congleton Town 1

1986–87: Rnd 1: Runcorn 2, Macc. 0

1987–88: Rnd 4: Macc. 1, Stalybridge Celtic 0
SF: *First leg*: Northwich Vics. 1, Macc. 2
*Second leg*: Macc. 3, Northwich Vics. 1
(*Aggregate*: W 5–2)
F: Runcorn 2, Macc. 1   Finalists

1988–89: Rnd 4: Vauxhall GM 1, Macc. 1
*Replay*: Macc. 2, Vauxhall GM 0
SF: *First leg*: Altrincham 0, Macc. 1
*Second leg*: Macc. 1, Altrincham 1
(*Aggregate*: W 2–1)
F: Runcorn 3, Macc. 1   Finalists

1989–90: Rnd 3: Northwich Vics. 2, Macc. 2
*Replay*: Macc. 1, Northwich Vics. 1
(*Macc. won 5–2 on penalties*)
SF: *First leg*: Macc. 1, Witton Albion 0
*Second leg*: Witton Albion 0, Macc. 1
(*Aggregate*: W 2–0)
F: Hyde Utd. 1, Macc. 0   Finalists

1990–91: Rnd 3: Warrington Town 0, Macc. 1
SF: *First leg*: Altrincham 1, Macc. 0
*Second leg*: Macc. 2, Altrincham 0
(*Aggregate*: W 2–1)
F: Macc. 2, Witton Albion 0   Winners

1991–92: Rnd 3: Macc. 3, Hyde Utd. 2
SF: *First leg*: Winsford Utd. 1, Macc. 3
*Second leg*: Macc. 3, Winsford Utd. 1
(*Aggregate*: W 6–2)
F: Macc. 1, Witton Albion 1
*Replay*: Macc. 2, Witton Albion 0   Winners

1992–93: Rnd 3: Macc. 0, Warrington 2

1993–94: Rnd 2: Altrincham 0, Macc. 1
Rnd 3: Macc. 7, Colwyn Bay 1
(*Macc. disqualified for fielding ineligible
player – see text*)

1994–95: Rnd 3: Caernarfon Town 2, Macc. 1

1995–96: Rnd 3: Vauxhall GM 0, Macc. 4

SF: *First leg*: Hyde Utd. 2, Macc. 1          (*Macc. won on away goals rule*)
*Second leg*: Macc. 1, Hyde Utd. 1            F; Macc. 1, Runcorn 0                    Winners
(*Aggregate*: L 2–3)

1998–99:  Rnd 1: Macc. 5, Vauxhall GM 0
1996–97:  Rnd 2: Congleton Town 1, Macc. 3    Rnd 2: Runcorn 4, Macc. 2
SF: *First leg*: Macc. 7, Nantwich 0
*Second leg*: Nantwich 1, Macc. 2     1999–    Rnd 3: Macc. 2, Chester 1
(*Aggregate*: W 9–2)                  2000:    SF: Macc. 2, Crewe Alexandra 1
F: Hyde Utd. 3, Macc. 0      Finalists          F: Macc. 2, Altrincham 1                Winners

2000–01:  Rnd 1: Macc. 2, Tranmere Rovers 1
1997–98:  Rnd 2: Macc. 2, Cheadle Town 0      Rnd 2: Macc. 5, Woodley Sports 1
SF: Northwich Vics. 2, Macc. 2        SF: Macc. 5, Stockport County 8
*Replay*: Macc. 1, Northwich Vics. 1


# (c) FA Cup

| | | | | | |
|---|---|---|---|---|---|
| 1882–83: | Rnd 1: Lockwood Brothers | H L 3–4 | 1897–1907: | *did not enter* | |
| 1883–84: | Rnd 1: Davenham | A L 0–2 | 1907–08: | Rnd 1q: Wigan Town | H W 4–1 |
| 1884–85: | Rnd 1: Hartford St John's | H W 9–0 | | Rnd 2q: Buxton | A D 0–0 |
| | Rnd 2: Leek | H L 1–5 | | *Replay – match abandoned*: | H 1–2 |
| | | | | *2nd replay – at Stockport*: | W 3–2 |
| 1885–86: | Rnd 1: Northwich Victoria | H W 4–1 | | Rnd 3q: Atherton | A L 0–5 |
| | Rnd 2: Davenham | A L 1–8 | 1908–09: | Rnd 1q: St Helens Town | A L 1–3 |
| 1886–87: | Rnd 1: Goldenhill | A L 2–4 | 1909–10: | Rnd 1q: Heywood Utd. | H L 0–1 |
| | (*FA ordered match to be replayed at Leek*) | | 1910–11: | Rnd 1q: Chapel-en-le-Frith | H W 7–2 |
| | *Replay*: | L 2–3 | | Rnd 2q: St Helens Town | A L 0–3 |
| 1887–88: | Rnd 1: Shrewsbury Town | A L 1–3 | 1911–12: | Rnd 1q: Hurst | A L 1–6 |
| 1888–89: | Rnd 1q: Chester | A D 2–2 | 1912–13: | Rnd 1q: St Helens Town | H W 1–0 |
| | (*Chester awarded tie*) | | | Rnd 2q: Rochdale | H L 3–5 |
| 1889–90: | *did not enter* | | 1913–14: | Rnd 1q: Hurst | H W 2–0 |
| 1890–91: | Rnd 1q: Cliftonville | A L 3–4 | | Rnd 2q: Stalybridge Celtic | A L 0–1 |
| 1891–92: | Rnd 1q: Newtown | H W 4–2 | 1914–15: | Prelim: Hyde | A D 1–1 |
| | Rnd 2q: Nantwich | A W 3–2 | | *Replay*: | H W 4–3 |
| | Rnd 3q: Northwich Victoria | A L 0–5 | | Rnd 1q: Atherton | A W 2–1 |
| | | | | Rnd 2q: Altrincham | H L 1–3 |
| 1892–93: | Rnd 1q: Northwich Victoria | A L 0–4 | 1915–19: | *no competition* | |
| 1893–94: | Rnd 1q: Newtown | H D 5–5 | 1919–20: | Rnd 1q: Garston Gasworks | H L 1–2 |
| | *Replay*: | A W 5–1 | 1920–21: | *did not enter* | |
| | Rnd 2q: Chester | H W 6–1 | | | |
| | Rnd 3q: Crewe Alexandra | A L 2–3 | 1921–22: | Prelim: Harrowby | A L 0–2 |
| 1894–95: | Rnd 1q: Chester | A W 2–1 | 1922–23: | Prelim 1: Nantwich | H W 3–0 |
| | Rnd 2q: Wrexham | A L 1–7 | | Prelim 2: Ellesmere Port | A L 1–2 |
| 1895–96: | Rnd 1q: Glossop North End | A L 1–5 | 1923–24: | Prelim 1: Witton Albion | H W 6–1 |
| 1896–97: | Rnd 1q: Glossop North End | A L 0–5 | | Prelim 2: Northwich Victoria | A L 1–3 |

1924–28:  *did not enter*

1928–29:  Prelim: Colwyn Bay Utd.          A  D 2–2
    *Replay:*                               H  W 3–1
    Rnd 1q: Flint Town                   A  W 2–1
    Rnd 2q: Connah's Quay                H  W 2–1
    Rnd 3q: Rhyl Athletic                A  D 2–2
    *Replay:*                               H  D 0–0
    *2nd replay – at Crewe:*                   L 0–2

1929–30:  Prelim: Bangor City             H  W 6–0
    Rnd 1q: Rhyl Athletic                H  W 4–3
    Rnd 2q: Caernarfon                   H  D 2–2
    *Replay:*                               A  L 2–4

1930–31:  Prelim: Rhyl Athletic           A  D 0–0
    *Replay:*                               H  L 1–3

1931–32:  Prelim: Nantwich                H  W 2–0
    Rnd 1q: Congleton Town               H  W 3–1
    Rnd 2q: Winsford Utd.                A  D 1–1
    *Replay:*                               H  W 1–0
    Rnd 3q: Altrincham                   A  L 4–6

1932–33:  Prelim: Congleton Town          H  W 4–1
    Rnd 1q: Altrincham                   H  L 2–3

1933–34:  Prelim: Barnton Victoria        H  D 3–3
    *Replay:*                               H  W 4–3
    Rnd 1q: Colwyn Bay                   H  W 3–0
    Rnd 2q: Rhyl Athletic                A  W 1–0
    Rnd 3q: Altrincham                   A  L 1–2

1934–35:  Prelim: Bangor City             H  W 5–1
    Rnd 1q: Colwyn Bay                   H  W 3–1
    Rnd 2q: Northwich Victoria           A  L 1–2

1935–36:  Prelim: Altrincham              A  L 3–4

1936–37:  Extra prelim: Haslington Villa  H  W 4–1
    Prelim: Linotype                     H  W 4–3
    Rnd 1q: Barnton Victoria             H  W 5–1
    Rnd 2q: Runcorn                      H  L 1–2

1937–38:  *did not compete*

1938–39:  Extra prelim: Timperley         H  W 7–1
    Prelim: Moulton Verdin               H  W 2–0
    Rnd 1q: Bangor City                  A  L 1–3

1939–45:  *no competition*

1945–47:  *did not compete*

1947–48:  Prelim: Buxton                  A  L 1–6

1948–49:  Prelim 1: Shell-Mex             H  W 6–3
    Prelim 2: Northwich Victoria         H  L 0–3

1949–50:  Extra prelim: Port Sunlight     H  W 3–2
    Prelim 1: Congleton Town             H  L 1–2

1950–51:  Prelim: Droylsden               A  D 5–5
    *Replay:*                               H  W 7–2
    Rnd 1q: Altrincham                   A  L 1–3

1951–52:  Prelim: Buxton                  H  D 0–0
    *Replay:*                               A  L 0–2

1952–53:  Rnd 1q: Congleton Town          H  W 3–0
    Rnd 2q: Winsford Utd.                A  L 0–1

1953–54:  Rnd 1q: Stalybridge Celtic      A  L 0–1

1954–55:  Rnd 1q: Lostock Gralam          A  W 5–2
    Rnd 2q: Hyde Utd.                    A  L 1–3

1955–56:  Rnd 1q: Northwich Victoria      H  L 0–4

1956–57:  Prelim: Ellesmere Port Town     H  W 2–1
    Rnd 1q: Altrincham                   A  W 3–1
    Rnd 2q: Winsford Utd.                A  D 2–2
    *Replay:*                               H  W 4–2
    Rnd 3q: Hyde Utd.                    H  D 4–4
    *Replay:*                               A  D 3–3
    *2nd replay – at Stockport:*               L 3–5

1957–58:  Prelim: Winsford Utd.           H  W 5–4
    Rnd 1q: Altrincham                   A  L 3–4

1958–59:  Prelim: Ellesmere Port Town     H  L 1–3

1959–60:  Prelim: Ellesmere Port Town     H  L 2–3

1960–61:  Rnd 1q: Northwich Victoria      A  W 3–0
    Rnd 2q: Linotype                     H  D 1–1
    *Replay – at Broadheath, Altrincham:*      W 3–0
    Rnd 3q: Congleton Town               A  W 3–0
    Rnd 4q: Nelson                       A  W 3–2
    Rnd 1: Southport                     A  L 2–7

1961–62:  Rnd 1q: Droylsden               H  W 4–0
    Rnd 2q: Northwich Victoria           A  L 0–1

1962–63:  Prelim: Droylsden               A  D 2–2
    *Replay – match abandoned – poor light:* H  2–2
    *2nd replay – at Stockport:*               L 2–3

1963–64:  Rnd 1q: Winsford Utd.           H  W 1–0
    Rnd 2q: Mossley                      A  W 5–0
    Rnd 3q: Northwich Victoria           A  D 1–1
    *Replay:*                               H  W 1–0
    Rnd 4q: Frickley Colliery            H  L 1–3

1964–65:  Prelim: Oswestry Town           H  W 2–0
    Rnd 1q: Northwich Victoria           H  W 4–1
    Rnd 2q: Rhyl Athletic                A  W 2–0
    Rnd 3q: Witton Albion                H  W 2–1

|  |  |  |  |  |  |
|---|---|---|---|---|---|
| | Rnd 4q: Ellesmere Port Town | H W 2–1 | 1977–78: | Rnd 1q: Mossley | H L 0–2 |
| | Rnd 1: Wrexham | H L 1–2 | | | |
| | | | 1978–79: | Prelim: Marine | H L 2–4 |
| 1965–66: | Rnd 1q: Winsford Utd. | H W 7–0 | | | |
| | Rnd 2q: Witton Albion | H W 9–0 | 1979–80: | Prelim: New Brighton | A W 7–1 |
| | Rnd 3q: Oswestry Town | A L 2–3 | | Rnd 1q: St Helens Town | A W 2–1 |
| | | | | Rnd 2q: Mossley | H D 0–0 |
| 1966–67: | Rnd 1q: Alfreton | H W 2–1 | | *Replay:* | A L 2–3 |
| | Rnd 2q: Matlock | A D 2–2 | 1980–81: | Rnd 1q: Stourbridge | A L 2–6 |
| | *Replay:* | H W 6–1 | | | |
| | Rnd 3q: Worksop Town | H W 3–1 | 1981–82: | Prelim: Witton Albion | A L 1–3 |
| | Rnd 4q: Nuneaton Borough | H D 1–1 | | | |
| | *Replay:* | A L 1–3 | 1982–83: | Rnd 1q: Bangor City | H W 3–1 |
| | | | | Rnd 2q: Hyde Utd. | A W 5–2 |
| 1967–68: | Rnd 1q: Bacup Borough | H W 7–0 | | Rnd 3q: Ashton Utd. | A W 2–0 |
| | Rnd 2q: Witton Albion | A W 2–0 | | Rnd 4q: Stafford Rangers | H W 3–1 |
| | Rnd 3q: Hyde Utd. | A W 2–0 | | Rnd 1: Worcester City | H L 1–5 |
| | Rnd 4q: Wigan Athletic | A D 1–1 | | | |
| | *Replay:* | H W 3–0 | 1983–84: | Rnd 1q: Tamworth | A W 6–1 |
| | Rnd 1: Stockport County | A D 1–1 | | Rnd 2q: Marine | A W 3–0 |
| | *Replay:* | H W 2–1 | | Rnd 3q: Congleton Town | H W 6–0 |
| | Rnd 2: Spennymoor Utd. | H W 2–0 | | Rnd 4q: Horwich RMI | A D 0–0 |
| | Rnd 3: Fulham | A L 2–4 | | *Replay:* | H W 4–3 |
| | | | | Rnd 1: York City | H D 0–0 |
| 1968–69: | Rnd 4q: Retford | A W 2–0 | | *Replay:* | A L 0–2 |
| | Rnd 1: Lincoln City | H L 1–3 | | | |
| | | | 1984–85: | Rnd 4q: Bishop Auckland | A W 2–1 |
| 1969–70: | Rnd 4q: Altrincham | H W 3–0 | | Rnd 1: Port Vale | H L 1–2 |
| | Rnd 1: Scunthorpe | H D 1–1 | | | |
| | *Replay:* | A L 2–4 | 1985–86: | Rnd 4q: South Bank | H W 3–1 |
| | | | | Rnd 1: Hartlepool Utd. | H L 1–2 |
| 1970–71: | Rnd 1: Bradford City | A L 2–3 | | | |
| | | | 1986–87: | Rnd 4q: Southport | H L 0–1 |
| 1971–72: | Rnd 4q: Ellesmere Port Town | H L 2–3 | | | |
| | | | 1987–88: | Rnd 1q: Stalybridge Celtic | A D 1–1 |
| 1972–73: | Rnd 1q: Emley Moor | A W 2–1 | | *Replay:* | H W 5–1 |
| | Rnd 2q: Glossop | H W 3–0 | | Rnd 2q: Chadderton | H W 5–0 |
| | Rnd 3q: Bradford Park Avenue | H W 1–0 | | Rnd 3q: Marine | H D 0–0 |
| | Rnd 4q: South Liverpool | H L 0–1 | | *Replay:* | A W 2–1 |
| | | | | Rnd 4q: Whitby Town | H W 3–1 |
| 1973–74: | Rnd 1q: Ashton Utd. | A W 3–0 | | Rnd 1: Carlisle Utd. | H W 4–2 |
| | Rnd 2q: Leek Town | A D 2–2 | | Rnd 2: Rotherham | H W 4–0 |
| | *Replay:* | H W 4–2 | | Rnd 3: Port Vale | A L 0–1 |
| | Rnd 3q: Stalybridge Celtic | H W 2–1 | | | |
| | Rnd 4q: Merthyr Tydfil | H D 0–0 | 1988–89: | Rnd 4q: Altrincham | H D 0–0 |
| | *Replay:* | A L 1–2 | | *Replay:* | A L 0–4 |
| | | | | | |
| 1974–75: | Rnd 1q: Congleton Town | H W 2–0 | 1989–90: | Rnd 1: Chester | H D 1–1 |
| | Rnd 2q: Stafford Rangers | A L 0–3 | | *Replay:* | A L 2–3 |
| | | | | | |
| 1975–76: | Rnd 1q: Sutton in Ashfield | H D 0–0 | 1990–91: | Rnd 4q: Altrincham | H D 2–2 |
| | *Replay:* | A W 1–0 | | *Replay:* | A L 0–3 |
| | Rnd 2q: Sutton Coldfield Town | A W 1–0 | | | |
| | Rnd 3q: Arnold | H W 3–1 | 1991–92: | Rnd 1q: Skelmersdale Utd. | A W 4–0 |
| | Rnd 4q: Mexborough | A W 2–1 | | Rnd 2q; Borrowash | H L 1–2 |
| | Rnd 1: Sheffield Wednesday | A L 1–3 | | | |
| | | | 1992–93: | Rnd 1q: Glossop | A W 1–0 |
| 1976–77: | Rnd 1q: Rhyl | A D 1–1 | | Rnd 2q: Hucknall | A D 1–1 |
| | *Replay:* | H L 1–2 | | | |

|  |  |  |  |
|---|---|---|---|
| *Replay:* | H W 4–1 | 1996–97: Rnd 1: Rochdale | A L 0–2 |
| Rnd 3q: Horwich RMI | H W 1–0 | | |
| Rnd 1: Chesterfield | H D 0–0 | 1997–98: Rnd 1: Hartlepool | A W 4–2 |
| *Replay:* | A D 2–2 | Rnd 2: Walsall | H L 0–7 |
| *(Macc. won 3–2 on penalties)* | | | |
| Rnd 2: Stockport County | H L 0–2 | 1998–99: Rnd 1: Slough Town | H D 2–2 |
| | | *Replay:* | A D 1–1 |
| 1993–94: Rnd 4q: Southport | H W 5–3 | *(Macc. won 9–8 on penalties)* | |
| Rnd 1: Hartlepool | H W 2–0 | Rnd 2: Cambridge Utd. | H W 4–1 |
| Rnd 2: Crewe Alexandra | A L 1–2 | Rnd 3: Coventry City | A L 0–7 |
| 1994–95: Rnd 4q: Bishop Auckland | A D 2–2 | 1999– Rnd 1: Hull City | H D 0–0 |
| *Replay:* | H L 0–1 | 2000: *Replay:* | A L 0–4 |
| 1995–96: Rnd 4q: Northwich Victoria | H L 0–1 | 2000–01: Rnd 1: Oxford Utd. | H L 0–1 |

# (d) Cheshire League Challenge Cup

*(For neutral venues, where applicable, see text)*

1921–22: Rnd 1: Congleton Town 3, Macc. 1
*(Congleton Town disqualified for fielding ineligible player)*
Rnd 2: Macc. 5, Nantwich 1
SF: Macc. 2, Stalybridge Celtic 2
*Replay:* Stalybridge Celtic 3, Macc. 0

1922–23: Rnd 1: Congleton Town 1, Macc. 1
*Replay:* Macc. 1, Congleton Town 1
*2nd replay:* Macc. 4, Congleton Town 0
Rnd 2: Macc. 2, Stalybridge Celtic 1
Rnd 3: *bye*
SF: Macc. 1, Sandbach 1
*Replay:* Sandbach 2, Macc. 0

1923–24: Rnd 1: *bye*
Rnd 2: Macc. 1, Crewe Alexandra 2

1924–25: Rnd 1: *bye*
SF: Macc. 2, Northwich Vics. 1
F: Macc. 4, Manchester North End 2    Winners

1925–26: Rnd 1: Macc. 6, Mossley 2
SF: Macc. 5, Congleton Town 3
F: Northwich Vics. 2, Macc. 0    Finalists

1926–27: Rnd 1: Macc. 1, Congleton Town 1
*Replay:* Congleton Town 4, Macc. 2

1927–28: Rnd 1: Congleton Town 4, Macc. 1

1928–29: Rnd 1: Macc. 1, Port Vale 1
*Replay:* Port Vale 5, Macc. 4

1929–30: Rnd 1: Macc. 3, Nantwich 1
Rnd 2: Altrincham 2, Macc. 3
Rnd 3: Congleton Town 4, Macc. 0

1930–31: Rnd 1: Macc. 3, Congleton Town 0
Rnd 2: Port Vale 4, Macc. 1

1931–32: Rnd 1: Macc. 4, Congleton Town 2
Rnd 2: Macc. 5, Manchester North End 1
SF: Macc. 5, Hurst 0
F: Macc. 1, Port Vale 0    Winners

1932–33: Rnd 1: Macc. 4, Congleton Town 1
Rnd 2: Macc. 5, Hyde Utd. 1
SF: Altrincham 5, Macc. 1

1933–34: Rnd 1: Macc. 2, Altrincham 1
Rnd 2: Macc. 1, Stalybridge Celtic 1
*Replay:* Stalybridge Celtic 3, Macc. 3
*2nd replay:* Macc. 2, Stalybridge Celtic 2
*3rd replay:* Stalybridge Celtic 3, Macc. 4
SF: Stockport County 2, Macc. 2
*Replay:* Macc. 3, Stockport County 4

1934–35: Rnd 1: Stockport County 8, Macc. 1

1935–36: Rnd 1: Macc. 5, Congleton Town 1
Rnd 2: Runcorn 2, Macc. 3
SF: Macc. 1, Wigan Athletic 2

1936–37: Rnd 1: Macc. 6, Congleton Town 3
Rnd 2: *bye*
Rnd 3: Macc. 1, Buxton 1
*Replay:* Buxton 1, Macc. 2
SF: Winsford Utd. 3, Macc. 1

1937–38: Rnd 1: Macc. 3, Congleton Town 0
Rnd 2: *bye*
Rnd 3: Macc. 0, Port Vale 1

| | |
|---|---|
| 1938–39: | Rnd 1: Macc. 3, Congleton Town 2 |
| | Rnd 2: *bye* |
| | Rnd 3: Port Vale 2, Macc. 0 |
| | |
| 1939–46: | *no competition* |
| | |
| 1946–47: | Rnd 1: Macc. 2, Congleton Town 0 |
| | Rnd 2: Macc. 1, South Liverpool 2 |

1947–48: Rnd 1: Macc. 2, Congleton Town 0
Rnd 2: Wellington Town 1, Macc. 2
SF: Macc. 3, Mossley 3
*Replay*: Mossley 2, Macc. 3
F: Altrincham 3, Macc. 3
*Replay*: Macc. 3, Altrincham 1                    Winners

1948–49: Rnd 1: Macc. 4, Congleton Town 4
*Replay*: Congleton Town 3, Macc. 1

1949–50: Rnd 1: Macc. 0, Congleton Town 4

1950–51: Rnd 1: Congleton Town 1, Macc. 2
Rnd 2: Macc. 4, South Liverpool 2
SF: Ellesmere Port 2, Macc. 5
F: Altrincham 1, Macc. 0                            Finalists

1951–52: Rnd 1: Macc. 3, Congleton Town 1
Rnd 2: Macc. 0, Mossley 0
*Replay*: Mossley 2, Macc. 1

1952–53: Rnd 1: Congleton Town 0, Macc. 2
Rnd 2: Buxton 1, Macc. 2
SF: Macc. 2, Bangor City 1
F: Hyde Utd. 2, Macc. 1                             Finalists

1953–54: Rnd 1: Macc. 2, Congleton Town 0
Rnd 2: Stafford Rangers 2, Macc. 1

1954–55: Rnd 1: Congleton Town 1, Macc. 4
Rnd 2: Macc. 0, Mossley 1

1955–56: Rnd 1: Macc. 0, Congleton Town 1

1956–57: Rnd 1: Macc. 1, Congleton Town 1
*Replay*: Macc. 3, Congleton Town 3
*2nd replay*: Macc. 2, Congleton Town 1
SF: Wellington Town 6, Macc. 0

1957–58: Rnd 1: Macc. 1, Congleton Town 2

1958–59: Rnd 1: Crewe Alexandra 2, Macc. 4
Rnd 2: Macc. 2, Wrexham 3

1959–60: Rnd 1: Mossley 0, Macc. 2
Rnd 2: Macc. 2, Oswestry Town 0
SF: Hyde 2, Macc. 1

1960–61: Rnd 1: Buxton 4, Macc. 1

1961–63: *no competition: see (e) below*

1963–64: Rnd 1: Ellesmere Port Town 0, Macc. 0
*Replay*: Macc. 3, Ellesmere Port Town 1
Rnd 2: *bye*
Rnd 3: Frickley Colliery 0, Macc. 2
SF: Macc. 2, Stalybridge Celtic 1
F: *First leg*: Altrincham 0, Macc. 0
*Second leg*: Macc. 2, Altrincham 4
*(Aggregate: L 2–4)*                               Finalists

1964–65: Rnd 1: Macc. 6, Chester 0
Rnd 2: Altrincham 3, Macc. 2

1965–66: Rnd 1: Ellesmere Port Town 0, Macc. 2
*(match abandoned after 84 mins. – tie
awarded to Macc.)*
Rnd 2: Macc. 3, Frickley Colliery 0
SF: Macc. 0, Wigan Athletic 1

1966–67: Rnd 1: Macc. 3, Frickley Colliery 3
*Replay*: Frickley Colliery 1, Macc. 3
*(Cheshire FA ordered match to be
replayed – see text)*
*2nd replay*: Frickley Colliery 0, Macc. 0
*3rd replay*: Macc. 4, Frickley Colliery 1
SF: Macc. 1, Northwich Vics. 1
*Replay*: Northwich Vics. 0, Macc. 2
F: *First leg*: Runcorn 0, Macc. 1
*Second leg*: Macc. 2, Runcorn 0
*(Aggregate: W 3–0)*                               Winners

1967–68: Rnd 1: Oswestry Town 0, Macc. 1
Rnd 2: Witton Albion 5, Macc. 1

## *(e) Inter-League Challenge Cup*

1961–62: Rnd 1: Macc. 7, Prescot Cables 1
Rnd 2: Macc. 6, Earlestown 3
Rnd 3: Macc. 1, Marine 1 (*at Crewe*)
*Replay*: Marine 3, Macc. 0 (*at Southport*)

1962–63: Rnd 1: Darwen 0, Macc. 0
*Replay*: Macc. 6, Darwen 0
Rnd 2: *bye*
Rnd 3: Macc. 1, Fleetwood 0
SF: Wigan Athletic 2, Macc. 1

## (f) Northern Premier League Challenge Cup

1968–69: Rnd 1: Bangor City 2, Macc. 0

1969–70: Rnd 1: Boston Utd. 0, Macc. 2
Rnd 2: Macc. 3, South Liverpool 1
SF: *First leg*: Gainsborough Trinity 2, Macc. 2
*Second leg*: Macc. 2, Gainsborough Trinity 2 (*Aggregate*: 4–4)
*Replay*: Macc. 0, Gainsborough Trinity 0
*2nd replay*: Macc. 2, Gainsborough Trinity 1
F: *First leg*: Altrincham 1, Macc. 1
*Second leg*: Macc. 1, Altrincham 2
(*Aggregate*: L 2–3)                    Finalists

1970–71: Rnd 1: Macc. 4, Northwich Vics. 1
Rnd 2: Macc. 4, Stafford Rangers 2
SF: *First leg*: South Liverpool 2, Macc. 2
*Second leg*: Macc. 2, South Liverpool 0
(*Aggregate*: W 4–2)
F: *First leg*: Fleetwood 1, Macc. 1
*Second leg*: Macc. 0, Fleetwood 0
*Replay*: Macc. 0, Fleetwood 1 (*at Wigan*) Finalists

(Watney NPL Challenge Cup)
1971–72: Skelmersdale Utd. 6, Macc. 0

1972–73: Rnd 1: Mossley 1, Macc. 3
Rnd 2: Macc. 0, South Liverpool 0
*Replay*: South Liverpool 4, Macc. 0

1973–74: Prelim: Macc. 0, Altrincham 2

1974–75: Rnd 1: Great Harwood 3, Macc. 0

1975–76: Rnd 1: Macc. 2, Bangor City 2
*Replay*: Bangor City 1, Macc. 1
*2nd replay*: Macc. 1, Bangor City 0
Rnd 2: Macc. 1, Worksop Town 2

(Greenalls Northern Premier cup)
1976–77: Rnd 1: Mossley 2, Macc. 1

1977–78: Rnd 1: Rnd 1: Buxton 1, Macc. 0

(John Smith Northern Premier Cup)
1978–79: Rnd 1: Mossley 7, Macc. 1

1979–80: Rnd 1: *bye*
Rnd 2: Macc. 2, Frickley Athletic 1
Rnd 3: Macc. 1, Matlock Town 3

1980–81: Rnd 1: *bye*
Rnd 2: Macc. 2, Buxton 2
*Replay*: Buxton 1, Macc. 0

(Bass Northern Premier Cup)
1981–82: Rnd 1: *First leg*: Tamworth 0, Macc. 2
*Second leg*: Macc. 3, Tamworth 1
(*Aggregate*: W 5–1)
Rnd 2: Workington 2, Macc. 2
*Replay*: Macc. 0, Workington 2

1982–83: Rnd 1: *bye*
Rnd 2: Macc. 1, Tamworth 0
Rnd 3: Macc. 3, Hyde Utd. 0
SF: *First leg*: Witton Albion 2, Macc. 1
*Second leg*: Macc. 2, Witton Albion 0
(*Aggregate*: W 3–2)
F: Burton Albion 2, Macc. 1
(*at Maine Road*)                    Finalists

1983–84: Rnd 1: *bye*
Rnd 2: Macc. 2, Matlock Town 2
*Replay*: Matlock Town 1, Macc. 2
Rnd 3: South Liverpool 3, Macc. 1

1984–85: Rnd 1: *bye*
Rnd 2: Worksop Town 2, Macc. 1

1985–86: Rnd 1: *bye*
Rnd 2: Macc. 2, Oswestry Town 1
SF: *First leg*: Macc. 0, Hyde Utd. 0
*Second leg*: Hyde Utd. 4, Macc. 1
(*Aggregate*: L 1–4)

1986–87: Rnd 1: *bye*
Rnd 2: Mossley 0, Macc. 0
*Replay*: Macc. 2, Mossley 0
Rnd 3: Macc. 4, Hyde Utd. 0
SF: *First leg*: Caernarfon Town 1, Macc. 3
*Second leg*: Macc. 2, Caernarfon Town 1 (*Aggregate*: W 5–2)
F: Macc. 2, Burton Albion 0
(*at Maine Road*)                    Winners

# (g) FA Challenge Trophy

1969–70:   Rnd 1: Macc. 1, Burscough 0
           Rnd 2: Macc. 2, Gainsborough Trinity 0
           Rnd 3: Bangor City 1, Macc. 1
           *Replay*: Macc. 1, Bangor City 0
           Rnd 4: Burton Albion 1, Macc. 1
           *Replay*: Macc. 4, Burton Albion 2
           SF: Macc. 1, Barnet 0 (*at Stoke*)
           F: Macc. 2, Telford Utd. 0 (*at Wembley*) Winners

1970–71:   Rnd 1: Macc. 2, South Liverpool 1
           Rnd 2: Macc. 0, Scarborough 0
           *Replay*: Scarborough 2, Macc. 3
           Rnd 3: Macc. 1, Dover 0
           Rnd 4: Hereford Utd. 2, Macc. 0

1971–72:   Rnd 1: Macc. 2, Bilston 1
           Rnd 2: Macc. 3, Burton Albion 0
           Rnd 3: Macc. 2, Morecambe 1
           Rnd 4: Stafford Rangers 1, Macc. 1
           *Replay*: Macc. 0, Stafford Rangers 3

1972–73:   Rnd 1: Scarborough 3, Macc. 1

1973–74:   Rnd 1: Macc. 2, Tamworth 1
           Rnd 2: Worksop Town 2, Macc. 2
           *Replay*: Macc. 4, Worksop Town 0
           Rnd 3: Macc. 3, Buxton 0
           Rnd 4: Stafford Rangers 0, Macc. 0
           *Replay*: Macc. 2, Stafford Rangers 0
           SF: *First leg*: Macc. 1, Dartford 2
           *Second leg*: Dartford 0, Macc. 0
           (*Aggregate*: L 1–2)

1974–75:   Rnd 1: Macc. 1, Mossley 3

1975–76:   Rnd 1: Macc. 1, Runcorn 3

1976–77:   Rnd 3q: Macc. 3, Stalybridge Celtic 0
           Rnd 1: Macc. 1, Gateshead 0
           Rnd 2: Willington 3, Macc. 1

1977–78:   Rnd 3q: Dudley 1, Macc. 0

1978–79:   Rnd 1: Macc. 0, Witton Albion 0
           *Replay*: Witton Albion 3, Macc. 1

1979–80:   Rnd 1q: Macc. 5, Kirkby Town 2
           Rnd 2q: Macc. 1, Ashton Utd. 0
           Rnd 3q: Witton Albion 1, Macc. 3
           Rnd 1: Macc. 1, Matlock Town 2

1980–81:   Rnd 1q: Macc. 3, Sutton Coldfield Town 4

1981–82:   Rnd 1q: Heanor Town 1, Macc. 0

1982–83:   Rnd 1q: Moor Green 3, Macc. 0

1983–84:   Rnd 1q: Macc. 0, Horwich RMI 1

1984–85:   Rnd 1q: Macc. 3, Leek Town 0
           Rnd 2q: Macc. 2, Congleton Town 1
           Rnd 3q: Macc. 0, Kettering Town 2

1985–86:   Rnd 1: Kings Lynn 1, Macc. 1
           *Replay*: Macc. 3, Kings Lynn 0
           Rnd 2: Leek Town 2, Macc. 1

1986–87:   Rnd 3q: Macc. 1, Grantham 1
           *Replay*: Grantham 1, Macc. 0

1987–88:   Rnd 1: Macc. 2, Bishop Auckland 1
           Rnd 2: Rhyl 0, Macc. 2
           Rnd 3: Leyton Wingate 1, Macc. 2
           Rnd 4: Wokingham Town 2, Macc. 0

1988–89:   Rnd 1: Marine 2, Macc. 2
           *Replay*: Macc. 4, Marine 1
           Rnd 2: South Bank 0, Macc. 3
           Rnd 3: Macc. 2, Gravesend and
           Northfleet 0
           Rnd 4: Macc. 1, Welling Utd. 0
           SF: *First leg*: Dartford 0, Macc. 0
           *Second leg*: Macc. 4, Dartford 1
           (*Aggregate*: W 4–1)
           F: Telford Utd. 1, Macc. 0 (*at Wembley*) Finalists

1989–90:   Rnd 1: Boston Utd. 0, Macc. 0
           *Replay*: Macc. 3, Boston Utd. 0
           Rnd 2: Darlington 1, Macc. 0

1990–91:   Rnd 1: Macc. 0, Gretna 2

1991–92:   Rnd 1: Macc. 0, Boston Utd. 0
           *Replay*: Boston Utd. 0, Macc. 2
           Rnd 2: Macc. 1, Bangor City 0
           Rnd 3: Northwich Vics. 0, Macc. 1
           Rnd 4: Yeovil Town 1, Macc. 2
           SF: *First leg*: Colchester Utd. 3, Macc. 0
           *Second leg*: Macc. 1, Colchester Utd. 1
           (*Aggregate*: L 1–4)

1992–93:   Rnd 1: Macc. 0, Witton Albion 0
           *Replay*: Witton Albion 0, Macc. 0
           *2nd replay*: Witton Albion 2, Macc. 1
           (*at Witton*)

1993–94:   Rnd 1: Boston Utd. 1, Macc. 1
           *Replay*: Macc. 1, Boston Utd. 0
           Rnd 2: Worcester City 0, Macc. 0
           *Replay*: Macc. 3, Worcester City 2
           Rnd 3: Macc. 0, Billingham Synthonia 1

1994–95:   Rnd 1: Macc. 2, West Auckland Town 1

Rnd 2: Ashton Utd. 0, Macc. 5
Rnd 3: Gateshead 0, Macc. 1
Rnd 4: Macc. 0, Woking 1

1995–96:  Rnd 1: Macc. 1, Runcorn 0
Rnd 2: Macc. 2, Purfleet 1
Rnd 3: Macc. 1, Sudbury Town 0
Rnd 4: Gresley Rovers 0, Macc. 2

SF: *First leg*: Macc. 3, Chorley 1
*Second leg*: Chorley 1, Macc. 1
(*Aggregate*: W 4–2)
F: Macc. 3, Northwich Vics. 1
(*at Wembley*)                                    Winners

1996–97:  Rnd 1: Kidderminster H. 3, Macc. 0

## (h) Bob Lord Challenge Trophy

1989–90:  Rnd 1: Darlington 5, Macc. 2

1990–91:  Rnd 1: *bye*
Rnd 2: Barrow 2, Macc. 1

1991–92:  Rnd 1: *bye*
Rnd 2: Telford Utd. 1, Macc. 2
Rnd 3: Macc. 1, Altrincham 1
*Replay*: Altrincham 3, Macc. 1

(Drinkwise Cup)
1992–93:  Rnd 1: *First leg*: Altrincham 1, Macc. 3
*Second leg*: Macc. 0, Altrincham 0
(*Aggregate*: W 3–1)
Rnd 2: Witton Albion 0, Macc. 1
Rnd 3: Macc. 3, Kidderminster H. 1
SF: *First leg*: Northwich Vics. 2, Macc. 0
*Second leg*: Macc. 1, Northwich Vics. 1
(*Aggregate*: L 1–3)

1993–94:  Rnd 1: *First leg*: Witton Albion 1, Macc. 2
*Second leg*: Macc. 4, Witton Albion 1
(*Aggregate*: W 6–2)
Rnd 2: Runcorn 0, Macc. 4
Rnd 3: Halifax Town 1, Macc. 2
SF: *First leg*: Macc. 2, Northwich Vics. 1
*Second leg*: Northwich Vics. 0, Macc. 1
(*Aggregate*: W 3–1)
F: *First leg*: Macc. 4, Yeovil Town 1
*Second leg*: Yeovil Town 0, Macc. 0
(*Aggregate*: W 4–1)                          Winners

1994–95:  Rnd 1: *bye*
Rnd 2: Macc. 4, Runcorn 2
Rnd 3: Macc. 2, Altrincham 1
SF: *First leg*: Macc. 2, Bromsgrove
Rovers 1
*Second leg*: Bromsgrove Rovers 4,
Macc. 1 (*Aggregate*: L 3–5)

(Spalding Cup)
1995–96:  Rnd 1: *bye*
Rnd 2: Macc. 4, Kidderminster H. 1
Rnd 3: Morecambe 1, Macc. 4
SF: *First leg*: Southport 4, Macc. 4
*Second leg*: Macc. 2, Southport 1
(*Aggregate*: W 6–5)
F: *First leg*: Macc. 1, Bromsgrove
Rovers 1
*Second leg*: Bromsgrove Rovers 3,
Macc. 1 (*Aggregate*: L 2–4)          Finalists

1996–97:  Rnd 1: *bye*
Rnd 2: Altrincham 0, Macc. 1
SF: *First leg*: Morecambe 0, Macc. 2
*Second leg*: Macc. 4, Morecambe 1
(*Aggregate*: W 6–1)
F: *First leg*: Macc. 1, Kidderminster H. 1
*Second leg*: Kidderminster H. 0, Macc. 0
(*Aggregate*: 1–1)
(*Kidderminster won on away goals rule*)    Finalists

## (i) Football League Cup

(Coca-Cola Cup)
1997–98:  Rnd 1: *First leg*: Macc. 0, Hull City 0
*Second leg*: Hull City 2, Macc. 1
(*Aggregate*: L 1–2)

(Worthington Cup)
1998–99:  Rnd 1: *First leg*: Macc. 3, Stoke City 1
*Second leg*: Stoke City 1, Macc. 0
(*Aggregate*: W 3–2)
Rnd 2: *First leg*: Macc. 0, Birmingham
City 3

*Second leg*: Birmingham City 6, Macc. 0
(*Aggregate*: L 0–9)

1999–
2000:     Rnd 1: *First leg*: Macc. 1, Stoke City 1
*Second leg*: Stoke City 3, Macc. 0 (*Aggregate*: L
1–4)

2000–01:  Rnd 1: *First leg*: Bolton 1, Macc. 0
*Second leg*: Macc. 3, Bolton 1
(*Aggregate*: W 3–2)

Rnd 2: *First leg*: Middlesbrough 2,
Macc. 1
*Second leg*: Macc. 1, Middlesbrough 3
(*Aggregate*: L 2–5)

2001–02:  Rnd 1: Macc. 1, Bradfors City 2

## *(j) Auto Windscreens Shield*

1997–98:  Rnd 1: *bye*
          Rnd 2: Macc. 0, Preston North End 1

1998–99:  Rnd 1: Macc. 0, Wrexham 1

1999–     Rnd 1: *bye*

2000:      Rnd 2: Macc. 2, Rochdale 3

(LDV Vans Trophy)
2000–01:  Rnd 1: *bye*
          Rnd 2: Chesterfield 4, Macc. 2
2001–02:  Rnd 1: Darlington 2, Macc. 1

# The Dream Team?

*I offer the following as a basis for discussion, and no more.*
*The years given indicate the debut of each player.*

John Cooke
(1965)

Efe Sodje
(1997)

George Sievwright                    James Bates                    Jess Robinson
(1965)                              (1879)                        (1906)

Lennie Butt              Billy Bolton
(1931)                  (1890)

Warren Bradley              John Askey              Keith Goalen
(1962)                    (1984)                  (1957)

Brian Fidler
(1966)

Subs: Wilf Hall (1963), Elfyn Edwards (1986), Albert Leake (1961), Chris Byrne (1997), William Bromley-Davenport (1884)

Choosing the goalkeeper was an almost impossible task, given the great tradition the club has enjoyed. In the end I opted for the hero of Fulham '68. Besides, the number of goals conceded by the team during his stay, in the supposedly free-scoring 'sixties, is an eloquent statement in Johnnie Cooke's favour.

I then went for defenders who could score goals, some of them unforgettable. 'O rare Jim Bates' would have shone in any age, although possibly having a bit to learn about modern-day positional sense. I could not resist including Jess Robinson; the great bulldog could perhaps cover for the ebullient Mr Sodje during the Nigerian's unsettling raids into opposition penalty areas. And of course, along with Sievwright, Robinson was capable of spectacular long-range goals.

Automatic choice for right midfield was Lennie Butt, with a willing workhorse of a partner in Billy Bolton. Both players were inventive, forceful, and highly attack-conscious: truly a marriage made in heaven.

The forward line gave me the biggest headache. How to justify omitting the prolific Valentine? The irrepressible Glazzard? The old warhorse 'Mush' Howarth? Record holder Kelly? Young, Lyon and Dennis Fidler from the 'sixties wonderteam?

More recent favourites Richie Barker, Lee Glover, Damien Whitehead, Richard Tracey and Kyle Lightbourne? The list is almost endless.

In the end I chose ex-Manchester United and England Warren Bradley on the right; a deeper-lying John Askey as schemer; on the left Keith Goalen in his fleeter, winger years; and the inimitable Brian Fidler as central striker. Valentine and Kelly, after all, did not have to deal with the crowded defences that Fidler managed to outwit so often, and so consummately.

There you have it, my dream team from the élite of the ages at Macclesfield Football Club. I welcome disagreements.

# Bibliography

*Fifty Years of Football, The Origins and History of the Macclesfield Club*, John Earles (Courier and Herald Office 1925)

Club History, Mike Griffiths, Clare Swift, Nikki Walton (Website: www.mtfc.co.uk)

Also see Gary Jackson's club history on www.thesilkweb.com

*Against All Odds*, Paul Atherton, Neil Howarth, David Lafferty (More Than Ninety Minutes 1998)

*Physical Recreation in Macclesfield 1900–1914*, Peter Berry Sadler (Macclesfield Local History Library 1971)

*Streets and Houses of Old Macclesfield*, John Earles (MTD Rigg 1915, reprinted 1990)

*Pen Pictures of Macclesfield's Public Men* (Courier 1907)

*A History of Macclesfield*, Ed. Stella Davies (E. J. Morton 1981)

*Portrait of Macclesfield*, Doug Pickford (Sigma 1988)

*Golden Days: A Macclesfield Life*, Paul Maybury (Sigma 1995)

*An Alphabet of Silkmen Memories*, Harry Williamson, in *Old Macc* (magazine), issues 3, 4 and 5 (Bawdstone Press)

All of the above may be found in the Reference Section of Macclesfield Library.

*The Guinness Non-League Football Fact Book*, Tony Williams (Guinness 1993)

*The History of Non-League Football Grounds*, Kerry Miller (Polar 1996)

*The Guinness Record of the FA Cup*, Mike Collett (Guinness 1993)

*A Team for All Seasons: A History of Northwich Victoria FC*, K. R. Edward (Cheshire County 1992)

*Sons of Albion*, George Haspell (George Haspell 1996)

*Football in Sheffield*, Percy M. Young (Sportsman's Book Club 1963)

*Football and the English*, Dave Russell (Carnegie 1997)

*The People's Game*, James Walvin (Mainstream 1994)

*The Book of Football*, Ed. Clive Leatherdale (Desert Island Books 1997 – original magazine 1905–06)

*Macclesfield Courier and Herald* 1873–1952

*Macclesfield Times* 1910–1958

*Macclesfield (County) Express (Advertiser)* 1958-present

*Staffordshire Sentinel* 1873–1915

*Northwich Guardian* 1880–1915

*Manchester Courier* 1900–1914

Author's e-mail address: gphyth@btinternet.com

# List of Subscribers

Matthew Cooper, Macclesfield
Haydn King, Bollington
Terry Jordan, Macclesfield
Mr J.D. Swindells, Macclesfield
Mick McConkey, Luton
Phil Davies, Poynton
Jude Davies, Poynton
Rob Cooper, Henbury
Arthur Grace, Poynton
Clive Wright, Congleton
Paul and Clare Etchells, Family, Macclesfield
Mr J. Bate, Leeds
David and Helen Swindells, Macclesfield
John Clark, Sutton
Peter Ingley, Bollington
Roger Wash, Newmarket
Peter Newman and Richard Brindley, Buxton
Richard Gibbons, Gawsworth
John T. Kearns, Macclesfield
Lynette Dobson, Macclesfield
Ashley O'Regan, Macclesfield
Patrick O'Regan, Macclesfield
John D. Souness, Macclesfield
Mr and Mrs C.T. Riley, Chelford
John Land, Poynton
Francis Pyatt, Macclesfield
Mr Neil W. Jackson, Sutton
Anthony Holland, Macclesfield
David Bancroft, Macclesfield
Nick Phythian, Macclesfield
Robert Edge, Macclesfield
Bernard Jordan, Hazel Grove
J.R. Knight, Macclesfield
Terry Hill, Macclesfield
Roger Goulden, Macclesfield
Mr Philip Gibbons, Bollington

Patrick Jervis, Stoke-on-Trent
Ed Perry, Macclesfield
Geoff Findlow, Macclesfield
Bernard Offiler, Chesterfield
Matthew Lenton, Macclesfield
Dr Brian Green, Macclesfield
Clare Griffiths, London
Colin Garlick, Macclesfield
Stephen Barnes, Macclesfield
Chris Buxton, Macclesfield
Ian Percival, Walkeringham
Neil Percival, Enstone
Matthew Bardsley, Bollington
Mr Don Riseley, Macclesfield
Margaret and Bill Milligan, Macclesfield
Alan Maguire, Macclesfield
Tom Read, Macclesfield
Chris Edge, Macclesfield
Mike Rance, Macclesfield
Mr Derek Leonard, Hurdsfield
Norman Gosling, Macclesfield
John Thomason, Grange-over-Sands
Graham Brinkhurst, Macclesfield
Geoff Thorley, Stockport
Dave Thorley, Stockport
Carl Wood, Macclesfield
Barry Cox, Congleton
Michael Bell, Gawsworth
Andrew Kirk, Congleton
Michael Thomason, Macclesfield
James Foreman, Macclesfield
Steven Higginbotham, Thirsk
Mr Anthony James Drabble, Tytherington
David Blakeley, Ripley
Neil Hayes, Macclesfield
Mr Paul Hulme, Macclesfield

Steven Hulse, Crewe
John Burgess, Macclesfield
Peter Wilkinson, Macclesfield
Thomas Haddock, Nottingham
A.V., R.P., P.H., A and F. Bradley
Matthew Todd, Macclesfield
Simon Rollinson, Macclesfield
David Steele, Carlisle
C.A. Horsfall, Macclesfield
J.B. Horsfall, Macclesfield
Mr Colin Askey, Milton
Mr Geoff Molyneux, Macclesfield
R. Goulsbra, Manchester
W. Osbaldiston, Bollington
Leigh Edwards, Bransgore
Mr M.J. Walker, Aldridge
Sandra Downton, Poole
Brian Kemp, Macclesfield
Adrian Steele, Walthamstow
Jon Bowers, Tytherington
Tom Virtue, Macclesfield
Anthony Eastwood, Langley
Anthony Holmes, Bollington
David A. Smith, Macclesfield
Allan McNeil, Tytherington

Ian Buxton, Macclesfield
Kenneth Buxton, Macclesfield
Lis Garforth, Bollington
Patricia Massey, Manchester
Zoë C. Lloyd, Sandbach
Peter Wilkinson, Macclesfield
Phillip Reece, Macclesfield
Russ Bailey, Macclesfield
Kelly Cross, Macclesfield
John David Moss, Macclesfield
George Whittaker, Gawsworth
Mike Jones, Runcorn
Mr and Mrs P. J. Mann, Nottingham
John Hughes, Macclesfield
John Kearns, Macclesfield
Michael Gillibrand, Macclesfield
Peter Clark, Macclesfield
Michael Clark, Macclesfield
David Clark, Macclesfield
Andrew Farrer, Macclesfield
David J. Jackson, Macclesfield
Alan Hayward, Macclesfield
Trevor Surtees, Macclesfield
Lars Erik Pedersen, Oslo, Norway
John Dines, Eaton